THE FINANCE AND ANALYSIS OF
CAPITAL PROJECTS

Other published work

BUSINESS ECONOMICS AND STATISTICS

A. J. Merrett with G. Bannock

London, Hutchinson, 1962

HOUSING FINANCE AND DEVELOPMENT

An Analysis and Programme for Reform

A. J. Merrett and Allen Sykes

London, Longmans, 1965

A. J. MERRETT & ALLEN SYKES

The Finance and Analysis of Capital Projects

1724

LONGMANS

LONGMANS GREEN AND CO LTD

48 Grosvenor Street, London, W.1.
*Associated companies, branches and representatives
throughout the world*

© *A. J. Merrett and Allen Sykes, 1963*

First published 1963
2nd Impression 1965

*Printed in Great Britain by
J. W. Arrowsmith Ltd., Bristol*

To Dorothy and Huyèn-Trân

CONTENTS

✓ INTRODUCTION   xi

PART ONE

1. Basic Discounting and Compounding   3

2. Methods of Investment Appraisal   33
   Appendix A – The Present Value of Tax Allowances on Capital Expenditure

3. The Cost of the Individual Sources of Capital   58
   Appendix A – Basic Accounting Principles

4. The Cost of Capital and the Analysis of Projects under Alternative Financing Policies   108

5. Methods of Investment Appraisal Compared   148
   Appendix A – The Extended Yield Method

6. The Analysis of Risk   176

7. Conventional Methods of Investment Appraisal   219

8. Leasing Decisions and Property Analysis   241

9. The Timing and Scale of Expansion   269

10. Assessing the Purchase Price of a Firm I –
    Principles of Valuation   294
    Appendix A – Stock Appreciation

11. Assessing the Purchase Price of a Firm II –
    A Case Study   311

12. Assessing the Purchase Price of a Firm III –
    Miscellaneous Problems   330
    Appendix A – Some Traditional Methods of Business Valuation

13. Evaluating an Overseas Mining Project and Some General Problems of Evaluating Overseas Projects   348

14. The Capital Budgeting Organization   372

PART TWO

15. Optimal Financing   393

16. Capital Budgeting under Cash Surplus Conditions   423

17. Cost of Capital and Analysis of Projects When Shares are Undervalued   433
    Appendix A – The Derivation of Cost of Capital Under Conditions of Short Term Undervaluation

18. The General Principles of Valuation   466

19. Valuation, Depreciation and Replacement   485

Contents

APPENDIX

TABLE A: The present value of 1 from 1 to 50 years, and from 1% to 50%   510

TABLE B: The present value of 1 per annum from 1 to 50 years, and from 1% to 50%   520

TABLE C: The amount of 1 per annum from 1 to 50 years, and from 1% to 50%   530

INDEX   541

ACKNOWLEDGEMENTS

In producing this book we are conscious of our indebtedness to many friends and colleagues. We would particularly like to thank Professor W. T. Baxter and Professor H. C. Edey of the Department of Accounting of the London School of Economics and Political Science for their constant encouragement since the work was first conceived, and also for their help in arranging for the Statistical Research Division of the School to compile the comprehensive discount and compounding tables reproduced at the end of the book. For this latter task we are particularly indebted to Miss J. May and her team of assistants. We should like to thank Jack Bennett of the Standard Oil Company (New Jersey) and Alastair K. Hanton of Unilever Ltd., with whom a number of the more complex topics in the book have been fruitfully discussed; Barbara Lever and Margaret Walton for checking the bulk of the calculations; and Antony Hichens for reading and checking the proofs. We should also like to thank our many patient typists who have had the unenviable task of producing a readable manuscript from our innumerable untidy drafts. Finally we owe a very special debt of gratitude to our wives for their help, encouragement and many sacrifices which have made this book possible.

INTRODUCTION

The selection and financing of capital projects are indisputably two of the most important and critical business decisions. As such they are almost invariably the preserve of top management: the Cabinet itself sanctions the major investment projects of the Nationalized Industries. This is not surprising considering the magnitude of the sums involved. In 1961 the Nationalized Industries spent some £900m., the Standard Oil Company (New Jersey) $795m., General Motors $503m., Royal Dutch Shell £374m., I.C.I. £65m., and Unilever £60m. But it is not only the magnitude of these investments which is important–typically comparable sums are invested in working capital–it is the greater complexity of the investment decision and the cost of mistaken decisions. Investment in working capital to supply an existing market (the occasion for the major part of working capital investment) is largely routine and involves few complications or risks. Investment in fixed capital, however, often involves complex choices between alternative capital assets, dates of commencement, and methods of financing. These choices are both complex and critical given the scope for, and very high cost of, erroneous decisions. In complex industrial societies most fixed capital investments are in very specific forms such that their value in alternative uses is low or negligible. If a major refinery or factory is wrongly sited or sized, the mistaken decision is largely irredeemable in that the cost of correcting it is greater than the cost of simply bearing the cost of the mistaken decision. This is in marked contrast to a mistaken investment in working capital. Where a firm has built up say extra stocks in anticipation of a sudden rise in sales which does not materialize, it is usually possible to recoup the major portion of the investment either through resale or a temporary reduction of purchases or production. A significant loss may be involved but rarely as large as the losses which commonly follow from mistaken investment in fixed capital. The contrast between capital investment in specific fixed assets, and in current assets such as stock, can be likened to the risk of making a single false move in boxing compared to a mis-hit in tennis. In the former case one's scoring opportunities may be ended, whereas the latter need involve but a temporary setback. Moreover, fixed capital outlays often have a serious bearing on the direction and pace of a firm's future growth. As such, they determine the opportunities open to a firm and the directions in which it can move in the same way that track laying determines the opportunities open to a locomotive and the directions in which it can move.

Probably the most important effect of a moderate or poor investment performance is the failure of a firm to realize fully the profit and growth potentialities open to it, and this disadvantage is largely hidden. Any management is on strong grounds in defending its record against those who urge that something better might have been expected. Such allegations can be refuted as the uninformed criticism of those who 'don't know the industry'. Even comparisons with more successful firms in the same industry can usually be dismissed because of 'special factors', and 'unusual conditions'. All too often, for managements to avoid criticism it is enough to show a reasonable improvement on their own past performances, however moderate they may have been.

But whereas individual firms and individual industries may escape notice and criticism with an inadequate rate of growth, an individual nation is not in this position. Of no important Western nation is this more true than Britain where criticism and concern over our inadequate rate of growth has reached significant proportions. While this low rate of growth since the war, and particularly in the last decade, is commonly thought to be due primarily to an inadequate amount of investment, the evidence suggests (see particularly reference [1]) that it is rather the quality of the investment which is at fault. Many detailed examples of mistaken large scale investments, drawn from a wide variety of major industries, have been set out by Duncan Burn [2]. The published reports of the Select Committee on the Nationalized Industries, on two of which we have commented elsewhere [3], afford similar disquieting evidence of seriously inadequate methods of investment appraisal. On these and other sources of evidence, and also on the basis of our own fairly extensive experience, there are serious reasons for examining critically the investment appraisal procedures practised throughout British industry, in the public and private sectors alike.

THE SCOPE AND METHOD OF CAPITAL BUDGETING

Depending as it does on the successful forecasting of future events, logical analysis alone frequently cannot yield the complete answer to take view in addition to

A using any method.

a capital investment problem. But omniscience is not the prerequisite of scientific method. That all the facts relevant to business decisions cannot be known is no justification for abandoning a rational approach or making do with rough and ready rules of thumb, which too often conceal a serious lack of professional competence. Progress in management depends on applying logic to experience, to known or assumed facts in order to enlarge the area of understanding, and investment decisions are no exception. For this analysis to be justified despite uncertainty and imperfect estimates, it is merely necessary that the extra effort involved should yield a worthwhile improvement in the quality of the decision taking. Providing this condition is met, it is completely irrelevant that the analysis cannot reduce the problem to an exercise in pure logic.

A strong body of opinion particularly in Britain holds what we shall refer to as the traditionalist view, that the possible range of errors involved in forecasting sales, costs, technological development, etc., is such that only a very rudimentary economic and financial analysis is justified. While there is an element of truth in this argument as applied to a few specific types of capital projects, its generality has been much exaggerated. The argument is rarely based on an informed unprejudiced assessment of the facts. Too often it is simply a pretext for enjoying the pleasures of major decision taking while irresponsibly refusing to devote to these decisions the detailed and serious consideration they require.

It is important to be clear as to the type of project to which the traditionalist argument applies. Perhaps the clearest instance is investment in research. It is often the case that such investment is largely in the nature of a speculation. By its very nature it is often impossible to forecast the results of detailed research into new products or processes. Another situation where the role of financial analysis is relatively slight is one that relates to a product which is subject to rapid and unpredictable obsolescence – as for example in many chemical projects.

We would argue, however, that over a wide range of capital projects (in our experience, well over half those that come up for serious consideration) the basic data can be estimated to a useful degree of precision, and in many cases the data is highly certain – as for example with cost-saving projects, lease or buy decisions, contractual arrangements, etc. These will be discussed in detail in the text. Further, some features of the financial analysis of any project will apply over a range of possible outcomes, as, for example, will the analysis of alternative methods of financing the project and, perhaps to a lesser degree, the effect on a firm's tax position.

The advantages flowing from financial analysis also are not necessarily vitiated by errors in basic data. Widely different assumptions concerning the data may all point to specific changes (such as size of plant, choice of sites, dates of commencement) which would improve the financial outcome of the project. And it is too often forgotten by academics and businessmen alike that many so-called 'imponderables' may be pinned down to definite ranges. This, combined with the fact that the alternatives as regards size of plant, date of commencement, etc., often involve discontinuously large changes in costs or revenues, may indicate conclusively the specific changes that could be made to improve the financial return offered by the project. It should also be noted that without considerable experience of financial analysis it is extremely difficult to tell what possibilities exist for improvement in the financial return from a project of even moderate complexity.

Not least of the shortcomings of the traditionalist view is a failure to realize that financial analysis has anything to contribute to assessing the risks involved in the project. Thus even where it is impossible for financial analysis to improve the actual fortunes of a particular project it may nevertheless be able to delineate the risks involved in the project, highlight the salient factors, and possibly suggest methods by which these risks might be reduced. This is the area in which financial analysis has a great deal to contribute to sound decision taking. That a particular product may suffer differing degrees of price competition, or its productive processes become obsolete, are matters for marketing and technical estimation. But given such estimations only financial analysis can indicate the real cash significance of these eventualities. (It should be noted that the word 'obsolete' has no meaning unless defined in financial terms, and even then is consistent with a wide range of outcomes for the financial return on a project.)

In the literature on capital budgeting very little has been suggested that is of practical use in assessing or analysing risk. Such assessment and analysis are frequently dismissed as being necessarily subjective and hence not amenable to improvement. While accepting that part of risk appraisal, perhaps the larger part, will remain subjective, and that unquantifiable experience alone may be of some help, we feel there is still much to be said on this subject of a practical nature. For instance it is useful to distinguish between future cash flows at manifestly different levels of risk. Sales revenue is typically at a significantly higher level of risk than, say, tax concessions on capital expenditure which will be recouped so long as a firm has sufficient taxable income from whatever source. Contractual obligations such as loan interest and repayments are at no risk at all if the firm concerned is to remain in business. They are as certain a type of cash flow as can exist in the business world. Given this situation, where different cash flows are at indisputably different levels of risk, we hope to demonstrate the considerable advantage of using suitable methods of evaluation.

In the course of this book we have tried to develop many methods and techniques which are somewhat complex in relation to those currently in use in business. In practice it will often be possible to ignore many of the complexities, either because it is apparent that they can have little influence on the result, or because other non-economic restraints, such as top management policy decisions, automatically preclude certain profitable alternatives. But there will be many occasions when the complexities must be faced and it is for these occasions our methods have been developed. We have been particularly concerned to avoid all technicalities which, in our fairly wide experience, have not clearly justified their usefulness. This book can be said to be the result of our having attempted to solve many basic and often complex problems which, to our knowledge, have never previously been adequately considered. For despite the importance of assessing capital projects, the many practical problems posed thereby have received relatively little attention. Most of the attention they have received is the product of the last dozen years and is the work of a handful of applied economists, almost all American, led by Professor Joel Dean and G. Terborgh.

The reasons for this neglect probably spring from the very nature of capital budgeting decisions. These are extraordinarily diverse, ranging from the banal and obvious to problems of gruelling conceptual and administrative complexity, lying at the intersection of involved problems of pure finance, forecasting, taxation, law, and market strategy. These problems involve more than the use of formally correct financial techniques: they require the imaginative consideration of the potentialities of the project and the delineation of its salient risk characteristics. These problems should naturally fall to the financial executive as the individual closest to the financial potentialities of the project. The financial executive is essentially engaged in conflating the estimates and ideas from the various disciplines of marketing, technology, accounting, taxation, and law, in order to reveal their financial implications. Thus he is uniquely well placed to see the relevance of possibilities which these disciplines have to offer to a particular capital budgeting decision, potentialities which other disciplines can only imperfectly evaluate given their lack of integration and acquaintance with the contributions of other disciplines. But hitherto, the analysis of capital projects has fallen between the disciplines of accountancy and economics and in consequence has failed to be covered adequately by either.

We hope in the course of this book to present the fundamentals of the subject and the techniques for solving a number of the basic problems. In addition we have endeavoured to develop techniques for solving some of the complex hitherto unsolved problems in capital budgeting. In particular we have tried to break away from the usual assumptions of equilibrium analysis and deal with the problems of, for example, the cost of capital and the analysis of projects when shares are undervalued or the firm is following a non-optimal financing policy. Given that this involves breaking new ground to a substantial degree it is inevitable that errors and omissions will later come to light. It has been part of the object of the book to throw open the problems of capital budgeting and consider them in a realistic degree of diversity and complexity for both British and American conditions. If as an outcome of this book there is a wider comprehension of these problems with the incidental result that its errors and omissions are made good, we will consider the effort of writing it well spent.

METHOD AND OUTLINE
OF THE BOOK

This book has been written with the intention of being of use both to specialists (financial executives, accountants, and business economists) and to the non-specialist business executive. To this end the book has been split into two parts, with the more difficult and advanced topics relegated to the second part, which takes up a quarter of the space. Further, many of the chapters have also been split into two parts with the more difficult and specialized aspects relegated to the latter part. By means of these devices it should be possible for the general reader to obtain a broad and practical outline of the subject and for specialists to have their more complex problems dealt with adequately. Even for specialists we would recommend a quick first reading of the whole of Part I of the book, ignoring the second parts of the more difficult chapters.

While of necessity we make use of mathematical techniques these seldom involve more than a knowledge of elementary algebra, and all formulae are fully explained in the text, which also contains many fully worked out examples based on actual problems. It is another feature of this book that we have set out many short cut approaches which permit the simple handling of complex data. We have also developed graphical techniques where appropriate. To aid in the assessment of capital projects we have included as appendices present value and annuity tables in unit percentage increments from 1 per cent to 50 per cent, and in yearly steps from 1 to 50 years. By all these various means we hope to demonstrate that no heavy or difficult computational burdens need be involved in the application of the appropriate techniques.

In addition to a knowledge of elementary algebra, we also assume some general acquaintance with the basic principles of accountancy. For readers without such knowledge and for those whose knowledge is in need of revision, we have summarized these basic principles in the appendix to Chapter 3. While no substitute for a proper detailed study, it should serve as a brief outline of the main tenets of the subject which comprises the language of business.

The book begins with a comprehensive description of discounting and compounding formulae, and this first chapter serves as reference for all subsequent chapters. There follows (Chapter 2) an elementary discussion of the main discounting methods that have been developed for and applied in business. (In this same chapter we show the importance of tax concessions in enhancing the profitability of investments, and in the appendix we develop several short-cut formulations which permit the full complexities of current British capital allowances to be evaluated quickly and simply.) This provides the necessary introduction to the two basic chapters (3 and 4) which are concerned with basic company finance and measuring a firm's cost of capital. Alternative theories are critically examined in conjunction with the new approach we are putting forward. Chapter 5 is devoted to a much more detailed and critical examination of the common discounting methods. We argue that the internal rate of return approach, which has been the subject of considerable academic criticism, is capable of modifications which meet the several objections raised against it. Further, we argue that it has certain administrative and descriptive virtues which are fairly conclusive grounds for its general use in business.

Chapter 6 considers the effect of the allowances to be made for risk and uncertainty in the assessment of capital projects. There is also a full discussion of inflation, which significantly distorts the recording and appraisal of economic facts. Accountants have not yet developed their art to make full and realistic allowances for this situation. But as capital is in part raised in fixed money terms, as costs and income can be differently affected by changing prices, the problems raised by inflation are often of considerable importance. The general problem is discussed there, while the specific problems are discussed in subsequent chapters devoted to case studies.

Finally there is a chapter (7) devoted to a critical examination of the conventional business methods of appraising capital projects, notably 'rate of return' and 'payback'. The simplicity of applying such methods is shown to be quite inadequate compensation for their many serious defects. There is also demonstrated the weaknesses and inadequacies of conventional accounting ratios (principally annual profits to annual capital employed) for the assessment of a firm's performance, a subject of particular relevance to the control of the nationalized industries. This chapter concludes the discussion of principles in Part I, the remainder of which is devoted to specific capital budgeting problems.

The first applied chapter (8) is concerned with the common problem of whether to lease or buy capital assets – a choice which commonly arises with buildings, ships, and plants. This problem is bound up with tax and financing complications and prone to distortion from the effects of inflation. Various other leasing problems, including 'lease and lease-back' arrangements are examined as are various other problems arising in property analysis. Chapter 9 examines the important and complex problem of deciding when and by how much to expand productive capacity, office accommodation, etc., when faced with an expanding demand for a firm's services or products. This is followed by three chapters (10, 11, and 12) devoted to the problems of take-overs and mergers. The first chapter sets out the detailed principles to be used in assessing the purchase price of a business, and by definition, the selling price for the existing owners. There follows a detailed case study to give flesh to the skeleton of theory. Finally comes a chapter devoted to the important incidental problems that arise in connection with take-overs, such as evaluating alternative methods of payment (shares, or cash, or some combination of the two), the consequences of failing to achieve 100 per cent ownership, and the effect of inflation upon the valuation to be placed on a firm. This chapter also contains an appendix devoted to a brief description and appraisal of some conventional methods of business valuation, notably the 'super profit' method. Chapter 13 is a specialized chapter devoted to consideration of some of the financial problems of mining ventures and the financing of overseas companies generally. The final chapter of Part I (14) comprises our recommendations on the setting up and staffing of an efficient capital budgeting organization for the analysis investment proposals, general financing, and *post mortem* analysis of past investment decisions in order to learn how to improve future decisions. One notable omission from Part I is a discussion of the recurring problem facing nearly every firm of when to replace an existing asset. This problem is inextricably bound up with that of valuing existing assets and both subjects are fully discussed in Part II.

Part II of the book consists of the more advanced topics of interest primarily to specialists. The first chapter (15) considers some of the problems of optimal financing for a typical joint stock company under normal conditions. It contains a detailed assessment of whether or not debt capital can lower a firm's weighted average cost of capital. There is also an analysis of convertibles (conversion options). Chapter 16 examines the cost of capital to a firm under cash surplus conditions. The subsequent chapter (17) examines the problems facing a management when they consider their firm's shares to be significantly undervalued at the current market price. The cost of capital is examined under these conditions, especially when the raising of further capital by way of rights issues or new issues is contemplated. Also considered is the relevance of accounting or 'book' profits in the assessment of capital projects.

The last two chapters of the book are devoted to valuation problems and allied topics. The first chapter comprises a detailed discussion of asset valuation under the wide variety of conditions commonly met with in practice. From the discussion, formulae are derived which permit the meaningful valuation of assets under these conditions. The same chapter also considers the effect of second-hand prices on asset valuation and examines the significant factors which influence second-hand markets. The final chapter consists of the application of the valuation formulae in determining the optimal life of assets and hence the optimal time of replacement, the meaningful calculation of annual depreciation, the calculation of residual asset

value, and the effect on all such calculations of taxation, capital allowances, changing prices, immediate and future obsolescence.
London, October, 1962

REFERENCES

1. P.E.P., *Growth in the British Economy*, George Allen and Unwin, London, 1960.
2. DUNCAN BURN, 'Investment, Innovation and Planning in the United Kingdom', *Progress*, September 1962.
3. A. J. MERRETT and ALLEN SYKES, 'The Financial Control of State Industry', *The Banker*, March–April 1962.

Part One

CHAPTER ONE
Basic Discounting and Compounding

The defining characteristic of an investment is the outlay of valuable resources in the expectation of future gain. In the simplest case it is the outlay of cash in one period in the expectation of the return of a larger sum in the following period. In the most common case, an investment comprises a planned series of capital expenditures undertaken in anticipation of their generating a larger series of cash flows (generally uncertain) at various times in the future. The main problem of investment appraisal follows quite simply from this defining characteristic: it is the evaluation of uncertain future cash flows in relation to cash outlays (possibly also uncertain) in the immediate and near future. The solution of this general problem involves an understanding of the basic techniques of discounting and compounding as applied to *certain* cash flows, and the adaptation and extension of these techniques to *uncertain* cash flows, that is cash flows subject to risk.

This chapter is devoted entirely to an exposition of the basic discounting and compounding techniques as applied to cash flows known with certainty. Situations in which cash flows are known with a high degree of certainty are fairly common in commercial investment (as for instance, in 'lease or buy' decisions discussed in Chapter 8), but they are more common in the field of fixed interest investment. In giving priority to the evaluation of certain cash flows, we do not wish to minimize the evaluation problems arising from uncertainty. These are given detailed treatment in later chapters, particularly in Chapter 6. The formal techniques of discounting and compounding are, however, sufficiently extensive and complex in themselves to warrant a detailed exposition under these simplifying conditions. This chapter covers the basic techniques used in the remainder of the book where it is extensively used as a reference. For the comprehension of individual subsequent chapters it is not necessary to read this chapter in its entirety. It may be found more convenient merely to read the sections found in Part I, and to refer to later sections as required.

3

I

1. THE BASIC ASSUMPTIONS OF DISCOUNTING AND COMPOUNDING

The basic assumption of discounting and compounding is that money has a time value: that a given sum of money now is normally worth more than an equal and certain sum at some future date because it permits profitable investment or consumption in the interval. Put formally, a sum of money P now is held to have the same value as the sum $P(1+r)$ one period from now. In other words the assumption is that the exchange rate between money now and money one period in the future is as the rate of 1 now to $(1+r)$ one period hence. Because present money is almost invariably at a premium compared with future money, the value of r is almost invariably positive. It is usual to refer to r as a rate of interest expressed in percentage terms related to a period of a year. (For the present we shall adopt the common convention of discounting or compounding for discrete periods of a year.)

Consider the case of a firm, at present borrowing at the rate r per annum on a British type bank overdraft, which is able and planning to meet all its likely future cash requirements in this way. (With the British type of bank overdraft interest is paid only on the balance of the loan outstanding, and any part of the loan may be repaid at any time.) As the firm can exchange future money for present money via the bank overdraft facilities, the rate r per annum sets the firm's exchange rate between present and future money. If the firm is offered the sum $P(1+r)$ one year away, it should logically value it as worth P now. For guaranteed $P(1+r)$ one year away, the firm could obtain (i.e. borrow) P from the bank now and freely use this sum for whatever purpose it chose, by sacrificing the $P(1+r)$ one year hence – that is use the $P(1+r)$ to extinguish the loan of P plus the year's interest Pr. The firm should be prepared to sacrifice money in the future for present money at least at the rate of $(1+r)$ to 1 since this is effectively what it is doing by its existing borrowing from the bank. Similarly, the firm should accept the sum of P now in settlement of a debt of $P(1+r)$ due one year from now.

In this case the exchange rate between present and future money is determined by the supply of a specific type of capital to the firm. In the majority of cases the supply of capital to the firm and the demand for it is much more involved, with the result that the exchange rate between present and future money is considerably more complex so that either modification of the cash flows themselves or adaptation of the conventional discounting techniques is required. For the present, however, we are only concerned with this simple basic case.

So far we have established the basic proposition that the sum P now is worth the sum $P(1+r)$ one year from now. Similarly, the sum $P(1+r)$ one year from now must be equivalent to (can be exchanged for) $P(1+r) \times (1+r) = P(1+r)^2$ two years from now, and to the sum $P(1+r)^n$ n years from now. It follows that any given sum now is worth $(1+r)^n$ more by n years from now.

In discounting/compounding terminology the symbol S is used to identify a sum arising in the future, just as P is used to identify a sum at the present time. Using these symbols, and where the sum S arises n years from now, we can formally express the results so far established in the following way:

$$S = P(1+r)^n \tag{1.1}$$

and

$$P = \frac{S}{(1+r)^n} = S(1+r)^{-n} \tag{1.2}$$

Equation (1.2)[1] is of course merely a restatement of equation (1.1).

These two equations are the foundation on which all discounting and compounding theory is based (equation (1.1) relating to compounding, i.e. the ascertainment of terminal values, and equation (1.2) to discounting, the ascertainment of present values).

For ease of computation, compound interest tables have long been calculated from both these expressions. Table A at the end of this book reproduces the second formulation, which is conventionally written[2] as $v_{n|r} = (1+r)^{-n}$, where v is the present value of the sum 1 (standing for £1, $1, etc.) at the end of n years, discounted at the annual interest rate of $r\%$. The table gives all values of r for 1% to 50%, and of n for 1 to 50 years. It will be apparent that all the entries in this table will have a value of $< 1 \cdot 0$; thus $v_{2|5\%} = 0 \cdot 907029$.

It should also be apparent that this table may be used to give

---

[1] The value of $1/x^n$ is also conveniently written as x^{-n}.

[2] The upright stroke between the subscripts n and r is conventionally written as an inverted capital L but throughout this book use will be made only of the single upright stroke.

the 'amount' to which 1 for n years would accumulate at $r\%$. If $v_{n|r}$ is the present value of 1, then 1 is the 'amount' of $v_{n|r}$ at the end of n years at $r\%$, and accordingly the amount of 1 in these circumstances is simply $1 \div v_{n|r}$, i.e. the reciprocal of $v_{n|r}$. Hence Table A may be used for calculating amounts of 1 as well as giving present values of 1. A detailed discussion of the meaning to be attached to the present values is given in Section 1a of Chapter 2.

2. COMPARING A SERIES OF CASH FLOWS – PRESENT VALUES

We have now established that to obtain the present value of a sum arising n years hence at a rate of interest r, it is necessary merely to divide by $(1+r)^n$. Most problems, of course, involve more than the comparison of a future sum with a present sum: usually the problem is to relate a series of future cash flows to a present invest-ment outlay, or perhaps even a series of outlays. For the moment we will consider only the case where a series of future cash flows is compared with a single present outlay.

Suppose that the present investment of a sum C will result in the sums $A_1, A_2, A_3 \dots A_n$ arising respectively at the end of years $1, 2, 3 \dots n$. Given the appropriate rate of discount, r, we can express their aggregate present value as

$$P = \sum_{i=1}^{i=n} \frac{A_i}{(1+r)^i} \qquad (1.3)$$

where Σ is the conventional sign for indicating the summation of the sums A_i, from the first, A_1 (indicated by $i = 1$) to the n'th, A_n (indicated by $i = n$). To determine the attractiveness of any in-vestment in the very simple conditions postulated it is necessary merely to compare P with C.

In the case when the cash flows vary from year to year in an irregular manner, there is no formula that will enable the present value of the series to be computed in one embracing calculation. If there are ten such annual cash flows, it is necessary to perform ten separate discount calculations in the manner described above and add together the ten separate present values. Where the series of cash flows follows a regular pattern however, short cut formulations can be used. Consider first the case where the cash flows are constant for all years: this series is known as annuity.

a. *Constant Periodic Cash Flows – Annuities*

The problem of reducing these cash flows to a present value is simply the problem of calculating their present value P, where

$$P = \frac{A}{(1+r)} + \frac{A}{(1+r)^2} + \frac{A}{(1+r)^3} \cdots + \frac{A}{(1+r)^n}$$

and where A is the constant end-year cash receipt received for n years and discounted at $r\%$. This equation (which is a geometric progression) can be simplified as follows. Multiply both sides of the equation by $1/(1+r)$. Therefore

$$\frac{P}{(1+r)} = \frac{A}{(1+r)^2} + \frac{A}{(1+r)^3} \cdots \frac{A}{(1+r)^n} + \frac{A}{(1+r)^{n+1}}$$

If this second equation is subtracted from the first, only the first term of the series P, and the last term of the series $P/(1+r)$ fail to cancel out, leaving:

$$P - \frac{P}{(1+r)} = \frac{A}{(1+r)} - \frac{A}{(1+r)^{n+1}}$$

Multiplying both sides by $(1+r)$, the expression simplifies into

$$P(1+r) - P = A - A(1+r)^{-n},$$

therefore

$$Pr = A[1 - (1+r)^{-n}]$$

whence

$$P = \frac{A[1 - (1+r)^{-n}]}{r}$$

When A is a series of $1(£1, \$1, \text{etc.})$, the formula is conventionally written,

$$a_{n|r} = \frac{1 - (1+r)^{-n}}{r} \tag{1.4}$$

where $a_{n|r}$ is the conventional symbol for the present value of an annuity of 1 ($£1$, $\$1$, etc.) a year for n years at $r\%$ p.a. This formula comprises Table B at the end of the book for values of n from 1 to 50 years and values of r from 1% to 50%.

To illustrate the application of the $a_{n|r}$ formula, consider the following simple problem. A firm is offered the choice of a 20 year lease on a building by a property company.

Alternative (a) £10,000 down and £4,000 p.a. for 20 years.
Alternative (b) £15,000 down and £3,000 p.a. for 20 years.

Annual payments are assumed to be made end-year, and the relevant rate of interest is assumed to be 5%. Ignoring all problems of risk, inflation, tax, etc., this problem can be considered in the following way. Alternative (b) involves the firm in putting up £5,000 more at the beginning of the lease than alternative (a), but results in an annual end-year saving of £1,000 for 20 years. From Table B it is seen that the present value of a 20 year annuity of 1 at 5% is 12·4622, hence the present value of £1,000 p.a. for 20 years is simply £12,462·2. There is therefore a gain of net present value by taking alternative (b) equal to £12,462·2 − £5,000 = £7,462·2, and this alternative is clearly to be preferred.

b. *Constant Periodic Cash Flows – Perpetuities*

When the series is expected to go on perpetually, that is $n \to \infty$ (the symbol for n tending to infinity), then in the annuity formula (1.4), the expression $(1+r)^{-n}$ tends to zero, and the formula becomes simply

$$P = \frac{1}{r} \tag{1.5}$$

This case of a perpetual annuity is referred to as a 'perpetuity'.

It is also useful to consider the present value of a perpetual series of constant cash flows occurring at regular intervals of the multiple of a year. For example, suppose the sum A occurs every k years beginning k years hence. The present value of this series is evidently

$$P = \frac{A}{(1+r)^k} + \frac{A}{(1+r)^{2k}} + \frac{A}{(1+r)^{3k}} \cdots \frac{A}{(1+r)^{\infty}}$$

Multiplying both sides of the equation by $(1+r)^k$ we obtain

$$P(1+r)^k = A + \frac{A}{(1+r)^k} + \frac{A}{(1+r)^{2k}} \cdots \frac{A}{(1+r)^{\infty}}$$

Subtracting the first equation from the second, we get

$$P(1+r)^k - P = A$$

therefore

$$P[(1+r)^k - 1] = A$$

whence

$$P = \frac{A}{(1+r)^k - 1} \qquad (1.6)$$

If we define $(1+r)^k - 1 = z$ we can rewrite (1.6) as

$$P = \frac{A}{z} \qquad (1.6)$$

c. Cash Flows Growing at a Compound Rate

In investment appraisal it is not uncommon to require to find the present value of a series of cash flows which are expected to grow at a compound rate, e.g. the present value of a series of dividends, or revenues, or costs from an expanding market growing at say 5% *per annum*.

Suppose the end period cash flows are expected to grow by $g\%$, then the series would be

$$A, A(1+g), A(1+g)^2 \ldots A(1+g)^{n-1}$$

The present value P, of this series is then

$$P = \frac{A}{(1+r)} + \frac{A(1+g)}{(1+r)^2} + \frac{A(1+g)^2}{(1+r)^3} \ldots \frac{A(1+g)^{n-1}}{(1+r)^n}$$

Multiplying both sides of the equation by $(1+g)$,

$$P(1+g) = \frac{A(1+g)}{(1+r)} + \frac{A(1+g)^2}{(1+r)^2} + \frac{A(1+g)^3}{(1+r)^3} \ldots \frac{A(1+g)^n}{(1+r)^n}$$

If we define the term $(1+g)/(1+r) = 1/(1+r_0)$, the series can be written as,

$$P(1+g) = \frac{A}{(1+r_0)} + \frac{A}{(1+r_0)^2} + \frac{A}{(1+r_0)^3} \ldots \frac{A}{(1+r_0)^n}$$

This is clearly equivalent to the present value of an annuity of A per period, discounted at the rate r_0. Hence

$$P(1+g) = A a_{n|r_0}$$

therefore

$$P = \frac{A}{(1+g)} a_{n|r_0} \qquad (1.7)$$

where $r_0 = (r-g)/(1+g)$, and A is the first term of the series.

This formula can, of course, also be used to determine the present value of a series *declining* at a compound rate (i.e. where g is negative).

Where $r > g$, use may be made of $a_{n|r}$ tables, although interpolation will often be necessary if the exact value of r_0 is not given in the tables.

Where $r = g$, $r_0 = 0$, and the formula becomes simply

$$P = \frac{An}{(1+g)}$$

Where $r < g$, r_0 becomes negative, and it becomes necessary to work out the $a_{n|r}$ formula by logarithms as annuity tables are not calculated for negative values of r. Alternatively, amount tables i.e. tables for equation (1.1), can be used from the simple fact that $1/(1+r_0) = 1+d$ where d is a positive number.

To illustrate the formula derived above, consider the following example. A dividend stream commencing one year hence at £110 is expected to grow at 10% per annum for ten years and then cease. If the rate of discount is 21% p.a., what is the present value of this expected series?

$$P = \frac{A}{(1+g)}a_{n|r_0}, \quad \text{where} \quad r_0 = \frac{r-g}{1+g}$$

hence

$$r_0 = \frac{0 \cdot 21 - 0 \cdot 10}{1 \cdot 10} = \frac{0 \cdot 11}{1 \cdot 10} = 0 \cdot 10$$

and

$$\frac{A}{(1+g)} = \frac{£110}{1 \cdot 10} = £100$$

Therefore

$P = £100\, a_{10|10\%}$. From Table B, $a_{10|10\%} = 6 \cdot 14457$ and therefore

$$P = £100 \times 6 \cdot 14457 = £614 \cdot 457.$$

d. *Cash Flows Increasing or Decreasing at a Linear Rate*

situations in which cash flows grow linearly, that is by a constant *amount* in each period, are probably rather less common in investment appraisal than series growing at a compound rate which we have already considered. Cases of linear growth, however, occur sufficiently often for a formula method of obtaining its present value to be of practical use.

Suppose the series to be of the form

$$A, \quad A+B, \quad A+2B \ldots A+(n-1)B,$$

that is, A is the constant amount in the cash flow and B is the amount by which the series increases in each period.

By considering first the amount to which this series will accumulate at the end of the period and then reducing this amount to present value, the present value of the series is found to be

$$P = a_{n|r}\left(\frac{B}{r} + A\right) - \frac{nB(1+r)^{-n}}{r} \tag{1.8}$$

For illustration, consider the ten year cash flow where $A = 100$ and $B = 10$. The series is 100, 110, 120 ... 190, and its present value at 10% is

$$P = a_{10|10\%}\left(\frac{10}{0\cdot10} + 100\right) - \frac{100(1\cdot10)^{-10}}{0\cdot10}$$

$$= 6\cdot14457(100+100) - \frac{100}{0\cdot10} \times 0\cdot385543$$

$$= 1228\cdot914 - 385\cdot543$$

$$= 843\cdot371$$

The formula (1.8) with the B taken as negative applies equally to a series decreasing by B per period.

So far in this section we have been comparing the present value P of a series of future cash flows with a single investment outlay C, to ensure $P > C$. It will now be clear that, where the investment outlay occurs in more than one period, it too can be reduced to a present value by use of the formulae derived above.

3. COMPARING A SERIES OF CASH FLOWS – TERMINAL VALUES

So far we have examined methods of calculating the *present* value of different series of end year cash flows. For some purposes it is more useful to consider the *terminal* value of a series, i.e. the amount to which a series of end-year cash flows will grow over a period at a given interest rate, r. To determine this value it is necessary to find the aggregate amount of each separate cash flow, grossed up at the rate $(1+r)$ for the time interval between the respective cash flows and the end of the period. More formally the terminal value S of a series can be expressed as

$$S = \sum_{i=1}^{i=n} A_i (1+r)^{n-i} \qquad (1.9)$$

To determine whether an initial capital investment, C, would be justified, it is necessary to compare $C(1+r)^n$ with S in the above formulation.

In the case where the cash flows vary from period to period in an irregular manner, there is no simple formula that can be derived that will enable a simple algebraic computation of the terminal value of the series. As in the case of discounting, if there are ten such annual cash flows, it is necessary to compound each cash flow separately (using the reciprocals of the values in Table A), and aggregate the resulting terminal values. Where the series of cash flows follow a regular pattern however, again as in the case of present values, some algebraic short cuts can be used.

Before considering any specific formulations, it is useful to consider the basic relationship that exists between present and terminal values. As was demonstrated in Section 1, the present value P of a single sum S arising n years in the future is simply equation (1.2),

$$S(1+r)^{-n}$$

and conversely, the terminal value at the end of n years of a sum P is of course equation (1.1)

$$P(1+r)^n$$

Once the present value of a *series* of cash flows has been computed, it follows that this single value can be turned into a terminal value, simply by multiplying it by $(1+r)^n$. Hence, it will be seen that

$$(1+r)^n \sum_{i=1}^{i=n} \frac{A_i}{(1+r)^i} = \sum_{i=1}^{i=n} A_i (1+r)^{n-i} \qquad (1.10)$$

From this it is clear that all the formulae derived for present values can be turned into terminal value formulae by increasing them by $(1+r)^n$.

a. *Constant Periodic Cash Flows – Annuities*

Suppose the sum A is set aside at the end of every year for n years, and is invested to earn r p.a. The sum A arising at the end of the first year will have grown by $(1+r)^{n-1}$ having been invested at r for $(n-1)$ years. Similarly the sum A arising at the end of the second year will have grown by $(1+r)^{n-2}$, and so on for all the remaining cash flows. At the end of n years the sums set aside and their compound interest will amount to a terminal value of S, where

$$S = A(1+r)^{n-1} + A(1+r)^{n-2} \ldots A(1+r) + A.$$

This is seen to be a declining geometric progression. By means of the device illustrated previously in Section 2(a), if we multiply both sides of the above equation by $(1+r)$, and subtract the first equation from the second, we obtain

$$S(1+r) - S = A(1+r)^n - A$$

therefore

$$Sr = A[(1+r)^n - 1]$$

therefore

$$S = \frac{A[(1+r)^n - 1]}{r}$$

Where A is a series of 1 (£1, $1, etc.), the formula is conventionally written

$$s_{n|r} = \frac{(1+r)^n - 1}{r} \qquad (1.11)$$

where $s_{n|r}$ is the conventional symbol for the terminal value of an annuity of 1 per year, end year, for n years at $r\%$ p.a. This formula comprises Table C at the end of the book for values of n from 1 to 50 years, and values of r from 1% to 50%.

As stated above (1.10), the present value P of a series when increased by $(1+r)^n$, equals the terminal value of that series at the end of the n'th year. Hence $a_{n|r}(1+r)^n = s_{n|r}$.

This can be shown as follows for a series of 1

$$a_{n|r}(1+r)^n = \frac{1-(1+r)^{-n}}{r}(1+r)^n$$

$$= \frac{(1+r)^n-1}{r}$$

which is the formula

$$s_{n|r} \qquad (1.11)$$

In financial terminology, the terminal value of a constant or regular annuity is usually referred to in terms of a 'sinking fund'. This latter is a fund to which periodic payments are made and then invested to accumulate to a given amount by a certain date, often for the purpose of redeeming a loan. Hence one may be required to find out how much must be regularly set aside say yearly for ten years at 5% to accumulate to £1,000,000. This can be found simply as follows. From Table C $s_{10|5\%} = 12.5779$. Therefore the amount to be set aside annually

$$= \frac{£1,000,000}{12.5779} = £79,505.$$

b. *Constant Periodic Cash Flows – Perpetuities*

It will be apparent that no meaning can be attached to the terminal value of a series which never terminates.

c. *Cash Flows Growing at a Compound Rate*

As shown above (1.10), the terminal value of any series is simply the present value P of that series increased by $(1+r)^n$. The present value P of a series growing at $g\%$ p.a. was shown to be

$$P = \frac{A}{(1+g)}a_{n|r_0} \qquad (1.7)$$

where $r_0 = (r-g)/(1+g)$. Therefore the terminal value,

$$S = P(1+r)^n = \frac{A(1+r)^n}{(1+g)}a_{n|r_0} = \frac{A}{(1+g)}s_{n|r_0} \qquad (1.12)$$

d. *Cash Flows Growing at a Linear Rate*

Similarly, the terminal value S of a series of cash flows increasing at a linear rate can be found by increasing the present value P of that series by $(1+r)^n$. The present value of a series commencing with the term A, and increasing each period by the amount B,

$$= P = a_{n|r}\left(\frac{B}{r}+A\right) - \frac{nB(1+r)^{-n}}{r} \qquad (1.8)$$

therefore

$$S = P(1+r)^n = a_{n|r}(1+r)^n\left(\frac{B}{r}+A\right) - \frac{nB}{r}$$

therefore

$$S = s_{n|r}\left(\frac{B}{r}+A\right) - \frac{nB}{r} \qquad (1.13)$$

4. CALCULATING YIELDS

a. *The Basic Approach*

In the preceding sections we have been concerned with the evaluation of various cash flows by means of finding their present or terminal values at a *given* rate of interest, and comparing these values with capital outlays to determine whether or not a certain investment is attractive. There will be many occasions, however, when it is more useful to know the rate of interest which will equate capital outlays and their resultant cash flows. This rate of interest is known as the *investment rate*, or more commonly, the *yield rate*.

The yield rate is that rate of interest which discounts the future cash flows generated by an investment down to the present value which exactly equals the cost of that investment. Put more formally, the yield rate is the solution r to the equation (1.3) where C is substituted for P.

$$C = \sum_{i=1}^{i=n} \frac{A_i}{(1+r)^i} \qquad (1.3)$$

where C is the initial capital, and A_i is the cash flow in year i.

Consider the following simple example. The outlay of £169 gives rise to a cash flow of £100 at the end of each of the next two years. What is the yield, i.e. what is the value of r in the following equation?

$$£169 = \frac{£100}{(1+r)} + \frac{£100}{(1+r)^2}$$

As the result of trial and error it will be found that $r = 12\%$ i.e. $£100/1\cdot12 + £100/1\cdot12^2 = £169$ approximately.

In this example, the periodic cash flow is constant, and so it is possible to derive the yield rate from $a_{n|r}$ tables. In all other cases, i.e. where the cash flows are irregular, it is necessary, by a process of trial and error, to discount each separate cash flow from $v_{n|r}$ tables until the rate of interest is found which exactly discounts the cash flows to the cost of the investment. With practice, it will be found that the yields of even the most irregular cash flows can be found after no more than three or four attempts. (Usually this will involve interpolation from the tables provided, and this matter is discussed further in Part II of this chapter.) An example will make this clearer.

Consider the following end year cash flows originating from an investment costing £6,273.

Years

1	2	3	4	5	6	7–11 inclusive	Total
£600	£1,000	£1,500	£1,800	£1,600	£1,400	£1,000 per year	£12,900

This is an irregular cash flow for the first six years, followed by a five year period of constant cash flows. To determine the true yield, it is necessary to estimate the likely yield, and discount at that rate of interest to see how close the resulting present value is to £6,273, and repeat the process until an accurate answer is achieved. Suppose the approximate yield is estimated at 17%. Using this rate, the cash flow would be discounted as follows:

Years	(1) Cash Flow	(2) 17% Discount Factors (from $v_{n|r}$ and $a_{n|r}$ Tables)	(3) Col. (1) × Col. (2)
	£		£
1	600	0·854701	512·8
2	1,000	0·730514	730·5
3	1,500	0·624371	936·6
4	1,800	0·533650	960·6
5	1,600	0·456111	729·8
6	1,400	0·389839	545·8
7–11	1,000 per year	1·24723*	1,247·2
Total	12,900		5,663·3

* (As the annual cash flow in the final five years is constant, a short cut is possible. The present value at the beginning of year 7 of £1,000 p.a. for five years is simply $£1,000 \times a_{5|17}$. Reducing this to the present value at the beginning of year 1, it is necessary to multiply by $v_{6|17}$. Thus $v_{6|17} \times a_{5|17} = 1\cdot24723$, which can be used as the discount factor for the years 7–11 inclusive.)

Comparing the resulting present value, £5,663·3 with the capital cost, £6,273, it is clear that too high a discount factor has been used. Hence, for the next calculation a lower factor would be selected. Suppose 14% is used. Using a procedure identical to that just shown, the resulting present value is £6,406·9 – i.e. more than the capital cost of £6,273. Clearly the correct answer lies between 14% and 17%, but nearer the former. Suppose therefore a 15% discount rate is used: the resulting present value will be £6,143·3. The answer is thus between 14% and 15%.

Using the method of linear interpolation (see Section 7b below)

Present value at 14%	=	£6,406·9
Present value at 15%	=	£6,143·3
Difference	=	£263·6
Present value at 14%	=	£6,406·9
Actual capital cost	=	£6,273·0
Difference	=	£133·9

Therefore, by linear interpolation, the unknown rate lies

$$\frac{133·9}{263·6} \times 1\% = 0·508\%$$

of the way between 14% and 15% = 14·508%, which should be rounded to the nearest tenth of a per cent. Hence the yield = 14·5%.

Bracketing the unknown yield with the smallest spread will, of course, provide the greatest possible accuracy, i.e. 1% in the tables provided in this book. Had we interpolated from the present values discounted at 14% and 17%, i.e. a 3% spread, the apparent yield would have been 14·540% compared to the 14·508% derived above. The correct yield is actually 14·500%.

Resort to tables to determine the yield is not simply a matter of convenience: for any investment giving rise to a cash flow in more than one period it is a matter of necessity as the value of *r* cannot be derived separately from equation (1.3). In certain cases it is possible, however, to obtain an approximate answer by use of certain formulae. A good example of this is the calculation of the yield to redemption on a bond.

b. *Yield to Redemption on a Bond*

A bond is a long term debt contract whereby the borrower agrees

c

to make a given number of constant fixed interest payments, at stated (usually regular) intervals, and to repay the sum borrowed at the end of the contract. For example, a company might issue £100 twenty year debentures at 5%, whereby it would make twenty end-year payments of £5, plus a terminal payment of £100 at the end of the twentieth year to repay the debt. This would be described as a 5% debenture or bond, and would be said to have a coupon or *bond rate* of 5%. The coupon or bond rate relates to the interest paid on the *face* value (or par value) of the bond.

When a bond is purchased for exactly its face value, then the yield rate will be equal to the bond rate. It will be apparent, however, that an investor may buy a bond at a price above or below its face value, in which case the yield rate and the bond rate will diverge. It can also diverge because not all bonds are redeemed at their face value, but at a premium to make them more attractive investments. Suppose an investor buys a twenty year bond with a face value of £1,000 and a coupon rate of 5%, when the bond has exactly ten more years to run, and suppose the purchase price is £926·4, i.e. less than the face value. For this expenditure the investor will receive ten end-year payments of £50 and a terminal payment of £1,000, giving rise to a capital gain of £73·6 over the purchase price. It is clear that this purchase will result in a yield greater than the 5% bond rate. The actual yield will be the solution r in the following equation:

$$£926·4 = £50\ a_{10|r} + £1,000\ v_{10|r}$$

It will be found that the value of r which satisfies this equation is 6% – that is the yield to redemption on this bond is 6%.

As stated above this equation has no exact algebraic solution, but because the cash flow is a series of regular payments plus a single terminal payment, this regular pattern permits the use of approximation formulae which can give sufficiently accurate answers for most purposes.

Three formulae will be given, beginning with the simplest but least accurate. The formulae have the following terms in common.

p_0 = the purchase price of the bond,
p_n = the redemption or terminal payment on the bond,
n = the period of the bond at which interest payments are made,
A = the amount of the interest payments per period, and
r = the annual yield on the bond.

(*i*) *Method of Averages*

$$r = \frac{nA + p_n - p_0}{\frac{1}{2}n(p_0 + p_n)} \qquad (1.14)$$

This method compares the average period gain (i.e. the interest payment plus the proportion of the capital gain per period) with the average capital invested (i.e. the straight average of the purchase price and the redemption payment).

In most cases where $r < 7\%$, the answer is accurate to within 1/10th of a per cent.

(*ii*)
$$r = \frac{A - \left(\dfrac{p_0 - p_n}{n}\right)}{p_n + \dfrac{n+1}{2n}(p_0 - p_n)} \qquad (1.15)$$

Where $r < 7\%$, this formula is accurate to within 1/100th of a per cent.

(*iii*)
$$r = \frac{A - \left(\dfrac{p_0 - p_n}{2}\right)\left(\dfrac{1}{s_{n|r_1}}\right)}{p_0} \qquad (1.16)$$

The r_1 in this expression is the best guess that can be made of r and should be found from either of the two previous formulae. This formula gives a very accurate estimate of the yield.

Where sufficiently detailed tables of $a_{n|r}$ and $v_{n|r}$ can be utilized, interpolation from the tables[1] to find r in the equation

$$p_0 = Aa_{n|r} + p_n v_{n|r}$$

can be the most practical method. Where use is made of this method, the tables should be entered for the value of r given by the first formula, the method of averages.

c. *The Yield on Shares*

The yield on shares is a term used in a number of senses, but most frequently it is used to refer to 'dividend' yield and 'earnings' yield. The dividend yield is the current (or more properly the *forecast*) dividend, gross of tax in the hands of an investor, as a proportion of the current share price. Similarly, the earnings yield is the current

---

[1] For a further brief discussion of interpolation see Part II of this Chapter.

(or more properly the forecast) earnings available for distribution as dividend as a proportion of the current share price. The two yields will, of course, differ as long as a firm is retaining any of its earnings which is the normal case. In share investment circles, particularly in Britain, both yields are sometimes referred to in terms of £100 invested at the current share price. Thus a 5% dividend yield would be referred to as £5%. The two concepts are also referred to as the 'dividend price ratio' and the 'earnings price ratio'. The latter is sometimes described as the 'price earnings ratio'. Thus a 10% earnings price ratio would be described as a 10 to 1 price earnings ratio.

It should be evident that the dividend yield means very little as a guide to the attractiveness of a share if the dividends of the company are expected to change significantly in the future. A shareholder will normally be anxious to know the return he can expect on his investment taking into account any possible change in future dividends and any capital appreciation or depreciation when he sells out. Similarly, but on a larger scale, a firm considering buying the shares of another firm will want to know the yield on its investment in these shares when it takes into account the future dividend stream it may receive from the company taken over. Indeed the attractiveness of the return will be the main reason for purchasing these shares.

In what follows we shall try to give some broad generalizations – in the shape of a formula – of the factors determining the rate of growth of dividends and on the yield offered by shares under certain general conditions. It is not suggested that these generalizations are ineluctable rules but only that they serve as useful guide posts to thinking about the highly complex and varying problems that arise in practice.

Consider the case of a firm retaining and re-investing a fixed proportion of its net of tax earnings. Assume

(i) the net of tax profitability of the existing business of the firm remains constant;
(ii) depreciation is realistically calculated (so that earnings are neither inflated nor deflated thereby);
(iii) that retained profits can be invested to earn a constant net of tax return.

Let the net earnings of the firm in some future year t be E_t, the proportion of earnings retained be p, and the yield on retained earnings be r. On the above assumptions, the net earnings in the following year, $t+1$, will be $E_t + prE_t$, where prE_t are the earnings resulting from the investment at r of the retained earnings pE_t of the previous year. Hence $E_{t+1} = E_t + prE_t = E_t(1+pr)$ and similarly $E_{t+2} = E_{t+1}(1+pr)$, etc. etc. Thus, the net earnings of each period are $(1+pr)$ greater than the net earnings of the previous period, and so net earnings are growing at the rate of pr per annum. In short, the rate of growth of net earnings is equal to the proportion of retained earnings times the rate of return earned thereon. Since dividends are assumed to be proportional to earnings, it follows that dividends are growing at the same rate.

Suppose a firm retains 50% of its earnings, and that the firm can earn 6% net of taxes on such re-invested funds, then earnings and thus dividends are growing at the rate of $50\% \times 6\% = 3\%$. Thus the problem resolves itself into a series of cash flows growing at a constant rate which terminates with the price received for the share when it is finally sold. The net of tax 'yield to redemption', or rather the net of tax yield as previously defined to mean the *discounted* yield, is the solution r to the equation

$$p_0 = \frac{A}{(1+r)} + \frac{A(1+g)}{(1+r)^2} + \frac{A(1+g)^2}{(1+r)^3} \cdots \frac{A(1+g)^{n-1}}{(1+r)^n} + \frac{p_n}{(1+r)^n}$$

$$= \frac{1}{(1+g)} \sum_{i=1}^{i=n} \frac{A(1+g)^i}{(1+r)^i} + \frac{p_n}{(1+r)^n} \tag{1.17}$$

where: p_0 is the price of the share at time $t = 0$;
$\quad$ p_n is the price of the share at time $t = n$, net of any tax levied thereon;
$\quad$ A is the dividend per share (net of tax in the hands of an investor) in the base period; and
$\quad$ g is the rate of growth of dividends derived by the method described in the previous paragraph.

If the share is not to be sold until some very distant date in the future, that is $n \to \infty$, then from the analysis of Section 2c, equation (1.7), $p_0 = A/(1+g)r_0$, where $r_0 = (r-g)/(1+g)$, therefore

$$r = \frac{A}{p_0} + g \tag{1.18}$$

By definition, A/p_0 is the dividend yield and we have therefore shown that the true yield on the shares is the existing yield plus the rate of growth.

Assume now that n is any positive number (that is, the shares are sold at any time in the future) and that the dividend yield of the shares remains constant. For the dividend yield to remain constant when dividends are growing at the rate g, it is obviously necessary for the price of the share also to increase at this rate. Hence $p_n = p_0(1+g)^n$. Substituting this value in (1.17) we obtain

$$p_0 = \frac{1}{(1+g)} \sum_{i=1}^{i=n} \frac{A(1+g)^i}{(1+r)^i} + \frac{p_0(1+g)^n}{(1+r)^n}$$

therefore

$$p_0 = \frac{A}{(1+g)r_0} \left[1 - \frac{1}{(1+r_0)^n} \right] + \frac{p_0}{(1+r_0)^n}$$

therefore

$$p_0 \left[1 - \frac{1}{(1+r_0)^n} \right] = \frac{A}{(1+g)r_0} \left[1 - \frac{1}{(1+r_0)^n} \right]$$

hence

$$p_0 = \frac{A}{(1+g)r_0}, \quad \text{where } r_0 = \frac{r-g}{1+g}$$

and

$$r = \frac{A}{p_0} + g$$

This is precisely the same result as was obtained in the previous case (1.18) when the purchaser of the share held the share for an infinitely long period. In other words we have shown that, providing the dividend yield of the shares remains constant, then the return to the shareholder is the same *irrespective of when he sells out*.[1]

It frequently arises, of course, that the dividend yield will not remain constant. The most frequent reasons for this are that the share was originally undervalued, or its future prospects appear to be markedly different from recent past experience, or alternatively that there are general new factors influencing the supply and demand for shares. The generalization can be made, however, that if (given all the other assumptions enumerated above) the dividend yield at the time the share is sold, is lower than in the base period (implying

[1] See also reference (1) for a similar derivation of the same formula and an extended discussion of its applications.

that the share price has risen at a higher rate than the growth in dividends), then the return will be more than the initial dividend yield plus the rate of growth. Conversely, if the dividend yield at the time the share is sold is higher than the base period, then the return will be lower than the initial dividend yield plus growth. It should be noted however, that substantial deviations are required from the dividend yield if the return is to be affected by a share price say more than 8–10 years hence.[1]

5. CONCLUSIONS

The above discussion provides a sufficiently detailed exposition of compounding and discounting appropriate to most of the subject matter of this book. Part II of this chapter deals with certain points in somewhat greater detail, including compounding and discounting for periods of less than a year and also continuous compounding and discounting. There is also a discussion of practical discounting matters, including interpolation and the accuracy of yearly discounting. But it does not deal with many of the complex and detailed matters necessary for a full understanding of financial mathematics, in particular the handling of fractions of periods, interest payments occurring at other than the exact end of the period to which they refer, short cut methods, and other variables. For an understanding of these matters, readers should consult any basic textbook on financial mathematics.[2]

II

6. THE COMPOUNDING AND DISCOUNT PERIOD

a. *Compounding at Discrete Intervals of other than a year*

In Part I of this chapter we adopted the convention of discounting for a yearly period. All capital outlays were assumed to occur at exactly the start of a year, and all cash flows at the end of a year.

---

[1] For tables computing discounted yields under a variety of assumptions concerning growth, readers are recommended to consult reference (2).

[2] For this purpose the authors' preference is for the lucid and comprehensive work by Hummel and Seebeck, reference (3). An important feature of this book is the comprehensive tables for fractional rates of interest up to 8%. It also contains a very large number of problems (and answers) for the practice of readers.

To denote this yearly interest rate we adopted the symbol r. We shall now consider how to deal with discount periods of less than a year, and we shall make use of the following standard notation:

P = the initial outlay, or present value of S;

S = the compound amount of P, or terminal value;

n = the total number of years;

m = the number of compoundings or conversion periods per year;

j = the nominal yearly interest rate to be converted m times per year; and

i = the interest rate per conversion period = j/m.

Suppose it is desired to find the amount to which £10,000 would grow in one year at 6% compounded semi-annually. We should describe the yearly nominal rate (usually referred to as simply the nominal rate) j as equal to 6%, but to distinguish the fact that interest is to be compounded semi-annually, we should write $j_2 = 6\%$. As the interest is to be reckoned twice yearly, i.e. $m = 2$, then the interest rate per conversion period is $j/m = 6\%/2 = 3\%$, i.e. $i = 3\%$. We have already shown that for a yearly interest rate r that $S = P(1+r)^n$, so by extension for any other interest rate $S = P(1+i)^n$. Thus the amount S to which £10,000 will grow in one year at $j_2 = 6\%$ is simply

$$S = £10,000\,(1+i)^2 = £10,000(1 \cdot 03)^2 = £10,609$$

It will be clear that £10,000 will grow in one year at 6% compounded semi-annually to the same sum as it would grow in two years at 3% compounded annually – in both cases the principal would be increased by $(1 \cdot 03)^2$. It will also be clear that any sum will grow more rapidly at any given nominal interest rate the more conversion periods there are per year. Had the £10,000 been compounded only once at 6%, i.e. $r = j_1 = 6\%$, it would have grown only to £10,600, compared to the £10,609 for semi-annual compounding. Compounded quarterly, i.e. $j_4 = 6\%$, it would have grown to £10,613·6, and monthly, i.e. $j_{12} = 6\%$, to £10,616 etc., etc. The reason why an amount at a given notional interest rate increases the more conversion periods per year is that the interim interest payments themselves attract interest. In the case of the semi-annual conversion, the mid-year interest payment of £300 itself bears interest at 3% in the second period to account for the £9 difference compared to the yearly 6% compounding. All this is fairly obvious, just as it is fairly obvious that the tables for values of r per year are interchangeable with the tables for values of i per period.

Consider now the relationship between j and i on the one hand, and r on the other. So far we have designated r as the yearly interest rate, and by this we have meant, although we have not stated this explicitly, the yearly *effective* rate – i.e. the amount by which a sum would grow during a year, regardless of the number of conversion periods. In the example just quoted, for instance, where $j_2 = 6\%$, the £10,000 increased to £10,609, i.e. by $6\cdot09\%$. Thus where $j_2 = 6\%$, $r = 6\cdot09\%$, where $j_4 = 6\%$ it is $6\cdot136\%$, etc., etc. From this it is clear by definition that

$$(1+r) = \left(1+\frac{j}{m}\right)^m = (1+i)^m$$

therefore

$$r = \left(1+\frac{j}{m}\right)^m - 1 = (1+i)^m - 1 \qquad (1.19)$$

and conversely

$$\frac{j}{m} = i = {}^m\sqrt{(1+r)} - 1 \qquad (1.20)$$

By using these relationships, it is possible to convert all previously derived formulae for yearly effective rates of interest into formulae where interest is converted more frequently. Thus the formula for the present value of an annuity of a nominal interest rate of j_m, =

$$P = \frac{1-\left(1+\dfrac{j}{m}\right)^{-mn}}{j/m} \qquad (1.21)$$

In the example we considered compounding on a semi-annual basis, but from the formula it is apparent that we can adapt them to compounding at shorter intervals, e.g. quarterly, monthly, weekly, and even daily. In the limit compounding may be performed for such vanishingly small intervals of time that the compounding becomes continuous.

b. *Continuous Compounding*

For interest to be compounded continuously is equivalent to saying it is compounded m times per period where m tends to infinity.

Where this occurs it can be shown that

$$\left(1 + \frac{j}{m}\right)^{mn} = e^{jn} \tag{1.22}$$

where e is the conventional symbol for the number $2 \cdot 71828$ known as the exponential function which forms the basis of natural or napierian logarithms. Thus in the example we have been using, where $j_m = 6\%$ and $n = 1$, it can be shown that where $m \to \infty$, the £10,000 will increase to £10,000 $\times e^{jn}$,

$$= £10,000 \times 2 \cdot 71828^{0 \cdot 06},$$

$$= £10,618 \cdot 4.$$

This compares with £10,600 resulting from compounding annually at 6%.

It is important to be clear as to the significance of continuous compounding or discounting in capital budgeting. It is extremely rare that lenders ever express their interest requirements in continuous form. A firm however, may conceivably have such use for its funds that it can effectively compound continuously by its continuous re-investment in projects. An example may make clear the numerical effect of continuous re-investment.

Suppose a firm has a one year project offering a return (on the basis of end-year discounting) of 6%. The project consists of an outlay of £100,000 now and a cash flow over the following year of £106,000, this amount arising evenly over the period – e.g. at the rate of £106,000/365 per day.

Suppose the firm could obtain borrowed capital at a cost of 6% (paid annually) and that it could re-invest funds generated by the project at 6%. It might seem that the firm would exactly break even on this project – that is the £106,000 would exactly repay capital and interest at the end of the year. But from our previous discussion it is apparent that if the funds arise continuously throughout the year and the firm re-invests them at 6% these funds will have accumulated to £106,184 by end year. The firm therefore will not exactly break even but will show a profit of £184.

This points to the fact that where continuous discounting is used the standard of comparison – in this case the cost of capital – should be expressed in terms of continuous discounting also, although the difference this makes will seldom be of any significance. The other point to be borne in mind is that the validity of continuous discounting in capital budgeting turns on the assumption that a firm has some continuous use for its funds. This point is taken up in the following sub-section.

c. *Choosing the Appropriate Discount Period*

In the previous discussions we have considered compounding and discounting for the discrete period of a year, for discrete periods of fractions of a year, and finally on a continuous basis. The problem now to be considered is how to choose between these various alternative methods.

i. Yearly discounting. This approach, that of assuming all sums arise end-year or mid-year on average, is the one we recommend for the appraisal of most capital projects. Used sensibly, in the way to be discussed below (Section 7), it is sufficiently accurate for the appraisal of virtually all types of capital projects subject to risk, and tables A, B, and C at the end of the book will suffice for nearly all likely calculations.

ii. Discrete Discounting for Periods of less than a Year. This approach is appropriate to calculating the interest on loans, especially short term loans, the yield to redemption on bonds etc., in fact in all those situations where risk is at a minimum and it is therefore important to know the exact effective rate of *fixed* interest being paid or earned. This is essentially the province of financial mathematics (see reference (2)), and is not therefore the direct concern of this book.

iii. Continuous Discounting. This is the approach used in theoretical economics primarily for its convenience in mathematical analysis. It is sometimes considered, however, that continuous discounting would be a more accurate way of evaluating the cash flows. While this is generally true, it is not true in the sense that continuous discounting based on the assumption of regular accrual over the year would necessarily give a more accurate answer. This might be seen if we reflect on the exact incidence of cash payments associated with a cash project and the effect this may have on its evaluation. Many of the cash flows both in and out of a business will, of course, be markedly irregular. For example, customers will normally pay at discrete intervals of one month. Similarly, suppliers will normally need to be paid at roughly the same interval (although there may typically be as much as one to three weeks difference in 'phase' between these payments, depending on a firm's credit policy). Employees' wages will need to be paid regularly at weekly or monthly intervals, etc. . . . Tax payments, at least in Britain, will occur at markedly discrete intervals, usually of the order of six months. To evaluate this real situation as compared with that of assuming all payments to occur mid-year or end-year would require a careful analysis to determine precisely what the firm would be prepared to pay mid-year or end-year for the advantages (if any) of receiving the actual irregular series of cash flows associated with the project compared with the assumed mid-year or end-year payments. If the actual inflows and outflows were exactly in phase, a firm would have a regular amount of cash over the year, rather than simply mid-year or end-year. The question to be considered would then be the use to which the firm would put such cash. The answer to this will depend very much on the seasonal and irregular variations in the company's supply and demand for cash. For example, the incidence of capital expenditure may be particularly high in the first half of the year and at end-year. The firm may use a bank overdraft to tide it over these periods of irregular demands on capital. If this were the case, the advantages accruing from a regular series of net payments (rather than mid-year or end-year) might be that it would help even out this irregularity, thus saving bank over-draft interest. At the other extreme, a firm might immediately be able to plough the cash into investments earning considerably higher returns. The correct rate of discount to assume will probably be between these two extremes but varying according to circumstances. In fact, as we have noted, there will be marked irregularities in the series of cash flows from most projects. The most important of these will be tax, dividend, and interest payments. Strict accuracy would demand that these marked irregularities be taken into account particularly in their effect on a firm's overall supply and demand for cash.

From these considerations it will be seen that simply assuming that the net cash flow arises regularly over the year and assuming that the rate of return advantages accruing from this are as high as the normal return on equity capital may give a result of no greater real accuracy than mid-year or end-year discrete discounting and indeed may be even less accurate. For this reason we recommend using annual discounting only, unless special circumstances justify a shorter interval (see Section 7 below). Where cash flows arise fairly regularly over a year, we would recommend assuming that they arise mid-year on average. This will be found to be quite accurate for all practical purposes especially when it is borne in mind (see Chapters 3 and 4) that a firm's cost of capital can seldom be defined to an accuracy greater than one half of one per cent.

7. PRACTICAL DISCOUNTING

a. *The Accuracy of Yearly Discounting*

In practice it seldom happens that the capital outlay necessary to commence a project is spent at a single moment of time, and that income starts to flow from it immediately. Typically, capital outlays will be made over a period of months or even years, and income will only arise after a period during which the new equipment will be installed, run in, and slowly put on a full production basis. From this it will be seen that some adaptation of the actual data is necessary if the yearly discounting tables provided are to be used satisfactorily.

Consider first how to deal with capital outlays spread over a period. Suppose £1,000,000 is being spent fairly evenly over a two year period. For convenience, we need to be able to find the equivalent capital sum which would have to be spent at the very start of the two years. Suppose our cost of capital is $r = 8\%$. As an approximation to the fact that £1,000,000 is spent fairly evenly over two years, let us assume whether this is equivalent to £500,000 spent mid-year in each of the two years. We can discount the expenditure in the middle of the second year down to the middle of the first year by discounting at $8\% = £500,000v_{1|8} = £462,963$. Thus the equivalent expenditure of £1,000,000 over two years can be equated at $r = 8\%$ to £500,000 + £462,963 = £962,963 in the middle of the first year. This sum in turn can be reduced to the start of the first year by discounting for 6 months at the discount rate equivalent to the yearly rate $r = 8\%$. This rate as set out in equation (1.20) $= \sqrt{(1 \cdot 08)} - 1 = 3 \cdot 923\%$.

Therefore the equivalent capital sum at the start of the period

$$= \frac{£962,963}{1 \cdot 03923} = £926,612.$$

As $\sqrt{(1 \cdot 08)} - 1 = 0 \cdot 03923$ is so close to $(0 \cdot 08 \div 2) = 0 \cdot 04$, it is an unnecessary refinement to justify the bother of calculating, especially when it will be seen later (in Chapters 3 and 4) that it is seldom possible to define the cost of capital to the accuracy of the nearest tenth of a per cent, or indeed the nearest half of a per cent. As it also gives a spurious impression of accuracy, it will be dispensed with in the practical applications in this book.[1]

In even the best planned projects, the timing of capital outlays is subject to significant errors. Few engineers would care to be held to a narrower band than $\pm 10\%$ in any particular month of a yearly forecast, or $\pm 5\%$ in the yearly forecast as a whole. Hence, if it is desired to err on the side of caution in finding the present value equivalent of a series of capital outlays, such outlays should be assumed to occur somewhat earlier than planned. For instance, if capital outlays are forecast on a quarterly basis for say two years, with expenditure occurring on average at the middle of the periods, they could be assumed to occur at the beginning of the periods and discounted accordingly. Just how much forecast capital outlays should be advanced is a matter of judgement to be acquired with experience.

A similar procedure should be followed in discounting the forecast income or cash flows from an investment. When they can be forecast to occur fairly evenly over a year, it is usually satisfactory for most purposes to assume that they actually occur mid-year. The accuracy of forecast cash flows hardly ever justifies a greater refinement than this.

In the interests of caution, it is sometimes advisable to assume that cash flows arising on average mid-year are discounted on an end-year basis to give a somewhat lower present value or yield. As just mentioned in the discussion of discounting capital outlays, the amount of such an allowance is a matter of experience. Some simple examples will illustrate the point.

Consider the sum of £1,000 arising during the course of a year. If the yearly discount rate is $r = 10\%$, and the sum is assumed to arise mid-year, its present value is £953·5. If the sum is conservatively calculated to arise at the end of the year, the present value falls to £909·1, i.e. by 4·65%. Conversely, if the present value of the

---

[1] Had we assumed that the capital expenditure was incurred evenly at the end of every month for the two years, then by discounting at the rate $i = {}^{12}\sqrt{1\cdot08} - 1 = 0\cdot006434$, the present value equivalent at the start of the two periods would have been £923,874, a difference of £2,738 to that computed on a mid-year basis, a difference of less than a tenth of a per cent. Given that r can almost never be defined to an accuracy as great as the tenth of a per cent, and that capital expenditure can seldom be forecast accurately on a monthly basis, it is clear that a mid-year refinement is accurate for most practical purposes.

£1,000 is given as £953·5, but the single cash flow of £1,000 is conservatively assumed to arise end-year, the yield drops from $r = 10\%$, to $r = 4·9\%$.

If the £1,000 is assumed to arise each year for ten years, its present value at $r = 10\%$ is £6,444·5 if the £1,000's are assumed to arise mid-year, compared to £6,144·6 if arising end-year – again the present value falls by 4·65%. Conversely, if the cash flow cost £6,444·5 to initiate and the £1,000 cash flows arose only end-year, the yield would be $r = 8·9\%$.

Finally, a perpetuity of £1,000 p.a. would at $r = 10\%$ have a present value of £10,488 on a mid-year basis compared to £10,000 on an end-year basis, again a decline of 4·65%. Assuming this perpetuity cost £10,488 to initiate, the end-year cash flow case would give a yield of $r = 9·53\%$.

Thus, it will be seen that the percentage difference in present value in the case of a regular net cash flow is constant, regardless of the period assumed as between mid-year and end-year series, but the difference in yield declines as the period increases.

As in the case of capital outlays, the use of end-period discounting rather than mid-period discounting on grounds of caution is a matter for experienced judgment. The difference it makes can easily be quantified in cases of doubt.

b. *Interpolation*

The discount and compounding tables provided in the Appendix are for values of r in 1% steps. Sometimes it will be found necessary to find present values or compound amounts for intermediate values of r and n, e.g. 13·2% or $7\frac{1}{2}$ years. Also, when using the tables to determine yields, the value of r will usually fall between the entries provided in the tables, and sometimes the period will not coincide exactly with the period of n. In these cases three courses are available.

(i) For values of r up to 8%–10%, reference can be made to standard financial tables which give a large range of intermediate values for r, and conversion periods in excess of the 50 provided in this book.

(ii) In all cases, but especially those in excess of $r = 10\%$, resort can be had to seven figure logarithms in solving for appropriate values of $v_{n|r}$, $a_{n|r}$, and $s_{n|r}$.

(iii) The approximate method of linear interpolation (as set out in Section 4 above) can be used from the tables provided.

For the practical purposes of the assessment of investments in risk situations, this last method will be found sufficiently accurate.[1]

[1] To estimate the amount of error involved in any particular calculation, readers are referred to [3] especially pp. 177–194, or any similar textbook.

REFERENCES

1. MYRON J. GORDON and ELI SHAPIRO, 'Capital Equipment Analysis: Required Rate of Profit', *Management Science*, October 1956.
2. GEORGE E. BATES, 'Comprehensive Stock Value Tables', *Harvard Business Review*, January–February 1962.
3. PAUL M. HUMMEL and CHARLES L. SEEBECK, *Mathematics of Finance*. Second edition, McGraw Hill, 1956.

CHAPTER TWO
Methods of Investment Appraisal

The previous chapter was concerned with the strict derivation of basic discounting and compounding formulae. This chapter is concerned with describing and illustrating the three main discounting methods of investment appraisal recommended in economic theory and extensively used in practice, and with rigorously defining all the terms basic to these methods such as 'cash flows'. A detailed comparison of the uses and advantages of the three methods is postponed to Chapter 5, for much of the discussion turns on our understanding of the cost of capital to a firm which is itself dependent on the firm's financial policy. This forms the subject of the two intervening chapters.

Every firm must pay its shareholders, bond holders, and short term lenders for the amount of the capital they provide, and for the period that it is so provided. Establishing a firm's cost of capital is often a complicated matter. For our present purposes, however, it will be assumed that the firm's relevant cost of capital has been determined and, further, that this cost of capital is constant over all relevant future periods. Armed with this cost of capital, which is effectively the exchange rate between present and future sums of money, it is possible to evaluate future cash flows associated with different investment projects.

1. THE MAIN DISCOUNTING METHODS

There are three main discounting methods recommended in economic theory and used in practice: the net present value method (referred to henceforth as NPV), the yield method, and the annual capital charge method. The last named is probably much less commonly used than either of the other two, but it is used in certain types of industries where long term operating costs tend to be stable. Further it is commonly employed in the Nationalized Industries in Britain.

The areas in which all three methods can be used continuously overlap, especially NPV and yield, which for the most part are interchangeable. To aid in their exposition we shall consider them in relationship to a simple example. A three year project involves a net capital outlay of £1,000 at the start of the first year and gives rise to annual *incremental* cash receipts (called 'net cash flows') of £388 arising on average end-year for each of the three years. Consider how this project will be evaluated by each of the three methods in turn, assuming the firm has a 5% net of tax cost of capital. (All calculations will be rounded to the nearest £.)

a. *Net Present Value*

This is the classic economic method of investment appraisal and is of impeccable ancestry. The *present* value P of any project is found by discounting at the firm's cost of capital all future net cash flows to their present value equivalent. Assuming a project gives rise to end-year cash flows designated by the symbol A at the end of each of three years, and that the firm's cost of capital is $r\%$, then

$$P = \frac{A_1}{(1+r)} + \frac{A_2}{(1+r)^2} + \frac{A_3}{(1+r)^3}$$

This can more conveniently be written as

$$P = \sum_{i=1}^{i=3} \frac{A_i}{(1+r)^i}$$

where, to repeat, Σ, known as the summation symbol, sigma, indicates that the numbers are to be added up. The $i = 1$ beneath the sigma indicates that A_1 is the first of the numbers, and the $i = 3$ indicates that A_3 is the last of the numbers in the sum. It is understood that the numbers to be added run through all the numbers from 1 to 3 inclusive. More generally, the present value formula is written as

$$P = \sum_{i=1}^{i=n} \frac{A_i}{(1+r)^i} \tag{1.3}$$

where A_i is the net cash flow at the end of year i, where the project has a life of n years, and r is the firm's cost of capital. The *net* present value is found by subtracting the capital cost C of initiating the project, thus the net present value = $(P-C)$. The equation can thus be rewritten to give the NPV as

$$\text{NPV} = \sum_{i=1}^{i=n} \frac{A_i}{(1+r)^i} - C \tag{2.1}$$

Where the capital outlays occur over more than one period, the C in the above equation should refer only to the initial capital outlay, all other capital outlays being incorporated into the net cash flows of future periods, thus some of the A_i's could be negative.

Where the net cash flows arising from a project are risk free (or at a degree of risk adequately reflected in the rate of discount), then any project giving rise to a positive NPV should be accepted in that it will increase the profitability of the firm. (Where two or more projects are mutually exclusive it may pay the firm to accept one of the other projects instead, which would increase profitability even more. This is fully discussed in Chapter 5, Section 1b.ii.)

Applying the above formula to the example where $C = £1,000$, $A_i = £388$ for all years, $n = 3$, and $r = 5\%$, then

$$\text{NPV} = \frac{£388}{1 \cdot 05} + \frac{£388}{1 \cdot 05^2} + \frac{£388}{1 \cdot 05^3} - £1,000 = £57$$

i.e. the project has a positive NPV and should therefore be accepted.

Because the A_i's are constant for each year, the same result could have been calculated by using the formula for the present value of an annuity (1.4). Thus

$$\text{NPV} = A a_{n|r} - C$$
$$= (£388 \times a_{3|5}) - £1,000$$
$$= £1,057 - £1,000 = £57$$

It is important to be clear on the meaning that can be attached to the NPV of £57 in the above calculations. Continuing the assumption that the net cash flows are risk free, then £57 represents the immediate increase in the firm's wealth which will result from accepting the project. It is equivalent to a capital gain as yet unrealized. It represents the price at which the firm would be willing to sell to a third party the right to initiate or exploit the project. Finally, if the firm could freely raise capital at 5% interest,[1] it

[1] This assumption is of course unrealistic but this fact has no bearing on the simple point of interpretation of the NPV method which we are trying to establish here.

represents the amount the firm could raise (in addition to the initial capital outlay C) to distribute immediately to its shareholders and by the end of the project's life have paid off all the capital raised plus interest on it at 5%. This can be appreciated as follows.

The firm borrows £1,057, spends £1,000 of this on initiating the project, and pays the remaining £57 out to its shareholders. The net cash flows are exactly sufficient to pay off the total debt of £1,057 plus interest at 5% on the outstanding balance in three equal annual instalments, thus:

Years	Opening Balance	Plus Interest at 5%	Total Debt Outstanding Year End	Less Repayments from Net Cash Flow	Closing Balance
	£	£	£	£	£
1	1,057	+53	1,110	−388	= 722
2	722	+36	758	−388	= 370
3	370	+18	388	−388	= —

Where the net cash flows are at risk, these interpretations must be modified. Under these circumstances the NPV represents the firm's *prospective* increase in wealth from undertaking the project, the *prospective* unrealized capital gain. It also represents the maximum value the firm could place on its rights to exploit the project, and the maximum amount it could borrow for distribution to its shareholders and break even by the end of the life of the project.

b. *Yield*

The yield method[1] (see Chapter 1, Section 4) is of later derivation in economic theory (late 19th century) than present value, but it has an impressive pedigree including both Fisher and Keynes amongst its exponents. One of its variants, the yield to redemption on a bond (Chapter 1, Section 4b), has an even longer pedigree, having been used for centuries in banking and investment circles.

The yield on an investment project is defined as the rate of 'interest' which discounts the future net cash flows of a project into equality with its capital cost; that is, it is the rate of 'interest' which results in a zero NPV. Put formally, the yield on an investment is

---

[1] The method is known under a variety of names including rate of return (Fisher), marginal efficiency of capital (Keynes), discounted cash flow (Dean), internal rate of return (Boulding), actuarial return, interest rate of return, and the investor's method.

the solution r to the following equation:

$$C = \sum_{i=1}^{i=n} \frac{A_i}{(1+r)^i} \qquad (1.3)$$

where the symbols are as previously defined.

As with NPV, when the capital outlays occur over more than one period, the C in the above equation should refer only to the initial capital outlay, all other capital outlays being incorporated into the net cash flows of future periods. This means that some of the A_i's could be negative. As long as *all* the negative net cash flows always occur prior to the positive net cash flows, the above equation can be used with complete confidence. But where any negative net cash flows occur subsequently to positive ones care must be exercised since in certain cases this may deprive the yield of any useful meaning. This possibility, which is often held to be a serious shortcoming of the discounted yield, is discussed in Chapter 5, Section 2, where the problem is fully considered and a method of satisfactorily overcoming it set out. In the rest of this chapter it is assumed that the rather rare conditions which would result in the yield becoming meaningless do not hold.

Subject to the qualification just mentioned, when the net cash flows from a project are risk free, then any project giving rise to a yield greater than the firm's cost of capital should be accepted on the grounds that it will increase the profitability of the firm. More realistically, a project should be accepted if the degree of risk is held to be adequately compensated for in the resulting yield. (Where two or more projects are mutually exclusive a simple comparison of yields may well lead to accepting the wrong project. In this situation it is necessary to subtract the capital outlays and net cash flows on one project from those of another and compute the differential yield. This too is fully discussed in Chapter 5, Section 1b.)

Applying the above formula to the example, it is found that the value of r which satisfies the equation

$$£1,000 = \sum_{i=1}^{i=3} \frac{£388}{(1+r)^i}, \quad \text{is } 0{\cdot}08 \text{ or } 8\%$$

Where the net cash flows are irregular, it is necessary, as pointed out previously (Chapter 1, Section 4), to solve for r by trial and error using the $v_{n|r}$ tables (Table A at the end of the book). In this particular case where the net cash flows are constant, it is of course possible to interpolate from the $a_{n|r}$ tables (Table B) by finding the nearest value of C/A_i for the period of the project.

It is important to be clear of the meaning that can be attached to the yield of 8% on the project. Assuming the net cash flows to be risk free, 8% represents the highest net of tax rate at which the firm could raise money on this project and not lose thereby, *providing* the firm has the option to repay the capital at will. This is equivalent to saying that it is the break even net of tax rate of borrowing on bank overdraft terms. An alternative interpretation, which amounts to the same thing, is that the yield on a project is the rate of return on capital outstanding per period while it is invested in the project. These interpretations can be demonstrated as follows.

Suppose the firm borrows £1,000 on bank overdraft terms (i.e. paying interest only on the outstanding balance of the loan) at 8% net of tax to finance the project. It can be shown that it will exactly break even.

Years	Opening Balance (Capital Outstanding in Project)	Plus Interest at 8%	Total Debt Outstanding Year End	Less Repayments from Net Cash Flow	Closing Balance
	£	£	£	£	£
1	1,000	+80	1,080	−388	= 692
2	692	+55	747	−388	= 359
3	359	+29	388	−388	= —

Thus the firm would exactly break even on an 8% overdraft type loan, and as each £ of outstanding loan earned 8%, then by definition, the return per unit of capital was 8% per period outstanding.

This interpretation of yield may be demonstrated more generally. Each A_i may be thought of as representing a repayment of capital, X_i, plus the compound rate of return earned on this capital for the i years for which it has been invested in the project. (The return or interest of earlier years is notionally deferred, and added to the amount of capital outstanding.) Thus $X_i(1+r)^i = A_i$, and $X_i = A_i/(1+r)^i$. From equation (1.3) the sum of the n capital payments, X_i, is equal to the initial capital invested, C, and thus this interpretation leads logically to the full repayment of capital. Each element of capital X_i still outstanding in the project is earning the rate of return r. It thus follows that r is the rate of return earned per unit of capital per period, and is the break-even rate for financing the project on conventional bank overdraft terms.

c. *Annual Capital Charge*

Whenever a capital investment is made which gives rise to a constant (or approximately constant) net cash flow it is possible to make use of the annual capital charge method (also known as the annuity method) of discounting.[1] As such it is commonly used in public utilities, in the British nationalized industries and in some property companies.

The annual capital charge method, in common with the other two discounting methods, recognizes that these are two costs associated with the use of capital, 'interest' on the capital employed and depreciation (the recovery of capital apart from any residual values). To determine whether any investment is profitable, it must be calculated whether the net cash flow is sufficient to cover the depreciation and the minimum acceptable 'interest' cost (cost of capital). The present value method does this by discounting the net cash flows at this minimum 'interest' rate to determine whether the present value of the future net cash flows exceed the initial cost of investment. The yield method consists in finding the 'interest' rate which reduces the net cash flow into equality with the initial cost, and then comparing this rate with the minimum 'interest' rate. If the first method results in a net present value over initial cost, or the second method results in a yield in excess of the minimum cost of capital, then, subject to the qualifications mentioned, the project is acceptable.

The annual capital charge method achieves the same result by calculating the average annual charge (depreciation plus interest) and comparing this with the annual net cash flow (which is of course assumed to be constant from year to year). If the net cash flow exceeds the capital charge then the project is acceptable.

In simple terms, the annual capital charge formula aims at charging depreciation on a sinking fund basis such that the full capital invested in a project will be recovered *at the end* of the project's life. (Depreciation need only be charged on the sinking fund basis – which involves the aggregate annual depreciation provisions being less than the total initial capital to be depreciated – because, notionally,

---

[1] The method can in fact be used even when investments give rise to irregular cash flows, by turning such cash flows into constant annual equivalents – see Chapter 5, Section 3b. But where cash flows are irregular it is more common to use either the NPV or yield method.

the annual depreciation provisions can be re-invested at the firm's cost of capital in the interval between being set aside and the end of the project's life – see Chapter 1, Section 3a.) Also, it charges 'interest' on the full initial capital. The reason for this is that, as the initial capital is deemed to be recovered only at the end of the project's life, 'interest' is due on it for every year of the project's life.

The essentially different feature of the annual charge method is its use of the sinking fund method of depreciation. This probably derives from the fact that the enterprises using it typically are largely, if not entirely, financed by debt capital and often make formal provision for the redemption of capital via sinking funds. The realism of the method in view of the special financial position of the industries using it will be briefly considered in Chapter 5, Section 3b.

The annual capital charge is built up as follows.

Provision of annual depreciation on a sinking fund basis

It has been shown that the investment of £1 per annum, end-year, for n years accumulates to the sum s according to the formula

$$s_{n|r} = \frac{(1+r)^n - 1}{r} \tag{1.11}$$

therefore the annual investment necessary to accumulate £1 at the end of n years is simply

$$\frac{1}{s_{n|r}} \tag{2.2}$$

therefore the annual investment necessary to provide the sum C at the end of n years is simply

$$\frac{C}{s_{n|r}}$$

which when fully written out

$$= \frac{Cr}{(1+r)^n - 1}$$

The interest cost of capital

As the whole capital sum C is not returned until the end of the project's life, the sum C is continuously invested, and so the annual interest charges is a constant Cr.

The total annual capital charge

This is found simply by adding together the depreciation charge and interest cost. Using N as the symbol to denote this total annual capital charge, then:

$$N = \frac{Cr}{(1+r)^n - 1} + Cr$$

$$= \frac{Cr(1+r)^n}{(1+r)^n - 1}$$

Assuming $C = 1$, the formula would be written generally as

$$N = \frac{r(1+r)^n}{(1+r)^n - 1} \tag{2.3}$$

In applying the above formula, it should be noted that it assumes that the whole of the initial capital C is depreciated. Where any of the initial capital is recovered at the end of a project's life (such as working capital, land, scrap value of machines) then the true annual cost is found by using the above formula for the depreciable capital, and adding to it the annual interest charge for the non-depreciable element. Thus where the total capital C can be split into a depreciable element C_d and a non-depreciable element C_n, the total annual cost is simply

$$N = \frac{C_d r(1+r)^n}{(1+r)^n - 1} + C_n r \tag{2.4}$$

Consider now the example used to demonstrate the other two discounting methods. As the residual value of the assets is assumed to be zero, the formula (2.3) is the appropriate one to use. Thus the annual cost is

$$N = \frac{(\pounds 1{,}000 \times 5\%)(1 \cdot 05)^3}{1 \cdot 05^3 - 1}$$

$$= \pounds 367$$

As this is less than the annual net cash flow of $\pounds 388$, then in the absence of risk the project should be accepted. (The same remarks concerning mutually exclusive projects which were made previously in connection with the NPV method apply here.) Where the net cash flow is at risk, it is necessary to consider whether the margin between the net cash flow and the annual capital charge is sufficient to compensate for the risks involved.

A further discussion of the annual charge method and in particular its relation to the other main discounting methods is given in Chapter 5, Section 3. This subsequent discussion is likely to be of interest only to specialists, particularly those who apply the method, or a variant of it, in practice.

We turn now to the task of rigorously defining the basic terms used in the discounting methods.

2. DEFINING THE BASIC TERMS

The logic underlying the methods of analysis discussed in the previous section determines the precise data to be used in their application. Thus all three methods take explicit account of the need to recover the capital outlays in full. In the NPV method all future cash receipts are brought to a present value equivalent from which the initial capital outlay is deducted, thus ensuring the full recovery of capital. Similarly, the yield method involves determining the maximum rate of return the project will generate and still provide for the full recovery of the initial capital. Hence, as both methods automatically imply the full recovery of capital, there is no need to deduct any allowance for depreciation from the cash flows entering into the discussion. The same is true of the annual capital charge method which involves a single charge embracing 'interest' and a sinking fund depreciation provision to recover initial capital outlay in full.[1]

It is also apparent that the time element is critical to all the methods. Hence, cash receipts and payments must be considered at the time they actually occur rather than at the time accounting provision is made for them. For example, in Britain income tax is collected from companies some 12 to 18 months after the date on which the liability is incurred. Accounting provision is normally made at the end of the period (usually of a year) in which the liability

[1] As long as the annual cash flow is sufficient to cover the total annual charge for a zero rate of interest – at which rate the depreciation charge would of course be the same as for straight line depreciation, that is, initial capital divided by the number of years of the project's life – the method will provide for the full recovery of initial capital and so no further deduction from the annual cash flow is called for.

was incurred. If the cash flows entering into the present value or yield calculation were based on the accounting figures, therefore they would not reflect the fact that the firm does not actually pay the tax until some 12 to 18 months after provision has been made for it and hence would not fully reflect the actual advantage in the timing of cash outlays associated with the project. With these basic principles in mind, we can now define more fully the precise elements entering into the formulae.

a. *Cash Flows*

The cash flows or, to use the more common term, the 'net cash flows', associated with a given capital project, may be defined as the *incremental* cash receipts and expenditures solely attributable to the commencement of the project. Cash expenditures, or negative net cash flows, typically comprise the capital outlays necessary to commence a project or replace major capital items during the project's life. They can also consist of operating losses or terminal expenditures of a capital nature such as restoring agricultural land after open pit or strip mining operations. Cash receipts, or positive net cash flows, comprise the incremental cash inflows such as profit, rent, and depreciation. These two types of net cash flows are considered in turn.

i. Capital outlays. Henceforth, negative net cash flows will typically be referred to as 'capital outlays', and the term net cash flow will generally be used to indicate only cash *receipts* or *positive* net cash flows.

In determining all the relevant capital outlays associated with a project, it is important to have regard only to the incremental outlays attributable to it. For example, if a firm buys a large new factory to manufacture a new product, but part of the factory is used to increase the production of an existing product, the whole cost of the new factory should not necessarily be attributed to the new product. Suppose the new factory costs £100,000 but it can be shown that if it is decided not to go ahead with the new product the firm would spend only £20,000 buying a smaller factory to provide the extra manufacturing capacity for the existing product. In such a case, the capital outlay attributable to the new product would be only the incremental or net outlay involved, the £80,000. Conversely, if no extra capacity would otherwise be bought to increase the output of the existing product, but it merely happens that the large new factory has spare capacity that will not otherwise be utilized and no other cheaper factory is available which is suitable for the manufacture of the new product, then the whole £100,000 should be treated as the relevant capital outlay for the new product.

Where actual expenditure will occur to purchase capital equipment, or to finance an increase in working capital in connection with a contemplated new project, then the identification of the relevant incremental capital outlays is a fairly straightforward matter. But it sometimes happens that a firm need not be involved in such expenditures, for it will allocate to the new project existing assets which it already owns. For instance, it might make spare land available for a new factory, or release an office building or spare productive capacity. In such cases, where no cash changes hands, it is necessary to value the assets made available for the new project. This value will seldom correspond, save by coincidence, to the book value of the assets in the firm's accounts. In valuing such assets, it is necessary to determine their worth to the firm in the most profitable alternative employment.

For instance, when a firm puts up a new factory on land it already owns, then the minimum value to be assigned to the land would be its resale value. If, by using the land to build a factory on this year, the firm is forced to buy new land for another factory it planned to put up on the land next year, then the appropriate minimum value would be this replacement cost taking into account the fact that the extra expense would not occur until next year. In either case, the original price paid for the land is quite irrelevant. The aim of this valuation approach is to identify the actual sacrifice a firm makes through assigning to a project assets which the firm already owns.

Asset valuation involves many special problems which are frequently misunderstood. Where such valuation is thought to be a significant factor in the analysis, the reader is strongly recommended to consider the methods of valuation set out in Chapter 19.

Finally, it sometimes happens that a firm acquires part of the assets for a new project by issuing its own shares. This involves valuing the shares, often a complicated matter. This problem is discussed in Chapter 12, Section 2 (see also Sections 1 and 2 of Chapter 17), but suffice it to say, here, that the sacrifice of the firm will not necessarily be measured by the market price of its own shares on the date of issue. The firm is not giving over a cash sum equal to the current market value of the shares in question, nor is it giving up the shares with the option to re-purchase them at any time at the current market price. Rather, it is giving up *permanently* a share of all its future profits and the current market price is only the measure of this sacrifice when it adequately reflects profitability, a condition that is frequently unfulfilled. The need arises to value the means of payment, when other than by cash. It also arises when the firm pays for assets by way of granting loans, preference shares, or conversion options (convertibles). These problems are considered later in the book (particularly in Chapter 12 Section 2, Chapter 15 Section 2e, and Chapter 17 Sections 1 and 2).

ii. Cash receipts – or net cash flows. Net cash flows (in the *positive* sense) comprise the net cash receipts to which a project gives rise. Formally, they comprise profits less taxes when actually *paid*, plus the depreciation provisions less replacement capital expenditures when actually *made*, plus net changes in working capital, plus the recovery of any net residual values from assets at the end of a project's life, plus miscellaneous cash receipts which fall into none of the preceding categories. Further, it will often be found convenient to consider the net cash flows after allowing for any changes in working capital between the provision of the initial working capital by way of a capital outlay, and the recovery of all, or a proportion, of the residual working capital. Each of these items will be considered more fully below, but first a brief justification for using cash receipts rather than more conventional figures such as 'book' profits.

An individual or a firm can make use of 'income' from an investment for purposes of consumption or reinvestment, only when it is turned into cash in one form or another. Therefore, to earn profits in an overseas company which is prevented by restrictions from paying them out by way of dividend or a return of capital, is effectively to receive no profits, unless the share value of the company quoted on the home market rises to reflect at least part of the increased wealth. This possibility apart, profits should be valued only from the time they can effectively be received. Suppose that, because of balance of payments difficulties, the government of a country temporarily suspends dividend remittances to overseas investors. The 'frozen' profits, however, can still be freely re-invested within the country, pending an easing of remittance restrictions. Such profits should be taken into account only when actual remittance is possible. Thus, suppose a company with a cost of capital of 10% after tax has an overseas subsidiary which is expected to earn £100,000 net profits a year hence. The parent company wants these profits remitted in full, but the subsidiary will be prevented from remitting them until a year later, after which time they will have grown to £103,000 through being invested in short term securities in the overseas country. The cash flow to the parent company is then £103,000 two years hence, not £100,000 one year hence. (The discounted values to the nearest thousand £'s are respectively £85,000 and £91,000 – a significant difference.) For investment purposes, it is more useful to know this net cash flow than to know that profits, as recorded in the subsidiary's annual accounts, will be £100,000 a year hence. In short, the net cash flow gives the *opportunity* value of a project's earnings because it reveals when the opportunity for consumption or re-investment will arise.

Finally, we would again emphasize that the net cash flows comprise only the *incremental* net cash receipts solely attributable to the project and must be calculated from the same base case as their associated capital outlays.

PROFITS LESS TAXES WHEN PAID. As we have argued, profits must be valued for the net of tax incremental wealth involved. Hence, it is appropriate to take account only of net of tax profits. It seldom happens that taxes on profits are collected simultaneously with the earning of those profits. Usually there will be a delay, varying from a matter of months to a year or more. In Britain, income taxes on company profits are collected with an average delay of 18 months and profits taxes after 12 months. For this reason, net of tax profits, as required for computing the net cash flow, will not necessarily correspond to profits after tax as prepared for annual profit and loss account purposes. A simple example will suffice. Suppose a three year project gives rise to a gross profit of £100, £150 and £200 at the end of each of the next three years. Tax is levied at the rate of 40% and collected one year in arrears. Net of tax profits as prepared for profit and loss account purposes will be:

Years	1	2	3	4	Total
	£	£	£	£	£
Gross profits	100	150	200	—	450
Less tax at 40%	−40	−60	−80	—	−180
Net of tax of profits	60	90	120	—	270

The same information for net cash flow purposes would be:

Years	1	2	3	4	Total
	£	£	£	£	£
Gross Profits	100	150	200	—	450
Less 40% tax *when paid*	—	−40	−60	−80	−180
Net cash flow	100	110	140	−80	270

While the totals of profits and taxes are the same, the incidence of cash receipts differs significantly from the accounting version of net of tax profits. The present value at 10% of the former is only £219·1, compared to £232·4 of the latter. This arises because the tax authorities have effectively granted an interest free loan of the annual tax bills in each of the three years, a tangible and significant advantage.

The incidence of tax collection is thus relevant to assessing the profitability of any investment project. Because it is such a commonly encountered matter, and as many regular tax allowances have rather complex patterns, it is desirable to develop short cut formulae to handle them. This has been done for British tax allowances in Appendix A, which also contains simple tables to aid in their evaluation, tables which can easily be extended in scope. Similar formulae can be derived for other countries from making use of the basic formulae given in the previous chapter; in particular, those which relate to flows changing at linear or compound rates. The Appendix also contains references to the sources of tables for evaluating United States' capital allowances and the modifications required to these tables to allow for investment credits.

DEPRECIATION PROVISIONS LESS REPLACEMENT CAPITAL EXPENDITURES. At first sight it might be thought incorrect to include the depreciation provision as part of the net cash flow on the grounds that it constitutes the recovery of capital as opposed to income. The sentiment is correct, but the conclusion is false. As we have seen, both the method of net present value and of yield, because they embrace all the incremental cash receipts of an investment, automatically allow for the depreciation element. The same applies to the annual charge method. A simple example may help to clinch this point. Suppose a project involves buying a machine which costs £200, lasts two years only, has a net scrap value of zero at the end of the period, and gives rise to a net cash flow of £111 (£100 straight line depreciation +£11 net profit) at the end of the first year and £121 at the end of the second year. 10% is the firm's cost of capital and it will be seen that the present value of the cash flows at this rate is

$$\frac{£110}{1 \cdot 1} + \frac{£121}{1 \cdot 1^2} = £200.$$

In other words by taking up the investment the firm would fully recover its original capital of £200 (i.e. depreciation has been allowed for fully) while earning 10% on the capital invested in the project. Had the respective cash flows been only £100 each (i.e. consisted simply of depreciation with no profit element) the yield would have been zero. Depreciation would have been fully recovered but no profit earned to meet the cost of the invested capital. Thus discounting net cash flows which include depreciation automatically allows for capital recovery.

One important advantage of including the depreciation provision in the net cash flows instead of considering merely profit as a ratio to initial or average capital (see the discussion of the accountant's rate of return – Chapter 7, Section 1) is that the assessment of profitability is quite unaffected by the chosen method of depreciation. Many accountants and business men are convinced that by writing off capital costs quickly, or alternatively, over a very long period with perhaps no charge in the early years, they are somehow affecting the profitability of the project concerned. It will be apparent that the rate of depreciation shown in the firm's accounts has no effect whatsoever on the amount of cash a project will generate each year and thus it can in no way affect its attraction as an investment. By concentrating on the relevant facts, the use of the net cash flow avoids the confusions arising from arbitrarily chosen depreciation policies.

The one modification necessary to the use of the depreciation provision is capital expenditure on replacements for the capital assets being depreciated. When a project is being appraised over a given life, the replacement of fixed assets within that period should be set off against the depreciation provision, provided it has not already been charged as an expense in computing profits. Where assets, such as many manual tools, have a very short life, say under a year, they are not depreciated at all in annual accounts, but merely charged as an expense. Assets with lives longer than a year are, however, depreciated. Where the less important of such assets, as for instance vehicles, will automatically be renewed once or more before the main assets come to the end of their estimated useful life, it will usually be found convenient to deduct the replacement expenditure involved from the depreciation provision and, of course, from 'profits' where the depreciation provision is insufficient, rather than treat it as a separate capital outlay. The reason the same treatment is not recommended for the main assets is that when their useful life ends they should not be renewed automatically. Any major replacement expenditure should be treated like any other project, something to be justified on its prospective profitability.

NET CHANGES IN WORKING CAPITAL. Working capital is here defined to embrace stock (inventories), plus debts (accounts receivable), plus cash, less creditors (accounts payable). (See also the appendix to the subsequent chapter which comprises a brief exposition of basic accounting principles.) Just as capital outlays include expenditure for working capital, so also should the net cash flows include any net changes in working capital, including the recovery of some or all of the working capital when a project terminates. Net changes in the working capital typically arise when output can be forecast to change over the years. For instance, if output is expected to increase, working capital is likely to increase also. This means that a part of net earnings will necessarily be tied up in financing the net increase in working capital. Conversely, a falling output with a corresponding decline in working capital will release cash previously locked up, provided either by initial capital outlays or by past retained profits, or both. These changes have cash implications and must therefore be considered in the computation of the net cash flows.

Working capital as here defined is not taken net of any bank loans or overdrafts, so that the exact amount of financing which needs to be arranged will be apparent. (Creditors are here taken as an *automatic* source of short term finance although a choice is often possible in this relation and the different choices have different associated costs which call for specific evaluation (see Section 1 of the next chapter).) It is quite satisfactory, however, when drawing up the capital outlays to be financed by long term debt and equity funds (see next chapter) to include bank loans as a part of working capital and to consider only the increases in net working capital which have to be financed by long term capital and, in the case of reductions, to consider only the increase in the net cash flows net of any reductions in bank loans.

An alternative method of taking into account working capital

E

requirements and changes therein would be to set out forecast revenue receipts and payments exactly as regards timing. Thus we should take into account in the revenue receipts the fact that, with the granting of say six weeks average trade credit, payment for output sold would not be received until an average of six weeks after delivery. We should also take account of the lag between actual production and payment to suppliers, for transport, for power, and so on.

This is an entirely valid method of taking account of a project's requirements for working capital, for these are in essence nothing more than leads and lags in payments and receipts. The first method described above will, however, usually be found to be more convenient, in that the relatively small leads and lags involved in working capital are computationally awkward to take into account and of little significance in project evaluation. Where initial working capital is treated as capital expenditure and all subsequent changes in it as net cash flows, the important thing is not then to double-count by also taking into account leads and lags of the kind already reflected in the deductions made from the cash flows for working capital. The cash flows should entirely ignore these particular leads and lags.

NET RESIDUAL ASSET VALUES. At the end of any project's life, it will often be possible to recover some value from the residual assets, either through resale or through employing them to advantage elsewhere. These residual values should be calculated net of any dismantling or handling charges, and should include any balancing tax allowances or tax charges (see appendix, and especially Section 1 of Chapter 19).

MISCELLANEOUS RECEIPTS. Finally, some projects give rise to miscellaneous cash receipts which do not truly fall into any of the above categories. Profits may be remitted from an overseas subsidiary in the form of repaying parent company loans (see Chapter 13), in the form of the issue of free loan stock (see Chapter 16), or even in the form of an equity capital repayment. Shipping goods with shipping companies which subscribe to a conference agreement may give rise to periodic rebates, providing that goods have been shipped over a sufficiently long period. Other examples may well occur to the reader.

b. *Cost of Capital*

The definition of the cost of capital is properly the subject of subsequent chapters, particularly of the next two chapters, but here one basic point must be made. To be consistent with the definition of net cash flows being on a net of tax basis, the cost of capital is always to be taken on a net of tax basis also, as this represents the true net burden to a firm. Where the cost of capital to a firm comprises, say, borrowed funds, the true cost of such funds is clearly only the net burden involved in paying for them. Where the interest cost can be set off as a charge against taxable income, then the incremental cost is reduced by the amount of tax saved; hence, the net of tax cost is the relevant and therefore correct cost. (Where no such taxable income exists, it is still correct to say that the interest cost is 'net of tax', but here the effective tax rate is zero and there is no difference between the gross of tax and the net of tax costs.)

One final important point to appreciate is that *if* tax payments are treated as deductions from net cash flows at the time they *occur* (which is our practice throughout this book) it would be double counting also to take credit for any delays in tax payments as a source of short term finance in computing the weighted average cost of capital (see page 118 *et seq.*).

APPENDIX A

The Present Value of Tax Allowances on Capital Expenditure

In many of the discounting problems arising in capital budgeting it is useful to be able to evaluate separately the present value of future tax allowances, on the assumption that a firm will have a sufficient taxable income to make full use of such allowances. Usually these allowances fall into regular patterns and in such cases the computation of their present values can be reduced to a formula and hence tables.

Tabulations of the present values of United States' depreciation write-offs (capital allowances) are given in reference (1), hence the analysis to be set out below relates only to British capital allowances. But before leaving the subject of American capital allowances we would point out that the tabulations referred to require adjustment in view of the provision for a 7% tax credit introduced in the 1962 Tax Bill. This credit is the right to deduct from a firm's tax *liability* (as opposed to *taxable income*) 7% of the cost of an asset which is then to be written down for tax purposes by this amount. The present value which, multiplied by the firm's percentage tax rate t, gives the combined present value of the tax saving from both the depreciation provisions and the investment credit is found from the following expression where C is the initial cost of the asset and D is the tabulated present value of the depreciation allowance:

$$(0 \cdot 93 \, D + 0 \cdot 07 \, C/(1+r)t)$$

Most capital assets in Britain attract capital allowances whereby the depreciation of the asset, as agreed by the tax authorities, is an allowable expense in compiling the tax liability of a firm. The main capital allowances are the following.

INVESTMENT ALLOWANCE. This is the right to set against tax a given proportion of the initial cost of an asset. This is an outright gift from the Revenue and a firm is not required to depreciate the asset by this amount for the purposes of computing other future tax allowable depreciation charges.

INITIAL ALLOWANCE. This is a special allowance permitting an asset to be depreciated for tax purposes by an exceptionally large amount in the first year (compared with the subsequent years). The asset, however, must be written down by this amount in computing future allowable depreciation.

ANNUAL ALLOWANCES. These are annual amounts by which an asset may be depreciated each year for tax purposes. The most commonly used method in Britain is for an asset to be depreciated each year by a fixed proportion, specified for different types of assets, of its written-down value at the end of the preceding year. This is known as the reducing balance method. It is also optional for a firm to choose between this method and the straight line method, i.e., writing the asset down by a given proportion each year of the asset's initial cost. In the case of some assets, notably industrial buildings, annual depreciation for tax purposes is only permitted on a straight line basis. (Non-industrial buildings, such as, shops, offices, hotels, garages, attract no capital allowances.)

BALANCING CHARGES AND ALLOWANCES. When an asset is disposed of by a firm at a price different from its written down value for tax purposes, there are tax consequences. If the selling price is less than the written-down value, then a tax allowance is given in respect of the difference. If the selling price is above the written-down value, then a balancing charge is made on the difference; i.e., tax is levied on the 'profit' that arises on the transaction. Where the selling price exceeds the initial cost, the balancing charge is restricted to the difference between initial cost and written-down value.

Present values of these capital allowances can be computed from the formulae derived in Sections 1 and 2. These sections are for reference only and readers should now turn to Section 3 containing practical applications.

1. REDUCING BALANCE METHOD

Consider the present value P of the following tax allowances that arise in the case of the reducing balance method of tax depreciation allowances, assuming tax relief to arise at yearly intervals from the purchase of the asset, discounted at the rate r.

End Years

$$
\begin{array}{cccc}
0 & 1 & 2 & 3
\end{array}
$$

$$
P = tC(V+R+d) + \frac{tdCm}{(1+r)} + \frac{tdCm(1-d)}{(1+r)^2} + \frac{tdCm(1-d)^2}{(1+r)^3} \cdots
$$

$$
+ \frac{tdCm(1-d)^{n-1}}{(1+r)^n} + \frac{t(W-S)}{(1+r)^n}
$$

where C = initial capital cost,

n = life of the asset in years,

t = percentage rate of tax,

d = percentage rate of depreciation on the reducing balance method,

V = percentage investment allowance,

R = percentage initial allowance,

S = the lower of the resale value at end year n, and C,

W = written down value at end year n, and

$m = (1-R-d)$.

This series arises in the following manner. Each £1 of depreciation saves a firm tax at rate t. In the first year (assumed initially to be at the start of the first year, that is, the time of purchase of the asset) the firm is allowed as an expense for tax purposes $(V+R+d)\%$ of the capital cost C. Thus the tax saved is $tC(V+R+d)$. The written down value of the asset for tax purposes is then the initial cost C, less the initial and annual allowance only, i.e., $C(1-R-d) = Cm$. At the end of the first year, the firm is allowed for its annual tax depreciation the proportion d of the written down value Cm. Hence, the tax saving is $tdCm$. Since the allowance of proportion d has been received, the written-down value for the end of the second year becomes $Cm(1-d)$, and at the end of the third year $Cm(1-d)^2$, to $Cm(1-d)^{n-1}$ at the end of the nth year.

The series can be rewritten as

$$
P = tC\left\{(V+R+d) + \frac{dm}{(1-d)}\left[\frac{(1-d)}{(1+r)} + \frac{(1-d)^2}{(1+r)} \cdots \frac{(1-d)^n}{(1+r)^n}\right]\right\} + \frac{t(W-S)}{(1+r)^n}
$$

If we now put $1/(1+k) = (1-d)/(1+r)$, so that $k = (r+d)/(1-d)$, the formula reduces to

$$
P = tC\left[(V+R+d) + \frac{dm}{(1-d)}(a_{n|k})\right] + \frac{t(W-S)}{(1+r)^n}
$$

The balancing allowance, or charge, $(W-S)$, is the difference between S (the lower of initial cost and resale value) and the written down value of C for tax purposes at the end of the nth year, that is $W = Cm(1-d)^{n-1}$. Thus the present value of the balancing allowance, or charge, can be rewritten as

$$\frac{t[Cm(1-d)^{n-1}-S]}{(1+r)^n} = \frac{tCm(1-d)^n}{(1-d)(1+r)^n} - \frac{tS}{(1+r)^n}$$

$$= \frac{tCm}{(1-d)(1+k)^n} - \frac{tS}{(1+r)^n}$$

If this expression is substituted for $t(W-S)/(1+r)^n$ in the full series, and allowance is made for the fact that the average delay between capital expenditure and receipt of tax relief from capital allowances is assumed to be two years,[1] then the series can assume the final form of:

$$P = \frac{tC}{(1+r)^2}\left\{(V+R+d)+\frac{dm}{(1-d)}[a_{n|k}+(1+k)^{-n}]-\frac{S}{C(1+r)^n}\right\}$$

$$(2.5)$$

Consider a simple example of an asset costing £10,000, owned for ten years, where the investment allowance is 20%, the initial allowance 10%, and the annual allowance is 10% on the reducing balance of written off expenditure. Assuming the asset is sold for £1,000 at the end of the tenth year, that the rate of discount is 5% and the tax rate is 50%, the present value P of the tax concessions would be found by substituting in (2.5) as follows:

$$k = \frac{(r+d)}{(1-d)} = \frac{(0.05+0.1)}{(1-0.1)} = \frac{0.15}{0.9} = 0.1667$$

$$P = \frac{0.5 \times 10,000}{1.05^2}\left\{(0.2+0.1+0.1)+\frac{0.1(1-0.1-0.1)}{(1-0.1)}[a_{10|16.67}+1.1667^{-10}]\right.$$

$$\left.-\frac{1,000}{10,000(1.05)^{10}}\right\}$$

---

[1] The period of delay between capital expenditure and the benefit felt in reduced tax payments varies with circumstances. A common delay is 18 months as opposed to the 2 years illustrated in the formula. Where this occurs the formula should be $P = tC/(1+r)^{1.5}\{\text{etc.}\}$. The expression $(1+r)^{1.5}$ is sufficiently accurately rendered as $(1+r) \times [1+(r/2)]$ (See Chapter 1, Section 7a).

$$= \frac{5,000}{1\cdot1025}\left\{0\cdot4+\frac{0\cdot08}{0\cdot9}[4\cdot717+0\cdot214]-\frac{1}{10(1\cdot6289)}\right\}$$

$$= 4,535\left\{0\cdot4+0\cdot0889(4\cdot931)-\frac{1}{16\cdot289}\right\}$$

$$= 4,535(0\cdot4+0\cdot43837-0\cdot06139)$$

$$= £4,535(0\cdot77698) = £3,524$$

In many cases firms elect to forgo the balancing allowances and simply continue to write the asset down indefinitely on the aggregate value of all their tax depreciated assets. Where this happens a firm pays slightly more tax than it need, but this may be justified by the saving in clerical costs required to process the claiming of the balancing allowance. In such a case $n \to \infty$ and the formula would be rewritten with all the terms subsequent to the first as a perpetuity of k, thus:

$$P = \frac{tC}{(1+r)^2}\left\{(V+R+d)+\frac{dm}{(1-d)}\left[\frac{1}{k}\right]\right\}$$

$$= \frac{tC}{(1+r)^2}\left[(V+R+d)+\frac{dm}{(r+d)}\right] \qquad (2.6)$$

2. STRAIGHT LINE METHOD

For the straight line method of tax depreciation a slightly different formula is necessary, as the annual allowance is a constant proportion of the original capital cost, rather than a declining one. Using the same symbols as for the reducing balance method, the series of allowances excluding the balancing allowance for the moment is:

End Years

0	1	2	3
$P = (V+R+d)tC$	$\dfrac{dtC}{(1+r)}$	$\dfrac{dtC}{(1+r)^2}$	$\dfrac{dtC}{(1+r)^3}\ldots$

This series of d does not continue to year n necessarily as the annual allowances go on only until they equal $1-(R+d)$ – i.e., until year $\{1-(R+d)\}/d$. Hence, the series of d is an annuity for j years where j is defined as the lesser of n and $1-(R+d)/d$. Thus, the series is now

$$P = tC\{(V+R+d)+d_{j|r}\}+\frac{t(W-S)}{(1+r)^n}$$

Hence, with the assumed 2 year tax delay the series can finally be written as

$$P = \frac{tC}{(1+r)^2}\left\{(V+R+d)+d_{j|r}+\frac{(W-S)}{C(1+r)^n}\right\} \qquad (2.7)$$

3. SHORTCUTS

It will usually be convenient for firms to compile tables based on (2.5), (2.6), and (2.7) to permit the quick evaluation of projects which, in the absence of tax allowances, would have fairly even net cash flows. By treating the tax allowances separately the evaluation of the net cash flows becomes a simple matter.

Set out below for illustrative purposes as Table 2.1 is such a tabulation

Table 2.1

Percentage Present Value of Capital Allowances and Net Revenue or Costs after Tax—1963 Basis

Rate of Discount	Capital Allowances – V = Investment R = Initial d = Annual				Effective Net of Tax Factor
	I (Ships) $V = 40\%$ R = nil $d = 15\%$	II $V = 30\%$ $R = 10\%$ $d = 25\%$	III $V = 30\%$ $R = 10\%$ $d = 15\%$	IV $V = 30\%$ $R = 10\%$ $d = 20\%$	$1-0\cdot5375\,(1+r)^{-1\frac{1}{2}}$
r	P	P			
2%	·6784	·6533	·6324	·6452	·4783
3%	·6472	·6328	·6044	·6217	·4859
4%	·6192	·6137	·5791	·6000	·4933
5%	·5938	·5958	·5563	·5800	·5006
6%	·5706	·5790	·5354	·5614	·5077
7%	·5494	·5632	·5163	·5441	·5147
8%	·5300	·5483	·4987	·5279	·5215
9%	·5120	·5342	·4824	·5128	·5281
10%	·4954	·5208	·4674	·4986	·5346
11%	·4800	·5082	·4534	·4852	·5410
12%	·4656	·4961	·4403	·4726	·5473
13%	·4522	·4847	·4281	·4607	·5534
14%	·4396	·4738	·4166	·4494	·5594
15%	·4278	·4635	·4059	·4388	·5652
16%	·4167	·4536	·3957	·4287	·5710
17%	·4062	·4441	·3861	·4190	·5766
18%	·3963	·4350	·3771	·4099	·5821
19%	·3869	·4264	·3685	·4011	·5875
20%	·3780	·4181	·3603	·3928	·5928
21%	·3696	·4101	·3525	·3848	·5980
22%	·3615	·4024	·3452	·3772	·6031
23%	·3539	·3950	·3381	·3699	·6081
24%	·3466	·3880	·3314	·3629	·6130
25%	·3396	·3811	·3249	·3562	·6178

based on (2.6.) The first four columns set out commonly encountered tax allowance cases introduced in the April 1963 Budget. The table is drawn up for a tax rate of 53·75% and an average delay in tax payments of $1\frac{1}{2}$ years.

Also included in Table 2.1 (right-hand column) is the 'effective net of tax factor' to be applied to taxable earnings or costs when the tax rate is 53·75% and the delay in liability for tax is $1\frac{1}{2}$ years. This is defined as $1-t(1+r)^{-k}$ where t is the tax rate and k is the delay in tax liability. Thus applied to a revenue stream, the longer the delay and the higher the rate of discount, the greater the value of a delay in tax payments. When an expense is being set against taxable income, the reverse is of course true. The 'effective net of tax factor' is a shortcut which could be applied to the present value of a gross of tax cost or revenue stream to reduce it to the desired net of tax basis. (The present value of the cost or revenue stream would of course have been calculated using a *net of tax* cost of capital as the aim of the calculation is to find the present value of the cash flow net of all taxes.) By subtracting the 'effective net of tax factor' from 100% there results the 'effective tax *rate*' a firm is paying.

As an example of the application of these short cuts consider the net present value at 7% of a project costing £100,000, the whole of which sum attracts capital allowances at the rates of $V = 30\%$, $R = 10\%$, and $d = 20\%$ (column IV of Table 2.1). The project has a *gross* of tax cash flow of £15,000 a year for 20 years. Using the factors from the last two columns of the 7% row in Table 2.1, the present value of the project is

$$(£15,000 \times a_{7/20} \times 0·5147) + (£100,000 \times 0·5441) = £136,200.$$

Therefore the net present value is £136,200 − £100,000 = £36,200.

REFERENCES

1. HAROLD BIERMAN and SEYMOUR SMIDT, *The Capital Budgeting Decision*, The Macmillan Company, New York, 1960.

CHAPTER THREE

The Cost of the Individual Sources of Capital

The charge – the interest rate – at which investors or lenders are prepared to exchange funds at the present for funds in the future is determined by a number of complex factors. When a firm raises a loan it is essentially buying current funds with a promise to repay a larger sum in future (i.e. the original capital sum plus interest thereon). A firm is willing to do this because it expects to invest the borrowed capital to such advantage that it can earn sufficient to repay the loan and interest, and still make a profit for itself. It is this expectation which gives rise to the demand for capital.

On the supply side are the private and institutional investors (insurance companies, pension funds, banks, etc.). But behind the institutional investors stand other private investors so that private investors comprise the ultimate source of private capital. (Similarly behind most sources of government capital there stands ultimately the private investor but we are here more concerned with private capital for industrial and commercial investment.). What factors then cause private individuals to lend their funds to business or to a government? Of itself lending spending power to others without compensation seldom results in anything but disadvantage for the lender who is deprived of purchasing power for the period of the loan. Of course the majority of private lenders are prepared to forego present consumption in order to provide for future needs for themselves or their dependents, that is they are already inclined to *save* for the future. But what inducement have they to invest or *lend* their savings, as opposed to storing them safely in the form of cash? Cash is the most liquid of all forms of saving and by acquiring shares or debentures etc., liquidity and hence flexibility are being sacrificed. Expense, inconvenience, and delay are involved in converting other investment assets into cash. Further there is the uncertainty concerning the full return of lent funds and dividends or 'interest' thereon. These factors make it inevitable that under almost all circumstances a lender or investor will require compensation in the form of interest or participation in profits to overcome the disadvantages of investing or lending. The need for such compensation sets the lower limit

58

to the premium or charge required for the use of savings. The actual demand for the limited supply of savings may, however, drive this premium up considerably above its minimum level.

In barest outline this is the mechanism which gives rise to the fact that a firm must pay interest on its borrowed capital and hold out a reasonable promise of a return on its equity capital comparable to that available from other similar equity investments.

In the simple case considered in Chapter 1, the firm was assumed to have a sufficiently large supply of bank credit available to it (relative to its foreseeable demand) for the firm to consider its cost of capital as constant at the rate r per year over all the relevant future. From this derived exchange rate of 1 to $(1+r)$ per year, followed all conventional discounting theory. In order to establish the basis of discounting where a firm is operating under conditions of more realistic complexity concerning its supply of capital, we must consider that supply with detailed reference to the methods by which capital is raised and their place in the context of the firm's general financing plan. A company will normally have several available sources of finance ranging from creditors and short term advances, through medium and long term loans, up to equity finance. Typically a company will draw on several or all of these sources concurrently. To determine such a company's cost of capital we must examine first the cost of each individual source of finance. In the following chapter we will consider the problems of measurement when funds are obtained from several sources jointly. In neither of these chapters are we specifically concerned with the problems of optimal finance (which is dealt with primarily in Chapter 15) and only very broad generalizations will be made comparing the alternative sources of funds.

The following sources of finance will now be considered:

> Short Term Funds
> Medium and Long Term Loans
> Preference Shares
> Equity Funds

Some idea of the relative importance of these different sources of capital in Britain can be had from Table 4.1A of the following chapter relating to 3,000 of the largest public companies. Similar information for the United States is given in Table 4.1B. Percentages from this source will be quoted throughout this chapter.

For ease of comparison the separate costs of all these sources of finance will be reduced to an effective annual equivalent rate of interest. This is defined (see Section 6a of Chapter 1) as the amount that would be payable at the end of a year, less the sum borrowed at the beginning of a year, on any funds borrowed assuming that any interest payable in the course of the year could be reborrowed on identical terms to be repaid at the year end. The need for this rather long-winded definition will be apparent later.

Because of the constant and necessary reference to accounting terms in this chapter, and indeed throughout this book, a brief exposition of the basic principles of accountancy is included in Appendix A to this chapter, for the benefit of readers lacking this knowledge.

1. SHORT TERM FUNDS

These can be subdivided into four main categories: trade credit, bank borrowing, bills of exchange, and deferred tax payments.

a. *Trade Credit*

Goods and services are seldom supplied to companies on 'cash on delivery' terms. More usually there is a period of grace in which to settle the account. There may be a discount offered for prompt payment, e.g. $\frac{1}{2}\%$ off for payment within fourteen days. Or there may be an extra charge if the account is not settled within a month of say 1% per month compound. In these cases it is a relatively straightforward matter to compute the annual equivalent rate of interest implied (see Chapter I, Section 6a). For instance the rate of $\frac{1}{2}\%$ for payment within a fortnight is equivalent to

$$\frac{0 \cdot 5\%}{100 \cdot 0\% - 0 \cdot 5\%} = \frac{0 \cdot 5\%}{99 \cdot 5\%} = 0 \cdot 5025\% \text{ per fortnight.}$$

(The reason for using 99·5% as the denominator rather than 100·0% is that 99·5% represents the present sum or capital value on which interest cost should correctly be calculated. 100·0% in this example represents the terminal sum, which includes both the assumed capital, here 99·5%, and the interest, 0·5%.) This rate per fortnight is equivalent to an effective annual interest rate of

$$1 \cdot 005025^{26} - 1 = 14 \cdot 0\%.$$

This represents the annual equivalent cost of *not* settling such an account within a fortnight. In the case of the penalty of 1% per month, assuming this refers to calendar months, the annual equivalent rate of interest is $(1 \cdot 01^{12} - 1) = 12 \cdot 7\%$. As the cost of goods and services supplied can universally be charged as an expense for tax purposes these rates should be reduced by the company's effective tax rate to give the net burden of the implied interest charges. If a company's effective[1] tax rate were say 40%, the interest charges just quoted would be reduced by this amount to 8·4% and 7·6% respectively.

Trade credit is of course a *specific* source of finance limited to the supply of certain goods (and services). It sometimes happens that no charge at all is made for trade credit, i.e. there are no discounts for prompt payment, and no extra charges for delayed payment. In these cases there is no interest charge as such, but in order to maintain good business relations it pays a company not to abuse the privilege and to pay such accounts within a reasonable period. Such 'free' credit is thus not available for an indefinite period.

In 1960 trade credit provided 16·0% of the total capital of British quoted companies, and 5·2% for United States companies.

b. *Bank Borrowing*

The British type of bank overdrafts are probably the most flexible possible form of borrowing. The borrower is usually granted an agreed credit line, that is a maximum up to which he may borrow, and generally has the right to repay the overdraft in whole or in part at any time. (It is common, however, for banks to require a firm to make certain agreed use of its overdraft line in order to ensure that such credit is extensively employed. Alternatively, in times of credit stringency, the bank may require a firm to make only very temporary use of the credit line.)

In Britain banks sometimes require a given sum related to the extent of the credit line and the administrative services which the bank performs for the firm, to be considered as being on permanent deposit with the bank, attracting no interest. In the United States these 'compensating balances' as they are called, are a quite common arrangement. Apart from this, however, interest is normally charged only on the actual balance outstanding as computed weekly, or more often daily, with the result that a borrower is not required to pay for any unused part of a credit line.

[1] The effective tax rate is defined in the Appendix to the previous chapter. In brief it takes account of the *average* delay in the payment of company taxes and thus gives an *approximation* to the net interest burden on any loan or credit transactions which is sufficiently accurate for all practical purposes.

The effective annual equivalent interest rate on a bank overdraft is simple to determine. As noted, the interest may be computed on the daily or weekly balances, but this will be at rates equivalent to a nominal annual interest rate payable quarterly or, more commonly, half yearly. This means that the effective annual equivalent interest rate is slightly higher than the nominal rate at which the overdraft is granted. An example will make this clear. Assume that the nominal rate is 6% per annum and that interest is charged half yearly. The half yearly rate will be 3% and the annual equivalent rate is simply $1 \cdot 03^2 - 1 = 6 \cdot 09\%$. As such interest is normally an allowable deduction from taxable income, it must be reduced by the effective rate of the company's tax to give the net burden as was described in Section a. above.

In the United States the overdraft form of bank borrowing is virtually unknown and loans are typically in the form of promissory notes of a fixed period of at least 30 days. Interest is deducted from the actual proceeds of the loan, that is the note is discounted; the procedure for converting such interest to an equivalent annual basis is as for bills of exchange which are considered below.

The principal limitation on the extent of a bank borrowing which a firm of good standing may obtain is usually its 'current ratio', that is the ratio of its current assets to its current liabilities (see Appendix A). This ratio should preferably be of the order of 2: 1, with 1·5: 1 as the likely desirable minimum.

Subject to this and the general restriction of overall credit worthiness, bank lending is extremely flexible. This is essentially because of the very small degree of risk involved compared, for instance, with long term debentures. While it is frequently stated that bank loans 'finance' working capital (current assets less current liabilities) and not the long term fixed assets, and that in this fact lies the security of a bank, such a view is somewhat naïve. Funds received from banks go into the general pool of a firm's financial resources and the particular use to which specific funds are put cannot be meaningfully determined. In the event of liquidation banks normally have no legal claims whatever on specific assets such as the working capital which their overdrafts allegedly finance, and in such liquidations will rank after the secured creditors who normally include the debenture holders.

A bank's real security lies in the fact that its loans are largely of a temporary nature and can be withdrawn, at least in part, at short notice. Should a firm run into financial difficulties the bank can quickly take steps to withdraw its loan. Debenture holders typically have no such option as long as their interest payments are not currently in arrears (and interest payments are seldom more frequent than half yearly, and sometimes only yearly – periods in which a firm's position can significantly deteriorate). They must simply take their chance in any possible liquidation of the company. A bank's ability to withdraw at least part of its loan is enhanced by the fact that it should nearly always be possible to oblige the ailing company to run down its working capital to pay off the short term bank loan. But this is rather remote from the oversimplified belief that such loans finance working capital.

From the viewpoint of the borrowing company the British type overdrafts have the advantage of being a fairly high interest bearing outlet for any temporary funds, as such funds can be used to reduce the amount of the overdraft thus saving interest.

A United States corporation, however, could achieve much the same effect albeit at lower interest 'saving' by investing its temporary surplus funds in short term securities while waiting for the dates of maturity of the promissory notes.

Against these advantages of short term bank borrowing must be set the possibility that such borrowing is likely to be withdrawn at the first sign of serious difficulties, thus aggravating those difficulties. To avoid this possibility it is in the interest of both a company and its bank to raise a proportion of loan capital on a longer term basis, and on terms which compensate for the extra risks associated with such lending.

In 1960 bank overdrafts and other short term loans provided 4% of the total capital of British quoted companies and 1% of United States companies.

c. *Bills of Exchange*

The third main form of short term borrowing is the trade bill, or bill of exchange. Such a bill is essentially a post dated cheque which a vendor draws in his own favour for signature by the purchaser. By signing the purchaser formally 'accepts' the bill, which normally refers to specific goods received and is made out against the cost value of such goods. A bill is generally made payable at a date 3 to 6 months after purchase of the goods and its function is to enable the vendor to obtain cash prior to the date of payment on the bill. This is done by selling (discounting) the bill to a third party such as a bank or discount house at a price below the face value. The bank or discount house can sell the bill in turn or hold it until the due date of payment when it would be presented to the original purchaser of the goods for settlement within three days.[1] This method has the advantage of allowing the vendor to receive cash without requiring earlier settlement by the purchaser.

The difference between the discounted value and face (maturity) value of the bill sets the interest cost to the vendor. Suppose a £100 bill payable exactly 3 months hence is discounted for £1·5, that is the vendor receives £98·5. The true *three monthly* interest rate is then £1·5/£98·5 = 1·5228%. The corresponding annual equivalent interest rate is then simply $1·015228^4 - 1 = 6·232\%$. The interest rate thus calculated is of course the gross of tax interest rate. To determine the net effective interest rate the effect of taxes, if any, must be considered. In selling a trade bill rather than holding it for eventual settlement, the vendor in the example just quoted is receiving £1·5 less for his goods than would otherwise be the case. This effectively reduces taxable income by the same amount. For this reason it is necessary to reduce the interest rate previously calculated by the vendor's effective tax rate to give the true net burden of interest.

d. *Deferred Tax Payments*

Another source of short term funds essentially similar in character to trade credit are the credits automatically extended by tax authorities due to the interval of time which elapses between the earning of income and the payment of taxes thereon. For many firms this can comprise a significant amount of short term finance, particularly in Britain where the average period between the earning of profits and the payment of taxes is 18 months for the major tax, income tax, and 12 months for the profits tax. (In 1960 the provisions for future current taxation accounted for 8% of the total capital of British quoted companies and $6\frac{1}{2}\%$ for United States companies.) As long as a firm continues to earn stable or expanding profits, such deferred tax payments comprise a virtually permanent source of finance as each year a new deferred tax payment replaces that of the previous year. Typically tax authorities make no interest charge for what amounts to a short term loan and so this source of finance is without cost to a firm. Useful as this form of finance is its value does not lie within the control of a firm save to the extent that it can increase

---

[1] There are many variations on this basic theme. See particularly reference 1.

its profits. (This source of finance should *not* be used for computing the weighted average cost of capital for evaluating net cash flows based on delayed tax payments—see page 118 *et seq*.)

2. MEDIUM AND LONG TERM LOANS

Most medium and long term loans are granted on fixed interest terms and are repayable on specified dates. The interest payments are normally payable quarterly or semi-annually, so that in precisely the same manner as described for bank overdrafts the nominal rate needs to be adjusted to give the true annual rate of interest. These interest payments are also deductible for tax purposes and should also be reduced by the effective rate of tax.

The additional risks borne by longer term lenders have already been noted and these follow essentially from the fact that they are lending long term. Long term loans for substantial borrowers will normally take the form of mortgage debentures secured on specific assets, or floating charge debentures which only become a fixed charge on the assets of the corporation in the event of certain contingencies. In American financial parlance these are known as mortgage bonds and debenture bonds respectively. Both are commonly controlled by a debenture trust deed which is an agreement between the borrowing corporation and the trustee (usually a trust company, insurance company, bank, or similar institution) who acts on behalf of the possibly numerous holders of the debentures. The debenture trust deed will detail the precise conditions of the loan and in the case of a floating charge debenture will specify the conditions (usually non-payment of interest or principal on the due dates) which will cause the floating charge to 'crystallize' and become a fixed claim on the assets of the corporation. The trust deed will also normally lay down various conditions safeguarding the debenture holders. These conditions often include limitations on the firm's right to create further debt ranking prior to or *pari passu* with these debentures, and restrictions to be imposed on the dividends paid by the firm in the event that the security provided (in terms of assets or earnings cover) becomes inadequate. These restrictions on the firm's general financing will normally be more detailed the larger the reliance of the debenture holders on the firm's general credit rather than on the pledge of specific assets.

Sometimes fixed interest loans are raised on the understanding that they will be repaid as a first charge on the income of a business.

F

No dividends at all will be permitted until the loans are completely paid off, or perhaps unless net liquid assets (debtors plus cash less creditors) exceed the balance of the outstanding loans *after* the payment of the dividends. Such terms are common in the mining industry where, because of the nature of mining risks, no long term debt capital is generally available (see case study in Section 1 of Chapter 13).

Given the additional liquidity and security to be derived from short term loans it would seem likely that longer term loans would normally command a somewhat higher interest rate than say bank overdrafts. In fact, of course, the longer term interest rate is strongly influenced by views as to the probable pattern of interest rates in the future. Owing to mistaken views on this point (though particular historical factors such as the manipulation of the market by government authorities may also be influential in this respect) some outstanding debentures conceded in the past may be at a lower interest rate than current shorter term loans such as bank overdrafts.

It is common practice in Britain to issue debentures at a slight discount, that is £100 of debenture stock may be issued at £95, although the interest rate (generally known as the coupon rate) relates, of course to the face value of the debenture, the £100. The true yield on the debenture will naturally take into account the capital appreciation occurring when the debentures are redeemed and is calculated as described in Section 4b of Chapter 1. It is thus possible to issue at a yield interest rate finely adjusted to the prevailing market without the arithmetical inconvenience of a cumbersome decimal in the coupon rate. The second reason for this practice is that it fits into the general scheme of the gilt edged market where it is common government practice to issue at a discount.

A special form of debenture deserves brief mention, namely the convertible option (or convertible). This is a fixed interest loan which carries with it the right to convert into equity shares on fixed terms at some future date. Often the terms will vary at different future dates, each £100 of loan stock, for example, being convertible into 17 paid up equity shares in four years' time, 16 in five years' time, and 15 in six years' time. It aims to give subscribers a one way option, guaranteeing an attractive fixed income with the option to convert into equity shares on favourable terms at a time when higher profits are expected to be an established fact rather than a mere promise. Should such profits fail to materialize, the subscriber can always continue with the loan. This form of finance has found increasing favour in Britain in recent years, particularly with certain large companies such as I.C.I. and B.P. Analytically it poses some difficult but important problems for optimal financing, the discussion of which is postponed until Chapter 15.

In 1960, medium and long term loans provided 7·6% of the total capital of British quoted companies, and 21·4% of United States companies.

3. PREFERENCE SHARES

Preference shares are a source of long term or permanent finance and are similar in some respects to loan capital. The important distinction is that they are *shares*, i.e. they carry the title to part ownership of the business. As such they participate in profits or surplus on liquidation only when all creditors and lenders have been paid in full. Their profit participation is usually restricted to a given percentage on their nominal or face value, and no profits can be distributed to the ordinary or equity shareholders until the preference dividend has been met in full. Commonly preference shares are permanent in that they are irredeemable. Sometimes, however, preference shares are redeemable either at the company's option (i.e. effectively at the option of the equity shareholders) or at a given time, in which case they approximate to long term debt. In these cases preference shares have the advantage from the viewpoint of the equity shareholders in that no payment need be made if profits are insufficient. The preference shareholders, unlike the debenture holders, cannot force the company into liquidation when this happens. In the case of 'cumulative' preference shares, the dividends not paid are deferred until profits permit their payment. In the case of liquidation, such deferred dividend payments would be added to the nominal value of the preference shares, and would have to be settled in full before any payment could be made to the equity shareholders.

Because preference shares are at greater risk than fixed interest loans in regard both to income and ultimate repayment, their right to profit participation or annual interest cost is usually higher than in the case of such loans. Compared to equity shares, however, preference shares are cheaper because they are both at less risk and participate in profits only to a limited extent.

The effective interest rate is easily ascertained. Where preference shares are redeemable, the effective interest rate is found as for fixed interest loans. Where the preference shares are irredeemable they approximate to perpetuities, and the effective cost is net of tax dividends divided by the issue price (see Section 2b of Chapter 1). (This presupposes we are examining the cost of preference shares prior to raising capital this way. Once preference shares or loans have been raised the cost of continuing them is the cost of servicing them.)

The tax treatment of preference share dividends can be different from that applicable to fixed interest loans. In many countries the preference dividend is paid gross of any personal income taxes. In Britain both preference and ordinary dividends are paid net of income tax at the standard rate, but preference share dividends, unlike loan interest, cannot be claimed as an expense for profits tax purposes. This is because preference dividends are a division of profits, not an expense in earning such profits. Thus preference capital at any given interest rate is considerably more costly to service than a bond or debenture carrying the same rate. With the British profits tax at 15%, preference share interest must be nearly 25% less than debenture interest to give the same after tax (income and profits tax) cost. In the United States with a corporate profits tax of 52% the preference interest would need to be 52% less. This tends to make preference shares less popular than debentures as a means of raising prior charge capital. (It should be noted, however, that this comparison with debentures is only valid if these are the realistic alternative in the firm's financing policy; in some cases it may be possible and profitable to have both forms.)

As in the case of long term loans, care must be taken in budgeting for future capital requirements, as surplus cash cannot usually be applied to repaying preference shares at will. In the case of irredeemable preference shares it cannot be applied at all. These considerations are seldom of importance for an expanding company, especially in times of inflation when the burden of servicing preference capital falls.[1]

In 1960 preference shares represented 5·3% of the total capital of British quoted companies, and 3·9% of United States companies.

[1] See Section 7, Chapter 6 for the effect of inflation on equity capital and capital raised on fixed interest terms, and also Section 3, Chapter 12, where the problem of assessing the future burden of fixed interest capital when inflation is expected is discussed with reference to a business being purchased which has such capital outstanding.

4. EQUITY CAPITAL

a. *The Nature of Equity Capital*

In 1960 equity capital (including retained profits) accounted for over 60% of the total capital of British quoted companies and 57% of United States companies. Thus the major part of long term business finance is provided in the form of equity capital, the residual source of finance. Equity funds are also residual claimants to earnings in that they can participate in earnings only when all creditors and other suppliers of funds have received their interest payments, etc., in full. Similarly equity investors receive only the residue (if any) on funds realized on the winding up of a business after all creditors, lenders, etc., have been paid in full. Because they are entitled only to residual participation in earnings and realized proceeds on winding up, equity funds are subject to the greatest risk of all forms of capital. For this reason equity funds are forthcoming only when profit prospects are sufficiently attractive to compensate for the risks involved, and this makes equity capital the most expensive source of finance. But equity capital is also the one essential source of finance. It is possible, if not usually desirable, to dispense with all other sources of credit or finance, but never with equity. No one in normal circumstances[1] will supply all the funds required by an enterprise on fixed interest terms, with the prospect of only a moderate return if all goes well, and perhaps nothing if the business fails. In short, equity finance is the one essential source of finance, it is subject to the greatest risks, and it is the most expensive.

b. *The Cost of Equity Capital*

The direct cost of loan capital to a firm is a clearly defined legally binding interest rate. In contrast, the cost of equity capital to a firm is a conceptual construct, the purpose of which is to enable the firm's management to take decisions in the best interests of the equity

---

[1] Exceptions to this rule are companies built around long term contracts from larger companies, such as tanker finance companies. An example is Tanker Finance Ltd., a British company formed in 1957 with £1,000 of equity and £26m. of debt capital. The company's entire activities consisted of long term chartering of tankers to Shell Petroleum Ltd. (the latter effectively, although not legally, controlling the tanker company). Such companies in effect draw on the equity capital of larger companies via the chartering.

shareholders, the owners of the firm. Its purpose is to indicate the minimum rate of return which projects must obtain if their acceptance and the raising of equity capital to finance them is to be in the interests of the equity shareholders, that is, lead to an increase in the net present value of their future income.

It will generally be accepted that one of the main objectives of a firm's management is to maximize the profits of the owners, the equity shareholders. The cost of equity capital is thus held to be the cost of capital to the collective body of such shareholders. For this purpose the company should be regarded as merely the legal form of this collective body, not an entity independent of it. The cost of capital to the shareholders is considered to be the *net of tax return* they could obtain from investing their capital to the best advantage elsewhere, making due allowance for any risk differential.[1]

By 'return' is meant the prospective net of tax yield on the current market value of their shares, i.e. the rate of discount which will reduce all prospective future dividends into equality with the current market price of the shares (see Chapter 1, Section 4c). This is clearly the net of tax rate of return which the firm must earn on equity funds if it is to improve the income prospects of the shareholders. By definition the shareholders on average are not interested in yields below this or they would have bid up the price of the company's shares till they gave a lower yield.

This prospective return or yield will rarely equal either the dividend yield[2] or the earnings yield[2] (respectively the current dividend per share and the current earnings per share expressed

---

[1] If the prospective discounted return or yield on investment in a similar firm is 10%, and this return is the most attractive alternative investment open to the shareholders, then 10% defines the cost of capital. If the most attractive alternative investment promises a yield of, say, 15%, but in a more risky industry, this 15% yield would have to be scaled down to give the risk equivalent yield, and this latter yield would be the relevant cost of capital.

[2] These yields are usually given gross of personal income tax deduction. In Britain, companies deduct income tax at the standard rate from the dividends, so the dividends are actually received net of tax. In the United States and most other countries dividends are paid net of company taxes, but income taxes are then levied on the individual shareholders. In either case it is the net of tax yield that concerns most individuals. As we are concerned with the net income of shareholders we shall intend all references to 'yields' to be understood as net of all taxes, corporate and personal, unless the contrary is specified. For an exposition of yields and related matters readers should consult one or more of references (3)–(7) inclusive.

as percentages of the current share price) beloved of investment analysts. Neither measure purports to embrace *all* future dividends which are the relevant determinants of the cost of equity capital, so both must be rejected for this purpose. This point is implicitly conceded by investment analysts who constantly qualify references to these measures (in particular their references to dividend yields) by stressing 'growth' possibilities.

The relevant yield calculation requires a forecast of *all* future dividends. On the face of it this would appear to be a formidable, if not impossible, task. Due to the effects of discounting for long periods at even low rates of interest (see especially the case study in Chapter 11, which contrasts the effect on the valuation of a business assuming a life of 20 years, 50 years, and a perpetual life) any income arising more than say twenty years hence, has but a minimal effect on present valuation. Hence all that is required in practice is a long term dividend forecast. Usually it is possible to forecast specific actual dividends for only a few years ahead; thereafter approximations are necessary. For example those with a good knowledge of a particular firm's prospects may be able to say that the dividend is likely to grow at 10% a year for five years, and thereafter to be stable, or perhaps to grow at an average rate of only 2% a year. Such forecasts are easily translated into the appropriate prospective yields (Chapter 1, Section 4c and reference 2 of that chapter).

A more general approximation will be found to be very useful when specific year by year forecasts are not easily made, or for the inevitable period some years ahead when only the *average* rate of dividend increase can be estimated. This concept is implied in equation (1.18), i.e. $r = (d/p) + g$, where d is the current net of tax dividend, p the current market price of the share, and g the forecast rate of increase in dividends. The g in its turn can be considered (on broad assumptions) to be governed by the amount of retained income (i.e. total income less dividend) and the rate at which it is reinvested. The basis of this is discussed in Chapter 1, Section 4c, but as an example consider the case where current net of tax profit per share is £2, the dividend £1, the current share price £20, and the retained income can be invested to earn a constant 6% after tax. So long as dividends remain 50% of income, the implied cost of capital r is:

$$r = \frac{1}{20} + 50\%(6\%) = 5\% + 3\% = 8\%$$

This formula provides a useful framework for quantifying long term dividend forecasts when a firm's dividend policy and investment opportunities are likely to be fairly stable over a long period. (The formula is, however, of doubtful value when earnings and dividends are low, and not applicable if they are zero, or negative).

So far the cost of equity capital on which a firm's management should act has been defined as the prospective yield obtainable by the equity shareholders on comparable alternative investments. An evident difficulty is that the cost of capital to the various types of equity shareholder – the small scale private investor, the large scale private investor, and the institutional investors – may well differ given the different range of alternative opportunities and expert advice open to them. Also, those shareholders paying a high rate of tax may be more concerned to receive capital gains rather than dividends,[1] the converse being true for those with a low rate of tax, or as in the case of charities, pension funds, and other non-profit making bodies, which in both Britain and the United States are generally exempt from taxation.

There is thus no unique cost of capital applicable to all the shareholders if their investment opportunities, tax status, dividend requirements, etc., vary widely. Where a company has been following a fairly consistent dividend policy, however, and where conditions in the industry are stable (i.e. the risks associated with the industry through government regulations, tariff policies, technological developments, competition, etc., are not felt likely to alter significantly over the next five years or so and thus the character of the firm is not likely to be subject to unforseeable changes) the cost of equity capital in future can reasonably be taken as the yield *achieved* on an investment in the firm's shares over the last 5–10 years. This is a reasonable presumption in that investors with similar requirements will have been attracted to become shareholders. Some of the problems arising when this assumption no longer holds good are discussed in Section 3 of Chapter 17.

c. *Ascertaining the Cost of Capital to Shareholders*

Before examining whether the cost of capital to the shareholders and the cost of capital to the firm are always synonomous a brief consideration of the likely average order of magnitude of the shareholders'

---

[1] This is especially true of Britain where at the time of writing no effective long term capital gains tax exists. But it is also true of any country where the tax rate on capital gains is less than the income tax rate of many individual investors, as is the case in the United States.

cost of capital is appropriate. Determining the cost of equity capital resolves itself into first determining the yield the firm's shareholders could obtain on alternative investments of comparable risk, and second making due allowances and corrections for the method by which the equity capital is obtained by the firm – e.g. by depreciation provisions, retained profits, rights issues or new issues. It is the first part of this problem with which this subsection is concerned.

In general the cost of capital to the shareholder in a given firm is the net of tax yield investors could obtain on comparable firms in the same industry. As the definition implies, the cost of capital will vary from industry to industry according to the risks involved, hence the following discussion relates to the average cost of capital to the shareholders of firms engaged in manufacturing industry only.

The value of the return on alternative investments – which defines the cost of capital to the shareholders – is also best considered in terms of its real purchasing power, that is corrected for inflation. For this reason the following returns are based on that obtained when dividends and capital gains received have been deflated by an index of consumer prices. (For example, suppose the yield on shares over a given period in money terms has been fairly constant at 10% and inflation fairly constant at 3%, then the yield on shares in *real* terms has been approximately $10\% - 3\% = 7\%$, or to be strictly accurate $1 \cdot 1 \div 1 \cdot 03 - 1 = 6 \cdot 8\%$.)

While difficult to determine with any exactitude a number of considerations pin down the shareholders' cost of capital for the average British industrial corporation to the range 8% to 11% after all taxes. The cost in money terms should be at least 3% over the 3% or so after tax return obtainable on government securities or first class debentures, so that the minimum is almost certainly above 6%. Historically the return in dividends and capital gains (on the discounted yield basis described in Chapter 1, Section 4c) from investing in equities in the post war period has been in the region of 11% to 12% in money terms and in real terms $7\frac{1}{2}\%$ to $8\frac{1}{2}\%$, or say 8%.[1] An analysis of the period 1919–1963 shows that the return

[1] This is based on the comprehensive analysis of the results of all 53 British Unit trusts (mutual funds) over the period 1948–62 (see 'Which?' for May 1963). The 11%–12% results from assuming an equal annual investment over the period realized at the end of the period, with all dividends assumed to be re-invested, and is the rate of discount which equates the constant annual investment with the terminal capital gain received.

from investing a constant amount of money per year in equities, and selling out at the start of 1963, would have given a return of 7·9% after tax in money terms. This period encompasses 20 years of relative stagnation and 6 years of war. With the greater economic stability and higher rate of growth expected in the future, we would estimate the return over the next decade to average 7–8% after tax and in real terms.

Analysis of American common stocks – in particular the Moody's 125 Industrials – over the decades since the first world war suggest that the yield to shareholders in dividends and capital gains has been of the order of around 11% in money terms (before personal taxes) for the medium and long term investor. Appreciably higher levels of return have been obtained over particular periods. Assuming an equal annual investment over the period 1948–62, the yield on common stocks was around 15% in money terms and 13% in real terms (both before personal taxes). Having regard to the special circumstances of the post war period, a lower yield – say 9% in real terms and 11% in money terms – might reasonably be expected for the future.

The British rates of return (and cost of capital figure) is net of personal tax at the standard rate of personal tax (38·75% in 1963) which probably represents the average rate of tax paid on dividend income.

The forecast American figure of 11% in money terms is before all personal income taxes and capital gains tax. At average rates of personal tax on dividends the shareholders' cost of capital is probably in the region of 9% in money terms and 7% in real terms after tax.[1]

---

[1] The after tax computation is complicated by the tax on realized capital gains. Assume that the before tax yield of 11% in *money* terms is made up of a 5% dividend yield plus a 6% growth (see Section 4c of Chapter 1). This implies that the average annual rise in stock prices will be 6% and hence a shareholder will have an ultimate capital gain of this amount. The maximum rate of capital gains taxation is 25%, and taking into account the delay between the accrual of the capital gain and tax payment thereon, the net present value of this tax might be taken as 10%. If personal income taxes on dividends average 30%, then applying the rule that the discounted yield on common stock equals net of tax dividend yield plus the growth rate on dividends, the net of tax yield arising from the above mentioned 11% pre-tax yield, is as follows:

$(5\% - 0·3 \times 5\%) + (6\% - 0·1 \times 6\%) = 9\%$ approximately. This, as given in the text, comes down to 7% in real terms.

d. *Cost of Capital to the Shareholders and Cost of Capital to the Firm*

The purpose of the concept of the cost of equity capital is that it will aid a firm's management in making financial decisions in the best interests of its equity shareholders. The practical result of the theory as outlined above is that if a firm's cost of capital is held to be synonymous with the cost of capital to the shareholders, the firm, by accepting all investment opportunities offering a rate of return in excess of the shareholders' cost of capital, will improve their financial position by providing investments for their capital superior in yield to those obtainable elsewhere. It is at this point, however, that the theory fails to pass the test of general application, and considerable development is required before it can do so. The limitations of the theory can best be seen from the following examples.

Assume the cost of capital to equity shareholders, both existing and potential, to be r, and that *the* firm proposes to invest in certain new projects offering just this rate of return and no more, obtaining the necessary funds from a new issue of equity shares to subscribers of whom the majority are not existing shareholders. Will the financial position of both the existing shareholders and the new subscribers necessarily be improved by the firm undertaking the new investments yielding the rate of return r? This will depend on whether the price at which the new issue was made implied a rate of return r on the then existing investments of the firm. Clearly the new shares merely entitle their holders to a share in the profits of the whole company, both on the assets it already possesses and on the new assets bought out of the proceeds of the new issue. If the issue price implied a *higher* yield than r on existing assets then despite the fact that the new investment has achieved the acceptable return of r, the old shareholders will be worse off as a result, while the new subscribers will be better off. This arises from the fact that the prospective income per share before the new issue was greater than r, say $(r+s)$, while the prospective income after the new issue is a mixture of $(r+s)$, on the old assets, and only r on the assets acquired from the new issue funds. Hence the average prospective income per share (there is of course no distinction in income entitlement between old and new shares) must now be less than $(r+s)$, but greater than r, to the detriment of the old shareholders, and to the benefit of the new.

Conversely, if the issue price to new subscribers had *over-valued* the shares on the basis of prospective income the old shareholders must benefit at the expense of the new subscribers who would of course have a prospective income of less than r.

From this discussion it is apparent that whenever the shares of a company are incorrectly valued (that is valued at any price other than that giving them the same prospective yield as other comparable investment opportunities), *and* a share issue is made which involves the introduction of new shareholders (both conditions are necessary),[1] then the cost of capital to the shareholders and the cost of capital to the firm will diverge.

Whether a firm's shares are correctly valued at their quoted price is a matter of great importance whenever new equity capital is being raised from outsiders, but the price of a firm's shares should always be a matter of great concern to its management. Whenever shares are significantly undervalued this is to the detriment of the existing shareholders. Those shareholders who are aware of the under-valuation may be unable to hold on to their shares until their true worth is recognized by the market. Those who are unaware of the undervaluation may unwittingly sell. In both cases existing share-holders suffer a loss while outsiders stand to make a windfall gain.

The extent to which shares are commonly wrongly valued is difficult to determine, but from the fact that investment trust shares frequently stand (both in Britain and the United States) at sub-stantial discounts (and sometimes premiums) over the market value of their assets is a *prima facie* case for supposing that incorrect valuations are not uncommon.

In our experience it is fairly frequent for the shares of companies to be undervalued, particularly progressive expanding companies – if the 'correct' valuation is taken to be that of their own managements. Whether or not their assessments are correct is of course a matter of opinion: – the opinion of the investing public on the basis of publicly available information: the opinion of the managements on the basis of more detailed and often confidential information. As managements are more intimately concerned than the investing public with the opportunities open to their firms, and perhaps more important, their plans to exploit such opportunities, their estimates of future profitability are likely to be more accurate. In support of this

---

[1] Where new investment is financed by the existing shareholders' funds (that is by the depreciation provisions and retained profits, and by rights issues – see below) and no new shareholders are brought in, then so long as the new investment earns a return in excess of or equal to the shareholders' cost of capital, the shareholders must gain from the investment.

contention it can be argued that if the market held reasonably accurate views, then many of the erratic fluctuations so common in share prices would cease to exist. Rather price changes would occur slowly and smoothly as long term prospects were gradually judged to alter.

When managements consider their firm's shares to be significantly wrongly valued it would seem to be their obvious duty to their shareholders to do all in their power to publicize their own views to help the market form a more accurate opinion of future prospects. Even where dividend forecasts by management are explicitly prohibited (as is the case in the United States[1]) there are many ways of influencing opinion and it is desirable that this should happen. (That a management can sometimes produce a significant increase in share values was demonstrated by the spectacular increase of 75% achieved by Courtaulds when fighting off the I.C.I. takeover bid in early 1962.) This is obvious when a management considers its firm's shares to be significantly undervalued, as shares change hands at the wrong price to the detriment of the existing shareholders to whom management owes a clear duty. Where management considers its shares significantly overvalued (and this would seem to be uncommon in practice) it may not be in the best interests of its present shareholders to publicise the management's estimates of profitability. Whether management does so is more a question of commercial morality than economics. But it can be argued that as overvaluation cannot long be sustained it can be in the interests of existing shareholders to publish information on future profitability, even though share prices fall, otherwise shareholders may hold on to their shares and pass up more profitable investment opportunities elsewhere.

In a number of cases such public statements may not have the desired effect because of public scepticism, or more commonly because directors are unwilling to make forecasts save in the most guarded form in view of the public criticism to which they may be exposed in the event of errors. (In this last connection it has to be remembered that frequently a firm, for reasons of commercial secrecy, cannot make known to the public the grounds for its forecasts or the reasons why past forecasts have not been realized.)

The techniques required to evaluate the cost of capital to a firm where this diverges from the cost of capital to the shareholders

[1] Formally dividend and profit forecasts are forbidden by S.E.C. regulations although the letter of the regulations in this case is not rigidly enforced.

necessitate extended analysis and for this reason discussion of these techniques will be deferred to Chapter 17.

In this chapter we briefly outline only sufficient of the analysis to enable an assessment to be made of the effect on the cost of capital of undervaluation of shares in the case where a new issue is being considered.

e. *The Cost of the Different Forms of Equity Capital*

So far we have considered in general terms the cost of equity capital in a public quoted company. We must now widen the discussion and consider in detail the cost of different sources of equity capital. There are four such sources: depreciation provisions, retained profits, rights issues, and new issues. For the moment we shall continue to assume the company draws all its financial requirements from equity sources. We would repeat that it is not the object of these sections to discuss optimal methods of finance under the great variety of conditions which arise in practice. We are merely concerned here to indicate the main elements of the cost of equity and to make a few broad generalizations regarding the relative cost of the different types of equity capital.

For readers who are content to accept the broad conclusions of this section without reading the detailed justifications we estimate, as a rough order of magnitude, the average net of tax cost of the different forms of equity capital for Britain and the United States in *real* terms (i.e. after allowing for inflation) will be as follows for the typical medium and large size firms.

Forecast Average Net of Tax Cost of the Different forms of Equity Capital in Real Terms

	Britain After Corporate and Average Personal Tax	United States After Corporate Tax only	After Corporate and Average Personal Tax
Retained Funds			
Depreciation Provisions	8%	9%	5%
Retained Earnings	8%	9%	5%
Newly Raised Funds[1]			
Rights Issues	8½%+	10%+	7%+
New Issues[2]	9%+	11%+	7½%+

[1] In the case of newly raised funds the costs are minimum costs assuming a firm's shares are not significantly undervalued at the time of issue.

[2] Non-rights issues by established companies are rare: the figure is included merely for completeness.

i. *Retained profits and depreciation provisions.* The main source of funds available for investment by a firm are normally current retained profits and depreciation provisions. The 'cost' of the current retained earnings to the firm is determined by the fact that these funds can be returned to the shareholders as further dividends. Similarly the current depreciation provision can also be returned to shareholders. As long as there are sufficient reserves of past retained profits (known as revenue reserves – see Appendix A) the current depreciation provision can be returned to the shareholders in the form of dividends – that is the current depreciation provision effectively provides the cash for dividends formally declared out of past retained profits. When such retained profit reserves have been exhausted dividends can be returned to shareholders only if there is a formal reduction of capital. It is the possibility of paying out current retained earnings and depreciation provisions to shareholders which (subject to certain tax considerations analysed below) causes them to have an opportunity cost equal to the net of tax return which the shareholders might obtain from the use of these funds in alternative investment. This opportunity cost, however, must be defined more exactly in the light of the taxes imposed on firms and on their shareholders.

Suppose for example that the tax levied on or deducted by the firm at source in anticipation of personal taxes is proportion t of the firm's *earnings* and that any amount received by the shareholder as dividends is taxed at his additional personal rate of tax p. If the firm has earnings of x and distributes these to the shareholders they will receive net of tax $x(1-t)(1-p)$ and will have this amount available for investment. If the firm retains the earnings x it will have net of tax $x(1-t)$ and avoid payment of the personal taxation $xp(1-t)$. Hence the firm can accept a return on its investments less by the proportion p than the return open to shareholders on their alternative investment opportunities. It follows therefore that the cost of equity retained capital from earnings is less than the shareholders' cost of capital (the rate of return they can obtain on alternative investments) by the proportion p.

In Britain tax at the standard rate of personal tax is deducted at source by the firm on all *earnings*. When such earnings are paid out in dividends, this tax on the earnings is credited by the individual against his personal tax which will include tax on the gross (before tax) amount of the net of tax dividends received. Additional tax is then effectively paid or refunded to the individual depending on whether he is in a tax bracket above or below the standard rate of tax which has been deducted at source. The standard rate of tax, however, covers such a wide range of taxpayers, and with the offsetting effect of those above and below the standard rate, p the average additional tax actually paid by or credited to the individual is probably negligible.

In the United States, however, with no deduction of personal income taxes at source, p is probably quite high and for firms whose shares are not held to an exceptional degree by tax exempt institutions it is probably around 30%. Hence this factor might make the cost of retained earnings some 30% less than the cost of externally raised equity. A qualification to this general line of argument as regards the United States is that retained earnings, by increasing the price of the stock (each unit of stock now represents more invested capital), make the shareholders subject on realization of the stock to additional capital gains tax on this increase in price. This tax, however, had a maximum (in 1963) of 25% and if payment of this tax can be postponed though postponing realization for a number of years the effect of inflation and discounting will reduce this to a substantially smaller figure. This figure will evidently vary from person to person and period to period, but as an order of magnitude it might be hazarded that it would on average be around 10%. Hence if the average rate of personal tax is, say, 30%, the equivalent of an *immediate* tax saving of 20% results from this. Taking the shareholders' cost of capital as 9% net of personal taxes (see the end of Subsection C above) in *money* terms, the net of tax cost of equity capital from retained earnings is therefore $0.8 \times 9\% = 7.2\%$, less 2% for inflation, $= 5.2\%$ or say, 5% in *real* terms.

The British figure, which requires no such adjustment, is simply the shareholders' normal cost of equity capital, namely around 8%.

Given that retained funds obviate the issue costs of externally raised equity (and in the United States reap an appreciable tax advantage), there would seem to be some justification for the view that no dividends should be paid when investment opportunities are open to the company in excess of the shareholders' yield requirements. In a perfectly rational world this would be true, but in practice it would be unrealistic to recommend a company to follow such a course. Shareholders and the market generally place a high value on regular dividend payments, and whenever a company fails to pay a dividend, share prices are liable to fall in consequence. If a company persists in such a policy – i.e. its dividend fluctuates appreciably, and is occasionally withheld altogether even though profits are quite adequate – then the market price of its shares will probably be permanently lower than would have been the case with a stable[1] dividend policy. Where this happens the cost of capital to the company may permanently increase.

The emphasis the market places on the dividend rate is based on some quite sound reasons. Many institutions and individuals depend on a regular cash income from their equity investments. If in any year the dividend is withheld or reduced (even for the purpose of retaining more funds for profitable reinvestment) such shareholders may have to sell part of their holdings. This depresses the market price of the shares to the detriment of those shareholders who must sell, especially if many shareholders are in this position and are thus forced to sell at short notice and at the same time. There is also the fact that the dividend rate is often held to indicate the management's own view of future prospects on the grounds that managements are generally reluctant to raise a dividend rate unless it can be maintained in future. Finally, shareholders may view with not unreasonable scepticism the profitability of a stream of investment projects for which a firm's management is unwilling to make a direct approach to them via a rights issue, or by a new issue in the equity market. Examples of retained profits being used for basically uneconomic purposes – to finance 'empire building' or maintaining loss making activities for reasons of tradition or even the largely personal gratification of directors – are not unknown.

Finally let us consider in somewhat more detail the cost of the depreciation provisions. As already noted this turns on a realistic assessment of the alternative use of these provisions. Normally they can effectively be paid out to the shareholders in the form of dividends by declaring dividends out of past retained earnings and this will normally define their opportunity cost as identical to that of retained earnings. A qualification to this, however, is that such a reduction in the capital of the company may necessitate the repayment of some outstanding debt since insufficient assets are available

---

[1] By a stable dividend policy is meant not so much a fixed dividend, but rather a dividend which is typically at least as high as in the previous year, and rising as profits increase. As with any such general rule there are many exceptions. Mining companies often make a practice of distributing quite a high proportion of their profits, even though such profits fluctuate quite widely with changing metal and mineral prices. But broadly speaking companies do not like to declare dividends at a rate above that which they can hope to maintain in the future, or at least for the next few years.

to support it or alternatively because this is simply management policy. In this case it would be necessary to consider the cost of the depreciation provisions as equal in part to that of the debt and in part that of retained earnings. Thus if this particular *tranche* of retained earnings will be used (if it is not invested) 30% to repay debt costing $2\frac{1}{2}\%$ after tax and 70% distributed as dividends when retained earnings have a cost of 9%, the 'cost' of the depreciation provisions should be considered as

$$0.3 \times 2.5\% + 0.7 \times 9\%$$

or approximately 7%. (This matter is fully discussed in Section 8 of the following chapter.)

ii. *New issues.* By new issues we mean new issues of equity capital made to the public in general with no special rights (pre-emptive rights) of subscription for the existing shareholders. Such non-rights issues are considerably less common in both Britain and the United States than rights issues. Indeed many states in the United States automatically confer pre-emptive rights on existing shareholders unless this right is specifically withheld under a corporation's charter. New issues, however, are still fairly common – particularly for relatively recently established companies whose capital needs have outgrown the resources available from existing shareholders or for private companies converting to public companies. For this reason, and also because they are somewhat simpler to understand than rights issues, they will be considered first.

Before considering the descriptive data it is necessary to establish the correct conceptual framework to which this data is to be applied. Consider first the method for computing the cost of such equity capital to a firm, that is the minimum rate of return it must earn on this capital in order for the raising of the capital to be in the best interests of its existing shareholders.

Conventional theory assumes that prior to a new issue shares are correctly valued by the market such that these shares offer a yield y, equal to that of all other firms of comparable risk, thus y correctly measures the existing shareholders' cost of capital. It is normally assumed that a new issue will need to be issued at a discount (say proportion d) off this pre-issue price, and hence that the shares of the firm will be undervalued at the new issue price. In addition to this discount the new issue will involve issue and administrative expenses (equal to proportion e of the pre-issue price). The minimum yield which a firm needs to obtain on any new capital raised, if this capital raising is to be in the interests of existing shareholders, is then held to be

$$\frac{y}{1-d-e}$$

If this minimum return is earned on the new capital then the new capital will have contributed its full proportionate share to the firm's profits such that existing shareholders have exactly the same income prospects as before the new issue. (It is additionally assumed that the undervaluation of the firm's shares is only temporary so that pre-issue shareholders selling out after the new issue suffer no losses, that is the post issue price soon rises to equal the pre-issue price.)

This criterion can be shown to give an unduly high cost of capital where it can be shown that any of the new capital has been subscribed by existing (i.e. pre-issue) shareholders. Suppose for example the whole of a new issue is subscribed by the existing shareholders in exact proportion to their existing holdings. In this case it would be immaterial at what discount the new shares were issued. The number of shares or the price at which they are issued will not in the least way alter the level or the proportionate participation of the shareholders in the firm's profits. Hence all that the firm needs to earn on the capital raised is simply $y/(1-e)$. As long as it does this all the existing shareholders will be as well off as they were before, and as well off as they would be investing their funds elsewhere.

At the other extreme, if all the capital is subscribed by 'outsiders', that is individuals who own none of the existing shares, the price at which the new shares are issued is no longer immaterial, but a vital factor determining the welfare of the existing shareholders. This issue price is the price at which the firm's existing profits are being shared with outsiders. On reflection it will be apparent that it is to this situation that the cost of capital as given by $y/(1-d-e)$ refers.

Almost invariably some capital will come from existing shareholders and some from new shareholders. It is intuitively fairly obvious that the cost of a new issue should be the two costs so far established weighted by the proportion, say, p subscribed by existing[1] shareholders and $1-p$ subscribed by new shareholders. For convenience of later discussion, however, it will be preferable at the cost of insignificant error, first to calculate the cost of capital

---

[1] Capital from 'old' shareholders is fully defined in Chapter 17, Section 1.

gross of issue expenses and then to arrive at the cost of net issue expenses by dividing by $1 - e$. The cost of capital gross of issue expenses is therefore given by:

$$\text{yield at new issue price} \times \frac{\text{capital from new shareholders}}{\text{total capital raised}} + \text{shareholders' cost of capital} \times \frac{\text{capital from old shareholders}}{\text{total capital raised}}$$

$$(3.1)$$

If the shares of the firm were correctly valued to give the yield y prior to the new issue, the yield at the new issue price is simply $y/(1-d)$. In the general application of the formula where shares are undervalued (in view of the firm's management – here accepted as correct) in the first place, then the yield at the new issue price used in the formula is simply the management's estimate.

Suppose for example that the normal market yield (and the shareholders' cost of capital) is 10% on this type of stock, but that the firm contemplating the new issue has reasonable grounds for supposing that its shares are already undervalued and that the additional undervaluation due to the new issue will cause the shares to show a yield of around 12·5% at the new issue price. If 40% of the new issue is subscribed by 'old' and 60% by 'new' shareholders the cost of capital before issue expenses will be

$$12 \cdot 5 \times 0 \cdot 6 + 10 \cdot 0 \times 0 \cdot 4 = 11 \cdot 5\%.$$

As seen from the formula the firm's cost of capital will be lower the smaller the degree of undervaluation of its shares at the new issue price and the larger the proportion of the new capital subscribed by existing shareholders. This points to the importance of keeping the undervaluation in the issue price at a minimum and endeavouring to obtain as much as possible from the existing shareholders.

It is nevertheless often the case that new issues are priced appreciably below what the market will bear and rapidly rise to a substantial premium above their issue price. This is generally undesirable since it means that the new issue price was below what the market was prepared to pay; the result is that those subscribing to the new issue have gained by this underestimation of the market price rather than the firm gaining this amount (in the form of a higher issue price) for the general benefit of *all* existing shareholders. Thus the settling down of the share price at much above the new issue price is not a cause for congratulation to the company's management and their financial advisers, but an indication of underestimating the acceptable new issue price at the expense of the existing shareholders.

For a number of reasons, however, it may be desirable or necessary to place the new issue price appreciably under the market price. One reason is the considerable difficulty of estimating the market price for the often little known or not widely marketed stocks which are usually the subject of new issues. It is also extremely difficult to estimate the equilibrium new issue price exactly, especially when it is remembered that the issue price must be agreed several weeks prior to the actual announcement to obtain the consent of the underwriters and to allow time for printing, etc. As share prices can move significantly in several weeks the issue price must be low enough to allow for contingencies. A further practical reason for issuing at a price rather below that which the firm would otherwise choose, is that the alternative may be higher underwriting commissions or even failure to obtain underwriting for the new issue at all.

Failure of an issue to be fully subscribed, with a consequent fall in price as the underwriters eventually dispose of the stock at the lower market price, may weaken the general market for the stock through this unfavourable publicity and the disappointed expectations of those who subscribed at the higher issue price. Hence the cost to the firm from a failure of the new issue heavily weights the decision in favour of issuing at something of a discount on the market price.

Finally the mere force of supply and demand and the need to attract shareholders who have not found the existing price sufficiently attractive may necessitate issuing the new shares at an appreciable discount.

The above considerations point to the possibility of the new issue price being appreciably under the market price. Whether or not this will represent an undervaluation of the firm's shares at the new issue price will evidently depend on the degree of the discount off the pre-existing market price and the extent to which this price represented a reasonable valuation of the firm's shares. In some cases it may be possible for the firm to chose the time of issue at a date when its shares are somewhat overvalued so that the discount induced by the new issue merely causes the shares to assume their correct valuation. From the frequent examples of new issues rapidly rising to a premium, however, an appreciable undervaluation would seem to characterize a substantial proportion of new issues.

The cost of new issues in terms of the discount at which the shares are issued, underwriting and administrative expenses, will evidently vary greatly with the widely varying circumstances of new issues. These may range from issues by substantial already quoted companies to issues by little known companies which are obtaining a quotation for the first time as they make the new issue.

Very little British data is available to make any assessment of the influence of different factors on the costs of new issues and as regards the vital element of the discount in the price at which the shares are offered, almost no published collated data is available at all. Information [8] relating to the years 1945–47 indicates the underwriting and administrative expenses of companies as averaging 12% of the capital raised, for companies simultaneously obtaining a market quotation and making the new issue. This figure was based on a sample of 19 companies making issues with an average size of £229,000. The costs for 17 companies making a new issue by means of a stock exchange placing (i.e. sale of the securities through a stock exchange broker to large investors on an individual basis) were 23% of the £136,000 average amount of capital raised. In recent years the more stable market in new issues and the effect of increasing prices in inflating the average size of new issues would appear to have reduced appreciably administrative and underwriting costs as a percentage of the capital raised.

Considerably more information is available on the costs of new issues in the United States and some data for United States manufacturing industries is set out in Table 3.1.

Table 3.1

Issue Costs for United States Manufacturing Industry 1951–1955

Size of Issue ($ million)	No. of Issues	Total Cost	Underwriters' Compensation	Other Expenses
		%	%	%
Under 1·0	11	14·87	11·71	3·16
1·0– 4·9	27	9·90	8·34	1·57
5·0– 9·9	4	7·14	6·41	0·74
10·0–19·9	1	4·53	3·99	0·54

Source: 'Cost of Flotation of Corporate Securities 1951–1955, S.E.C.'

Unfortunately almost no information at all is available on the proportion of the new capital subscribed by 'new' and 'old' shareholders. If, however, we take the proportion of 'old' and 'new' shareholders subscribing to the new issue as 50%, the average undervaluation at the new issue price as 7%, the after tax shareholders' cost of capital in real terms as 8% (the British case), this would suggest a cost of equity capital from new issues as of:

$$\frac{8\%}{0\cdot 93} \times 0\cdot 5 + 8\% \times 0\cdot 5 = 8\cdot 3\% \text{ gross of issue costs.}$$

Taking issue costs as 10% the net cost of capital is 9·35%. This compares with the simple 8% cost of equity capital from retained earnings.

iii. *Rights issues (privileged subscriptions)*. Rights issues or privileged subscriptions are issues of capital in which existing shareholders of the corporation are given the pre-emptive right to subscribe to the whole of the new issue; these pre-emptive rights are usually in proportion to existing shares held and at a price appreciably below the existing market price of the firm's existing shares. The shareholders can sell their right to subscribe if they themselves do not chose to exercise them.

Consider first the correct method by which investors should evaluate rights issues in a specific hypothetical example.

Example 1. Company X has 2,000,000 issued shares which now stand at a market price of £10 each, making a total market capitalization of £20m. At this price the shares are estimated by the market to offer, say, a 10% long term yield. To take an extreme case, suppose the firm now announces a 1 for 1 rights issue at £5, thus raising £10m. on which it forecasts a return equal to that on its existing capital. Ignoring all issue costs, consider first (a) the price the investor should be prepared to pay for the rights (i.e. the value of the 'right' to subscribe for a new share at a cost of only £5) and (b) the share price after the rights issue.

As might be expected the critical factor is the expected yield on the new capital. If the market behaves rationally, the total market value of the firm's shares after the rights issue should be equal to the capitalized earnings of the firm at the market's normal rate of capitalization for a firm of this type. If, for example, the market expects the same earnings on the new capital as on the old, the total value of the firm's shares should be their value before the new issue (£20m.) plus the value of the newly subscribed capital (£10m.). The value per share would, therefore, be this amount divided by the number of shares, or $$\frac{£30,000,000}{4,000,000} = £7\cdot5 \text{ each.}$$

This is a special case, however.

Suppose in fact the market estimated that the return on the new money would be less than that on the existing capital and only, say, 6%. (If the market's expectations were correct, then of course the firm would not be justified in raising money to invest at a rate below the shareholders' cost of capital.) If these yields could be expressed as a constant amount per year, the total yield on all the firm's capital would be:

$$0\cdot10 \times £20,000,000 + 0\cdot06 \times £10,000,000 = £2,600,000.$$

If the shares are to give the market yield of 10%, they must have a total value of

$$\frac{£2,600,000}{0\cdot10} = £26,000,000.$$

As there are now 4,000,000 shares the value per share must be

$$\frac{£26,000,000}{4,000,000} = £6\cdot5 \text{ each.}$$

For convenience this can be reduced to the simple formula
Ex-rights price of shares =

$$\text{pre-issue price} \times \frac{\text{no. of old shares}}{\text{total no. of shares}} + \text{issue price} \times \frac{\text{no. of new shares}}{\text{total no. of shares}} \times \frac{\text{yield on new capital}}{\text{yield on old capital}} \tag{3.2}$$

Thus in the previous example,

Ex-rights price of shares

$$= £10 \times \frac{2,000,000}{4,000,000} + £5 \times \frac{2,000,000}{4,000,000} \times \frac{0\cdot06}{0\cdot10} = £6\cdot5$$

In the earlier case, where the yield on the new and old capital was expected to be the same, the formula gives as before £7·5 per share as the ex-rights price of the shares. The usual assumption of the market, or at least the basis of normal calculations of the ex-rights price of the shares, is that the yield on the new and old capital will be the same.

It should be clear that determination of the ex-rights price determines the value of the rights. Thus if the value of the shares ex-rights is £7·5 it will pay an investor to offer for the subscription rights to one share, up to the difference between the £7·5 and the price of the privileged subscription to the new shares. The latter price in Example 1 was £5, hence the rights to subscribe at only £5 are worth £7·5 − £5 = £2·5. At this price the investor is indifferent whether he pays £7·5 for shares ex-rights (i.e. after their rights have been used) or pays £2·5 for the rights and acquires shares for £5. It is normally to be expected therefore that supply and demand will push the rights price towards this figure.

Consider now the effect of the rights issue on the existing shareholders. The price of the shares held by them will drop from £10 to £7·5 when the rights issue is over. Despite this, however, they will be no worse off *providing* they either exercise their rights and subscribe, or alternatively sell their rights for the calculated price of £2·5 per share. For if the shareholder sells the rights he obtains £2·5 per share to compensate for the £2·5 fall in the value of the shares after the rights issue. Alternatively if he subscribes then he obtains a share worth £7·5 for only £5 (the new issue price) and thus is compensated in this way for the £2·5 fall in the price of the shares he already holds. (It is increasingly common for firms to sell off the rights of non-subscribing shareholders who fail to do so on their own behalf, distributing the net proceeds to them.)

Providing the market behaves rationally, it is in fact invariably the case that the existing shareholders are always compensated in this way for the fall in value of their shares. Where this is the case it will always be immaterial, in this respect, at what discount (on the existing market price) the firm issues the new shares. This point is often mis-understood but it arises inevitably from the conditions under which the rights issues are made. A correct understanding of this point, however, is essential if the true cost and relative merits of this main source of externally raised equity are to be appreciated. Moreover as will be noted below certain advantages will normally follow from issuing at an appreciable discount on existing market price.

From the viewpoint of the firm the equity cost of capital from rights issues is determined by much the same considerations as for a straight new issue without pre-emptive rights, namely yield on the new issue price and costs of the new issue, and the proportion subscribed by outsiders. A new factor in the case of a rights issue, however, is the amount received by old shareholders for the sale of any rights which they do not themselves take up. The following formula which is justified in detail in Section 2, Chapter 17, can be shown to give the approximate cost of equity capital obtained by a rights issue.

$$\text{yield at new issue price} \times \frac{\substack{\text{capital subscribed} \\ \text{by new shareholders}}}{\substack{\text{total new capital} \\ \text{subscribed}}} +$$

$$\text{shareholders' cost of capital} \times \frac{\substack{\text{capital subscribed} \\ \text{by old shareholders} \\ \text{less capital received} \\ \text{for sale of rights}}}{\substack{\text{total new capital} \\ \text{subscribed}}} \quad (3.3)$$

By 'yield at new issue price' is meant (as always) the firm's best estimate of this on the total capital (old and new) valued at the price of the new issue.

The application of this formula is demonstrated in the following example.

Example 2. Suppose the facts to be as in Example 1 and that the market correctly estimates the yield on the old and the net new capital at 10% with the result that the ex-rights price is £7·5 and the rights sell for £2·5. Assume also that each old shareholder sells half of his rights for £2·5 each and exercises the other half in subscribing to the new issue. If we also assume the shareholders' cost of capital to be 10% we should expect the above formula to give the cost of capital as 10% since in this case the new issue causes no under-valuation of the shares.

The components of the formula are as follows. First the yield on new issue price. Treating the long term yield (10%) as if it were accruing currently at a constant annual amount (i.e. at 10% on the £30m. capital) is a valid simplification for the purpose of this calculation. On this assumption the yield is 10% on both new (£10m.) and old (£20m.) capital and is therefore £3m. At the new issue share price of £5 this represents a yield of 15% on the 2m. shares. The 'new' shareholders are those who have bought the rights, and since half the rights have been sold, these 'new' shareholders must have contributed half of the total subscription of £10m. The 'old' shareholders have subscribed the other half and have also received £2·5m. for their rights (1m. × £2·5). On this data the formula gives as the cost of capital (before issue expenses)

$$0{\cdot}15 \times \frac{\pounds 5\text{m.}}{\pounds 10\text{m.}} + 0{\cdot}10 \times \frac{\pounds 5\text{m.} - \pounds 2{\cdot}5\text{m.}}{\pounds 10\text{m.}} = 10\%$$

as expected. It will be found in this case, since there is no undervaluation of the shares, that the cost of capital will always be 10%, irrespective of the proportions subscribed by 'old' or 'new' shareholders.

Example 3. This example illustrates the effect of a rights issue in causing an undervaluation of the firm's shares. Suppose the firm anticipates that the pressure of the new share issue causes such a depression in the price level so that after the new issue they stand at a 12% yield instead of the pre-issue yield (and shareholders' cost of capital) of 10%. At the pre-issue price the shares are assumed to have been correctly valued. The other facts are as assumed in Example 2.

The post issue total value of the 4m. shares should be

$$\frac{\pounds 3\text{m.}}{0{\cdot}12} = \pounds 25\text{m. or } \pounds 6{\cdot}25 \text{ per share,}$$

On these assumptions the price of the rights, if the firm has correctly estimated the market's post new issue (ex-rights) price of the shares, will be the difference between the £6·25 and the new issue price of £5, that is £1·25.

The amount received for rights will therefore be

$$1\text{m.} \times \pounds 1{\cdot}25 = \pounds 1{\cdot}25\text{m.}$$

This amount and the yield at the new issue price (now 12%) are the only figures to change compared with the previous example of the formula.

The firm's estimate of the true yield on the new issue price is precisely as before, that given by the £3m. divided by the number of shares at the new issue price (£5 × 4m., that is £20m.) or 15%.

Substituting these values in the formula we obtain:

$$\frac{15\% \times \pounds 5\text{m.}}{\pounds 10\text{m.}} + \frac{10\%(\pounds 5\text{m.} - \pounds 1{\cdot}25\text{m.})}{\pounds 10\text{m.}} = 11{\cdot}25\%.$$

The cost of capital is now seen to be critically dependent on the proportion subscribed by 'old' shareholders. In the limiting case, however, where the latter subscribe to *all* the new capital, the cost of capital reverts to 10%,[1] the normal shareholders' cost of capital.

The costs of new issue itself can, of course, be allowed for by simply taking the cost of capital as determined by the formula and dividing by $1-e$ where e is the percentage of total capital raised comprised of issue expenses.

Rights issues have a number of advantages over non-rights issues. The mere fact that they are aimed at existing shareholders (rather than the investing public at large) probably produces greater response from this group of investors and thus should result in a larger proportion of the capital subscribed coming from existing shareholders. This, as we have seen above, is most important in that it should minimize the cost of capital by minimizing the adverse effect of the undervaluation which often accompanies a new share issue. The rights issue by the same token is also somewhat cheaper in administrative costs since it can rely primarily on contacting existing shareholders, rather than advertising to contact potential shareholders.

Table 3.2
Issue Costs of Rights Issues U.S. Manufacturing Industry 1951–1955

Size of Issue	No. of Issues	Total %	Underwriters' Compensation %	Other Expenses %
Under 1·0	3	8·17	5·44	2·74
1·0– 4·9	6	6·21	4·53	1·68
5·0– 9·9	3	3·19	2·38	0·81
10·0–19·9	3	2·96	2·24	0·72
20·0+	2	1·65	1·28	0·38

Source: 'Cost of Flotation of Corporate Securities' S.E.C.

[1] In the other limiting case where all the capital is subscribed by 'new' shareholders, the formula is seen to give the cost of capital as 12·5%. This can be shown to be incorrect due to the approximative nature of the formula. It can be corrected by recognizing the element of recursiveness in the formula – if the first estimate of the cost of capital is 12·5% then if the firm achieves this the yield at the £5 share price is 16·75%. Substituting this in the formula the cost of capital is estimated at 13·75%. As may be verified, a yield of this magnitude will almost exactly compensate them for 'giving up' 50% of the firm's earnings, assuming they invest the £2·5m. of rights money they obtain for so doing in investments giving the market yield of 10%. This correction, however, is rarely significant except, as in the present case, a substantial undervaluation is conjoined with a relatively large new issue and a large proportion is subscribed by 'new' shareholders. For a full discussion of all this see Chapter 17.

Moreover as will be clear from the later analysis (in the following subsection) the 'auction' element in rights issues (where the issue price is sufficiently below the market) is such as to make the possibility of the issue failing to be subscribed quite negligible. In Britain, where the new issue price is commonly well below the market, this enables underwriting either to be dispensed with altogether in a large proportion of the cases or for it to feature as a very small cost (appreciably less than 1% for established companies) for the outside risk of the share price falling below the low issue price.

In the United States where it would appear more common to make the new issue price closer to the existing market price, the risks of the issue failing to be subscribed are considerably greater, and for this reason underwriting would relatively seem more frequent. Table 3.2 gives some information on United States rights issues; comparing this with Table 3.1 it is seen to indicate clearly the lower costs of rights compared with new issues.

iv. *Comparison of rights issues and new issues.* Consider now the relative merits of rights and new issues. If the shares are correctly valued by all concerned at the issue price of a non-rights issue or at the expected ex-rights price which determines the value of the rights in a rights issue, then the choice is a straightforward one and depends only on the actual administrative and underwriting costs of the two alternatives. An appreciable advantage of raising the new funds via a rights issue is that the issue expenses are cheaper; also the final aggregate market value of the shares after the rights issue should be marginally higher than in the case of a new issue. Both factors benefit the existing shareholders whose interests should be the chief concern of the firm's management. The reason for the aggregate value of the shares being higher in the rights issue case is based on the assumption that even when the value of the shares is universally agreed, existing shareholders must value their shares marginally higher than non-shareholders. If the latter are to take up shares they should do so only at a price marginally below that acceptable to existing shareholders. This discussion pre-supposes that the rights issue, if made, would be taken up primarily by the existing shareholders, while the new issue if made would be taken up primarily by investors who are not already shareholders. Where the proportion of existing shareholders and new investors is the same regardless of whether the issue is a rights issue or a new issue, then the aggregate market value of all the shares should be the same regardless of which alternative is chosen. Even in this case, however, a rights issue retains the considerable advantages of lower costs of issue.

The most important reason for preferring rights issues to new issues arises where there is reason to suppose that the shares in question will be undervalued. If a firm's shares are correctly valued prior to raising new funds, and the firm's management are confident that they can choose the new issue price with such exactitude that the market price of all shares settles down at the new issue price, there is no problem. But for the reasons set out in the previous sub-section iii, in practice it is extremely difficult to determine this equilibrium new issue price and so the new issue price invariably tends to be made at a lower price to allow for contingencies and to meet the underwriters' requirements. The difference between the new issue price and the higher equilibrium price represents a loss to the existing shareholders. Rights issues at a significant discount, however, do not require any such valuation as they will exactly equate the supply and demand for the firm's shares without involving any loss to existing shareholders, for whatever the premium on the rights, it accrues to the existing shareholders. In effect the issue is at a 'floating' price consisting of (a) the actual issue price plus (b) the value of the rights to subscribe to one new share. Part (b) of the price is determined by the market forces of supply and demand. In this way the firm is ensured of obtaining the capital it requires while shareholders are compensated by the cash received in the form of the freely determined market value of the rights. The issue then takes place at the price which is just sufficient to clear the fixed number of shares on offer. It is seen therefore that the issue need not involve any appreciable (or indeed any) underwriting commission providing it is issued at a significant discount on the market price thus giving supply and demand a substantial margin on which to operate. This type of consideration must be qualified, however, by stressing that a strong and rational market in the shares is a pre-requisite. Underwriting even at a high cost may still be worthwhile where the market for the share is weak or irrational, in order to provide a stabilizing element in the market.

So far we have been presuming that a firm's shares are correctly valued prior to raising new funds, but that its management could not choose the new issue price as closely to the equilibrium price as would be desirable, and must therefore choose a somewhat lower price to be sure of a successful issue. This lower price would of course be more to the detriment of the existing shareholders than would be the case in a rights issue. The advantages of a rights issue are even more apparent in those cases where the firm's management considers the *pre-issue* market price to be a significant undervaluation of the firm's true prospects. A new issue by definition allows and encourages third parties to participate in a large way in the under-valued prospective income of the existing shareholders. New share-holders are of course always benefiting even without the new issue by buying out existing shareholders, and this will be accentuated in a rights issue as some rights are sure to be sold off. But a rights issue of a given size should result in far fewer outsiders benefiting than would a similarly sized new issue.[1]

From the above discussion it is apparent why rights issues are to be preferred to new issues. Indeed, in sum, there are good reasons for supposing that new issues are always less preferable than rights issues even when a rights issue would result in the majority of existing shareholders selling off their rights to third parties because they are unwilling to increase their own stake in the company. For the rights issue, as has been argued, is essentially an auction which ensures that the eventual market price is always for the benefit of the existing shareholders. Only a new issue made on the auction system would be an acceptable substitute.

As we have shown, rights issues are cheaper than new issues, and in turn, depreciation provisions and retained profits are cheaper than rights issues. (For a graphical presentation of these facts see Section f below.) These facts find their reflection in market conduct. Since the war the majority of equity funds have come from retained profits and depreciation provisions: rights issues come next, and last of all new issues. This is true both of Britain and the United States.

v. *Bonus issues (stock splits) and stock dividends.* To conclude the discussion of the different sources of equity capital some brief mention of bonus (scrip) issues or stock splits should be made. Such issues are not a source of finance as such, but a book-keeping transaction. They represent a 'free' issue of shares to existing

[1] While it seems likely that existing shareholders retain the bulk of the shares made in a rights issue, very little is known about this subject. If enough companies were willing to co-operate it would be a fairly straight-forward sampling exercise to determine the facts in this matter. It is to be hoped that this research may be carried out in the interest of a realistic discussion of the cost of capital.

shareholders made by capitalizing existing reserves, usually retained profits, which are of course already 'owned' by the shareholders. (By 'capitalizing' is meant renaming such reserves as shares of exactly the same type as the existing shares.) In other words shareholders are issued with more share certificates, in strict proportion to their existing shareholdings, such that an unchanged entitlement to the income and assets of the company is now represented by a greater number of pieces of paper. Each shareholder's percentage shareholding is unaffected.[1] At first sight such issues would appear to be pointless but they can serve some useful purposes, the most important of which are as follows.

When a company is contemplating a sizeable medium or long term loan and it has a large amount of retained profits represented by non-cash assets, the lenders may well be reluctant to lend funds which in theory could all be used to pay out dividends instead of being invested. In these circumstances the borrowing company may turn most of such retained profits into capital reserves (as opposed to revenue reserves – see Appendix A) out of which (under British company law) no dividends can ever be paid, or alternatively into bonus shares, a similar irrevocable step.

A more common reason for issuing bonus shares is to reduce the market value of each share unit which is held to increase their marketability. When companies have been established for a longish time their market value can become many times higher than their nominal value, such that each share represents an unwieldily large amount. It may only be possible to buy such shares in units of say £25 to £50, whereas most shares have a market value of less than £5 a unit. For the convenience of the shareholders, especially the smaller shareholders, bonus issues can be made to overcome this difficulty. This can also be achieved by reducing the value of each existing share, e.g. issuing two shares of the nominal value of ten shillings in place of each one pound share, but bonus issues are more flexible, especially when it is desired to increase the number of shares by odd amounts. (The judicious use of rights issues reduces the need for bonus issues on these grounds.)

A further reason for issuing bonus shares is simply for public relations. Left wing commentators, and often the general public,

---

[1] Because entitlement to wealth and income is unchanged such shares in no way represent income or even a capital distribution and should not therefore be taxable. While such shares result in no *additional* tax liabilities in Britain or the United States, this is not universally the case abroad.

are prone to claim that annual dividends, which are normally expressed in terms of the nominal value of the shares to which they relate, are excessive when they exceed say 50%, a view which ignores the retained profits which have been re-invested to help produce this result. To avert unnecessary criticism, the periodic issue of bonus shares is most useful.

Finally, bonus shares may be used as an indirect method of increasing dividends. Some firms like to keep their dividend rate (the ratio of the dividend to the *nominal* value of the share) constant. When they wish to increase their dividends by say 10%, they make a bonus issue of one new share for every ten existing shares, and maintain the same dividend rate on the increased capital. This practice also has the advantage that the market value of the shares need never rise to unwieldy units as long as the dividend rate reasonably reflects future prospects.

From this brief discussion it can be seen that bonus issues have their uses. They may sometimes seem a little pointless on their own but this is usually because they are part of a larger package, and not the whole package.

These same considerations all apply to the predominantly American practice of issuing 'stock dividends' which are new shares issued to the existing shareholders representing the capitalization of retained earnings. The position here, however, is slightly complicated by the tax implications. Stock dividends, like retained earnings, may substitute a *potential* capital gains tax liability for the *certain* and usually higher direct tax on dividends. The advantage, however, resides in retaining earnings as such and hence, as was seen above, attracting capital gains tax and not income tax. Nothing is added by then formally issuing further share certificates. In sum the sound arguments for stock dividends are really arguments for more retained earnings.

f. *Supply Schedule for Equity Funds*

It may be useful to summarize diagrammatically the conclusions of this chapter as regards the costs of the various types of equity capital, and this is done in Figure 3.1 below, with the vertical scale, the minimum percentage yields required on the various types of equity capital, being notional rather than an exact portrayal of fact.

Figure 3.1 is meant to cover the planning period relevant to the firm's capital budget. The first two segments of the curve, (a) the depreciation provision (equity portion only – see Section 8 of next

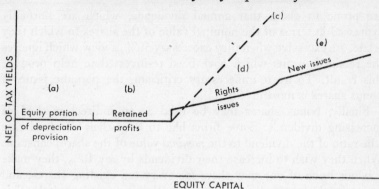

Fig. 3.1. Annual supply of equity capital – British conditions

chapter) and (b) retained profits, are shown net of the normal dividend and net of any funds sanctioned for expenditure in previous planning periods and are assumed not to provide any tax advantages over externally raised equity (the British situation). The level of these two segments represents the net of tax yield shareholders require on their funds.

The dotted line represented by (c) indicates the steep rise in the cost of capital that would occur if the normal dividend is significantly reduced or dispensed with altogether. The share price would fall, and the long term level of the share price might well be depressed in consequence, thus raising the long term cost of capital. If the dividend were reduced often, in an arbitrary or unforeseeable way, the share price might be permanently depressed.

Segment (d) represents rights issues and the slight break in the curve signifies the increased yield required to compensate for the issue cost of the rights issue. This segment will tend to rise as shareholders become less and less willing to increase their investment in any one company. In the extreme situation, where segment (d) merges into (e) which represents new issues, this curve too will tend to rise as new investors will only be persuaded to subscribe more funds to the company if shares are issued at an increasing discount.[1]

[1] See 'Measuring a Company's Cost of Capital' by Ezra Solomon, *Journal of Business*, Vol. XXVIII – October 1955, for a similar diagrammatic presentation. The main difference between the two diagrams is that Professor Solomon uses earnings per share as the measurement on the vertical axis, on the assumption that current income continues indefinitely, and all new investments also give rise to perpetual or indefinite incomes.

This diagram broadly indicates the cost curve facing a British registered company with shareholders subject to British tax. Where the tax system is different, as in the United States, different treatment is called for.

In the case of a country where dividends are taxed again at substantial rates in the hands of shareholders, there is a greater incentive for companies to retain funds for reinvestment to the shareholders' benefit. Assuming say a 30% rate of personal income tax the relevant diagram would be set out as in Figure 3.2 below.

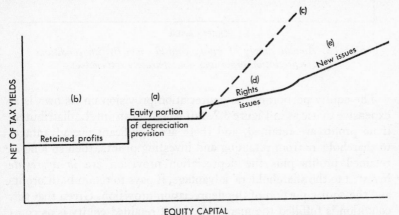

Fig. 3.2. Annual supply of equity capital – non-British conditions (Depreciation provision separately returnable)

Figure 3.2 differs from Figure 3.1 in only two respects:
(i) Retained profits need earn less than the prospective yields on other types of funds due to the fact that reinvested profits do not involve the shareholders in personal income tax.
(ii) On the assumption that the equity portion of the depreciation provision can be returned to the shareholders without tax consequences even when profits are retained for reinvestment, they are more expensive to reinvest than retained profits, being nearly as expensive as rights issues.

Where the depreciation provision cannot be returned to shareholders without being taxed as income so long as the company still has past retained profits, and this is the position in the United States and most other countries where dividends are taxed again in the hands of the shareholders, then as long as any profits are retained, the diagram alters to that depicted in Figure 3.3.

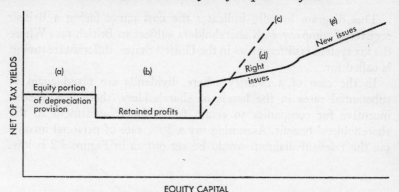

Fig. 3.3. Annual supply of equity capital – non-British conditions
(*Depreciation provisions not separately returnable*)

The equity portion of the depreciation provision on its own is as expensive to use as in Figure 3.2. But where it can only be distributed, if no profits are retained, and there are significant tax advantages to shareholders from retaining and investing profits, then so long as retained profits plus the depreciation provision are *in aggregate* invested to the shareholders' advantage, it pays to retain both profits and the equity portion of the depreciation provision. Given that this condition is fulfilled the marginal cost of retained equity is as computed in the text and less than the cost of depreciation provisions. This is illustrated in Figure 3.3. If this condition is not fulfilled, that is the firm's overall rate of return on the depreciation provision plus retained profits is less than the shareholders' cost of capital, then the firm should be seriously considering either major measures to increase profitability or returning its retained earnings and capital to the shareholders despite the taxation on retained earnings.

Figure 3.3. is based on the proposition that the firm has such limited past retained profits that the cash provided by depreciation provision can be paid out to the shareholders as a return of capital (and not payment of dividends from past retained profits) for tax purposes. (Procedurally the firm should first of all consider what projects are acceptable using the cost of depreciation provisions as the cost of capital and then, if sufficient projects are accepted to justify retaining the whole of the depreciation provisions, it can then go on to reconsider all the projects so far rejected, in order to establish whether they would be acceptable using the now justified lower cost retained earnings as the marginal source of finance.)

In practice this will seldom be the case: most firms will have substantial past retained profits. In this situation it will be possible to return the depreciation provision to the shareholders only when this balance of retained profits has been reduced to nil. Until this happens the realistic annual supply curve of capital will be as set out in Figure 3.4, with the depreciation provision being as cheap to invest as the retained profits.

In sum, the annual supply curve of equity capital for a company subject to the British type of company taxation is as set out in Figure 3.1. For the typical American type case, the annual supply curve of equity capital is as set out in Figure 3.4, with Figures 3.2 and 3.3 representing special cases. Figure 3.4 is similar to Figure 3.1, but there is a larger difference between the cost of retained profits plus depreciation and externally raised funds, owing to dividends being taxed again in the hands of shareholders.

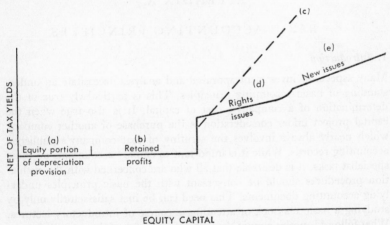

Fig. 3.4. Annual supply of equity capital – non-British conditions (Depreciation provision effectively non-returnable—the typical situation)

REFERENCES

1. F. W. PAISH, *Business Finance*, Second Edition, Pitman, London, 1961.
2. F. W. PAISH, 'The London New Issue Market', *Economica*, February 1951.
3. B. J. GRAHAM and D. L. DODD in collaboration with C. TATHAM Jr., *Security Analysis*, Third edition, New York, 1951.

4. HARGREAVES PARKINSON, *Ordinary Shares*, Third edition, Eyre and Spottiswoode, London, 1949.

5. GILBERT HAROLD, *Corporation Finance*, Revised Third edition, Barnes and Noble, New York, 1956.

6. DOUGLAS A. HAYES, *Appraisal and Management of Securities*, Macmillan, New York, 1956.

7. DOUGLAS H. BELLMORE, *Investment Principles, Practices, and Analysis*, Simmons–Boardman Publishing Corporation, New York, 1960.

8. R. F. HENDERSON, *The New Issue Market*, Bowes and Bowes, Cambridge, 1951.

9. F. E. ARMSTRONG, *The Book of the Stock Exchange*, Fifth edition, 1957.

APPENDIX A

BASIC ACCOUNTING PRINCIPLES

1. *Introduction*

Many aspects of investment appraisal and analysis necessitate an understanding of basic accounting principles. This is particularly true of the determination of a company's cost of capital. It is also true when the capital project under consideration is the purchase of another company which nearly always involves the scrutiny of that company's published accounting records. While it is important to employ accountants on these specialist tasks, it is desirable that all who are concerned with the evaluation procedures should be conversant with the basic principles underlying accounting documents. This need can be met satisfactorily only by studying a basic textbook or attending a course of introductory lectures. What follows is nothing more than a brief summary of the more important accounting principles.

Accounting records are designed to record systematically all the monetary transactions of a business. Whenever a cost is incurred or a sale agreed, the fact is recorded in the appropriate account. From this it follows that such documents constitute a comprehensive *historical* record of the transactions of a business.

Published accounting documents fall into two categories; a statement about net earnings (the profit and loss account) and a statement about wealth (i.e. assets and liabilities, known as the balance sheet). In most countries these documents must be published annually by all joint stock limited liability companies, especially those with stock exchange quotations. Their contents are the following.

2. Profit and Loss Account

This account shows the net earnings[1] arising during a year, and how it is divided up between the debenture holders and any other suppliers of long term loans, the different classes of shareholders, and the tax authorities. It begins with a statement of operating or trading profit before tax. Sometimes the annual depreciation charge is given also, but often profit is shown only after the deduction of depreciation. (In an increasing number of countries it is usual to give sales revenue and total costs incurred in earning that revenue, broken down into broad groupings. This practice can be expected to spread as amendments to company law compel the fullest disclosures of information.) The next piece of information is the tax liability *incurred* on the profits earned by the company. Since in most countries tax payments during a year are based on profits earned in the previous year, the tax liability shown in the profit and loss account does not correspond to the tax payment made during the year. Hence, the current net cash flow usually cannot be derived simply from the current annual profit and loss statement. After deducting the tax liability, we have net profit after company tax. From this are deducted fixed interest payments and preference share dividends, which leaves net profits available to the ordinary or equity shareholders. Any interim dividend or proposed final dividend is subtracted, leaving the balance of profits to be retained in the business.

The profit and loss account will also state the balance of retained profits from previous years which are also available for payment of dividends. Hence, in any year the dividend payment can exceed the profits earned for the ordinary shareholders.

The profit and loss account shows the increase in 'wealth' during the accounting period, but not the form it takes. This is shown in the balance sheet. It will be apparent that profits earned will not necessarily take the form of cash: they can have been used for investment in other assets, or to reduce liabilities such as debts.

---

[1] By 'net earnings' is meant the income arising from running the business rather than any increase in the value of the assets employed to produce that income. An example will make this clearer. Suppose a firm runs a chain of supermarkets, many of them occupying prominent sites whose value is rising. Unless one of the sites were actually sold off, normal accounting practice would ignore this increasing value. Hence, the profit and loss account would contain only the net profit from running the supermarkets as supermarkets. If one of the sites were sold off during a year, the difference between its sale price and its value as recorded in the accounts would not be recorded in the profit and loss account as it is a 'capital' as distinct from a 'trading' profit. Further, it would not usually be regarded as available for distribution as a dividend.

3. *Balance Sheet*

A balance sheet is a statement of a company's wealth, and of the aggregate claims on that wealth by those lending funds to the company, such as creditors, banks, debenture holders, etc., and residually by those investing in the company, the preference and equity shareholders. It is in two halves, known respectively as the statement of assets and liabilities. All the assets are due to some claimant; hence, the two sides of the balance sheet will, by definition, be equal. After the claims of all third parties have been satisfied – tax authorities, creditors, debenture holders, etc. – the residue belongs to the shareholders of the company. The prior claim on this residue is held by the preference shareholders (if any) in proportion to the paid up value of their shares. The balance, if any, belongs entirely to the ordinary shareholders.

The various items which go to make up a balance sheet are comprised in the following main categories.

Assets

(i) *Intangible Assets* – e.g. goodwill, trademarks, licensing agreements, patents, etc., usually at original cost less any subsequent write-offs.

(ii) *Fixed Assets* – land, buildings, plant, machinery, tools, vehicles, furniture, fitments, etc. – usually shown at original cost (occasionally at a revaluation) less total depreciation written off to date.

(iii) *Trade Investments* – usually investments in subsidiary or associated companies, both equity and loan, usually shown at cost at the time of acquisition plus net loans made since, and hence often revealing little information.

(iv) *Current Assets* – assets which will normally be turned into cash within a year – even where the cash is normally reinvested in the same assets, e.g. stocks, trade debtors and cash. Also included are quoted investments (i.e. investments quoted on a Stock Exchange), and payments in advance, e.g. on account of rents, etc.

Liabilities

(i) *Share Capital etc.*

Ordinary Shares – at par (i.e. nominal) value.[1]

Preference Shares – at par (i.e. nominal) value.[1]

Capital Reserves – reserves arising from 'capital' profits, such as issuing shares at a premium, or from capital gains.

Revenue Reserves – i.e. retained profits – (distributable as dividends).

[1] This assumes that the shares are fully paid up, i.e. that cash or equivalent assets are deemed to have been paid into the firm to the full value of the shares. Shares are not always issued fully paid. It is possible to issue a share with, say, a 10 shilling nominal value on which only 5 shillings has to be

[*footnote continued on page* 105

(ii) *Long Term Liabilities*
    Loans, Debentures, etc.

(iii) *Current Liabilities* (i.e. liabilities which fall due within a year)
    Bank overdrafts and other short term loans
    Tax payments
    Trade creditors
    Prospective dividend and interest payments

(iv) *Contingent Liabilities* – these comprise such items as legally contracted obligations to pay money in certain cases – e.g. capital expenditure; also such items as potential damages in a law suit. It should be noted that 'Contingent Liabilities' do *not* form part of the total liabilities but appear in the form of a note to the balance sheet. In short, they comprise supplementary information.

The total value of the 'Assets' will, of course, equal the total value of the 'Liabilities'.

The balance sheet usually shows asset values at cost of acquisition less any depreciation written off in the case of fixed assets, and sometimes of intangible assets also. Stocks are valued at original (historic) cost, or market value, whichever is lower, but accounting principles permit a choice in the way these costs are computed. The main variants are FIFO, LIFO, and average cost.

FIFO is the abbreviation for 'first in first out'. This is the traditional method which assumes that items are withdrawn from stock in the strict order in which they were put in; i.e. the oldest item of stock is always assumed to be withdrawn first. LIFO, or 'last in first out' is the opposite of FIFO, the newest item of stock is assumed to be consumed first. Average cost, or AVCO, is, as its name implies, an average of all past costs. An example will highlight the differences. Suppose that, at the start of our accounting period, a firm has 4 tons of material all of which cost £10 a ton. During the period 10 more tons of material are bought for £12 a ton, and 10 tons are sold. Under FIFO, the 10 tons sold would be assumed to be 4 tons from the opening stock at £10 a ton, and 6 tons newly added to stock. Hence, the cost of materials used would be

---

[*footnote continued from page* 104

paid at the time of issue, the remaining 5 shillings being available to be called at some future date. Such shares are said to be only 'partly paid up'. Where such shares exist, only the value paid up is shown in the balance sheet. Partly paid up shares occur most commonly in new companies which prefer to receive their initial equity funds in instalments. They are very rare in established companies as they constitute an unwelcome contingent liability for the equity shareholders. Should such a company go into liquidation (of its own choice or otherwise) with insufficient resources to pay off all creditors, lenders and preference shareholders in full, the equity shareholders are liable to pay up the balance outstanding on the partly paid shares.

$(4 \times £10) + (6 \times £12) = £112$, and the value put on closing stock would be $(£4 \times £12) = £48$.

Under LIFO, the 10 tons sold would be assumed to come from the newest stock, i.e. 10 tons at $£12 = £120$. The value of the closing stock would then be the 4 oldest tons, i.e. the original stock costing $£10$ a ton $= £40$ in all.

Under AVCO, opening stock and purchases would be averaged, e.g. $[(4 \times £10) + (10 \times £12)] \div 14 = £160 \div 14 = £11 \ 3/7$ per ton. Then the cost of materials used would be $10 \times £11 \ 3/7 = £114 \ 2/7$, and the value of closing stock would be $4 \times £11 \ 3/7 = £45 \ 5/7$.

These systems can all be used regardless of the physical order in which these items were drawn from stock. This departure from 'facts' is held to be a justified 'accounting fiction'. It is apparent that there is a choice in the 'cost' of materials and the 'value' of closing stocks which accountants report. (It will also be apparent to those readers who experiment with the LIFO and AVCO examples that the actual resulting 'costs' given are not uniquely determined; they depend on the accounting period. A LIFO account prepared once a year could be quite different from the sum of 12 monthly LIFO accounts if stocks had fluctuated from month to month. Similarly, average costs over a year will depend on how often costs are in fact averaged.) As will be explained in Appendix A on stock appreciation in Chapter 10 it will often be necessary to correct past profit and loss statements to determine the real trend in profits.

Whichever variant is being used, when a business is being valued for the purpose of purchase, stocks should be valued on a current basis. This will normally be at replacement cost, assuming the continuance of the business. Where the business is not to be continued, resale value is the appropriate valuation.

Clearly, none of the values contained in a balance sheet, save perhaps the cash balance, need be worth the sums stated. For this reason the balance sheet is merely a starting point for the ascertainment of current values.

4. *The Relationship between the Balance Sheet and the Profit and Loss Account*

It is not always clear to non-accountants just how the profit and loss account and the balance sheet are related. A brief explanation may help to clarify this. The balance sheet is a statement of the wealth of a business at a given time. The profit and loss account records the changes in wealth during a given period, due to the interaction of costs and revenues. Hence, it helps to explain the changes between balance sheets. It will not explain all the changes in wealth as some of these are of a capital nature. For instance, if the business raises more capital, or uses its cash to buy machines or repay debts, none of these items affects the costs or revenues of the business hence, they would not appear in the profit and loss account but would show up only in the balance sheet. Because of the rules governing the drawing up of the balance sheet, all these transactions will have a twofold effect so that both the assets and liabilities remain in equilibrium. If the business raises more capital, then the liabilities side of the balance sheet will increase, and will be counterbalanced by an exactly similar increase of cash on the assets side. When cash is used to buy machines, then the amount of cash will fall by exactly the amount by which the value of the total fixed assets will increase; i.e. the two changes both happen on the same side of the balance sheet and cancel out. When cash is used to repay creditors, then both assets and liabilities are reduced by the same amount.

So much for changes which affect only the balance sheet. Consider now changes which affect the profit and loss account also. Suppose an asset costing £1,000 is being depreciated by 10% in a given year. This £100 of depreciation appears in the profit and loss account as a cost, reducing profits accordingly. In the balance sheet, the value of fixed assets is reduced by £100, and profits as we have already seen, have been reduced, so the balance sheet remains in equilibrium. Similarly, when wages are paid, cash (an asset) is reduced, and so are profits (a liability). The relation of the two accounting documents is thus simple and direct.

5. *The Effect of Balance Sheet Statements on Debt Capital*

Certain balance sheet ratios are important in financial appraisals, notably net worth to long term debt capital. (These ratios are discussed in detail in Section 1 of the next chapter.) Net worth is usually defined to mean total net tangible assets less *current* liabilities, third party loans, and minority interests. It is usually the case that the amount of long term debt capital a business can raise is restricted to a certain proportion of its net worth, often around 30%–35%, although the actual amount varies from industry to industry, and country to country.

It is clear that where such rules are being applied, the way in which accounts are drawn up can affect the total borrowing open to a firm. Where fixed assets are written down as fast as possible, however laudable this may be on some grounds, it is to the detriment of a company's ability to raise money as cheaply as possible. Similarly, where there has been marked inflation and fixed assets are shown only on the written down historic cost basis, a wide gap exists between this value and the current value of the assets in question. To the extent that the assets are not written up to reflect their current value, the scope for borrowing cheaply is necessarily reduced.

REFERENCES

1. H. C. EDEY, *Introduction to Accounting*, Hutchinson, London, 1963.
2. H. C. EDEY, *Business Budgets and Accounts*, Hutchinson, London, 1960.

CHAPTER FOUR

The Cost of Capital and the Analysis of Projects under Alternative Financing Policies

The previous chapter set out the basis for calculating the cost of the individual sources of capital available to a firm. This chapter considers how the cost of capital to a firm should be calculated when it is drawing on two or more of these sources concurrently, which is of course the typical situation. Alternative methods of analysing projects are then considered in the light of differing cost of capital conditions, and some basic recommendations made regarding the most appropriate methods of analysis. Part II of the chapter explores some of the special difficulties arising from the varied policies and situations which arise in practice, including the problems raised by capital rationing. An understanding of the problems outlined in this chapter is essential for a sound grasp of the relationship between general financing of the firm and the impact of this on particular capital projects.

Before proceeding to the main subjects of this chapter we must briefly consider some elements of security analysis to establish the main factors limiting the amount of debt capital available to the firm. The factors are primarily expressed in the form of certain financial ratios based on firms' published accounts. (Readers who are not familiar with the basic accounting terminology on which these ratios are based are referred to Appendix A of the previous chapter on 'Basic Accounting Principles'.)

I

1. FINANCIAL RATIOS

The main sources of loan capital are the institutional lenders such as banks, insurance companies, pension funds, etc. Partly because of the low level of fixed interest rates after tax and inflation, and partly because of the need for these institutions' sources of income to be free from risk to either capital or income, very rigorous standards of creditworthiness are usually required by them of prospective borrowers. These standards are generally expressed in terms of certain financial ratios which firms are required to attain. It is primarily by these ratios that the creditworthiness of the firm will be assessed and the limits set to its borrowing. A firm itself will often be following a policy of maintaining these financial ratios at certain levels in order to establish a given credit rating or to maintain a measure of financial strength in reserve. The principle ratios are given below and, for assessment of the relative magnitudes of the quantities referred to, Table 4.1A sets out the aggregate 1960 balance sheets for 3,000 of the largest British quoted companies, excluding financial companies and companies whose main interests are overseas. Similarly, Table 4.1B gives the aggregate 1955 balance sheet for 295 large United States corporations.

Where reference is made below to the values and ratios in the following two tables, they will refer to the British figures (Table 4.1A) unless the contrary is specified.

a. *Ratio of Current Assets to Current Liabilities: Current Ratio*

Current assets comprise cash and those assets which can be, and usually are, turned into cash within a short period (and certainly well within a year). The main current assets (see Table 4.1) are stock (inventories), debtors (accounts receivable), and cash, but the term embraces other liquid assets such as quoted investments. Conversely, current liabilities embrace those liabilities which fall due for settlement within a year, principally trade creditors (accounts payable), tax liabilities, all short term borrowing (particularly from banks) and dividends payable to shareholders. The ratio of current assets to current liabilities is an indication of the cover available on the short term liabilities. Consequently, it is this ratio which is the principal concern of all the short term lenders, the suppliers giving trade credit, the banks providing overdraft facilities, and the banks and discount companies lending on trade bills. A current ratio of around 2:1 would generally be considered very good (the current ratio of Table 4.1 is slightly higher than this) and 1·5:1 would probably be considered the normal acceptable minimum. The more liquid the assets (i.e. the more easily they can be converted into cash) the lower the acceptable ratio.

Table 4.1A

1960 Balance Sheet: U.K. Manufacturing and Distribution £m.
(Quoted Companies)

Share capital and Free Reserves			Fixed Assets, etc.		
1. Ordinary Shares	4,165		Goodwill, etc.	374	
2. Preference Shares	968		Tangible Fixed Assets	7,394	
3. Capital & Revenue Reserves	5,850		Trade Investments	560	
		——10,983			—— 8,328
4. Future Tax	686		*Current Assets*		
5. Long Term Loans	1,400		Stocks & Work in Progress	4,883	
6. Minority Interest	426		Trade and other Debtors	3,682	
		—— 2,512	Marketable Securities	838	
Current Liabilities			Cash	683	
7. Bank Overdrafts & Loans	737				——10,087
8. Creditors	2,944				
9. Dividends & Interest Due	312				
10. Current Taxation	795				
11. Provisions	133				
		—— 4,920			
12.	£18,415m				£18,415m

Source: 'Economic Trends'. April 1962. Table 1B.

Table 4.1B

1955 Balance Sheet: 295 Large U.S. Corporations in Selected Industries $m.
(Quoted Companies)

Share Capital and Free Reserves			Fixed Assets, etc.		
1. Common Stock	30,332		Miscellaneous Assets including Goodwill	9,692	
2. Preferred Stock	5,439		Plant and Equipment	77,809	
3. Surplus and Surplus Reserves	49,959				
		——85,730			——87,501
5. & 6. Long Term Loans and Minority Interest	30,012				
		30,012	*Current Assets*		
			Inventories	20,998	
			Receivables (net)	12,448	
Current Liabilities			Government Securities	12,181	
7. Short Term Notes Payable to Banks	1,102		Cash	7,329	
8. Trade Notes and Accounts Payable	7,307				——52,956
9 & 11. Dividends and Interest Due and other Current Liabilities	7,342				
10. Accrued Federal Income Taxes	8,964				
		——24,715			
12.	$140,457m				$140,457m

Source: 'Federal Reserve Bulletin'. June 1956. Page 586.

b. *Ratio of Long Term Debt to Net Worth*

The net worth referred to here is the net worth of the equity and preference shareholders' interest in the firm at its book value. This is represented by items 1, 2, and 3 of Table 4.1, that is total share capital plus 'free reserves', – i.e. reserves resulting from the retention of profits or from capital gains. Put another way, the net worth is the total assets of the company, – item 12 of the table, – less all third party claims on those assets; that is, items 4 to 11 inclusive. This would evidently leave the sum of items 1, 2 and 3 as before. The long term debt is precisely what its name implies and is given as item 5 of Table 4.1. The ratio of long term debt to net worth, in this case, therefore is only 12·7%. The relevance of this ratio is that it is an indication of the extent to which the assets of a company could fail to realize their book value in the event of liquidation but still realize in aggregate sufficient to meet outstanding debt.

c. *Net Tangible Assets Ratio*

This ratio is essentially intended, like the net worth ratio, to give some indication of the asset cover available to debenture holders. The tangible assets in this case consist of total tangible assets less current liabilities and minority interests. This asset figure is then divided by long term debt to obtain the ratio of tangible assets to funded debt. A similar ratio can be, and sometimes is, computed to give the tangible assets per ordinary share, although in this case the tangible assets would be less the total of long term debt and preference capital.

It should be apparent from their definitions that the net worth ratio and the net tangible asset ratios are essentially numerical variants of the same concept and that (apart from the usually insignificant goodwill element etc.) the net tangible assets ratio of

$$\frac{\text{debt}}{\text{net worth} + \text{debt}} = \frac{\text{net worth ratio}}{1 + \text{net worth ratio}}.$$

The maximum ratio of long term debt to net worth which it is commonly thought practical for a normal manufacturing or distributing firm to maintain is about 1/3 to 1/2. Where this ratio is 1/3 it implies that the net tangible assets ratio is 1/4. Thus if, of the total assets created by a project, a balance of £1,000 remained after deducting all other liabilities associated with it (i.e. items 4, 6, 7, 8, 9, 10 and 11 of Table 4.1), £250 of these assets could be financed by long term debt. (A common use of the value 'net assets' is in comparing the total annual earnings (profit plus loan interest) on long term capital (i.e. 'net assets') of different firms with varying proportions of debt finance to fixed assets.)

d. *Ratio of Times Covered*

This is the ratio of the gross income available to the suppliers of long term capital (both debt and equity) to the interest charges on the long term debt. Gross income is profit after allowing for interest due to the suppliers of short term credit (bank overdraft and bill interest, etc.) This ratio shows the amount of income cover available to meet the long term interest charges, preference dividends, etc. A ratio of 5:1 of profits to loan interest would indicate that profits could fall by 80% and still be adequate to meet the total loan interest. Sometimes the ratio is calculated on income gross of tax, and sometimes net.

The loan interest times covered is often satisfactorily calculated on a gross of tax basis as it is a charge on a business prior to any tax claims. Where the company concerned has overseas subsidiaries, however, which retain profits abroad on which further taxes would be due when remitted to the parent (i.e. taxes that would rank prior to the parent company's loan interest), it is necessary to estimate this further tax and deduct it from gross income to determine the true cover. This situation commonly arises with British based international companies.

The cover for preference dividends and equity dividends can usually be better calculated net of tax, certainly net of profits tax which is a charge on a British company prior to the payment of any dividends. (Similarly, in the United States loan interest cover can be calculated on income gross of tax, but dividends cover on income net of tax – i.e. net of company tax.)

The above ratios can be calculated for total debt, and also for specific debt. When calculating the latter, it is necessary to include in both the asset and income cover all debt with prior or equal claims. Considerable stress (see especially reference [3] of previous chapter) is put upon the *total* long term debt being adequately covered as regards both assets and earnings. This is based on the reasonable contention that any threat to meet the interest obligations to junior issues would react more adversely on the market price of senior issues than is implied by the actual magnitude of the fall in the assets and earnings cover.

It should be apparent that in principle the times covered ratio indicates the number of times the fixed charges (short and long term interest, the 'interest' portion of lease commitments, etc.) are covered. It is in this form that the ratio is normally used in the United States (see Table 4.2B below).

The credit status of a firm will generally be evaluated in the light of the above ratios in conjunction with the firm's past record and future prospects. The investment analysts of the main institutional lenders will also employ various subsidiary tests and ratios as are needed to suit their special requirements. It is probably the case, however, that most manufacturing firms would find it very costly to raise further long term debt, if the ratio of long term debt (including the proposed new debt) to net worth significantly exceeded $1:2$ (that is, if total long term debts exceed 33% of net assets or capitalization) or if the times covered were less than 5–6. (For businesses with very secure and stable earnings, and with highly marketable assets – e.g. property companies – considerably larger proportions of debt capital can be raised.) The high cost of additional debt under these circumstances would arise partly from the high underwriting costs involved, but primarily from the fact that interest costs would tend to be higher on all future debt raising; hence, the marginal cost of debt in excess of conventional ratios can be very high.

Where there is any significant element of risk associated with the additional borrowing (e.g. where there is any doubt whether the firm can continue to meet all its debt repayments and interest), further debt capital would be extremely difficult to obtain on any terms. This is partly because the higher interest rates offered increase the risks of liquidation for which they are intended to compensate and partly because of strong institutional influences militating against such debt issues.

Finally, Table 4.2A shows the net worth, net asset, current, and times covered ratios for a fairly random selection of large British companies. These ratios are well within the limits mentioned above, apart from the first two companies. In these two cases special factors would appear to explain the remarkably high debt to net worth ratios. For example, in the case of Vauxhall its credit worthiness must be dominated by the overwhelming security offered by the support of its American parent company, General Motors. Table 4.2B gives similar information for a selection of United States companies for the period 1955–59.

Table 4.2A

British Financial Ratios (1960)

	Long Term Debt to Net Worth	Long Term Debt to Net Assets	Current Assets to Current Liabilities	Interest Times Covered
	%	%		
Bowaters	70·0	41·1	2·17	4·0
Vauxhall Motors	50·8	33·7	2·13	14·4
English Electric	37·6	27·3	1·76	6·8
Imperial Tobacco	36·4	26·7	3·2	18·5
Dunlop	31·6	24·0	1·88	11·7
Beecham Group	27·2	21·4	1·6	14·7
Vickers	20·5	17·0	1·62	12·4
Tube Investments	19·7	16·5	2·83	33·9
Metal Box	19·5	16·3	6·2	17·0
United Steel	11·2	10·1	1·94	47·3
I.C.I.	10·8	9·8	1·95	26·2
Rolls Royce	9·3	8·5	1·95	34·6
Distillers	8·1	7·5	1·76	59·0
G.K.N.	7·9	7·3	3·26	41·6
Unilever	7·3	6·8	2·64	64·6
Associated Portland Cement	4·8	4·6	2·11	205·0
Courtaulds	3·9	3·8	3·25	50·7
B.M.C.	0·6	0·6	1·86	1335·0

Table 4.2B

United States' Financial Ratios (1955–59)

	Long Term Debt to Net Worth	Long Term Debt to Net Assets	Times Fixed Charges Earned*
	%	%	
General Motors	6	6	92
Standard Oil (N.J.)	11	10	21
General Electric Co.	18	15	24
Borg-Warner	5	5	37
U.S. Steel	11	10	38
Bethlehem Steel	15	13	22
General Foods Corps.	19	16	27
National Steel	25	20	17
Owens–Ill. Glass Co.	30	23	14
Continental Oil Co.	32	24	13
Allied Chemical Corp.	43	30	8
Aluminium Co. of America	56	36	7
Consolidated Coal Co.	6	6	36
Sterling Drug Stores	28	22	18
Safeway Stores Inc.	32	24	10
Westinghouse Electric Corp.	39	28	6
Boeing Airplane Co.	11	10	5
Celanese Corp.	41	29	6

Companies are listed in descending order of their bond credit rating.

* (Fixed charges includes all interest, and amortization of debt premium or discount. Sources: *Long Term Financing*, John F. Childs.)

2. DEBT RAISING POTENTIAL

a. *General Points*

In our subsequent discussion the main emphasis will be on asset cover (ratio of long term debt to net worth and current ratio) as the effective limiting factors on the amount of debt capital raised. This is based on the view that earnings cover as regards capital projects is generally adequate, given the level of return normally expected on capital projects, and hence asset cover is the effective external limitation as regards the amount of debt raised. Some evidence of this is given in Table 4.2A. It is seen there that all the companies with a ratio of debt to net worth of 33% or less had a times covered ratio of at least 11·7. In both Britain [1] and the United States net income (after interest and taxes) averages around 10% of net worth. On the basis of a debt to net worth ratio of 33% and an interest rate of, say 3% after tax, this typically implies a times covered ratio of 10. Thus taking an acceptable times covered as, say, 5 or more, normal proportions of long term debt would appear primarily limited by asset cover rather than earnings cover.

If earnings cover on the existing assets of the firm is adequate (so that a proportion of the assets have not been used to support debt) then the 'surplus' earnings cover of capital projects under consideration may enable debt to be raised, using these existing assets for asset cover. Normally, however, inadequate earnings on existing assets will be only temporary and such earnings may eventually be expected to recover sufficiently to enable debt to be raised (or more probably maintained) on the existing assets, so that at most it could be argued that the surplus earnings cover on new capital projects simply accelerated the raising of debt. For these reasons we have assumed that asset cover is the principal limitation on the amount of debt raised. The case of a firm with earning cover as the effective limitation on debt raising is, however, discussed later in Section 6b.

b. *Debt Capital Associated with Individual Capital Projects*

The additional debt which may be raised as a result of taking on a particular capital project can broadly be assessed on the following lines. Consider first the short term debt raising possibilities as represented by the change the project brings about in the ratio of current assets to current liabilities. The project will usually result in an increase in current assets, principally stocks and debtors. In part this will be offset by a corresponding increase in current liabilities, primarily bank and other short term loans, creditors, dividends payable, current (ie. payable within 12 months) taxation etc. Table 4.1A, which sets out the aggregate balance sheet for certain British quoted companies at the end of 1960, illustrates their relative magnitude. (See Table 4.1B for American firms.)

Although the acceptable current ratio of $1 \cdot 5 : 1$ implies that £2 of short term debt could be raised for every £3 of current assets, as regards actual projects this will normally not be possible because of the change in current liabilities brought about by the project. From Table 4.1A it is seen that with the creation of the total current assets of £10,087m. went the creation of current liabilities (other than short term debt) of £4,183m. This implies that of the £10,087m. current assets, $1 \cdot 5 \times £4,183\text{m.} = £6,274\text{m.}$, would be required to provide current asset cover for the other current liabilities thrown up by the projects. This leaves only £10,087m. $-$ £6,274m. $=$ £3,813m. to provide current asset cover for direct short term debt in the form of bank overdrafts, bills, etc. The maximum amount of short term debt consistent with the $1 \cdot 5$ current ratio is therefore £3,813m./$1 \cdot 5 = $ £2,542m. or $25\frac{1}{4}\%$ of the total of current assets.

The proportion of long term debt to net assets (total tangible assets less current liabilities) that it is normally practicable to maintain is around 25%. If a firm is attempting to maintain a current ratio of $1 \cdot 5$, this will leave *net* current assets (current assets less current liabilities) of £0·33 for every £1 of current assets. Hence for every £1 of current assets typically $(0 \cdot 25 \times £0 \cdot 33) = £0 \cdot 0825$ or $8\frac{1}{4}\%$ could be raised as long term debt. The total of long and short term debt will therefore be of the order of $8\frac{1}{4}\% + 25\frac{1}{4}\% = 33\frac{1}{2}\%$, or, say, one third of the current assets created for the capital project.

In general discussion of company finance, creditors, dividends due, tax provisions, etc. are normally regarded as sources of finance. While this is certainly true these are all simply delays in payments and as such will already be taken into account in discounted yield or present value calculations (see Chapter 2, Section 2a ii). Thus, if taxes are paid, say one year in arrears, then on a 10 year project with a constant tax bill, the Revenue are effectively granting the first year's taxes as a 10 year interest-free loan. This will be clear if we consider the cash flows of the project with no delays in tax payments, and the project if tax payments are all delayed one year. The difference between the two sets of cash flows is that, in the latter case, the first cash flow is higher by the unpaid taxes of the first year and this is offset by an equal outflow of taxes in the eleventh year, – precisely the situation which would obtain if we took the delay of tax payments into account as a form of interest-free debt finance (see Example 1 of Section 4a below). Hence, wherever the actual net cash flow reflects the actual timing of cash inflows and outflows, it already reflects the 'financing' due to delays in payments. In considering the debt capital attributable to a project, therefore, we must exclude all 'loans' already taken into account in the actual pattern and timing of the cash flows.

We would stress, however, that what we are concerned with is the *effective* limitation on the firm's borrowing. In many cases (see in particular the case studies of reference 2) manufacturing firms are operating with debt at less than the 25–30% conventional debt level and could often raise substantially more debt than this figure at an incremental cost which it would be well worth paying. Frequently, however, firms prefer, for reasons of financial conservatism, maintaining large emergency borrowing powers in reserve, etc., to maintain their borrowing at levels lower than that acceptable to lenders. Given this is the case these internal restrictions are the effective limitation on borrowing to be evaluated in the analysis of capital projects in the same way as effective external limitations.

It should be noted that individual projects may differ substantially in the amount of debt capital that they will enable a firm to raise. Three special types of investment may be distinguished in this category. First, projects involving large amounts of capital expenditure to create intangible assets. The main example of this is capital expenditure on advertising or other sales promotion, or on research. This is often required to establish a product but it is almost universal accounting practice to write off such capital expenditure against revenue and not to allow it to be represented on the published balance sheet. As a result, this expenditure provides no assets on the published balance sheet to support debt and projects involving a large proportion of such expenditure will be financed by a relatively small proportion of debt. (Even if a firm kept such expenditures on its books as assets to be written down over an appropriate period of years, lenders would almost invariably disregard it in determining the amount of asset cover available.)

The second type of investment is that of cost saving capital projects. These projects normally involve very little change in working capital (hence, that proportion of capital which can normally be readily financed by short term debt is absent) and they may also involve the writing-off of existing assets which these projects replace. The particular project must be considered in the light of the *net* increase in the assets of the firm, also taking into account the actual type of assets involved.

The third type of project is the normal type of marketing project. These frequently involve a substantial increase in working capital (in the shape of stocks and trade credit allowed to customers) which, as we have seen above, will support an exceptionally large proportion of debt capital.

It should be clear from the preceding discussion that it is not generally possible to consider all debt as allocated in any meaningful economic way to specific projects so that they are *entirely* financed by debt capital. The debt may be raised as a specific charge on particular assets of a project but this is usually simply as a matter of legal convenience and at best simply secures the same amount of debt (or marginally more) than would otherwise be raised, although possibly on rather more favourable terms.[1] The qualifications to this arise out of special financing policies pursued by the firm: these are considered later in Section 5.

3. THE WEIGHTED AVERAGE COST OF CAPITAL

In the light of the preceding discussion we are now in a position to consider the joint cost of capital where a firm is drawing funds concurrently from a number of different sources – the typical situation. Suppose in fact the firm plans to finance its capital expenditures over the next decade or so from the following sources:

	Proportion of Total Capital (a)	Cost After Tax % (b)	Weighted Average Cost of Capital (c) = (a) × (b)
Short and Long Term Debt	·20	3	·6
New Equity Capital	·10	10	1·0
Retained Earnings	·30	9	2·7
Depreciation Provisions	·40	7·5	3·0
			7·3

The only factor calling for comment here is the 7·5% cost attributed to the depreciation provisions. It is argued briefly in Section 4 of Chapter 3, and at greater length in Section 8 of this chapter, that

[1] The relevance of debt capital raised on specific assets is discussed in more detail in Chapter 8, Section 2.

the cost of this capital must be considered as made up of the cost of the alternative uses to which it could be put. In this case it is assumed that the alternative use is to use ·10 to repay debt (costing 3%) and to distribute ·30 as dividends (and hence having an opportunity cost of 9% as for retained earnings). The average cost of this capital is therefore:

$$\frac{10}{40} \times 3\% + \frac{30}{40} \times 9\% = 7.5\%.$$

This weighted average cost of capital may be used over a fairly wide range of conditions as the cut-off point for investments, that is the minimum return which investments must earn in order to be acceptable. Projects which show this minimum return (on a discounted cash flow basis and taking into account all lags in payments which are not taken into account in the weighted average cost of capital computed above) will *normally*[1] then earn sufficient, if their forecast return is achieved, to pay each component of the capital which has jointly financed it with the full return appropriate to that capital. In the above example a return of 7·3% would normally be sufficient to provide a return of 3% for the short and long term debt, 10% for the new equity capital, 9% for retained earnings, and match the 7·5% opportunity cost of the depreciation provisions.

A matter for care here is allowing for non-interest bearing credit (accounts payable and future tax). Non-interest bearing credit, as we have argued previously, is only to a limited degree within a firm's control, and often varies from project to project. For this reason it is best treated in the analysis in the form of delays in cash flows.

As regards interest bearing short term loans, these may be included either in the weighted average cost of capital, or alternatively in the net cash flows. The choice between these two alternatives may vary from firm to firm depending on the relative magnitude of the short term debt and the extent to which this short term debt is being used as a substitute for longer term indebtedness. Where a firm's short term borrowing is closely related to the current assets created by projects it is generally preferable to exclude short term debt from the

---

[1] The use of the weighted average cost of capital as a cut-off rate is least accurate for short term projects (4–7 years) where the required equity return is 8% or lower. In such cases the weighted average cost is too high as a cut-off rate. An example of this is given in Section 4a below where a 5 year project with a weighted average return of 6·25% has a return on total capital (debt plus equity) of only 5·4%, which is significantly lower.

weighted average cost of capital and take it into account in the net cash flows. It should be clear, however, that there is no valid *conceptual* reason for uniformly excluding short term debt from the weighted cost of capital.

In our view, the weighted average cost of capital must be based on a factual estimate of a firm's future financing plans. Where the firm is working at high levels of gearing or at ceiling levels of gearing determined by policy considerations, this is not too difficult a task. It is necessary to determine how projects will be financed in the future, through retained profits, depreciation provisions, additional debt raising, etc., and on this basis compute the weighted average.

It is sometimes suggested, (see reference [3]), that the weighted average cost of capital should be based on the relative *market value* of the equity and debt capital. For example, if the market value of the firm's equity capital stood at £45m., its debt at £30m., the cost of equity capital was 10% and the cost of debt capital 3% (both after tax) then the weighted average cost of capital should be computed as:

$$\frac{45}{75} \times 10\% + \frac{35}{75} \times 3\% = 7{\cdot}4\%.$$

Basing the analysis on the market value of the equity and debt has difficulties of its own. There would appear to be some confusion between what (under certain assumptions) is *possible* and what will *actually* occur as regards future capital raising: the two are assumed to be identical. If the market assumed that a firm could find new investments which on average were exactly as profitable as the old, then it might be possible (subject to the qualification noted in the following paragraph) for the firm to issue debt and equity in the same proportions as their present market values. Whether the firm will in fact do so, even where this is possible, is another matter. For example, it is entirely possible say, that the firm normally raises debt and equity (including retained profits) in certain given proportions but that fluctuations in share prices (and interest rates) often cause the proportions based on current market value of its debt and equity to differ widely from these normal *capital raising* proportions. If the value of book assets were the effective limitation on debt raising, this would inevitably occur.

Finally we should note that the weighted market value approach would lead to the bizarre conclusion that a slump in the market value of the firm's equity (due, say, to a decline in the firm's profitability) would lead to a fall in the weighted average cost of capital! For the cost of equity capital remains constant (the shareholders revise the value of the stock downwards to give the required, say, 10% yield, given the new profit expectations) but, since by market value the proportion of debt in the total value of debt plus equity has increased, then the weighted average cost is now lower. The true situation could well be that the firm has now so little earnings cover that it will be unable to raise any debt for some years to come. Hence, its future weighted average cost of capital is higher than it was formerly. Conversely, if the market value of its equity increased markedly, relative to its debt, the cost of capital to the firm would appear to increase!

In our view then, satisfactory analysis must be based on (a) a careful consideration of the firm's *future* financing policy and (b) the debt raising potentialities of particular projects in the light of this policy. This will permit a more realistic approach to the problem of debt financing and will also reveal some of the conceptual weaknesses of the weighted average cost of capital approach generally.

The general application of the weighted average cost of capital as a cut-off rate, however, is subject to some important qualifications which will only be outlined here, but developed further in the Part II of this chapter.

The first qualification concerns the case in which a firm is raising new equity capital at a cost significantly in excess of its other sources of equity capital (retained earnings, and in part at least, depreciation provisions). This case can arise where a firm's shares are undervalued at the time of the new issue or because of high underwriting and other expenses of the new issue. This situation is essentially one in which the firm has a temporarily high cost of capital since in the longer term it can normally expect to have its requirements for capital met from internal sources and debt. Under these circumstances a special method of analysis is required for the capital budgets around the period when the new issue is contemplated. This is described in detail in Chapter 17.

The second qualification concerns the debt raising policy of the firm. The situation may be that, in total, the firm proposes to finance, as in the previous example, 20% of its future expenditures by debt capital, but this proposition is entirely consistent with the debt capital being used only as the *marginal source of finance*. In other words the firm may not raise debt and equity in relatively fixed proportions to finance each batch of projects, but rather it only uses debt capital when it has exhausted internally generated sources of funds. In this situation the firm is effectively financing the marginal projects entirely with debt capital. Where the firm is in this situation – that of residual debt financing as we shall term it – a very careful reconsideration of capital budgeting procedures will often be called for. This problem is considered in more detail in Part II of this chapter in Section 6.

Finally, and in general, it is essential that a realistic account be taken of a firm's financial position and a realistic assessment made of the true opportunity costs of the firm's capital sources. It may often be the case that the firm is not prepared, at least for a considerable period, to pay out a larger proportion of its earnings in dividends, and still less is it prepared to consider paying out depreciation provisions in the form of dividends paid out of retained earnings. There may or may not be substantial justifications for this policy, but, given that it exists, financial analysis must recognize it to the extent that improved decision making will follow from such a recognition. These issues are also discussed at greater length in Part II of this chapter (Section 6) and the general problem of capital budgeting under cash surplus conditions is discussed at length in Chapter 16.

4. THE RELATION OF THE SUPPLY OF CAPITAL TO THE ANALYSIS OF PROJECTS

a. *Isolating the Equity Net Cash Flows*

In analysing a capital project it should be apparent that we are attempting primarily to ascertain its advantages to the *equity* shareholders. From this it would appear that, in strict logic, we should in every case set out the net cash flows from and to the equity shareholders. In this analysis, the debt which could be raised on the assets of the project would be regarded as an inflow reducing the total capital required from the equity shareholders, and in the subsequent years of the project's life the interest and debt repayments should be regarded as normal cash outflows. The net present value at the equity cost of capital and the yield on these equity net cash flows we shall refer to as the equity net present value and the equity yield respectively. An example of the method of calculation in a simple hypothetical case is as follows.

Example 1. To illustrate the logic of the equity cash flows, consider the extreme and simple case where the firm is borrowing up to the maximum amount permitted by maintaining asset cover at 35% of book assets. The closest a firm could approach to this in practice would be for it to raise extensive amounts of short term debt in between major issues of long term debt. The long term debt could then be used to pay off the temporarily 'excessive' element in the short term debt and the cycle could begin again. This implies peaks and troughs in the actual gearing but this will be ignored in the present example. The cash flows of the project being analysed are set out in Table 4.3.

Table 4.3

£'s Years	0	1	2	3	4	5
1. Book Value of Asset	100,000	80,000	60,000	40,000	20,000	0
2. Net Revenue before Interest		23,346	23,346	23,346	23,346	23,346
3. Capital (Outlay)	−100,000					
4. Debt Inflow	35,000					
5. Debt Outflow		−7,000	−7,000	−7,000	−7,000	−7,000
6. Interest 3%		−105	−84	−63	−42	−21
7. Residual Inflow (Outflow) of Equity Funds = 2+3+4+5 +6	−65,000	16,241	16,262	16,283	16,304	16,325

The project is assumed to be written down on a straight line basis (20% p.a.) over its working life. The book value of the project is given in line 1. The firm is assumed to be raising debt at a level equal to 35% of the book value of its assets. Hence, initially the project will support debt of £35,000. As the asset is written down, the amount of debt it will support is correspondingly reduced: this results in the debt outflows of £7,000 in each subsequent year.

In effect, as the project is depreciated on the firm's books, the depreciation provisions flow into the general pool of financial resources. Of course, providing the depreciation provisions remain within the firm (that is are not effectively paid out in dividends), then its net worth remains the same and no actual debt repayments are required to maintain its financial ratios. For purposes of analysis, however, we must consider the depreciation funds generated by the project as being debt and equity in the normal proportions. That is, we must consider the *project's* initial debt capital being reduced, as the project is depreciated on the books and becomes able to support less and less debt. If the analysis is not based on this assumption, we should be forced to argue that a given project retains to the end of its life the debt capital with which it initially started and that depreciation provisions when used to finance other projects contain no element of debt capital. (A more detailed discussion of this point is given below in Section 8.) This method of analysis results in the attribution to the project of a given level of debt capital at any time starting with £35,000 in the first year and running down by amounts of £7,000 p.a. to zero. Corresponding to this declining amount of debt attributable to the project is the declining amount of interest given in line 6 of the table. Finally by adding lines 2, 3, 4, 5, and 6 we arrive at the residual, the pure equity cash flow of line 7. These are the pure equity cash flows in that they are the cash flows entirely attributable to the equity shareholders and could all be paid out to them without involving any further debt outflows.

The final stage of the analysis is to calculate the yield on these pure equity cash flows and compare this with the equity cost of capital. It is found in this case that the discounted yield is 8%, which compares with the yield of 5·4% on *total* capital.

b. *General Recommendations*

It should be evident that either the yield or the net present value method of analysis on the *equity* cash flows should be the basic criterion for the evaluation of capital projects. Their advantages over alternative methods will be apparent from the many examples of its use throughout this book. At this point, however, we wish to frame some general recommendations for methods of analysing projects and to discuss alternative methods in the light of these proposals.

We must stress at the outset that there are certain industries such as property and mining where the importance or the peculiarities of gearing are such that there is no alternative to detailed calculation of returns or net present values based on the equity cash flows. Several examples of the application of this technique in the field of property investment are given in Chapter 8 and an example of the special features of gearing in mining ventures is given in Chapter 13. In what follows we shall be discussing normal industrial enterprises, excluding such special categories.

It will be agreed that any method of analysing capital projects which, in a serious degree, failed to reflect in a consistent way its attractiveness to the equity shareholders, would be seriously defective. This attractiveness to the equity shareholders evidently depends on the numerical return offered to the equity shareholders and the risks to which this is subject. The method of assessing the return on projects should preferably perform both functions. Any uniform, rigid system applied to all projects is likely to be inefficient. Careful use should be made of well considered approximations where these produce worthwhile savings in administrative convenience and cost to counterbalance the errors involved. We therefore recommend two distinct methods of analysing as follows.

FOR INITIAL SCREENING AND FINAL PRESENTATION OF NON-MARGINAL PROJECTS. For this type of project we advocate the use of the discounted yield on the total or combined (equity plus debt) net cash flows throughout. These discounted yields should then be compared with the appropriate cut-off rate which will usually be the firm's weighted average cost of capital (defined in Section 3 above). This will often reveal conclusive orders of magnitude which eliminate the need for further analysis such as specifically considering the equity yield.

FOR MARGINAL OR NEAR MARGINAL PROJECTS. For these projects we would suggest that the *final* analysis be performed in terms of the equity cash flows throughout (with a realistic assessment of debt financing) wherever the effect on the project of debt capital raised is likely to be significant. This yield should, of course, be compared with the firm's equity cost of capital.

These two lines of approach form part of our suggested administrative procedure discussed in Chapter 14, Section 5.

The main reason for preferring the discounted yield on total capital is that it provides a more useful method of assessing the return offered for risk than does any net present value method. The question of risk is discussed in more detail in Chapter 6 and we can only touch on it briefly at this point. The primary issue with many projects will frequently be the total amount of capital which is at risk and the return per unit of capital per unit of time that it is at risk. As we have seen in the discussion in Chapter 2, Section 1, the discounted yield represents the rate of return per unit of time on the capital outstanding in the project. Hence, this method is advantageous under these conditions. In this respect, the approach of calculating the yield on total capital also has the advantage of simplicity and ease of application compared with computing the discounted yield return in the equity element alone. The use of net present value as a method of risk assessment is unsatisfactory in that it is an absolute amount unrelated to the amount of capital involved in the project and the length of time that it is so involved. In our experience this has proved a major difficulty in its general practical application.

The second reason for preferring the discounted yield on total capital is that there exists a strong linear relationship between the return to total capital and the return to equity capital, wherever the firm is following a reasonably uniform debt raising policy. The

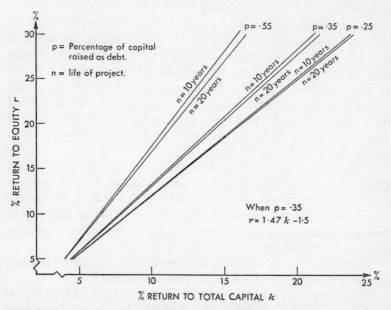

Fig. 4.1. To show the relationship between the return to equity and the return to total capital

effect of debt capital in raising the return to the equity shareholders is illustrated in Figure 4.1. The individual lines of the graph show the relation between the return to the total capital and the return to the equity capital for different proportions of debt capital and life of project. The capital is assumed to be raised at the time zero and 80% to be repaid in equal annual instalments as the asset is written down over the life of the project. The remaining 20% is taken to be working capital repaid at the end of the life of the project. The interest rate is assumed to be 3% after tax for both types of debt capital and the total net cash flows before debt repayments and interest are taken as constant throughout the project's life.

The relationship between the return to total and the return to equity capital is seen to be almost exactly linear. Moreover it is found that the linear relationships differ only slightly as the life of the project increases.

In the transition from the total to the equity return, the debt element is effectively being deducted (present value of debt inflow and outflow of debt repayments plus interest) and the remaining cash flows discounted at a higher rate. Empirical examination would suggest that it would require a very pronounced trend in the cash flows over an appreciable time to make any significant difference to the relationships shown in Figure 4.1. For this reason, the relationships shown in this diagram can be taken as applying to a broad range of capital projects. A qualification to this, however, is that the cash flows in each period should not fall to a level such that the debt repayments must be met out of fresh injections of equity capital. The complication that in the initial period there may be more than one year of capital outlays does not appear to disturb appreciably the relationships shown.

The simple relationships of Figure 4.1 lend themselves readily to assessing the returns on equity capital corresponding to differing returns to total capital. Thus it may be concluded (subject to the qualifications of Section 3) that the weighted average cost of capital meets all the main criteria of practical application.

II

In this second part of the chapter we consider first three related topics concerning the weighted average cost of capital. The subsequent sections deal with some of the more complex diverse financing situations which are frequently met with in corporate financing including the commonly encountered problem of capital rationing. Finally we discuss the split of depreciation into its debt and equity components.

5. WEIGHTED AVERAGE COST OF CAPITAL

a. *A Qualification in the Asset Cover Limiting Case*

The basic situation in which the weighted average cost of capital can be employed to give the minimum rate of return required from capital projects, is the asset cover limiting situation. By the latter term we mean the situation in which a firm's borrowing powers, either because of external restrictions imposed by lenders, or more generally because of its own policy restrictions in the light of its limited borrowing powers, are effectively limited by the book value of its assets. Hence each capital investment which creates or replaces assets tends to be financed by a given proportion of debt capital. In this situation the debt raised by the firm in the case of individual projects can be assessed, given the financial policy of the firm, along the lines of Section 3 above.

When the financial situation of a firm deviates substantially from the asset cover limiting case, the weighted average cost of capital approach will often need substantial modification. In this subsection, however, we are concerned to indicate that the weighted average cost requires an important qualification even when applied to the asset cover limiting situation.

If asset cover is the limiting factor on the firm's debt raising, then the assets associated with a given project (at their book value) form the basis on which further debt capital can be raised and in this sense debt can be allocated to specific projects. The limitation of asset cover on debt raising means that, although a firm can finance *assets* by debt and equity, it cannot replace all *cash flows* by raising debt and equity in the usual proportions. This basic point is best illustrated by the following extreme example.

Example 2. Consider the case of a firm in an equilibrium situation, raising capital normally as 50% debt at 4% interest and 50% equity, on which it wishes to maintain a return to its equity shareholders of 10%. For the purposes of the example, the complications of taxation will be ignored, and it will be assumed that the firm is operating at a high level of financial efficiency, in that it maintains its borrowing to the fullest limit of its 50% of total capital or 100% of net worth. Assume the firm now takes on a project costing £100,000 in year 0 and producing the cash flows set out in line 1 of Table 4.4. The firm is assumed to write down its assets on a straight line basis so that £25,000 of the original assets are written off each year. (Working capital is assumed to be zero.)

In the situation described in the previous paragraph, we must consider, because each year the project is depreciated by £25,000 (i.e. the asset's value on the books is reduced by this amount), that

50% of this represents debt capital, so this amount of debt must accordingly be considered as withdrawn from the project.

Consider the relevant cash flows of the above example as set out in Table 4.4.

Table 4.4

£'s

Years	0	1	2	3	4	Total
1. Net Revenue before Interest	—	14,000	14,000	14,000	82,920	—
2. Capital Outlay	100,000	0	0	0	0	—
3. Debt Inflow	50,000	0	0	0	0	—
4. Debt Outflow	0	−12,500	−12,500	−12,500	−12,500	—
5. Interest 4% of Outstanding Debt	0	−2,000	−1,500	−1,000	−500	—
6. Residual Inflow (Outflow) of Equity Funds = 1+2+3+4+5	−50,000	−500	0	500	69,920	—
Discounted at 9%	−50,000	−459	0	386	49,531	−540
Discounted at 8%	−50,000	−463	0	397	51,393	1,327

The weighted cost of capital in this example is assumed to be $0.5 \times 10\% + 0.5 \times 4\% = 7\%$ and it will be found that £14,000 p.a. for 3 years, plus £82,920 at the end of year 4 for an initial capital expenditure of £100,000, exactly represents a return of 7%. It would follow, therefore, by the rule that the weighted cost of capital only had to be achieved or exceeded for the shareholder's to obtain their required return (10% in this case) or more, that the project should be accepted. It is found, however, that the return to the shareholders as represented by the cash flows of line 6 in Table 4.4 is in fact only 8·71% on the cash funds which they are required to contribute over the life of the project.

The manner in which this comes about can be seen from Table 4.4. As the asset is depreciated on the books by £25,000 p.a., 50% of this amount of the debt outstanding must be repaid. In addition, each year the interest payments of the debt outstanding at the beginning of the previous year must also be repaid. All these payments must come either from cash generated by the project or (where this is insufficient) from equity funds; that is, by withholding dividends that would otherwise have accrued to shareholders or, alternatively, absorbing what would otherwise have been fresh equity capital. In the first year, for example, cash generated is insufficient by £500 and this sum must be entirely met by *more equity capital*. It is not possible for the firm to borrow further funds for this specific project, since it has already borrowed the maximum possible on the initial book value of the assets and no further assets have been created by the subsequent injection of £500 of equity funds on which any further debt could be raised.

In years 2 and 3 the cash generated by the project is barely sufficient to cover the interest and debt repayments and there is certainly not sufficient remaining for the equity to give 10% on the £50,000 equity capital outstanding in the project at the end of the first year. Taking the equity funds involved in the project as being invested capital plus return due on this capital to date, we can put the matter another way and say that what is happening is that effectively the proportion of equity capital invested in the project *increases each year*. It is in the nature of the weighted average cost of capital that no allowance can be made for this: the weighted average rate of return remains the minimum rate, despite the fact that particular projects may involve greater (or lesser) proportions of equity capital as their life proceeds.

It will be apparent from a consideration of the above example that, wherever asset cover is the effective limitation, the schedule of interest and debt repayments must be considered as governed by the change in the net book assets which results from the particular project under consideration.

It is a corollary of this fact that the firm under these conditions cannot replace all *cash flows* by drawing proportionately on debt and equity but can only finance *book assets* by drawing proportionately on debt and equity. Thus, the net present value, as determined by the weighted average cost of capital, is invalid. The net present value obtained under these circumstances is essentially (but only approximately) that which would apply to the combined equity and debt holders if they were in partnership together, dividing all the cash flows in the proportions in which the debt and equity figures are taken in the weighted average cost of capital, (a situation which it hardly needs to be said, never exists).

The point which must consistently be borne in mind is that all net of tax funds in excess of debt repayments and interest *accrue solely to the equity shareholders*. Any increase in these funds will flow to the equity shareholders either in the form of dividends or increased retained profits increasing the net worth of the company, and any diminution of these funds is a corresponding loss. Moreover, these funds cannot be replaced in any measure by borrowing, since there are no further assets other than those originally created on which to borrow. From this it follows that the time value of these funds must be the cost of equity capital to the shareholders (10% in the above example). As a result, discounting these should be at the equity cost of capital and not the weighted average cost. This is particularly important as regards any proposals for modifying the cash flows from the project – as, for example, choosing between alternative pricing policies for the output from the capital asset involving, say, greater future revenues at the expense of current revenues. The only change in the debt raised on this project will be a possible marginal change in the working capital owing to the change in the value of working capital represented by accounts receivable from customers. Effectively, however, the proposed change looked at on an incremental basis is a change in the cash flow to and from the equity shareholder and hence should be evaluated by discounting at the equity cost of capital.

The situations discussed in the preceding paragraphs, of course, only apply exactly where the firm is at or near its policy or conventional financial ratios. If a firm is well below these ratios – that is, the firm is undergeared – then this raises special problems of its own (see Section 5). The impact that any given project and pattern of cash flows will have on future debt finance will depend on the specific debt raising policy being pursued by the firm and on the effect of these cash flows on the firm's demand for and supply of capital. Under these conditions, neither the return to total capital nor the net present value based on the weighted average cost of capital bear any consistent relationship to the return or net present value of the equity shareholders.

b. *Relationship Between NPV on Total and on Equity Capital*

Again assuming an asset cover limiting situation, consider the relationship between the net present value as given by the weighted average cost of capital applied to the debt plus equity cash flows and the net present value as given by applying the equity cost of capital to the equity cash flows. The latter present value, of course, represents the true numerical attractiveness of the project to the equity shareholders.

The relationship is illustrated graphically in Figure 4.2.

This represents the relation between the net present values for the same type of projects as in Figure 4.1, that is, constant net cash flows, with the debt reducing by a constant annual amount as the asset is written down for depreciation purposes.

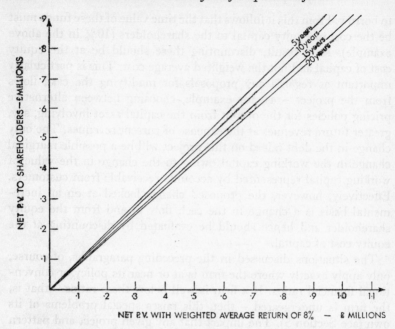

Fig. 4.2. The relationship between total net present values and equity net present values for projects of different lives, where the cost of equity is 10% and the cost of debt capital is 4%. Initial debt capital is 50%, giving a weighted average cost of capital of 7%

For a given life, the relationship between the two net present values is approximately linear and passes through the origin. The slope of the lines however varies with the life of the project such that a net present value of £600,000 at the weighted average cost of capital corresponds to a £497,000 equity net present value for a 20 year project and to £565,000 in the case of a 5 year project. Thus conversion of weighted average present values into equity present values requires reference to the different linear relationships connecting the two present values according to the life of the project.

From this analysis it is apparent that the weighted average cost of capital for projects with a constant net cash flow on total capital will pass the criterion of reflecting numerical attractiveness to equity shareholders, albeit with some administrative inconvenience in referring to a number of graphical relationships.

Finally we must examine the use of the weighted cost of capital, either in present value or yield calculations, as a simple accept or reject criterion for marginal projects involving relatively slight degree of risk, and hence projects which are only required to show on the equity capital involved a return in excess of the cost of equity capital. In this context we need to consider the extent to which a project with a return to total capital just equal to (and hence with a zero net present value at) the weighted average cost of capital gives a return to the equity capital equal to the cost of equity capital. From an analysis of numerical examples it would appear that, in general, providing either that the life of the project exceeds say, 10 years or alternatively the cash flows are relatively regular, the error involved is negligible for all practical purposes. In the case of relatively short term projects with markedly irregular cash flows, however, the error can be appreciable (see Example 2 above).

c. *Disequilibrium Problem*

We must now refer to an implicit contradiction which runs through the use of the weighted average cost of capital as a cut-off rate. This is the simple fact that, if a firm's equity cost of capital is, say, 10%, and its weighted average cost of capital is, say, 8%, then this last figure should *never* become effective as a cut-off rate. For, by assumption, the firm's shareholders have an opportunity cost of capital of 10%; that is, they can invest freely at this rate of return, and if this is the case then *so also can the firm*. In other words the firm has an infinite supply of projects offering the equity cost of capital (investing in the equity capital of other firms); hence, there can never be any justification for its investing at any lower rate.

On purely theoretical grounds, the only objection which can be levelled at this rather disturbing conclusion is that it would involve the firm's shareholders in investments which may be excessively geared. The firm itself is geared up and so also are the shares of the firm it is buying. At conventional levels of gearing, however, it is unlikely that this will be of any significant importance, and in any event it is clearly apparent that there is a large number of inadequately geared firms in which the firm could invest if this double gearing were considered an objection.

In a perfectly competitive market and in the absence of restricting institutional pressures, this contradiction would be removed by market forces. Investment trusts would be formed and, by raising debt capital, would bring to operate such additional gearing on the general range of shares that any further gearing would result in no net advantage to the equity shareholders. This would be due to the additional risk of bankruptcy to which the investment trust would be subject because of its high burden of fixed interest charges which have first claim on any dividends received by it. The forces which might bring about this result are discussed in detail in Chapter 15. We will only say here that, in our view, major institutional imperfections do not permit the equilibrium which pure theory would suggest.

While we are faced with this contradiction and unresolved problem on a theoretical level, on the level of practical policy, for analysis to proceed, it is only necessary to know the policy on which the firm has decided to operate. If, as in the majority of cases the firm will not contemplate investing in the equity capital of other firms, then the weighted average cost of capital (where its use is appropriate) stands as the effective cut-off rate for investments. The policy decision not to invest in the equity of other firms wipes out this the troublesome alternative. If the firm does consider investing in the equity capital of other firms, it is unlikely that this will be to a sufficient extent to make these investments the effective floor below which the firm cannot invest.

In all of the following analysis we shall assume that a firm is not prepared to invest to such an extent in the equity capital of other firms that the rate of return obtained thereon forms the effective opportunity cost of capital. This is reasonable in that, as shareholders have the opportunities to invest in geared investment trusts, but have instead invested in a firm's equity shares, it must be assumed that they do not wish the firm to become an investment trust.

d. *Conclusions*

In the preceding discussion we have tried to show that the use of the weighted average cost of capital is subject to certain definite limitations. We have also tried to show that the net present value calculated from the weighted average cost of capital has no definite meaning wherever the conditions required for the validity of the weighted average cost are not met. It is however possible, as we have demonstrated, to convert the net present values derived from the weighted average cost of capital into net present values of the equity cash flows to the equity shareholders, under certain simplifying assumptions. We have also contended that the net present value method, – including that based on the weighted average cost of capital, – is a clumsy means of considering the return offered for risk bearing. Given this, and the complication of converting this to equity net present values, we would conclude that the NPV method has little to commend it in real simplicity of application to the circumstances met with in most day to day applications of discounting methods (see also Chapter 5).

6. NON OPTIMAL FINANCING SITUATIONS

a. *Temporarily High Levels of Debt Financing*

In this section we will deal with the case in which firms are either in a position of temporary financial disequilibrium or deliberately pursuing a 'non-optimal' financing policy. It may frequently arise that a firm will have appreciable unused debt raising capacity. This may occur where the firm has been financed in an inefficient manner in the past, or where conditions in the past have been unpropitious for raising debt capital (e.g., because the firm has been too small, only recently established, or has had an inadequate earnings record). In these circumstances, the firm may find that it is able and willing to raise exceptionally large amounts of debt to finance its current capital projects. The question now arises, how should this exceptionally large proportion of debt finance be taken into account in the analysis of the capital projects?

The exceptional quantity of debt raised is essentially being raised on the assets created by *past* investments of the firm. These investments must have been financed by an exceptionally large proportion of *equity* capital, and the debt now being raised on these assets represents an opportunity to back out some of the equity used to finance these projects. This equity can essentially be backed out by declaring exceptionally large dividends out of retained profits (i.e., profits retained from previous projects). (Declaring the dividend out of retained profits is, of course, merely an accounting fiction since the retained profits will normally have been invested in capital projects: essentially, the cash for the dividends is coming out of the debt currently being raised. It is conceptually useful, however, to regard equity capital as being withdrawn from the projects represented by these assets and being replaced by debt.)

The point to be noted is that there is usually no legal impediment to a firm following this procedure. Under British company law it is generally necessary for a firm to have retained profits of at least the same amount as is now being distributed as dividends out of reserves but this will rarely represent an impediment in the case we are considering. For, if the firm has existing assets on which it can raise debt, it will normally be the case that these assets have been financed substantially by retained profits. The exception to this is, of course, the firm which has only recently become established and has been substantially created by directly raised equity capital. Such a firm is not likely to have sizeable retained profits. Where it is both desirable and possible to back out equity capital, it can seldom be done solely by way of declaring larger dividends for a year or two. Apart from the general undesirability of declaring extra large dividends when of necessity they cannot be maintained at that level, it may be impossible to get sufficient funds out solely by this route. But other alternatives are possible such as declaring capital bonuses (effectively returning share capital) or even issuing 'free' redeemable loan stock (*pace* Courtauld's tactics when rebuffing the ICI take over bid early in 1962). This latter alternative would be open to a firm which had no free reserves. (For a full discussion of the problems of a firm in a cash surplus position see Chapter 16.)

Directly backing out equity, however, is not common. More usually, a firm with this opportunity, as by definition it must be a successful firm if debt capital is now available to it, will be concerned to expand its activities. Thus any debt raised will be used for this purpose rather than for releasing equity funds from the business. But, in raising such debt capital, it would be quite wrong to regard it as entirely or even mainly attributable to the new projects being financed. The only reason so large a proportion (perhaps even 100%) of the finance for new projects can be raised in the form of debt is the existence of a large amount of equity financed assets which form the bulk of the asset cover for the debt now being raised. In this case, the debt should be considered in two parts; that attributable to the existing assets and that attributable to the new. The former must logically be regarded as equity capital in that it represents the amount of equity capital that could have been backed out if desired. Similarly, the new assets should only be considered to be debt financed to the extent that they genuinely enable the firm to raise further debt capital by the additional assets and earnings they create. If with the cost of capital set at this level the firm is unable to find sufficient investment opportunities to absorb the available capital, then it should seriously reconsider the possibility of backing out the excess capital in one of the ways described in the previous paragraph. If the 'cheap' capital is expected to be absorbed in a reasonable period over the next few years, the firm could also consider reducing its short term cut-off rate along the lines set out in Chapter 16.

b. *Alternative Debt Financing Policies*

The analysis of the previous section was based on the assumption that the objective of management was to pursue a policy of high gearing. In this section we consider alternative policies that are sometimes pursued and also the position where the firm has surplus cash or debt raising capacity which it is unwilling, or unable, to distribute by the methods touched on in the previous section.

It was argued in Section 1 that the normal external limitation on debt raising will be asset cover. Hyper-conservatism or relatively low earnings, however, may make earnings cover the effective limitation for a number of firms. Where this is the case, the debt capital associated with a given project will be related to its earnings over its life and the project may retain its debt capital (possibly increasing it as earnings increase) throughout its life. This involves no particular difficulties in calculating the net equity cash flows although, of course, it makes the relationships of Figures 4.1 and 4.2 inapplicable. Projects under these financing conditions would need to be analysed in the light of their actual earnings, the appropriate debt computed and the whole project finally analysed in terms of its equity cash flows.

An alternative policy which is sometimes pursued is what we shall refer to as the policy of residual debt financing. Firms following this policy, instead of considering debt as the cheapest source of finance and borrowing up to conventional limits, tend to resort to debt finance only when internally generated sources are insufficient. Such firms normally have a tradition of retaining a high proportion of profits and this, combined with depreciation and other provisions, is regarded as the first line of financing. If these resources prove adequate the firm may continue for years with little or no debt financing. Such a policy can rarely be in the best interests of the equity shareholders and is generally indicative of considerable financial inefficiency. Given that such a policy is being followed, however, it is important to consider what effect such a gearing will have on individual projects and consequently on the method of analysing them.

In fact, the effect of individual projects on gearing will generally be complicated and may differ widely with circumstances. Three main situations can arise. The first is where the firm is temporarily short of capital and is resorting to debt as its residual source of finance.

In this case taking on a project may result in raising debt equal to the whole capital cost of the asset, that is in 100% gearing. This debt, however, may be rapidly run down (if it is in the form of overdrafts or other long term debt which is maturing) if the firm generates surplus funds over the course of the next few years.

The second situation is where the firm finances the project by retaining funds which would otherwise have been distributed as dividends. Initially, therefore, the project is 100% equity financed. But if, over the life of the project, the firm is running into a capital deficit as regards internally generated funds, the fact that this project has been taken on may result in actual gearing being *reduced* compared with what it would have been if the project had not been taken on. This can arise because the project itself generates cash which reduces the capital deficit and hence reduces the extent to which the firm has recourse to debt finance. The project therefore goes from zero to negative gearing. In both these cases, the important factor is the effect that the project has on the firm's present and future cash capital surplus or deficit from internally generated funds. It should be noted that in this situation, where the restraint on debt raising is not the asset cover, this does not make assessment of net present values by the weighted average cost of capital more viable. In fact it should be clear that exactly how much debt will be associated with a given project will vary markedly depending on whether the first or second situation applies and on the exact effect of the cash flows of the project on the particular pattern of supply and demand for capital thrown up by the firm. Exact analysis of capital projects under these conditions requires a forecast of the firm's supply and demand position for capital over the future life of the project and the relation of this to the cash generated by the project to determine precisely the effect on debt financing which the project may have. Where the amount of debt financing is relatively large, there would appear to be no alternative to this detailed special analysis. A particular problem in this case is the method of analysis to be used where the project is 100% debt financed in the early years. This is best treated by regarding it as a situation where the firm has a temporarily low cost of capital (the interest cost of the debt capital). The appropriate technique for this case is developed in Chapter 16. Where the amount of debt is relatively small (as will often be the case), or very considerable uncertainty surrounds future financing plans, it may be possible to ignore the effect of debt capital entirely and regard all projects as 100% equity financed.

The third situation is where the firm is drawing on an existing cash surplus to finance the project. In this situation, the firm has accumulated cash which it is unwilling to distribute to its shareholders, preferring to retain the cash until it can find some suitable investment opportunity. In the interim the cash will generally be invested in secure but low yielding portfolio investments. This case is also considered in detail in Chapter 16; but, broadly, the situation is that the firm has created a situation in which the short run opportunity cost of capital is extremely low, – the return which can be obtained on short term loans. This, and the subsequent effect of the project on gearing, need to be taken into account explicitly by the method developed in that chapter.

7. THE CAPITAL RATIONING SITUATION

In this section we consider a commonly encountered financing situation termed capital rationing. This is a situation in which a firm either cannot or will not raise capital beyond a certain limit. Such a firm has a supply curve of capital which in the relevant range becomes vertical, as illustrated in Figure 4.3.

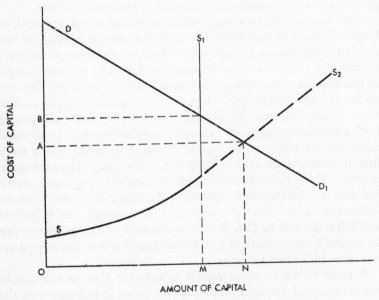

Fig. 4.3. Annual cost of capital under capital rationing

SS_1 and DD_1 are respectively the supply and demand curves for capital for a given period, say a year. OM represents the maximum funds available to the firm. Beyond that limit no funds are available and the supply curve of capital accordingly becomes vertical. This means that the cost of capital in the simplest case is determined by the return available on the marginal project that the firm can accept, – OB in the diagram.

A number of factors can give rise to a capital rationing situation. The most common cause as regards larger firms is that the firm is passing through a period of relatively low profitability due to exceptionally severe competition. This competition, while reducing the profits available for re-investment, may nevertheless create a need for exceptionally heavy 'defensive' investment. The poor profit record, however, may make it extremely costly if not totally impractical to raise further equity capital. Attempts to float a new equity issue at a time when the market is doubtful whether the firm can earn a worthwhile return on the new equity may lead to a serious collapse in the price level of the firm's shares. At the same time, the poor record may also make it extremely difficult for the firm to obtain further debt capital. In Britain an important example of externally imposed capital rationing is that imposed by the government on the nationalized industries from time to time.

More commonly, however, capital rationing is self imposed. A board of directors are unwilling to borrow money because of the restrictive conditions lenders will impose on the firm; or they are reluctant to raise more equity capital for fear they will lose control of the firm; or even because they do not wish to grow too fast and prefer the quiet life. These reasons apply particularly to smaller firms. (Such firms will in any case frequently be in the position of having inadequate access to externally supplied capital.) In all these conditions of self-imposed capital rationing, it is important for a firm to calculate the cost of its policy. This cost is clear from the diagram. If the policy is abandoned, the firm's cost of capital curve becomes SS_2 and with this cost curve the firm will be able to invest MN more funds with advantage, and its marginal cost of capital will fall from OB to OA. Before any capital rationing scheme can be justified, an estimate of profits sacrificed on investment projects not taken up should be made.

A point to notice about capital rationing is that, as the supply curve of capital becomes vertical at the point it typically cuts the demand curve for such capital, then the marginal cost of capital is liable to fluctuate more than if no such restriction existed. This means that to assume a constant cost of capital over future years is a less tenable assumption under capital rationing conditions than under normal conditions. This is especially so when capital rationing takes the form of raising no further capital at all, relying entirely on self generated funds, i.e. depreciation provisions and retained profits. These latter can fluctuate significantly from year to year. To calculate the marginal cost of capital in such circumstances, however, involves forecasting all likely investment projects for many years ahead, together with all the funds which they in turn would generate. This poses a fairly complicated programming problem which, although it could be handled on a computer, would involve a number of thorny conceptual problems (these are briefly considered below). Given these complications, and the very imperfect forecasting on which the analysis will probably be based, it will generally be the best policy simply to estimate the firm's average opportunity cost of capital over the next few years, that is, the return offered by the marginal projects that will be accepted over the next few years, and use this as the cost of capital in the normal way. This is not quite so unsatisfactory as might first appear because it is probable that most projects, after allowing for risk, cluster fairly thickly around the margin. Thus the demand curve for capital is fairly flat. So, even with the supply curve of capital fluctuating, the marginal opportunity cost of capital may not alter greatly.

In some cases, however, a firm may expect to emerge from this period of capital rationing into a period when either an increase in self generated funds, or rewon access to the capital market, cause a fall in the cost of capital to a more normal level. In this case, the firm has a temporarily high opportunity cost of capital up to year, say, k and thereafter the cost of capital drops to its more 'normal' level. The main problem in this case is to establish the opportunity cost of capital which applies up to year k, and this is best achieved by an adaptation of the present value method. All the cash flows after year k are discounted back to year k at the 'normal' cost of capital which is assumed to obtain after that year. Various trial rates of discount are then applied to bring these and their preceding cash flows back to year zero and establish the present value of the projects. The trial rate of discount, which, applied in this way to all the projects, results in the elimination of sufficient projects to equate the supply and demand for capital is then the true opportunity cost of capital over the period up to year k. This line of approach may in this case give an improvement in accuracy over the simpler approach of merely estimating the average cost of capital over the period, although it is probably rare that this will be sufficient to outweigh the evident administrative difficulties of its application.

It sometimes arises in capital rationing situations that the firm, due to changing availability of capital and investment opportunities, has an opportunity cost of capital which changes markedly from year to year. The best way of attacking this problem is to abandon the attempt to determine the *firm's* changing opportunity cost of capital and rephrase the problem in terms of the *shareholders'* cost of capital. The problem is thus one of directly evaluating at the *shareholders'* cost of capital *all* the investment possibilities open to the firm, and their timing, in terms of the flow of dividends which they and their re-invested earnings will ultimately produce. The maximization of the net present value of the shareholder's dividend stream at their cost of capital is the first principle of financial analysis (see Section 4a of the previous chapter), and the return to first principles in this case will be found to cut through many of the difficulties.

8. DIVIDING CURRENT DEPRECIATION INTO ITS DEBT AND EQUITY COMPONENTS

In this concluding section we develop further the arguments given in Section 3a for considering current depreciation provisions to be part debt and part equity, whenever asset cover is the effective limitation on debt raising.

Commonly a firm's depreciation provision is regarded as always being a source of equity funds in its entirety. As we have briefly argued above, we regard this view as mistaken. The main reason for our view that often the depreciation provision can be meaningfully split into debt and equity portions is simply this. Where the depreciation provision is used for re-investment, as it certainly is in most expanding firms, it obviates the need to repay debt and to the extent that it does this it must be regarded as a source of debt capital. And, in the case where debt is actually being repaid, this must be regarded in the first instance as a set-off against depreciation. In short, when the opportunity cost of using part of the depreciation provision is effectively the repayment of debt, that part of the depreciation provision can meaningfully be regarded as attributable to debt and should be so regarded. Accordingly, it need only be invested at a rate of return sufficient to service debt capital. Having stated our position we must now justify it. To aid in this a simple example will prove useful.

Suppose a taxi firm runs two taxis. Each taxi is presumed to cost £200, to have a life of only two years after which its scrap value is nil, and to be depreciated on a straight line basis of £100 a year. It is possible to borrow up to 50% of the net assets of the firm at 4% net of tax, the remaining finance coming from equity funds for which the cost of capital is 10% net of tax. Each taxi earns a constant £$110\frac{2}{3}$ net of tax income each year after meeting all expenses save depreciation and loan interest. All profits are assumed to be paid out as dividends. When the taxi firm commences business, it starts off with only one taxi for its first year. At the beginning of the second year it buys a second taxi, and thereafter it replaces one taxi a year as taxis wear out after a two year life. Consider the firm's accounts for the first three years. Closing Balance Sheets are drawn up after loan interest and dividends have been paid.

Opening Balance Sheet £'s

Year 1

Share capital	100	Taxi 1	200
4% Loan	100		
	200		200

Profit and Loss Account

Depreciation	100	Net Income	$110\frac{2}{3}$
Loan Interest	4		
Profit	$6\frac{2}{3}$		
	$110\frac{2}{3}$		$110\frac{2}{3}$

Closing Balance Sheet

Share Capital	100	Taxi 1	200	
4% Loan	100		−100	
				100
		Cash		100
	200			200

Year 2

The firm buys a second taxi at the start of the year costing £200. This is paid for £100 from cash (representing the first year's depreciation provision, £50 from new debt at 4%, and £50 from a further injection of share capital).

Opening Balance Sheet £'s

Share Capital	150	Taxi 1	100
4% Loan	150	Taxi 2	200
	300		300

Profit and Loss Account

Depreciation	200	Net Income	$221\frac{1}{3}$
Loan Interest	6		
Profit	$15\frac{1}{3}$		
	$221\frac{1}{3}$		$221\frac{1}{3}$

Closing Balance Sheet

Share Capital	150	Taxi 1	100	
4% Loan	150		−100	
				−
		Taxi 2	200	
			−100	
				100
		Cash		200
	300			300

Year 3

The firm buys a third taxi at the start of the year to replace the first taxi which has been retired. This is paid for entirely from the available cash equivalent to the previous year's depreciation provision of £200.

Opening Balance Sheet £'s

Share Capital	150	Taxi 2	100
4% Loan	150	Taxi 3	200
	300		300

Profit and Loss Account			*Closing Balance Sheet*		
Depreciation	200	Net Income 221⅓	Share Capital	150	Taxi 2 100
Loan Interest	6		4% Loan	150	−100
Profit	15⅓				200
					Taxi 3 −100
					100
				Cash	200
	221⅓	221⅓		300	300

This set of accounts will be repeated for all future years. The firm's profit and capital structure will remain constant, and every year the depreciation provision will be used to purchase a replacement taxi.

Before examining the implications of this example, it should be noted that the income of the firm is exactly sufficient to pay off the loan interest and enable the equity funds to earn a 10% discounted return. Consider the equity net cash flow.

Years	0	£'s 1	2	3	... n
Outlays	−100	−50	—	—	—
Income	—	+ 6⅔	+15⅓	+15⅓	+15⅓
Net	−100	−43⅓	+15⅓	+15⅓	+15⅓

This series has a discounted return of exactly 10%.

It should also be noted that the discounted return on the equity capital involved in each single taxi is also 10%. This can be demonstrated on the basis that the firm only operates the first taxi for two years, buying no other taxis, and ceasing operations at the end of the second year, repaying the loan in two equal end-year instalments of £50. (This assumed pattern of loan repayments is critical to the argument and is justified later.)

Years	0	1	2
Equity Outlay	−100	—	—
Debt Outlay	−100	—	—
Total Net Income	—	+110⅔	+110⅔
Less Loan Interest		− 4	− 2
Less Loan Repayment		− 50	− 50
Equity Net Cash Flow		56⅔	58⅔

This equity net cash flow gives rise to a discounted return of exactly 10% on the original equity outlay of £100.

It will be apparent from this that as each taxi costs the same and gives rise to the same income, then each taxi, looked upon as a separate investment, would give rise to a constant 10% return on the equity investment it involves, and to a constant return (fractionally above 7·0%) on the total investment of debt and equity combined that it involves. This, of course, presumes that each taxi is financed in the same way, 50% debt and 50% equity. But consider how each of the first three taxis was actually financed.

	£'s New Equity	New Debt	Depreciation Provisions
Taxi 1	100	100	nil
Taxi 2	50	50	100
Taxi 3 etc.	nil	nil	200

If it can be shown that the depreciation provision can meaningfully be split 50–50 into debt and equity portions, however, then it follows that each taxi was financed in the same way, namely half debt and half equity.

Consider the position of the firm at the end of the first year. It has £100 in cash representing the first year's depreciation provision. What is the alternative use for these provisions if they are not used for re-investment? The firm could of course retain the cash, and invest it in, say, short term securities and by so doing it would obviate the need to repay any debt as the net assets would suffice to cover debt twice over. But to keep the money invested in low yielding portfolio investments would evidently be inefficient. The firm could then consider three possible uses of the surplus funds.

(i) It could repay the whole £100 to the equity shareholders for investment outside the business at 10%.

(ii) It could repay the entire loan, so averting the interest cost of 4%.

(iii) It could repay part of the loan, paying the balance out to the equity shareholders to re-invest at 10%.

Choice (i) offers the highest return on the funds from the viewpoint of the equity shareholders, but in practice it would not be possible to implement it. The firm would be left entirely debt financed and in the absence of adequate asset cover the lenders would call in their loans as soon as it becomes possible to do so. Hence, choice (i) must be rejected as impractical.

L

Choice (ii) is possible but it represents a very low return (4%) on the funds involved.

The best practical course is then choice (iii). The best choice the firm could make, in the interests of returning the maximum sum to its equity shareholders for re-investment elsewhere at 10%, is to split the £100 equally between debt and equity, which would leave unimpaired the net asset cover on the debt remaining. This is the maximum possible equity distribution which is consistent with maintaining the required asset cover.

We have thus established that, if the firm does not re-invest the depreciation provision at the end of the second year, the most acceptable course is to return it to the equity shareholders and lenders in such a way that the net asset cover on the remaining debt does not fall below the minimum acceptable to the providers of debt capital.[1] In our example, that acceptable ratio is 50% debt and 50% equity. Hence, by re-investing the depreciation provision in full, the opportunity cost to the firm is repaying £50 of debt and returning £50 to the equity shareholders. This being so, it is meaningful to say that in this case half of the depreciation provision should be considered the equivalent of debt capital. Similarly, at the end of year 2, and all years thereafter, the depreciation provision should be thought of as 50% debt and 50% equity.

As final confirmation that in this case part of the depreciation provision should be thought of as debt capital, consider the return that each of the taxis earns. If the depreciation provision were all equity then taxi 3, and all subsequent taxis, would have had to earn more than taxi 2, which in turn would have had to earn more than taxi 1. Yet all taxis earn the same net income of £110$\frac{2}{3}$ a year and the return on the total equity investment is the required 10%. This can only be because the depreciation provisions must realistically be said to comprise 50% debt and 50% equity. Re-investing the depreciation provision in its entirety every year effectively avoids the necessity of repaying any debt, and to the extent that it does so, part of the depreciation provision, 50% in this case, must be considered attributable to debt rather than to equity.

This breakdown of current provisions into debt and equity applies only, however, where asset cover is the limiting factor in the

[1] In all this we are assuming that debt can be repaid at the borrower's behest. In practice, even if a loan is for a fixed period, it is usually possible to repay it sooner if the borrower so desires, although a small premium may be necessary to compensate the lenders for any inconvenience caused.

firm's debt raising. Consider, for example, the position of a firm which has not fully exploited its debt raising potential. A firm in this position must regard its current depreciation provisions as equity capital to the extent that it can return the depreciation to its equity shareholders (by way of a return of capital declaring dividends out of past retained profits, etc.) without being forced to repay any of its existing debt. In short, the depreciation provision can be regarded as equity to the extent that the opportunity cost of paying it out to the shareholders is not debt repayment in any form. (It will be apparent that a firm which has raised its full potential debt could never be in this position.)

We have demonstrated that the depreciation provision often contains a debt element and we have shown how this may be identified in different situations. In conclusion, we would emphasize that for the firm which has raised debt capital on the strength of depreciating assets, where, as typically happens, the depreciation provision is retained in the firm to finance replacement and expansion investment, then the debt element in the depreciation provision is effectively being transferred to the new assets acquired, and should be so regarded. In the example used of the firm with two taxis, the re-investment of the depreciation provision at the end of the first year in taxi 2 represented a pure expansion investment. Thus re-investment of the depreciation provision at the end of the second and all subsequent years represented pure replacement investment. In both situations it is realistic and meaningful to regard debt as being repaid on the depreciating taxis each year, and new debt being raised on the new taxis being purchased. Thus, the depreciation provision can be regarded as the source of funds for notional debt repayment which identifies the debt proportion of the depreciation provision. We have already demonstrated that, but for the profitable re-investment of the depreciation provision, such debt repayment would actually occur.

REFERENCES

1. 'Economic Trends', April 1962. See especially Tables E, F, and 1A.
2. GORDON DONALDSON, *Corporate Debt Policy*. Division of Research, Harvard Business School, Boston, 1961, and 'New Framework for Corporate Debt Policy', *Harvard Business Review*, March-April, 1962.
3. HAROLD BIERMAN, JR., and SEYMOUR SMIDT, *The Capital Budgeting Decision*, p. 139, Macmillan, New York, 1960.

CHAPTER FIVE

Methods of Investment Appraisal Compared

The three main economic methods of analysing capital projects, net present value, discounted yield, and annual capital charge have already been discussed in outline in Chapter 2. The methods of present value and yield were also considered in relation to a firm's financial policy in Chapter 4. In this chapter we propose to conclude the analysis by a critical examination of the methods themselves and some of their applications.

The general reader will probably find the whole of Sections 1 and 2 of interest. Section 3 is rather specialist in character, in that it consists of a fairly full discussion of the annual capital charge method and its applications, and this will probably be of interest only to the particular industries using this method.

I

1. YIELD *Vs*. NET PRESENT VALUE

It should be evident from the previous discussion that yield and net present value represent two alternative economically viable methods of analysing capital projects and in this section we will consider their relative merits.

It will be convenient to state at the outset our broad conclusions (particularly since part of the conclusions must await demonstration until later chapters dealing with special subjects). Our main conclusion is that, for the vast majority of simple capital budgeting decisions (the exceptions will be apparent from our following discussion), we consider that yield is both technically and practically superior to net present value. In these relatively simple situations, the disadvantages of net present value considerably outweigh its technical simplicity. Over a certain range of problems, – as, for example the changing cost of capital situation discussed in Chapter 17, – neither simple discounted yield nor simple net present value is satisfactory. Both

148

methods, however, can be extended to cover these special cases without undue difficulty. In certain special applications, such as in valuation and determining the optimal life of assets (see Chapter 19), the flexibility and technical simplicity of the method of present value give it decisive advantages over yield.

a. *A General Comparison of the Two Methods*

The first and fairly obvious point to be noted is that, as a formal accept or reject criterion, both yield and present value would lead to the same selection of projects. All projects which have yield in excess of the cost of capital must also have a positive net present value. Hence, accepting all projects which have a yield in excess of the cost of capital or accepting all projects which have a positive net present value must lead to the same selection of projects. (Certain exceptions to this rule, however, are considered below.)

Because the two methods are both formally correct the choice between them must be largely decided on grounds of their convenience in other respects and the administrative facility with which they can be employed. We must state at the outset that, where either method can be used without giving rise to the technical difficulties discussed below, we strongly prefer the yield method. This is for three main reasons. The first is that yield is a more useful measure of profitability when we are endeavouring to assess the return offered for risk bearing for the following reasons. An essential characteristic of the type of risk normally encountered in business is that it is related to time (generally increasing with time) and relates to the amount of capital 'outstanding' in a capital project at any time. Thus a rate of return per unit of capital outstanding in the project per unit of time (the figure provided by the discounted yield method) is essentially measuring return in the same dimensions (time and quantity) as risk, and thus facilitates the task of determining whether the return offered is adequate, given the risks involved. Net present value as an absolute quantity lacks this very important advantage.

Second, the yield method, despite its being in some respects the more complicated is, in our experience, more easily understood and accepted by businessmen than the method of net present value. There would appear to be a strong tendency for businessmen to think in terms of a rate of return on capital in many contexts and this is primarily connected with its convenience in facilitating the assessment of the return for risk bearing. Because the present value method runs so contrary to this ingrained inclination to assess projects in terms of a rate of return on capital, businessmen find it difficult to make advantageous use of it. There is a strong tendency for them either explicitly or implicitly to modify the method into some eccentric perversion of yield. For example, the net present value of a project is sometimes divided by the project's expected life and the result expressed as a percentage of the initial capital outlay. This is a form of rate return on capital but without the discounted yield's relevance to the cost of capital. It reproduces the disadvantages of the yield method but only very imperfectly reproduces its advantages.

Finally, the yield method has the advantage of obviating needless dispute about a firm's cost of capital. As we have noted, it is often very difficult to determine the cost of capital with any exactitude. The effect that changing the estimated cost of capital will have on a particular net present value is difficult to determine without performing the actual calculation, depending as it does on the life of the project and the pattern of the net cash flows. If the net present value is used therefore, it is necessary to give a number of net present values covering the range of estimates of the cost of capital. It is descriptively simpler, particularly where a project already involves a mass of complex information which must be digested by top management, to avoid adding to this proliferation of data by quoting merely the yield. This can be related to the reviewer's estimate of the cost of capital and, if sufficiently above this estimate for the risks involved, further analysis of this particular point is obviated. As we will argue in Chapter 6 on Risk, it is generally desirable to consider the profitability of a range of alternative outcomes. This being so, it is important to be able to indicate the profitability of each outcome by a single figure, which the yield method permits. Present value, on the other hand, would require a range of profitability estimates for each of these outcomes, which makes for a cumbersome and confusing presentation.

b. *Objections to the Yield Method*

A number of objections have been levelled at the yield method. In this section we briefly consider these objections and the modifications necessary to the yield method to overcome them. We should state in advance, however, that none of these objections appear in our estimation to be sufficiently important to invalidate the general superiority of yield over present value.

i. The Ranking problem. A common objection levelled in academic discussion against the yield method is that it does not rank projects in their true order of attractiveness. The true order of attractiveness in this context is taken to be the order of the magnitude of their net present values. An example is given in Table 5.1.

Table 5.1

Project	Annual Cash Flow	Capital Cost	Life	Discounted Yield	Net Present Value at 8%
	£	£	Years	%	£
A	100	750	30	13	376
B	200	1,004	10	15	338
C	100	502	10	15	169
D	52 (plus 259 at end of year 4)	259	4	20	104
E	100	259	4	20	72

It is seen in this extreme case that the order of attractiveness given by the magnitude of the net present value is the reverse of the order of attractiveness given by the magnitude of the yield. The reason for this difference in ranking is fairly obvious. The yield is related to the *amount* of capital and the *period* over which it is invested: it is possible for a high yield (100% per day) to be produced by investing £1 on one day and receiving back £2 the following day. Present value, however, is an absolute quantity: it is the difference between the present value of the net cash inflows and the present value of the capital outlay – a mere £1 in this latter example.

Table 5.1 illustrates how the ranking order may be reversed, depending on the lives and initial capital cost of the project. It shows that where two projects (D and E) have identical capital costs, lives and yields, the ranking order given by yield and present value can be different, depending on the pattern of cash flows over time. This should also be apparent from reflecting that a project with, say, a negligible cash flow after the 10th year of its life, while formally having a life of 20 years, is very close to being a project with a 10 year life. For this reason a project from which virtually all the capital and profit had been recovered by the end of the 10th year might have a lower present value than a project with the same yield but whose cash flows, say, were spread evenly over the whole 20 years.

While it is generally true that the yield method gives a different ranking from that of net present value, the question needs to be asked: Has this any practical significance? Before proceeding to consider this point, we should first note that ranking as given by the estimated net present value is valid only in the absence of risk. If the projects were subject to different degrees of risk, their order of attractiveness could well be different from that given by their apparent net present values. More important than this is the fact that the capital budgeting decision (with an important exception discussed below) is generally simply one of acceptance or rejection. It is immaterial to this decision whether a particular project is first, third or thirtieth in the order of attractiveness. It may still be either accepted or rejected, depending solely on the return it alone offers compared with the firm's cost of capital. Involved in any investment decision there will normally be a great deal of interesting information which is nevertheless generally irrelevant to the decision: the ranking position of a project is generally in this category.

A situation in which the ranking order is sometimes of relevance is in the capital rationing situation described in Chapter 4, Section 7. Two basic situations can be distinguished. The first is where the firm's opportunity cost of capital (the yield on the least attractive of its acceptable marginal projects which can be financed by available capital resources) is constant over the relevant future. This case essentially reduces to the normal situation in which the firm has a well defined cost of capital with which to evaluate its projects on a yield basis. The second situation is where the firm has a changing opportunity cost of capital due to its changing investment opportunities or availability of capital. This indeed poses complex ranking problems in that it is necessary to choose between mutually exclusive (or partially mutually exclusive) investment *programmes*. In this, as in a number of complex investment problems, the method of net present value (albeit in a more complicated form than its normal application) is probably the only practical method of analysis. This inadequacy in certain recognizable special cases, however, in no way detracts from the general superiority of the yield method over the wide range of commonly encountered capital budgeting situations.

ii. Mutually exclusive projects. The most typical situation in which mutually exclusive choices arise in capital budgeting is where there are alternative means of achieving a given objective, – for example, different types of equipment to produce a given product or alternative means of utilizing a given building site. It is an essential feature of the problem in these cases that it is not possible, or at least not desirable, to accept more than one of the investment opportunities offered, hence the problem is not one of accepting or rejecting but of choosing between the alternative possibilities.

This is a situation in which the argument that the yield method fails to give a satisfactory ranking of projects has some real force. It is evidently possible that the alternative having the highest yield may involve a relatively small amount of capital or be for a more limited period of time than another lower yielding investment which, as a consequence, has a higher net present value. While it would be possible in these cases to discriminate between the alternatives on the basis of net present value, the use of this method in this connection brings out in greater relief the weakness of the present value method in risk situations. For simply choosing whichever alternative has the highest net present value could involve a firm, say, in taking the alternative which is far more capital intensive in return for a totally inadequate *improvement* in the net present value compared with that offered by a less capital intensive and less risky alternative. It is a fairly common characteristic of additional capital outlays that they are at a rather higher risk than the base outlays. For example, the typical situation in which a firm finds itself with mutually exclusive projects is that it has a variety of processes to produce a given output or it has the choice of alternative sizes of plant it might build to cope with future demand. Frequently (although not always), the more capital intensive processes are less well tried and thus subject to the risk of 'teething troubles', etc. Similarly, building larger plants in anticipation of distant future demand is almost invariably more risky than building smaller sized plants based on more conservative assessments of demand.[1]

This type of problem, for reasons which are illustrated in the course of the following example, is generally most satisfactorily analysed in terms of the *incremental* net cash flows resulting from choosing one alternative compared with another.

---

[1] It might be objected that if demand is equally likely to be higher or lower than estimated, building a smaller plant involves the risk of being obliged to build another plant after a few years and thus lose the economies of scale. This would be true if we possessed firm knowledge that it was equally as likely that demand would be higher as lower than forecast. It is often the essential nature of the problem that we do not have such knowledge and it is this absence of knowledge that is a part of the inherent inescapable risk. Moreover, in so far as any knowledge is available on this point, it would be to the effect that the unknown in these situations is more likely to be unfavourable than favourable because of the asymmetric pressure of competition which tends to destroy profit opportunities rather than create them.

Example 1. The following example (like others in this chapter) is not meant to be thoroughly realistic (tax complications, for example, are entirely omitted), but is merely designed to illustrate the principle of the incremental approach. Assume that a firm has two mutually exclusive projects, with the characteristics set out in Table 5.2, and has a cost of capital of 8%.

Table 5.2

£000's

Project	Annual Cash Flow	Capital Cost	Life	NPV at 8%	Yield
A	100	502	10 years	169	15%
B	144	780	10 years	186	13%
B–A	44	278	10 years	17	9·4%

The incremental yield approach simply consists of subtracting the net cash flows of the cheaper alternative from those of the dearer to establish the incremental cash flows which result from accepting the alternative involving the higher initial capital outlays. These net cash flows are set out in the last row of Table 5.2. It will be found that the incremental yield given by a cash flow of £44,000 for 10 years, in return for an initial capital outlay of £278,000, is only 9·4%. Whether or not this return is acceptable turns essentially on the degree of risk involved and either A or B may be preferable depending on this factor. Thus if the returns are fairly assured, B is better than A despite its lower return, since it *offers all that A offers* plus the chance of an incremental investment of £278,000 at 9·4% – appreciably above the 8% cost of capital. If the incremental cash flows are at a higher degree of risk, requiring a return in excess of 9·4%, then A is to be preferred. It is, of course, essential in any incremental cash flow calculation that the base case (project A in this example) and its return are clearly stated, since if this level of return is unacceptable then the project with the higher capital cost (B in this case), may be rejected despite the fact of a high level of return on the incremental investment of B–A.

Consider now the very real practical problem of how this project is to be presented for top management approval. It is very difficult to know in advance what level of return will prove acceptable to top managment in the light of their particular assessment of the project's risks and rewards. Under the yield method they would be advised that the yield on A was 15% and that on the incremental investment B–A was 9·4%. These returns can then readily be assessed by them in the light of the cost of capital and the risks involved in the two alternatives. It may well be in this case that A is acceptable, but that given its higher degree of risk and lower return, the incremental investment B–A is not.

The application of the formally simple present value criterion to this problem, namely that of simply accepting the project with the higher NPV at the firm's cost of capital, is not practical because of the need to allow for risk. A choice therefore, has to be made as to the particular modification of NPV that is required in this case. The choice is between (a) presenting the project simply in terms of the NPV of Table 5.2, or (b) varying the rate of discount to allow for what is thought might be the top management's rate of discount for each alternative in the light of the risks they involve. The latter is administratively clumsy since it is difficult to assess what top management's views might be as regards the often differing appropriate rates of discount for each project. Indeed were it possible to know the appropriate discount rates in advance, the decision of top management to accept or reject would be unnecessary since it could be foreseen in advance. But the alternative of presenting management with the NPV of Table 5.2. is also administratively cumbersome. Top management are required to balance these net present values against the capital involved and life of the project, and are then left to speculate on what the effect would be on these net present values of allowing for risk by higher rates of discount. (This effect could of course vary appreciably from project to project depending on its life and pattern of cash flows.) The yield has the particular advantage in this latter respect that, if desired, it can be looked on as the maximum rate of discount which can be applied to the cash flows before the net present value becomes zero. In this way it is ideally suited to accept or reject decisions which only need to establish not some generally agreed relevant magnitudes such as net present values, rates of discount, or rates of return (a much more complicated process), but simply whether the magnitudes do or do not exceed the figure which is regarded as acceptable.

Thus the financial simplicity of NPV in discriminating between mutually exclusive alternatives is lost wherever the alternatives involve risk, and indeed the problem under these circumstances becomes one of allowing for the administrative inadequacies of the NPV criterion.

The incremental yield approach as a method of discriminating between alternatives will generally be found to be the most satis-factory method of solution, particularly since the added complexity of the different risks in the alternatives strongly favour using a method which aids this task. Even where it is decided to employ the net present value method, this will generally require that risk projects be expressed in an incremental form, e.g. the incremental net present value resulting from the incremental capital outlay.

The problem becomes more complicated when there are more than two choices. This problem is generally simply solved on a practical level by a process of elimination. Beginning with the project involving the smallest initial capital outlays, the incremental return involved in moving from this to the project with the next largest initial capital outlays is first calculated. If this incremental return proves satisfactory, this second alternative becomes the basis for further comparisons and the first alternative is rejected completely. A third course is then chosen and this should be the choice involving the smallest additional capital outlays more than the new basis for comparison – that is, the second alternative. If this incremental return proves satisfactory, the second alternative as wel las the first may be abandoned entirely in favour of the third. If this incremental return proves unsatisfactory the third course would be abandoned and further analysis would proceed still using the second alternative (the undefeated champion so far) as the basis. In this way, the analysis proceeds step by step towards better solutions until the optimum is reached.

A particular case of mutually exclusive investments arises where there is a choice between alternative dates of commencing a given project. It is evidently impossible to commence the same project at more than one time. Hence, the choice between alternative dates of commencement is, by its own nature, one of the choices which are mutually exclusive. This problem can be tackled by the incremental yield method, simply considering the incremental gain from undertaking the capital outlay now compared with some alternative later date. This problem can arise only where the project's cash inflows will be higher (or the capital outlays lower) if the project is postponed. For example, capital outlays on new plant will often need to be postponed until an increasing level of repairs or operating diseconomies on the old plant make for profitable replacement (see Chapter 19, Section 1). The following example may clarify the problems involved.

Example 2. Assume the firm has a marketing capital project which, because of the rate of growth of the customer's offtake, has a series of cash flows as set out in Table 5.3, row A. The pattern of the cash flows suggests that a later date of commencement might result in a higher level of profitability. The customer in this case agrees to use alternative sources of supply for three years in return for a price concession of 20%.

Table 5.3

£000's

Years		0	1	2	3	4	5	6	7	8	9	10
A	Start now	−289	20	50	70	100	100	100	100	0	0	0
B	Start in 3 years	0	0	0	−289	80	80	80	80	80	80	80
A–B		−289	20	50	359	20	20	20	20	−80	−80	−80

Line B of the table shows the cash flows which result from the proposal that the project be delayed three years. To determine whether or not the project would be better postponed we can use the incremental method, subtracting the cash flows of row B from those of row A. These are given in the row marked A–B.

If the firm had a cost of capital of 8%, the series of cash flows set out in row A–B would offer a net present value of − £10,000, thus indicating that postponing and starting in three years is the better alternative.

This problem and the data illustrated in Table 5.3, however, highlight a general weakness of the yield method, which is that it cannot generally be applied to give meaningful results to a pattern of cash flows of the types set out in row A–B of the table. The difficulty resides in the series of negative cash flows at the end of the project A–B, in the years 8, 9 and 10. (Nor of course could it have been solved from knowing simply the separate yields of the two projects, 15% for A and 20% for B as A and B, as previously mentioned, are obviously mutually exclusive projects.)

This problem and a method of solving it, − the extended yield method, − are considered below. By using the extended yield it is possible to perform a yield calculation on the cash flows which has essentially the same usefulness as the normal discounted yield. As this method involves some additional computation, however, it will as a matter of practical computational convenience, usually be preferable − at least in the preliminary stages of the analysis − to use the net present value method on the incremental cash flows.

II

2. SITUATIONS IN WHICH THE DISCOUNTED YIELD HAS NO MEANING

a. *The Problem*

We must first make clear that the presence of negative cash flows in the later life of a project is quite consistent in the majority of cases with the normal useful interpretation of the cash discounted yield holding; i.e. with there existing only one positive value for this yield. This is best illustrated in the following example.

Example 3. The project has the cash flows set out in Table 5.4.

Table 5.4

£'s

Years	0	1	2	3	4	5	6	7	8	9	10
Cash Flow	−6,418	1,000	1,000	1,000	1,000	−6,780	3,000	3,000	3,000	3,000	3,000

These cash flows are found to give rise to a discounted yield of exactly 9%. It is seen in this case, however, that the project has a negative cash flow of £6,780 in the 5th year. Nevertheless, the present value (at the 9% yield rate) at the start of year 5 of all the subsequent cash flows from and inclusive of year 5, is still positive – in fact, it is £4,888. To show that the normal interpretation of the discounted yield still holds, we can note that the cash flows from this project can be split up in the manner shown in Table 5.5.

Table 5.5

£'s

Years	0	1	2	3	4	5	6	7	8	9	10
Cash Flows A	−6,418	1,000	1,000	1,000	1,000	0	1,257	1,257	1,257	1,257	1,257
B						−6,780	1,743	1,743	1,743	1,743	1,743

The two rows (A and B) are seen to add up to exactly the series of cash flows shown in Table 5.4, but A and B can be regarded as (and could equally well arise from) two separate projects, one with an initial capital cost of £6,418, and one with an initial capital cost (in year 5) of £6,780. Both of these projects will be found to earn

9%, as does the combined project shown in Table 5.5. This notional breakdown of cash flows is always possible providing that at no time in the life of a project the sum of the remaining *discounted* cash flows become negative when discounted at the yield rate. It is therefore possible in these situations to regard the project as being one in which each successive injection of capital earns the overall discounted yield return found for the project as a whole in the normal way. Evidently, providing this interpretation holds, the presence of net cash outflows in the future life of the project does not impair the usefulness or validity of the discounted yield.

The usefulness of the discounted yield turns on this validity of its interpretation as the return being earned on capital outstanding in a project each year. In some circumstances, however, this interpretation no longer holds and the definition of the discounted yield must be extended in order to give a meaningful result for these cases. This situation arises when there are *sufficiently large* negative net cash flows in the later period of a project's life. In these cases it will be found, discounting at the apparent yield of the project, that after a certain period of its life a project is a liability in the sense that the sum of the discounted net cash flows from that period onwards is negative. An example of this is given in Table 5.6.

Table 5.6
£'s

Years	0	1	2	3	4	5	6	7	8	9	10
(a) Net Cash flows	−2,000	1,000	1,000	1,000	1,000	−1,600	−2,000	1,000	1,000	1,000	−1,110
(b) Net cash flows discounted at 11%	−2,000	901	812	731	659	−949	−1,070	482	434	391	−391
c) Cumulative discounted net cash flows	−2,000	−1,099	−287	444	1,103	154	−916	−434	0	391	

Line (b) gives the present value at time zero of the individual net cash flows set out in line (a). Line (c) gives in each column the cumulative discounted net cash flows of line (b) up to the year denoted at the head of the column. Thus in year 1 there is shown the cumulative total of − £2,000 from time zero plus £901 from year 1, = − £1,099.

Discounting at 11% the cumulative total of the net cash flows is seen to have a net present value of zero, hence 11% is the normal discounted yield. As the cumulative total of the discounted cash flows by year 3 is positive at £444, it will be apparent that the sum of all the discounted cash flows arising *after* year 3 must be correspondingly negative (i.e. $-£444$). This implies in effect that some of the net cash flows recovered from the project to date will afterwards be re-absorbed as the later negative cash flows arise. Where the cumulative total of the discounted net cash flows in such cases as this changes from negative to positive and finally back to zero we effectively have only *temporary* use of some of the funds generated by the project during the period in which the cumulative total of the discounted cash flows is positive. Comparing this situation with the normal case, the difference in the present case is that at a certain stage in the project's life we have recovered from the project *more* than the initial capital plus the rate of return it has earned, and *this excess is later re-absorbed in the net cash outflows of the project.*

In extreme cases the presence of large negative net cash flows in the later life of the project can give rise to more than one discounted yield, that is to multiple solutions of r in equation (1.3). For example, consider a project with a 3 year life and the net cash flows given in Table 5.7. This project has discounted yields of 0%, 20%, and 40%, and the cumulative discounted net cash flow position is shown for 20% and 40% as in Table 5.6 above.

Table 5.7

£'s

Year	0	1	2	3
(a) Net Cash Flows	-100	360	-428	168
(b) Net Cash Flows discounted at 20%	-100.0	300.0	-297.2	97.2
(c) Cumulative net cash flows				
discounted at 20%	-100.0	200.0	-97.2	—
(d) Net cash flows discounted at 40%	-100.0	257.2	-218.4	61.2
(e) Cumulative net cash flows				
discounted at 40%	-100.0	157.2	-61.2	—

Some further light[1] can be thrown on the problem by the graphical analysis.

Figure 5.1 illustrates the normal situation in which the only negative net cash flow is the initial capital expenditure at the start of the

---

[1] See also Bailey, reference 1, for an alternative way of looking at the phenomenon of multiple solutions. This consists of regarding each consecutive pair of periods as a hypothetical investment or borrowing situation, at various rates of interest, which will give rise to the net investment or withdrawals of the actual project under consideration.

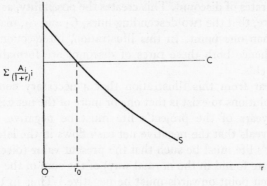

$$\Sigma \frac{A_i}{(1+r)^i}$$

Fig. 5.1.

first year. The horizontal axis of the figure is the rate of discount applied to the cash flows and the vertical is the resulting magnitude of the present value of the net cash flows. The horizontal line C represents the magnitude of the discounted negative net cash flows (a horizontal line in this case since the cash outflow C at year zero is not affected by discounting). The line marked S represents the present value of all the positive net cash flows. The point at which these two lines intersect, r_0, is the normal discounted yield.

Figure 5.2 shows the situation in which there is more than one negative net cash flow. In this case, the line C must fall with

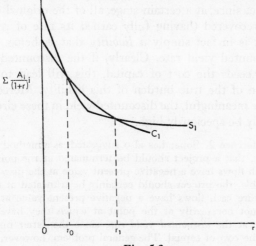

$$\Sigma \frac{A_i}{(1+r)^i}$$

Fig. 5.2.

M

increasing rates of discount. This creates the possibility, as illustrated in the figure, that the two descending lines, C_1 and S_1, may intersect at more than one point. In this illustration, intersection occurs at r_0 and r_1 hence both these rates of discount are formally the discounted yields.

It is clear from this illustration that a necessary condition for multiple solutions to exist is that one or more of the net cash flows in the later years of the project's life must be negative. Algebraic analysis reveals that the negative net cash flows in the later years of the project's life must be such that the present value (discounting at the yield rate found in the normal way) of the sum of the cash flows from a given point onwards must be negative.[1] Thus in the project given in Table 5.7, it is seen that the sum of the discounted cash flows is negative after year 1 at both of its yield rates of 20% and 40%. This is the *necessary* condition for multiple solutions to exist, although it is not *sufficient* of itself to cause multiple solutions.

Multiple yields are certainly very rare in actual practice although it is this disadvantage of the yield method which has received most attention. A more common but equally serious aspect of the problem arises in those situations in which the discounted net cash flows, – as in Table 5.6, – show a negative present value at the yield rate from a given point onwards. If this factor is not explicitly recognized and the discounted yield method adapted to take it into account, the conventional discounted yield becomes meaningless. It can no longer be the return earned on initial capital while it was invested in the project since, at a certain stage, all of the original capital will have been recovered (having fully earned its rate of return), and thereafter it is in fact simply *a liability* that is being discounted at the discounted yield rate. Clearly, if the discounted yield rate markedly exceeds the cost of capital, this will lead to an undue minimization of the true burden of this liability. Moreover, while ceasing to be meaningful, the discounted yield in these circumstances will generally be speciously high.

[1] Soper, reference 2. Soper has also suggested, as a method of resolving this difficulty, that a project should be terminated at the point at which its future cash flows have a negative present value at the discounted yield rate. If possible, the project should certainly be truncated at the point at which its future cash flows have a negative present value at the *cost of capital*, but not necessarily at the point at which they have a negative present value at the *discounted yield rate* since the latter may be much higher than the cost of capital. The general problem, however, is that it is is not usually possible to truncate the project at all.

It can in fact be shown that a high discounted yield in these circumstances is entirely consistent with a project having a negative net present value at a firm's marginal cost of capital. The example whose net cash flows are detailed in Table 5.8, illustrates this point.

Table 5.8

£000's

Years	0	1	2	3	4	5	6	7	8	9	10
Net Cash Flows	−419	292	100	100	100	100	100	100	100	100	−891

This project has a major capital outlay at the end of its life, – a situation that may arise where a project requires, say, major restoration of land or property when the project terminates. The discounted yield on this project is 20%, and this might appear an eminently satisfactory return on a project for a firm with an equity cost of capital of say 10%. It will be found, however, that far from being profitable by a comfortable margin, the project is in fact submarginal. The net present value of the project at 10% is actually negative, – i.e. −£12. In short, the project is submarginal on a present value basis. This situation can arise despite the fact that a project has a *unique* yield. In other words, multiple yields are only an occasional symptom of a more common and therefore more significant disease. Having identified the problem, we turn now to considering a solution.

b. *The Extended Yield Method*

A method of resolving the problem described above is to extend the definition of an apparent yield. Such an extension of the definition is given below, and it will consequently be referred to as the 'extended yield' method.[1]

In its simplest and probably most common application, the method is quite straightforward. It consists of finding the point from which the future cash flows (discounted at the yield rate) are negative. These cash flows are then all discounted at the normal cost of capital to bring them back in time to the point at which they are largely absorbed by the preceding positive cash flows. A revised yield calculation is then performed on the cash flows modified in this way. This is best demonstrated in an example.

[1] We are indebted to Dr. John Laski for explaining the implications of this method and for a detailed proof that it gives rise to a unique meaningful solution.

Example 4. The project has the cash flows set out in Table 5.9.

Table 5.9

£'s

Years	0	1	2	3	4	5	6	7	8	9	10	Yield
Cash Flows	−4,277	1,000	1,000	1,000	1,000	1,000	1,000	1,000	1,000	1,000	−2,000	15%
Adjusted Cash Flows	−4,277	1,000	1,000	1,000	1,000	1,000	1,000	1,000	188	0	0	14·6%

The yield calculation gives an *apparent* yield of 15%. It is seen however, that the discounted cash flows are negative after year 9. In this case, all that is required is to discount the negative cash flow of £2,000 back until this condition no longer holds. If we assume the firm's cost of capital is 7%, discounting the £2,000 back one year at 7% and subtracting it from the positive cash flow of that year we obtain the adjusted cash flow for that year of

$$£1,000 - \frac{£2,000}{1·07} = -£869.$$

This is still negative; hence, we discount this amount at 7% back a further year and subtract it from the cash flow of that year to obtain

$$£1,000 - \frac{£869}{1·07} = £188.$$

This cash flow is positive and the adjusted cash flows in this way are now as given in the second row in Table 5.9. The normal yield calculation is then performed on these cash flows: the yield is found to be 14·6% but for 8 years as opposed to 15% for 10 years.

The logic of this approach is best seen from the following interpretation. The firm can be regarded as recognizing the fact that the project becomes a liability in the last year of its life. It would be natural to consider coping with this liability by setting up some realistic provision to meet it. This suggests that the firm should allocate all that may be required of the *immediately preceding* cash flows into a *sinking fund* (see Chapter 1, Section 3a) which, accumulating at the firm's normal cost of capital, will be sufficient to pay off the liability of £2,000 which the project becomes at the end of its life. This is, in effect, what has happened in the above example. The sums deducted from the cash flows of years 8 and 9, £812 and £1,000 respectively, will in fact grow to £2,000 by the end of 2 years. Thus the £812 becomes £812$(1 \cdot 07)^2$ = £930, and the £1,000 becomes £1,000$(1 \cdot 07)$ = £1,070, making £2,000 in total, which is precisely the amount required to offset the £2,000 liability owing in year 10. We shall refer to this as the sinking fund interpretation.

The revised discounted yield in this situation is based on the period over which the project is *an asset*, and after making provision for meeting the future liabilities associated with the project. There is of course a certain element of arbitrariness in this. It may well be asked – why not set up a sinking fund from the first year onwards, deducting a constant amount from the cash flows in each year? Against this, it can be argued that the method proposed has two advantages. First, it has a simple interpretation which, in its emphasis on actual *cash*, is nearer to that of the normal discounted yield because no deductions (which are not strictly cash deductions) are made from the cash flows until the latest possible date. Second, the cash flows immediately preceding the offending cash outflows are also usually more similar in risk than the earlier cash flows, particularly, of course, where errors of forecasting increase with time. Hence, it will normally be the case that provision is being made *for* negative cash flows *from* positive cash flows of comparable risk. This would not normally be the case if provision were made out of cash flows in the immediate and relatively certain future.

The example given above demonstrates the application of the method in the normal and relatively simple case in which the problem arises. For completeness, however, a detailed example is given of a more complex case in Appendix A to this chapter.

To sum up: first there is no danger whatever in using the yield method unless a project has substantial negative net cash flows in its later years. Second, where this occurs the project should be tested at the apparent yield rate to establish whether it has a negative net present value from *any* point onwards in its life. Third, only if this latter condition is met does the yield cease to be meaningful, and resort must therefore be had to the extended yield method.

3. ANNUAL CAPITAL CHARGE METHOD

The annual capital charge method was described in Chapter 2, Section 1 and in this Section we shall consider the sinking fund return variant (as that most commonly used) critically in its relation to the other methods and its general usefulness. The sinking fund return is normally defined as being simply the net profit ('surplus') after sinking fund depreciation, expressed as a percentage of the initial capital cost of the project.

a. *Relationship to Yield and NPV*

The relationship between the sinking fund return (henceforth SFR), and yield is best illustrated in terms of a simple numerical example. Consider a capital project with cash flows set out in Table 5.10. This reproduces the standard example used in Chapter 2.

Table 5.10

£'s

Years	0	1	2	3
Net Cash Flows	−1,000	388	388	388

Net present value at 8% = 0, Yield = 8%.

The return as given by the SFR variant of the annual charge method is shown in Table 5.11 on the basis of a 5% sinking fund, and also 8% and 10% sinking funds.

Table 5.11

£'s

Sinking Fund Return at 5% SF

Years	0	1	2	3
Net Cash Flow	−1,000	388	388	388
SF Depreciation at 5%	—	−317	−317	−317
'Surplus'		71	71	71

SF Return = 71/1,000 = 7·1%

Sinking Fund Return with 8% SF

Years	0	1	2	3
Net Cash Flow	−1,000	388	388	388
SF Depreciation at 8%	—	−308	−308	−308
'Surplus'		80	80	80

SF Return = 80/1,000 = 8%

Sinking Fund Return with 10% SF

Years	0	1	2	3
Net Cash Flow	−1,000	388	388	388
SF Depreciation at 10%	—	302	302	302
'Surplus'		86	86	86

SF Return = 86/1,000 = 8·6%

This example illustrates the basic connection between discounted yield and the annual charge method. It is seen that if on a particular project the sinking fund is assumed to accumulate at the same rate as the discounted yield then the numerical magnitude of the return as given by the sinking fund variant of the annual charge method is *identical* with that given by the discounted yield.

The general relationship between the SFR and discounted yield can be summarized by saying that the SFR bears the same relationship to the yield as does the 'interest' rate used in the SFR, – i.e. if the sinking fund interest rate is *less* than the discounted yield so also is the SFR less than the discounted yield; if the sinking fund interest rate is *equal* to the discounted yield, so also is the SFR; and if the sinking fund interest rate is *more* than the discounted yield so also is the SFR. From this it will be seen that, if the sinking fund is assumed to accumulate at the firm's cost of capital, then accepting all projects with a discounted yield more than the cost of capital will give the same selection of projects as accepting all projects with an SFR in excess of the cost of capital.

Given that discounted yield and net present value would formally result in the same selection of projects, it follows that discounted yield, net present value, and the SFR all give the same selection of projects, where each method is handled in the correct way.

b. *Advantages and Disadvantages of the SFR*

If the SFR method is based on a sinking fund accumulating at the firm's cost of capital, then it can be interpreted quite usefully as the surplus (expressed as a percentage p.a. of the initial capital) that is available for distribution if the firm wishes to set aside enough to recover its capital in full at the end of the life of the project. It can also be regarded as the return offered for risk bearing expressed as a percentage of the initial capital. This interpretation only holds, however, if the sinking fund is based on the firm's marginal cost of capital. From the standpoint of economic logic, the sinking fund must be assumed to accumulate at the firm's marginal cost of capital, since this is the rate being earned on marginal projects. The sinking fund must be thought of as going into *marginal* projects (or backing out from raising new capital at the same cost) since all better than marginal projects will be accepted anyway, regardless of the funds available from the sinking fund. If the sinking fund is not assumed to accumulate at the firm's cost of capital, then no useful meaning can be attached to the SFR. For the firm will end the period with either more or less than the amount of capital with which it started the project. Hence, the keeping of capital intact interpretation does not hold. Either more or less of the return fund could be regarded as the surplus and the compensation offered for risk bearing, depending on whether the sinking fund rate was respectively lower or higher than the firm's cost of capital.

It is true, – as was seen from the second set of cash flows of Table 5.11, – that the yield itself could be regarded as an SFR return with a sinking fund at the yield rate. But this interpretation becomes devoid of useful meaning when the yield (and hence the sinking fund in question) becomes other than equal to the marginal cost of capital. For example, to take an extreme case, what useful meaning is to be attached to saying a project with a 30% yield can be regarded as a project with an SFR of 30% using a 30% *sinking fund*? No sinking fund either notional or actual is conceivable at this rate in a firm normally earning, say, 10% on its marginal projects and so having a marginal cost of capital of this rate.

The SFR method, however, does possess the useful meaning already noted when the sinking fund is set at the firm's marginal cost of capital. It also has the advantages of simplicity of computation and presentation. Offsetting these advantages, however, is the fact that the method would appear to combine all of the disadvantages of present value and some of the yield method, together with some particular difficulties of its own. As a form of yield method it should be apparent that the annual charge method has all the difficulties of the yield method. On the other hand, it lacks the useful simple meaning of the discounted yield method as the rate of return on the capital outstanding in the project.

As a firm's cost of capital must be used in computing the sinking fund, the method is involved in the administrative difficulties of obtaining an agreed specific definition of the cost of capital, in the same way that the use of present value involves such a general agreement.

Wherever there is any irregularity in the cash flows, the method is forced into the difficulty of either turning them into regular cash flows of the same present value or, alternatively, of ignoring the irregularity. Even where a project, once begun, may have reasonably regular positive cash flows there is still the difficulty that many projects will have a relatively long gestation period requiring a series of capital outlays spread out over a number of years. These considerations, and the inevitable irregularity of most projects net of tax cash flows resulting from the incidence of capital allowances,[1] would constitute a significant disadvantage to the general use of the method in industry.

Other difficulties of the method are best considered in relation to the industries which make extensive use of the method, namely state industries and property.

c. *The Use of the SFR Method in State Industries in Britain*

The preceding analysis demonstrated that the annual capital charge method would qualify as a formally correct economic method, if correctly used. It is fairly common, however, that the basic condition for this, – that the sinking fund should be at the cost of capital, – is not met. In the case of some of the state owned enterprises (which are 100% financed by debt capital), it would appear common to calculate the sinking fund on some assessment of the long term borrowing rate. The realism of using borrowing rates at all as indicative of the cost of capital to the community is discussed briefly below.

Of more immediate importance than this, however, is the problem of correctly assessing the cost of capital in these industries. It is a common feature of state enterprises that they are frequently subject to a form of government imposed capital rationing, – that is, they cannot obtain all the capital they require at the interest rate used in the return calculation. In these circumstances, the interest rate has no economic meaning as the cost of capital since the latter has a scarcity value in excess of this 'interest' cost. In these circumstances, the firm is in a capital rationing situation and the methods described in Chapter 4, Section 6, should be applied.

Even where a firm can obtain all the capital it requires at this interest rate, it is a serious question for economic policy whether or not the interest rate paid reflects the true cost of capital to the community on whose behalf the nationalized industry is operating. It would appear unlikely that the opportunity cost of capital to the community could be as low as the interest rate on which this debt is raised, given (a) the rationing of capital which applies in many other activities of the public sector because of the burden of raising further finance through government channels, and (b) the fact that private industry must inevitably look for a higher return than this

---

[1] This particular objection does not of course apply in the case of the nationalized industries, since these are rarely in a tax paying position.

interest rate. We therefore suggest that nationalized industries should (a) determine their opportunity cost of capital and (b) use this as their cut-off rate with yield as their basic method of analysis. Social benefits may properly be included in the returns on capital but are no reason for obscuring the true cost of such capital.[1]

d. *Use of the SFR Method in Property Analysis*

Property analysis (see reference 4) is the second main field in which the annual charge method is commonly used, and standard sinking fund return tables exist for this specific purpose. There are two main difficulties in using the method in this field. The first is the irregularity of the net cash flows, and the second is the special conditions of gearing which apply to property ventures. Where a property company is primarily concerned with assets which do not attract capital allowances (and this is generally true at the present time in Britain), this certainly removes one of the commonest sources of irregularity in the cash flows. In a world of inflating property prices and rents, however, it is frequently the case that increasing cash flows from increasing rents is a major consideration in the analysis of property ventures.

Reference was also made in (b) above of the need to set up the notional sinking fund at the firm's cost of capital. Frequently, however, where the method is used in property calculations, it will be the case that the sinking fund is at some conventional interest rate, or the interest rate at which the majority of the capital has been raised. Further the sinking fund will be related, not to the life of the project, but rather to the term of the debt capital. If a formal sinking fund is set up and the cash in it is not available to the firm for its normal activities, and a large proportion, say, 80% or more of the capital is raised as debt on this specific asset, the method constitutes a somewhat clumsy way of assessing the gross return (equity profit plus interest payable) in relation to the total initial capital.

Where the firm is not in fact setting up a sinking fund, but has free use of the capital, then the method will understate the real return as long as the 'interest' rate used in the sinking fund is less than the firm's cost of capital.

Where the debt is not secured on specific assets, and the firm is

[1] A discussion of the desirable investment criteria for the nationalized industries is given in reference 3.

raising debt capital in a general way on all its assets, it may be possible to employ the weighted average cost of capital as the relevant cost of capital to use in the sinking fund. Where, as is frequently the case, the debt capital is raised primarily through mortgages or special arrangements on specific projects, the method becomes difficult to operate in a useful way. For in this type of situation the gearing is specifically related to individual projects and consequently a different cost of capital may relate to each project. The capital flowing into the sinking fund, however, is rarely available to the firm in general. Additional complications are that the gearing will probably be renewable, at least to some extent, given that many properties will tend to appreciate, and that the institutions providing the debt capital will often demand a share in the equity of the company in general, or the rental profits received from this project in particular. Given these complications and the predominating importance of gearing in property ventures, it will often be simpler, more flexible, and less likely to result in error if the whole analysis is in terms of the equity cash flows, in the manner outlined in Chapter 4, Section 3a. A detailed discussion of the approach specifically related to property is also given in Chapter 8.

REFERENCES

General Reference – Ezra Solomons, *The Management of Corporate Capital*, The Free Press of Glencoe, Illinois, 1959.

1. MARTIN J. BAILEY, 'Formal Criteria for Investment Decisions', *Journal of Political Economy*, October 1959.
2. C. S. SOPER, 'Marginal Efficiency of Capital: A Further Note', *Economic Journal*, March 1959.
3. A. J. MERRETT and ALLEN SYKES, 'The Financial Control of State Industry', *The Banker*, March–April 1962.
4. W. A. LEACH and E. G. WENHAM, *Investments in Land and Property*, Sweet and Maxwell, London, 1961.

APPENDIX A

The Extended Yield Method

In this appendix, we set out the detailed working of a more complicated example of the extended yield method. It was shown in Section 2 that it was possible for a project to have negative cash flows in the later life of a project without this necessarily invalidating the meaningful interpretation of the discounted yield. In other cases the presence of negative cash flows in the later life of a project did invalidate the meaning of the discounted yield. In this appendix we demonstrate how it is possible to turn projects in the latter category into projects in the former category by converting *some*—but not necessarily all—of the later negative cash flows by setting up a sinking fund to absorb part of these later net cash flows. Simply discounting the whole of the later negative cash flows at the firm's cost of capital back to the point at which they were absorbed, is not always necessary since, as we have seen, negative cash flows of certain magnitudes are entirely compatible with the discounted yield retaining its normal useful interpretation. To eliminate the *whole* of the later negative net cash flows will typically result in a modified yield which is unduly conservative. The procedure illustrated in this appendix is designed to eliminate just sufficient of the later negative cash flows to permit the resulting modified yield to have its normal useful interpretation. The procedure to be followed is illustrated below in Table 5.12. For simplicity, in this example, we shall use the sinking fund interpretation but it should be apparent from the discussion in the text that the analysis could equally well be in terms of discounting at a firm's cost of capital.

The cash flows of the example are set out in column A and their discounted cumulative total (discounting at the apparent discounted yield rate) in column B. In this more complex example, it is easier to work by using a trial extended yield rate, and use this to determine those points at which the project becomes a liability and a sinking fund adjustment is required. Column C for the first two years gives the normal cumulative total discounted net cash flows at the trial rate of 9%. It is apparent from the figures that with the income of year 3 ($£1,000/1·09^3 = £772$), the cumulative sum of the net cash flows will become positive, – that is, the flow of funds from the project will exceed the initial capital plus the 9% return. The excess is therefore to be deducted from the net cash flow and placed in a sinking fund. Of the net cash flow in year 3 then, $£x$ appropriately discounted (multiplied by $0·772 = 1/1·09^3$), is required to offset the ($£241$) and complete the repayment of the $£2,000$ initial capital and the 9% return. Hence, it is required that $0·772£x = £241$ so that $x = 241/0·772 = £311$. The balance of the net cash flow, namely $£1,000 - £311 = £689$, goes into the sinking fund to offset future negative net cash flows. For purposes of this example, the sinking fund will be assumed to cumulate at 5% per year (i.e. the firm's cost of capital is taken at 5%).

Year 4, Column C. In this year there is a further *positive* net cash inflow of $£1,000$. This is absorbed into the sinking fund. As the sinking fund has grown by 5%, this makes the total fund at that date of

$$£689 \times 1·05 + £1,000 = £1,723.$$

Year 5, Column C. In this year there is a net cash outflow of $£1,600$ to be offset by the sinking fund. At this date, the sinking fund is 1·05 times its value in the previous year and stands at £1,809. Of this £1,600 is absorbed by the negative net cash flow, leaving £209.

Year 6, Column C. The net cash outflow this year is £2,000, and deducting from it the sinking fund (grown at 5% to £219), a negative net cash flow of £1,781 results. At this stage, therefore, we have completed one phase of investment (ending in year 3), carried forward the excess funds to offset later negative net cash flows, and are now called upon to make a new net capital outlay of £1,781. This is effectively the beginning of a new investment project and, since it begins 6 years hence, we discount it at the trial rate of 9% making it (£1,061).

Year 7, Column C. The £1,000 inflow in this year is discounted for 7 years at the trial rate of 9%, since we are effectively considering the return to the investment of the previous year. The cumulative discounted cash flow of Column C becomes (£514).

Year 8, Column C. The £1,000 inflow of this year is also discounted at 9%, and this makes the cumulative total of Column C equal to (£12).

Year 9, Column C. The cash inflow of £1,000 in this year discounted at 9% is £460, and this will obviously make the cumulative total positive, – that is, we shall have received more from the project (effectively the net £1,782 invested in year 6) than the capital invested plus the 9% rate of return. As in year 3, the excess is placed in a sinking fund to meet the future negative net cash flows. Again, the cash flow in year 9, £x multiplied by 0·460 = 1/1·09⁹, must equal £12, where £x is the amount required to complete repayment of capital and earn a 9% return on the capital invested to date. Hence £x = 13/0·460 = £26. The balance of the cash flow = £1,000−£26 = £974, goes into the sinking fund.

Year 10, Column C. A cash outflow of (£1,110) occurs in this year and this is only partially offset by the sinking fund of £1,023 (= £974×1·05). The balance of (£87) indicates that the trial rate of 9% is too high.

Column D. This column is computed by the same method as Column C, but using the lower trial discount rate of 7%. This is seen to result in a terminal sum of positive £82.

Column E. Interpolating between the terminal figures of (£87) found with the 9% rate, and the £82 found with the 7% rate, a new trial rate of 8% is suggested, and this is given in Column E. This is seen to result in a zero terminal sum; hence 8% is the true 'extended' yield.

This type of complex discounting calculation, with its many repetitive calculations and trial runs, is, of course, ideally suited to being processed on a computer, as it could easily be handled by a simple standard programme as recommended in Chapter 14, Section 1.

Table 5.12
The Modified Yield

Year	A Project Cash Flows	B Cumulative Total of Column A discounted to Year 0 at 11% – the Conventional Discounted Yield	9% Trial Rate	C 9%	D 7%	E 8%
0	−2,000	2,000		−2,000	−2,000	−2,000
1	1,000	−1,099	$-2,000+\dfrac{1,000}{1\cdot09}$	−1,083	−1,065	−1,074
2	1,000	−287	$-1,083+\dfrac{1,000}{1\cdot09^2}$	−241	−192	−217
3	1,000	444	$-241+\dfrac{1,000}{1\cdot09^3}>0$	689	765	726
			therefore $1,000+\dfrac{1,000}{1\cdot09^3}$			
4	1,000	1,103	$689\times1\cdot05+1,000$	1,723	1,803	1,762
5	−1,600	154	$1,723\times1\cdot05+-1,600$	209	293	250
6	−2,000	−916	$209\times1\cdot05+-2,000<0$	−1,061	−1,130	−1,094
			therefore $-2,000+209\times1\cdot05$			
			$\dfrac{1}{1\cdot09^6}$			
7	1,000	434	$1,061+\dfrac{1,000}{1\cdot09^7}$	−514	−507	−511
8	1,000	0	$-514+\dfrac{1,000}{1\cdot09^8}$	−12	129	54
9	1,000	391	$-12+\dfrac{1,000}{1\cdot09^9}>0$	974	1,135	1,057
			therefore $1,000+\dfrac{1,000}{1\cdot09^9}$			
10	−1,110	0	$974\times1\cdot05+-1,110<0$	−87	82	0
			therefore $-1,110+974\times1\cdot05$			

< 0 means number preceding this sign is negative. > 0 means number preceding the sign is positive.

CHAPTER SIX
The Analysis of Risk

Risk and uncertainty are the inevitable concomitants of many forms
of investment. Investment appraisal techniques which cannot be
adapted to this state of affairs are likely to be of little practical use.
This chapter is concerned with examining the more important
of the common methods recommended for dealing with risk, as well
as suggesting alternative methods. The very first section consists
of a general justification for analytical methods in investment
appraisal, despite the existence of risk. The second section deals
with a firm's policy towards risk. Subsequent sections explore the
nature of risk, and the final sections, with the exception of the last
which deals with inflation, comprise a discussion of methods for
drawing out and highlighting the risks involved in investment
projects.

1. JUSTIFICATION FOR ANALYTICAL METHODS UNDER CONDITIONS OF UNCERTAINTY

Before discussing the methods and techniques we recommend for
dealing with risk and uncertainty, it is desirable to consider the
justification for the analytical methods of the type put forward in
this book *vis-à-vis* the traditional methods commonly employed in
business.

It is sometimes urged that errors in the data and the general
uncertainty surrounding most investment decisions are usually such
that it is not worthwhile engaging in any complex ('sophisticated')
methods of analysis. There are probably some situations in which
this is to a degree true, but it is important that the limited application
of this view should be recognized. Omniscience is not the pre-
requisite of scientific method in this or any other field of decision
taking. Risk in particular capital budgeting decisions generally
derives from the following five sources. (See Section 3 below for an
extended discussion of these sources of risk.)

(i) Risk from undertaking insufficient numbers of similar investments;

(ii) risk from misinterpretation of data;

(iii) risk from bias in the data and in its assessment;

(iv) risk from a changing external economic environment invalidating much of the usefulness of past experience; and

(v) risk from errors of analysis.

The final source of risk includes errors of financial analysis. Essentially, the argument that extended analytical methods are not justified will be valid whenever there is good reason to suppose that the risks arising from faulty analysis are of such an insignificant magnitude that it is not worth the effort involved in attempting to eliminate them. The point to be noted is that it is not the magnitude of the other risks, nor their magnitude relative to the risk due to errors of analysis, that is relevant. To justify itself, a method designed to reduce these errors of analysis merely has to be a worthwhile expenditure of effort in its own right. Thus the fact that the data is already subject to error cannot of itself be a valid reason for adding to it further errors due to faulty analysis.

A factor of great and general importance is the emphasis that is placed on intuitive judgment. It is clear that a great deal of perception and logical activity is not capable, in the present state of knowledge, of explanation in terms of conscious logical processes, or of imitation on a purely conscious level. For example, the understanding of the complex mechanism of consumer demand and the reactions of rival producers which a good marketing executive possesses, his method of assessing what will sell by evaluating the relative importance of different features of a product, etc., are generally too complex to formulate in purely logical terms. It is easier to ride a bicycle then to explain the complex mechanism by which this is achieved. A similar type of unconscious analysis occurs in almost every form of creative mental activity. The same activity enables a good engineer to perceive the solution to a technical problem, or a mathematician to a logical problem.

It is useful, however, to distinguish between two types of activity here. In many marketing decisions, the activity would seem to be an understanding of the emotional and psychic needs or reactions of other people; this is essentially an ability for unconscious evaluation and may be entirely divorced from any conscious ability to reason consistently or to consider in a logical manner all the relevant aspects of a situation. In the case of the mathematician and the engineer, the activity would appear to be one of choosing from all the possible series of logical alternatives that lead to a useful

N

result in a given situation, and hence would seem to be a form of unconscious rationalization. Financial analysis, where it is involved in discovering worthwhile areas for financial negotiation or financing possibilities or implications within the institutional framework of the firm, industry, and capital market, is involved in both types of activity, as well as the activity of straightforward logical analysis.

In our view, the analysis of treatment of risk in the analysis of investment decisions must start from the basic premise that, in the vast majority of cases, the risk arises from bias, inadequate knowledge and external change, which can be evaluated only by 'intuitive' rational processes. It is not argued that no method exists for evaluating such factors; for it would appear evident, from the fact that some firms are consistently successful in evaluating these factors, in so far as they achieve the objective of making profits, that method is employed. We are merely stating that it cannot be achieved by an agreed process of logic in the same way, for example, as we can obtain the solution to an algebraic equation. No conscious logical process exists by which it is possible to produce great works of art, but there are nevertheless great works of art and there are people consistently successful in producing them.

It is important to recognize, however, that sound intuitive judgment, while a necessary part of a sound decision, is not sufficient to guarantee it. Analysis is then required to ensure that no other factors have been omitted from the basic premises, to examine and even extend its possibilities. The object of analysis is not to replace intuitive judgment in its proper field but to exploit its possibilities more fully and ensure that its implementation is not vitiated by errors and omissions. Analysis is no substitute for sound intuitive judgment, but neither is such judgment a substitute for analysis.

2. POLICY TOWARDS RISK

The pre-requisite to allowing for risks in investment decisions is for a firm to determine its own policy towards risk. The amount of risk a firm is prepared to undertake to secure a given actual or apparent monetary return is a general question of values: there is no rational or logical criterion by which the choice can be made. The lines of policy in this respect will largely be determined by the reputation of the firm and the preferences of its shareholders, and the amount of risk to which it is already exposed. For these reasons, a firm may opt for a policy of conservatism demanding a very high return for risk, or alternatively for a policy of taking greater risks. The choice is one of value judgments in which, once the issues are clearly stated and understood, the financial adviser has no special competence. The essential qualification, however, is that the issues are clearly stated and understood by those making the judgment. In many cases, a policy of conservatism is simply inconsistent within its own assumptions, in that, by rejecting some forms of risk investment, it merely exposes itself to risks of a different type. This occurs most frequently where a firm refuses to undertake risky investment expenditure in research, new products, or new methods, while failing to recognize that this policy exposes it to even greater risks of loss through the successful investment expenditures of this type that its rivals may undertake. In an industry which is fast changing technologically, no haven of safety is to be found by simply refusing to undertake risky investment. In private life, where personal fortunes are less subject to the risk of erosion by competitive pressures, safety can be found by forswearing risk, but in a competitive industry the maximum safety generally lies in the intelligent balancing of risks. Because of this, a policy of conservatism in business is by no means simple and generally depends on the same intelligent balancing of risks as do more adventurous policies.

Once a firm has decided on its general policy towards risk it needs to make this attitude clearly understood at all levels where capital projects are under consideration. It is generally helpful to set up specific rates of return requirements for different types of projects. (This is discussed more fully below, in Section 6.) For example, a firm might lay down that it is prepared to invest in relatively risk free projects if these offer a return on total capital in excess of, say, 7% after tax. Projects in this category would include routine cost saving investments (which are relatively immune from the risks involved in the sale of the final product), and projects involving revenues or saving expenditures which are largely determined by contractual obligations (e.g. lease or buy decisions). These acceptable return figures are not merely helpful in respect of the particular projects to which they apply, but are also useful bench marks for more risky projects. The aim of this procedure is not to favour one type of project rather than another, but to try to ensure that all projects are afforded equal consideration once due allowance for the differential risks involved has been made. We do not suggest that this is either an easy or an exact task, but we hope to show that it is worth attempting.

3. PROBABILITY CONCEPTS AS AN AID TO RISK ASSESSMENT

It is generally helpful in analysing the risk involved in investment decisions to regard these decisions as being single trials of a given game of chance. The game of chance, or rather the probability mechanism, is a complex one and generally involves considerable scope for skill. The risk associated with investment decisions is the danger of the profit outcome being inadequate, and this risk arises primarily from the fact that an investment is a single trial of the probability mechanism, of which we have only imperfect knowledge. Consider the sources of this risk.

a. *Sources of Risk*

Five main sources of risk can be distinguished:

i. Risk from insufficient numbers. This risk arises from the fact that. as a rule, a firm will have only a few investments of a particular type, Hence, even if the firm had estimated all the probabilities associated with the project (this particular game of chance) with complete accuracy, it would still be exposed to the risk that the average or mean profit from this type of project might fail to materialize simply because of the failure of the law of averages (law of large numbers) to operate with so few trials of the probability mechanism. It is possible, for example, to lose at the game of spinning a coin, despite the fact that one knows the probability of each of the two outcomes is exactly 0·5.

The risk from insufficient numbers may not be of particular importance where the investment decision being considered is small, relative to the total operations of the firm. If all the risks borne by the firm were of this type, then the firm could be seen as involved in a large number of trials of different known probability mechanisms, and the outcome would be that, while profit from *individual* projects might vary widely from their expected value, the realized total profit from all the different projects would have a high probability of being the *total* expected profit.

ii. Risk from misinterpretation. This is the risk that the probability mechanism may be of such complexity that its method of working and its relationships may be misunderstood. In most investment decisions, for example, an attempt must be made to estimate the future course of sales for a particular product. This involves understanding the complex relationships governing consumer demand for the product; that is, the effect of changing tastes, incomes, prices, and the influence of rival products. In the present state of knowledge concerning these relationships, great scope for error of forecasting exists and such error is often the main element of risk involved in a capital project.

iii. Risk of bias. It frequently arises that some individuals are prone to biases towards optimism or pessimism, or are unconsciously influenced by factors other than those with which they are ostensibly concerned, as, for example 'empire building', or fear of responsibility. The presence of biases of this type is always possible because methods of estimating the future are not susceptible of exact objective verification.

The risk from bias can to some extent be safeguarded against by careful observation of the judgment of the individual concerned, particularly in those situations where there is strong, reasonably objective evidence. Careful follow-up procedures of the type discussed in Chapter 14, Section 6, are also helpful in this.

iv. Risk from external change. This is the risk due to changes in the probability mechanism itself. Any all-embracing probability mechanism would by definition include the possibility of change, since it would contain within itself all possibilities of future development. Such a mechanism is, of course, impossible to estimate and businessmen are invariably engaged in trying to assess that particular part of the probability mechanism which governs, say, the demand, price, etc., for a particular product. This mechanism itself may be subject to basic external changes to it: for example new revolutionary products, changes in consumer tastes, variations in government policy, etc. Some attempt may be made to bring these factors into the probability mechanism, but generally they must be regarded as resulting from larger, more complex forces outside the mechanism on which the analysis is based.

v. Risk from errors of analysis. This is essentially a risk of error in the technical and financial analysis of the project. Examples of faulty technical analysis are very common where the technical process being used is unusual, with the result that expensive teething troubles develop and operating costs are appreciably different from those forecast. Faulty financial analysis is also of very common occurrence. Where the financial implications of a project have not been fully thought out, some items of investment (e.g. working capital), or some of the cash advantages, may have been omitted. Or the financial analysis may have been performed in a way that arbitrarily presents projects in an unjustifiably attractive or unattractive way. This is inevitably the consequence of using crude methods such as payback or RR (the ratio of average profit to initial or average capital) – see subsequent chapter.

A point that is worth noting as regards these risks is that they are risks of both commission and omission. Particularly important in the case of errors of technical and financial analysis, is the danger that they may lead to the adoption of the wrong alternative. The choice between alternatives (different types or sizes of plant, alternative types of contractural arrangements with customers and suppliers, etc.) is often more complicated than the basic decision to go ahead with a project at all.

b. *Risk and Probability Analysis*

We have so far discussed risk by reference to probability mechanisms. The analogy with classical probability can be stretched a little further to throw light on the basis of thinking which lies behind the process of forecasting the future. Errors in these forecasts are, of course, the immediate origin of the risk involved in capital projects, and it is important to be quite clear as to the basis on which these forecasts are drawn up. This will enable us to make clear our considerable reservations concerning the extended use of probability analysis as a method of analysing risk.

There are, in fact, two quite different probability bases on which forecasts can be drawn up, – a point which is often misunderstood by businessmen and which forecasters frequently fail to make clear. Suppose the problem is to assess the gross sales revenue from a project. This can be based on establishing what, in the opinion of the forecaster, is the *most likely* revenue. Alternatively, it can be based on the mean or average expected revenue; that is, the revenue which would result from different outcomes weighted by the probability (again in the opinion of the forecaster) of these outcomes occurring. The meaning and possible divergence of the two bases is illustrated in the following example. Suppose that for a given product there are three main eventualities as given in Table 6.1.

Table 6.1

Eventuality	Probability of Occurring	Gross Sales Revenue Realization	Weighted Realization
	(1)	(2) £000's	(3) = (1) × (2) £000's
A. Competition continues as at present	·25	120	30
B. Competitors reduce prices	·50	100	50
C. New product made obsolete by rival's new project	·25	40	10

Mean Realization = 90

The data in the table relates to a simple hypothetical example which is designed to illustrate certain basic issues. In the example, it is supposed that a firm is considering the introduction of a new product and trying to assess the gross sales revenue it might obtain, given the alternative competitive conditions A, B and C. The most optimistic assumption it can make is that competitors will simply continue as at present; the most pessimistic outcome it can foresee is that rival firms will introduce a highly competitive new product of their own which they are rumoured to be developing.

In the assessment of the forecaster the most probable outcome is B (£100,000), with a probability the forecaster assesses at 0·5, and the whole analysis of profitability could be conducted in terms of the realization which would result from this outcome. An alternative basis of forecasting is to use the mean realization of £90,000, – the sum of realizations weighted by their respective probabilities of occurring.

A point that should be noted is that the most probable outcome and the mean outcome differ in this case, despite the fact that the probabilities are symmetrical, – that is, both A and C are equally likely. The mean and the most probable can diverge either because the probabilities are asymmetrical or because the realizations are asymmetrical; they may also diverge because both these conditions obtain. For these reasons, it is probable that it frequently arises that the mean and the most probable outcomes diverge. Despite this evident divergence of meaning, the two terms are often confused and used interchangeably in the description of estimates.

At this point we must make clear our reservations concerning the use of classical probability analysis in this connection. Our main reservation is the practical meaning that can be attached to subjective probabilities. These probabilities, unlike the probabilities of classical analysis, are not objectively verifiable. Moreover, the evidence for any given probability used in the analysis may differ markedly in both quality and quantity from that for any other probability. Uncertainty is not eliminated by the use of these probabilities, turning the problem into one of probability analysis; the uncertainty is merely pushed back to being uncertainty connected with the probabilities on which the whole analysis is based. The fact that individual probabilities may be subject to different degrees of certainty involves two difficulties. The first is best seen from the simple example of Table 6.1. Suppose that, in eventuality C, the realization would have been zero and that, in this case, the firm would have been involved in very substantial losses, – losses so large that the mean profit from the project is reduced to a level at which the project is not acceptable. Suppose now the forecaster qualifies his statement that the probability associated with C is 0·25, by saying that he is really very uncertain as to the magnitude of this probability and that it is largely a shot in the dark. Is this probability, then, and this outcome to be given the same importance as the other probabilities, the relative magnitudes of which he can estimate with a large degree of confidence? The answer to this is, surely no. But manipulating probabilities according to the classical rules and producing, for example, mean profit figures, involves exactly this assumption; namely, that probabilities subject to different degrees of certainty can be treated as equally significant (given their relative numerical magnitude).

Moreover, since the sum of the probabilities must be unity, the uncertainty attaching to one probability must logically be reflected in the remaining probabilities. Thus, in our simple example, the forecaster may say he is certain that B is twice as probable as A; but what this implies in terms of the absolute magnitude of these figures (as opposed to their size relative to each other) depends on the probability assigned to C. In our example, the probability of A was 0·25 and B was 0·50 because the probability of 0·25 was assigned to C. If the probability of C could equally well have been 0·4 (the forecaster just didn't know) then the probability of A and B could equally well have been 0·2 and 0·4 respectively.

A further objection to the extended use of probability analysis arises when it is applied to major capital budgeting decisions involving a limited number of markedly different outcomes. If, for example, a project's profitability could vary by 50% depending upon whether a sales contract would be renewed, then an average of these two extremes has little practical meaning. (This objection does not hold where a firm has *many* projects of this type, for in this case they could be regarded as many different trials of different games of chance from which the mean outcome of *all* the trials of all the different 'games' would be the mean of all the different 'games'.)

It is because of these (in our view rather serious) shortcomings of classical probability analysis in this connection that it seems inadvisable for the analysis of projects to be based on extended methods of probability analysis which either conceal or do not adequately reflect the reservations which need to be made concerning the individual probabilities.[1]

4. GENERAL METHODS OF DESCRIBING AND ANALYSING RISK

a. *Confidence Levels*

While we have argued against the extended use of classical probability analysis in investment appraisal in the present state of knowledge, we nevertheless believe that certain broad probability estimates and terminology can be extremely useful when assessing the likely outcomes of investment outlays. In a later sub-section, we shall argue the need for top management to consider a range of profitability outcomes for most projects. Here we shall be concerned with the method for attaching some useful probability estimate to the range of outcomes.

The assessment of the likelihood or probability of different profitability outcomes occurring should not be the task of the financial analyst as such. There will of course be some estimates on which he will be qualified to offer an opinion, such as the likely cost of debt and equity funds in future, and the consequent financial advantages and disadvantages associated with postponing a project to a time when funds may be cheaper (see Chapter 3, Section 4, and Chapter 17, Section 2). This type of estimate apart, the financial analyst as such will not be qualified to comment on the range of error inherent in the technical, cost and marketing estimates prepared elsewhere in the firm. The subjective assessment of the differing probabilities

[1] We must briefly refer to the more recent developments embodied in modern 'Decision Theory'. While we would have reservations regarding the application of this technique where it involves the extended manipulation of subjective probabilities, it may well present advantages for certain capital budgeting decisions. This, however, is too specialist a subject to be considered here and interested readers are advised to consult references 1 and 2.

is ultimately the task, – albeit with advice from specialist departments, – of top management. This is pre-eminently the area of decision to which their judgment and experience are relevant, including their estimation of the capabilities of the senior staff who will be appointed to run the new project, should it be accepted.

While the assessment of the likelihood of different outcomes is ultimately the responsibility of top management, there is nevertheless much which can be done to help them in this critical task. It is desirable that all persons or departments responsible for the different estimates (capital costs, production costs, distribution costs, sales, etc.,) should give their opinions on the confidence they have in their various estimates. It is evidently important that top management should have the opinions of the senior technical and marketing executives as to the likelihood of cost being kept to a certain level, or of sales achieving a given volume. But, if such opinions are to be truly useful, they must be presented in an unambiguous and systematic form. Opinions couched in vague terms such as 'most likely', 'most optimistic', and 'most pessimistic', suffer from a serious degree of ambiguity. The 'most likely' outcome may be thought to have a 10% chance of occurring, while ten other outcomes may each have a 9% chance. The fact that the 'most likely' outcome is estimated to be only slightly more probable than ten other equi-probable outcomes is not a fact to be concealed, but rather to be brought out for the benefit of all concerned. Similarly, what does 'most pessimistic' mean? Does it mean that the estimator would never expect a worse result under any conditions, or only in one such investment in a hundred or in a thousand? Even without the qualifying adjective 'most' such phrases leave vital questions unanswered, as do the terms such as 'reasonably pessimistic' or 'moderately optimistic' etc.

To render probability concepts useful it is imperative that a terminology is established which is free from the ambiguities just noted. A satisfactory method of doing this is for the person or department responsible for each of the major estimates to state the percentage degree of confidence with which they expect estimates to be achieved or exceeded. Thus, a sales manager might describe his sales estimates as follows:

Average Sales over next Ten Years	Estimated Chance of being Achieved or Exceeded
1,000 tons	90%
1,300 tons	70%
1,600 tons	40%
1,900 tons	10%

A works manager might estimate his variable costs per ton of a new product as follows:

Variable Cost per Ton of New Product	Estimated Chance of being Equal to or *Less* than stated
£20	90%
£18	75%
£16	50%
£15	20%

The above type percentages will be referred to as 'confidence levels'. It will be apparent that, if a sales estimate is taken low enough, or a cost estimate high enough, the chances of the estimates being respectively too low or too high are negligible. Thus, whatever the uncertainties connected with specific estimates may be, it should be possible to produce estimates of any desired broad confidence level. By using this approach, top management can set up appropriate standards to which basic estimates should conform.

The use of this particular confidence level approach enables the confusion and uncertainty resulting from the conflation of estimates of different and *unstated* levels of confidence to be avoided. Consider, for instance, the confidence level to be assigned to a profit figure which is the result of two *separately estimated factors*, sales revenue and operating costs. By interpreting the confidence levels as probabilities, then the sum or difference of such estimates must possess *at least* the same confidence level as is given by the product of the two confidence levels of which it is composed. For example, suppose that the chance of a given cost estimate being equal to or less than $£x$ is 80%, and the chance of the corresponding given sales revenue equalling or exceeding $£y$ is also 80%.

The relevant outcomes and their confidence levels are shown in Table 6.2 below.

Table 6.2
Confidence Levels

	Outcome for Revenue	C.L.	Outcome for Costs	C.L.	Outcome for Combined Estimate	C.L. of Combined Estimate of Net Revenue = product of C.L.'s for Revenue and Cost
(1)	$\geq y$	0·8	$\leq x$	0·8	$\geq y-x$	0·64
(2)	$\leq y$	0·2	$\geq x$	0·2	$\leq y-x$	0·04
(3)	$\geq y$	0·8	$\geq x$	0·2	?	0·16
(4)	$\leq y$	0·2	$\leq x$	0·8	?	0·16
					Total:	1·00

($\geq$ means more than or equal to; $\leq$ means less than or equal to)

The table sets out all the relevant outcomes and it is seen that the probabilities add up to unity. The confidence levels (probabilities) of combined independent events are equal to the product of the confidence levels of the independent events, – e.g. revenue higher than y and costs lower than x, has a confidence level equal to the confidence level of y multiplied by the confidence level of x, namely $0\cdot8\times0\cdot8 = 0\cdot64$. The combined effect of outcome (3) is uncertain. If revenue is sufficiently greater than y, to compensate for the fact that costs are greater than x, then the outcome would be net revenue higher than $(y-x)$. If the higher revenue is more than offset by the higher costs, then net revenue may be lower than $(y-x)$. With the data given, therefore, the effect of outcome (3) on net revenue is indeterminate. Similar considerations lead to the same conclusion for outcome (4). It is clear, however, that outcome (1) is certainly that a net revenue higher than $(y-x)$ has a confidence level of $0\cdot64$. This then is the minimum confidence level of the net revenue.

Where half the expected outcomes (3) and (4) are favourable, i.e., give a net revenue equal to more than $(y-x)$, then the confidence level of the net revenue figure would be $0\cdot64+0\cdot08+0\cdot08 = 0\cdot80$. On these general considerations it would seem reasonable to assume that, where the confidence level of the separate estimates is reasonably high (say in excess of $0\cdot7$), then the combined estimate can fairly safely be taken as having the same confidence level.

It should be noted that the use of probability concepts in this connection is not open to the objections noted at the end of the previous section. For in the case of confidence levels the estimator is focusing his attention on a given composite outcome (his assessment of a given figure being exceeded). There is no mechanical manipulation of different probabilities (as in determining the mean outcome). Such manipulation of 'probabilities' as occurs is performed *subjectively* by the estimator and takes account of the particular qualifications he attaches to each probability.

We have made use of a probability interpretation of confidence levels, but the approach will generally be accepted simply on its merits of practical usefulness. No techniques can of themselves overcome the difficulty that individuals or departments responsible for estimates may be mistaken in the assignment of confidence levels. Such mistakes can generally be revealed only by *ex post* enquiries several years or more afterwards. This is examined more fully in Chapter 14 dealing with the desirable arrangements for a firm's capital budgeting organization. But it should be noted in passing that the likely use of confidence levels is to cause individuals to be over cautious. Responsibility for projects wrongly rejected through over caution is very much less likely to come home to roost than in the case of projects wrongly accepted through over optimism. It is the task of top management to guard against this possibility when making its own final assessments of projects.

We would stress, in conclusion, that in recommending the confidence limits approach we are not suggesting that it should supersede written or verbal reports giving the background of the various estimates and the reasons for holding given views. These reports are essential for top management. What we do say is that such reports should be quantified as far as possible and the confidence level approach is often a good practical method of doing this. This does not involve an extra step in the decision making process because top management will inevitably quantify the verbal or written reports submitted by their subordinates. But in so doing they may well interpret their subordinates' unquantified intentions incorrectly. It is to avoid this possibility of adding to the uncertainty by the use of ambiguous terminology that the method is recommended.

b. *Calculating the Relevant Return on Capital*

i. The return on equity capital and the return on total capital. The principle objective of a firm's management will generally be that of maximizing the return on the equity shareholders' capital, within the framework of contemporary social and political restraints. This being so, it can be argued that the critical figure in any investment appraisal is the return on equity capital. While accepting that this is the critical figure in the sense that this is what is to be maximized, and that where this figure is unsatisfactory no project is of itself worth undertaking, we consider there is a strong practical case for *also* considering the return on total capital. The two returns are really complementary.

There are two main reasons for this view. First, consideration of the return on total capital shows whether or not a project is viable in its own right, regardless of how it is to be financed. It helps to indicate whether or not the project *of itself* will give rise to a sufficient income to provide the requisite earnings cover for debt capital (see Chapter 4, Section 2). Also it duplicates the calculation that lenders, particularly institutional lenders, make when considering lending funds, and is therefore a useful indication of the financeability of the project.

The second reason for considering the return on the total capital involved in a project, as well as the equity return, is that in the last resort the equity shareholders stand behind the debt capital. Should the project turn out to be less profitable than was estimated, or should it fail entirely, then the debt capital will have to be repaid out of equity capital or equity income if the firm is not to become bankrupt. This being so, a firm's management, on behalf of the equity share-holders, should be concerned with the return on total capital, as in the last resort all the capital involved can be regarded as effectively guaranteed by the equity capital unless a firm is prepared to go into liquidation.

ii. The return on capital at risk. In deciding on the relevant returns on the various categories and sub-divisions of capital, it is some-times helpful to consider how much of the capital committed to any project is actually at risk, and further, how much of future income is also at risk. Consider first the capital situation.

Where all or part of the capital committed to a project has some significant value in alternative uses, then it is apparent that the total initial capital sum invested is not entirely at risk. Should the project fail, some of the capital could be recovered. This means that, for purposes of risk assessment, it is necessary to consider only that portion of the invested capital which could not be recovered if the project were abandoned. For some projects, nearly all of the capital investment is at risk. This is true of most research projects, most forms of oil and mineral exploration, and of most mines, especially those in remote places where even the general purposes assets, such as houses and office buildings, have no value if the mine is abandoned. It is also true of any assets of a very specialized nature. Blast furnaces, wind tunnels, oil refineries, etc., if not used for the purposes for which they have been designed, are worth only their scrap value. Even this may be non-existent if the cost of dismantling and disposing of the assets exceeds the resale value. And, of course, some projects will have a negative scrap value in that, if abandoned, continuing costs are incurred. A railway which has closed a branch line may have to continue some upkeep of say its bridges where these cross roads, as they cannot be allowed to collapse. Nuclear power stations abandoned because of radioactivity, etc., require continuing ex-penditure to render them safe.

But cases where scrap values are non-existent or negative are comparatively rare. Most projects involve assets which retain some value if the project is abandoned. This is nearly always true of a part of working capital (cash of course, usually most debtors, and often part of stocks and work in progress), of land and property, of ships and vehicles, and of much general purpose plant and equipment. Where an abandoned project will result in some significant residual value in the assets originally committed to it, the following method of analysis will be found useful for risky projects.

First an estimate must be made of the likely residual value of the assets. Frequently (particularly with land, property and working capital), this residual value is likely to be fairly constant over a long period. In such cases, this value can simply be subtracted from the initial capital and the difference is the capital at risk in the project, representing the maximum capital loss if the project is a failure. Often, however, this residual value can be expected to decline with time as the assets concerned deteriorate physically or become obsolescent. In these circumstances, it is necessary to relate the residual value to several estimated lives of the project. Thus it is only possible to talk of the capital at risk with reference to a particular period of time: the longer the period, the greater the capital at risk. This range of values need be no handicap because for most projects there will be a definite time span during which the project will either be seen to be profitable and worth continuing, or to warrant abandoning. The residual value to use is then clearly that which could be realized at the end of the chosen trial period. For many projects the latter will be a matter of only two or three years.

Having selected the residual value for the appropriate period, the next step is to consider splitting the income to which the project gives rise. Consider first the case where the residual value is estimated to be constant over a fairly long period, perhaps for the whole of the estimated life of the project. Suppose, for instance, that a ten year project costs £1,000,000 and is expected to involve assets with a constant residual value of £200,000. Suppose further that the project is entirely equity financed and that the firm's cost of capital is 10%, this being the return which the firm must expect to earn on relatively risk free projects. The project is estimated to have a constant (but very risky) annual net cash flow of £189,300 arising on average end-year for the ten years, plus the recovery of the £200,000 residual value at the end of the tenth year: this gives a yield of 15% on the initial £1,000,000 investment. The annual net cash flow should now be considered in two separate parts. The first part consists of 10% of the constant residual value = $10\% \times £200,000$

= £20,000. Once the project has been commenced, as long as it gives rise to a minimum £20,000 a year, it will pay to continue the project. The £20,000 annual income represents the opportunity cost to be earned from abandoning the project, realizing the £200,000 residual value of the locked-up capital, and investing it elsewhere at 10%. Thus £20,000 of the project's annual net cash flow can be regarded as safe: the remaining £169,300 represents the return on the remaining £800,000 of capital which is at risk. This offers a yield of 16·6% over the ten years. (The annual net cash flow of £169,300 relates solely to the £800,000 of capital at risk, and thus includes an element for the recovery of this amount of capital. The £20,000 and the ultimate recovery of £200,000 relates to the 'safe' capital. Because this safe capital is recovered in full, there is no element of capital recovery in the annual net cash flows relating to the safe portion of capital.) It is this yield of 16·6% on £800,000 which must be considered in determining whether or not the project offers a sufficient return for the risks involved.[1]

Where the residual asset value declines with time, the same procedure would be used but would be related to the different trial periods being considered. Suppose, in the above example, the residual value were estimated to be £500,000 at the end of two years, and £300,000 at the end of four years, reverting to £200,000 from the end of the fifth year onwards. If the project were being judged over two years, the annual net cash flow would need to exceed 10% of the appropriate residual value of £500,000 – that is it would have to exceed £50,000. If it failed to do this, unless better conditions could be expected in later years (i.e. sufficient to better a 10% yield on the £500,000 residual value to be recovered from abandoning the project), this would be a signal to abandon the project. Thus, £500,000 would be seen to be at risk in a two year trial period and £700,000 for a four year trial period. Any longer trial period would involve risking £800,000 of capital.

Considering residual values at different dates is generally a useful practice in that it focuses attention on the alternative yield to be had

---

[1] This approach can, of course, be readily adapted to the use of the net present value method for those who prefer it. The only change involved is that the £169,300 net cash flow relating to the capital at risk would be reduced to a present value at 10% (the firm's cost of capital) from which would be subtracted the risk capital. The resulting net present value is the prospective reward for risk. In this case the figures are £169,300$a_{10|10}$ −£800,000 = £1,040,000 −£800,000 = £240,000.

from terminating projects as opposed to continuing them to the end of their technically feasible lives.

We have so far considered how to determine the amount of capital at risk and seen how this involves notionally splitting the estimated net cash flow into a safe and a risk portion. We must now consider the implications for those projects where it is reasonable to regard at least part of the estimated net cash flow as relatively free of risk for reasons unrelated to the residual value of the assets employed. Such a situation might arise from a firm sales contract, or some form of rent or leasing arrangement with a reputable firm. Where part of the net cash flow can be so regarded, it can usefully be considered separately from the remainder of the net cash flow *providing it exceeds the safe element calculated on the residual value basis*. This distinction is important. Where the assured[1] income from continuing with the project is equal to or less than the safe[1] income calculated on residual values (which of course exists independently of the continuation of the project) its existence adds nothing to the security of the project. Additional security arises only when the assured income significantly exceeds the safe income, for they are in no way additive. Where the assured income does exceed the safe income (or, more strictly, where the value of the assured income, discounted at the firm's cost of capital, exceeds that of the safe income where both incomes include the ultimate residual value recovered from the project), it will never pay to abandon the project once commenced. Hence the assured income gives the minimum return on the total capital investment. When this return on total capital equals or exceeds the firm's cost of capital, then essentially none of the capital invested in the project is at risk.

Where the discounted value of assured income exceeds that of safe income it should be subtracted from the initial capital investment to give the proportion (if any) of the capital at risk. It should then be determined whether or not the difference between the total prospective net cash flow and assured income is sufficiently high to justify committing the capital that will be at risk.

One final point needs considering in relation to the secure elements of income, and this is the place of tax concessions in the analysis. Most investment projects involve capital expenditure on which

---

[1] The term 'assured' income will be used to denote safe or secure income arising from the continuance of the project, while the term 'safe' income will be restricted to income dependent for its security upon the opportunity to abandon the project and invest the residual value of the assets elsewhere.

capital allowances can be claimed. Such allowances are often substantial. (The present value of such allowances at, say, a 7% discount rate, often amount to nearly a half of the cost of the assets to which they relate, – see the table at the end of the appendix to Chapter 3 for the present value of certain standard British capital allowances.) They have the further advantage that they can be claimed even if the project fails to generate any taxable income as long as they can be set off against other income of the firm. Similarly, if a project is a total failure, the assets concerned can usually be written off for tax purposes at once and set against the firm's other income. Thus, it is seen that, where a firm has other taxable income, then capital allowances guarantee some recovery of any new capital invested, thus reducing the amount of capital at risk. This must be allowed for accordingly. As the present value of the capital allowances will typically differ if the project is abandoned rather than continued, we recommend the following procedure. The part of the capital allowances which will accrue as long as the project continues should be added to the amount of assured income. The part that will arise through abandoning the project (the balancing allowance) should be added to the residual value of the project at the end of the chosen trial period where it will effectively increase the amount of safe capital.

iii. The return on total capital reconsidered. In view of the discussion in the preceding sub-section it is appropriate to consider the place of debt capital in the analysis of risk and to determine whether the return on total capital, or simply on equity capital, should be used. In general, we would stress the usefulness of considering the return to total capital as well as the return to equity capital. Our reasons for this were, first, that the return to total capital reveals whether or not a project is viable in its own right without regard to any special financing possibilities, and, second, because ultimately the equity capital, to the extent of the equity resources of the whole firm, guarantees that the debt capital will be repaid.

The fact that it is possible to break down total capital into a risk portion and a safe portion does not obviate the need to consider the return on total capital in order to determine whether or not a project is viable as a whole and justifies financing on its own merits. We therefore consider it important for those appraising a project to know this figure in the preliminary stages of the investigation.

Our second reason for justifying consideration of the return on total capital, that the equity shareholders were ultimately responsible for it to the extent of their total investment in the company, loses much of its force when capital can be split into a safe and a risk element. If the safe element has been properly estimated, then the liability of the equity capital will be restricted to the risk element and it is only this latter figure that need be considered. But even the best estimates can be wrong and it is therefore desirable to know that the maximum commitment of the equity resources of the firm, should the very worst happen. In short, we recommend that a firm should consider both the return on total and the return on the capital at risk in addition to the return on equity capital. Each figure throws a different but useful light on the attractiveness or otherwise of a project.

It is also occasionally useful to relate the return on risk capital to the amount of debt and equity involved. In some projects, such as property investments, the greater the safe element of capital the more debt it is possible to raise, because the firm can offer more security. As the providers of debt have the first claim on the capital in a project the safe portion of capital should first be considered as debt financed with short term debt ranking before long term debt. Only if the safe capital exceeds the debt capital should any part of it be thought of as being equity financed. (Similarly, in the unlikely event of the debt capital exceeding the safe capital, the excess should be thought of as financing risk capital. Put the other way round, the risk portion of total capital should first be thought of as being equity financed, and any surplus as being debt financed.) Looking at the break-down of capital in this way it is possible to see the relationship between the equity investment and the amount of risk capital which represents the true extent of the effective equity responsibility.

Consider a simple example. Suppose a firm is considering investing in a £1,000,000 project. The safe portion of capital is estimated to be £450,000. It is possible to raise £150,000 short term debt (bank overdrafts, creditors, etc.) and £250,000 long term debt. The remaining £600,000 represents the amount of the equity contribution. The £450,000 safe portion of the total investment should be thought of as being allocated first to short term debt (£150,000) and then to long term debt (the next £250,000). This leaves £50,000 of safe capital which effectively is being financed by equity. Hence the *effective* equity commitment at risk is the £550,000. A further £50,000 of equity money is invested in safe capital. This safe portion should be regarded as having to earn only the risk-free minimum equity return. The risk portion must of course promise more. (In the unlikely event that part of the debt capital is being used to finance the risk element of capital – a common occurrence in mining ventures – then the equity return on funds at risk should be looked for on the debt element as well as the equity. Thus if, in the above example, the safe capital had amounted to only £350,000 against the total debt of £400,000, the equity risk return should also be looked for on the last £50,000 of debt.)

To sum up, in cases of this kind, the total capital investment involved in a project should be split up into its safe and risk portions, and the latter considered to be the sum on which the prospective return must be adequate to justify commencement in view of the risks involved, regardless of whether this is entirely financed by equity capital or by a combination of debt and equity.

c. *Identifying the Critical Variables*

It is seldom that an investment project can be adequately appraised on the basis of a single set of figures, reflecting as they do but a single set of assumptions. For most projects there is a degree of uncertainty surrounding such assumptions as selling price, operating costs, length of life of the project, capital costs, etc. Often there will hang over a project a question mark concerning what will happen some years off, as for instance, whether a certain tariff will be reduced, an import quota altered, or a currency devalued. Faced with such uncertainties in a project, and there are few projects without any, it is impossible to do justice to its appraisal unless all the significant likely combinations of the variables are set out side by side. Only some such procedure enables analysts and senior management to identify the critical assumptions. The presentation of only one or two combinations may lead to projects being wrongly accepted or rejected on erroneous surmises as to the impact on profitability of these alternative outcomes.

We therefore recommend that all combinations of the main variables be considered and set down in tabular presentation. Consider an example. Suppose a project costs £600,000, on which the safe element is estimated to be £250,000, and suppose for simplicity that the total debt which can be raised also equals £250,000, of which £100,000 represents short term debt, and £150,000 long term debt. The project's estimated output of 1,000 tons a year will be sold half on a 10 year fixed price contract of £1,000 per ton, and the remainder on the free market where the price is currently

£1,200 per ton. This is felt to be the likely maximum future price but the price could average as low as £800 per ton. The technical life of the project is thought to be 20 years, but because of the possible development of new products, it might be only 10 years. Also, there is no information on the likelihood of renewing the fixed price contract after ten years, so all sales thereafter are estimated to be at the free market prices then prevailing. As this is a fairly well established process, operating costs can be accurately estimated and the likely variations are too small to warrant separate consideration. The firm looks for a 9% net of tax return on equity funds and a 7% net of tax return on total funds where the proportion of total debt raised is around 40% as in this case. A tabular presentation of such a project might be as follows:

Table 6.3

Estimated Returns on Total Capital Investment

Selling Price per Ton of Free Market Sales	10 year life	20 year life
£1,200	9%	11%
£1,000	7%	$8\frac{1}{2}$%
£ 800	4%	5%

Estimated Returns on Risk and Equity Capital*

Selling Price per Ton of Free Market Sales	10 year life	20 year life
£1,200	12%	14%
£1,000	9%	12%
£ 800	6%	6%

* Where the risk capital and equity capital differ, separate presentations would, of course, be required.

(For those who prefer it, the above net of tax yields could, of course, be replaced with their net present value equivalents.)

From the above table it is apparent that the project is unacceptable regardless of the period of life assumed if the selling price averages £800. Even at an average selling price of £1,000, the project is only marginal unless the assumed life significantly exceeds 10 years. For the higher average selling of £1,200, the project is acceptable even for the shorter life period, always assuming 12% is an adequate return for the other risks still inherent in the project and not represented in the tabular presentation (strikes, distribution hold-ups, interrupted raw material supplies, etc.).

This presentation helps to identify the crucial variables at a glance. The average selling price is clearly the dominant consideration, with the assumed length of life being of much less importance. To reduce the remaining risks inherent in the project still further, it would be necessary to consider more variables, and, in marginal projects involving relatively large amounts of capital, this will often yield further worthwhile results, even though time consuming. Apart from the fact that much of the work can be handled by reasonably skilled clerical labour, the cost of getting a more complete picture should not be begrudged. Often projects are put up for consideration which have involved hundreds or even thousands of hours work by skilled technical and marketing staff. A further few hours of appraisal by the financial department drawing out the full financial implications of this work is likely to represent a very worthwhile incremental investment.

It should be borne in mind that, when it is felt that many combinations of variables can usefully be considered, a firm will often justify securing time on an electronic computer. It is desirable to set out standard computer programmes for such work, into which can be incorporated the relevant basis of taxation charges, loan repayment schedules, etc. In this way the cost of using a computer can be kept very low.[1] It will be realized that this all ties in with the initial problem of deciding the optimal size, method and timing of capital projects; hence, all the work can conveniently be dovetailed.

It may well be objected that all these various combinations would bewilder rather than help top management in its task of decision taking. This is true, but there is no need to pass all the information up. The finance department should consider and assess far more information than they pass upstream. Their task is to identify the critical variables and pass up a small edited selection for decision. Just how much is passed upstream depends on the extent to which top management wish to delegate their responsibility and the time they have at their disposal.

When it is necessary to present a rather large amount of detailed information to top management, it will often be advisable to have resort to graphical methods of presentation. We give below in Figure

---

[1] In one complex investment project known to us costing over £30 million' the total costs of hired time on a computer – over a year in which many hundreds of combinations of possibilities had to be analysed – was less than £500.

6.1 a typical graph of this type showing a range of equity yields[1] on a project for two given estimates of both selling prices and costs, considered against a range of possible lives of the project which is estimated to have a maximum possible life of 12 years. Such a project might represent an investment in a certain type of plant which was expected to become obsolete over such a period. Also shown (vertical dotted lines) are the minimum breakeven or capital recovery periods (see Section 5 below).

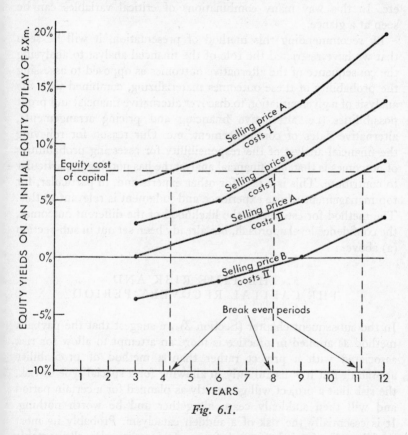

Fig. 6.1.

This diagram quickly reveals the critical assumptions and shows the estimated breakeven periods for the different combinations of costs and selling prices. The results of 16 calculations are thus easily

[1] Instead of equity yields the graph could easily be made to show equity net present values if this presentation is preferred.

summarized and presented. Top management can easily see that the firm must achieve Costs I and preferably Selling Price A if the project is to be worth accepting.

Similar diagrams could be drawn to illustrate the effect of inflation at different estimated rates on the equity return in *real* terms (see Section 7 below) – the effect of a fall in sales volume as contrasted with a fall in selling prices, the effect of the imposition of tariffs on exports after a certain period, or of tariffs on imported materials, etc. In this way many combinations of critical variables can be seen at a glance.

By recommending this method of presentation, it will be seen that we have restricted the role of the financial analyst to analysing the consequence of the alternative outcomes as opposed to assessing the probability of these outcomes materializing, combined with the analysis of a given situation to discover alternative financial and profit possibilities (i.e. alternative financing and pricing arrangements, alternative dates of commencement, etc. Our reason for relieving the financial analyst of the responsibility for assessing probabilities of outcomes is that, *qua* financial analyst, he has nothing in particular to contribute. This is a task for other experts and, in particular, for top management whose experience and judgment is relevant to this. The method for estimating the likelihood of the different outcomes, the confidence level approach, has already been set out in sub-section (a) above.

5. THE TIME RISK AND THE CAPITAL RECOVERY PERIOD

In the subsequent chapter (Section 2) we suggest that the payback method as applied in practice is more an attempt to allow for risk associated with a project rather than a method of profitability appraisal. But it is useful only in allowing for a special type of risk, the risk that a project will go exactly as planned for a certain period and will then suddenly cease altogether and be worth nothing. It is essentially the risk of a sudden cataclysm. Probably its most useful application in business is for investments in politically unstable areas. A nation may suddenly collapse under revolution or civil war in which case all business activity may cease, certainly foreign business activity, and it may never be allowed to restart. Another such risk is the risk of nationalization or expropriation with negligible compensation. Another business risk of this type is the risk arising from the fairly sudden development by a rival firm of a new technique or product such that much of an existing investment suddenly becomes worthless.

Such risks as these are risks related almost solely to time and, since they exist, it is desirable to develop some method of assessing them. This is the one type of risk for which the payback method is suited.[1] Providing some way can be found for overcoming its serious drawbacks. The two main drawbacks are that payback, as commonly applied, makes allowance for neither the time costs of money involved, nor the amount of the initial capital recovered. The former drawback is obvious, while the latter can be appreciated if we imagine a project in which 90% of the initial capital investment is recovered in say four years, whereas the remaining 10% takes a further two years to be recovered. Evidently after four years the main risk is over, but merely describing the project as one with a six year capital recovery period is very misleading. Similarly, two projects with, say, a five year payback are at very different risks if in one case the capital is recovered evenly over the five years, while in the other it is recovered only in the last two years. Should both projects cease after three years, the former would have recovered over half its capital but the latter would be a total loss.

A further drawback arises in deciding on the time from which to measure the period of capital recovery. As many projects have a long gestation period, often of five years or more, with perhaps only small expenditures in the early stages, it is evidently unsatisfactory to measure the capital recovery period from the day the first penny is spent to the day the last penny is recovered. But the alternative date which is nearly always chosen instead, the commencement of operations, is also unsatisfactory in that it completely ignores the pre-production period. Two projects with the same capital recovery periods measured from the start of operations could have very different gestation periods such that capital is at risk for a much longer time in one case than in the other. The significant period of risk is from the time of expenditure, not from the commencement of operations.

Fortunately, all these drawbacks can be overcome simultaneously

---

[1] It is important to appreciate that the method is most unsuited to the more normal business risks, say that sales will decline, costs rise, taxes be increased, etc.: risks in short, that profits will turn out to be rather less than expected over a period. Payback assumes profits continue unchanged for a time then suddenly cease completely.

by use of a simple technique allied to a diagrammatic presentation. The technique is notionally to charge an 'interest' rate (the firm's equity cost of capital) on any equity funds involved and to set out the result on a block diagram showing the amount of capital outstanding (including 'deferred interest') on an annual basis until it is completely recovered. By charging fully for the use of capital while it is invested in a project, it is possible to calculate the significant break-even period. This is the time that must elapse (assuming annual profits to be as forecast) before the firm will have suffered no actual loss from undertaking the project. An example will illustrate the technique.

Suppose a firm is contemplating a £1,000,000 project with an estimated life of eleven years. The project is estimated to require a three year construction period with expenditure occurring fairly evenly at the rate of £300,000 a year, plus £100,000 working capital at the end of the third year. It is estimated that the firm can raise a £300,000 6% loan (3% net of tax which is assumed to be 50%) over eleven years of operation, to be repaid in ten equal instalments of £30,000 starting at the end of the second year. (It should be noted that for a fully geared company this is exactly equivalent to raising a loan for ten years or more to be repaid at the end of the loan period if the project's assets, on which security the loan is being raised, are being written down on a 10% straight line basis from the second year onwards. In having to write down the assets, and yet not repaying the loan, the firm is effectively transferring the loan to its other assets which are being financed out of the debt element of the depreciation provision – see Chapter 4, Section 8.) The reason for not starting loan repayments in the first year of operation is to give the firm time to build up to full output and to sort out teething troubles, etc. As equity money must be committed to the project first, the £300,000 loan will be raised last, in the third year of construction. It is assumed that it will be raised £100,000 at the start of the year, and £200,000 mid-year. Interest is paid end-year, and in this case cannot be deferred until operations commence. The working capital of £100,000 required at the end of the construction period just prior to the commencement of operations is assumed to be financed to the extent of £65,000 by a 6% bank overdraft which is likely to be indefinitely renewed. The remaining £35,000 is financed by equity capital. The total net cash flow is estimated to be £36,000 in the first year and £210,000 in each of the remaining ten years, all assumed to arise end-year on average.

Table 6.4

Net Cash Flow – £000's

	1	2	3	4	5
Years of Operation	Interest*	Loan Repayments	Total Debt NCF (1 & 2)	Equity NCF	Total NCF (3 & 4)
1	11	—	11	25	36
2	11	30	41	169	210
3	10	30	40	170	210
4	9	30	39	171	210
5	8	30	38	172	210
6	7	30	37	173	210
7	7	30	37	173	210
8	6	30	36	174	210
9	5	30	35	175	210
10	4	30	34	176	210
11	3	95	98	177	275†

* Net of tax basis, including £1,950 interest on bank overdraft in all years.

† Includes £65,000 for estimated recovery of working capital. The net residual value of other assets is nil.

The firm's equity cost of capital is 8% net of tax. The net of tax yield on total capital is 10%, and on equity capital 14%. Hence, if the project lasts for the eleven years of operation, it is of sufficient profitability to justify investment. The only risk is one of time – whether the project will enjoy an uninterrupted existence.

The first step in our recommended presentation is to set down the respective equity and debt outlays prior to the commencement of operations. They are set out in Table 6.5 as follows where time 0 represents the beginning of the first year of operations, and −1 the time one year prior to the commencement of operations, −2, two years prior to commencement, etc.

Table 6.5

Reproduction Outlays

Years	−3	−2½	−2	−1½	−1	−½	−0	Totals
Average Equity Outlays	—	300	—	300	—	—	41	641
Debt Outlays	—	—	—	—	100	200	—	300
Bank Loan Outlays	—	—	—	—	—	—	65	65

The equity outlay of £41,000 at time 0, the end of the final year of construction, consists of a £35,000 outlay to finance the balance of the working capital, plus loan interest at 3% net of tax on the debt raised at the beginning and middle of the year. (It is a viable procedure to charge only net of tax interest if the firm can set off the interest charge against the taxable interest of other projects. This will generally be the case unless the new project is put into a separate firm where interest must be borne gross until that firm itself has a taxable income.)

The next step is to charge the equity outlays interest at 8% (net of tax). In the pre-production period this will be done on a half-yearly basis at 4% per half-year (which is sufficiently accurate for this purpose), and thereafter on an annual basis as in Table 6.6.

Table 6.6

Cumulative Investment during Pre-production Period – in £000's

Time End Half-Year	(1) Total Outlays Plus Interest Out-standing	(2) Plus Interest at 8%	(3) Cumu-lative Interest	(4) Total (1 & 2)	(5) Next Period's Plus Outlay	(6) Cumu-lative Outlays	(7) Total Carried Forward (4 & 5)
-3	—	—	—	—	300	300	300
$-2\frac{1}{2}$	300	12	12	312	—	300	312
-2	312	12	24	324	300	600	624
$-1\frac{1}{2}$	624	25	49	649	—	600	649
-1	649	26	75	675	—	600	675
$-\frac{1}{2}$	675	27	102	702	41	641	743
Cumu-lative Position at time 0	743	102	102	—	641	641	743

From this it can be seen that the *equivalent* equity outlay to £641,000 spread out over three years is £743,000 at the end of the three years. All this is set out in Figure 6.2 below. The next step is to determine how long it takes to recover this sum from the *equity* cash flow. But before passing on to this, it is pertinent to consider how to treat the debt outlays and recovery. These will be treated exactly as the equity case but no interest element need be shown in this case as interest is paid as it arises, by equity outlays in the construction period and out of the net cash flow once operations commence. Had interest been deferred during the construction period, it would be added to the debt outlays to give the total sum outstanding (just as the notional equity 'interest' cost is added to the equity outlays). Debt recovery raises certain problems. In the case under consideration, some debt will be outstanding to the very end of the project whereas the total net cash flow will permit total capital to be recovered in a shorter period. If the debt and equity net cash flows are separately allocated as we are suggesting, to reduce their separate outstanding totals, the equity will be recovered (with 'interest') before the debt. This difficulty can be dealt with in one of two ways. Either the equity cash flow can be used notionally to repay debt once the equity capital has been recovered, or the equity capital recovery period alone can be calculated where it is felt that even if the net cash flow were suddenly to cease for any reason, the residual assets could be realized to repay any outstanding debts. The former course of action is appropriate where the project, should it end, is likely to be a complete write-off leaving outstanding debts to be repaid from equity resources: this might be true of a project subject to essentially political risks. The latter course is more appropriate where assets will retain significant residual value. In practice, some compromise between the two approaches is usually called for. The capital recovery period should be calculated for the time it takes to recover all capital outlays, both debt and equity, from the combined net cash flow *plus* the likely residual value of the assets involved. It will be appreciated that there is no point in calculating a recovery period which excludes residual values.

Consider now how to handle the capital recoveries. Debt outlays are recoverable at the scheduled loan repayment rate, and this presents no problem. Nor does the treatment of the bank overdraft which remains constant for the life of the project to be recovered out of the realization of the working capital. Equity outlays are recovered as fast as the equity net cash flow permits. Essentially the calculation is the reverse of that used in the construction period. This is set out in Table 6.7 on an annual basis as follows:

Table 6.7

Recovery of Equity Outlays at 8%

£000's

Year	1 Total Outlays Plus Interest Outstanding at Beginning of Year	2 Plus Interest at 8%	3 *Less* NCF	4 Cumu- lative Interest	5 Cumu- lative Capital	6 Total End-Year Carried Forward (4+5)
0	743	—	—	102	641	743
1	743	59	−25	136	641	777
2	777	62	−169	29	641	670
3	670	54	−170	—	554	554
4	554	44	−171	—	427	427
5	427	34	−172	—	289	289
6	289	23	−173	—	139	139
7	139	11	−173	—	−23	−23

In this table it will be seen that the equity net cash flow is always first set against the cumulative interest charge including the current years interest. Only the balance is used to reduce the original capital outlay. This helps to show how long it takes to recover the initial capital outlays after allowing for the notional interest cost of equity capital.

From this table, it can be seen that just before the end of the seventh year the equity capital is fully recovered having earned the firm's minimum acceptable return on equity funds of 8% net of tax. Assuming the debt capital then outstanding (£185,000 at the end of the seventh year including the bank loan) could be repaid from the residual value of the assets if the project were suddenly terminated, the meaningful capital recovery period is nearly seven years after the commencement of operations, and nearly ten years after the commencement of the project. If none of the capital could be recovered if the project suddenly terminated, then nearly another full year would need to elapse before all the capital, including the debt capital outstanding at the end of the seventh year, could be said to be fully recovered. Conversely if the residual value of the assets exceeded the amount of loans outstanding by a constant amount, say, £139,000, the effective capital recovery period would have been a year earlier, at the end of the sixth year of operations, as the project could be terminated at this time, both debt and equity capital would have been fully recovered, and would have earned fully their respective 'interest' costs for every year they were invested.

All this can be better presented diagrammatically, with the annual amounts outstanding being shown *after* the year's net cash flow has been allocated to interest and capital repayment. This is done in Figure 6.2 below.

A brief glance at this diagram reveals the amount of loan and equity capital at risk at any one time as it shows comprehensively both the build-up and the recovery periods. It is much more helpful than merely reporting the total capital recovery period as nearly eight years after the start of operations. It distinguishes between projects of a similar nature, cost, and capital recovery period where the timing of the capital recovery is significantly different. It permits answers to the question of what is lost if the project ends after only 5 years instead of 7, etc. The diagram is capable of several variations to suit analysts' requirements. For some projects it may well be worth having a separate diagram for each type of capital, but even so, one diagram containing all the different sources combined will probably still be found useful as well.

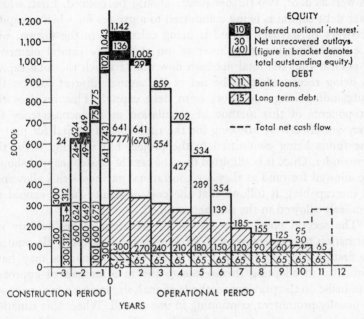

Fig. 6.2.

This approach brings out several interesting points. It shows that the period when the maximum amount of capital is at risk is the start of the second year by which time some capital has started to be recovered. It also shows up the effect of payback as normally used without allowing for the time cost of money. The normal calculation would say £1,000,000 is invested and is recovered after 5½ years of operation, ignoring residual values, and only just over 4 years if allowance is made for them being equal to outstanding debts. This compares with the more meaningful calculation of nearly 7 years – the time it takes to reach a meaningful break-even position, i.e. a position where the firm is no worse off for having undertaken the project. This throws a rather different light on a risky project. It is seen that the project under consideration would need to run *uninterruptedly* for nearly two-thirds (instead of half) of its estimated life just to break even. The high overall return on the project is thus seen to depend critically on the possibility that the project will continue uninterruptedly until well into the final third of its life.[1]

Concerning the use of a notional interest rate for equity capital as well as debt, two further points should be noticed. First, whenever debt capital is being committed to a project for which a capital recovery or payback period is being calculated in the normal way (i.e. excluding charging 'interest' on the equity capital element), it is clear that the total net cash flow out of which the total capital is being recovered must be net of the annual interest cost on the outstanding long and short term debt capital. This involves the proponents of this method of calculation in an inconsistency for they are effectively allowing for the time cost of capital for part of the funds being committed to the project but ignoring it for the remainder. Once it is admitted that the cost of all debt capital should be allowed for (and as they are contractual payments this allowance is inescapable), it follows that the cost of equity funds should be similarly allowed in the manner outlined.

The second point concerns the presentation of profitability information to top management. Whenever the concept of discounting is first introduced into a firm many senior managers may have difficulty in adapting themselves to the new method of approach and insist on the previous methods of analysis, among which payback is usually prominent, continuing in use as well. Where this situation prevails it is useful to introduce discounting in steps and the first step is to demonstrate the superiority of payback plus 'interest' over simple payback. Once this has been accepted it is but a short step to showing that the yield on equity funds or total funds over a whole period, assuming no interruptions, is the amount the firm earns for a payback period equal to the length of a project's life, and the excess of this yield over the cost of capital indicates profitability. Suppose a firm is considering a project with a 12 year life, and a payback period of 6 years when the firm's equity cost of capital is taken as 7%. The profitability information could be presented thus:

Life of Project	Return on Equity Capital
6 years	7% – break-even rate
9 years	10%
12 years	14%

[1] An even greater contrast results for projects with a longer construction period as is common in the mining industry – see Chapter 13, Section 1.

It could be explained that the project breaks even after
has a payback period of 9 years for a 10% cost of capital,
for a 14% cost or return, the payback period is 12 years
project's whole life.

As we have argued, the calculation of a project's capital recovery
period as an aid to risk assessment is only useful when the project
is subject to significant risks of a time nature. As many projects
are not subject to such risks, the technique is not one to be applied
universally to all projects.

6. RISKS ASSOCIATED WITH DIFFERENT TYPES OF PROJECTS

It will be generally accepted that the riskier a project is the higher
the apparent return it must promise to warrant acceptance. With this
in mind it may be useful to list some of the main types of projects
and comment on the different types of risk to which they are subject.
The ultimate aim would be to determine the differential risk allowances which would reduce all such projects to a common basis. This
cannot be done in general terms for such a list will vary from industry
to industry, indeed from firm to firm, for it will be affected by the
technical and managerial skills and resources available to each firm.
And in the last resort, the compilation of differential risk allowances
is very much a matter of subjective judgment. Even so, some useful
generalizations can be made from examining the different types of
investment projects from the standpoint of the risks to which they
are subject, and it is to the examination of such a list that we now
turn. In considering such a list it should be borne in mind that
the categories are not necessarily exclusive; they often overlap and a
given project may well fall simultaneously into two or more
categories.

a. *Cost Saving Investments*

Cost saving investments should be considered in two categories;
those which apply to established operations and those which apply
to planned operations. Where a cost saving investment is being
considered in relation to an established operation *which will continue
regardless of whether the cost saving investment is made or not* then
it is clear that there will be a continuous and virtually risk-free
demand for the services or output of the proposed investment. This
reduces the risks associated with such an investment to the usually

P

quite minor risks that the capital cost and resultant cost savings (the incremental net cash flow attributable solely to the investment) have been estimated too optimistically. Thus such an investment need promise a return only slightly more than the cost of capital involved to be justified. An example of such an investment would be the installation of mechanical loading arrangements in a factory with an assured future, or the electrification of a railway line which the railway authorities were pledged to keep open. Where the continuance of the existing parent operation is in doubt, or dependent on the profitability of the cost saving investment under consideration, then the problem is equivalent to that met with in planned projects which is considered next.

Where a proposed cost saving investment is only part of a larger planned investment, then it must be judged with the larger investment and promise a commensurate return. Thus if it is proposed to open up a mine in mountainous country twenty miles from a railhead which can only be reached by road, and an aerial ropeway is being contemplated as an alternative to shipping the output of the mine by the road, then clearly the capital invested in the ropeway must offer a return comparable to that invested in the mine. Both investments are subject to the same risks. If the mine is forced to operate at half capacity, or close down, the worth of the aerial ropeway declines correspondingly because it has no alternative uses. Similarly, if the mine is in existence but making little or no profits because of the high road transport costs, and an aerial ropeway is being contemplated as a means of keeping the mine in existence, it is subject to the full risks of the mine and must offer the same type of return as any other mining project. Mining costs, sales, fixed asset renewals, etc., must all be considered to determine whether the ropeway investment can keep the mine going for a sufficiently economic period.

A particular category of cost saving investments are where the capital expenditure 'saves' or avoids some series of contractual outlays. The commonest case here is that of choosing the buying alternative in lease or buy decisions (see Chapter 8). The savings in lease payments, in view of their contractual nature, are highly certain, but for this reason may have significant financial implications as regards the firm's debt raising capacity. A full discussion of these problems is given in the chapter referred to.

Allowing for the inflationary risks in cost saving investments is also important and this factor is discussed in Section 7 below.

b. *Replacement Investments*

It should be apparent that no replacement investment should occur automatically just because a building or a piece of equipment has come to the end of its life. Replacement investments must be justified on their merits of future profitability in the same way as all other investments (see Chapter 19, Section 1). Even so, in a large number of cases detailed analysis will not be required because it will be obvious that a replacement is overwhelmingly justified. Without it a whole production line or process would have to close down. The gain from making such replacements at once is so obviously profitable that any allowance for risk is irrelevant. But this is not true of all replacements, especially replacements where there is some choice about the date of replacement due to the possibility of repairs prolonging its working life. The method of analysing the optimum time for replacement is fully discussed in the chapter reference just cited. Here it is sufficient to note that replacement investments are often akin to cost saving investments in that where they form part of larger *continuing* projects they do not add to the firm's main risks and that therefore replacement will be justified whenever the projected return exceeds the firm's cost of capital by quite a small margin. Further, when the continuance of the parent project is dependent on the replacement expenditure of one of the parts, that expenditure is subject to the risks of the future of the whole project and must be analysed accordingly.

To sum up on cost saving and replacement investments, both types of investment, when forming part of a continuing project, are subject to very few of the risks associated with normal investments and need offer a return only marginally in excess of a firm's cost of capital. In these circumstances fine calculations are both possible and justified. In all other circumstances, however, they are subject to the normal business risks and must offer a commensurately higher return. One other point should be noted. Whereas many types of investment projects require additional highly skilled personnel which a firm may not have or be able to obtain, cost saving and replacement investments usually require none. The existing engineers, etc., can usually be relied on to operate the new investments. And even when extra engineers and technicians are required they are often more easily obtained than say highly skilled marketing executives. For these reasons, when a firm is going through a period of consolidation or retrenchment, or is prevented from taking on expansionary new projects through lack of sufficient managerial talent, there is much to be said for concentrating on cost savings and replacement investments.

c. *Market Expansion Investments*

Often amongst the riskiest type of investment projects are those designed to expand a firm's markets, particularly if this involves fighting highly organized and skilled competitors who possess large resources. This process often involves intensive and costly advertising and sales campaigns for a new product which can be a total loss should it fail to gain a significant share of the market. Not infrequently test marketing will give rise to false optimism due to the inadequacy of the tests or the failure of the factories to deliver in bulk at the quality achieved on small batches. In addition, considerable expenditure may be involved in developing and test marketing a product before it is apparent that it should be abandoned. Because of all these inherent uncertainties, market expansion investments must often promise the highest of investment returns to justify acceptance. These returns, however, may often include substantial intangible items – such as helping to consolidate the firm's marketing position – and the apparent tangible return may be quite small.

d. *Investments Required by Regulations*

Most firms will be required to undertake some investments because these are required by government regulations or under an insurance policy. The provision of safety equipment, of dust control equipment, or fire escapes and fire fighting equipment, of toilet and washing facilities, etc. all come into these categories. As such investments are compulsory if the firm is to operate at all, little or no analysis is called for. Similarly, no risk attaches to investments of this type save in the rare circumstances that a firm may have a choice between long and short lived investments under this heading – the long lived investment being the cheaper providing it will be utilized for a long period. A choice of this nature involves the firm deciding on the likely time it will need such facilities in a given locality.

e. *Welfare Amenity Investments*

Most firms undertake welfare amenity investments of some kind. These may range from the provision of canteens and rest rooms, to convalescent homes and sport and social clubs. Clearly investments of this type tend to improve morale and enable a firm to attract and retain a higher quality staff. To some extent it may reduce the need to pay higher wages and salaries. The task of evaluating these investments is of course largely a subjective exercise in employee relations. The personnel department can hardly carry out experiments on the effect say of two years with a canteen followed by two years without. Once an amenity has been provided its discontinuance at least for a long period, will usually be impracticable. This being so, welfare amenities must be justified largely on the basis of subjective judgments. Usually the minimum provision is fairly easily determined as a firm which fails to provide the minimum facilities equal to those of nearby firms will have difficulty recruiting staff. But above the minimum, *objective* justification of amenity investments is well nigh impossible. A firm may risk the complete waste of its money if it provides what the staff accept but little value.

7. ALLOWING FOR INFLATION

Inflation may be regarded as a special type of risk – that of changing prices and costs – to which projects are exposed. For this reason it will be convenient to consider the subject in this chapter. General inflation, albeit of a mild variety, would seem to be almost endemic in post-war Western economies. As such it is a risk factor to be allowed for in the evaluation of many investment projects. Its effects will be dealt with under three headings, the cost of equity and debt capital, changes caused to net cash flows, and the increase in a firm's debt raising potential.

a. *The Cost of Capital*

i. Equity. It is probably true to say that most equity investors expect that firms will maintain the rate of return on equity capital during periods of general inflation at a level which adequately compensates in real terms for the opportunities – of consumption or alternative investments – foregone. It would also appear from the available evidence that firms are broadly successful in realizing this expectation. The majority of firms would probably accept that it should be an object of policy in investment to try to maintain/obtain a worthwhile real rate of return on equity capital invested.

Before we consider how this policy can be put into practice, however, we need to consider the policy more carefully to clarify the meaning of 'real terms' in this context. Initially at least, only the profit element from a given project will be distributed to the shareholders and a substantial proportion even of this may be retained by the firm. The capital and the retained profits arising from a project will be spent on the assets and services normally purchased by the firm. Obtaining a return which was adequate in real terms in relation to the price level of these assets and services however may not necessarily be an acceptable policy. For example if the assets and services normally purchased by the firm fell in price while the general price index rose the shareholders might not receive an adequate return. For if the assets and services required by the firm are falling in price it is possible (and in the long run, probable) that due to competitive pressures this will be reflected in a reduction in the firm's selling prices and hence in its profits. It would be small consolation to an investor that funds arising from a project were adequate to purchase identical assets if, because of a fall in the price of these assets, the firm's, and hence the investor's income prospects were now much worse.

While the exact solution to this problem is rather complicated and depends on the circumstances of particular firms and industries the investor would probably consider his wealth to be maintained intact if the firm obtained an adequate real rate of return with reference to the investor's normal cost of living index. Following this policy then, whatever may be happening to the cost of investment opportunities to the particular firm, the shareholder is at least being 'maintained whole' as regards his normal consumption alternatives.

Consider now the method of allowing for inflation in assessing the cost of equity capital. Let r equal the cost of equity capital in the absence of inflation. With no inflation, when a future payment is being converted to its present value equivalent, it is discounted at r. Thus the present value of the sum A due in n years $= A/(1+r)^n$. But when money values are not fixed, then discounting A at the rate r will not indicate the present value equivalent of A received in n years time. A must be modified by the general price level change that is expected to occur over the n years. Suppose prices are expected to rise at a rate d every year for the n years, then to translate A into money units of the same worth as present units, A must be reduced by the factor $(1+d)^n$. (If general prices were expected to decrease by d per year then A would have to be multiplied by this factor.) This sum can then be discounted at the rate r to reduce it to its present value equivalent. Thus the present value of a fixed money sum, A due in n years, when the equity cost of capital is r, and the expected rate of inflation is d, is simply

$$\frac{A}{(1+r)^n(1+d)^n}$$

This is equivalent to

$$\frac{A}{[(1+r)(1+d)]^n}$$

Thus the equity cost of capital in *money* terms, r_i under inflation at rate d is simply

$$r_i = (1+r)(1+d)-1 \qquad (6.1)$$

In other words, the rate of inflation should be *multiplied* by the equity cost of capital, and their product used to discount future payments. Suppose the equity cost of capital is 4% and a 3% cumulative rate of inflation is expected. The appropriate discount factor is $(1\cdot04\times1\cdot03)-1\cdot0 = 7\cdot12\%$. When both factors are low, very nearly the same result is achieved by *adding* the rate of inflation to the equity cost of capital, thus $4\%+3\% = 7\%$. While the adding is not strictly correct, the result is so little different from multiplying that it can be used with confidence for low values of r and d, especially when it is remembered that neither factor can be estimated with great precision.

ii. Debt. The rate of interest and terms of repayment of loan capital will normally be fixed in money terms. With persistent general inflation it is of course to be expected that interest charges on loan capital will tend to increase to compensate for this. In Britain however, the fixed interest loan market is seriously influenced by institutional factors and the measures taken by the monetary authorities to limit the cost of long term government borrowing. As a result of these factors and indeed ignorance on the part of private lenders, interest rates are probably only partially adjusted to offset inflation, and this with a pronounced time lag.[1]

[1] Assume the effective rate of personal income tax is say 40%. Debenture holders have been receiving interest at say 5% gross and thus 3% net. The 3% net of tax rate is of course the relevant figure as the burden of inflation is felt on *net* income. If inflation is at the rate of 2%, then i debenture holders are to receive the same real income as before, the *gross* interest rate on debentures would need to rise to $(0\cdot03+0\cdot02)/0\cdot60 = 8\frac{1}{3}\%$ i.e. by 2% plus 40/60ths of 2%. With inflation in Britain averaging $3\%-4\%$ a year, it is an observable fact that long term fixed interest rates have failed to rise by an amount sufficient to maintain the real income of debenture holders.

iii. The gain to equity shareholders. When general inflation occurs and a firm has a significant amount of debt capital, a gain accrues to the equity shareholders, and this gain is supplemented by the raising of further debt in future years at a lower cost in real terms than would exist with stable prices. Consider the magnitude of such gains.

Suppose for example a firm has a £1,000,000 debenture outstanding at 6% due to be repaid in a single instalment 15 years hence. Suppose the annual net of tax interest burden on the debenture is $3\frac{1}{2}\%$ (i.e. £35,000 a year), the firm's cost of equity capital is 8% in real terms, and the expected annual rate of general inflation over the period is 3%. Without inflation the net interest payments and the final redemption payment represent a present value burden of

$$a_{15|8}£35,000 + v_{15|8}£1,000,000 = £615,000$$

With 3% inflation, the appropriate discount factor is 8%+3% = 11% (strictly 11·24%). Thus the present value burden under inflation becomes

$$a_{15|11}£35,000 + v_{15|11}£1,000,000 = £461,000$$

or a reduction of £154,000 (25%).

On new loans negotiated during continuing general inflation, the gain to the equity shareholders is the difference between the real burden of interest under inflation compared with that which would rule under stable prices. In post-war Britain, the average annual inflation of 3–4% has typically equalled the net of tax cost of interest payments, thus reducing the effective cost of debt capital to nil.

b. *The Effect of Inflation on the Net of Cash Flows*

It is sometimes the case that inflation can be expected to have a significant effect on the net cash flows arising from a project, and this is particularly true of projects involving sales at a contractual price agreed some years in advance. The effect of inflation in these cases depends on the particular circumstances and the provisions (if any) for price escalation in the contract. In the extreme case of contracts with no price escalation provisions but providing only for sales at prices fixed in money terms, it is evidently most important to take account of this factor in the analysis. Perhaps the most common instance of this type of problem is in the case of leasing or chartering agreements: long term ship charters for example are often fixed in money terms (with any escalation agreements usually being limited to crew labour costs) and often extend over most of the life of the vessel. Taking account of inflation in these cases presents no computational or conceptual difficulties and it is only necessary to discount all the cash flows at a rate higher by the estimated rate of inflation, or reduce the yield by this amount.

In the case of contracts which provide for a limited degree of price escalation, or where the extent of inflation of the selling price or costs can be estimated to a useful degree of accuracy, the process of taking this into account presents somewhat more difficult computational problems. Some elements of the net cash flows almost invariably remain constant and one of the most important of these is tax concessions on capital expenditure. These tax concessions are of course based on historical cost and remain fixed (apart from actual changes in tax legislation) whatever the degree of inflation. This, however, presents no particular computational problems where the tax formulae of the appendix Chapter 3 are being used. These formulae automatically segregate the cash flows attributable to the tax concessions, and since these remain constant in *money* terms, they are simply discounted (using the formula provided) at the higher rate of discount appropriate to the estimated degree of inflation.

Escalation for other elements of costs such as labour or certain raw materials will often be specifically provided for in the contract. A relatively simple computational method of allowing for inflation is then to discount that part of the revenue on which escalation is allowed at the normal cost of capital and that part of the price on which no escalation is possible at a cost of capital appropriately increased by the estimated rate of inflation. In some cases, however, it may be necessary to make a full scale computation of the estimated real net cash flows by calculating the increase in selling price permitted under the escalation agreement given the estimated degree of inflation in the indices on which escalation is based. Given these net cash flows, it is, of course, extremely simple then to perform the required discounting at the cost of capital appropriately inflated for the degree of general inflation.

c. *Increase in Debt Raising Potential*

For the sake of completeness one further effect of inflation should be mentioned. When general inflation continues a firm will be justified in revaluing the fixed assets in its balance sheet from time to time (say at five yearly intervals for the mild rates of inflation experienced in Britain or America post-war) to reflect more truly the current position. Strictly speaking, such assets should be revalued not on the basis of a general price index but rather on the basis of specific replacement cost indices appropriate to the assets concerned. But under the conditions postulated it is assumed that all price indices are generally moving upwards, and hence specific replacement costs are also likely to be rising at a time of general inflation. As replacement costs rise significantly, such that it becomes worth revaluing fixed assets, then when such revaluations occur it will be possible to raise extra debt on the amount of the revaluation (save perhaps to the extent that specific assets are mortgaged as security for particular loans). This is not likely to be of much importance in practice if only because it is difficult to forecast continued inflation at a given rate with confidence, but on occasion it may be of some importance.

REFERENCES

1. C. F. CARTER, G. P. MEREDITH, and G. L. S. SHACKLE
   Editors, *Uncertainty and Business Decisions*, Liverpool University
   Press, Liverpool, 1954.
2. G. L. S. SHACKLE, *Decision Order and Time*, Cambridge University
   Press, Cambridge, 1961.

CHAPTER SEVEN

Conventional Methods of Investment Appraisal

In this chapter we shall briefly consider the most common conventional methods of investment appraisal. We shall be concerned to examine the suitability of these methods compared to the more rigorous and complex discounting methods. If it could be shown that the conventional methods were sufficiently accurate for most practical purposes then clearly there would be little point in using more complex methods for an insignificant gain in accuracy. We shall demonstrate our contention that conventional methods are inadequate substitutes for discounting methods in most circumstances and often produce capricious results. Their simplicity of application will be shown to arise only from oversimplifying the often complex problems of investment appraisal.

Our second concern will be to consider the rationale of the common conventional methods for the light they throw on the practical requirements of businessmen. We hope to show that these requirements are more satisfactorily met by the methods recommended in the remainder of this book.

The three most common of the conventional methods will be considered, 'rate of return', 'payback' and 'postponability'. Finally, we shall examine the validity and usefulness of that common yardstick of the profitability or efficiency of a whole enterprise, or division of a business, the annual return on capital employed, that is, the ratio of annual profits to capital. The discussion of the relevance of 'book' profits to capital budgeting decisions is postponed to Section 3 of Chapter 17.

1. RATE OF RETURN

a. *Definition*

The rate of return on capital (henceforth referred to as RR) is defined as the ratio of profit (net of depreciation) to capital. This rate of return is to be compared to some estimate of a firm's cost of capital including, where appropriate, some allowance for risk. The method has a host of variants but in the interests of fairness and objectivity we shall consider only the most plausible. Profit can either be gross or net of tax. In view of the fact that the general aim of investment is to maximize net of tax income we shall consider only the net of tax case as being the more useful variant. Net of tax profits can be either initial profits, that is the profits from the first year of operation of a project, or some form of average profits, either an average over the whole life of the project or of only the first 5 or perhaps 10 years of operations. Use of initial profits which could be completely unrepresentative of the profits of later years is manifestly so unsatisfactory that we shall consider only the use of average profits. Finally, capital is defined either as the initial capital outlay on a project including working capital, or less commonly, average capital employed, the average usually being a straight average of capital in the first and last years of a project's life.

b. *Shortcomings*

Failure to allow for the incidence of capital outlays and earnings. Consider three simple investment projects, *A*, *B*, and *C*, all costing £500 to initiate, having a life of 5 years, with income arising end-year on average, and the residual value of the assets being zero. Depreciation both for tax purposes and for management accounting purposes is on the straight line basis of £100 a year. Tax is at the rate of 50% and is levied and collected simultaneously at the end of each year. The details of earnings, depreciation, tax and profitability are given in Table 7.1 below.

Table 7.1
£'s
Annual Earnings, etc.

Years	1	2	3	4	5	Total
Project A						
Gross earnings	200	200	200	200	200	1,000
Less Depreciation	−100	−100	−100	−100	−100	−500
Profits before tax	100	100	100	100	100	500
Less tax at 50%	−50	−50	−50	−50	−50	−250
Profits after tax	50	50	50	50	50	250
Project B						
Gross earnings	100	150	200	250	300	1,000
Less Depreciation	−100	−100	−100	−100	−100	−500
Profits before tax	—	50	100	150	200	500
Less tax at 50%	—	−25	−50	−75	−100	−250
Profits after tax	—	25	50	75	100	250
Project C						
Gross earnings	300	250	200	150	100	1,000
Less Depreciation	−100	−100	−100	−100	−100	−500
Profits before tax	200	150	100	50	—	500
L ss tax at 50%	−100	−75	−50	−25	—	−250
Profits after tax	100	75	50	25	—	250

Project *A* has stable profits, Project *B* rising profits, and Project *C* falling profits, but all three result in the same total profits and thus the same average profits. The RR method, based as it is on average profits, would result in all three investments being classified as equal, i.e. as offering a 10% return on initial capital (£50/£500) or a 20% return on 'average' capital (£50/£250). But clearly all three investments are not equally attractive even though their total earnings are the same. Project *C*'s earnings arise earlier than *A*'s which in turn arise earlier than *B*'s. As the differences in annual earnings can be employed elsewhere to advantage (either as dividends or investment) in the years before the end of the projects' lives, then *C* is preferable to *A* which in turn is preferable to *B*. This highlights one of the main weaknesses of the RR method compared to discounting methods: it takes no cognizance of the *incidence* of cash flows and so fails to reflect the advantages of near as opposed to distant cash flows (reference 1). Projects with the same capital cost, life, and total profitability are inevitably ranked equally. Applying discounting method to the three projects the results are as follows:

	Yield*	NPV at 7%
C	$17\frac{1}{2}$%	£129
A	$15\frac{1}{4}$%	£115
B	$13\frac{1}{2}$%	£101

* (It is interesting to note that none of the discounted returns are near either of the two RR variants, i.e. 10% and 20%.)

These differences in the three projects would have been even more marked had it been assumed that tax payments were made with a realistic time delay of say 12 to 18 months, a fact which the RR method, based as it is on an accounting concept of profit as opposed to a cash concept, would not take into account.

Another factor neglected by the RR method is the gestation or pre-production period between the commencement of a project and the time when it begins to produce an income. If all the above projects had taken two years before the commencement of earning instead of one year, their 'rates of return' as typically calculated would be unaffected. Some proponents of the method try to overcome this particular drawback by charging interest on capital outlays during the pre-production period, usually at a nominal rate of interest such as the rate at which loan capital may be borrowed even though projects must usually be financed with a large proportion of equity capital.

Although the RR method is recognized by some of its adherents as an approximation to more refined methods it is frequently justified on the grounds that it is sufficiently accurate for business purposes. This view turns on some implicit assumption regarding the correct method of calculation and the size of the errors involved in this particular approximation to it. It is our contention that the correct method of calculation involves discounting and so we shall consider

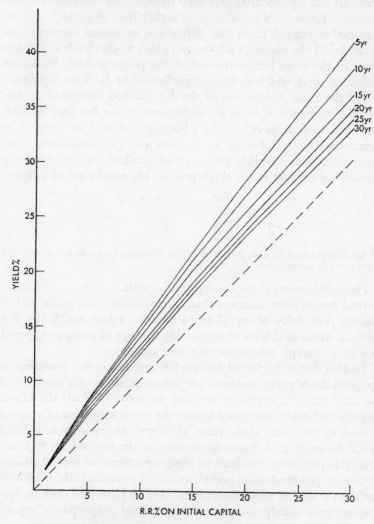

Fig. 7.1. Discounted yield and rate of return (on initial capital) compared for projects with constant earnings

the RR as an approximation to yield, the discounting method it most closely resembles. Further, we shall concentrate on the version of the RR based on initial as opposed to average capital.

c. *Accuracy Compared with Yield*[1]

Consider first the case in which the net cash flows are constant and the capital assets have negligible resale values at the end of the projects' lives. It is simple to show from its definition that the RR always underestimates yield. The size of the error depends on the size of the yield and the life of the project. It is negligible for a project with a life of less than one year or more than, say, fifty and rises to a peak within these two extremes of project life. These facts are illustrated in Figure 7.1.

In this diagram the yield is given on the vertical axis against the RR on the horizontal. Each curve gives the relationship between these two rates for capital projects of different lives. Thus the curve marked '10 year' gives the relationship for an asset with a ten year life. As the scale of percentages is common to both axes, if the two methods of calculating the rate of return gave the same answer the points would all lie on the dotted 45 degree line. The vertical distances between the curves and this dotted line indicate the error in the approximation. The curves for one year projects and projects with a life of more than 50 years (neither of which are shown separately) lie on the dotted line. The remaining curves are seen to depart from the 45 degree 'equality' line with decreasing length of life of asset.

The net of tax rates of return within which the majority of capital projects probably falls is 6%–10%. The error in this range as a percentage of the RR is 50% for a 10 year project falling to 40% for a 20 year project. The size of the error involved in the general case when the net cash flows are different from year to year cannot be assessed precisely save by a consideration of each individual case. Some idea of the nature of the approximation can be given, however, by considering the cases in which the net cash flows are increasing or decreasing at a constant (geometric) rate per annum. Net cash flows are frequently estimated to increase in this manner when the return on the asset is linked to an expanding market or output. The case of decreasing net cash flows frequently arises when the calculation is made after tax and where initial tax allowances, such as

---

[1] (See reference 2).

accelerated depreciation, are available in the early years. The comparison between the two methods of calculating the rate of return is given in Figure 7.2. In this figure the RR is given on the horizontal

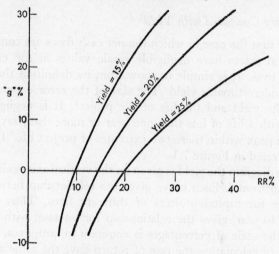

Fig. 7.2. Discounted yield and rate of return (on initial capital) compared for projects with earnings increasing or decreasing at a constant rate of g% per annum.

axis against the rate of growth or decline g of the net cash flows on the vertical. The curves of the figure give the relation between g and the RR for a project with a life of 15 years and different discounted rates of return. For example, the curve marked 'yield = 20%' gives the relationship for a yield of 20%. It is seen that in cases with a rate of growth of the net cash flows of 8·5%, the RR and the yield are equal. For a yield of 15%, however, a rate of growth of 10% is required for both methods to give the same results. More generally it is seen that the difference between the yield and the RR diminish up to a certain rate of growth beyond which the RR increasingly overestimates the yield. When the net cash flows are decreasing over time, however, it is seen that the RR is an underestimate and becomes increasingly so with the rate at which the net cash flows are falling over time. Similar conclusions hold for projects of different lives and for which the net cash flows are increasing or decreasing fairly regularly.

It is informative to consider the reasons for the different effect of increasing or decreasing net cash flows over time on the two methods of calculation. It is due to the fact that any changes in the net cash flows in the later years have a vastly greater effect on the RR compared with the yield. In the former, a pound in ten years time has precisely the same weight in the calculation as a pound one year from now, while in the yield the sums arising in the early years are vastly more important. It is found, in fact, that, when the yield is above 10%, substantial changes in the net cash flows arising after, say, the seventh year have relatively small influence on the yield as ultimately calculated. This is a point of considerable importance in favour of the yield and of course other discounting methods. For while this characteristic follows from the economic logic of the concept, it means that errors of forecasting and uncertainty, which are generally more serious in the later years, are of much less importance than with the RR, because the yield results in progressively larger reductions in the present value of the more distant net cash flows.

From this it is apparent that the RR method strongly discriminates against short term projects (say up to ten years) in favour of long term projects since the absolute error is always larger for the former. The underestimation is also larger for projects which pay off more heavily in the early than in the later years (as many projects do due to favourable capital allowances and other methods of accelerated depreciation) and so the method strongly discriminates against this type of project also. The result of these two factors will be to cause firms using the RR to fail to take up some projects of these two types. This is particularly undesirable since such projects are particularly attractive from the point of view of risk (when of a time nature) and liquidity. It is a curious feature of the RR that it discriminates strongly against types of projects which its proponents – who generally favour a conservative concentration on short run returns – are primarily concerned to accept.

So far we have been comparing the RR variant based on *initial* capital with yield. The conclusions for the other RR variant, based on some form of *average* capital, are typically the opposite of those so far arrived at. In the case of constant net cash flows, the RR based on average capital employed will typically be half that based on initial capital.[1] As such it will tend significantly to overestimate the attractiveness of projects, particularly short lived ones, or those with large cash flows in the early years. Hence, it will tend to result in firms accepting projects with a prospective yield below their

[1] Firms using this variant of the RR method will of course be aware that it gives higher returns than the variant based on initial capital.

costs of capital after allowing for risk. Thus either variant of the RR tends to result in firms making the wrong selection of investments.

d. *Comparability with External Investment Opportunities*

A further important weakness of the RR method is that it cannot simply be used for the purpose of comparing external investments with internal investments. (This criticism, and what follows, applies equally to both the initial capital and average capital variants of the RR.) It will generally be accepted that the rate return offered by projects within a firm should be compared continuously with external opportunities. This is especially the case where a firm is financing expansion by retained profits. For unless in this case a firm can improve on the rates offered by external investment, it is performing no service to the shareholders which they could not equally perform for themselves and can have little justification for retaining profits.

The reason for the inadequacy of the RR for purposes of this comparison is due to the fact that external investments are likely to differ markedly as regards the relevant incidence of income over time from internal investments. The external investment opportunity which defines a firm's cost of capital will consist typically of investment in equity shares of other firms over a given period. The resulting cash flows will take the form of a dividend stream (usually increasing with time) plus a large terminal sum when the shares are realized. This is evidently a pattern of cash flows which would be very difficult to value by the RR method. Application of the RR to internal and external investment for purposes of comparison is thus likely to give rise to somewhat misleading figures. Yield gives a flexible and quite satisfactory basis for comparison, and it should be remembered that the yield method is also the method generally used to calculate the yield to redemption on redeemable government securities and other bonds (see Chapter 1, Section 4b).

This drawback of the RR method is of significance because the rationale of the method, which distinguishes it from the other common conventional methods, is that it makes allowance for the cost of capital in that the rates of return calculated by it are intended to be comparable with a firm's cost of capital including the occasions when such a cost is measured by external investment opportunities. This allowance for a firm's cost of capital is of course an essential attribute of any satisfactory method of investment appraisal but it is clear that the RR method fails by this very test. The need, which is real enough, can only be adequately met by the discounting methods.

e. *Difficulties of Application*

It is clear that neither variant of the RR method will equal yield save by coincidence. The chief exception (ignoring one year projects) is very long-lived projects with constant earnings. In the case of a perpetual project of course, depreciation is zero and profits = net cash flow, and the RR exactly equals the yield. But long lived projects with constant net cash flows are not a common occurrence, and the fact that a method works occasionally is an insufficient recommendation. As has been remarked, even a stopped clock is right twice a day.

The fact is that most projects, after full cognizance has been taken of the start-up period, the incidence of actual tax payments, etc., have rather irregular cash flows especially in the important early years which are so critical to profitability. In these circumstances the RR gives rise to significant errors. This tendency is reinforced in those projects where there are heavy periodic replacement expenditures. Thus as a practical tool the RR is seriously defective.

Where the net cash flows for a firm's projects tend to be fairly regular or change at a fairly constant rate, then of course it would always be possible to make use of graphs such as those set out in Figures 7.1 and 7.2 to convert the returns of the easily calculated RR method into their equivalent discounted yields. In such circumstances the RR method would be useful as a shortcut. But it also happens that the calculation of yield in these circumstances, using the $a_{n|r}$ formula (Table B at the end of the book), is also very simple to perform so that the saving in calculation time is of little practical value.

One final point needs mentioning concerning the practical application of the method, and that is the choice of the appropriate cut-off rate. This problem exists of course with any rate of return method including discounted yield, and has already been discussed at length in Chapters 3 and 4. But there are certain widely held notions regarding this cut-off rate in relation to the RR method which deserve brief mention. Many businessmen hold that to establish a high RR cut-off rate is somehow a dynamic and progressive policy. This view, as Terborgh has pointed out in a notable refutation – [3], can lead to nonsensical results. To set a cut-off rate unduly high merely starves a firm of successful projects because too few projects ever qualify. In particular, it can cause a firm to wait far too long before embarking on certain investments (e.g. replacing old and inefficient equipment).

The optimal time to commence an investment requires the careful weighing of the relevant information (see Chapter 5, Section 1b *ii*) in conjunction with a realistic discounting method of investment appraisal.

One other choice of cut-off rate also needs treating with much caution, the average return the firm is earning on its capital. Quite apart from the difficulties of satisfactorily measuring both profits and capital (see Section 4 and also Chapter 19, Section 1), it should be apparent that the current return on capital can only correspond to a firm's cost of capital by coincidence. Successful firms earn much more than their cost of capital: to restrict them to projects which exceeded their average return would be to deny them the opportunity to invest their shareholders' funds to advantage. Similarly, in the case of unsuccessful firms, to permit them to take on any investment which raised their average return on capital even though it was below their cost of capital, would be a classic example of throwing good money after bad. In short, the policy has nothing to recommend it. All that can be said about it, especially in the case of successful profitable firms, is that it is self defeating. The more successful such firms are, the fewer projects they can find to raise their current average return on capital. This involves them in building up cash surpluses, perhaps in low yielding gilt edged or blue chip securities, which causes the average returns on their capital to fall to a level where more projects can be accepted. But before this happens the firms concerned will have passed up, to the detriment of their shareholders, many profitable investment opportunities.

2. PAYBACK

a. *Definition and Rationale*

The payback method (henceforth referred to as PB) is one of the most popular methods of investment appraisal. Defined as the time period it takes for an investment to generate sufficient *incremental* cash to recover its initial *incremental* capital outlay in full, its popularity is in no small part due to its simplicity of application. Unlike RR, but like the discounting methods, it makes use of the incremental net cash flow concept which has already been shown (see Chapter 2) to be the relevant concept in investment appraisal. This is a point in its favour. The drawback of the method is that it takes cognizance of the net cash flows only up to the point where they equal the initial capital outlay. It ignores any net cash flows arising after that point whether they go on forever, or for only a day. As such it is not, properly speaking, a profitability concept at all. Rather it is a time or liquidity concept. It answers but a single question – how long will it be before the absolute total of the original capital outlay is fully recovered? Where this question is of importance in assessing the attractiveness of a project the method has merit. Where this is not the case, and we will argue that this is typically the circumstance, PB is quite unsatisfactory. It causes assessors to concentrate on unimportant and often irrelevant characteristics of an investment project to the detriment of its significant character-istics. It has been harshly but not unfairly described as the 'fish bait' test, since effectively it concentrates on the recovery of the bait (the capital outlay) paying no attention to the size of the fish (the ultimate profitability) if any.

Before passing on to a more detailed critical appraisal of the method it is useful to consider, simplicity apart, why it is so popular. The reasons would seem to be two. First, it has obvious applications to industries subject to rapid technological changes. If new plants etc. tend to be scrapped long before the end of their technical or physical lives (see Chapter 19, Section 2) because of the advent of superior types of new plants, then for investment in them to be justified, they must promise sufficiently high profits over a very much shorter period, perhaps of only 2–4 years. The use of a well chosen payback period could be of considerable help in these cir-cumstances.

Second, the method, when used with a low payback period (the typical case), is sometimes referred to as a 'dynamic' investment policy – for the same reason as does the use of a high cut-off with the RR method. This is one of the most striking examples of the un-thinking irrationality that so often obscures serious consideration of investment policy. The type of policies referred to almost irresist-ably conjure up impressions of sweeping entrepreneurial initiative, scorning petty low yielding projects, and striving for rapid growth and expansion. While the sentiment behind these methods is com-mendable it is often naïve in conception and histrionic in application. Serious and complex economic problems do not yield before grand-iose and sweeping concepts. They can only be solved on their own terms by patient conceptual and logical effort. A firm restricting itself to investments with, say, a 2 year payback seems to have a progressive policy with high critical investment standards. In fact any such standard, in all but a handful of industries exposed to rapid technological change, is likely to be too high and to cause firms either to miss a wide range of profitable investments altogether or to wait overlong to implement them [3]. Far from being progressive and dynamic, it generally results in blind conservatism.

It seems clear the PB reflects a widely felt practical need to be able to cope with certain types of risk, and also the need to choose the investments most likely to enhance profitability and growth. Both needs can usually be met more adequately by other methods as will become apparent from subsequent discussion.

b. *Usefulness in Assessing Risk and Liquidity*

i. Risk. PB is usually justified as a practical method of assessing investment projects under risk conditions. It is of some importance to establish its usefulness for this purpose. As it is a time concept it would seem *prima facie* to be suited only to the assessment of risks of a time nature. Once a payback period for a project has been calculated the assessor and top management should compare it with their own assessment of the project's likely economic life, and if the latter exceeds the former, the project is acceptable. But essentially this is only a useful procedure if the estimated net cash flows from the project are likely to be unimpaired for a certain period after which they might suddenly cease altogether. This is akin to assessing the risk of a nuclear war, glorious peace for a certain period followed by complete annihilation. Risks of this type exist in business – the risk that a protective tariff will be completely withdrawn after a time, the risk of a competitor suddenly bringing out a new line which captures initially the whole market, the risk of a new unheralded revolutionary process, and the risk in an overseas project of sudden uncompensated expropriation by a nationalistic government. Such risks undoubtedly exist but they by no means constitute a large proportion of the commonly encountered business risks. The usual risk in business is not that a project will go as forecast for a period and then collapse altogether. Rather the risks are that a given project will have lower sales, higher costs, unsuspected teething troubles, etc. etc. – the risks that all will not go as well as planned. For risks of this type PB is evidently unsatisfactory for it is an 'all or nothing' indicator. While it would be possible to calculate a payback period for every likely variation to deal with such risks there seems little point in so doing. If a project has a forecast life of ten years, it is important to establish its profitability in all likely circumstances *over the ten years* rather than calculate a corresponding variety of payback periods for a project which, if worth commencing, is hardly likely to become suddenly so unprofitable that it will be worth abandoning.

This being so, we consider the main use of PB should be as an aid in the assessment of certain risks of a time nature. Even here the method needs adaptation. As it stands it only gives the time by which total capital is recovered.

Consider the data in Table 7.2 of two projects both of which have the same capital cost and payback.

Table 7.2

£000's

		Annual Net Cash Flows					
	Capital Cost	1	2	3	4	5	6
Project D	(100)	25	25	25	25	25	25
Project E	(100)	40	40	10	10	25	25

Both projects have a four year payback but after 2 years, 80% of the capital cost of E has been recovered compared to only 50% in the case of D. Where risks are of a time nature such differences are significant and need highlighting, something which PB as normally applied fails to do.

A further adaptation needed is to make due allowance for the cost of capital. PB purports to give the break-even time on a project but a firm will only have truly broken even when it recovers its initial capital outlay plus 'interest' at its appropriate cost of capital for the period the capital has been outstanding. For if as an alternative to this investment the firm could have undertaken other (marginal) investments yielding a fairly certain return equal to its cost of capital. then in no rational sense can the firm be said to break-even by just recovering its initial outlay.

Both these adaptations are more fully discussed in Chapter 6 on Risk (see Section 5) which shows that PB, suitably modified, is a useful technique for assessing certain risks of a predominantly time nature.

ii. Liquidity. The other need the PB method seems designed to meet is helping in the assessment of a firm's future cash position particularly in the case of firms which are short of funds. Where firms are in such a position it is obviously important to pay special attention to the flow of cash which projects generate, but liquidity is not a virtue in its own right. The aim of firms is to maximize profits not to be liquid as such. Liquidity is only an important consideration in so far as a certain amount of liquidity is essential if a firm is not to be driven bankrupt despite good prospects, and also to preserve sufficient flexibility to enable the firm to take on some unusually attractive investment at short notice. It may ease the problem temporarily but only at the cost of creating a larger problem for the future.

If a firm in fact has a liquidity problem this can better be tackled directly and by other methods. Forward cash budgeting for several years ahead is an obvious measure and one that in any case should be a standard practice for all firms. Other measures to be examined are revising the firm's capital structure, changing its pricing policies, streamlining and rationalizing its existing activities, etc. These approaches are likely to be more efficacious than resorting to a policy of insisting on, say, a 3 year payback in the hope that this of itself will ease the liquidity problem.

Finally, if a firm is genuinely restricted by liquidity to a capital rationing position, appropriate methods for selecting capital projects are available (see Chapter 4, Section 7) without resort to Procrustean methods. Certainly the case of an arbitrary payback requirement in such circumstances will not result in a satisfactory outcome save by unlikely coincidence.

c. *Shortcomings* (See particularly reference 4)

i. Failure to measure profitability. By concentrating on a project's net cash flows only up to the point where they equal initial capital outlay, PB ignores overall profitability. A project can have a quick payback and a zero or very low discounted yield, or a high payback but a high discounted yield, particularly where the net cash flows are increasing with time. A method which neglects these possibilities is deficient and can have but a limited field of application as a method of appraising investment opportunities.

This stated, it is only fair to point out that where projects give rise to fairly constant net cash flows and have fairly constant lives (both conditions are necessary), there is a relationship between the payback period and profitability. In these circumstances the lower the payback period the higher the profitability. Alternatively, even when lives are not constant, as long as the payback period is considered in relation to overall life a rough indication of profitability is provided. But these are the circumstances where the calculation of yield or NPV is also very simple (by using $a_{n|r}$ tables such as Table B at the end of the book).

ii. Lack of versatility. For the same reason that PB is an unsatisfactory method of measuring profitability it is also unsatisfactory as a means of comparing projects. If, for example, the problem is deciding how best to replace an inefficient ferry service across a river by (a) a bridge which might last a century or more, (b) a road tunnel with a similar life, or (c) a modern ferry service the ships of which would require replacement at 20 year intervals, then knowing the paybacks of the three propositions would not permit an intelligent choice.

Similarly when a firm is deciding on the optimal time to commence a project, or the optimal size plant capacity to install where the demand for the plant's end product is increasing, or the optimal time to replace an asset, PB is a totally unreliable guide. No method which so oversimplifies the complexities of investment decisions can hope to answer usefully questions of this sort, and yet answers to such questions are commonly required. For the same reasons the method is defective when comparing internal investment opportunities with external ones, which, as already mentioned (Section 1b above), tend to have very different net cash flow patterns.

Finally, as pointed out in b. *i.* above, PB is lacking in versatility as a method of risk appraisal being suited only to the assessment of certain risks of a strictly time nature.

d. *Some Useful Limited Application*

i. As an approximate measure of profitability (see reference 5). Where a project has a short gestation or pre-production period such that the aggregate capital outlays are concentrated in a short period of say a year or less, and these capital expenditures give rise to a fairly constant annual net cash flow, then the reciprocal of the payoff period will give a useful approximation to discounted yield. Providing a project has a life of ten years or more the approximation is fairly accurate, and for projects of 20 years or more, very accurate. In the case of a perpetual project the reciprocal of the payout period exactly equals discounted yield. For projects with a life of less than ten years, however, the approximation is too inaccurate to be useful.

This relationship is interesting and could be useful in leading executives who have used PB as their sole method of investment appraisal, to discounting methods involving calculating a meaningful return on capital. Apart from this the relationship would seem to have little practical application because, as has already been pointed out in the discussion of the RR, the calculations of yields or net present values is extremely simple in the case of projects having constant annual net cash flows. Further, probably the majority of projects in most firms will fail to have constant annual net cash flows and an estimated life in excess of ten years.

ii. As an initial screening device. One other limited application of PB is as a crude initial screening device. Any project which fails to pay for itself over, say, 10–15 years is unlikely to be a profitable attractive investment save in exceptional circumstances (such as perhaps a bridge across or a tunnel underneath the English Channel, the utilization of which might reasonably be expected to go on increasing with time). This being so there might be some advantage in using PB to save the detailed consideration of any projects which could not pass such a test [1].

Alternatively, on very small projects, where it could be shown that the payback period was very short compared to the useful life of the recommended investment (e.g. a fork lift truck with a 5 year life which paid for itself in six months) the method could be used fairly safely to economize executives' time [4].

e. Summary

PB is seriously deficient as a method of profitability appraisal where its sole uses should be confined to serving as a crude screening device to eliminate obviously unacceptable projects and for sanctioning obviously profitable investments involving small outlays. The assessment of time risks apart (see Chapter 6, Section 5), the PB method can do nothing which methods based on discounting cannot do very much better. Further, there are many commonly encountered investment decisions involving optimization to which it has no applicability whatsoever. Perhaps its worst fault is its very simplicity of application which results in it being widely used in the most inappropriate circumstances. If executives are to perform their capital budgeting responsibilities competently it is essential that they should relegate PB to a minor role and become familiar instead with the common discounting techniques discussed elsewhere in this book. Only then will they be in a position to grapple successfully with the knotty complexities commonly involved in investment appraisals. Indeed, it is the most important single attribute of the discounting methods that they induce as well as make possible a suitably realistic approach to these problems.

3. NECESSITY – POSTPONABILITY

The necessity-postponability method of investment appraisal (henceforth referred to as NP) measures the attractiveness of projects on the basis of urgency. The less postponable a project is the higher the rating it gets, thus 'now or never' investments get the highest ratings of all, and indefinitely postponable projects, the lowest. The intelligent implementation of the method requires that some other method of profitability assessment (PB or RR) is used to establish the basic attractiveness of projects (thus weeding out submarginal investments) but that despite the use of this procedure a firm is faced with more projects than it has funds available. In short it is in a capital rationing situation. Projects are then finally selected on the basis of urgency on the grounds that to implement all the most profitable projects at once might cause the firm to lose the opportunity to invest in the less profitable but still attractive non-recurring investments which offer a higher return than the normal investment projects open to a firm. If some of the most profitable investments can be postponed a year or two, the firm might do better to defer them and accept the non-postponable projects first. In short, the rationale of the method would seem to be that by applying an urgency criterion a firm will choose that selection of projects which will most enhance long run profitability.

The existence of this measure of investment appraisal is evidence of the need for a method to deal with this very real problem. Sympathy with the problem should not, however, extend to this method of dealing with it. The unsatisfactory nature of NP has been convincingly set forth by Dean [1]. As he has pointed out, a firm may be faced with a continuing stream of once and for all opportunities to invest in marginal projects which it could only accept by indefinitely postponing a highly profitable cost saving project. Urgency is not necessarily synonomous with profitability. It is evident that many highly profitable investments are also very urgent. If a railway bridge on an important line is damaged so that traffic is suspended then repair expenditure should be a top priority. But this priority or urgency is the result of the loss of a significant revenue for every day the line is out of use. It is this high profitability of the quick repair expenditure which makes it a 'must' investment.

Where a firm is in a capital rationing situation, the problem of selecting the projects which maximize profitability is often much more complex than is implied in the NP method and reference should be made to the discussion in Chapter 4, Section 7. For a brief discussion of the optimal time to commence a project, reference should be made to Chapter 5, Section 1b *ii*, and to Chapter 19, Section 1 for the optimal time to replace an asset.

A General Comment on the Above Sections

The conclusions reached in this chapter as regards the many short-comings of conventional methods of investment appraisal must be qualified by saying that in many uses the protagonists of the methods are partly aware of these shortcomings. Thus it would be hard for a rational proponent of, say, a two year payback criterion, not to be influenced favourably by the fact that a project which, while having a three year payback, promises large profits in the third and later years of its life. Factors such as this will often be recognized and some attempt made subjectively to take them into account. Thus a low RR might be qualified by the phrase 'nevertheless the project has the advantage of profits concentrated in the early years'.

But clearly, these factors, if they are subjectively recognized as important, should be suitably assessed by using the correct economic method of analysis rather than be allowed for in a vague subjective manner which may vary from person to person. Practical experience of capital budgeting administration points to the great importance of keeping the assessment of projects as free as possible from these 'other' unquantified considerations. Some considerations of this kind will be inevitable, but to allow the assessment of projects to be made needlessly imprecise and vague is both inefficient and conducive to lax administrative control (see Chapter 14).

4. THE ANNUAL RETURN ON CAPITAL EMPLOYED

It is very common to assess the profitability of a business *as a whole*, or a major subdivision of it, with reference to the annual profit return (either gross or net of tax) earned on the capital employed during the year (i.e. the capital employed on the aggregate of past projects). While for a sufficiently large business with a fairly even age distribution of assets depreciated in a conventional manner the measure has a broad validity, its use as a general index of annual profitability for control or assessment purposes is unsatisfactory for a number of reasons.

First, by considering only the aggregate of the projects which go to make up a major subdivision of a business, the method throws little light on the profitability of individual projects. If used as the sole index of management efficiency it prevents the detection of dud investments as these are swallowed up with all the other investments. Further, the method is open to abuse. Where capital employed is measured as either end-year capital employed or an average of beginning and end-year totals, it is often possible deliberately to run down working capital to reduce the effect of one single year's low profits on the profit/capital ratio. By running down working capital below the minimum requirement profits in the following year will necessarily suffer. But by this means a divisional management can show two years of medium profitability instead of one poor year followed by a good year. Other abuses are also possible. The method is thus no substitute for post mortem procedures (see Chapter 14, Section 6) and other efficiency investigations.

Second, the method is unsatisfactory since it concentrates on a single year in isolation. Where projects have a longish gestation period they inevitably temporarily lower the annual return on capital ratio as they swell the amount of capital employed while temporarily making no contribution to profits. But if such projects are sufficiently profitable a firm is better off for investing in them regardless of the temporary decline this causes in the annual return on capital ratio.

Third, and most important of all, the method is unsatisfactory in that significant fluctuations in the return on capital ratio can result which are quite independent of the efficiency with which a firm is run. This arises from the way that assets are conventionally valued and depreciated in firms' accounts. The best way to appreciate this is to consider a very simple example.

Suppose a firm is entirely equity financed and starts off with £1 million of capital which is invested in a 10 year project which produces a constant annual net cash flow after tax of £200,000. Depreciation is on the typical straight line basis of £100,000 a year, leaving net of tax profits also of £100,000 a year. All profits are fully distributed as dividends, but the depreciation provisions are re-invested *end-year* to earn the same return as the original project, that is to give rise to a constant annual net cash flow equal to 20% of the initial capital outlay over the ten subsequent years. Assuming the original project is renewed by fresh injections of equity capital of £1 million every 10 years then the annual return on capital will fluctuate as depicted in Figure 7.3.

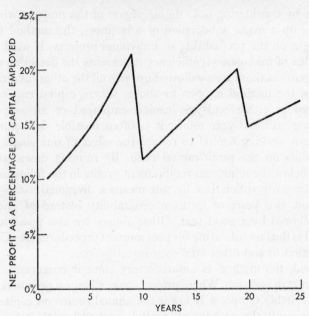

Fig. 7.3. 10 year projects
Initial project costs £1,000,000 – renewed every 10
years by fresh injections of equity capital – all profits
are distributed, all depreciation provisions are rein-
vested to earn an identical return to initial project.
Annual earnings per project constant at 20% of which
half represents profit and half straight line depreciation

If no further equity capital is raised, however, that is the first project
is *not* renewed at the end of its life, the firm continuing to invest
only the depreciation provisions thrown up by all the smaller projects
commenced subsequently, then the annual return on capital will
fluctuate as depicted in Figure 7.4.

These fluctuations exceed 100% and yet it is apparent that the
efficiency of the firm is the same every year in that earnings are both
identical for all projects and constant! These fluctuations derive
from the method of asset valuation[1] and depreciation, and unless
this is corrected, it is impossible to deduce much useful information
from the annual return on capital employed. Meaningful methods
of valuation and depreciation (as set out in Chapter 19, Section 1)

[1] In both diagrams annual capital is taken as the end-year figure *after*
all profits have been paid out as dividends.

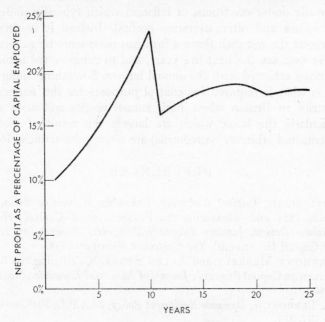

Fig. 7.4. 10 year projects
Same assumptions as in Fig. 7.1 except that there are no
further injections of equity capital

would overcome these difficulties and if applied would result in
the annual return on capital ratio being constant at 15·1% for both
the examples set out in Figures 7.3 and 7.4. This annual return
also equals the discounted yield on all the projects undertaken.
The same valuation and depreciation methods make full allowance
for the distorting effects of taxes such as uneven or irregular capital
allowances.

In fairness it must be pointed out that we have used rather extreme
examples to establish the point that the annual return on capital is
often an unsatisfactory index of annual efficiency and profitability.
In practice, as we have mentioned, where firms are sufficiently
large and have a fairly even age distribution of assets (which causes
the effect of unmeaningful asset valuations to cancel out), their
annual returns on capital, especially if averaged over a long enough
period, will give a broad indication of the discounted average yield
on investments. As conventionally applied, however, this method
is far too crude a tool for purposes of control or measuring efficiency

(especially under conditions of inflation which typically understate asset values and often overstate profits). Instead it is necessary to forecast the net cash flows a firm can reasonably be expected to achieve over say the next five years, and to compare the actual net cash flows achieved with the annual targets. Something along these lines is what is required for control purposes for the nationalized industries in Britain where both annual profits and asset values (particularly the latter which are largely the result of historical accidents and arbitrary writedowns) are often quite artificial [6].

REFERENCES

1. JOEL DEAN, *Capital Budgeting*, Columbia University Press, New York, 1951 and 'Measuring the Productivity of Capital', *Harvard Business Review*, January–February 1954, and 'Profitability Indexes for Capital Investment', *The Controller*, February 1958.
2. ANTHONY MERRETT and ALLEN SYKES, 'Calculating the Rate of Return on Capital Projects', *Journal of Industrial Economics*, November 1960.
3. G. TERBORGH, *Dynamic Equipment Policy*, M.A.P.I., 1949, especially pp.187–213.
4. HERBERT E. DOUGALL, 'Payback as an Aid in Capital Budgeting', *The Controller*, February 1961.
5. MYRON J. GORDON, 'The Payoff Period and the Rate of Profit', *Journal of Business*, October 1955 – reproduced in Ezra Solomon's *The Management of Corporate Capital*, The Free Press of Glencoe, Illinois, 1959.
6. A. J. MERRETT and ALLEN SYKES, 'Financial Control of State Industry', *The Banker*, March–April 1962.

CHAPTER EIGHT

Leasing Decisions and Property Analysis

I

This is the first of four chapters dealing with the applied problems of capital budgeting. Lease or buy and allied problems have been chosen for the first applied chapter because of their relative simplicity, which arises from the fact that the cash flows concerned are usually known with a high degree of certainty, and tend to be constant over long periods. The problem in one form or another is of very frequent occurrence and so will be of interest to the majority of readers. Finally, lease or buy problems will serve to illustrate some of the complex realities of financing and the intimate connection between financing and the assessment of capital projects.

The problem of whether to lease or buy capital assets, and the allied problem of analysing the profitability of projects involving lease commitments, arise frequently for almost all firms. Virtually every firm will be involved in deciding whether to lease or buy its head and branch offices. For companies such as those controlling large chains of stores, oil companies controlling service stations, shipping companies obtaining ships on long term charters, lease or buy decisions and analysing the profitability of investment projects involving these leased assets, are fundamental and recurring problems. While the alternative of purchasing rather than leasing assets can be looked on as a cost saving investment (the costs saved being the lease payments), these leasing problems differ from normal capital projects in their often extensive financial implications. For example, if a company takes the purchasing rather than the leasing alternative it will sometimes be the case, because of the highly marketable character of assets involved, that the company will be able to raise an exceptionally high proportion of debt capital secured on this specific asset. On the other hand, if the leasing alternative is taken, the existence of extensive lease commitments may have serious repercussions on the firm's credit status since the fixed nature of the lease obligations may be held to be a substantial impairment of the security which the firm can offer to other direct lenders.

In sum, the lease or buy problems and the analysis of lease projects frequently involve special financial complications and in many cases the analysis is inseparable from the evaluation of these financial considerations. For simplicity of exposition, however, we shall first consider lease or buy problems in which these financial considerations are relatively unimportant. This will serve to illustrate the basic problems and techniques into which the complication of more realistic financing can be later introduced.

1. THE BASIC ANALYSIS

In what follows we assume that a firm has shown adequate justification for obtaining effective ownership of the asset either by leasing or buying, hence the only question is which of these two forms of effective ownership would be the more economical.

In most lease or buy decisions, it is necessary to compare the period of the lease with the period of likely ownership which is typically longer. If a company buys a new office block, this asset may have an economically useful life of 50 to 60 years but it may be offered a lease on the building for only 20 years. It is not possible to compare such alternatives without reducing them to a common time period. In the case under consideration, there are two possibilities. The company can compare the value of ownership over the same period as the lease. To do this it must estimate the likely value it will place on ownership of the building in 20 years' time (or the replacement cost at that time if this is lower). Alternatively it can consider the likely costs of its necessary office accommodation for the 30–40 years subsequent to the ending of the lease which will normally amount to much the same thing. (See also Chapter 19, Section 1.) In the following example the former alternative is adopted.

Example 1. Lease or buy. Suppose X Ltd. have the choice of buying a small recently erected office block for £200,000 or leasing it for 21 years at an annual rent of £30,000 payable annually in arrears. If they lease it, they will also be responsible for rates, repairs and maintenance. There is no tax allowance for depreciation on the office block (since it is not an industrial building, which alone attracts British tax allowances), but the annual rent would be a deductible expense for tax purposes. Income tax and profits tax combined are assumed to be at the rate of 53·75 % (paid 1·5 years in arrears) and to remain at that figure. In these circumstances, should X Ltd. lease the office block, or buy it outright?

Consider first the question of risk. The acquisition of an office block, whether by way of a lease or outright purchase, has its attendant risks in the same way as any other investment project. The value of its site, its appearance, its suitability in later years compared with more modern buildings then existing, etc., can all affect its economic value. But the point to be borne in mind is that there is no significant difference in the risks associated with owning and with leasing the same building *over the same period* – the resale of both lease and freehold will be fairly closely related over time. It is true that taking the lease alternative the firm avoids risks associated with the residual value of the building at the end of the lease but this is usually of negligible significance where the lease is of, say, more than 15 years' duration. (If the choice was between leasing one building in location A, and buying another in location B, then some differential risk allowance might be called for.)[1]

The firm expects that with normal expansion of its activities over the years the office block will become too small and that if the purchase alternative is taken that it must expect to sell the building at some relatively distant future date. Taking the date of sale as the 21st year (the year in which the proposed lease terminates), the sale price of the building (which has no tax consequences) is estimated at £160,000.

The method of analysing this problem is to regard the payment of £200,000 now to purchase the building as a cost saving investment which saves lease payments of £30,000 p.a. (after tax) for 21 years and gives rise to a final capital gain of £160,000 at the end of the 21st year from the sale of the building. In this example we shall assume that the firm would be unable to raise a significant amount of debt capital on the building and hence that the purchase would have to be entirely financed by equity capital. The cost of this equity capital is set at 7% after tax.

Using present value the method of analysing the purchase alternative as a cost saving investment is as follows. The present value of the after tax cash savings is:

$$(1 - 0 \cdot 5375 v_{1 \cdot 5|7}) a_{21|7} 30,000 + 160,000 v_{21|7}.$$

[1] An important qualification arises because of tax complications. Where, as in Britian, non-industrial buildings do not attract capital allowances a reduction in company tax rate in the future would appreciably increase the net of tax cost of leasing compared to owning. This arises because the tax deduction on the tax deductible lease payments becomes less while no corresponding loss would result in the ownership case.

The bracketed expression on the left is the 'effective net of tax factor' explained and tabulated in the appendix to Chapter 2, and giving the net present cost of an outlay of 1 which attracts relief of tax amounting to $53 \cdot 75\%$ in $1 \cdot 5$ years' time. With $r = 7\%$, the 'effective net of tax factor' is found to be $51 \cdot 47\%$. The present value of the whole expression is then found to be £205,953, and subtracting from this the initial capital outlay of £200,000 the net present value is found to be £5,953. On the net present value criterion, therefore, the purchasing rather than the leasing alternative is marginally preferable.[1]

Analysing the problem on a discounted yield basis and calculating the return offered by this 'cost saving' investment poses no difficulties. It is merely necessary to ascertain the rate of discount which will bring the discounted savings into equality with the initial capital outlay. This rate is clearly somewhat in excess of 7% and trying 8% the net present value is found to be $-£11,502$. Interpolating linearly between 7% and 8% the discounted yield is found to be

$$7 + \frac{5953}{5953 + 11,502} = 7 \cdot 34\%.$$

In this example it was assumed that the asset attracted no capital allowances. Where the assets do attract capital allowances – as in the case of industrial buildings or plant, or in the case of the United States, any commercial building – the capital allowances are included in the savings which would result from taking the purchase alternative. Thus using the present value approach we should have included in the present value of the savings the present value of the relief from taxation afforded by the capital allowances. In this the use of the tabulated present value of the different types of capital allowances (see Appendix to Chapter 2) will be found extremely useful.

Example 2. Sale and leaseback. Suppose a firm owning a large store is considering, as a method of raising capital, selling the store and leasing it back from the purchaser. This type of transaction is very common both in the United States and Britain.

While the firm owned the building (now some 25 years old) it

---

[1] Had the payment been annually in *advance* then the annuity factor, $a_{21|7}$, would have become $(1 + a_{20|7})$. More commonly, lease agreements provide for quarterly payments in advance in which case pedantic accuracy would require the annuity factor to be for 3 monthly periods.

held the ground on which it stood on a lease due to expire 30 years hence. A property company which was interested in the long term development of the site had acquired the land lease some years before. At the end of the term of the land lease, the residual value of the building is expected to be negligible and the property company, which would then become the legal owner, has plans to demolish it. The firm has approached the property company and offered to sell it the store and lease it back for the remaining term of the ground lease – that is, for 30 years.

The property company offers the following terms. Purchase price of the store £1,150,000, a rent of £150,000 for the next 15 years followed by a rent revision. The rent for the last 15 years was to comprise a minimum of £230,000 or a higher figure to be agreed from an independent valuation. The property company has argued for a considerable increase in rent for the last 15 years on the grounds that rents generally could be expected to appreciate. Inflation in rents at the rate of $2\frac{1}{2}\%$ p.a. would justify raising the rent by 45% at the end of 15 years and with the developments planned for areas adjoining the store, a considerably greater increase in rents could be justified. The firm accepts this argument and considers that its own development of the store combined with these other factors would result in an independent valuation giving a rent of £260,000 or so.

Retaining the building in the face of this offer would essentially mean that the firm is forgoing the sale price of £1,150,000 in order to 'save' rents of £150,000 p.a. for 15 years and £260,000 for the following 15 years. Looking at this as *investing* £1,150,000 to make these savings, the return with a tax rate of 53·75% (paid 18 months in arrears) is the r in:

$$1,150,000 = (1 - 0.5375v_{1.5|r})(150,000a_{15|r} + 260,000a_{15|r}v_{15|r}).$$

At $r = 7\%$ the present value is $-£5,060$, and to pedantic accuracy, $r = 6.96\%$. This is the after tax rate of return from this cost saving investment. To put the matter another way the firm could afford to pay up to 6·96% to raise the capital from another source.

The firm is nevertheless rather concerned at the level which the rent might reach in the last 15 years and has bargained for a uniform rent throughout the whole 30 years. The property company was reluctant to concede this and refused to go lower than a flat rent of £176,000 p.a.

Before considering whether either rental alternative is acceptable, a choice must first be made between them. The most revealing way of comparing the alternative of the flat rental with the alternative of the increasing rental after 15 years, is to set out the incremental cash flows from accepting the immediately more expensive project – the flat rental of £176,000. To do this we subtract the cash flows of the first offer (£150,000 for 15 years followed by an estimate of £260,000 for 15 years) from those of the second (the flat £176,000). On this basis the firm is paying £176,000 – £150,000 = £26,000 *more* before tax for the *first* 15 *years* to *save* around £260,000 – £176,000 = £84,000 before tax for the *last* 15 *years*. The return this represents to the additional outlay of £26,000 for 15 years is the *r* in

$$(1 - 0 \cdot 5375 v_{1 \cdot 5|r}) 26,000 a_{15|r} = (1 - 0 \cdot 5375 v_{1 \cdot 5|r}) 84,000 a_{15|r} v_{15|r}.$$

Cancelling out the factors common to both sides and dividing both sides by 84,000 the rate of return is seen to be the *r* in $v_{15|r} = 0 \cdot 3095$. The value of *r* is found to be $8 \cdot 14 \%$ after tax. In other words the firm is effectively earning just over 8% p.a. after tax on each of the fifteen additional annual outlays of £26,000 in the first fifteen years.

The return in total to the flat rental alternative, that is, the return from forgoing £1,150,000 now to save £176,000 for 30 years, is $6 \cdot 75\%$ after tax.

It is possible to look at these returns in two ways, both of which would lead to the same decision. Assume the firm's only other source of capital is by raising more equity, say by retaining more profits than it otherwise would. Its equity cost of capital is assessed at $7\frac{1}{2}\%$. Now we can look upon the return figure found, namely $6 \cdot 75\%$, *as the cost of the capital raised by the leaseback transaction*. This interpretation is entirely valid since, as was shown in Chapter 2, Section 1b, the yield return means that a firm could afford to pay this return on the capital and just break even. On this way of looking at things, the firm would conclude that the £1,150,000 is slightly more cheaply raised by the leaseback than by direct raising of equity. On these grounds it would accept the offer of the leaseback.

The alternative method of looking at the transaction is as a cost saving investment. Thus if the firm is prepared to sacrifice the £1,150,000 it can avoid paying lease payments of £176,000 p.a. for 30 years. Looked at in this way we can say that avoiding the lease-back is a cost saving investment which *earns* $6 \cdot 75\%$. As the firm's cost of capital is $7\frac{1}{2}\%$ the cost saving investment offers too low a return, hence this cost saving investment should be rejected. The firm should prefer to accept the costs of the lease rather than forgo the £1,150,000, that is the firm should accept the leaseback offer. Thus both ways of looking at the project lead to the same conclusion.

We should also note that of the two offers it is in fact the flat rental alternative which should be chosen. For as we have seen, the incremental return from paying this higher rent in the earlier years to avoid the still higher rents of the later years, offers a return of 8%. This is higher than the cost of equity capital: hence this is the alternative which should be accepted. This of course assumes that the 8% return is a worthwhile compensation for the risks involved – namely that the rents in the last fifteen years might be less than the estimated £260,000, or that a fall in the tax rate might occur. Such points evidently deserve careful consideration.

It would, however, be most extraordinary if raising equity capital were the only other alternative source of capital. The mere fact of having a building suitable for such a leaseback transaction will normally mean that the firm has open to it the alternative of obtaining a mortgage secured on this specific asset, and this, in the majority of such transactions, is the alternative with which the leaseback should properly be compared. As this involves some analysis of the special financing possibilities in this type of transaction it will be postponed until the end of the following section which considers the implications of raising debt capital on specific assets.

2. THE EFFECT OF SPECIFIC DEBT FINANCE

In many lease or buy problems the underlying assets are of a highly marketable nature, and if purchased, can be used to raise substantial amounts of debt capital in the form of mortgage debentures secured on these specific assets. Now it is important to consider fully the implications of securing debt capital on specific assets. In many cases this will not mean that the firm can raise significantly more loan capital than could be obtained by the normal methods of raising other forms of debt capital – e.g. floating charge debentures, bank overdrafts, etc. This is simply because the presence on the firm's balance sheet of additional debt secured on specific assets will normally result in a reduction of the debt which the company can raise in these other ways. This follows from the fact that the specific debt will affect the interest times-covered and net worth ratios in the same way as any other form of long term debt, and thus result in less non-specific debt being raised either when existing debt becomes due for renewal or when (in an expanding firm) new debt issues are planned.

In a number of cases, however, it may be possible to secure additional debt capital that would not otherwise have been possible by securing the debt on specific assets. The most common situation will perhaps be that in which debt capital raised as a specific charge on assets is the main source of debt capital to the company. This may arise where the company is unwilling or unable to meet the conditions imposed by a major debenture issue in the form of a debenture trust deed, or simply has inadequate financial standing for such an issue.

There may also be situations in which the firm will follow the policy of securing all its long term debt on specific assets on the grounds that in the nature of its business it can obtain more debt in this way where a fixed charge debenture (i.e., a charge secured on specific assets) confers substantially greater real security to the holders than a floating charge debenture. The floating charge debenture is a weaker form of security in that such debentures normally permit the firm a wider degree of freedom in respect of the mortgaged assets than does a fixed charge. Thus under a floating charge a firm might make heavy losses which caused a running down of the assets possessed by the firm and which would be available to meet the claims of the debenture holders when the floating charge crystallized (i.e. when the firm went into liquidation). The assets could effectively waste away in this case simply because the firm did not make sufficient profits to provide for their replacement as they depreciated. Alternatively, the firm might sell off assets (as it is normally permitted to under a floating charge debenture) to provide the cash required to meet its losses.

Thus where the assets of the firm are suitable for a fixed charge debenture—as in the case of land, buildings, and ships, etc., – the greater security offered by a fixed charge debenture secured on specific assets may genuinely result in the firm's being able to raise more debt capital than would be the case with a floating charge. Its actual quantitative importance would, however, depend in part on the overall credit standing of the firm. The additional risk to the lender on a floating charge as opposed to the fixed charge might be negligible in the case of a large first class company, but considerable in the case of a small less soundly based firm.

The basic question which must always be asked is: how much additional debt can the firm raise because of taking on a particular project? If the firm's only source of debt capital is that which is raised as a specific charge on particular assets, then clearly any project which provides such assets should have attributed to it all the debt capital raised on those assets. Where the amount of capital which the firm can raise is limited not by the assets which it has available to bear specific charges, but by other considerations, e.g. policy, earnings cover, etc., the fact that the firm may, at this juncture, choose to raise debt on assets associated with a specific project does not mean that all this debt can be thought of as attributed to this specific project. For example, suppose the overall policy of the firm is to maintain long term debt at 25% of total assets, but, as a matter of financial policy, to raise it on specific assets. The debt capital attributable to the assets of a specific project would always be 25% of the total assets, regardless of the fact that these assets might be those chosen to bear a specific charge amounting to a considerably larger proportion.

Where a firm can from the nature of its assets raise more debt (or debt at a lower interest cost) by securing the debt on specific assets it should of course do so. Firms with assets suitable for leaseback transactions will nearly always be in a position to consider this alternative. A case of a firm following such a policy will be considered in Example 3 below.

Now the risks involved in lease or buy problems are generally relatively small. The cost savings associated with taking the purchasing route are principally the lease commitments saved, and these are known with certainty for a relatively long period from the specific terms now being offered. Because of this, and because of the relatively large amounts of debt capital which it may be possible to raise on assets which are the subject of lease or buy transactions, it will be found useful to work on the basis of the pure equity return as described in Chapter 4, Section 4. This procedure and some of the financing considerations are illustrated in the following example.

Example 3. Consider the case of a large retailing company, the expanding part of whose assets consists primarily of stocks and properties. The stocks can be efficiently financed primarily by bank overdrafts (and possibly bill finance). In the case of the properties, the greatest amount of debt can be raised through the creation of specific charges on the individual properties. The company is considering acquiring a large centrally located building suited to its needs in an expanding city. It can acquire building and site outright for £2·4m., or it can lease it for 21 years at £300,000 p.a. with the option to renew the lease at £200,000 p.a. for a further 21 years, all lease payments to be made yearly in advance. If the firm purchases the property, it expects to be able to raise a first mortgage loan of £1·5m. for 21 years at 8%, followed by a 21 year loan for £1.0m., also at 8%. At the end of 42 years the property is estimated to be worth a minimum of £1·1m., due mainly to its site value (this is of very minor importance in the computation but is given here primarily for completeness). For simplicity in this example we shall assume that the firm's effective tax rate is 50%, and that taxes are paid with no time lag. If the firm assesses its equity cost of capital at 7% net of tax, which alternative should it choose?

The first step is to ascertain the net of tax payments and receipts. The annual lease payments can be reduced by 50% to £150,000 p.a. for the first period and £100,000 p.a. for the second period. Similarly the net interest burden is 4% of £1·5m. = £60,000 p.a. for the first period, and 4% of £1·0m. = £40,000 p.a. for the second period. It is always of great help in clarifying the analysis of complicated alternatives if their relevant cash flows are set out in tabular form. The relevant cash flows of this example (the capital and revenue receipts and outlays) are set out in Table 8.1 below, from which the *equity* net cash flow (that is the cash flows to and from the equity shareholders which follow as a result of buying rather than leasing) is derived.

Table 8.1

£000's

Years	0	1–20	21	22–41	42
1. *Revenue Flows*					
Net interest Payments	—	−60	−60	−40	−40
Lease Payments Saved	150	150	100	100	—
Net Revenue Flows	150	90	40	60	−40
2. *Capital Flows*					
Purchase and Realization of Asset	−2,400	—	—	—	1,100
Debt Inflow	1,500	—	1,000	—	—
Debt Repayment	—	—	−1,500	—	−1,000
Equity Outlay	−900	—	−500	—	100
3. *Net Cash Flow* (1+2)	−750	90	−460	60	60

The items in the above table are self-explanatory, and for simplicity, as noted above, we have ignored tax delays. It is quite possible to evaluate this project by the net present value method, discounting the equity net cash flows at 7%. This would have resulted in a net present value of £249,000, thus indicating that the net equity outlay of £750,000 would be a profitable investment and that the firm should buy the building rather than lease it. In this case, however, it is also instructive to value the project on a discounted yield basis, and it is to this we now turn.

The first point to notice is the presence of a large negative net cash flow of £460,000 in year 21. This should put the analyst on guard against the possibility of obtaining a meaningless yield (see Chapter 5, Section 2). The first step is to compute a discounted yield in the ordinary way that is to find the solution r to the equation

$$£750,000 = a_{20|r} \, £90,000 - v_{21|r} \, £460,000 + v_{21|r} a_{21|r} \, £60,000$$

For $r = 10\%$ the net present value is £24,000, and for $r = 11\%$ it is $-£31,000$ (both results being given to the nearest £1,000). By linear interpolation the yield is found to be 10·44%, or say $10\frac{1}{2}\%$. Providing this yield is meaningful, it is clear that the project offers a return well in excess of the equity cost of capital, and as little differential risk is involved, the company should accept the project, that is it should purchase the property rather than lease it.

The test of whether the yield is meaningful or not, as set out in Section 2, of Chapter 5, is to find the present value *at the time of the negative cash flow* of *all* the net cash flows subsequent to that negative cash flow at the apparent yield rate, here $10\frac{1}{2}\%$. As long as the present value of the subsequent net cash flows exceed the negative cash flow, the yield has its normal useful meaning. Thus we find the value of $a_{21|10\frac{1}{2}} \, £60,000$, which is £502,000 compared to the negative cash flow of only £460,000, thus indicating the yield has its normal interpretation and can be used with full confidence. In short, the purchasing alternative yields $10\frac{1}{2}\%$ net of tax on the capital outlay involved, and should be accepted.

By examining the solutions at 11% and 10% of the net cash flow expression, it is clear how unimportant are the second 21 years which comprise a mere 10% of the discounted values, making errors of estimation for this period of little consequence.

When a firm is faced with several choices of financing plans for the same project, e.g. loans of differing amounts for differing periods, or perhaps a larger loan repaid in instalments, it must

discriminate between a series of cash flows to select the one in its best
interests. All these cash flows are of course mutually exclusive, and
in such cases, bearing in mind that the risk element is not significant,
it is sometimes simpler to make the selection on the basis of net
present value.

Another fairly common situation will be where a firm has the
opportunity, if it purchases the asset from the present owners rather
than leasing it, to arrange a leaseback arrangement with a third
party as an alternative to a straightforward loan. This last approach
presents no new difficulties for the analysis. It is again simply a
question of setting out, as in Table 8.1, the cash flows resulting
from such an arrangement and calculating their present values for
purposes of comparison with the other alternative – e.g. using some
of the firm's own capital.

Example 2, continued. Comparing the leaseback with direct debt. As
was pointed out at the conclusion to our previous analysis of Example
2, the evaluation of a leaseback should be in terms of other capital
raising alternatives open to the firm, and particularly to the alternative of retaining the asset and attempting to secure specific debt
finance on it. The procedure used in the Example 2 provides the
basic analysis required.

In this case suppose the company has approached an insurance
company to negotiate a mortgage on the store. The insurance company values the store at £1·15m. – the same as the sale price offered
by the property company on the leaseback alternative – but on this
valuation will lend only 60%. It offers to lend the firm the sum of
£700,000 at 7% secured by a first mortgage which, in view of the
declining value of the property, is to be repaid in equal annual
instalments of loan and interest over years 16 to 25. Thus the choice
between the mortgage loan and the leaseback is complex in that the
alternative with the lower annual cost (the mortgage) provides a
smaller capital sum and this for a shorter period.

Again the basic line of approach in discriminating between these
alternatives is to establish what additional cash flows are involved in
taking one alternative rather than the other. In this case we assume
that if the firm takes the leaseback route it will take the flat rental
alternative (of £176,000 for 30 years) on the grounds that its equity
cost of capital is rather less than 8% and that this alternative shows
an incremental return (compared with the other offer) of 8%.

Taking the mortgage alternative it would be able to raise only the

£700,000 offered under the mortgage. Thus it would be obtaining £450,000 more initially by taking the leaseback offer. To decide between these alternatives we must now consider what the firm is required to sacrifice in the future in taking the leaseback rather than the mortgage and thus obtaining the additional £450,000. The cash flows under the two alternatives are set out in Table 8.2.

Table 8.2

Years	0	1–15	16–25	26–30
Leaseback		£000's		
1. Capital	1,150	0	0	0
2. Lease payments		−176t	−176t	−176t
Mortgage				
3. Capital	700	0	−70	0
4. Interest 7%		−49t	−29·7t*	0
5. Net cash Flows = 1+2−3−4	450	−127t	−(146·3t−70)	−176t

[1] (The annual interest payment for each year is fixed at £29,700, that is a constant sum of £99,700 is paid each year to redeem the loan of which £70,000 is deemed to be loan repayment and £29,700 is deemed to be interest. This latter sum is simply one tenth of the total interest that would be paid over ten years to redeem a £700,000 loan on normal mortgage loan repayment terms.)

In this table the t against the tax deductible amounts indicates that they have to be taken after tax: thus 176,000t is 176,000 less tax (with appropriate time delay in the actual discounting procedure). This device will often be found useful in setting out complex patterns of cash flows where it is required, at a later stage to take realistic account of the amount of and delays in tax payments.

Subtracting lines 3 and 4 from 1 and 2, we ascertain the additional cash flows the firm will be involved in over the years in order to obtain the *additional* £450,000, that is the cost of raising this extra £450,000 by accepting the leaseback. For each of the first fifteen years it is simply the difference between the lease payment of £176,000 t and the mortgage interest payment of £49,000 t – a net outflow of £127,000 t. Over each of the subsequent ten years the extra cost is £176,000 t less the loan repayments of £70,000 and the reduced interest payments of £29,700 t. In the final five years the extra cost of the leaseback is the whole of the lease payments of £176,000 t.

To compute the discounted yield on the net cash flows of line 5 of Table 8.2, we endeavour to find the value of r in the equation

$$£450,000 = £127,000\, t\, a_{15|r} + a_{10|r}\, (£146,300\, t - £70,000)\, v_{15|r}$$
$$+ a_{5|r}\, £176,000t\, v_{25|r}$$

If t is taken as $1 - 0.5375\, v_{1.5|r}$, that is the present value of £1 which affords relief from taxation at the rate of 53·75% one and a half years later, the solution to this equation is found to be 14·4%. In other words, the cost of raising the extra £450,000 capital by accepting the leaseback has a net of tax cost of 14·4%. As this markedly exceeds the firm's net of tax cost of equity capital of $7\frac{1}{2}\%$, the leaseback alternative should be rejected in favour of the mortgage loan.[1]

The preceding examples have all related to property and it should be fairly clear that precisely the same type of analysis would be required from a property company's standpoint – the cost saving investments examined above are simply revenue earning examples looked at from their standpoint.

Finally, we should perhaps note that in these problems where specific debt finance is so important, the weighted average cost of capital approach (working on the total cash flows to debt and equity) is completely inapplicable. The relevant cash flows are by their very nature the pure equity cash flows.

3. THE EFFECT OF INFLATION

A general discussion of inflation was given in Section 7 of Chapter 6. In this section we briefly recapitulate and touch on some of the points which specifically relate to the problems discussed in this chapter. In evaluating contractual economic obligations fixed in money terms some attention must always be given to the effect on them of inflation. This is as true of leases as of loans, both of which must be evaluated in choosing between leasing and buying. The general effect of inflation is, of course, to reduce the real burden of future money payments which tends to increase the relative attractiveness of the leasing alternative. This arises because all the outlays connected with leasing are commonly fixed in money terms. If inflation is ever conceded to be endemic in western society, this situation will almost

---

[1] Had the mortgage loan to be repaid in a lump sum, say at the end of the twentieth year, the equation to be solved would have had to be solved by means of the extended yield method – see Chapter 5, Section 2 – or else by the net present value method.

certainly change, and we can expect lease payments either to be geared to some specific price index or set at a level which offsets the effect of inflation. At the present time the majority of lessors expect some inflation and take this into account when setting the level of their lease payments. Whenever lease payments are fixed in money terms, however, it is important to evaluate the impact on them of price inflation.

When a series of future payments is being converted to their present value equivalent, they are discounted at the appropriate marginal cost of capital. This is straightforward when money values are constant, thus the present value of sum A due in n years $= A/(1+r)^n$, where r is the marginal cost of capital. But when money values are not fixed, then discounting A at the rate r will not indicate the present value equivalent of A received in n years' time. A must be modified by the price level change that is expected to occur over the n years. Suppose prices are expected to rise at a rate d every year for the n years, then to translate A into money units of the same worth as present units, A must be reduced by the factor $(1+d)^n$. (If prices were expected to decrease by d per year then A would have to be multiplied by this factor). This sum can then be discounted at the rate r to reduce it to its present value equivalent. Thus the present value of a fixed money sum, A due in n years, when the marginal cost of capital is r^1, and the expected rate of inflation is d, is simply $A/[(1+r)^n(1+d)^n]$. This is equivalent to $A/[(1+r)(1+d)]^n$. In other words the rate of inflation can be *multiplied* by the marginal cost of capital, and their product can be used to discount future payments. Suppose the marginal cost of capital is 4% and a 3% cumulative rate of inflation is expected. The appropriate discount factor is $(1 \cdot 04 \times 1 \cdot 03) - 1 = 0 \cdot 0712$. When both factors are low, very nearly the same result is achieved by *adding* the rate of inflation to the marginal cost of capital, i.e. $\cdot 04 + \cdot 03 = \cdot 07$. While adding is not strictly correct, the result is so little different from multiplying that it can be used with confidence for low values r and d, especially when it is remembered that neither r nor d can ever be estimated with absolute precision. Having established the procedure for evaluating the present worth of future sums when price level changes are expected, let us consider some examples.

[1] r is assumed to be fixed in real terms on the basis that equity shareholders expect their income to be maintained in real terms during an inflation – see Chapter 6, Section 7 and Chapter 3, Section 4.

Example 4. Suppose a firm is considering leasing a building for 21 years at a cost of £200,000 p.a. payable in advance. The alternative is to buy it outright now for £1,300,000. At the end of 21 years it is assumed to be worth £1,000,000. Purchase of the building gives rise to no capital allowances. Tax is at the rate of 50% and for the sake of simplicity we shall ignore the effect of any tax delays. Running costs are assumed to be the same for either alternative. Assume first that if the building is purchased it will be financed entirely by equity capital, and that the firm's cost of capital is 7% net of tax. In the absence of inflation the choice between these alternatives is quite straightforward.

The cost of the lease is simply the present value of a series of 21 annual payments in advance of a net £100,000 each (£200,000 less the tax saving of 50%) which equals $£100,000 + a_{20|7}£100,000$ = £1,159,401. The cost of purchasing is equivalent to an outlay of £1,300,000 less the residual value of £1,000,000 some 21 years hence, which equals $£1,300,000 - v_{21|7}£1,000,000 = £1,058,487$. From a comparison of the two present value equivalents, purchasing is clearly the cheaper alternative.

Suppose now, however, that general inflation at the rate of 3% a year is expected over the 21 year period, how will this affect the calculation? Assuming the residual value of the building keeps in step with general inflation the net cost of purchasing the building is unaffected, i.e. the residual value remains fixed in real terms, hence the purchasing calculation is unaffected. The lease payments, however, are fixed in money terms and so the effect of inflation is to reduce their burden. The correct discount rate to use is $(1 \cdot 07 \times 1 \cdot 03) - 1 \cdot 0$ = 10·21%. This is so close to 10·0% that we will make use of the latter figure as sufficiently accurate for our purpose. (This implies a 2·8% inflation.) The present value of the lease payments under inflation is then $£100,000 + a_{20|10}£100,000 = £951,356$. This swings the balance firmly in favour of leasing as it is substantially less than the £1,058,487 equivalent cost of purchasing.

Instead of calculating whether at a given expected rate of inflation leasing is cheaper than purchasing, it is sometimes more useful to calculate the critical or break-even rate of inflation. This is a straightforward task. We merely need to solve for *b* in equation

$$C = L(1 + a_{n-1|b}) \tag{8.1}$$

where C = the net equivalent purchase price, and L the effective net of tax lease payment, assuming payments yearly in advance, and then the break-even rate of inflation d, is given by $d = [(1+b)/(1+r)]$ -1, where r is, of course, the cost of capital.

Substituting the facts in our example

$$\pounds 1,058,487 = \pounds 100,000 + a_{20|b}\pounds 100,000,$$

therefore $\qquad a_{20|b} = 9 \cdot 58487.$

By interpolation $b = 8 \cdot 3\%$.

As $\qquad\qquad d = \dfrac{(1+b)}{(1+r)} - 1$

therefore $\qquad\qquad d = \dfrac{1 \cdot 083}{1 \cdot 07} - 1 = 1\frac{1}{4}\%$ approximately.

Thus for any expected rate of annual inflation of up to $1\frac{1}{4}\%$, purchasing is cheaper than leasing. Above $1\frac{1}{4}\%$, leasing is the cheaper alternative.[1]

Consider now the complication of debt capital being available to finance part of the purchase price if this alternative should be chosen. In the interests of exposition we shall assume the annual lease payment to be reduced to $\pounds 135,000$ but all the other facts to be unchanged. Suppose that 50% of the cost of the building can be raised by way of a loan at 6% repayable at the end of 21 years. Assuming there is no inflation the calculation would be as follows.

If the building is purchased, the equity cash flow would consist of a $\pounds 650,000$ outlay, plus the raising of a $\pounds 650,000$ loan, with annual interest at 3% net ($\pounds 19,500$) for 21 years, followed by a repayment of the loan. At the end of the 21 years the building would still be worth $\pounds 1,000,000$. This is equivalent to

$$\pounds 650,000 + a_{21|7}\pounds 19,500 + v_{21|7}\pounds 650,000 - v_{21|7}\pounds 1,000,000$$
$$= \pounds 650,000 + \pounds 211,292 + \pounds 156,983 - \pounds 241,513$$
$$= \pounds 776,762.$$

(This, as would be expected, is significantly less – some 27% – than the effective purchasing cost for the 100% equity case.)

The leasing alternative present cost equivalent is simply

---

[1] This solution has been worked out on the assumption that whatever the expected rate of inflation it would be constant every year. Where this is not expected, the solution should be quite apparent even though the arithmetic is slightly more complicated.

s

£67,500 + $a_{20|7}$£67,500 = £782,595. Thus with no inflation, purchasing is slightly cheaper than leasing, although there is very little in it.

Let us now introduce the complication of a general inflation of approximately 3% per annum (2·8% to be exact), and recalculate the alternatives accordingly.

The purchasing alternative will now cost

$$£650,000 + a_{21|10}£19,500 + v_{21|10}£650,000 - v_{21|7}£1,000,000$$

$$= £650,000 + £168,650 + £87,835 - £241,513 = £664,972.$$

The leasing alternative is also reduced, to

$$£67,500 + a_{20|10}£67,500 = £642,165.$$

Thus the effect of inflation has been to swing the choice very slightly in favour of leasing.

In short, when substantial debt finance is involved in the purchasing alternative, there is a gain from inflation which tends to affect the marked gain from leasing under an inflation. Compared to an asset which is completely or mainly financed by equity, inflation does not cause nearly so marked a swing in favour of leasing. The exact effect of inflation in any given case is a matter of fact, but the higher the proportion of available loan finance solely attributable to the asset providing the security, the less the relative attractions of leasing during an inflation.

One final point. The relative attractions of leasing would be even less pronounced if inflation permits a firm periodically to revalue its assets such that it could raise additional debt capital as a result of such revaluations. This effect too is a matter of fact to be specifically evaluated when debt raising potential and the degree of inflation can be forecast with reasonable accuracy.

4. SOME GENERAL CONSIDERATIONS REGARDING LEASE PROJECTS

There are general grounds for supposing that it will rarely be in the best interests of companies which do not have an exceptionally high marginal cost of capital to undertake lease commitments on plant and machinery, or indeed on any assets which are subject to normal commercial risks of obsolescence or vagaries of profitability in particular industries. It would hardly be necessary to demonstrate this point in detail but for the general misconceptions that have arisen from one-sided presentation of the facts by firms primarily interested in leasing out their equipment.

If the equipment in question is subject to normal commercial risks then it will not normally be possible for the lessor company to raise capital more cheaply than the lessee company. The only exception to this would be where the lessee company operated in an exceptionally risky industry, had a poor profit record, or was so small that it could not raise capital on terms as favourable as the lessor company. In the case of marketable property the situation is very different and scope will often exist for a mutually advantageous leasing transaction. For in this case it will often be possible for the company leasing out the building to secure a higher proportion of debt capital to finance the building than could the normal commercial firm (see Section 2 above). It is thus possible for the leasing company to accept a rental which makes leasing attractive to the lessee.

In Britain at least, no net gains arise from tax reliefs on hiring transactions. The lease payments are an allowable expense against tax for the lessee, but taxable income in the hands of the lessor. As both parties will normally be taxed at the same rate no arrangement is possible whereby the two parties can benefit at the tax authorities' expense. It is true that the capital allowances accruing to the lessor company in some degree offset the fact that the income received as lease payments is taxed. It will be found, however, on any numerical examination of the case, that the charge to the company hiring the asset must be at least as high as the annual 'cost' (depreciation plus required profit) net of all tax reliefs that the company would be involved in by actually purchasing the asset. This of course assumes that both the lessor and lessee company require the same profit margin and that neither is able to buy (or sell) the assets concerned on especially favourable terms. Where such conditions do not obtain, there can be a real advantage to both parties in leasing. A good example of this arises in the motor trade where many dealers who have an agency with a large manufacturer also hire out cars on favourable terms to individuals and companies. They obtain their cars about 15% cheaper than the public, and are protected in this by resale price maintenance. Also at the end of a year or two of hiring out, such dealers are well placed to sell the second-hand cars at the most favourable prices. In these circumstances a gain to lessor and lessee alike is possible.

It is sometimes argued that the leasing of assets obviates losses from obsolescence. This is true in the obvious sense that an insurance policy will obviate specific risks. The implied conclusion that this is a net advantage evidently depends on the 'premium' that has to be paid for this 'insurance'. Only if the lessor company has some special advantage of foresight will it be able to accept the risks of obsolescence at a lower cost than that which would be incurred by the lessee. In general it may be supposed that since the assets in question will be a much larger proportion of the capital employed of the lessor company, the latter will require a *higher* risk premium per asset for obsolescence than will companies which have only limited amount of their capital employed in these assets for their normal business purposes.

We conclude, therefore, that insofar as leasing is more profitable than purchase for some firms it will be due to the lease payments being reduced by some specific advantage of cheaper finance, lower profitability requirements or economies of scale or skill which are open to the lessor company.

II

5. FINANCIAL IMPLICATIONS OF LEASE PROJECTS

The examples so far considered were primarily designed to illustrate the logic of lease or buy problems ignoring the impact of lease commitments on a firm's credit status; this complication must now be taken into account. Discussion of the effect of lease commitments on the financial status of companies is unfortunately complicated by the absence, at the time of writing, of any uniform treatment of lease commitments by the security analysts of the main institutional lenders.

Substantial differences in attitude to lease commitments would appear to exist between the institutional lenders in the United States and those in Britain, and this difference in attitude is reflected in the fact that lease commitments in the United States must be disclosed in the form of a summary statement of the commitments to the Securities Exchange Commissions, available for public inspection. Some American companies reveal summary details of their lease commitments as a matter of course in their annual reports and accounts. In Britain, however, companies are at present under no general legal obligation to reveal their lease commitments and generally do not do so.[1]

In the United States security analysts tend to regard lease commitments as effectively the same as debt finance, and consider that a firm taking a lease is in practice engaged in the joint operation of purchasing the asset *and* raising capital to pay for it. For example, suppose a firm is offered the choice of either purchasing an asset which has a life of 20 years (and a negligible value thereafter) for £100,000 or alternatively leasing the asset for 20 years at £8,718 p.a. payable end-year. If the firm takes the leasing alternative it should be evident that the firm would then be in much the same position as if it had *bought* the asset for cash and *simultaneously* raised capital to obtain the requisite cash, the capital raised and interest (at 6%) being repaid in annual instalments equal to the annual lease payments. In both cases it would obtain possession of the asset and commit itself to payments of £8,718 per annum end-year for 20 years. Thus we can in some measure look on leases as a simultaneous purchasing and capital raising operation. The main difference is in the effect of such operations on the balance sheet. Where the firm actually raised capital and simultaneously purchased the assets, both assets and debt capital would appear in the firm's balance sheet. If the leasing alternative were taken, however, neither assets nor debt would be shown on the balance sheet despite the basic similarity of the transactions involved in the two cases.

Consideration of the financial ratios (described in Section 1, Chapter 4) of debt to net tangible assets and the number of times that interest charges are covered by earnings, will normally limit the company's ability to raise debt capital to about 25% or so of total capital employed, depending on the stability and prospects of the individual company and the type of industry. Providing that lease commitments are neither revealed nor treated by potential lenders to the company as a form of debt, it will be apparent that leasing offers a means of increasing the 'debt' of companies beyond what would normally be possible by means of direct raising of debt capital. By leasing assets it may therefore be possible (depending on the terms on which this debt capital is raised) for a firm to gear its return to its equity shareholders in the same way as if the additional assets were purchased by it with capital borrowed for the specific purpose. By

[1] In view of the Jenkins Committee Report which has recommended the disclosure of long term lease and rent payments, this situation may soon change.

leasing it would obtain for its equity shareholders, without requiring further capital from them, the surplus which those assets earn over and above the 'interest' and capital repayments (i.e. the lease obligations) assumed to finance them. It is clear that many firms under existing conditions in Britain can effectively raise more 'debt' capital via leasing than could be obtained by direct borrowing. The extent to which this is possible (or desirable) must vary from firm to firm. So, too, does the extent to which firms are already utilizing their direct borrowing powers and the terms on which this 'debt' capital is obtained. Where firms are already highly geared it is to be expected that even in Britain the addition of extensive further lease commitments will appreciably impair the firm's credit standing if the extent of their commitments becomes known to the institutional lenders. The extent to which the firm can obtain part of its capital through indirect borrowing on leases without impairing its direct borrowing powers will probably be found to be a critical factor in a number of lease or buy problems.

We consider the present treatment of lease commitments in Britain to be an undesirable anomaly for the following reasons. The similarity between lease commitments and debt secured on specific assets has been commented on above, but realistic assessment of the importance of lease commitments turns on a direct assessment of their economic and legal significance to other direct lenders to a company. Consider first the relevance of lease obligations to the yardstick used in determining the maximum amount of long term indebtedness open to a company, the ratio of long term debt to net tangible assets (see Chapter 4, Section 1). This ratio is meant to indicate the ostensible value of the assets available to meet the claims of the long term lenders in the event of liquidation. But this ratio specifically excludes lease commitments. The value of the lease is not included as part of the net tangible assets, neither are the capitalized lease commitments included in the long term loans. It might be thought that as the amounts to be added to each side of the ratio are the same, excluding them has no effect. This view neglects the proportional effect. Consider an example. Suppose the net tangible assets of a company amount to £250,000 and that the maximum debt it is practical to raise is 40%, or £100,000. If the company then leases an asset worth say £100,000, this is excluded from the ratio. Had it been included, the effect would have been to add £100,000 to both long term loans and net tangible assets in such a way that the ratio became £200,000 to £350,000, the loans now representing 58% of net tangible assets compared to the previous 40%. Had the company tried to raise a direct loan and purchase the building, and if the net tangible assets ratio had been enforced, it would have been able to raise only £40,000 compared to the £100,000 raised indirectly via the lease commitment. Thus the net tangible asset ratio as normally computed hides the true position. (The same is, of course, true for the net worth ratio.)

It might be argued that this is of little moment in that the lease commitment is fully covered by the value of the leased asset. If such assets can always be realized to cover fully the liability imposed by the lease, this would be true, and leased assets are often of an appreciably more marketable character (e.g. buildings) than normal business assets. Where, however, the leased asset cannot be realized to cover the full lease liabilities, the position of other long term lenders can be affected adversely. In the event of a company's liquidation the lessor would normally be entitled to retake possession of the leased asset and sue for any balance of profit lost through the default of the lessee company. (The balance of profit would probably be the difference between the capitalized value of the lease payments due from the lessee and the capitalized value of the lease payments to be obtained from re-leasing the asset elsewhere for the remaining period of the old lease.) In this respect the lessor is in much the same position as lenders who have advanced debt on the security of specific assets. Moreover, under British law, the lessor is entitled to surrender the actual lease and rank as a secured creditor to the full extent of any loss suffered. (The loss here suffered is the capitalized value of *all* future lease payments and is evidently equivalent to a debt of the same amount.) In short, where lease commitments exist the net tangible asset ratio fails to reveal the contingent creditors with claims to a firm's assets.

The ratio of interest times covered, that is the number of times current profit could pay the outstanding interest burden, is similarly deficient where lease commitments exist and such commitments are left out. If the firm simultaneously purchased the asset and raised debt capital of the same amount (repayable in equal annual instalments of interest and capital over the life of the asset) profits would be reduced by (a) the depreciation charge and (b) by the interest charge on the debt. Thus in the times covered ratio the numerator (profits before interest) would be reduced and the denominator (interest charges) increased. If the asset were leased for an annual rental exactly equal to (a) plus (b), then in the times covered ratio profit before interest would be reduced by this sum while the denominator (interest charges) would remain unchanged. It is clear, therefore, that the times covered ratio would change by a much smaller amount in the lease than in the purchase case. Given that the two alternatives are assumed to be effectively identical, this result is clearly anomalous and the times covered ratio needs to be adjusted to include the interest element of the lease so that the times covered ratio is the same in both cases.

In terms of the extent to which they impair the firm's financial strength, lease commitments generally constitute as serious a threat to the security of those lending to the firm as direct debt financing of the same assets. In both cases the same sum must be amortized, but in the leasing alternative the amortization is effectively fixed and inescapable each year in the form of a charge on profits *prior* to any loan interest, or of course loan redemption. Also, the lease payment is likely to be higher than the equivalent annual interest and sinking fund charge in the case of the 100% loan. The lease payment must cover the lessor's administrative charges and profit margin – which must include a return to his equity capital.

Given all these considerations, it is entirely justifiable that lease commitments should be regarded as at least as substantial an impairment of the security of those providing long term debt directly to the company as the capitalized value of such commitments discounted at the company's normal borrowing rate. Where investment analysts do so regard lease commitments as the equivalent of long term debt, the following method of analysis is suggested.

The analysis should be conducted in the terms of the equity cash flows associated with the project. In the case of the lease or buy problem considered in Example 2 above, the firm should consider what amount (if any) of debt capital it will, either as a matter of necessity or policy, be forced to forgo as a result of the lease obligations it is now being asked to undertake. This debt capital must be regarded as a form of *negative* gearing. Suppose, for example, the firm decided in Example 2 above, that if it undertook the lease commitment it would need, as a matter of financial policy in order to maintain its financial standing, to reduce its normal borrowing by £300,000 throughout the period of the lease. This sum must be considered an equity cash flow which would be *saved* by going the purchase route. Thus in the example being considered, a net outlay of £750,000 given in line 3 of Table 8.1 would be £750,000 − £300,000 = £450,000. Offsetting this additional disadvantage of the leasing route, however, would be the fact that, if the firm had reduced its borrowing by £300,000, it would be paying less interest each year that its borrowing was so reduced, hence the equity cash flows after year 0 would be increased by the interest saving. At the end of the period of the lease the firm could restore its borrowing to the level which would have existed if it had not taken the lease commitment. Thus in this example, there would be an *in*-flow to the equity shareholders of £300,000 in year 42.

The return on buying rather than leasing, calculated on these net equity cash flows would reflect the adverse financial effects of the lease payments and, hence, would be higher than the return calculated ignoring this adverse financial implication. The proposed procedure can, of course, be adapted to any given assessment of the adverse effect that the lease commitment might have on a firm's borrowing. The firm might consider that in view of its heavy lease commitments it should as a matter of course always relate its planned borrowing to the existing burden of lease commitments. This policy reduction in borrowing could evidently be assessed by the method just outlined.

6. RETURN ON LEASE PROJECTS

So far we have considered how to choose between leasing and buying the same asset assuming effective ownership of the asset by one of these two methods is clearly justified. Where this justification is in doubt, and leasing has been shown to be the better (or indeed the *only* alternative), a method is required to establish whether even leasing the asset is, of itself, viable compared with not undertaking effective ownership at all. In this case, if the return (in net revenue earned by the assets) is calculated in the normal way on the small amount of actual capital which the firm puts up – say the interior fittings for a leased retail outlet – the return on this small amount of capital will generally seem much higher than if the firm purchased *all* the assets outright and calculated the return on the *total* capital involved. Indeed in many cases where the actual capital put up by the firm is negligible the return will be infinitely high. This creates a return figure which it is difficult to assess and may also be spuriously high in that it ignores the effect of the lease on the firms credit standing and hence debt raising potential. Where the leases do appreciably impair the credit of the company and hence its effective debt raising capacity the burden of the lease commitments must be adequately taken into account.

A fairly simple and flexible method for achieving this is illustrated in the following example. The method of analysis is here based on the evident similarity between leasing an asset and buying an asset which involves the firm accepting – as a part of the deal – a loan equal to the value of the asset and involving debt repayments and interest equal to that of the lease payments.

Example 5. The main data is as set out in Table 8.3. A firm is considering undertaking a project by leasing all the required assets for a lease payment of £100,000 per year for 21 years. The assets could be purchased for £800,000 and have a life of 21 years with an insignificant residual value. Essentially we can regard this as a normal project tied to a loan of £800,000 which is being repaid in the form of the £100,000 p.a. lease payments – line (a) of the table. In addition to these actual lease payments, however, the firm also has to forgo the capital allowances (for simplicity of illustration straight line tax depreciation is assumed over 21 years) by going the leasing route rather than purchasing, hence this lost tax saving must be added to the lease payment to get the total annual cost of this 'loan'. This cost is given in line (b).

Table 8.3

Years		0	1–21
1. *Capital Cost of Asset*		−800,000	
2. *Net Revenue* (excluding lease payments)			$191,400\,(1-t)$
3. *Financing Charge*			
(*a*) Lease Payments	$100,000\,(1-t)$		
(*b*) Capital Allowances	$38,000\,t$		
Less			
(*c*) Loan Repayment	38,000		
(*d*) Interest	$30,000\,(1-t)$		
			$32,000\,(1-t)$
4. N.C.F.		−800,000	$159,400\,(1-t)$

t = tax rate   Yield (with $t = 50\%$) is 8%

The lease essentially represents a form of off-balance sheet financing and the next question to be posed is: how much is the firm prepared to pay – given its other financing opportunities – for off-balance sheet financing of £800,000? Suppose in fact because of its being off-balance sheet financing that the firm is prepared to pay rather more than its normal rate of interest on loan funds, say, 6% before tax. A 6% loan repayable over the period would cost £68,000 per annum. For simplicity and since the degree of error is of negligible importance, this alternative form of finance can be assumed to be repayable in equal annual instalments of interest and debt repayment over the same period as the lease, namely debt repayments of £38,000 and the interest of £30,000 after tax. These are given as lines (c) and (d) of the table.

The difference between the cost of the lease 'loan' finance and the cost of the comparable finance via the alternative loan is (a) plus (b) less (c) and (d) which is equal to the £32,000 $(1-t)$ of line 3. This is the amount by which the cost of financing via the lease is higher than the cost of alternative borrowing and hence this amount is a debit to the project and negative in sign.

The net revenue (*before lease payments* and taxes) is £191,400, and the after tax value of the sum is indicated by £191,400 $(1-t)$ in line 1 of the table.

The net cash flows of the projects are then as given in line 4 = 1+2+3.

The yield is now calculated on these cash flows in the normal way and compared with the normal cut-off rate for total capital. In the present example with a 50% tax rate paid concurrently the yield is found to be 8%.

From the layout of the figures in Table 8.3 it is seen that the calculation can be reduced to a simple rule: (1) compute the normal cash flows as for the purchase case including capital allowances but excluding the lease rental, (2) add into the cash flows the difference between the lease rental and the equivalent borrowing, (3) compute yield return in the normal way.

In its most common application the method presents no difficulties. Some extension of the analysis is sometimes required, however, to cover the case in which the assets are leased for substantially less than their normal life. In this case the firm is obtaining by the lease, not the whole asset, but a limited interest in the property of correspondingly lower value. If the appropriate alternative method of acquiring such an interest in the property would be to purchase a similar asset with the same life span as the lease, the analysis should be as in Example 5, but in terms of purchasing this particular asset with the same life span as the lease. For most practical purposes, however, this will give the same return as basing the calculation on the whole cost of a new asset and inserting the residual value of the asset as a final cash inflow. The reason for this is not hard to see:

the value of the lease interest will tend to be the cost of the asset now, less its residual value at the end of the lease discounted at the market cost of capital. As long as the return on the project is around this cost of capital or the residual value is a relatively small factor, basing the analysis on the value of the lease interest will amount, in present value, to much the same thing as basing it on the initial cost of the whole asset and inserting the residual value of the asset as a capital inflow at the end of the lease term.

The method has the difficulty of estimating the value of the assets being leased (i.e., the cost to the lessee of purchasing assets with the same financial characteristics). It will be found however that the proposed method of analysis is relatively insensitive to errors in this estimated value since, say, under-estimation of the value of the asset will result in an offsetting higher 'financing charge'.

The proposed method of analysis is extremely flexible in that it can be used to cover the wide range of situations where the effect of lease obligations on the firm's balance sheet is not as great an impediment as actual debt of the same amount. This can be allowed for by raising the rate of 'interest' which (in view of this fact) the firm is prepared to pay for off-balance sheet finance in the form of lease commitments.

REFERENCES

1. FRANK K. GRIESINGER, 'Pros and Cons of Leasing Equipment', *Harvard Business Review*, March–April 1955.
2. DONALD R. GANT, 'Illusion in Lease Financing', *Harvard Business Review*, March–April 1959.
3. RICHARD F. VANCIL and ROBERT N. ANTHONY, 'The Financial Community Looks at Leasing', *Harvard Business Review*, November–December 1959.
4. RICHARD F. VANCIL, 'Lease or Borrow – New Method of Analysis', *Harvard Business Review*, September–October 1961.
5. RICHARD F. VANCIL, 'Lease or Borrow – Steps in Negotiation', *Harvard Business Review*, November–December 1961.
6. W. A. LEACH and E. G. WENHAM, *Investments in Land and Property*, Sweet and Maxwell, London, 1961.

CHAPTER NINE
The Timing and Scale of Expansion

I

1. DEFINING THE PROBLEM

The problem of deciding when to undertake a major expansion of the production or marketing facilities, or even of office space, ranks as one of the major capital budgeting decisions. Its significance and importance derive from the relative magnitude of the capital outlays required and the often serious policy implications involved.

The problem may arise in the following form. A firm producing, say, soft drinks, is approaching the limit of capacity in its existing plant. As sales expand, especially in the more distant markets, consideration must be given to establishing a new plant nearer to these distant markets. This may be primarily to reduce transport costs, but technological advances in plant may also be an important factor. The alternative is to expand production at the existing plant either by installing increased capacity or resorting to increased shift work and overtime. Having chosen the best locality in which to establish the new plant should it be decided on, the firm must establish whether or not such a plant is a better alternative to expanding production at the existing site. If it is found to be economically superior, the next problem is to establish the best possible time to set up the new plant. These two problems are generally interdependent – the new plant is often economically advantageous, but not before some specific future date.

It should be clear that the same general problem arises if the expanding firm is, say, a purely marketing firm purchasing products for resale and is now considering going into production for itself. This is the common problem of 'make or buy'. In this case, instead of an existing plant it is faced with suppliers prepared to supply at given prices. Here part of the inquiry should be to establish how high prices of existing suppliers must be before 'own' production becomes economically viable. This information would then be used for bargaining with existing suppliers and for other decision purposes. Another guise in which the problem frequently arises is where a firm has overseas subsidiaries supplied by exports from the home country, and it is considering the possibility of setting up a factory in the overseas country.

A related general problem to those already discussed concerns the actual capacity of any contemplated new plant or facility. Where output is constant or only growing slowly, this is not a difficult problem; but where output is growing rapidly and there are significant economies of scale in the size of plant, the problem of choosing the optimum initial excess capacity can be highly complex and important, depending as it does on both the economies that can be obtained from different sizes of plant and the rate of increase of output.

While the general form of these two related classes of problems is similar, individual cases may involve many special complications. As with many other problems considered in this book it would be neither practical nor desirable to deal exhaustively with all the complications involved, but it is hoped that the particular complications considered will suggest the general line of attack for the remainder. In the subsequent analysis we start from the simplest case, and progress to the more complex.

2. THE FIRST APPROXIMATION

a. *The Basic Approach*

The first step towards a viable solution of the problem of when and where to expand productive capacity is to abandon the search for a total cost per unit of output. This is not a useful concept where, as in the present case, major cost discontinuities are involved. Instead we must consider the specific series of cost outlays that different expansion plans involve, and the timing of such outlays.

Consider the first problem referred to above, the problem of deciding if and when to install additional productive capacity on a site away from the existing plant and nearer important distant markets. Three choices exist:

(i) establishing a new plant away from the existing one;

(ii) continuing output at the existing plant without increasing its capacity (by working the existing plant more intensively, e.g. overtime, shift working, etc.); and

(iii) continuing output at the existing plant and also increasing its capacity.

For the moment we will ignore (iii) and establish how a choice is to be made between the other two choices.

Suppose it is decided to establish a new plant in three years time: what costs will be involved? The firm will incur, over the three years prior to establishing the new plant, the costs of producing and transporting the products to be sold in the area which is later to be supplied by the new plant. It will then be involved in the capital outlays of setting up the new plant (and at later dates in replacement expenditures), and thereafter in the current costs of producing and distributing the output from the new plant.

To simplify the problem initially let us make the following assumptions concerning the costs of supplying the distant markets:

  (i) that the current (non-capital) costs involved in both the new and the existing plant consist of a fixed element and a constant amount per unit of output over the relevant range of output;

 (ii) that all current costs on the existing plant will be avoided if and when production is switched to the new plant (i.e. there is no 'non-reversible' element in the current costs of production which are thus defined as 'incremental' costs);

(iii) that no new capital costs will be involved in continuing production in the existing plant; and

(iv) that output, and thus sales revenue, is given independently of whether or not a new plant is decided on, and the problem is therefore to minimize costs.

The initial capital outlays, and the series of replacement capital outlays (assuming output can be expected to continue long enough to justify such expenditures) which the firm will incur by establishing the new plant should be reduced to their present value at the time the series is commenced, net of the present value of any tax reliefs resulting from the capital expenditures (Chapter 2, Appendix A).

Thus the present capital outlay net of tax reliefs of our item of plant which is assumed to be renewed k times at regular intervals of n years is for the purposes of this chapter defined as C where

$$C = (A-R)+(A-R)\frac{[1-(1+z)^{-k}]}{z} \qquad (9.1)$$

and A is the amount of the capital outlay, R is the present value of capital allowances, $(1+z) = (1+r)^n$, and r is the weighted average cost of capital. (For the derivation of z as the interest rate for a period in excess of 1 year see Section 2b of Chapter 1.) It is assumed that the financing policy of the firm is such as to make the weighted average cost of capital a viable approximation in the present applications.

Where the new plant will enable the profitable disposal of some existing assets (e.g. the entire 'old' plant), the net realization from this should be deducted from the cost of the first of the series of new plants.

Where no replacements can be foreseen the expression becomes simply

$$C = (A - R) \tag{9.2}$$

For perpetual replacements it reduces to

$$C = (A - R) + \frac{(A - R)}{z}$$

which can be simplified to

$$C = \frac{(A - R)}{1 - (1 + r)^{-n}}. \tag{9.3}$$

In addition to the present value of the net capital outlays the firm will also incur total current production, administration, and distribution running costs over the life of the new plant, and its replacements if any. For convenience of notation let us denote the present value *now* of the capital costs and all future running costs on the new plant from the time of its inception t by $N(t)$, where N mnemonically indicates *new* plant (including all transfer costs, etc.) and the bracketed t serves to remind us that this present cost depends on the time t when the new plant is put into operation.

Similarly we may denote the total present value equivalent cost of producing and distributing the requisite output from the existing plant up to the time t by $E(t)$. This cost too evidently depends on the date of establishing the new plant. The object of our analysis is to find the value of t (the date of inception of the new plant) which minimizes

$$T(t) = E(t) + N(t)$$

where $T(t)$ represents total present value.

Figure 9.1 illustrates the simplest type of function $T(t)$ that may be found in practice. The horizontal axis gives the time the new plant comes into production, while the vertical axis gives the total

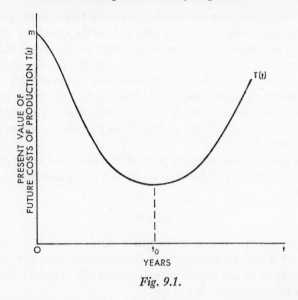

Fig. 9.1.

present cost on the existing values of t. Thus if the new plant could be put into operation immediately the total cost would be OM. If the plant is to be put into operation at a later date, the total costs will be less and it is seen that they reach a minimum for t_0, that is when the new plant is put into operation at time t_0.

It is generally inefficient to attempt to compute the function $T(t)$ for different values of t and find the minimum simply by inspection. Analysis reveals a simpler way of establishing this minimum and some other useful information.

The present cost $N(t)$ of the new plant over the rest of its life from the time of its inception at time t clearly must decrease as t increases – the further in the future the installation of the new plant is put the less its present cost. The present cost of continuing with the old plant, however, must increase with time – the longer the old plant is kept in operation the more is produced, hence the greater the cost in total current outlays. (There may also be some additional capital outlays required as time progresses to maintain the old plant in operation: this point is considered later.)

Prior to time t_0 in Figure 9.1, the curve of total costs $T(t)$ is decreasing. This must be due to $E(t)$ increasing less with time than $N(t)$ diminishes, leading to the observed fall in their total, $T(t)$. When $T(t)$ stops falling at point t_0, it is due to costs of the period in which

T

t_0 falls being such that the increase in costs from continuing for a further period with the old plant is exactly offset by the cost saving in postponing the commencement of the new plant for another period. Hence at the minimum point t_0, the *increase* in costs of $E(t)$ is exactly offset by the *decrease* in costs of $N(t)$. To find the minimum, therefore, we merely have to find the point at which the increase in the costs from going on with the old plant for one more year exactly equals the savings from postponing the new plant for one year.

Let us assume that costs *per year* on the old plant resulting from output x for the area to be covered by the new plant can be represented by:

$$ax+b \tag{9.4}$$

where a and b are constants. In other words there is a fixed cost per year of b and an additional or 'incremental' cost per ton, say, of a. Clearly then the cost of going on with the old plant for a year in which the output is x is $(ax+b)$.

The decrease in costs resulting from postponing inception of the new plant is a little more difficult to establish. As for the old plant we may assume that actual current outlays per year for an output x on the new plant is:

$$cx+d$$

where again d and c are constants, being respectively annual fixed costs and additional or 'incremental' costs per ton. The capital costs over the future life of the plant, if the plant is established in year t, are computed by the method outlined above in formulae (9.1) to (9.3), to be C. If the new plant is postponed a year, the firm will be involved in the same series of future capital outlays but all postponed one year. Hence, the total capital cost if the asset is postponed one year is $C/(1+r)$.

The saving from postponed erection of the new plant for one year is, therefore, $C-C/(1+r) = Cr/(1+r)$ or simply the 'interest' saving arising one year hence on the present cost of all future capital outlays involved in establishing and continuing the new plant. The total cost saving from postponing establishment of the new plant for one year is then

$$cx+a+\frac{Cr}{(1+r)} \tag{9.5}$$

The point of minimum cost in Figure 9.1 occurs where the costs incurred by continuing production on the existing plant are just offset by the cost saving from postponing the new plant for one more year. At the minimum cost point, therefore:

$$ax+b-\left(cx+d+\frac{Cr}{1+r}\right) = 0. \tag{9.6}$$

The only variable in this equation is x, the volume of output produced for the year that gives the minimum cost of Figure 9.1. Solving the equation for x we obtain:

$$x = \frac{d-b+Cr/(1+r)}{a-c}. \tag{9.7}$$

Thus, by solving for x it is possible to determine the optimal output for installing the new plant. It is important to appreciate that under the conditions assumed this optimal output is in no way affected by time. The new plant should be installed whenever the optimal output is reached be it next year or ten years hence.

If the new plant has an appreciable gestation period this can be allowed for by compounding the capital cost C forward to the date at which the plant comes into effective operation. Thus if the capital expenditures required for the new plant must be undertaken two years before the plant comes into operation the capital cost is taken not as C but $C(1+r)^2$.

Finally two points of interpretation should be noted. First there is no need to allow in the cost for depreciation on the new plant since this already effectively allowed for in the formula (9.3). Second, the analysis also automatically allows for a return on capital, that is the return from putting the new plant in operation at the optimum date shows a return compared with any alternative date of at least r (the rate of discount being used in the calculations).

Example 1. An example of the application of this formula is as follows. A firm is considering establishing a new plant in one of its distant markets at present supplied from its main plant. Assume the relevant current costs can be represented by £900x+£10,000 per annum for an output of x tons. Current running costs on the new plant, however, are £400x+£7,000. The present value of the estimated capital outlay C (defined above) is £1·9m. assuming perpetual renewals. Assuming a weighted average cost of capital of 8%, the 'interest' saving from postponing the erection of the plant for one year is £1·9m. × 0·08 ÷ 1·08 = £141,000. Inserting all these costs into equation (9.7) and solving for x, we find the value of $x = 276$ tons. Future costs of both the old and the new plant together will be minimized if the new plant is installed just prior to annual sales in the distant market rising to 276 tons. If sales forecasts in this market indicate such a rise in five years time, this would be the optimal time for having the new plant ready. As sales forecasts are constantly being revised the estimated optimal date will vary, but no final decision is necessary until sales can be forecast to reach the critical point by whatever period it takes to install the new plant and transfer staff, etc. Such a period is typically 12–18 months. It is usually possible to forecast sales with considerable confidence at so short a range when sales are expanding. In short, we are suggesting the calculation of when to expand is not a once and for all calculation indicating a future date at which plans should be put into operation without further consideration in the interim. Rather the calculation should be regarded as like a reading on a radar set to be used to give the estimated range of a target which will not necessarily always be drawing closer. Action is not necessary until the critical target range is reached.

Our second example illustrates a slightly different approach to the expansion problem, one which makes use of graphical presentation of information. It is particularly suited for situations in which there are major intangible costs and benefits to be considered and where the identifiable costs per unit of output are variable.

The problem is that of determining the optimal date on which to undertake a major expansion of head office accommodation. Problems of this type involve of course many questions of policy. The many policy factors such as personnel welfare, ease of communication, etc., can only be assessed subjectively. As we have stressed before, however, these subjectively assessed factors should be weighed against the tangible costs of the decisions before any rational solutions can be arrived at – the presence of intangible items in the costs and benefits are no grounds for declining to assess those costs which are identifiable.

Example 2: The head office problem. A firm at present owns a mort-gaged head office which accommodates 1,200 of its 1,600 staff, the remaining 400 being scattered in variously located pieces of leased accommodation. The staff numbers are growing fairly rapidly and the firm has previously acquired a suitable site on which to build an entirely new head office. This new site has planning permission for an office block accommodating 2,500, and as the firm can expect to see its staff grow to this figure sometime over the next 10 years, there appear to be fairly conclusive grounds for building to the maximum permitted size. If this is done prior to staff expanding to 2,500 it creates the difficulty of having to lease off some accommodation during the period when it is not required for the firm's existing staff. Arrangements can be made, however, for a suitable proportion of the surplus accommodation to be let out on short term leases to allow for the building being more fully occupied by the firm's existing staff as its numbers grow. The basic data of the problem when the costs involved are fairly regular is summarized in Table 9.1.

Table 9.1

Old Building		Symbol
	(All net of tax)	
Equity funds that will be realized from resale after repaying the outstanding mortgage	1,700,000	
Total operating costs (fixed and variable) with 1,200 staff	190,000	*b*
Cost per person of maintaining 400 additional staff in *leased* accommodation	150	*a*
New Building		
Total cost (excluding the cost of the site already acquired)	5,900,000	
Mortgage at 6½% before (3⅓% after) tax, repayable in 25 years (assume 50% renewed on same terms at end of first 25 years, making 50 years in all)	5,000,000	
Estimated value at end of 50 years, including site	2,500,000	
Annual Costs		
Variable costs per person	15	*c*
Fixed costs	225,000	*d*
Annual rent from leasing of surplus accommodation (average) per person	100	*p*

The question to be answered given these facts is when would be the optimal date at which to plan to sell the old building and to build and occupy the new? The answer to this problem evidently involves balancing the costs of the old building (plus the costs of the leased accommodation) against the costs of the new building (including capital outlays).

A point to be noted here is that the cost of the actual site which has already been acquired is not being taken into account in this calculation. Normally, when some expenditure has already been made its past cost is of course irrelevant, and only its opportunity cost – that is its value in some alternative use – needs to be taken into account. In this particular case it is assumed that the costs and uncertainties of the only practical alternative use – its resale and replacement at a later date by another site – are such that this alternative is quite unacceptable. This being so, the opportunity cost of the site is effectively zero in choosing the optimal date for constructing the new head office and for this reason is ignored in the subsequent calculations. Of course for the *initial* decision on whether to build a head office at all on this site, the firm should have taken all the relevant costs into account, both the construction costs of the building and the cost of acquiring the site. Where the site was already owned at the time of this decision the site cost would be taken as its opportunity cost (e.g. its resale value).

The general solution to this optimal timing problem could be established by the methods already used but it will be found rather more useful and revealing in this case, where large intangibles have to be measured against orders of magnitude, to present the costs and determine the solution graphically.

The old building given its fixed staff has total annual costs of £190,000, but the marginal 400 staff are maintained elsewhere at a cost of £60,000 or £150 per head. If we indicate the staff of the existing building by x_0 and let a be the cost of leased accommodation per head, then the total cost of continuing with the old building and a total staff of x is:

$$a(x - x_0) + b = ax + (b - ax_0)$$
$$= 150x + (190,000 - 150 \times 1,200)$$
$$= 150x + 10,000.$$

As regards the new office block it is assumed that the assets will enable the firm to obtain all the debt capital indicated in Table 9.1 as specific debt finance additional to the firm's normal debt financing. Hence the analysis is best conducted in terms of the equity cost of capital (assumed to be 8% after tax) and the equity cash flows. The net present value of the equity capital cost is set out in Table 9.2 below.

The only factor calling for further definition is b. This is the present value (at 8%) of $3\frac{1}{2}\%$ after tax interest on £5m. for 25 years followed by a *net* debt repayment of £2·5m., and $3\frac{1}{2}\%$ after tax interest on £2·5m. for a further 25 years, concluded by a debt repayment of £2·5m. which is assumed to be exactly offset by the

Table 9.2

	£000's
(a) Total capital outlay	5,900
(b) Plus net present value of future interest and debt repayments	2,370
Less	
(c) Total debt inflow from mortgage	−5,000
(d) Net equity realization from sale of old building	−1,700
(e) Net present value of the equity cost	1,570

residual value of the building at that time. The figures relating to the second 25 years are of course very tenuous but, as we have so often found before, the broad magnitude of these figures is of no material importance and are only included here for completeness.

In computing the capital charge $Cr/(1+r)$, see formulae (9.1) to (9.3), we could take into account the series of replacement expenditures (i.e. replacing the new office block) starting some 50 years or so after the new office block is built. But the difference between assuming a perpetual series of replacements at 50 year intervals and no replacements is insignificantly small and so will be ignored. Further, this accords with common sense in that no one can predict 50 years in advance whether replacement will in fact occur. We shall therefore simply use the value of £1,570,000 calculated in Table 9.2 above as the net equity value of C.

$$\frac{Cr}{1+r} = \frac{£1,570,000}{1 \cdot 08} \times 0 \cdot 08 = £116,296, \text{ or say } £116,000.$$

The total annual costs on the new building with a staff of x are: variable costs + fixed costs + capital charge − rent from letting surplus accommodation.

The last item can be written symbolically as $p(K-x)$ where p is the average rent (net of tax and allowing for periods of vacancy) and K is the capacity of the building (2,500). Total costs can therefore be written as:

$$cx + d + \frac{Cr}{1+r} - p(K-x)$$

$$= (c+p)x + d + \frac{Cr}{1+r} - pK$$

$$= 115x + 225,000 + 116,000 - 250,000$$

$$= 115x + 91,000 = \text{total costs per annum on the new building}$$

The two equations giving annual costs on the old and new buildings are depicted in Figure 9.2.

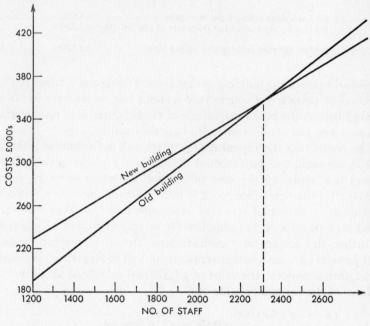

Fig. 9.2.

It is seen from Figure 9.2 that it would need staff numbers of around 2,300 to make the tangible annual cost of switching to the new building break even with continuing to accommodate staff in the old building and rented accommodation.

This type of graphical analysis is useful in a number of ways. By depicting the year by year difference in costs from switching over to the new building it gives an indication of the value that must be attached to the intangible benefits from shifting to the new building. For example, to justify switching immediately while the number of personnel is around 1,600, it would have to be argued that the intangible benefits of having the 400 staff gathered under the same roof as the other 1,200, of welfare and prestige, etc., would have to be valued at £25,000 p.a. after tax or nearly £16 per head of staff.

The graphical analysis also lends itself to a quick assessment of the effect of assuming different values for some of the estimated figures – e.g. assuming that the existing building will realize either more or less than the assumed price. In this latter case we would merely need to increase uniformly the line indicating the costs with the new building by $0.08/1.08$ of the reduction in the price realized, thus increasing the cost of moving into the new building.

Finally, the type of approach illustrated by Figure 9.2 conveniently extends to more complex cost situations. The preceding example assumed a fairly simple cost structure – in particular it was assumed that new accommodation could be acquired at a given uniform cost. This, of course, will often not be a viable approximation. The additional staff may have to be accommodated at an exceptionally high cost as the low cost accommodation available locally is exhausted. The firm may then have the choice of signing a lease for a fairly long period for a whole block of accommodation sufficient for a large number of additional staff. This can give rise to the type of situation depicted in Figure 9.3.

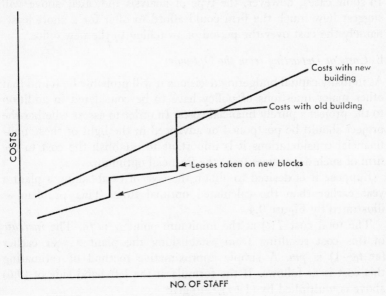

Fig. 9.3.

The effect of signing a lease for a given period for whole blocks of accommodation is to cause the discontinuous increases in costs of continuing to operate the old building and buying leased accommodation. While the firm has available spare capacity in the newly leased accommodation the additional costs of accommodating more staff may be very small – current operating costs only. This is shown by the line representing costs on the old building (see Figure 9.3) becoming virtually horizontal after increasing discontinuously by the amount of the rent on the new 'parcel' of accommodation. If the firm can sub-let the surplus accommodation, however, the cost per person of new staff would be operating costs plus rent foregone from sub-letting.

Where removing to the new building involves the firm sub-letting or surrendering leases, then any losses from this should be added to the cost of switching to the new building. This is of particular importance where the firm does not own its old office block but is merely leasing it. The lease payments will then bulk large in the fixed costs of continuing with the old building, and an imminent rent revision, through causing an abrupt rise in these costs, may be the obvious indication of it being time to switch to the new office. In some cases, however, the type of analysis indicated above will suggest how much the firm could afford to offer for a short lease, namely the cost over the period of switching to the new office.

b. *Costs of Departing from the Optimum*

As in many capital budgeting decisions it will probably be found that other major questions of policy have to be considered in addition to the project's purely financial costs. In order to assess whether the project should be postponed or advanced in the light of these non-financial considerations it is important to establish the cost to the firm of such departures from the financial optimum.

Suppose it is desired to obtain the cost of establishing a plant a year earlier than the calculated optimal time. This problem is illustrated by Figure 9.4.

The total cost $T(t)$ at the minimum point t_0 is *fn*. The *increase* in this cost resulting from establishing the plant a year earlier (at t_0-1) is *pm*. A simple approximative method of estimating this cost is as follows. If the formula at the left hand side of (9.6) above is multiplied by $(1+r)^{-t}$, to give

$$\left[ax+b-\left(cx+d+\frac{Cr}{1+r}\right)\right](1+r)^{-t} \qquad (9.8)$$

then this formula will give a highly accurate estimate of the slope of the curve $T(t)$ at the time t at which the output x is achieved. The slope is identical to the gradient except as regards the sign

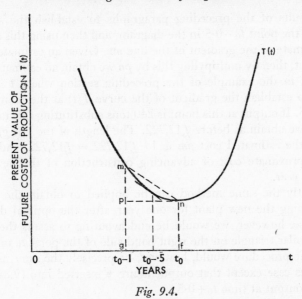

Fig. 9.4.

convention, that is the slope is taken as negative where the function, in this case $T(t)$, *decreases* with increasing values of t, and is positive where the function increases with the value of t. The gradient, however, is always taken as positive. Suppose, for example, it is desired to establish the slope of the curve $T(t)$ at the point $t = 4 \cdot 5$ in Example 1 where $t = 5$ represents the minimum point of $T(t)$, that is $t_0 = 5$. The required slope is found by establishing the output x at that date and substituting the resulting value of x into (9.8). Thus if output at $t = 4 \cdot 5$ is 240 substituting this in (9.8) we obtain $- £18,000/(1 \cdot 08)^{4 \cdot 5}$. Taking $(1 \cdot 08)^{4 \cdot 5}$ as $(1 \cdot 08)^4 (1 \cdot 04)$ we obtain $- £12,722$. This indicates that if the slope of the curve $T(t)$ remained constant from $t = 4$ to $t = 5$, then postponing the new plant one more year from $t = 4$ to $t = 5$ would *decrease* $T(t)$ by £12,722, and conversely advancing construction from $t = 5$ to $t = 4$ would *increase* $T(t)$ by £12,722. The slope found is negative, indicating that the curve $T(t)$ decreases around this value as t increases – as is apparent from the Figure 9.4. It is seen from this diagram that the gradient of the curve $T(t)$ is not constant but gradually *decreases* as t increases towards t_0. As we progress beyond the point t_0 the gradient increases again.

For present purposes we can estimate *pm* in Figure 9.4 by using the results of the preceding paragraphs to establish the slope of $T(t)$ at the point $t_0 - 0.5$ in the diagram, and then using this slope as an estimate of the gradient of the line *mn*. Given an estimate of this gradient, then by multipyling this by *pn* we obtain an estimate of *pm*. Hence, in the example of the preceding section where $t = 5$, we want to establish the gradient of the curve $T(t)$ at the point where $t = 4.5$. If output at this point is 240 tons substituting this into (9.8) above we obtain as before £12,722. The length of the line *gf* is 1.0, hence the estimated cost *pm* is $1 \times £12,722 = £12,722$, and this is the approximate cost of advancing construction of the new plant by one year.

Exactly the same method can be applied to obtain the cost of postponing the new plant for one year after the optimal date. In this case, however, we would be endeavouring to assess the height of a similar triangle on the right hand side of the point t_0 in Figure 9.4. The procedure would, however, be precisely the same as in the previous case except that output figure *x* inserted into (9.8) would be the output at time $t_0 + 0.5$.

II

3. EXTENSION OF THE ANALYSIS

a. *Additional Capital Outlays Required on the Old Plant*

The major simplifying assumption in the previous analysis was that no extra capital costs would be involved in expanding the production of the existing plant. This was not to say that no additional capital expenditure was expected to occur on the existing plant either by way of replacement or to meet expansion needs in other markets; but merely that such expenditure would in no way be affected by the growing requirements of the more distant market in question. This assumption will now be dropped and consideration given to the complexities involved when failure to establish a new plant nearer the distant market will necessitate additional capital expenditure at the existing plant.

This gives rise to the complication that there may be times of installation for which the total present value *now* of future capital and operating cost outlays, is of a lower value than the minimum value of the curve $T(t)$ in Figure 9.1. This is illustrated by the *discontinuous* curve $O(t)$ in Figure 9.5 where it is seen that there is no

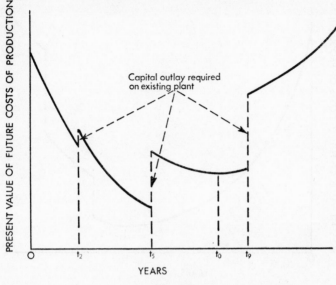

Fig. 9.5.

alternative to the somewhat more complex undertaking of attempting to determine the actual height of the curve $O(t)$ at its minimum point, i.e. a point where the slope or gradient is zero. (In mathematical terms the minimum point of the discontinuous curve $O(t)$ is not necessarily the point of lowest value since the slope is *not* zero at the points of discontinuity – e.g. t_2 and t_5 in Figure 9.5.) Once the minimum point has been determined, it is *then* necessary to compare the height of the curve at this point with the height at any *earlier* points of discontinuity (i.e. at which major capital outlays on the existing plant are required), to determine the time at which the total present value is lowest. At points of discontinuity which occur *after* the 'minimum' point of $O(t)$ the height of the curve must be greater than at the 'minimum' point and can therefore be disregarded. This is illustrated in Figure 9.6.

A formula and a numerical illustration are given below for the case in which, over the relevant period, current costs are linear with respect to output (or approximately so) and output from the plant is increasing at a constant compound rate per annum.

Example 3 – The discontinuous cost case. Consider first an algebraic example of the method required to determine the optimal date for

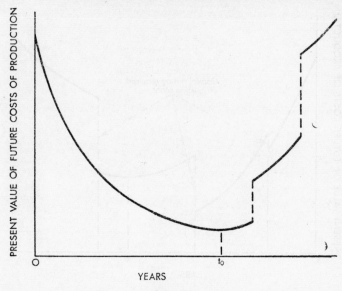

Fig. 9.6.

inception of the new plant in the case when the cost of operating the existing plant is subject to major discontinuous cost increases due to capital outlays for bottleneck removals on output or otherwise unavoidable delays.

The details are given in Table 9.3:

Table 9.3

Discount rate is r
Output at time t' is $x(t') = q(1+p)^{t'-1}$ where q and p are constants and t' is measured in years.

	Existing Plant	New Plant
Current outlays for output $x(t')$	$ax(t')+b$	$cx(t')+d$
	(a and b are constants)	(c and d are constants)
Capital outlays (net of the present value, at time of outlay, of tax concessions)	$A(t')$	C(see (9.3) above)

The details given in the table are largely self explanatory; several points, however, call for further comment. The output which will be transferred to the new plant, when it is established, is assumed to be increasing at the constant compound rate of $p\%$ a year from the initial output of q. The discontinuous capital outlays $A(t')$ call for special attention. It is important to ensure the extent to which capital outlays on the old plant can be avoided by establishing a new plant.

Where the existence of the new plant will simply lead to these outlays being postponed or diminished, the appropriate 'outlays' $A(t')$ are the present values of the additional costs due to advancing or increasing these capital expenditures. (The present value of replacements on the initial outlays should also be included where replacement will in fact be undertaken.) It is probable for some values of t, that $A(t')$ will be zero. For convenience of reference let us denote the sum of the present values of these capital expenditures up to year t (the year before the new plant comes into production) by $B(t)$.

The problem is again one of minimizing all future costs in so far as they are effected by the time at which the new plant comes into operation.

Assuming capital expenditures to bring the new plant into operation in year $t+1$ must be undertaken at time $t-n$, the present value of the costs on the old plant up to year t and the present value of the costs on the new plant from this date to, say, year m, can be written as:

$$O(t) = aqa_{t|s} + ba_{t|r} + B(t) + v_{t|r}(cqa_{m-t|s} + da_{m-t|r}) + v_{t-n|r} C \ldots (9.9)$$

where $s = r - p$. The first three expressions represent costs $E(t)$ on the old plant and the last two expressions represent $N(t)$ the costs on the new plant. Now m can be given *any* value sufficiently large to make certain that it is beyond the likely date of inception of the new plant, since costs beyond such a date are independent of the date at which the new plant is put into operation.

The problem for analysis is to find the minimum value of (9.9), and in this case this is normally most readily found by simply sketching out a few values of this equation for different values of t and ascertaining the minimum by inspection. This is illustrated in the following example.

Table 9.4

Discount rate $r = \cdot08$, $m = 30$, $n = 0$.

Output at time t' is $x(t') = 150(1 + \cdot05)^{t-1}$

	Existing Plant	New Plant
Current outlays for output $x(t')$	£900$x(t')$+17,000	£400$x(t')$+15,000
Capital outlays occurring only in years 2, 5 and 9 are:	$A(2) = $£12,500 $A(5) = $£50,000 $A(9) = $£87,500	£1,500,000

Substituting this data in (9.9) the successive values of $O(t)$ are computed as follows in Table 9.5:

Table 9.5

Year t	£-000's E(t)	N(t)	E(t)+N(t) = O(t)
1	147	2,610	2,757
2	299	2,393	2,692
3	436	2,194	2,630
4	569	2,010	2,579
5	731	1,841	2,572
6	855	1,685	2,540
7	974	1,542	2,516
8	1,090	1,410	2,500
9	1,246	1,288	2,534
10	1,354	1,176	2,530
11	1,459	1,074	2,533
12	1,560	979	2,539

The minimum cost point is seen to occur in year 8 and therefore the optimal date for the new plant to be put into operation is year 9.

b. *Optimal Type and Capacity of Asset*

So far we have assumed that there is only one size of new plant which can be put up and we have found the optimal date for its introduction. Where the plant is supplying an expanding market, however, there will certainly be more than one choice of plant depending on the extent to which the firm is prepared to carry surplus capacity in order to obtain the economies of scale from larger sized plants. If economies of scale are considerable and demand is growing rapidly the firm may find it profitable to construct plants of such size that they are of a capacity substantially in excess of *current* requirements. Where these choices exist, discriminating between them involves considerable problems of policy, concept, and computation – particularly if a large number of choices present themselves.

In practice the problems are simplified by the fact that the number of choices is likely to be limited to two or three serious possibilities, so the burden of calculation is not as onerous as might at first appear. Where two or more choices exist, the calculation, as set out, merely gives the optimal date for installing each. The first stage of the analysis required for choosing between them is to establish the optimal dates of commencement for the different sizes of plant — i.e. to perform the foregoing analysis on each alternative to establish the date of inception of the new plants.

It is at the second stage of the problem – that of discriminating between these choices, given their optimal date of commencement – that difficulties arise. The initial choice to build enough capacity to last, say, 8 years, or enough to last only, say, 3 years, will effect the productive capacity of the firm in all future years and thus change the timing of later expansion expenditure and possibly also the magnitude. Formally, therefore, the choice of alternative should be made in the light of the impact it will have on all future expansion expenditures. Assuming exponential or linear growth, and simple cost relationships governing the economies of scale, it is possible to set up a formal analysis[1] which takes some of these considerations into account. But for reasons which will become clear in the course of this section, it is generally better to use a less formal and more flexible approach along the following lines.

Whatever choice of plant is made initially there will generally be a date in the future at which, whatever plant building programme is followed to meet capacity requirements prior to that date, further capacity will be required. Suppose, for example, a firm is expecting output to increase over the next 12 years and to meet this capacity requirement it can either build four plants of size A at three yearly intervals (beginning immediately) or three plants of size B at four yearly intervals (also beginning the first immediately). What we shall describe as an *intersection of opportunities* comes at the point in time when following either policy, further new expansion investment is required, in this example at end-year 12. In choosing between plants A and B it is necessary, in these two simple strategies of keeping to plants of only one size, to consider only the next 12 years since at the end of this period the firm, by following either policy, can reconsider its investment strategy. If it has so far elected to build plants of size A it could go over to size B, or vice versa. Thus, the method of analysis proposed can use this date (end-year 12) as the time horizon for discriminating now between the two simple strategies considered.

If the future growth of demand were a constant amount per period, then any size plant which is optimal at the outset will normally remain the optimal size for successive increments to capacity. Where the growth of demand varies markedly from this, however, it may prove more desirable to follow a mixed strategy and instead of building all plants of size A, say, build the first of size A the second of size B, the third A, etc.

---

[1] See for example reference [1] where graphical relationships are given for the case of linear economies of scale in cost of the initial capital assets and exponential and linear rates of growth in demand. The method proposed there minimizes the cost of *new* capacity required to meet the expanding demand.

U

The problem of finding a point of intersection of opportunities becomes more difficult where, as in this case, three or more strategies might be worth considering. This however is usually not too difficult to overcome given that there is normally a considerable degree of 'elasticity' in the capacity of the plants so that without significant error the future timing of the new expansion of plant can be advanced or retarded, and given also the relative unimportance of the exact timing of cash flows many years hence.

A particular problem in using the first year in which an intersection of opportunities occurs as the time horizon is that at this date a firm will still have other plants in operation – in fact, in our above example, four plants of type A, or three of type B. These assets pose opportunities for further reconsiderations of policy when they in turn fall due for replacement. For example a firm may decide when an asset of type A comes up for replacement it will take this opportunity to build a plant of type B as being more suited to the estimated future growth from that time. (It is because new opportunities become possible as assets fall due for replacement that the policy of simply finding the optimal sizes for *new* plants erected at different dates in the future will often fail to be satisfactory.)

Ideally it would be desirable to follow through all these opportunities for reconsidering investment policies which are presented by the existing assets falling due for replacement but it will generally be found that the vast computational effort involved is not worth the effort as regards replacements outside the time horizon set by the intersection of opportunities. This is owing to (a) the relative unimportance of outlays so far in the future, (b) the greater flexibility, in particular the more frequent intersections of opportunities which occur as the firm expands in a particular direction, and (c) the extreme uncertainty which must surround both forecasts and company selling and replacement policy so far into the future.

For all practical purposes therefore, the point at which opportunities intersect can be taken as the effective time horizon. The value of the assets built up to that time can then be taken into account by the method discussed in Chapter 19. The costs associated with any particular investment policy up to this time are depicted in Figure 9.7.

This figure depicts by the continuous line the pattern of capital and operating outlays (and residual values) following the policy of building relatively large plants of type B which provide capacity for several future years. The dotted line shows the outlays and residual values which would result from following the alternative policy of

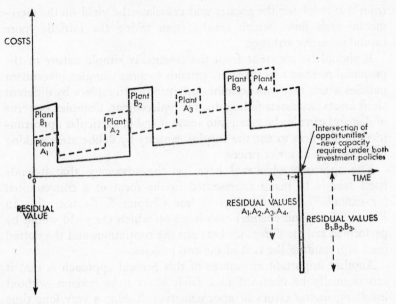

COSTS

Plant B₁
Plant A₁
Plant A₂
Plant B₂
Plant A₃
Plant B₃
Plant A₄

"Intersection of opportunities" –new capacity required under both investment policies

0   t→   TIME

RESIDUAL VALUE

RESIDUAL VALUES A₁, A₂, A₃, A₄.

RESIDUAL VALUES B₁, B₂, B₃.

Fig. 9.7.

building smaller plants of type A. As these provide less capacity their surplus capacity is more rapidly absorbed and consequently four plants of this type are required compared with only three of type B. It is also seen that the two types of plant differ in operating costs – those of type A are higher than type B. The operating costs will normally be increasing over time (as depicted in the figure) because of the increasing volume of output as expansion proceeds. The residual values of the plants which would result from either policy are shown on the far right of the figure and are, of course, to be considered as inflows.

A similar set of cash flows can be set out for each investment policy. Formally, of course, the optimal policy is that involving the lowest net present value. Where the risks connected with the latter period are very great the firm may however prefer to take a policy involving a higher present value and to build less capacity in anticipation of future requirements. In this respect the technique proposed is very flexible since it can readily be turned into a yield calculation. To do this we simply deduct from the cash flows of the policy involved the smaller series of capital outlays in the early years from that involving the greater and calculate the yield on the incremental cash flows which results from taking the initially more capital intensive strategy.

It should be apparent from the essentially simple nature of the proposed method that it readily extends to more complex investment policies which take into account opportunities to replace by different sized assets any assets falling due for replacement. Complex patterns of demand can also be taken into account and in particular opportunities for the firm to use the surplus capacity by deliberately seeking new business at lower prices.

The approach advocated here has the advantage that it lends itself readily to being represented in the form of a conventional (or extended) incremental yield (see Chapter 5, Section 2b). In Figure 9.7 the incremental cash flows on which the yield would be performed are the difference between the continuous and the dotted lines representing the cost of the two policies.

Another important advantage of this general approach is that it can normally be confined to a fairly short time horizon without involving undue errors of approximation. Taking a very long time horizon can present alternatives in a spurious light in that relatively small savings over a very long time are taken into account and appear to offer conclusive inducements to take a particular investment strategy, say, strategy A. The real situation may well be that some alternative strategy B would at some point produce an intersection of opportunities after which all the savings of strategy A could be acquired by changing to strategy A at that point. Again the saving arising in the very distant future may be very heavily discounted for uncertainty, and presenting a case for a particular investment strategy based on very distant cash advantages may for this reason be considered unsatisfactory. A particular weakness here is that it is extremely difficult for top management, presented with a present value calculation based on cash flows over a very long future period, to know how much of this present value arises from the very distant future which they may well be inclined to discount very heavily for uncertainty. This difficulty could only be overcome by using alternative discount rates and/or showing how much of the net present value comes from different time periods.

c. *The Limitations of the Cost Minimization Approach*

Two matters call for comment under this heading. First, all the above methods are of course cost minimization methods designed to choose the optimal new plant (if any) for installation away from the existing plant, and the optimal timing of that installation. But solving this problem does not automatically guarantee that even the optimal alternative is economic. It may well be that the distant market is unprofitable and all the method has done is to reveal the least unprofitable method of serving it. Where this is suspected it becomes necessary to find the present value of all future revenues to be derived from the market in question for comparison with the optimal alternative of meeting production requirements, i.e. to determine if there is a positive net present value in even the optimal case.

Second, there will be occasions when the assumption of a constant output and sales revenue is unrealistic simply because the installation of new capacity makes possible an increased output at a lower selling price. Where this possibility exists the cost minimization method must be abandoned and resort made to maximizing the present value of future net cash flows. In practice this requires but little modification of the method outlined, merely the subtraction of the cost outlays (both capital and revenue items) from the net of tax sales revenue stream.

Where output is constant, but tax treatment is different (as would often be the case if the new plant was set up overseas to manufacture locally what was previously imported from the existing plant, thus receiving special capital allowances and perhaps reduced import duties), it will usually be possible to treat the tax charges as cost savings either of a capital or revenue nature, thus permitting the much simpler cost minimization method to be used.

REFERENCE

1. Ian McDowell, 'The Economical Planning Period for Engineering Works', *Operations Research*, Number 4, Volume 8, July–August 1960.

CHAPTER TEN
Assessing the Purchase Price of a Firm

I

Principles of Valuation

This and the subsequent two chapters are concerned with the financial and analytical problems involved in assessing the purchase (or sale) price to be put on a going concern. This first chapter sets out the basic approach to be followed. The second chapter consists of a detailed case study to demonstrate the practical application of the recommended method. The third chapter is devoted to examining certain miscellaneous problems associated with take-overs, such as determining the most economical method of payment.

1. INTRODUCTION

One of the recognized methods of expanding a company, whether to increase profits, or to safeguard them by securing control of either supplies or outlets, is the purchase of another company.

Take-overs and mergers have long been part of the economic scene, but in the more advanced industrialized countries the pace appears to be accelerating: certainly the capital sums involved tend to be larger as more and more industries tend to be dominated by a few large firms. In the United States this has long been a normal process. In Western Europe, especially in Germany with its long tradition of cartels, the tendency has received even greater impetus from the impact of the Common Market. In Britain, this process has been actively fostered by the Government, e.g. in aircraft manufacture, in the cotton industry, and in shipbuilding. Indeed in many industries and economic activities the *sine qua non* of entry is the purchase of an existing firm with whom the government, as the main or only customer, is prepared to deal. Suppliers of telephone equipment to the G.P.O. are limited to seven firms: an electronics firm must buy one of them if it is to be allowed to compete with the others. Seventeen old-established merchant banks alone have access to the Bank of England for rediscounting bills of exchange, hence the discount market is effectively limited to these firms. Any up and coming merchant bank wishing to participate in this profitable activity, or extend similar facilities to its clients, must merge with one of the seventeen.

It should be apparent that the purchase of another firm is merely a particularly complex investment project. As such it must satisfy the same criteria and be justified on the same grounds as any other investment open to a firm. Purchase of an existing business, however, often involves special problems or problems at a greater level of complexity than commonly occurs with the normal internal investment.

In the case of internal investments the capital outlays involved are easily ascertained, and the chief problem lies in assessing the likely return on the investment. Where the proposed investment is to purchase another firm, the cost is seldom ascertainable in advance. The problem is to estimate both the future income *and* the range of prices it is worth offering to existing owners of the firm. The cost is usually open to negotiation, and cannot be taken as fixed. In ascertaining the cost it is necessary to establish the alternative values to the owners of the firm under consideration for purchase, i.e. the value from continued operation or selling out to some third party, and this calls for a rather different technique than that applicable to normal internal investment projects.

Buying an established company is usually a rather more complex affair than executing an internal capital project. A company may be bought with one or more objects in mind, e.g. acquiring additional manufacturing capacity, joint operation of a sales force or distribution organization, securing sales outlets for products, or safeguarding raw materials, etc. In practice, however, it is rare to find a company suitable for purchase which has just the assets desired, *neither more nor less*. Almost all firms engage in more than one simple activity. The firm with suitable manufacturing capacity to produce the purchasing firm's products may also have a substantial business in other quite different lines, which, in the interests of efficiency, ought to be continued – perhaps even expanded. The firm whose distribution organization could be dovetailed advantageously with the purchaser's may also have experience and established goodwill in outlets which do not or cannot cater for the purchaser's type of product. The firm with retail outlets which does handle the purchaser's type of product may not do so exclusively: in fact, that type of product might well amount only to a minority of its total sales, albeit a significant minority. The firm which produces the purchaser's basic raw materials in all probability produces much which it could not or would not want to use. In short, taking over another firm typically means enlarging the range of a purchaser's activities as well as the extent. To justify absorption, a purchaser may need to participate successfully in industries and markets of which it has little or no experience. When investing in an internal investment project a firm can often avoid expanding into activities which it does not choose: but when buying a firm, it can seldom choose to buy just the part that interests it, and not the rest.[1] It is this necessary but often involuntary expansion into diverse activities which is one of the chief factors separating the purchase of another firm from a similar internal investment. This is an important reason for devoting special attention to the problems of buying out existing companies.

There are other and related special problems involved in takeovers and mergers. The assets of going concerns usually include goodwill, i.e. the reputation a business enjoys with its customers, which gives the business value over and above the value of its physical assets. Indeed, the goodwill may well comprise the primary asset, as in the case of a newpsaper or well-known restaurant, and so constitute the chief reason for acquisition. This is scarcely ever true of any internal investment project. A firm may expand its range of lines, hoping its existing good name will help to sell the new lines, but this is exploiting its own 'goodwill' rather than acquiring the 'goodwill' of another company. The 'goodwill' that is being purchased will consist in many cases of an exploitable market position and access to other investment opportunities.

Going concerns nearly always embrace established contractual or traditional obligations to customers, suppliers, and, of course, staff. Certain customers may have received special terms, and to terminate them might prove costly in terms of public relations, yet to continue them may cause the existing customers of the purchasing firm to object to what they consider to be discrimination. The relationship with suppliers can be similarly complicated. A firm may always have bought from one or two suppliers, and be their main or indeed only customer. Yet one of the attractions of a merger may be the replacing of such suppliers from a cheaper source. This same problem can

---

[1] The *Daily Mirror* group in its bid for Odhams was primarily interested in the latter's magazine trade, and not its main newspaper, the *Daily Herald*, which was regarded as a significant liability.

arise with an internal investment project whose main purpose is to reduce or eliminate dependence on an outside supplier, but it seldom arises in such an acute form.

Special problems of staff relationships are frequently involved in take-overs. If a merger involves serious redundancy, the question of compensation arises because of a legal or moral obligation. Often the question of redundancy arises within the purchasing firm if some of the staff of the acquired firm are more capable or experienced. This problem can arise with internal investment projects, e.g. when an operation becomes more mechanized thus releasing labour. But it seldom arises in such an acute form, or with so many people, especially people with whom the firm's personnel department is unfamiliar.

Other major problems arising with mergers are the settling of outstanding financial obligations, and arranging the form of purchase, the rights of existing shareholders, minorities, etc. When a firm is purchased which has redeemable preference shares, debentures, secured or unsecured loans, bank overdrafts, etc., there is often the opportunity, and sometimes the obligation, to redeem such finance at the time of purchase. Then there is the basic problem of settling the terms of the merger itself, whether the shares will be paid for in cash, or with the shares of the purchasing firm, or some combination of the two, a matter which calls for very considerable skills. These complications do not exist in the case of internal investment.

Consideration must be given to the tax consequences of mergers, which are very often of a far-reaching nature. Indeed, in many countries they can constitute the prime reason for merging. The tax consequences of internal investments are usually straightforward and limited to obtaining some sort of investment allowances or accelerated depreciation. Whereas these allowances are standard and give little scope to the ingenuity of tax experts, mergers are often the framework for their best endeavours.

From this discussion it will be apparent that assessing the purchase price of a firm is typically a much more complicated matter than assessing an internal investment project: it is different in degree and also in kind. As a consequence, the problems it gives rise to require special analytical techniques.[1]

---

[1] For general background reading illustrated by case studies see references [1] and [2].

2. BASIC INFORMATION REQUIRED

This comes under four headings.

(i) Estimates of future profits (plus depreciation) available to the equity shareholders, net of tax, which can be expected to arise if the firm is operated in the most efficient way to further the interests of the purchasing company. The profits considered should be taken net of likely dividend payments to any minority shareholders.

(ii) The value of all surplus assets, that is, those assets not required to earn the profits referred to in (i) (e.g. cash reserves, investments, surplus buildings, unused land, etc.).

(iii) The replacement cost of non-surplus assets, and estimates of when replacement will be required.

(iv) The amount and timing of any loan or debt redemption.

These four constitute the basic information necessary to commence the evaluation of a company. All other information required can be used to elaborate one or more of the above. Before passing on to these detailed matters, consider first the relationship of the basic information.

Assume first that the firm will continue to operate indefinitely in the future. By taking (i), (iii) and (iv) together, it is possible to establish the net cash flow resulting from the acquisition of such a business. (It should be remembered that the net cash flow here referred to is the incremental net cash flow likely to result from the merger, that is it may include higher profits from the existing company where this is attributable to economies arising from the merger.) This net cash flow accruing to the purchasing firm should be discounted at the appropriate marginal cost of capital, after allowing for risk, to its present value. To this present value should be added the value to the purchaser of any surplus assets (item (i)), and the combined figure will set the maximum value to the purchaser from continued operation. Where the continued operation of the firm is justified, it will be worth offering up to this amount to acquire the business.

So far, it has been assumed that the purchased firm will continue to be operated indefinitely, but this may not be the case. Whether or not it is profitable to do this can be ascertained by comparing the present values of (i) (profits net of tax, plus depreciation) and (iv) (loan or debt redemption) with the present value of factor (iii) (replacement expenditure necessary to the continuance of the business). Where the present value of replacement expenditure exceeds that of net income, then clearly it would not be worthwhile to continue the business. This is true regardless of what is paid for the business. It does not mean such a business is not worth buying. It can still be profitable to buy, but only as an investment with a limited life. In these circumstances, the maximum purchase price is set by finding the present value of items (i) and (iv), and aggregating them with item (ii) (the value of surplus net assets). In calculating item (i) it is necessary to determine how long income can be earned by 'milking' the existing assets until revenues cease to cover operating expenses. (Care must be used in assessing this point of time. It may well be that in any one year the net cash flow may fail to cover the replacement cost of a given item of plant. This does not necessarily mean the business should be then terminated. The replacement of this one item of plant may give the whole business a few more years of profitable life before really major pieces of plant wear out. This is a matter for precise calculation.[1]) A business is usually worth continuing until major replacement expenditure can no longer be justified. Then the business should be closed down. Alternatively, it may be possible to reconstruct or sell it, in which case there is a terminal value. Where such a value exists, it should be expressly considered as part of the net cash flow for the limited life case.

Having considered the basic relationships, the requisite information for amplifying these basic categories will now be examined in some detail.

3. REQUISITE DETAILED INFORMATION

a. *Estimating Future Income*

Any business not on the point of being broken up, takes its primary value from the income it is expected to generate in future. It follows that the most important part of evaluating a business is the estimate of its future income. This calls for a rigorous and detailed analysis of what its potential owners estimate the net cash flows of the company will be when it is taken over. Usually they will be continuing to operate the acquired company in its existing line of activity and so a

---

[1] This matter is covered in Section 1 of Chapter 19 on replacement decisions.

logical starting point – and it can never be more than just that – is its past performance. Apart from its value as an aid to prediction, it is the best measure of the performance of its existing management. It is sometimes the case that they comprise the major asset being acquired.

The first step is to look at the firm's record over the recent past, usually the last five years, although often it will be instructive to consider a rather longer period, say ten years. It is rarely worth going beyond ten years as conditions are likely to be so remote from the present as to lack relevance, and the present management is unlikely to have held major responsibility at that time. In looking at the past record it is instructive to consider profits primarily on a net of tax basis as it is net of tax profits which management should have been striving to maximise. But where tax rates or allowances have been changing, or where a firm has been in receipt of unusual capital allowances it is also desirable to consider profits on a gross of tax basis.

In examining the trading profits for trends, etc., several corrections are called for. Firstly allowance should be made for the incidence of stock appreciation or depreciation,[1] a matter for expert handling. Usually exact information for this adjustment will be lacking, even when the firm under consideration for purchase freely makes available its detailed accounting records. What is required, however, is a broad adjustment and this can always be done. Secondly, attention should be paid to the trend of advertising and other sales promotion expenditure to be sure that they are not being run down in the interest of increasing short run profits at the expense of future profits. This is particularly a matter to watch when it is the directors or owners of the firm to be purchased who have taken the initiative in proposing the sale.

Thirdly, some attempt should be made to allow for the change in money value over the period being considered where this is likely to be of significance in interpreting trading profits. Disagreement will always exist as to which is the appropriate price index to use, retail prices (cost of living), wholesale prices, or a sales price index for the industry, etc., etc. No entirely satisfactory answer can be given on this problem, but on the basis that the object of raising income is to increase personal consumption, the cost of living index would seem to be the least objectionable price indicator. In applying such an

---

[1] For the benefit of readers unfamiliar with advanced accounting concepts, an explanation illustrated by a simple example is given in Appendix A.

index to the trading profits of past years, it should be used to convert them into current terms, rather than the money units of say five years ago, as the object of the exercise is to aid in predicting future trading profits starting from the present, and it is obviously more convenient to have the past trends set out in present day money values.

Having established 'corrected' trading profits for the firm under consideration, it is useful to compare this with other firms in the same industry (or industries) as a measure of the performance of the present management.

Once the firm's recent past history has been examined, the next step is to attempt to forecast the likely future trading profits.[1] This involves considering all the possible ways the firm could be developed and choosing the one that maximizes the present value of its future net cash flow, or rather the aggregate net cash flow of the firm acquired and the purchaser's present business. Thus the economies of joint purchase of materials, manufacturing, transport, selling, advertising, etc., must all be specifically evaluated. From the predicted gross trading profits, allowance must be made for the taxes which will be incurred, and of course the capital expenditure needed to maintain and expand the business. These two matters are considered below.

First, consider in more detail the questions of marketing the firm's products, and buying in raw materials, etc. Any appraisal of the future income of a firm turns on the estimated market for its products. Inevitably, this will be done in the first instance by the purchaser's own marketing experts. Indeed, it will usually be on the advice of such experts that any particular firm is being investigated with a view to purchase in the first place. But with the evaluation of so critical a factor it will often be advisable to take a second opinion from a capable market research firm. This is even more desirable where the purchasing firm has no experts of its own, and is taking

---

[1] In forecasting expected trading profits it should be remembered that this includes gross profits *after* they have been corrected for any likely stock appreciation or depreciation. Usually it is not possible to foresee these happenings in advance, but where there is a long term trend of, say, rising raw material prices, stock appreciation can and should be allowed for specifically. That this is sensible is apparent, for 'stock profits', to give stock appreciation its other name, are not available to the owners of the business as part of the net cash flow because they must inevitably be reinvested in the business if it is to earn the surplus represented by the net cash flow.

much on trust from the vendors. The market research survey [3] will be concerned with the firm's market potential and the risks associated with it. Risk associated with any business must depend overwhelmingly on the structure of the product market and the place the firm holds in it. The three factors of principal importance here are first the firm's market share and its trend over the past few years. Second, the rate of growth of the total market relative to capacity of the industry, for any slackening off in this growth would suggest that the industry was becoming more competitive, and hence more risky. Third, the effect of any relevant government action particularly as regards protection from foreign competition. An exactly similar analysis should be applied to the markets supplying the firm with its basic raw materials.

In evaluating the net cash flow, one final point must be made. It has already been stressed (Chapter 2) how the net cash flow to be evaluated is the *joint incremental* net cash flow of the purchaser and the acquired firm, i.e. the *differential* net cash flow which can be attributed to the fact of the merger alone. In so doing it is well to remember this should include any losses that might otherwise have occurred in the absence of the take-over. If firm A does not buy out firm B, and this gives C an opportunity to merge with B instead, then A might well suffer a loss of business (either by failing to expand as rapidly, or even actually declining). In such a case the net cash flow to be considered should properly include any loss or shortfall averted by the fact of the merger.

b. *Evaluating the Assets*

While a firm is bought primarily for its income prospects, the state of its tangible assets (as opposed to its goodwill) has an important bearing on this, and whenever possible, they should be specifically evaluated.

Those appraising assets have two functions to perform. First to ascertain whether any of the assets will be surplus to the requirements of the purchaser. Where surplus assets are identified, they must be valued from the purchaser's viewpoint. If the purchaser can make use of some of the assets, e.g. land or buildings, these assets are worth their replacement cost. Where the purchaser has no need or use for the assets they are worth at least their current resale value. They might be worth more than this sum if their resale value can be expected to appreciate more than the purchaser's cost of capital: this is often true of land, but seldom true of other assets.

The second function of the technical appraisers is to determine when those assets which are to be continued in their present use will wear out, and what it will cost to replace them. Obviously this cannot be done for each and every single asset, but it should be done in broad groupings of major assets, e.g. the main plants, buildings, etc. Items which are replaced regularly at frequent intervals, e.g. vehicles, are fairly easily valued. But the larger items call for more careful evaluation. Sometimes it is possible to treat assets in broad categories, but in many cases this can be a false economy. When, say, a brewery is considering buying out another brewery whose chief asset may consist of hundreds of public houses and hotels, many of them occupying prominent sites in the centres of towns, it may be worth having each one of them properly surveyed and evaluated. The fixed assets, land, buildings, plant and machinery, vehicles, etc., require the appraisal of technical experts, such as surveyors, property dealers, and engineers. Assets such as patents will generally require expert legal appraisal as well.

Net current assets (stock, debtors, and cash, less creditors, taxes due, etc.) are more easily valued, and this is usually best done by accountants. The same goes for contingent liabilities such as capital commitments, etc. Sometimes it will be possible to take this element of the purchase price of the firm as the value of the net current assets in the last audited balance sheet, with an adjustment payable on the basis of an *ad hoc* audit for the date of the purchase. This is most feasible when a private business is being purchased. When a public offer is being made for shares at a fixed price, no subsequent adjustment is possible. Finally, it is the job of all who are concerned with the vetting of assets to assign a resale or break-up value to *all* the assets, not just the surplus ones. By break-up value is meant the separate break-up value of the assets assuming they will be sold in sufficiently small lots such that the business is effectively discontinued. This usually involves the complete loss of any goodwill which usually attaches only to the business as a 'going concern'. Where assets have other profitable uses (notably land and buildings), the break-up value can yield the highest value of all – indeed this is inevitable at some time in the life of every declining business when it becomes more profitable to close down rather than continue. This assessment gives a minimum value to the business, not only to the potential purchaser, but also to the existing owners.

c. *Tax Aspects*

As has been stressed, a change of ownership in a business often has far-reaching tax implications. Sometimes the firm to be purchased will have tax losses on its books which can be used to offset tax on the purchaser's profits. Sometimes the purchased firm will have substantial capital allowances or other tax 'carry forwards'. These are very real and important factors justifying specific evaluation.

In the assessment of the expected net cash flow of the purchased firm, tax payments will need to be explicitly assessed. Once the tax specialist has been given the forecast trading profits, and the incidence and amount of capital expenditure, this factor is fairly easily estimated.

d. *Rate of Discount and Evaluation of Gearing*

The acquisition of another firm differs from normal investment projects by the fact that it may already have built into it some degree of gearing in the shape of outstanding preference shares or debentures of the firm taken over. To evaluate the equity cash flow of the company by the weighted average cost of capital is often unsatisfactory since it implies that the purchaser can bring yet more gearing to bear on an already geared equity stream – an assumption that may be the reverse of the truth if the gearing of the firm taken over is unduly high or if a substantial proportion of the purchase price will be reflected in the purchaser's balance sheet as 'goodwill' (see Chapter 12 Section 1). The actual opportunity for gearing which the new acquisition will permit will generally vary in fact with the outstanding amount of its indebtedness, the financial standing and policy of the purchaser, and the method and amount of payment. For these reasons it is generally most desirable that the analysis be conducted in terms of the equity net cash flows discounted at the purchasers equity cost of capital and for subsequent analysis to take into account any special financing advantages or disadvantages of the new acquisition.

e. *Financial Considerations*

When a business is acquired the purchaser becomes responsible for its debts and financial obligations. These can be divided into short term and long term debts. The former heading embraces those items which are shown in the balance sheet under the heading of 'current liabilities', an accounting distinction for debts falling due for payment within a year (see Appendix A, Chapter 3). These debts comprise trade creditors, dividends due, tax payment obligations, and any short term loans such as bank overdrafts. As has been mentioned above in section (b), the valuation of current liabilities should normally be done by accountants when current assets are being valued, and the net balance ('net current assets') struck. In many businesses, however, the amount of current assets can be expected to have significant seasonal fluctuations. This must be considered explicitly together with the likelihood of current liabilities, particularly trade creditors and bank overdrafts, expanding at the same time. Where any such expansion is insufficient, it is necessary to allow for the provision of additional short term finance which must be added to the purchase price of the business.

As short term liabilities by definition fall due within a year, little or no discounting is involved in their evaluation. For the evaluation of longer term liabilities, however, discounting is the essence of the procedure. Long term liabilities can be classified under two headings, preference shares, and loans of various types. Both represent fixed interest obligations, but there are important distinctions. Loans are regarded as an expense of the business; they are usually for a fixed period of years, and have a prior charge on the assets, i.e. they rank before preference shares in the event of bankruptcy or liquidation. Preference shares, by contrast, are deemed to participate in profits (after all expenses, including loan interest, have been met) albeit to a fixed extent; they are often irredeemable, and in the event of bankruptcy or liquidation they rank ahead only of the equity shares. Despite these differences, the same method is used in evaluating the two kinds of claim. The method is simply to discount all future expected net-of-tax outgoings involved in being responsible for the obligations incurred.

Consider first irredeemable preference shares. In this case the purchaser will be responsible for a net-of-tax interest charge in perpetuity. This is merely discounted at the net-of-tax equity cost of capital to give its present value. In the case of a loan that was to be redeemed say ten years hence, the net interest payments and the terminal capital repayment would merely be discounted to their present value. The capital repayment would only be discounted if the loan was not going to be renewed. If the loan would be renewed, the new loan would be used to repay the old loan, and so a new series of interest payments (at perhaps a different rate of interest compared to the present loan), commencing ten years hence, would take the place of the repayment of capital. Redeemable preference shares are similar to fixed period loans and should be treated accordingly. Sometimes preference shares are redeemable at the company's option, or over a long period. In such a case, alternatives must be evaluated to find which gives the lowest present value. If a firm had issued redeemable preference shares at a very high interest rate, the best course of action might be to redeem them at the earliest opportunity, and replace them either by cheaper preference shares or, more probably, by debentures. Such opportunities might arise in taking over old-established companies where the incidence of increasing profits tax has made the net-of-tax burden of preference shares significantly higher than that of debentures bearing the same 'gross' interest.

Sometimes preference shares carry the right to further participation in profits when equity shareholders have received a given amount of dividends. If this state of affairs is likely to obtain in future years, any such estimated extra payments must also be discounted and added to the cost of the financial obligation being incurred. Similarly, in the case of cumulative preference shares on which some past dividends are outstanding, allowance must be made for paying them off as soon as profits permit.

Another complication to be considered arises when preference shares or debentures have conversion rights into equity shares. Where such rights exist and are likely to be exercised, the purchaser must evaluate the cost either of buying out such shares, or being obligated to share the firm's equity dividends in perpetuity. The solution to this problem, which is similar to that of evaluating minority shareholdings, will be apparent from Chapter 12 dealing with the miscellaneous problems relating to take-overs.

Finally, it is necessary to consider the bearing of expected inflation (or deflation) on the evaluation of obligations fixed in money terms. This important problem is also discussed in the same chapter on miscellaneous problems. (See also Chapter 6, Section 7.)

f. *Personnel Problems*

Management and labour are often a critical factor affecting the profitability of the company and will often warrant thorough investigation in view of their financial implications. First the level of wages and salaries in the firm will need to be compared with those in rival and neighbouring firms as a prerequisite to assessing long term labour costs. The history of recent labour relations in the firm and the whole industry has an important bearing on this appraisal. If expansion is planned, the likelihood of obtaining adequate supplies of labour in future must be estimated. Alternatively, if any redundancy is likely in either the firm being purchased and/or the purchasing firm, the question of compensation payment must be considered, together with its effect on morale, future recruitment, etc. Finally consideration must be given to the pension arrangements in the firm to be purchased. Where such arrangements are less adequate than those obtaining for the purchasing firm's staff they will need improving: where more adequate, they could result in the purchasing company needing to increase the benefits of its existing staff.

It sometimes happens that the main asset of a firm is its existing staff, particularly its top management, in which case an assurance of their continuation for a period is required. With senior staff this will usually be a matter for special individual service contracts. With less senior staff it may be a matter of all-round salary increases. For a good research team it may involve primarily the provision of better facilities: for a good sales staff, better cars and more generous expense accounts. All these are matters for calculation.

g. *Legal Considerations*

Most of the tasks for lawyers in purchasing other firms are obvious. They must investigate the position of minority shareholders if any, preference shareholders, and the owners of debentures and other long term loans. They must consider the terms of any leases on land or buildings, both any leased by the firm, and to the firm. Their services will be required to vet the ownership of property, to appraise contingent liabilities of a legal nature such as pending lawsuits, etc., to investigate patent rights, licensing arrangements, contracts for the exchange of technical knowhow, etc., etc. Contracts to customers, or for the supply of raw materials, or components need scrutiny, as do any exclusive selling franchise rights held or granted by the company. The existing contract terms of the senior management, or any new terms to be drawn up, are clearly the province of the lawyers, as are pension fund arrangements for the staff. Where technical appraisal reveals the need to expand onto adjoining land in future, the feasibility of this must be examined, including the likelihood of obtaining planning permission. There will also be such matters as arranging the purchase or merger to minimize stamp duties, etc. And this list of legal tasks is by no means exhaustive.

h. *Aggregation of Information*

When all the separate factors which go to make up the business have been evaluated, the information thus obtained must be aggregated.

The resulting total should set the upper limit[1] to the *cash*[2] price it is worth paying to acquire the business. Obviously a purchaser should try to get the business for as cheap a price as possible – the valuation merely sets one of the limits for bargaining.[3]

The other limit is set by the vendor's valuation and it is worth going through the same valuation procedure as has been outlined above from the vendor's viewpoint. The lowest valuation the vendor can be expected to put on the business is its break-up value, see (b) above. If it is a public company, the lower limit is usually set by the current market value of its shares. It is possible that this market valuation is too high but no take-over bid would be expected to succeed with a lower price. Where the market valuation is too high, it will usually be necessary to wait upon events until the share prices fall significantly below the maximum offer the purchaser will make.

Another factor bearing on this process is the value of the business to any third parties who are potential purchasers. Frequently one take-over bid can be expected to call forth one or more counter-offers as rival firms see their market hegemony threatened. It is as well to attempt to assess the maximum bids they could make in advance of one's own bid so as to be fully prepared for a situation where developments could occur rapidly. With so much at stake, this is an elementary precaution.

These matters are best appreciated by considering a detailed example of valuing a business, and this is done in the next chapter. This example assumes that all relevant information is made available. In the majority of cases, of course, only a limited amount of information will be available, and approximations and guesses of orders of magnitude have to be made, and only part of the following method of analysis will be appropriate. It is important, however, to establish what is being approximated to so that errors of judgment as to fact are not compounded by subsequent errors of evaluation. The following

---

[1] This is not strictly true if some similar business could be acquired more cheaply. This point is examined in Section 4 of Chapter 12.

[2] Where the means of payment take the form of the purchasers' own shares in whole or part settlement, the problem is not quite so straightforward. This is dealt with in Section 2 of Chapter 12.

[3] This is only the upper limit to value if the purchase of the firm at this price offers a higher net present value than entering the industry and building up a new firm from scratch – a mutually exclusive alternative (see Section 4 of Chapter 12). As the cost of breaking into a new market from scratch is often very high, entry by purchase of an existing firm will usually be the cheaper alternative, but it is always worth investigating.

method of analysis is intended to demonstrate the appropriate techniques of evaluation, and also to serve as a checklist of possibly important considerations.

As a matter of general organization, however, it is well to remember that take-overs often represent the largest sums ever invested by firms. This being so, such expenditure should be taken in the light of the fullest knowledge that can be made available. The savings that can accrue for a given expenditure of time and effort are clearly very large in this situation. In the case of some prospective take-overs, the purchaser will have full access to the records and accounts of the vendor. This should result in the most realistic valuation. But even in a secret take-over bid considerable information can often be collected by diligent and imaginative research. If it be argued that in the normal course of business such appraisals have to be done hurriedly, then this is *prima facie* evidence of inadequate foresight. Wherever take-overs are possible (either of rival firms or one's own), highly competent staff should be constantly engaged in studying all the possibilities, increasing their information, checking their estimates, etc., etc. The allocation of key staff to so important a function will represent an investment with the highest of returns. Where, for whatever reason, a detailed appraisal is not possible before major decisions are taken, an understanding of the factors entering into such an appraisal will be of advantage in revealing the critical factors entering into this particular case.

The fact that much time of senior staff is often not made available for such studies cannot be rationally defended. It implies an extremely high valuation on the time of top management which few, if any, could justify.

REFERENCES

1. GEORGE BULL and ANTHONY VICE, *Bid for Power*, Third Edition, Elek Books, London, 1961.
2. J. FRED WESTON (Editor), 'Readings in Finance', *Fortune*, Henry Holt and Company, New York, 1958.
3. A. J. MERRETT and G. BANNOCK, *Business Economics and Statistics* – Parts Two and Three, Hutchinson, 1962.

APPENDIX A

STOCK APPRECIATION

Where a business normally carries stock equivalent to say three months' output, there will be a gap of three months on average between the purchase and sale of its goods. If the cost of the materials used rises or falls, the accounting records will charge against current sales the original cost of the materials consumed, which will be different from the current or replacement cost of those same materials, and this gives rise to a distortion in reporting real profits (see Section 3 of the Appendix to Chapter 3). A simple example will make this clearer.

Suppose a firm sells 40 tons of material a year, and always has a stock of 10 tons. At the start of a year it has 10 tons in stock which cost £10 per ton, or £100 in all. Suppose the replacement cost of the material rises to £12 at the start of the year, and stays there for the rest of the year. If net sales revenue were £15 a ton, and the firm purchased 40 tons of material during the year at £12 a ton, so that year end stocks were also 10 tons, ordinary accounts would report profits as follows:

Opening Stock – 10 tons at £10 a ton		= £100
Plus Purchases – 40 tons at £12 a ton		480
		580
Less Closing Stock – 10 tons at £12 a ton		−120
Cost of Sales		460
Profit		140
Net Sales Revenue – 40 tons at £15 a ton		= £600

i.e. Sales were charged with 10 tons out of stock at £10 a ton, and 30 tons at £12 a ton.

Had current replacement costs been used, the charge would have been 40 tons at £12 a ton = £480, and profit would be £600−£480 = £120, i.e. £20 less. This £20 difference is known as 'stock profit', or 'stock appreciation', as it is equivalent to the rise in the value of stocks during the accounting period from £100 to £120. The accounting records have treated this rise in stock value as a profit, whereas it is more properly regarded (by progressive accountants and economists) not as a profit, but an extra capital cost necessarily incurred to stay in business on the same scale as before. In other words, the business could only distribute £120 as profit if it is to continue to operate at its previous level. Stock depreciation arises when replacement costs have fallen, and closing stocks have a lower cost than opening stocks. In these circumstances, accounting records normally understate real profits.

Many more complications occur in practice in calculating stock appreciation or depreciation, but sufficient explanation has been given to indicate the nature of the problem and how it should be handled.

For evaluating past profits and estimating future profits it should be clear that the appropriate profit concept is profit corrected for stock appreciation or depreciation. This corrected profit, plus depreciation less tax payments and capital expenditures, amounts, to the net cash flow of a business.

CHAPTER ELEVEN

Assessing the Purchase Price of a Firm

II

A Case Study

This chapter is devoted to a detailed analysis of a hypothetical but fairly realistic take-over. For completeness it is assumed that the firm being taken over makes available to the prospective purchaser all the information required for it to determine the true worth of the business. Frequently, of course, such full information will not be available. Where a firm is unwilling to be taken over, the bidder will have to rely on published information and possibly market research reports, surveys of the firm's properties etc. In some cases it may not even be possible for extensive analysis to be undertaken because of the dangers of a leak of information resulting in harmful speculation in the shares of both the firm being considered for take-over, and the potential purchaser. Finally, a firm being taken over, while willing to provide some information, is not generally prepared to divulge information in the nature of trade secrets such as share of particular markets, profit margins on particular products, future plans, etc. For obvious reasons, this will normally be the case where the bidder is a competitor and there is any likelihood of the take-over not going through. In this case study, however, we are primarily concerned to establish the general method of approach and this is not altered in principle (only in scope) when the information available is less detailed and reliable.

On a number of points, particularly taxation, we have also simplified some of the problems to avoid discussion of specialist issues outside the scope of this book.

1. BASIC INFORMATION

All-Star Arctic Products Ltd. is a frozen food manufacturing company with a national distribution organization. Well known for its quality meats, fruits, vegetables and speciality foods, it desires to complete the range of its existing lines by handling fish products. It is thought that the ability to market the full range of frozen foods will be a valuable selling point both with retailers and the catering trade, and further, that there should be substantial economies in the advertising and distribution of the additional product. With no firsthand knowledge of the fishing industry, it decides it is advisable to buy up an existing firm with a competent management and experienced staff. From this viewpoint the most promising firm is thought to be the small but enterprising Northern Star Ltd. Founded forty years earlier, it was originally a family firm of trawler owners which expanded into the retailing business. In recent years it has gone into frozen fish production and marketing, partly through its own shops, but mostly through other retail outlets, including the catering trade. Its frozen fish has the reputation of being of the highest quality on the market, due primarily to its pioneering of factory trawlers where fish is caught, filleted, packed, and frozen, all within the space of a few hours.

This is all the information that is known initially to the management of All-Star Arctic Products Ltd. (henceforth referred to as ASAP). They consider that there is a *prima facie* case for investigating further to see whether or not Northern Star Ltd. (henceforth referred to as NS) can be purchased at a price which will make it an attractive investment. To this end negotiations are entered into with the directors of NS who prove willing to discuss the possibility of selling out to ASAP. As a result of the meetings the following information is forthcoming.

First, the published profit and loss accounts for the previous five years, and the latest balance sheet as set out in Tables 11.1 and 11.2.

This information would of course be available normally without access to a firm's internal accounts (unless it were an exempt private company). These should be carefully studied prior to opening any negotiations, as they will be the basis of the first estimated value.

The first and obvious piece of information to be gleaned is the number of equity shares and their current stock exchange quotation, as this will normally set the lower limit to the purchase price which is likely to be attractive to the existing owners. In the case of NS, there are one million £1 ordinary shares currently valued at £2·85. The current dividend is $7\frac{1}{2}\%$ gross on the nominal share capital which gives a current dividend yield (gross dividend ÷ current market price) of 2·63%. The significant point about the dividend

Table 11.1

Northern Star Ltd. Profit and Loss Account – Previous Five Years

£000's

	-1	-2	-3	-4	-5
Gross Profit before tax	286	448	266	206	202
Less tax: Profits tax – 10%	-25 } -139	-41 } -60†	-23 } -129	-17 } -99	-18 } -99
Income tax – 40%	-114	-19	-106	-82	-81
Gross Profit after tax	147	388	137	107	103
Less Net of tax payments: (paid under deduction of 40% income tax)					
(i) 400 – 5% debentures	-12 } -52	-12 } -52	-12 } -52	-12 } -52	-12 } -41
(ii) 300 – 6% debentures	-11	-11	-11	-11	nil*
(iii) 600 – 8% Preference Shares	-29	-29	-29	-29	-29
Net of tax profit available for Equity Shareholders	95	336	85	55	62
Dividends	-45‡	-45	-30	-25	-25
Retained Profit	50	291	55	30	37

(Stock Exchange value = 2·63% gross dividend yield = £75,000 ÷ 2·63% = £2·85m.)

* The 6% debentures are assumed to be raised at the start of year –4.

† Reduced by a 40% tax allowance on the purchase of a factory trawler for £800,000 in previous year.

‡ Dividend = $\begin{cases} 75 \text{ before income tax} \\ 45 \text{ after income tax} \end{cases}$

Table 11.2

Northern Star Ltd. Balance Sheet – End Year 5   £000's

		Gross (at cost)	Less Depreciation to date	Net
Share Capital; etc.				
1,000,000 – £1 Shares	1,000			
Capital Reserves	400			
Retained Profits	941			
Future Tax	139			
	2,480			
8% Irredeemable Preference Shares	600			
	3,080			
Long-Term Loans				
6% Debentures (redeemable yr. 21)	300			
5% Debentures (redeemable yr. 8)	400			
	700			
Current Liabilities				
Creditors	25			
Tax	60			
Dividend (net-of-tax)	45			
	130			
Fixed Assets				
100 freehold shops		150	−90	60
6 wholesale cold storage depots		180	−30	150
Factories: A		50	−40	10
B		150	−15	135
TOTAL PROPERTY		530	−175	355
Plant and Machinery		200	−50	150
3 Factory Trawlers		2,300	−645	1,655
Vehicles:				
10 ten-tonners		30	−15	15
20 five-tonners		40	−20	20
45 light vans		27	−17	10
TOTAL FIXED ASSETS		3,127	−912	2,215
Current Assets				
Stocks – frozen fish		705		
Trawler – ⅓ payment in advance		300		
Debtors		200		
Cash		490		
				1,695
TOTAL	3,910			3,910

yield is that it usually gives a broad indication of whether or not a firm is considered to have growth prospects. If the current yield on long dated gilt edged securities is say, 6%, the market, in valuing NS's shares such that it gives a dividend yield of less than half this amount, clearly expects profits and dividends to grow appreciably in future. So, in the case of NS, the firm is valued by the stock markets as a growth stock whose minimum purchase price can be expected to exceed £2·85 per share.

Having established an approximate minimum purchasing price, the next step is to consider what profits might be as the result of the contemplated merger. The relevant data here is the level to which NS's profits can be raised after takeover *net* of the capital expenditure needed to produce them. (It must be emphasized that it is quite erroneous to capitalize – as is often done – the *whole* of a growing stream of earnings when in fact a substantial proportion of the initial earnings must be reinvested to achieve the further growth.) Suppose, however, that ASAP estimate that they can increase net of tax profits from £100,000 to £200,000 within five years without significant capital expenditure in excess of the current depreciation provisions (by cost economies and exploiting ASAP's greater marketing outlets) and can then maintain profits at that level indefinitely. Taking ASAP's net-of-tax cost of capital for equity as 7%, the calculation would be as follows.

(i) First five years

net of tax profits expected to grow from £100,000 to £200,000 approximately, implies a compound growth rate of 14·9%. (This is found by interpolating in Table A in the 5 year row to determine the reading 0·50 – i.e. the present value £100,000 of a sum growing steadily to £200,000 in 5 years.) The present value (in £000's) at 7% of a five year series starting at £100 and growing at 14·9% p.a.

$$= \sum_{i=1}^{i=5} \frac{£100(1\cdot149)^i}{1\cdot07^i} = \sum_{i=1}^{i=5} £100 \times 1\cdot074^i = £623.$$

(ii) Year 6 onwards

$$= v_{5|7} \times \frac{£200}{0\cdot07} = \frac{£200}{0\cdot07} \times 0\cdot713 = £2{,}037.$$

Therefore total present value of income = £2,037 + £623 = £2,660, i.e. £2,660,000.

This is just about the current market price and so indicates that more detailed study will probably result in a higher valuation after allowing for surplus assets and the amount of the depreciation provision not actually required for new investment.

Having established that NS has possibilities the next stage is the detailed evaluation. This is done in three parts:

(a) Evaluating the assets[1] including future capital expenditure.
(b) Evaluating the liabilities.
(c) Evaluating the likely net cash flow.

The evaluation will be done on the assumption that NS has a life of 20 years, of 50 years and also a perpetual life which will be seen to come to very much the same thing. The results of all the separate detailed calculations are set out in Table 11.4 at the end of the chapter.

2. THE DETAILED EVALUATION

a. *Evaluating the Surplus Assets and Future Capital Expenditure*

i. The shops. NS have always had the policy of owning the freehold of all their shops. This makes them potentially very valuable if it should become policy to sell off some or all of these shops. ASAP do not themselves own any retail outlets, and have little desire to enter this field. From an examination of the detailed profit and loss account of NS, it transpires that the profit on all the shops together is only £50,000 gross (i.e. before tax). Fish retailing is thought to be a declining trade and this profit is consequently expected to

---

[1] This example will be *broadly* based on British tax law. The salient features assumed are as follows:

  (i) Tax payments are assumed to occur one year in arrears – i.e. tax on the profits of year 1 are assumed to be paid at the end of year 2.
 (ii) Depreciation for tax purposes is on a straight line basis – 5% on ships, plant, and machinery, and 2% on *industrial* buildings (commercial buildings attract no tax allowances). In addition, ships attract a 40% investment allowance over and above cost, and a 10% initial allowance, which is at the expense of the normal depreciation allowance in the final years of assumed life.
(iii) There is no effective capital gains tax on the sale of surplus capital assets.
 (iv) Income tax = 40% and profits tax = 10% – making 50% in all.

decline. ASAP are advised by property surveyors that if all the free-hold shops were sold they could confidently be expected to realize about £870,000. The current gross profit of only £50,000 represents a current gross return of only 5¾% on this resale value – and this is expected to fall. Hence ASAP feel they should sell off the shops. The shops employ a staff of some 300 employees who have served with NS for more than two years. In the circumstances ASAP would want to pay compensation averaging £200 per head – some £60,000 in all. It is estimated that it would take a year on average to sell off the shops and pay off the staff. This can be evaluated as follows:

One year hence – profit after tax	= say	£20,000
Add estimated net resale value of shops =		870,000
		£890,000
Less compensation payments		−60,000
Net value one year hence	=	£830,000[1]
Present value = £830,000/1·07	=	£776,000

[1] It is assumed that there are no tax effects from any of these transactions.

Because of the falling profit which is currently inadequate, it is better to sell off the shops now rather than to continue them in-definitely. But it may be even better to operate the shops for a few more years at a low profit, perhaps even at some loss, if the resale value of the shops can be expected to rise sufficiently to compensate for this. If the property values could be expected to rise at say 10% per annum for the next three or four years and then level out, it would be worth deferring the break-up of the retail side of the business till then. To discover whether this is worthwhile, it is necessary to discount net profits (or losses) up to the time the shops are to be sold, and the eventual net selling price, and to compare this with the valuation made above to determine the more profitable course.

In practice it is likely that it will not be a choice of selling off all the sites now or in a few years time, but of selling some now, and some later. But the principles of the calculations required are apparent.

ii. Wholesale cold storage depots. NS possesses six fairly new wholesale cold store depots, some of which are much under-utilized. These depots exist in an area where ASAP would be expanding in the next few years and the purchase of NS would save the cost of one new depot (£60,000) in a year's time, and two years hence the cost of a further two new depots also costing £60,000. It is assumed that these buildings would not qualify for any capital allowances so there are no tax consequences to consider. Hence the purchase of NS will save ASAP £60,000 expenditure one year hence, and £120,000 two years hence. The present value is

$$\frac{£60,000}{1 \cdot 07} + \frac{£120,000}{1 \cdot 07^2} = £161,000.$$

Depots are expected to have a life of around fifty years or more, and the fact that the NS depots are not quite new and might not last quite as long as brand new depots is immaterial with such long lived assets.

If the firm has a fifty year life the depots will not need to be replaced. Where the firm is assumed to have a perpetual life, however, and these depots are replaced at 50 year intervals, the cost would be say £60,000 per depot, (actually slightly less as the £60,000 includes some cost for the land but this can be ignored), or £360,000 in all. In perpetuity – see equation (1.6) – this has a present value of

$$\frac{£360,000}{1 \cdot 07^{50} - 1} = \frac{£360,000}{28 \cdot 46} = £13,000.$$

So small a figure can be safely ignored.

iii. Factories and plant. Factory A and its plant will be adequate for a further five years when it will need to be replaced. ASAP are planning a new factory in the same area as A, and can use the land on which A is situated. It is estimated that this will save ASAP about £20,000 in five years time, bearing in mind the rising cost of land. The remainder of the land, (A has rather a large site part of which is unoccupied) could be sold off immediately for £30,000, but if held for a further 5 years can be expected to be worth £50,000: thereafter its value is unlikely to increase significantly. Land purchase and sale are assumed to have no tax consequences, hence the evaluation of the land is as follows.

The present value to ASAP of the £20,000 saved on acquiring another site 5 years hence is simply $v_{5|7} \times £20,000 = £14,260$. The present value of selling the surplus land off now is £30,000 – its present resale value. Keeping it for five years and selling off for £50,000 has a present value of $v_{5|7} \times £50,000 = £35,650$ – hence the surplus land should be kept for 5 years. Therefore present value of the land = £14,260 + £35,650 = £49,910, or, say, £50,000.

The additional expenditure on ASAP's new factory and plant to supply the facilities at present supplied by factory A is estimated to be £50,000 for a larger building and £85,000 for additional plant, both with a life of say 25 years. On the basis of NS having only a 20 year life, and ignoring scrap value, the present value of this expenditure some 5 years hence is $v_{5|7} \times (£50,000 + £85,000)$ = £96,000.

If the firm is deemed to have a 50 year life, then factory A will need to be replaced once more some 30 years hence. Assuming the same costs of £135,000 in total, this replacement expenditure has a present value of $v_{30|7} \times £135,000 = £18,000$. Therefore the total present value of expenditure on factory A and its replacement = £96,000 + £18,000 = £114,000. Assuming the firm has a perpetual life, £135,000 would be spent at 25 yearly intervals forever, commencing 30 years hence. Spending £135,000 every 25 years at an *annual* cost of capital of 7% is equivalent – see equation (1.6) – to an annuity with an annual interest rate of $(1 \cdot 07^{25} - 1)$. Thus the present value now of spending £135,000 at 25 year intervals commencing 25 years hence = $£135,000/(1 \cdot 07^{25} - 1) = £30,500$. As the series does not actually commence until 5 years hence, its present value now is $v_{5|7} £30,500 = £22,000$. To this must be added the present value of £135,000 5 years hence £96,000 + £22,000 = £118,000.

Factory B and its associated plant are very modern and would be kept in use by ASAP. Its life is estimated at 25 years. If NS is deemed to have a 50 year life, it would need to be renewed once more 25 years hence, at an estimated cost of £150,000.

This has a present value of $v_{25|7} £150,000 = £28,000$. For a perpetual life, £150,000 would be spent at 25 year intervals

$$= \frac{£150,000}{1 \cdot 07^{25} - 1} = £34,000$$

an insignificant difference from a 50 year life.

iv. Factory trawlers. The new factory trawler on which £300,000 has already been paid will be required by ASAP to increase the output of quality fish for the expanded production which is planned. Thus a further £600,000 will become due one year hence which has a present value of £600,000/1·07 = £561,000. The following year there will be a once and for all tax relief from the 40% investment allowance and 10% initial allowance which = 50% × 50% × £900,000 =

£225,000. This has a present value of $£225,000/1\cdot07^2 = £196,000$. Thus, the net cost of the new trawler $= £561,000 - £196,000 = £365,000.$[1]

All trawlers are expected to have a working life of another 25 years. Thereafter, they would need to be replaced at about 25 year intervals. Such a course may well be unnecessary as it might become possible and profitable to buy quality fish from other factory trawlers under contract. If not, every 25 years there would be an expenditure equivalent to the net sum of $£900,000 - £225,000v_{1|7} = £900,000 - £210,000 = £690,000$. On 4 trawlers this would equal £2,760,000. If the trawlers are renewed only once this has a present value of $£2,760,000v_{25|7} = £508,000$. If this is done in perpetuity at 25 year intervals the present value of this expenditure would be $£2,760,000/(1\cdot07^{25} - 1) = £623,000$.

v. Vehicles. The ten 10 ton vans, and the twenty 5 ton vans will be required if NS is absorbed. As these assets have a fairly even age distribution the annual depreciation charge will be absorbed most years in replacement expenditure. In this case the replacement expenditure on the two sets of vans and their depreciation is expected to amount to £12,000 p.a. For 20 years this has a present value of $a_{20|7}£12,000 = £127,000$. For 50 years this has a present value of $a_{50|7}£12,000 = £166,000$. For this expenditure in perpetuity, the present value is $£12,000/0\cdot07 = £171,000$.

The forty-five light vans will become redundant with the sale of the fish shops. It is estimated that they can be sold for £9,500 in one year's time. (This figure is assumed to be the net of any balancing allowances or charges.) Redundancy compensation will be paid to ten of the drivers at £200 a head. The remainder of the drivers will not qualify for redundancy payments because of short service, or can be absorbed into ASAP's own organization which is currently short of good drivers. These cash flows have a present value

$$= \frac{£9,500 - £2,000}{1\cdot07} = £7,000$$

---

[1] For ease of calculation in this application it is convenient to evaluate unusual or irregular tax concessions by reducing the capital cost of the asset concerned. Regular tax concessions are evaluated in the net cash flow – see Section C below. Alternatively, all tax concessions on capital outlays could be evaluated using the formulae and tables of the Appendix to Chapter 2.

vi. Net current assets (i.e. current assets less current liabilities). It is extremely important to assess stocks and debtors most carefully. Often large sums of capital will be involved and a reduction in stocks (by more strict inventory control), or tighter credit control reducing debtors, can release substantial capital which would of course be available to the purchaser as surplus cash in the business. In this example, however, it is assumed that stocks, debtors and creditors are appropriate for their type and level of business and that the closing of the fish shops will result in negligible savings. Further, the book value of the stocks is accepted as being equal to replacement cost (see appendix to Chapter 3).

The tax payment and dividend must be paid within a month, therefore net cash without them = £490,000 − £105,000 = £385,000. Of this cash balance, £250,000 is regarded as the basic working balance, leaving a surplus of £135,000.

vii. Terminal value. If NS is deemed to have anything but a perpetual life, some allowance must be made for terminal value, if any, of the surviving assets. Normally, a company will not just be allowed to wind up: rather its owners will cause it to take up new activities gradually, and the business will continue along new lines. It is not possible to forecast how or what form this will take, but if the most drastic happening, the complete winding up of the company, is considered, a lower limit of terminal value (i.e. the value of the business in its present type of activity) can be set.

For either a 20 year or a 50 year life, ASAP estimate the following values.

1. Land for factories	£40,000
2. Net Working Capital (stock, debtors and cash less current liabilities)	£700,000
Total	£740,000

In the 20 year case, the cold storage depots are estimated to have a combined value of a further £100,000. All other assets are assumed to have no terminal scrap value in either case. Therefore, in the 50 year case, terminal value = $£740,000v_{50|7} = £25,000$. In the 20 year case it is $£840,000v_{20|7} = £217,000$.

b. *Evaluating the Liabilities*

i. £400,000 of 5% debentures redeemable in 3 years' time. To evaluate the liabilities of the company it is necessary to determine what will happen three years hence. (In all that follows, a continuation of the 50% tax rate is assumed.) If the debentures were redeemed and no further action taken, the liability would be a ($£400,000v_{3|7}$) capital repayment plus ($£10,000a_{3|7}$) in net interest payments. If, however, these debentures are to be redeemed by the issue of further debentures, (perhaps with short time interval and bridging operation) and this process is repeated *ad infinitum*, the liability under this heading is the present value of all future *net* interest payments. Suppose these 5% debentures are expected to be redeemed by issuing 7% debentures in their place, with the latter being renewed at every future redemption date. Then the present value of this liability is simply the following:

Net of tax interest payments next 3 years $£10,000a_{3|7} = £26,000$.
Net of tax interest payments year 4 onwards $= [£14,000/0·07]v_{3|7}$ $= £163,000$.

Therefore, the total liability has a present value of $£26,000$ $+£163,000 = £189,000$.

If the firm is assumed to have a life of 50 years, the liability would have the following present value.

First 3 years – as before $= £26,000$.

Interest payments, years 4–50 inclusive $= £14,000a_{47|7}v_{3|7}$ $= £156,000$.

Final redemption payment $£400,000v_{50|7} = £14,000$.

Therefore, the total liability has a present value of ($£26,000$ $+£156,000+£14,000) = £196,000$.

From this it is apparent that the difference in the present value of redemption in 50 years time, and perpetual renewal is insignificant.

If it is assumed, however, that the firm has only a 20 year life *and* that the debentures would have to be redeemed at the end of that period, the present value of the liability would reduce to the following.

Net interest payments for first 3 years as before $= £26,000$. Interest payments for years 4–20 inclusive $= £14,000a_{17|7}v_{3|7}$ $= £112,000$. Redemption 20 years hence $= £400,000v_{20|7}$ $= £103,000$. Therefore, the total liability has a present value of ($£26,000+£112,000+£103,000) = £241,000$.

Usually, even when it may no longer pay to continue a company's existing activities, it will be possible to keep the legal form of the company in existence. Where this is so, the parent company can continue to raise fresh debenture capital to redeem each issue, while it changes the field of operations in which the company is engaged. This amounts to a perpetual existence of the company, or to a 50 year existence which comes to very much the same thing.

ii. £300,000 of 6% debentures redeemable 16 years hence. On the same reasoning as above, the value of this liability depends on what happens at redemption date. Assume this debenture issue is also renewed by a further 7% debenture, and that taxes continue at the rate of 50%. For a perpetual life, then present value of net interest payments next 16 years $= £9,000a_{16|7} = £85,000$. Net interest payments year 17 onwards $= [£10,500/0·07]v_{16|7} = £51,000$. Therefore, the total net present value is $(£85,000 + £51,000) = £136,000$.

For a 50 year life, followed by redemption, the present value becomes the following:

First 16 years' net interest payments as before $= £85,000$. Net interest payments years 17–50 inclusive $= £10,500a_{34|7}v_{16|7} = £46,000$. Final redemption payment 50 years hence $= £300,000$ $v_{50|7} = £10,000$. Therefore the total net present value is $(£85,000 + £46,000 + £10,000) = £141,000$.

Again the difference is insignificant between perpetual renewal, and redemption in 50 years.

For a 20 year redemption, assuming the debenture would, in fact, be renewed for only four years at the end of the first 16 years, the present value would be:

First 16 years' net interest payments as before $= £85,000$. Net interest payments years 17–20 inclusive $= £10,500a_{4|7}v_{16|7} = £12,000$. Final redemption payment 20 years hence $= £300,000$ $v_{20|7} = £78,000$. Therefore the total net present value is $(£85,000 + £12,000 + £78,000) = £175,000$.

iii. £600,000 of 8% irredeemable preference shares. Preference shares are deemed to participate in profits albeit to a fixed extent, and as such they, unlike debentures, cannot be set off against profits tax under British (or United States) tax regulations. Hence, the net of tax burden of the preference shares is gross dividend less income tax at 40%[1]— i.e. $-£48,000 \times 60\% = -£28,800$.

[1] The reason for treating all debt capital liabilities net of tax is for convenience, as the net cash flow, which is to be evaluated below, will be gross profits before debenture interest and preference dividends, less *gross* tax deductions including tax deducted on account of debenture interest and preference dividends.

Assuming a perpetual life for the company, the present value of the preference share net dividend is simply $-£28,800/0 \cdot 07 = £411,000$.

If the shares were in fact redeemed in fifty years' time, the present value is as follows:

Net dividend payments for 50 years $= £28,800a_{50|7} = £398,000$. Redemption at end of 50 years $= £600,000v_{50|7} = £20,000$. Therefore total present value $= (£398,000 + £20,000) = £418,000$, i.e. an insignificant difference. If they had to to be redeemed in 20 years, the position would be:

Net dividend payments for 20 years $= £28,800a_{20|7} = £305,000$. Redemption at end of 20 years $= £600,000v_{20|7} = £156,000$. Therefore total present value is $(£305,000 + £156,000) = £461,000$.

iv. Pension scheme. ASAP runs a generous contributory pension scheme for its own employees whereas no such provision has been made by NS. If ASAP absorbs NS it will start a pension scheme for the NS staff to which it will make an initial contribution of £300 per head. If NS is absorbed, it is estimated that 500 employees will continue to work for ASAP, so the total cost will be an immediate outlay of $£300 \times 500 = £150,000$. Future contributions will be added into wages and salaries.

c. *Evaluating the Expected Net Cash Flow*

In evaluating all future capital expenditure an allowance has already been made for all irregular tax concessions. The regular tax concessions which NS is currently receiving can be expected to continue. Annual depreciation allowance for tax purposes are taken to be as follows:

Plant and Machinery 5% of £200,000	=	£10,000
Factory Buildings = 2% of £200,000	=	£4,000
Vehicles	=	£12,000
Factory Trawlers = 5% on 3 existing trawlers		
= 5% × £2,300,000	=	£115,000
Current total	=	£141,000
Plus new trawler, third year onwards		
= 5% × £900,000	=	£45,000
Total from third year onwards	=	£186,000

Given the estimated timing of asset replacements, actual annual tax allowances in some future years will vary somewhat from those assumed here but the differences will be too small to be worth taking into account specifically.

The current gross profit before tax is £286,000. An examination of the published profit and loss account over the previous five years indicates a rising trend. Two years ago profits were very large, but this was an exceptionally prosperous year for the whole fishing industry with record catches coinciding with a severe meat shortage. It was therefore a very unusual situation and one not likely to recur. In assessing future profit trends it can therefore be ignored.

ASAP feel they can improve strongly on the present profit position which is reproduced below.

	Current Year £000's
Gross Margin	427
Less Depreciation	−141
Gross profit before tax	286
Less tax	−139
Gross profit after tax	147

Selling off the fish shops will reduce the gross margin by £50,000 per annum, but this will be more than offset by the packaging and distribution economies made possible by the merger. Further, by putting in a team of top marketing men, stepping up advertising, etc., ASAP anticipate they can double the NS profit in five years. Thereafter it is expected that increased competition will prevent further expansion and that profits will probably become fairly stable. From this, the following estimates emerge.

Table 11.3 *Estimated Net Cash Flow*

	Current year	1	2	3	4	5	6 etc.
				£000's			
Gross Margin	427	380*	450	580	670	750	750
less additional advertising and development costs	nil	−150	−150	−100	−50	nil	nil
	427	230	300	480	620	750	750
Less regular depreciation	−141	−141	−186	−186	−186	−186	−186
Gross Profit before tax	286	89	114	294	434	564	564
Less tax (estimated 48% average) payable 1 year in arrears	−60	−139	−43	−55	−141	−208	−270
Therefore net profit after tax *paid*	226	−50	71	239	293	356	294
Add back depreciation	141	141	186	186	186	186	186
Net cash flow	367	91	257	425	479	542	480

* Excluding £50,000 of fish retailing profits already taken into account.

This expected net cash flow, assuming it is constant from year 6 onwards, has a present value at 7% of

£4,526,000 for 20 years,
£6,065,000 for 50 years,

and £6,298,000 assuming a perpetual life for the business.

Having calculated the present value of surplus assets, of future liabilities (including replacement expenditure) and of estimated net cash flows, the upper limit to the present value of NS for ASAP can now be determined by aggregating all the previous calculations. This is done in Table 11.4.

From this tabulation several important conclusions are apparent.

(i) The difference between valuing the firm on the basis of a perpetual life, and a 50 year life are negligible, not only in total, but virtually item by item. This will be found to be the case with any business, save one that can be predicted to expand at a phenomenal rate *after* 50 years – a case so rare that it can be disregarded.

(ii) The difference between a 20 year evaluation and the other two evaluations is not very great – the 20 year value being approximately 83% of the two higher values. Further, a very low scrap value was assumed for NS, virtually just net working capital and land. If the business had any future prospects its goodwill would be saleable. These two factors would raise the 20 year valuation closer to the other two evaluations, and may close the gap entirely. From this it is apparent that the length of life assumed for the company is not necessarily of great consequence provided it exceeds about 15 years, when the cost of capital is as high as 7% after tax.

(iii) Where the major assets fall due for renewal within a few years of one another, this sets the natural limit to the future life period to be considered. In the case of NS, the major assets, the trawlers and factories, will require renewal some 20–25 years hence. The big jump in future discounted capital expenditure (the major reason for the difference between the value of the business for a 20 year life and for a 50 year life) occurs between the 20 year life (£588,000) and the 50 year life (£1,181,000). Therefore, when these major assets fall due for renewal will be the time to reconsider the future of NS, whether it would be profitable to continue it in its present

Table 11.4

Valuation of Northern Star for a 20 year, 50 year, and a Perpetual Life

	Present Values at 7%				£000's	
	(1) 20 year life		(2) 50 year life		(3) Perpetual life	
	+	−	+	−	+	−
(a) Surplus Assets and future Capital Expenditure						
1. Shops	776		776		776	
2. Wholesale Depots	161		161		161	13
3. Factories and Plant						
A	50	96	50	114	50	118
B				28		34
4. Factory Trawlers						
New Trawler		365		365		365
Total Trawlers				508		623
5. Vehicles	7	127	7	166	7	171
6. Net Current Assets	135		135		135	
7. Terminal Value	217		25		n.a.	
Total	+1,346	−588	+1,154	−1,181	+1,129	−1,324
(b) Liabilities						
1. £400,000 – 5% Debentures		241		196		189
2. £300,000 – 6% Debentures		175		141		136
3. £600,000 – 8% Preference shares		461		418		411
4. Cost of Initiating Pension Scheme		150		150		150
Total	−	−1,027	−	−905	−	−886
(c) Expected Net Cash Flow	4,526	−	6,065	−	6,298	−
Totals	+5,872	−1,615	+7,219	−2,086	+7,427	−2,210
Net Totals	+4,257	−	+5,133	−	+5,217	−
or say	+£4·3 million		+£5·1 million		+£5·2 million	

form, or to change the nature of its activities, even to close it down as a last resort.

(iv) If there are no other factors to consider (see below) beyond the proposed changes in operations etc., set out above, it is worth ASAP bidding up to £4·3m.–£5·2m. to acquire the equity of NS. As the present stock market valuation of the equity shares is only £2·85m. there should be plenty of scope to obtain the shares at a fairly attractive price, say, £3·5m. At this price an investment in NS would offer an attractive return.

In this example we have valued the business at but a single rate, the purchasing firm's cost of capital. In practice it would be advisable to value the business at two higher rates as well to give the yields for a range of purchase prices. By taking three widely spread rates, the actual yield for any given purchase price could be found easily by interpolation.

A number of other factors, however, will often need to be considered before the valuation of the firm is completed. These will include the resale value of the separate assets of NS; the effect of expected inflation on the valuations; the likely purchase prices of other similar firms; the scope for the purchaser to raise additional cheap finance on the strength of the assets, etc. of the firm being purchased; the effect of obtaining less than 100% of the equity of the firm being purchased; and the considerations involved in making a bid for the preference capital and/or debenture loans as well as the equity. Most of these factors will be considered in the next chapter on miscellaneous problems. The bearing of one factor, the resale value of the separate assets, can be dealt with here.

Briefly, before deciding to buy up a firm and continue to operate it, it is worth checking its break-up value to be quite sure that it pays to continue it. In the example considered, it has already been demonstrated that ASAP prefer to sell off the retail side of the business rather than earn small and diminishing profits. It may, however, be better to consider breaking up the whole business now, or in a few years time. While this is seldom the case, it should always be checked where a business has valuable assets with alternative uses: property is the best example of this.

Valuation for break-up, say one year hence, might give the following results as set out in Table 11.5.

(Where this resale value is not expected to rise significantly with time, there is no need to consider resale at some future date, unless by 'milking' the business before resale, higher profits can be made. This possibility has been ignored here, but the calculations required will by now be self evident.)

As this value is below the present stock exchange value it can be

Table 11.5

Net Resale Value[1]

Fixed Assets		£000's	£000's
100 Freehold Shops		890	
6 Wholesale Cold Storage Depots		300	
Factory A		50	
Factory B		150	
Plant and Machinery		5	
Factory Trawlers		1,500	
Vehicles		15	
			2,910
Current Assets			
Stocks	300		
Debtors	200		
Cash	200		
		700	
Less Current Liabilities			
		−130	
			570
Trawler advance payment (assuming it can be recovered for a penalty payment of £50,000)			250
Net cash flow for one year of operation			150
			3,880
Less Liabilities			
8% Preference Shares		600[2]	
6% Debentures		300[2]	
5% Debentures		400[2]	
		1,300[2]	
Staff Redundancy Compensation payments		160	
Winding-up Expenses, terminal tax adjustments, etc.		200	
			−1,660
Therefore Net value one year hence =			2,220
Therefore Present value = £2,220$v_{1|7}$ =			2,075

[1] Values should always be net of any tax consequences.
[2] Assuming redemption at the time NS is broken up.

ignored in this case as having no influence on the valuation ASAP
will place on NS. Where it exceeds the present stock exchange
valuation (the likely lower limit to purchase price), it could have a
bearing on the NS purchase price in the sense that it is worth paying
up to its net break-up value. Where break-up value exceeds both
present stock exchange value and value from continued operation,
it sets the upper limit to purchase price and also determines the future
of the firm if the purchase is successful.

CHAPTER TWELVE

Assessing the Purchase Price of a Firm

I I I

Miscellaneous Problems

This chapter comprises four sections dealing with certain valuation problems which commonly arise in connection with the valuation of a firm for purchase. The first section deals with the valuation of any under-utilized debt raising capacity. The second deals with assessing the optimum means of payment (e.g. cash, shares, etc.). The third section discusses the effect of inflation, while the fourth deals with the relevance of alternative or mutually exclusive purchasing opportunities. An appendix to the chapter briefly examines some of the conventional methods of business valuation, notably the Super Profit method.

1. ALLOWANCE FOR POSSIBILITY OF RAISING ADDITIONAL DEBT CAPITAL

In the detailed case study in the previous chapter the discount rate used was of course the purchaser's net-of-tax equity cost of capital which was there assumed to be 7%. The use of the equity rate is appropriate when it is remembered that it is an equity investment which is being purchased. Sometimes, however, it will be possible for the purchaser to raise additional debt capital on the assets and earnings cover acquired through the purchase. Where this possibility exists credit should be taken for it.

The calculations allowing for this advantage are relatively straightforward. Suppose firm A has acquired the equity shares of firm B whose net tangible assets[1] are £2m., and whose debt capital (not

---

[1] Reference should be made to the appendix to Chapter 3 and Section 1 of Chapter 4.

acquired) amounts to £500,000. Because of the nature of B's assets, let us suppose that it is possible to raise debt capital to the extent of 40% of net tangible assets, i.e. to £800,000 and the earnings cover is adequate to support this amount of debt. In this case firm A can and should raise £300,000 worth of debentures. Suppose they can be raised for 7% *gross of tax* at 50%, i.e. $3\frac{1}{2}$% net-of-tax, and the appropriate equity cost of capital is 7% *net of tax*. On the basis of perpetual renewal, firm A receives £300,000 immediately for the price of paying a $3\frac{1}{2}$% net interest charge on the £300,000 into perpetuity. This net interest charge equals £10,500 per annum discounted at 7% $= £10,500/0.07 = £150,000$. Therefore, the net gain from this issue of debentures is £300,000 − £150,000 = £150,000 and this latter sum can properly be added to the value of B when being assessed from A's viewpoint. If the life of the business is uncertain, a lesser credit is appropriate. Suppose that only a 20 year life can be assumed. Then a 20 year debenture could be raised. For the immediate receipt of £300,000 firm A would take on the obligation to pay £10,500 net for 20 years, and £300,000 at the end of that time. At 7% this has a present value of $£10,500a_{20|7} + £300,000v_{20|7} = £111,000 + £78,000 = £189,000$. Thus the net gain is £300,000 − £189,000 = £111,000.

Similarly credit should be taken for the possibility of raising additional debt capital in future, for instance on new assets as and when purchased. In the case study in the previous chapter, the final instalment on the new factory trawler would provide just such an opportunity. Further, both inflation (with its effect on asset values) and the terms of payment for the purchase of a firm (e.g. in cash, in shares, or some combination of the two) affect the amount of debt capital which can be raised. These effects are examined in the two following sections.

2. TERMS OF TAKEOVER

So far we have considered the evaluation procedure only for the case of purchasing 100% of a firm's equity shares for cash. This section is concerned with the qualifications required when these simple conditions do not obtain; e.g. when less than 100% of the equity can be acquired, when all or part of the purchase price is to be paid in the purchaser's own shares, and where it is necessary or desirable to purchase the preference shares and debentures as well as the equity. But before discussing these matters let us examine the consequences of a cash purchase as it affects the purchaser's ability to raise debt capital.

In the previous section the method for taking credit for the possibility of raising future debt capital on the strength of the purchased firm's earnings and net tangible assets was set out. It is now necessary to extend this method to cover the consequences of the terms of payment (i.e. whether by cash, shares, or both) for future debt raising potentiality. (The example which follows presumes some basic knowledge of accounting. Those lacking this are referred to Appendix A of Chapter 3.)

a. The Effect of a Cash Payment

Firm A is considering making a cash offer for firm B of £200,000 for a 100% equity interest. Their respective pre-merger balance sheets are as follows.

Balance Sheet – Firm A

(all figures are in £000's)

Liabilities			Assets		
Capital & Reserves –			Fixed Assets		1,550
Ordinary Shares	300				
Reserves	900				
	—	1,200			
			Current Assets – Cash	300	
			Other	250	
Debentures		800			550
Current Liabilities		100			
		2,100			2,100

Balance Sheet – Firm B

Liabilities			Assets		
Capital & Reserves –			Fixed Assets		170
Ordinary Shares	80				
Reserves	40				
	—	120			
Debentures		80	Current Assets		60
Current Liabilities		30			
		230			230

Both firms are assumed to be in the same industry where debt capital can be raised to the value of 40% of net tangible assets. It will be seen from the above balance sheets that both firms have availed themselves fully of this opportunity (Firm A has raised £800,000 of loans on net tangible assets of £2,000,000. Firm B has raised £80,000 on net tangible assets of £200,000). If firm A's offer of

£200,000 for all the equity shares of firm B is successful, it will be paying this sum for an investment which appears on the books of firm B as only £120,000, the value of the equity share capital and reserves. The balance sheet of firm A after the merger will then show a goodwill item of £200,000 − £120,000 = £80,000.

Balance Sheet – Firm A (after absorbing Firm B)

Liabilities			Assets		
Capital & Reserves –			Goodwill		80
Ordinary Shares	300		Fixed Assets		
Reserves	900		1,550+170 =		1,720
		1,200	Current Assets		
Debentures 800+80 =		880	Cash 300−200 =	100	
Current Liabilities			Others 250+60 =	310	
100+30 =		130			410
		2,210			2,210

Combined net tangible assets (total *tangible* assets – i.e. excluding goodwill – less current liabilities), is now £2,000,000 (i.e. £1,720,000 + £410,000 − £130,000), and 40% of this = £800,000. In other words the maximum debt which could normally be raised on these net tangible assets is some £80,000 less than the debt actually outstanding. (The difference of £80,000 is 40% of £200,000, the amount of tangible assets withdrawn from the combined business as the result of the merger.) What are the consequences of this discrepancy?

None of the combined debt of £880,000 will have to be redeemed as the result of the merger (barring some special clause in firm A's debenture deed) but the next time firm A has to raise or to renew a debenture issue (something which will occur sooner for an expanding firm), its scope for so doing will have been reduced by £80,000. (This of course presumes that the lending market is very strict in its interpretation of the 40% rule. In the example taken, the difference between the normal maximum of 40% and the actual debt of 44% may possibly be ignored if firm A is regarded sufficiently highly, but the example serves for illustrative purposes.) Suppose firm A will have to renew £300,000 of its debentures in 5 years' time. If firm A's equity cost of capital is say 7% net of tax, and the 40% rule is strictly interpreted, then as a result of the merger firm A will only be able to renew £220,000 of the debentures. Thus, as a direct result of the merger A will then have to find £80,000 extra equity funds, which has a present value of £80,000$v_{5|7}$ = £57,000 which should be deducted from the net present value to be placed on firm B. Another possible consequence is that firm A's shares may be slightly depressed in value until the debt ratio is restored to 40% to reflect the greater risk on the equity shares.

If the assets of firm B are undervalued, however, it will be possible to revalue them with advantage.[1] To the extent that this can be done, the value of goodwill shown on the combined balance sheet will be reduced and the value of net tangible assets increased. This will directly reduce the amount that would otherwise have to be redeemed. Where asset revaluation exceeds the goodwill, the case reverts to that discussed in the previous section, where credit can be taken for the additional debt raising capacity open to the purchaser as a result of the merger.

From this discussion it will be clear that the allowance for debt raising capacity depends on current ratio of debt to net tangible assets in both firms, the scope for revaluation of the net assets in the firm being purchased, and the terms of the offer of purchase.

b. *Failing to obtain* 100% *of the Equity*

Firm A is considering buying up firm B. It values 100% ownership of B at say £1m., but it is going to be possible to buy only 80% of the shares. Does this necessarily mean that the 80% shareholding in B will be worth £800,000 to A?

Consider A's position. In valuing a 100% interest, it was valuing the *differential* net cash flow to which the merger would give rise. Assume for the moment that all of this differential net cash flow would derive from the net cash flow coming out of B rather than being made up, say, partly of lower costs in A. If A can still effectively make use of the net cash flow in B (i.e. assume B can always lend any surplus cash to A) then the *gross* value of B is still £1m. from which must be deducted the present value of all future dividend payments to the 20% minority shareholders. Suppose for instance that B will pay out £60,000 in net dividends every year in future, with any surplus cash not needed in the business being lent out to A for a reasonable rate of interest. If A's marginal cost of capital is deemed to be 7%, B's value will be reduced by £60,000 × 20%/0·07 = £171,500. Hence the value of B to A is simply £1,000,000 − £171,500 = £828,500.

[1] If the assets of firm A also happen to be undervalued, no credit can be taken for the additional debt raising potential involved, as this exists independently of the merger.

Under British and American law it is generally legal for subsidiaries to lend surplus cash to their parent company despite the existence of minority shareholders,[1] but in many countries it is not permitted and this inevitably affects the valuation of the business concerned. In such circumstances, the only way A could get cash out of B would be by way of dividends, and the minority shareholders would participate to the extent of 20% in all dividends declared. Under these conditions A would have to value B entirely in terms of 80% of future dividend payments (less any capital subscriptions or loans it may have to make to B to enable it to earn the profits). As dividends will nearly always amount to less than the net cash flow (principally because the latter will include depreciation provisions which the firm will generally have use of *temporarily* until they are required for any replacement expenditures), the value of B will be accordingly less. Suppose the advantages from retaining the depreciation provisions in B until required for actual replacement are negligible and that the *maximum*[2] net dividends from B remain at £60,000 per annum in perpetuity, then the value of B to A would be £60,000 × 80%/0·07 = £686,000, compared with £828,500 in the other case.

This is based on the assumption that the *differential* net cash flow from the merger could all be attributed to net income from B. Where, however, some of the benefits will accrue directly to A in the form of lower costs, reduced capital expenditure, higher profits from a stronger marketing position etc., the position is different. Suppose A estimates these direct benefits at a present value of £120,000. In this case, the value of B to A is £120,000 plus the discounted value of 80% of the maximum dividends to be expected from B. Assuming the same dividend rate as previously, i.e. £60,000 per annum, the merger with B is worth £120,000 + £686,000 = £806,000. Finally, A may prefer that B undertakes activities or pricing policies which, while in the overall interest of A, conflict with the direct interest of B. It may be difficult to adopt this policy in the face of opposition from the minority shareholders. This restriction can also

[1] Lending 'upstream' may be highly unpopular where the minority shareholders are receiving an inadequate return. Where this is not the case, it may still attract much adverse comment and so be impractical. In extreme cases minority shareholders could probably successfully challenge it in the courts.

[2] Maximum dividends are appropriate here because it is in A's interest to get the maximum out of B by this means, and with a majority shareholding A can ensure this happens.

be evaluated and plans made at a later date to offer a higher price to the remaining minority shareholders than is now being offered for the majority.

From this reasoning it is apparent that an 80% shareholding is unlikely to equal exactly 80% of the value of a 100% holding save by coincidence.

c. *Paying for the Purchase Price in Shares*

Frequently the purchase price of take-over bids is made partly or wholly in the shares to be issued by the purchaser, and this raises certain problems of evaluation. For simplicity we will consider first the case where A, the purchasing firm, is acquiring 100% of the equity of firm B and the purchase price is to be paid entirely in its own specially issued equity shares.

The first step is to value B in the normal way when 100% ownership is involved. This sets the upper limit to the *cash* price it is worth paying for B. But when payment takes the form of A's own shares, a second valuation problem arises, the valuation A should place on its own shares. It is incorrect to assume that the value of A's shares, when it is a public quoted company, is necessarily the current market value of those shares – this will only be true by coincidence. Apart from the obvious fact that even in the short term the market value of shares fluctuates and the value assigned to them will vary according to the date chosen, there is no reason to suppose the current market value of shares corresponds to the value of newly issued shares to the issuing company. The market price will be set mainly on the basis of shareholders' and potential shareholders' expectations of future dividends (or capital gains – which comes to the same thing as it results from future dividend expectations). These expectations would seem to depend primarily on the current dividend yield and on the earnings yield (which is held to indicate the scope for a higher dividend yield in future), and on the estimated growth prospects of the firm. These expectations will also be roughly qualified by the general vague view of trends in the industry and in the whole economy. It will be clear that such a valuation is likely to be much less meaningful and accurate from the company's viewpoint than that of its senior management based on expert detailed knowledge of the industry, the firm's future plans, and its future dividend policy.[1]

[1] Reference should be made to Chapter 3, Section 4 and Chapter 17, Section 2.

The correct criterion for A to use in valuing its own shares is the discounted value of all future dividend payments it will make on those shares in the light of the combined net cash flows of the two businesses. Suppose A has 400,000 £1 equity shares (whose current market value is £4 per share) and it is contemplating issuing a further 100,000 shares to acquire B, a firm which it values at £400,000. It estimates that on the combined net cash flow it will be paying out dividends in future at the rate of £0·35 per share net of tax. At a 7% marginal cost of capital the 100,000 shares have a present value of $(£0·35 \times 100,000)/0·07 = £500,000$. Hence A is paying £100,000 more for B than its value to A. Either A should offer fewer of its own shares, or should find some other way to raise the purchase price, perhaps by way of a loan. For example, the firm could explore the possibility of a medium term loan or bank overdraft to pay cash and later float either a long term loan of its own or make an issue of share capital when conditions were more favourable. For simplicity, this illustration made use of a constant future dividend rate. In practice the dividend rate is likely to be rising and specific allowance must be made for this if too high a price is not to be paid.[1]

Where the dividend rate is expected to rise in future at a constant rate, this is easily allowed for in simple formulae (see Section 4c of Chapter 1). For example, suppose the dividends net of tax after the acquisition of the new company were expected to grow at 2% p.a. The discount rate used in the previous illustration would be reduced by 2%, i.e. to 5% (more strictly to $1·07 \div 1·05$) and the present value of the dividends estimated at $(£0·35 \times 100,000)/0·05 = £700,000$.

Again, in the case where the purchaser's own shares are to be issued in whole or in part settlement for less than a 100% equity interest in a company, there is no difficulty. The valuation procedure outlined in (b) above has to be married to the method for valuing the purchasers' own shares. This requires care but is not inherently difficult.

Finally, it is instructive to consider the effect of a share, or part share offer on the debt raising potential of the purchased business. Taking the same facts as were used in the detailed example in (a) above, suppose firm A's offer to firm B consists entirely of its own shares (nominal value £1) whose value is agreed at £5 a share.

---

[1] It could well happen that the purchaser's evaluation of its own shares results in a lower value than the current market price. In these circumstances, if the vendor accepts the validity of the current market price, the purchaser stands to gain from the situation.

A thus offers to issue 40,000 of its own shares which are then valued in aggregate by both parties at £200,000. If the offer is accepted the balance sheet of firm A after the merger would be as follows:

Balance Sheet – Firm A (after absorbing Firm B)

(all figures in £000's)

Liabilities			Assets		
Capital & Reserves –			Fixed Assets		
Ordinary shares			1,550+170 =		1,720
300+40 =	340		Current Assets		
Reserves 900+80[1]=980			Cash	300	
		1,320	Others 250+60 =	310	
Debentures 800+80 =		880			610
Current Liabilities 100+30 =		130			
		2,330			2,330

Unlike the cash purchase method illustrated previously, the share purchase method has not affected A's scope for raising debt capital.

The aggregate debt to net tangible assets ratio, i.e. £880,000 to £2,200,000 = 40% is the same for A as before the merger, as the ratio in B was the same as in A. Unlike the cash purchase method, no net tangible assets have left A's possession, and so no goodwill has had to be incorporated in A's post merger balance sheet. (The only circumstance in which a goodwill figure *has* to be shown on the combined balance sheet is when the nominal value of the purchaser's shares is greater than the net tangible assets acquired, a very unlikely happening.)

[1] The £80,000 addition to reserves arises because 40,000 shares have been issued to acquire net tangible assets of £120,000 value in the accounting documents. As shares issued are always shown at their nominal value, the difference between this value and the value of the net tangible assets is shown as a reserve – known as a 'Share Premium Reserve'. This would be a 'capital' reserve, i.e. it would not be available for distribution as dividends. It will be appreciated that this accounting treatment, which effectively values the acquired assets at £3 per share issued, is at variance with the £5 value per share agreed by the two parties. It would be possible to show goodwill as £80,000 and increase the capital reserve by a similar amount to £160,000 to reflect the fact that the business acquired was held to be worth £200,000 but this is almost never done as accountants dislike having to show goodwill on the books. Where it exists they usually write it down at the first opportunity, either out of reserves – capital or revenue – or if necessary, out of profits. Not all capital reserves can be used for this purpose, but many types can be so used.

When an offer is partly in shares and partly in cash, the cash element can of course still result in a reduction in the net value which should be placed on the firm to be purchased, by the amount of any adverse effect on the purchaser's debt raising potential.

d. *Considerations Affecting the Purchase of Preference Capital, Debentures etc.*

When a take-over bid is under consideration, the problem arises of whether or not to make an offer for the preference capital as well as the equity. Sometimes there will be special circumstances which will be an incentive to this, as when the preference shares have votes and so exercise some measure of control over the business which could be troublesome. This is most likely to be the case when the purchaser is not able to obtain 100% of the equity shares. Similarly, when the preference shares have the right to participate in profits, it can be worth buying them out if the purchaser estimates that profits will be sufficiently increased in future. But apart from these rather special cases, what circumstances would normally justify the purchase of preference shares? The only circumstance is when the purchase price of such shares is less than the present value of future dividend payments on them. As the marginal cost of capital to a purchaser is always likely to be higher than the net prevailing interest rate on preference shares, this circumstance will rarely arise. The likelihood of inflation (see Section 3 below) will still further reduce this possibility.

The case for the purchase of debentures is similar to that of preference shares. Purchase in the normal course will be justified only by the purchase price having a lower value than discounted interest payments and eventual capital repayment. The eventual date of capital repayment will either be fixed at a single date or extend over a fixed period. The appropriate date for comparison with the present purchase price is whichever date, taken in conjunction with the interest payments, results in the lowest value. As for preference shares, it will seldom be worth buying out debentures in the normal course of events.

The special circumstances which would justify offering to buy up the debentures would be when they carried options for conversion into equity shares. (This consideration could also apply to preference shares.) Where this right exists, the purchaser must evaluate the consequences of this right being exercised. Clearly if the purchaser hopes to increase the profits of the business (which is the usual reason for the take-over), the option is likely to be exercised. This means the purchaser must discount all future estimated dividend payments that could be involved. Further, if the purchaser is acquiring 100% of the existing equity, the exercise of the options will reduce this 100% control and, as was set out in (b) above, this can reduce the valuation of the whole business to the purchaser. Both factors must be evaluated. It is almost certain that where 100% of the equity is being acquired it will be essential to purchase all options as well. Even where less than 100% of the existing equity is being acquired, it may be important to acquire the options, especially if the exercise of those options could cost the purchaser control of the company. Finally, it may be desirable to purchase the debentures when there is a restrictive trust deed which prevents the best use of the mortgaged assets or otherwise restricts the conduct of the business.

Whenever the purchase of preference shares or debentures is being considered, the correct comparison is between the present value of the net of tax interest payments (and redemption payments if necessary) on the existing shares or debentures, and the present value of the net-of-tax interest payments (and redemption payments if necessary) on the new loan capital raised to redeem them. Where less new loan capital can be raised than the amount of the old loans to be repaid, the difference must be made up by equity capital, and the cost of this equity capital must be allowed for. It will be appreciated that not much equity capital can be involved if it is to pay the purchaser to redeem the old loans.

3. THE EFFECT OF INFLATION

It is sometimes of importance to take explicit account of the probable effect of inflation on the value of the firm. Reference should be made to Chapter 6, Section 7, which deals generally with the issues raised by inflation. We shall only briefly recapitulate here and point out its relevance to the take-over problem.

The detailed example set out in the previous chapter was based on the assumption of all future prices being fixed at their present level. In practice, it is seldom possible to make this assumption with confidence. As has been pointed out, inflation, albeit of a mild variety, seems almost endemic in post-war Western society, and as such it affects many valuation problems. It is particularly important to allow for it in evaluating obligations fixed in money terms, such as preference share dividends, loan interest and redemption, lease payments, etc. Where future costs and revenues are not expected to move in exact step with general prices, some adjustment to future net revenues becomes necessary. Where tax payments are based on historic cost, and where such payments are made in arrears, again some allowance must be made for this. The clearest way of appreciating the effect of expected future price changes on the valuation of a business is to reconsider the cost of equity capital and *some* of the evaluation steps of the detailed example under these circumstances. It will be assumed that the general price level (retail prices) is expected to increase at 2% p.a. indefinitely. All assets, liabilities, and net revenues will be expressed in base year prices, i.e. all valuations will be reduced to real value terms.

First, the effect on the cost of capital. In the previous chapter, the purchasing firm's equity cost of capital was taken as 7% net of tax. Under inflationary conditions a firm, as we have argued previously, will be concerned to maintain the return to the equity shareholders at an acceptable level in real terms. Hence the rate of discount in *real* terms is not reduced. Further, the burden of existing fixed interest and loan redemption obligations will be reduced, as will future obligations to the extent that they do not rise in full step with inflation. Finally, it must be borne in mind that it will probably be possible to raise additional amounts of debt capital if assets are revalued in the light of inflation (see Section 1 above).

The next point to consider is the effect, if any, in real terms on the net cash flow of the prospective purchased firm. This is best appreciated by re-examining in the light of expected inflation, a selection of the valuations made in case study in the previous chapter.

a. *Evaluating Surplus Assets and Future Capital Expenditure*

The effect of expected future price changes on the valuation of surplus assets is likely to be small. Surplus assets will usually be disposed of very shortly after a business is acquired, at the most within a year or two. For this reason, the likelihood of a significant change in the real value of such assets is small as there is little time for a sharp divergence to develop between specific resale prices and general prices.

Future capital expenditures, however, can be significantly affected by the expectation of future price changes. As they typically extend over long periods, divergent price trends can become important. Whether this is true in any particular case is a matter to be determined, but the method of valuation is quite straightforward. Consider an example.

Suppose factory buildings and equipment are expected to become cheaper to replace in real terms at the rate of 3% per annum for ten years. How will this affect the value of Factory A and its plant? It was estimated that the plant and factory will be replaced in five years time for a combined cost of £135,000. This sum, expressed in real terms, must be reduced to its revised estimated cost in real terms, which $= £135,000v_{5|3} = £116,000$. This in turn, must be reduced to its present value equivalent at the cost of capital in real terms, i.e. $7\% = £116,000v_{5|7} = £83,000$, compared to the £96,000 calculated previously. (The practical usefulness of this consideration is of course limited by the extreme difficulty of predicting future relative prices.)

b. *Evaluating the Liabilities*

A company's liabilities for its debt and preference capital are nearly always fixed in money terms. Because of this, general inflation reduces the burden of such liabilities, and given the assumptions, this can be precisely evaluated.

If r is the firm's cost of capital, and d the expected rate of inflation, the correct rate to discount a fixed money sum as has been demonstrated, is simply $(1+r)(1+d)-1$. For low rates of inflation and costs of capital, this is almost the same as $(r+d)$. In the case under consideration the cost of capital is assumed to be 7% and the rate of inflation 2%. The approximate method is $7\%+2\% = 9\%$, compared with the correct method of $(1\cdot07 \times 1\cdot02)-1 = 9\cdot14\%$.

Armed with the revised appropriate rate of discount, it is a simple matter to recalculate the true burden of debt and preference capital. Two calculations from the detailed example will suffice to show the effect of even a mild rate of inflation.

i. £500,000 of 5% debentures redeemable in 3 years time. Assuming a 20 year life for the firm, with the present 5% debentures redeemed in 3 years time with a new issue of 7% debentures, to be redeemed in turn after 17 years, the present value equivalent of the annual net interest charge and redemption was shown to be £241,000.

The revised valuation would be as follows:

Net of tax interest payments next 3 years $= £10,000a_{3|9} = £25,000$, plus net of tax interest payments years 4–20 $= £14,000a_{17|9}v_{3|9}$ $= £92,000$, plus redemption payment 20 years hence $= £400,000$

$v_{2019} = \pounds71,000$. This amounts to a total of $\pounds188,000$, which is a saving of $\pounds53,000$ in real terms, or 22%.

ii. $\pounds600,000$ of 8% irredeemable preference shares. Assuming a perpetual life for the firm, and continued inflation, the annual net of tax dividend burden of $\pounds28,800$ has a present value of $\pounds28,800/0\cdot09$ $= \pounds320,000$. This compares with $\pounds411,000$, the burden assuming no inflation, a significant difference (also 22%) considering the very low rate of inflation assumed. If inflation is expected for only the next ten years, the present value of the preference dividend would be $\pounds28,800a_{10|9} + \pounds28,800/0\cdot07v_{10|9} = \pounds185,000 + \pounds174,000$ $= \pounds359,000$. This difference, though smaller (13%), is still significant.

c. *Evaluating the Expected Net Cash Flow*

The first matter to be considered is the effect of general inflation on the firm's income in real terms. It is a commonly held view that for most firms income rises in step with inflation. But, as we have argued (Section 7, Chapter 6), it sometimes happens that a firm's real income is distorted by the very process of inflation, due principally to the possibility that the demand for the firm's goods or services is changed by the accompanying redistribution of incomes. This possibility should be looked into for the firm, the take-over of which is being contemplated. It will be apparent that only a very rough correction can be made, but it might well be possible to say that persistent inflation is likely to increase (or decrease) the demand for the firm's output by say, $1-2\%$ a year.

d. *The Effect of Inflation on Debt Raising Potential*

One final point concerns the effect of inflation on the firm's debt raising potential. Whenever, purely as the result of inflation, it will be possible *in future* to revalue the net tangible assets of a firm, especially fixed assets, then it may be possible to raise more debt capital once the revaluation is shown in the balance sheet. To the extent that particular assets have been mortgaged as security for a particular loan, this possibility will not arise. In other cases, however, the possibility will exist and the value of the purchased business should reflect this credit item. Needless to say, this is only legitimate where future inflation can be forecast with sufficient confidence, and it relates only to the scope for revaluations in future. As was made clear in Section 1, credit should be taken immediately for the existing scope for *currently* revaluing assets over and above their present balance sheet values in the books of the company to be purchased.

4. THE RELEVANCE OF THE PURCHASE PRICE OF SIMILAR FIRMS

When a business has been evaluated with a view to purchase, it will be worth paying up to this price to acquire it. The fact that a similar business can be acquired more cheaply is irrelevant unless it can be shown that for technical or managerial reasons the two investments are mutually exclusive.[1]

For if the purchasing company's marginal cost of capital has been calculated meaningfully, then logically the company should acquire both firms. It may not be in a position to do this because of the strain involved on its own management, but this reduces it to the case of a mutually exclusive investment where the firm should accept whichever investment offers the highest net present value after allowing for risks.

There are several categories of mutually exclusive investments which can usefully be distinguished.

(a) The most obvious example of a mutually exclusive investment, which is present in nearly all cases, is the alternative of the firm entering the new industry itself and building up a new subsidiary from scratch. Or if it is already in the industry and wishes to expand its output, it can embark on aggressive marketing tactics rather than buy out an existing firm. If trained manpower is the critical factor of production in short supply, it can offer higher salaries to the skilled staff of its rivals, although this may probably involve having to pay higher salaries to its own staff. Whatever the advantages a take-over has to offer, it is usually possible to achieve those advantages by direct expansion, albeit often at a higher cost than that of a take-over or merger. It is merely a question of finding the cheapest way and self creation is always one possibility worth examination. Usually the chief advantage of the take-over route is the time that it can save by offering the opportunity to exploit a going concern with its existing goodwill. But it is an advantage to be evaluated and not merely accepted as conclusive.

(b) Another well known case of mutually exclusive investments

---

[1] Mutually exclusive investments are defined as investments whose values are not additive because the firm is concerned to invest in one but not both – see Section 1b *ii*, Chapter 5.

arises when an expanding firm wishes to acquire another smaller firm in the same industry to ease a production bottleneck. Suppose an engineering firm, *R*, needs additional manufacturing capacity. On investigation it is revealed that either firm *A* or *B* could supply this extra capacity, and the economies of joint operation would justify absorbing one of them, but not both, since *R* does not have the markets to utilize the capacity provided by both *A* and *B*. Having evaluated both *A* and *B*, *R* should buy whichever one offers the higher net present value over purchase price after allowing for risk. It cannot justify buying both as the valuations in this case are not additive.

(c) A similar case arises when the expanding firm, *R*, could absorb with advantage firms *D* and *E*, which are in different industries from each other, but has only sufficient managerial resources to exploit one or the other. Again, *R* should evaluate them, and buy whichever one offers the higher net present value over cost after allowing for risk.

(d) For the sake of completeness the case of mutually interdependent firms should be briefly considered. There could be a situation when the expanding firm *R* will consider buying two firms, *F* and *G* together, because of the economies that would result from the threefold combination, but not *F* and *G* separately. Here, the economies of *R* and *F*, or *R* and *G* alone, would be insufficient, – it is a case of both or neither.

Apart from these qualifications, it is worth paying up to the capitalized value of a business as illustrated in the previous chapter.

APPENDIX A

Some Traditional Methods of Business Valuation

The three previous chapters have been devoted to expounding and illustrating our approach to the problem of business evaluation, an approach based on the economic concept of discounting. It is perhaps appropriate that some attention should be given to outlining some of the traditional methods of business valuation.

In our experience most of these methods are based primarily on the value of net assets in a firm's current balance sheet with some rough allowance for future profit prospects. Almost invariably future profits are estimated on the basis of some mechanistic projection of past profits, often qualified by reference to what is vaguely termed 'normal' profits. A typical example is a German method known as the 'Berliner' method.

The Berliner method of valuation is to calculate the arithmetic average of 'intrinsic value' (net assets) and 'normal' profits capitalized at 8%. 'Intrinsic value' is defined as total assets less current liabilities and debt capital, i.e. the shareholders' funds as per the balance sheet, or net 'worth'. Where for any reason balance sheet values are thought to be unrealistic because of the existence of hidden reserves, non-adjustment for inflation, etc., it is in order to adjust the values to a current value basis, with no assets being valued above replacement cost. The sum of total assets, as in all these methods, is of course tangible assets, i.e. excluding goodwill.

The definition of 'normal' profits is to be taken as either average profits, or profits in a 'normal' year – neither of which is exactly precise. Once the valuer has decided on 'normal' profits, they are valued on the basis of a perpetuity, i.e. (normal profits/cost of capital), where the cost of capital = 8%. Then an arithmetic average is struck between 'intrinsic value' and capitalized profits, and that gives the value of the business. In the case where the business is not assumed to have a perpetual life, presumably only profits for its expected life are capitalized. This could obviously lead to ludicrous results, but perhaps the method would not be used in such circumstances.

Another typical method is based on the accountants' Rate of Return approach. First future profits are computed, usually on the basis of past average profits or 'normal' profits, perhaps adjusted for the future level of output. Then this is divided by what is regarded as an acceptable (i.e. maintainable) percentage return on capital (often the arithmetic average of the required rate of return on loan capital and equity capital in the proportions in which they are normally raised) to give a capitalized value. Usually the required rate of return and 'normal' profits are stated gross of tax, although they can both be on a net of tax basis. Here again, the business is implicitly assumed to have a perpetual life. Also, future profits are assumed to be either constant or fluctuating around a fixed level.

Perhaps the best known and most plausible of these rule of thumb methods is the 'Super' Profits Method [1]. This method is based on the proposition that a firm can only earn more than a 'normal' profit for a temporary period. It therefore capitalizes the difference between current or expected profits and normal profits – this difference is called super profits – for a given period of say 5 years, and adds this to the value of net assets on a balance sheet basis. The actual formula is

$$V = A + \frac{(P - rA)}{j}$$

V is the value of the business,
A is the value of 'net' tangible assets',
P is 'net maintainable profit',
r is the 'normal' rate of return appropriate to the business, and j

is the appropriate rate of capitalization of the 'super' profit. $(P-rA)$ is the annual amount of the 'super' profit, and $(P-rA)/j$ is the capitalized value of the 'super' profits.

The value of 'net tangible assets' is not defined but it is usually taken at balance sheet valuation corrected for any marked divergence between this valuation and current value. The term 'current value' is itself open to many interpretations but accountants (and the 'super' profits method like the other traditional methods were devised and are applied by accountants) define it to mean 'going concern value' by which is meant written-down replacement cost (see Section 1 of Chapter 19). For instance, if a machine is 50% depreciated in the accounts, and this is held to be realistic, then 'going concern value' is interpreted as 50% of replacement cost new. 'Net maintainable profit' corresponds to future average profits available for distribution as dividends.

The 'normal' rate of return in a business is based on the notion that industries have an accepted average expected rate of return on capital employed corresponding to the risks involved.

The appropriate rate of return for using in the capitalization of the 'super' profits is not defined, but is left as a matter for subjective judgment. Invariably, however, j is taken as greater than r.

The *raison d'être* of the method is simply that profits in excess of 'normal' profits are more risky than normal profits and they can never be more than a temporary occurrence. There is, however, some contradiction between this notion and the description of P as 'net *maintainable* profits'. If the profits can be maintained then j should equal r, and the value of the business would be simply P/r, with $(P/r)-A$ as the value of the intangible assets or goodwill.

We do not propose to criticize these various methods in any detail: indeed the whole of the three previous chapters can be read as sufficient criticism of such methods. It is enough to point out their more obvious shortcomings. None of them make allowance for cases of rising or falling profits or cases where a business has a limited life. As with all conventional accounting techniques, in the absence of discounting they must rely on a process of averaging with its inevitable distortions (see Chapter 7 Section 1 on the 'rate of return' method). The economies of the merger, the effects of tax allowances, the timing of capital expenditures, the cost of debt capital, the effects of inflation, the terms of purchase, the effect of less than 100% equity ownership etc., etc., are all neglected by these approaches, and yet they may all have a vital effect on the worth of the business to be acquired. For these reasons a full appraisal of their usefulness is not called for.

REFERENCE

1. 'The Super Profit Method' by H. C. Edey, *Accountancy*, January–February 1957.

CHAPTER THIRTEEN

Evaluating an Overseas Mining Project and Some General Problems of Financing and Evaluating Overseas Projects

The first part of the chapter is devoted to the assessment of a typical overseas mining project. The second part is concerned with the more general problems of overseas investment, in particular the assessment of earnings when there is a choice between re-investment in the overseas country and remittance of profits to the parent at the price of incurring tax liabilities, and some general financing problems.

1. EVALUATING OVERSEAS MINING PROJECTS

a. *The Preliminary Stages*

The mining industry may well be unique in the ratio of the number of projects seriously examined to the number commenced. Ratios of 20:1 are not uncommon, and 40:1 not unknown. This puts a premium on efficient investigation and much can be done on two fronts, the general approach to seeking out projects, and the evaluation of projects once found.

Concerning the general approach, it is desirable that any international mining company (and most mining companies of consequence tend to be international) have an overall exploration plan which identifies certain minerals and certain areas as being of interest. Some areas will be automatically ruled out as being too politically unstable, or as undesirable because any mineral export will have to go out via a politically unstable country. Similarly, many minerals will be ruled out because of oversupply. Bulk minerals such as iron ore and coal will be attractive only if found in areas sufficiently near the main markets to be able to stand the necessarily heavy transport costs, i.e. to be competitive with the production of existing established mines. The area will of course vary with the grade of the mineral - the higher the grade the greater the transport cost it will be able to bear. With low bulk minerals, gold, copper, nickel, etc., transport costs are relatively unimportant but grade, because of mining costs, becomes all important. Hence minimum economic grades can be established for ore bodies of a given size if they are to be of interest. In short, an efficient mining company should have clear specific criteria concerning which minerals will be of general interest and in which areas. This will enable it to investigate only those satisfying its basic criteria.

Once a prospect has satisfied the basic criteria (which ideally should be constantly revised in the light of market research reports, advances in mining or mineral processing techniques, political changes, alterations in mining tax concessions, etc.) it should then receive detailed attention. Test drilling will nearly always be essential, followed by detailed assaying to determine the exact metallurgical and chemical properties of the mineral concerned. Providing all these tests are satisfactory the next stage may well involve the establishment of a pilot plant particularly where a large orebody is concerned. All these are fairly obvious actions. But it is at this stage that much care should be exercised. Before a project can be satisfactorily planned and investigated it is necessary to determine the scale of operation. This is usually one of the most critical of decisions and yet often it is taken without sufficient consideration of the full range of choices. It is desirable to have a small study group comprising technical, transport, marketing and financial specialists studying the full range of possible outputs to ensure that the optimum one is chosen. Often there is no problem because the marketing outlets may be limited, or export licences or royalty agreements permit only a given annual output, or internal transport sets a natural limit, etc., etc. But in all cases the problem deserves full consideration.

The detailed approach set out in the case study below should be followed for all the important viable choices; only then is the optimum choice possible. It may be objected that this involves a great deal of work. So it does, but the time and effort involved is usually trifling compared with the potential gains, and this is the relevant test.

At this point it will be useful to consider a specific example, and this is done in sub-section (b) below. This case study is compounded from a large number of actual projects and therefore illustrates a number of points, some of which will, of course, be inapplicable in specific instances.

Table 13.1

Forecast Capital Expenditure

£ million

	−4 1st half	−4 2nd half	−3 1st half	−3 2nd half	−2 1st half	−2 2nd half	−1 1st half	−1 2nd half	−1 End Year	Total 4 Years
(a) Purchase of 2 year option	0.5	—	—	—	—	—	—	—	—	0.5
(b) Basic exploration, test drilling, pilot plant operation, engineering planning, etc.	0.5	0.5	0.5	0.5	—	—	—	—	—	2.0
(c) Exercise option	—	—	—	—	2.0	—	—	—	—	2.0
(d) Shaft sinking, etc.	—	—	—	—	0.8	0.8	0.8	0.6	—	3.0
(e) Refinery and surface facilities, etc.	—	—	—	—	0.4	0.6	0.8	1.2	—	3.0
(f) Mining Equipment and Stores	—	—	—	—	—	—	—	1.0	—	1.0
(g) Working Capital	—	—	—	—	—	—	—	—	1.5	1.5
Total:	1.0	0.5	0.5	0.5	3.2	1.4	1.6	2.8	1.5	13.0
Cumulative Total:	1.0	1.5	2.0	2.5	5.7	7.1	8.7	11.5	13.0	—

b. *The Ruristan Potash Project*

After spending £500,000 in preliminary exploration, test drilling, basic engineering and market research the International Mining Corporation (henceforth IMC) has reached the stage of deciding whether or not to go ahead with developing a large potash mine in Ruristan, a small Asiatic country on the Indian Ocean. The estimated future capital outlays over the 4 year pre-production period are set out in Table 13.1.

From this it is seen that IMC will be involved in a 2 year period of extended test drilling, to prove up the orebody in detail and determine the best way and place to sink a shaft, in pilot plant work to ensure that the mined material is suitable for refining, and in detailed planning of the refinery and other surface facilities, etc. Also during this period it will be involved in detailed marketing and financial negotiations such that a decision to go ahead can be taken at the end of two years. It is possible to negotiate a 2 year option period for £500,000 with the right to purchase the property outright for £2,000,000 at the expiry of the option. The first problem to decide is whether the detailed exploration and planning expenditure, some £2·5m., is warranted. Japan is known to need to import over 2 million tons of potash a year within 5 years and demand is expected to grow. The marketing department estimate a minimum price of £13 per ton can be achieved on an annual output of a million tons. The engineers and transport experts estimate that this amount of refined potash could be mined and shipped to Japan at a cost of £8 per long ton C.I.F. (Production would be 500,000 tons in year 1, 750,000 tons in year 2, and 1 million tons a year thereafter.) Mining operations are granted a tax holiday in Ruristan until all preliminary capital expenditure is recovered; thereafter profits are taxed at a rate of 30%, there being no further allowance for depreciation. Profits remitted to the parent company are taxed at 50% in the parent company's own country, but any Ruristan tax paid is allowed in full as a set-off. In both countries taxes are collected one year in arrears.

Given this information the IMC capital budgeting department calculates the net of tax yield on total capital employed for a ten year operation. For this purpose it is assumed[1] that all pre-production

---

[1] The return on capital under these assumptions will give a reasonably close approximation to the return on total capital when a project is financed in the normal way for mining projects, bearing in mind the pattern of tax allowances and loan repayments involved.

expenditures occur mid year on average, all income arises mid year on average, and that the whole project is financed by equity put up in the form of interest-free loans, and all surplus funds are immediately remitted to the parent company. The estimated net cash flows arising are as set out in Table 13.2 below.

The net of tax discounted yield on the future capital outlays assuming a ten year operation (the minimum period it is felt that the market forecasts would hold and the operation would be run without political interference) is 17%. This is sufficiently high, bearing in mind all the technical, marketing and political risks, and the decision is taken to purchase the 2 year option for £500,000 and commence the detailed test drilling, engineering planning, marketing and financing negotiations, etc.

All the preliminary work goes according to plan and 2 years later IMC is faced with the decision of whether or not to exercise the option to purchase the property outright for £2m., and spend a further sum bringing the mine into being. By this time IMC has spent £3m.; £0·5m. in preliminary exploration and £2·5m. in purchasing the option and doing detailed test drilling, planning, etc. The technical estimates have held up well. Capital costs remain as before and the total costs of producing a million tons of refined product delivered C.I.F. Japan have dropped slightly to £7·7m. (previously estimated at £8m.), or £7·7 a ton. The one estimate that has suffered in the two years is the selling price. A small low grade potash deposit has been unexpectedly found in one of the smallest Japanese islands which can make 500,000 tons of refined potash available annually at £11·5 per ton anywhere in Japan. Faced with this IMC have negotiated a twelve year contract to sell 11·4 million tons of refined product to a Japanese industrial consortium at a fixed price of £10·0 per ton. On the strength of this contract IMC have negotiated the right to raise non-guaranteed loan finance in the form of £7·0m. of first mortgage bonds at 8% from a European banking consortium, the money to go in after all the equity,[1] and to be repaid as a first charge on the project's net cash flow, with no dividends being payable until the loan is completely repaid. In addition, local Ruristanian banks are willing to finance

[1] In fact some equity capital will be put into the project concurrently with the loan capital to meet the half yearly interest payments on the loans during the construction period when no income is available. This is set out in line (b) of Table (13.3). Often, of course, it is possible to defer loan interest until a project is generating income.

Table 13.2

Preliminary Net Cash Flow Estimate

Years	1	2	3	4	5	£000's 6	7	8	9	10
Gross operating profit	2,500	3,750	5,000	5,000	5,000	5,000	5,000	5,000	5,000	5,000
Less combined tax at 50% collected 1 year in arrears on all profits after first £12m.†	—	—	—	—	−2,125	−2,500	−2,500	−2,500	−2,500	−5,000*
Net Cash Flow	2,500	3,750	5,000	5,000	2,875	2,500	2,500	2,500	2,500	—

† (The £12m. is made up of £0·5m. exploration expenditure to date, plus £11½m. forecast capital expenditure excluding working capital.)
* (Mine assumed to close down at end of year 10 and year 10's income used to settle tax payment due in year 11. All residual values ignored.)

2A

Table 13.3

Estimated Provision of Finance

£000's

Years	Prior to −4	−4 1st half	−4 2nd half	−3 1st half	−3 2nd half	−2 1st half	−2 2nd half	−1 1st half	−1 2nd half	End Year	Total
(a) Equity	500	1,000	500	500	500	—	—	—	—	—	3,000
(b) Loans from Equity Shareholders (Interest free)	—	—	—	—	—	2,500	28	84	148	260	3,020
(c) 8% First Mortgage Bond	—	—	—	—	—	700	1,400	1,600	2,800	500	7,000
(d) Bank Loan – at 6%	—	—	—	—	—	—	—	—	—	1,000	1,000
Total:	500	1,000	500	500	500	3,200	1,428	1,684	2,948	1,760	14,020

Table 13.4

Estimated Output and Operating plus Distribution Costs
(For an annual output of one million tons of refined potash)

Output:		Thousands of Tons		
Years	1	2	3	4 etc.
Amount of Crude Material Mined and Milled	1,800	2,400	3,000	3,000
Refined Potash Production	600	800	1,000	1,000
Less Stockpile Requirements	−150	−50	−50	—
Refined Potash Sales	450	750	950	1,000

Operating and Distribution Costs:		£000's		
Years	1	2	3	4 etc.
Mining – at £0·8 per ton crude	1,440	1,920	2,400	2,400
Milling – at £0·6 per ton crude	1,080	1,440	1,800	1,800
Start-up expenses	500	250		
Administration and other fixed charges	500	500	500	500
Total operating costs:	3,520	4,110	4,700	4,700
Loading and rail charges − £1·25 per ton	719	990	1,240	1,250
Port storage and handling charges − £0·25 per ton	144	198	248	250
Loading, sea freight and insurance − £1·5 per ton	787	1,163	1,463	1,500
Total operating and distribution costs	5,170	6,461	7,651	7,700
Less stockpile and stocks in transit cost	−1,180	−248	−247	—
Total Cost of Sales	3,990	6,213	7,404	7,700

the stockpile and stocks in transit up to a limit of £1·7m. at an annual charge of 6%. The estimated provision of finance over the 2 year construction period as well as over the previous years is set out in Table 13.3 in 6 monthly periods. For tax and political reasons (see Section 2) IMC will put in the remainder of its equity funds in the form of interest free loans to be repaid as a first charge on the project's net cash flow after the First Mortgage Bonds have been repaid.

From this table, which is drawn up on the conservative assumption that all funds are required at the start of the 6 monthly period to which they relate, it is seen that a further £11,020,000 must be found, comprising further capital expenditure of £9,000,000, the initial working capital outlay of £1,500,000 (comprising £1m. to finance initial stocks etc., and £0·5m. as a basic cash float), and interest on the 8% loan at six monthly intervals during the pre-production period.

Forecast output and operating costs are set out in Table 13.4, with the mining and milling costs including all capital replacement expenditures.

The calculations giving the cost of the stockpile and stocks in transit are set out in Table 13.5 below.

Table 13.5

Detailed Calculation of Annual Stockpile and Stocks in Transit

		£000's		
Years	1	2	3	4, etc.
Opening Stock (from previous year)	—	1,180	1,428	1,675
Plus total operating and distribution costs	5,170	6,461	7,651	7,700
	5,170	7,641	9,079	9,375
Less closing stock	−1,180	−1,428	−1,675	−1,675
Total cost of sales	3,990	6,213	7,404	7,700

Closing stock (assuming FIFO stock valuation system, see Appendix to Chapter 3) equals 12 weeks production, and as the mine is estimated to operate 48 weeks a year, this comprises one quarter of total annual operating costs, plus distribution costs incurred on stockpile at mine (2 weeks production), at port (4 weeks production), and on stocks in transit (6 weeks production), which averages £2 a ton.

Before IMC can decide whether the spending of a further £11,020,000 is justified (the £3·0m. spent to date is of course irrelevant in deciding whether or not to go ahead as this expenditure is irrecoverable whatever happens), it is necessary to compute the relevant net cash flows assuming the project is completed. As a step to drawing up these net cash flows the capital budgeting department produce a forecast profit and loss statement and the complementary source and application of funds statement, which, in effect, is a detailed cash account (see Section 5 of the next chapter). These statements are reproduced in Table 13.6 below. As the mine has sufficient proved reserves for at least another 20 years, and there is every likelihood of IMC continuing to be able to sell a million tons a year at around £10 a ton after year 12, both statements are drawn up on a 20 year basis. The taxation provision (lines f and j) and the taxation payment (line n) relate solely to Ruristanian taxes.

It is seen that the loss in the first year necessitates IMC putting up a further £115,000. This is put up in the form of an addition to the interest free equity loan.

Given the information in this table the capital budgeting department prepare the separate net cash flow statements for the bank loan, the long term loans, and of course the equity capital. From these three separate statements can be calculated the return on total capital, the return on *long term* capital (equity plus the long term loan), and the return on equity capital (see Section 3 of Chapter 6 for a detailed discussion of the uses and justification for these three returns). The reason for calculating the return on total capital is to determine whether or not the project as a whole is viable. The reason for calculating the return on equity capital is obviously to determine its attractiveness from IMC's viewpoint. The reasons for calculating the return on total long term capital are two. First, it happens to correspond in this case with the capital that is at risk. There is no need to include the bank loan in this calculation as even if the mine failed it is felt that the residual cash and working capital will suffice to repay the bank loan in full. The second reason for calculating the return on total long term capital although the bonds are not guaranteed (i.e. the bonds do not represent IMC's *legal* risk capital) is that IMC is concerned to ensure a good margin exists whereby the bonds can be repaid in full. It would harm its reputation to be associated with a project which failed to discharge its liabilities in full, and would adversely affect its prospects of financing other projects in future. Hence total long term capital in a meaningful sense represents IMC's 'risk capital'.

The net cash flow of the bank loan, assuming repayment at the end of year 20, is here taken as net of 50% tax on the interest elements,

Table 13.6

£000's

Years	1	2	3	4	5	6	7	8	9	10	11–19	20*
(i) Forecast Profit and Loss Account												
(a) Gross sales revenue	4,500	7,500	9,500	10,000	10,000	10,000	10,000	10,000	10,000	10,000	10,000	12,500
(b) Less: cost of sales (Table 13.5)	3,990	6,213	7,404	7,700	7,700	7,700	7,700	7,700	7,700	7,700	7,700	9,625
(c) Gross operating profit	510	1,287	2,096	2,300	2,300	2,300	2,300	2,300	2,300	2,300	2,300	2,875
Less:												
(d) Interest payments – (i) 8% Bonds	−560	−560	−478	−350	−200	−40						
(ii) 6% Bank loan	−65	−80	−95	−100	−100	−100	−100	−100	−100	−100	−100	−100
(e) Depreciation and Depletion on £12,520,000 – 20 year basis	−626	−626	−626	−626	−626	−626	−626	−626	−626	−626	−626	−626
(f) Taxation provision									−644	−660	−660	−833
(g) Net of Tax profits	−741	21	897	1,224	1,374	1,534	1,574	1,574	930	914	914	1,316
(ii) Forecast Source and Application of funds												
Sources												
(h) Net of Tax Profits (line g)	−741	21	897	1,224	1,374	1,534	1,574	1,574	930	914	914	1,316
(i) Depreciation (line e)	626	626	626	626	626	626	626	626	626	626	626	626
(j) Taxation provision (line f)									644	660	660	833
(k) Increase in bank loan	180	248	247									
(l) Increase in Equity Shareholders' Loan	115											−1,675
(m) Total Source of Funds	180	895	1,770	1,850	2,000	2,160	2,200	2,200	2,200	2,200	2,200	1,100
Applications												
(n) Taxation payment										644	660	1,493†
(o) Increase in Working Capital	180	647	1,523	1,850	2,000	980						−2,175
(p) Loan repayments		248	247									
(q) Equity surplus – (i) Equity loan repayments						1,180	1,955					
(ii) Dividends							245	2,200	2,200	1,556	1,540	1,782
(r) Total application of funds	180	895	1,770	1,850	2,000	2,160	2,200	2,200	2,200	2,200	2,200	1,100

* (Assumes sale of stockpile and stocks in transit and recovery of cash float)

† (Assumes the tax bill for year 20 is paid in year 20 along with the tax bill of year 19, rather than one year in arrears)

Table 13.7

Equity and Debt Net Cash Flows

£000's

Years	1	2	3	4	5	6	7	8	9	10	11–19	20
(i) Equity Net Cash Flow												
Equity dividends in Ruristan (net of Ruristan taxes)							245	2,200	2,200	1,556	1,540	1,782
Less: parent country tax collected 1 year in arrears								−123	−1,100	−456	−440	−949*
Add: tax free equity loan repayments	−115					1,180	1,955					
Total:	−115					1,180	2,200	2,077	1,100	1,100	1,100	833
(ii) 8% Bonds Net Cash Flow												
Interest payments less 50% tax	280	280	239	175	100	20						
Repayments		647	1,523	1,850	2,000	980						
Total:	280	927	1,762	2,025	2,100	1,000						
(iii) 6% Bank Loan Net Cash Flow												
Interest payments less 50% tax	33	40	47	50	50	50	50	50	50	50	50	50
Repayments	−180	−248	−247									1,675
Total:	−147	−208	−200	50	50	50	50	50	50	50	50	1,725
(iv) Combined Net Cash Flow to Risk Capital (i)+(ii)	165	927	1,762	2,025	2,100	2,180	2,200	2,077	1,100	1,100	1,100	833
(v) Combined Net Cash Flow to Total Capital (i)+(ii)+(iii)	18	719	1,562	2,075	2,150	2,230	2,250	2,127	1,150	1,150	1,150	2,558

* (Assumes tax bill for year 20 is paid in year 20 along with the tax bill of year 19, rather than 1 year in arrears)

i.e. the tax rate applying in IMC's home country rather than the 30% rate in Ruristan. This is because the calculation is being done notionally on the basis of IMC providing all the funds itself, some as loan and some as equity, and its own tax rate is therefore appropriate.[1] The net cash flow statement for the bonds is obviously the interest payments net of all taxes (again at IMC's 50% rate) plus repayments. To derive the equity net cash flow is not so straightforward. It comprises equity loan repayments which attract no taxes at all, and the dividends which are effectively taxed at 30% in Ruristan (i.e. they are paid out of company profits which have borne tax at 30%), and again in the parent company's own country if remitted there. If IMC has further projects in Ruristan it could of course use some of its earnings from the potash project to save sending out further capital, and also avoiding the extra 20% tax rate involved in remittance. The problem of evaluating earnings in this context is discussed fully in Section 2. Here it will be assumed that IMC can foresee no further use for surplus funds in Ruristan at this stage and accordingly all dividends will be remitted as soon as they are paid, hence further tax will be suffered in the parent country. Tax in the parent country is at the rate of 50% with Ruristanian tax allowed as a setoff in full. Hence, where dividends are paid out of profits on which Ruristanian tax of 30% has been levied, this will be notionally added back to the dividends which will be taxed at the rate of a further 20%. (Thus if a dividend of £70 is remitted to the parent company out of *taxed* profits, it will be notionally grossed up to £100 and a £20 levy will be made - thus bringing total tax up to 50% on the original profits.) Any dividends paid out of untaxed profits, however, will be subject to the full 50% tax if remitted to the parent country. This will apply to any dividends remitted out of profits up to year 9, plus £55,000 of any dividends remitted from the profits of year 9. (The amount of capital expenditure to be written off is the total pre-production expenditure - including

---

[1] The return on total capital varies with the proposed financing plan, as different financing plans have different tax consequences which affect the amount and timing of the aggregate net cash flows. The purpose of calculating the return on total capital and the capital at risk is to appraise the total risks being run by the equity shareholders. Hence the convention adopted here is to assume the equity shareholders put up all the finance in the form envisaged in the recommended financing plan and to calculate the return accordingly. The return to the equity shareholders if they did put up all the finance could be no worse than this. Hence it is a reasonable procedure.

bond interest - of £14,020,000, less the initial working capital, £1,500,000 = £12,520,000. This sum is to be written off out of gross operating profit less interest charges, whose cumulative total reaches £12,465,000 at the end of year 8, leaving a further £55,000 of tax free profits in year 9. Thereafter all profits are subject to Ruristanian tax at 30%, collected 1 year in arrears. All subsequent dividends, being paid out of taxed profits, will suffer a net loss of only 2/7ths when remitted to the parent country, and payment thereon will be 1 year in arrears. The relevant equity, debt, and total net cash flows are set out in Table 13.7, on the assumption that bank loan and bond interest are taxed at a combined rate of 50%, with tax payments coinciding with receipt of interest.

From this table it is possible to calculate the discounted net of tax yields on equity capital, 'risk' capital, and total capital, relating the net cash flows solely to the *future* capital expenditures. (Where any past expenditures could be recovered by not going ahead with the project they should of course be added to the present value of the future capital outlays. The same would apply to the sale of all rights in the project to another company.) They are as follows for operating periods of 12 and 20 years, assuming cash flows arise mid-year on average.

Net of tax discounted returns

	12 year operation	20 year operation
On Total Capital £11,020,000*	8%	10¼%
On Total 'Risk' Capital £10,020,000*	8¾%	11¼%
On Equity Capital £3,020,000*	12¾%	15¾%

* (These sums relate to absolute totals of expenditure over the two years construction period, i.e. they are not discounted although they were of course discounted in the actual calculation of the various returns.)

IMC, having regard to normal mining risks, feel that any project with which they are associated must promise a minimum net of tax return of 7% on total risk capital over a reasonable period. Given a firm 12 year fixed price contract,[1] and the very stable conditions in Ruristan, 12 years is considered to be a reasonable period. By this test the project is acceptable. And over the same period the

[1] No commercial contract of this type is absolutely 100% firm. If the buyers, through say a severe recession, cannot accept delivery, then deliveries would of necessity be reduced or postponed. But given this and the price concession given to obtain a fixed price contract, the contract is as firm as any commercial contract of this type can be, and hence it is reasonable to examine the operation over a 12 year period.

return on IMC's further equity investment is $12\frac{3}{4}\%$ net of all taxes. IMC's net of tax cost of equity capital is also 7%, and the $12\frac{3}{4}\%$ is considered to offer a sufficient margin allowing for the risks involved (e.g. of a capital overrun, of higher operating or distribution costs, of a temporary recession in Japan, etc., etc.) especially bearing in mind the likelihood of being able to continue to operate the mine profitably after the 12 year contract lapses which would increase the yield significantly. There is also the possibility of marketing some potash in Ruristan within a few years and the mine could be made to yield an increased output at little extra capital cost. Taking all these factors into account the project would be recommended for acceptance by the capital budgeting department.

There are several points of interest to be noted. First, had IMC known the likely price of the fixed contract which was eventually negotiated, it would never have commenced the £2·5m. detailed planning and testing as the project would have failed to give the necessary minimum return on total capital over the period of the fixed contract. Once the £2·5m. expenditure was made, however, (and the likely price for the contract was not apparent until this expenditure was nearly completed), it, like the £0·5m. original exploration expenditure, became irrelevant to the decision of whether or not to go ahead. The sole relevance of these two sums was that they still counted as capital expenditure which could be written off against profits for Ruristanian tax purposes, i.e. they still had a value if the project was commenced.

A second point to note is the significant increase in profitability if the project is continued for 20 years or more. This is best appreciated from considering the net of tax yields on equity, 'risk', and total capital over 20 years as set out in Figure 13.1.

This shows that the project requires just over 10 years to meet IMC's minimum requirement for a 7% net of tax yield on total capital at 'risk'. It also shows the conventional payback period to be nearly 7 years and the capital recovery period (i.e. the return of capital with 'interest' – see Section 5 of Chapter 6) to be over 8 years, the period by which all the 'risk' capital is recovered having earned its 'interest' in full, i.e. 8% gross of tax on the bonds, and 7% net of tax on the equity. The return on equity capital rises significantly if the project continues past 12 years, from $12\frac{3}{4}\%$ to $15\frac{3}{4}\%$ at 20 years. It should be appreciated that $15\frac{3}{4}\%$ over 20 years is quite an increase on $12\frac{3}{4}\%$ for only 12 years.

Third, it should be appreciated that for a venture of this kind where all long term debt is repaid as a first charge on the net cash flow the weighted average cost of capital can have no place in the assessment. In the initial period the whole net cash flow, both profits as well as all the depreciation provision, belong to debt, and thereafter entirely to equity. This being so, it is essential to work on the separate equity net cash flows in appraising a project of this type.

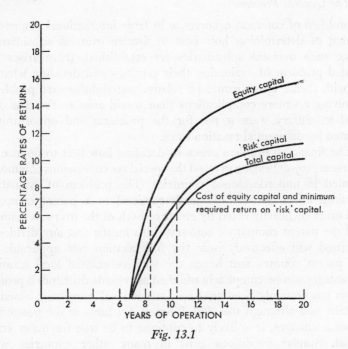

Fig. 13.1

Finally, the importance of using discounting methods should be appreciated in appraising projects such as this with a long pre-production period, unusual tax concessions, and a special form of financing. The irregularity of the net cash flows, see Table 13.7, especially the equity net cash flows which are of primary interest to the sponsors, would make conventional methods, particularly the rate of return (the ratio of *average* profits to initial or average capital) quite unsatisfactory.

After this consideration of a particular overseas project, we turn now to the more general financing and evaluation problems of overseas projects. Readers interested in the problems of presenting such projects to the international lending bodies, the World Bank, International Finance Corporation, the Eximbank, etc. are recommended to consult reference (1).

2. FINANCING OVERSEAS COMPANIES AND EVALUATING THEIR EARNINGS

a. *The General Problem*

A problem of common occurrence in large international companies is that of determining how best to finance overseas subsidiaries. Once such overseas subsidiaries are established, there arises the related problem of evaluating their earnings and deciding what to do with them. These would be relatively straightforward problems involving no more complications than would arise in the case of a local subsidiary were it not for the problems and opportunities created by differential taxation rates.

The financing problem arises in deciding how best to finance an overseas project bearing in mind the special tax concessions commonly granted in underdeveloped countries. The problem of evaluating earnings arises because dividends remitted to a parent company will often be heavily taxed by either or both of the overseas country and the parent company's country. This means that any dividends remitted will effectively bear the full taxation rate applicable in the parent country and hence the very substantial local taxation advantages can be completely nullified as regards distributed profits. (This has certainly been true for international companies based in Britain, and although the 1961 Finance Act hints at the possibility of some changes, it is likely to continue to be true for many years ahead. Similar conditions exist in many other countries with significant foreign investments.)

b. *Suggested Solutions*

Given these disadvantages of remitting profits there is a strong temptation for profits to be retained overseas even when there is little likelihood of reinvesting them profitably. This has led to two opposing schools of thought in evaluating overseas projects. One school holds that the relevant net cash flow from an overseas project should be evaluated net only of local tax as typically the funds so earned should be re-invested as this is likely to be the most profitable course of action. The other school holds that all overseas projects should be evaluated on the basis that all profits will be remitted to the parent company as this is the ultimate destination of all profits earned overseas, and this makes projects in different countries comparable both with one another and with investment opportunities in the parent company's country. Further, it is argued that it is impossible to estimate with any precision whether profits will actually have to be remitted or not and therefore it is prudent to evaluate overseas projects on the assumption that all profits will have to be remitted to the parent company as earned.

There is merit in both schools of thought but there is no simple answer concerning which is right. In certain circumstances one approach or the other is appropriate, but in other circumstances neither is adequate. It is certainly a point in favour of an overseas project if it is profitable enough to permit the full and immediate remittance of all its net earnings to the parent company even though this involves heavy tax payments. This being so we would recommend that every overseas project should be subject to this test because projects which can pass it are obviously very attractive. But any project failing this test should not automatically be rejected, especially if its earnings have a strong likelihood of being required for further and profitable re-investment overseas. Once this possibility exists then it is no longer possible to look at a particular project on its individual merits alone. It must be considered in conjunction with the other projects its earnings will be used to finance. One point, however, should be clearly appreciated. It is not possible to go on justifying projects *ad infinitum* on the basis that profits will be re-invested abroad rather than remitted to the parent. A bank account constantly increasing in size but on which one can never draw a cheque is hardly a satisfactory investment. In short, a company must be wary of constantly re-investing funds arising overseas on the grounds that remittance involves extra taxes, and no policy of 100% re-investment forever can be justified.

Before turning to a solution of this problem let us first briefly consider the *initial* financing problem of an overseas subsidiary.

c. *Initial Financing*

Once an overseas subsidiary is established, it is possible to consider its expansion partly in terms of re-investing its net earnings, but this possibility is better considered as part of the general problem of evaluating the net cash flows of overseas subsidiaries. Apart from the problem of deciding whether to raise debt capital locally or in the parent country, the solution to which is fairly obvious (e.g. raising loans at the cheapest rate, except when local inflation exists in which case local currency loans are usually preferable), there exists the problem of the best way to channel the parent company's own funds to the subsidiary. The normal method would be to put the parent company's funds in as straight equity but this method can have two disadvantages. First, when profits are remitted they will be in the form of dividends and are thus liable to suffer heavy taxation in the form of with-holding taxes in the overseas country, and also in the parent country if the tax effectively borne overseas is less than the rate in the parent country, a situation of common occurrence. (It is impossible to generalize on this matter as it is affected by the double taxation agreements etc., between countries, but the situation described holds true in some form or other for most foreign investments.) Second, the remittance of earnings in the form of dividends is often the cause of political unrest in underdeveloped countries where the benefits of foreign investment are often ignored, all attention being directed to the price paid, i.e. the remittance of dividends.

Both disadvantages can be partly overcome if the parent company puts up the bulk of its own funds in the form of loans. (This can often be best done by setting up a wholly owned holding company in the overseas country to which the parent company lends the full amount it is investing. The holding company is then free to put these funds into the operating subsidiary entirely as equity funds where this has advantages, e.g. on grounds of tax, public relations, etc.) Then as profits accumulate in the holding subsidiary they can be used to pay off these loans thus avoiding extra taxation either locally or in the parent company (because they are capital remittances and hence seldom taxed), and also incurring less political odium in the overseas country. There are obvious limitations to this device. The maximum the loan can amount to will be the capital sum the parent company is investing which by definition should be less than the total of expected profits if investment is to be justified. It is thus not possible to avoid extra taxes on all profits by this device. Also, as mentioned, a firm will often be well advised for financial and political reasons to put up a substantial proportion of its subsidiary's capital in the form of equity to indicate permanent investment, etc. These limitations apart, however, putting up as much of the capital as possible in the form of loan capital is usually a sensible course of action.

d. *Evaluating Overseas Earnings*

The two suggested solutions, see (b) above, set the limits to evaluating overseas earnings. If the earnings of an overseas subsidiary cannot be profitably re-invested abroad, then rather than leave them idle it pays to remit them home at once despite the extra tax burden incurred. No earnings can therefore be worth less than their net of tax remitted value to the parent company discounted to a present value in the same way as any earnings arising within the parent country. (Two cases where funds will have a minimum value in excess of this are discussed in the following paragraph.) Conversely, no overseas earnings can be worth more than the net value of capital funds remitted from the parent company, i.e. their replacement value. Thus if the parent company wishes to expand its activities in an overseas country in which it has a subsidiary then surplus funds arising from that subsidiary reduce the need to send out funds from the parent and are worth their face value. (In the rare cases when capital going into a country is taxed, overseas funds can be worth more than the face value of similar funds in the parent company. And overseas funds are always worth slightly more than funds to be sent out from the parent company by the amount of remittance and foreign exchange charges.) Where between these two extremes the actual value of funds earned overseas resides is a matter of fact. It depends entirely on the uses to which the funds can be put. Before examining this subject we shall consider briefly the cases where the minimum value of funds will be worth more than their remitted net of tax value in the hands of the parent company.

If funds arising overseas cannot be profitably re-invested there it will usually pay to remit them to the parent despite the net tax loss, as the funds can then be re-invested to advantage elsewhere. There is obviously no point in keeping a large sum permanently on bank deposit abroad. If it is to have any value at all to the parent company it must be remitted home one day and thus suffer tax. The longer that day is postponed the less the net of tax present value it will have as the sum itself will not be growing significantly. There are two obvious cases, however, where immediate remittance in these circumstances would not be in a firm's best interest. The first is where the tax loss on remittance is expected to be significantly reduced within a few years such that the present value at a firm's cost of capital (the net of tax cost of capital of the parent) of a sum remitted, say three years hence, exceeds the value of immediate remittance. The second is where the parent country's currency is likely to be devalued, or the overseas country's currency revalued. This situation is usually so difficult to predict that it is seldom of practical importance but there will be occasions when the possibility of revaluation or devaluation is sufficiently strong to justify retaining money idle in a particular country for a period. Conversely, the possibility of revaluation in the parent country or devaluation in the overseas country would make it worth remitting funds to the parent even when the opportunity for profitable re-investment abroad exists. In all these cases the correct solution will be obvious from comparing the present value of all the different choices at the parent company's net of tax cost of capital. We turn now to considering the appropriate technique for evaluating earnings in overseas subsidiaries in certain commonly encountered situations.

The optimal solution to the formal general problem of evaluating net cash flows arising abroad is an exercise in dynamic programming, the consideration of all possible alternatives allowing for re-investing net earnings, and re-investing the resultant net earnings etc., etc. This technique however is probably too cumbersome and expensive to apply to most practical problems and usually there will be insufficient data to justify it. Further, few firms can forecast their investment opportunities for more than a few years ahead. Much of the potential gain from the method can, however, be obtained by the application of more rudimentary methods. It is also desirable, as we have stressed before, that the technique should not obscure the risk situation, and an advantage of the rudimentary method proposed here is that it will give the individual applying it a good feel of the risks involved.

Consider a simple example showing the projects in an overseas country for a parent company in Britain, the basic data of which is set out in Table 13.8.

Table 13.8

Years	0	1	2	3	4	5	6	
Project A	$-I_1$	$-A_1$	A_2	A_3	A_4	A_5	A_6	...
Project B			$-I_2$	B_1	B_2	B_3	B_4	...
Project C				$-I_3$	C_1	C_2		...

The firm is assumed to have one major project A and to be planning two subsidiary projects B and C (but *no others*) in an overseas country.

The symbols I_1, I_2, and I_3 represent the capital outlays involved in projects A, B and C, respectively, and the symbols A_i, B_i and C_i are their respective subsequent cash flows before all taxes both local and British. The first net cash flow of project A is actually negative, representing an operating loss which must be financed in the same way as if it represented a further capital outlay. It is assumed in this case that no local taxes are levied up to year 6, but that funds would be subject to full British taxes if repatriated. The problem is to evaluate project A bearing in mind the alternative uses for its earnings because projects B and C are justifiable on the most pessimistic assumption that all their cash flows are subject to full British taxation, *and hence will be undertaken even if A is not.*

The basic line of approach to the problem is to consider simultaneously the cash flows involved in all three projects, and to ascertain what net cash flows would be required from the British parent after taking full advantage of the untaxed funds arising locally. Then the return on project A can be calculated to see if it is sufficiently attractive to justify commencement.

Table 13.9 shows the relevant cash flows on the basis that they are remitted home to the parent country and suffer aggregate taxes at the rate t, here assumed to be constant. Also given at the bottom of the table are the relative orders of magnitude of certain critical cash flows.

Table 13.9

Years	0	1	2	3	4	5	6	
Project A	$-I_1$	$-A_1$	A_2	$(1-t)A_3$	$(1-\cdot4t)A_4$	$(1-t)A_5$	$(1-t)A_6$	...
Project B			$-I_2$	$(1-t)B_1$	B_2	$(1-t)B_3$	$(1-t)B_4$	...
Project C					$-I_3$	$(1-t)C_1$	$(1-t)C_2$	...

where (a) $I_2 > A_2$, and (b) $I_3 = B_2 + \cdot6A_4$

The logic behind the table is as follows.

Year 1. A_1 is an outflow in the same way that I_1 is and requires in the same way the sacrifice of funds, i.e. a capital outlay by the parent company.

Year 2. Insofar as funds A_2 can be used to obviate capital of A_2 being sent from the British parent company they are worth precisely A_2 to the parent company. Tax free funds of £1m. in the overseas country saves the company sending £1m. of capital from

Britain. Since $I_2 > A_2$, all of the funds A_2 can be used in this way and hence are worth their full face value, hence the parent company need send out only $(I_2 - A_2)$ from Britain.

Year 3. Neither A_3 nor B_1 can be used to save capital being sent from Britain since, as can be seen, all the future capital requirements for I_3 can be met from the cash flows of the following year. Since there is no advantage in retaining A_3 and B_1 in the overseas country (as the firm has no other prospective investment projects here), both should be repatriated and suffer the full deductions of the taxes incurred through remittance.

Year 4. It is assumed that $I_3 = B_2 + 0 \cdot 6A_4$, hence all of B_2 and 60% of A_4 can be used to avoid capital expenditure from Britain. There are many other ways of splitting the sum I_3 between B_2 and A_4, e.g. it could have been done on a proportional basis, or I_3 could have first been set off against A_4 and only the balance (if any) set off against B_2. The justification for setting I_3 off against B_2 in its entirety first, and only setting off the balance against A_4, is that project B will be commenced even if A is not. As the problem is to determine whether or not to commence A it is correct to set off against A's cash flow only the residual capital requirements of other projects which could be financed only by remittances of capital from the parent company. Hence 60% of A_4 should be valued on a gross of tax basis (i.e. gross of taxes arising through remittance) and the remaining 40% on a net of tax basis. Hence the value of A_4 is $0 \cdot 6A_4 + (1-t)0 \cdot 4A_4 = (1 - 0 \cdot 4t)A_4$.

Year 5. All net cash flows arising in each project should be remitted, and valued accordingly.

Year 6 onwards. In this example it is assumed that the firm has no worthwhile investment opportunities in the overseas country after the 6th year so all cash flows arising thereafter should be valued as in year 5, on a net of tax remitted basis.

As a result of the above, the modified net cash flows of project A can be evaluated to determine whether or not the project is acceptable. An important complication must now be introduced into this simple example.

Suppose now that the investment I_3 exceeds $(A_4 + B_2)$ by an amount E (indicating excess). It is clear that the position could be improved by retaining some of the funds of year 3, namely A_3 and B_1. Assume that the marginal earnings of funds overseas (say on local lending) is at the rate of return of k, and that the parent firm could use any remitted funds to earn r (its normal cost of capital). Now by remitting $(A_3 + B_1)$ home in year 3 this sum will have a net present value to the parent company at that time of $(A_3 + B_1)(1 - t)$. By not remitting this sum home it would be re-invested at k to grow to $(A_3 + B_1)(1 + k)$ and we will assume this would exactly $= E$. This has a present value to the parent company in year 3 of $E/(1 + r)$. As long as $E/(1 + r)$ is greater than $(A_3 + B_1)(1 - t)$, and this is likely to be the case, the funds arising in year 3 are worth more retained abroad than remitted home for re-investment. A similar solution could be worked out when the profits of several years might need to be retained to finance a large capital outlay. As argued in the notes attached to Year 4 above, funds should first be thought of as coming from project B which will be commenced regardless of whether project A is started or not.

Normally a firm will have only the haziest impression of the capital projects that it will be worthwhile for it to undertake, given the frequent local complications of inadequate technical manpower, government restrictions, political and economic uncertainty, etc., etc. It is nevertheless common for firms to retain funds in an overseas country for long periods in order to avoid taxation and in the hope of finding a later worthwhile opportunity for local investment. The most efficient policy for a firm, however, will often be to re-patriate local profits as soon as they are earned and not begin accumulating them until it is necessary to do so in order to provide the capital sums required for the commencement date of a *known* investment opportunity. And sometimes it will pay a firm to postpone an investment opportunity a few years until it can be financed by profits retained from existing projects rather than by remittances from the parent company. Further, a firm can often obtain a substantial part of the advantages of retaining local funds for investment years hence by raising local loan capital where available.

REFERENCE

1. MURRAY D. BRYCE, *Industrial Development – A Guide for Accelerating Economic Growth*, McGraw-Hill, 1960.

CHAPTER FOURTEEN

The Capital Budgeting Organization

Attempting to lay down the principles of capital budgeting organization for firms in general is as impractical as trying to lay down the general principles of political organizations for countries in general, since firms are at least as diverse in their economic and administrative problems as are countries. To make the discussion usefully specific, therefore, we shall relate most of the following comments to the problems of the medium to large size firms in the general manufacturing or extractive industries. With some qualifications and adaptation, much of the proposed organization could apply equally well to primarily marketing or property companies, or to nationalized industries.

The problems of capital budgeting organization in any enterprise are both financial and political. It would be unrealistic to consider the financial aspects of capital budgeting organization in isolation from its political aspects since capital budgeting is inevitably involved in the major political issues of large firms. Even in the best organized firms there will always be powerful political pressures at work endeavouring to influence the financial assessment of capital projects because the future shape of a firm is essentially determined by the investment decisions of its top management.

The commonest type of capital budgeting organization is where the capital budgeting decision is largely taken – or at least almost all the investigation and analysis is performed – by that department, a producing or marketing department, primarily interested in the project. This has the obvious advantage of entrusting a project to the department most familiar with it and all the accompanying technical complexities. The disadvantage, however, and it is a major disadvantage, is that the investment appraisal of a project is conducted by the very people who are most concerned, and rightly concerned, to see the project accepted. It is inevitable and – to the relative exclusion of financial considerations – on balance desirable that manufacturing departments should be preoccupied with technical feats and marketing departments with sales volumes and questions of sales strategies. To require such departments to be both advocates and judges in their own cause is to require impossible objectivity.

Whatever may be said for the quality of sweet reasonableness, it is hardly conducive to the vigour and attack needed to advance the specialized objects of such departments. Impartiality and realism must be enforced, however, which requires a separate department. Also, as we have indicated throughout this book, rigorous investment appraisal calls for many specialist skills seldom found in technical or marketing departments, etc. For these reasons we consider it generally desirable to have a separate capital budgeting department functioning basically as a court, with all major project sponsors having the right of appeal to top management. It is to a consideration of the detailed organizational set-up of such a department that we now turn.

1. THE CAPITAL BUDGETING DEPARTMENT

For a capital budgeting department to function efficiently it must be able to call upon a staff with diverse special skills. It is of paramount importance that accounting skills are well represented even though a conventional accounting training is insufficient for adequate investment appraisal. Accountancy is the language of business and many investment projects will be presented in a form readily comprehended by accountants who are thus suited to turning it into the form relevant for appraisal, i.e. turning profit estimates into cash flows, etc. Further, accountants will be able to prepare estimated future balance sheets and profit and loss statements which are often needed if any external capital is to be raised to finance the project, or to determine the effect on the firm's reported profits, etc., etc. Finally, accountants will generally have a useful working knowledge of taxation and company law.

A second indispensable skill is that of the business economist. By training economists should instinctively appreciate the need to consider only the *incremental* effects of any course of action, the net capital outlays involved, the extra costs attributable solely to a given project, and the resulting incremental benefits. An understanding of the complexities raised by fixed and variable costs when considering a range of alternative outputs, an appreciation of the irrelevance of most allocated overheads, and an instinctive feel for opportunity costs enhance the contribution of a staff member soundly trained in economics. He is the essential complement to the accountant. Finally, the economist should be fully conversant with discounting techniques, and have a good understanding of what constitutes a firm's cost of capital in varying circumstances.

A third important contributing skill is that of the financial expert – the specialist in raising all relevant forms of capital from short term credit to equity funds. The desirability of any investment project depends in the last resort on whether or not it can and should be financed. It is the job of the financial expert to keep in close touch with the firm's finance department where one exists, or otherwise with the firm's financial adviser.

These are the three basic disciplines required for an efficient capital budgeting organization. It should be borne in mind that three skills does not necessarily imply three persons. Occasionally two, and sometimes even all three skills may be found in one person, although this latter combination is rare. But one thing is apparent and that is the general desirability that all senior members of a capital budgeting department should have some basic understanding and appreciation of the viewpoint and contribution of those trained in disciplines other than their own.

If accounting, economics, and finance provide the basic specialist knowledge in a capital budgeting department they will be much more effective if reinforced by two other specialized skills, those of the tax specialist and the mathematician. The contribution of a tax specialist will be obvious. The determination of net cash flows depends on being able to calculate accurately the incidence of tax payments which requires the detailed analysis of the tax allowances and liabilities thrown up by a project. Further, many new projects, especially those which lend themselves to the formation of new companies (particularly new overseas companies), offer considerable scope for tax savings if handled properly. And many forms of payment, e.g. the issue of shares, options, etc., have tax implications deserving full analysis. Indeed, it is not going too far to say that almost all major actions in business have significant tax implications. While it is not necessary for a tax specialist to belong to the capital budgeting department, it is most desirable that close links are maintained with such a specialist or specialists in the tax department. They in turn should appreciate the general approach of the capital budgeting department, and in particular the importance of discounting. Many recommended tax saving schemes seem to concentrate on maximizing the absolute magnitude of such savings, rather than their discounted present value.

The role of the mathematician in the capital budgeting department is not at first sight so obvious as that of other specialists, but he can provide two valuable services which are to some extent interlinked. First, the adequate consideration of many projects requires that a large number of approaches be examined. There may be several different ways of tackling the project initially, involving different starting dates and different output capacities, plus several assumptions concerning selling prices, sales volume, capital costs and operating costs. In some projects the number of possible combinations deserving study may well amount to 10 or more, and sometimes, as assumptions change, such combinations may have to be calculated half a dozen times or more before a project is ultimately accepted or rejected. Few capital budgeting departments will be prepared or indeed be able to produce so many calculations on a single project and thus there is always the possibility that the optimum plan or the effect of some critical factors will be overlooked. This is where a mathematician has a significant contribution to make because this problem of quickly processing many combinations of information in the same way is ideally suited to being handled by a computer. As most companies will be concerned with capital projects of a similar type, e.g. subject to constant tax allowances, etc., standard computer programmes can be drawn up to deal with them. Similarly, the constantly recurring problems of determining the optimal replacement policy for any given type of asset, optimal asset life, and annual depreciation (see especially Chapter 19), all lend themselves to handling by simple standard programmes. Computer time can be hired in nearly any medium to large city, and, once standard programmes have been written, itself not an expensive task, the cost of using a computer is very cheap.

The second valuable contribution of the mathematician is to be a link with or even a part of the operational research organization. This latter unit is almost invariably concerned with maximizing the profitability of complex operations where the correct course of action can seldom be determined by any other method. For the operational research approach to be useful it is necessary that the correct costs, tax allowances, discount rates, etc., are used (most such problems involve maximizing a net cash flow in one form or other) and close liaison with the capital budgeting department is thus essential. A mathematician familiar with capital budgeting problems is very suitable for this type of interdepartmental contact.

It will often be found desirable to have both a marketing and a technical executive on temporary secondment to the capital budgeting department as they will be in a position to question the project plans put up by the marketing and technical departments to ensure that all the relevant alternatives have been considered. Such suggestions are often better received in the departments concerned when coming from a specialist with a similar background. Also the regular staff of the capital budgeting department benefit from close contact with other specialists, and are more sympathetic to the problems involved. That secondment is only temporary is desirable on all counts. No marketing or technical specialist wants to be away from his field for too long, and indeed his value to the capital budgeting department would decline after too long a period. It is also an important department for any rising executive to have some experience of, especially if the department's potential is to be fully utilized in future.

The remaining staff of the capital budgeting department should include a number of highly trained calculators familiar with the full range of useful discounting techniques (see especially Chapter 1) and fully conversant with all kinds of accounting documents. While the use of a computer can supplement the work of such calculators the computer can never replace it. Whenever a problem is unusual, or an approximate answer needed quickly, then calculators are indispensable. Also such calculators ideally should become familiar with using the computer as just another of their tools, one especially suited to complex repetitive calculations.

2. THE NEED FOR A SPECIFIED FINANCIAL POLICY

It is essential to the fulfilment of a firm's objectives that there should be a clearly stated and understood policy towards general financing: this is the responsibility of the senior management. It is extremely common to find in many firms that uncertainty and ambiguity abound as regards the financial context within which individual capital budgeting decisions are taken. It is not uncommon to find in the same firm a belief on the part of some individuals that the firm must see very high returns (albeit high returns on which there is little numerical agreement), while on the other hand, an equally naïve belief to the effect that money costs only the interest rate at which it can be borrowed so that only this rate needs to be earned.

It is evidently impossible for most firms to lay down elaborate rules but the fairly rudimentary step of specifying the net of tax rate of returns expected on projects with a relatively minimal degree of risk is sufficient to give the requisite general guidance. This minimal return should reflect a realistic assessment of the firm's cash and financial position. For example if the firm is in a cash surplus position the minimum acceptable rate of return may be considerably lower than the situation in which say the firm is at maximum gearing and expects soon to be obliged to raise further equity capital. (See Chapters 4 and 16.) The special difficulties of analysis in these situations need not be known to those responsible for initiating projects. It is sufficient if they are told that a higher or lower rate of return than formerly can be considered for the current planning period. The specific details of the financial policy must of course be known to those responsible for the final financial analysis of the project.

3. NEED FOR A SPECIFIED RISK POLICY

Financial and risk policy are the two guide lines to the future development of the firm. The complications involved for the firm in considering risk have already been discussed (Section 2 of Chapter 6 on Risk) and we shall only briefly recapitulate and elaborate here. Policy towards risk is primarily a matter of relative values in which the main considerations must be what the shareholders have been led to expect as the risk policy of the firm and what the firm is itself capable of achieving. It would evidently be both wrong and foolish for firms whose shareholders had been led to expect a policy of slow but safe development and whose general management and organizational structure were geared to this end, to set out abruptly on a major policy of rapid but risky new developments. Such a course of action would require a clear mandate from the shareholders.

While any policy ranging from hyperconservatism to extreme adventurousness must be accepted as a policy decision to which technical analysis has nothing to contribute, such analysis has a great deal to contribute to ensure the *logical* and *consistent* development of that policy. A rationally applied policy of conservatism has at least as complex implications for financial analysis as a policy of high risk bearing. For example such conservatism must imply the concentration on and the careful sifting of relatively risk-free projects to establish those which are genuinely worthwhile. It must imply a special assessment of all projects which strengthen the security of the firm, for example marketing projects obtaining security of outlets, and research expenditure. The naïve 'conservative' policy of simply insisting on a high return from all projects will almost certainly result in increasing the risk of being borne by a firm if it results in the firm falling behind its rivals in the competitiveness of its marketing and investment in research.

4. CLASSIFYING PROJECTS INTO BUDGET CATEGORIES

For administrative purposes it is useful to distinguish five main categories of investment projects. These categories comprise obligatory, welfare, risk free, normal and speculative. Reference should be made to Section 6 of Chapter 6 on Risk.

a. *Obligatory Investments*

These investments consist of those required by law, by safety regulations, by insurance contracts, etc., and there is very little to be said about them. For the most part such expenditure must occur automatically and, as has been pointed out previously, the only occasion on which any choice exists is where there are several ways of complying with obligatory investment – e.g. by choosing long lived rather than shorter lived equipment. For most firms expenditure in this category will seldom reach significant proportions even in a single year so that its obligatory nature is not of material consequence for planning purposes.

b. *Welfare Amenity Investments*

There is little to be said about investments in this category, the amount spent on them being largely a matter of judgment. As with obligatory investment this type of investment seldom assumes significant proportions. There is, however, one important difference compared to obligatory investment: the fact that welfare investment need not occur in any one particular year. Rather it is fairly flexible both as to amount and timing.

c. *Risk Free Projects*

No projects are entirely free of any risks, but for most firms there will exist a significant proportion of relatively risk-free projects. This category will include a large proportion of cost saving projects and replacement outlays where these projects are generally free of all marketing risks. It is also convenient to include in this category all projects which are evidently acceptable in that they promise a worthwhile return on the most pessimistic of assumptions. Where such projects have significant intangible disadvantages (e.g. transferring staff to a cheaper but unpopular location), they should be excluded from this category (and put in one of the two remaining categories) for it is apparent that such disadvantages reduce the attractiveness of projects in the same way as do risks. Projects in the general risk free category should be subject to all the normal analysis outlined below but can normally be presented to top management as a special category requiring very little examination by them for risk and policy implications.

d. *Normal Projects*

The fourth category of investment is that involving appreciable risk and policy implications, but not such risk and uncertainties that detailed analysis is impractical. Such projects probably account for well over half the capital expenditure of most firms and should be subject to the appropriate risk analysis along the lines indicated in Chapter 6.

e. *Speculative Projects*

This final category arises out of a general policy recommendation that we would put forward. There are certain types of project, such as those involving new products or processes, which by their own nature are highly risky in the sense that there is simply inadequate information even to gauge with any accuracy the risks involved. Yet it will rarely be desirable for a firm to forgo projects of this type entirely. Some of these 'long shots' certainly do succeed, and equally important, often provide basic new products and processes which are essential if a firm is to maintain its market position. Analysed individually, however, such projects generally seem undesirable, or more often, there is simply inadequate information to assess their merits considered in isolation. These projects in fact need special consideration as an aggregate and the total amount of expenditure on them is a matter for a policy decision.

As a general procedure we would suggest that a firm decide on the total amount of money it is prepared to invest in projects of this type, basing its decision on the competitive activities of rival firms, its own needs to develop new products or processes, and possibly in the light of the historical record of such expenditure. For this type of expenditure we recommend that control and analysis is based on these considerations backed by adequate *ex-post* inquiries into the results of such expenditure, rather than by attempting the type of risk analysis appropriate to normal projects.

b. *Allocation of Funds Between the Above Categories*

The latter three categories enumerated above for risk-free, normal, and speculative projects, also form useful categories for control purposes, in that each category could be emphasized according to the policy objectives of the firm. (The control requirements for obligatory investments – choosing the cheapest adequate investments – and welfare investments – providing amenities comparable with those of other firms – are too obvious to require further discussion.) For example, a firm may consider that its past policy has been too conservative and that in the future it must try to put more of its energies into finding projects which fit in the normal or speculative categories. Alternatively, it may consider that it already has adequate resources directed to this end, and that it now needs to expend more effort consolidating its existing position and undertaking projects of assured if modest returns. In this case it would try to expand the proportion of its investment in the relatively risk-free category.

5. THE PRESENTATION AND ANALYSIS OF PROJECTS

a. *The Frame of Reference*

Before discussing the details of the presentation and analysis of projects it is worth considering the general frame of reference within which a capital budgeting department must make its recommendations. This primarily concerns a forecast of the firm's supply of and demand for funds over the next five years or so. By studying a detailed cash forecast (net cash flow of the firm on the basis of present knowledge) the department can determine which projects, bearing in mind their associated capital outlays and the incidence of the cash flows to which they will give rise, are particularly useful in overcoming years of marked imbalance, that is where supply significantly exceeds demand or vice versa. No cash forecast based on estimated known cash outflows (dividends, capital expenditures or committed projects, etc.) and likely revenues (from existing projects) is to be thought of as sacrosanct. It is merely the starting point for the department's work. Where the forecast demand for funds exceeds the estimated supply from internal sources, consideration must be given to the raising of further funds in the optimum manner, long or short term debt, or equity, or some combination of all three (see especially Chapters 4, 15, 16 and 17). Where there is a cash surplus, consideration must be given either to investing it internally to the best advantage of the shareholders, or returning it to the shareholders in the most suitable form, e.g. by increased dividends, return of capital, etc. (see especially Chapter 16). For any expanding firm this latter problem should almost never arise, but some profitable firms may well reach the limits of expansion in their present lines and be unwilling to diversify, or feel unsuited to it.

Whether the drawing up of a firm's cash forecast is done by the accounts department or the capital budgeting department is not a matter of any importance, but undoubtedly it is the latter department which will make the most use of it. This arises because the capital budgeting department has the primary responsibility for the firm's internal demand for funds. It is concerned to recommend the optimum selection of projects to absorb internal cash resources to the full, and, where necessary, to recommend the raising of additional funds externally, and, in the last resort, to recommend the return of permanent excess funds in the form that is in the best interests of the shareholders.

b. *The General Presentation of Information*

All capital budgeting problems can essentially be looked on as matters of choice. The three main choices connected with any project are:

(i) doing nothing,

(ii) different methods of achieving the same objects, and

(iii) different times of commencement.

In general the presentation of each capital project should contain the basic information (capital outlays, net cash flows, proposed method of financing, etc.) on the choices. In some cases, of course, the other choices may be obviously ruled out, but since it takes little time and space to point out this basic fact, it is worth putting it in the general presentation which will then always permit a systematic reference to all the relevant possibilities.

This basic information will generally be all that is required for projects in the risk-free category. In the case of projects in the normal category this information will need to be supplemented by information on the risk characteristics outlining the critical variables, the capital at risk, etc., along the lines suggested in Section 4c of Chapter 6. Projects in the speculative category will often not admit of much useful analysis, but such analysis as is practical and useful should be performed and the inadequacies of data and the purely speculative elements in the decision clearly pointed out.

So much for the general provision of information, we turn now to a consideration of the detailed forms on which such information should be provided.

c. *The Detailed Presentation of Information*

It is not possible to make detailed recommendations which will satisfy every type of business, but the capital proposal and basic information forms to be set out below are put forward as a general guide to the basic information that should be provided on any project, plus a suitable form of presentation.

For any system of central vetting and recommendation to work, it is necessary to set minimum limits to the value of projects to be considered by the capital budgeting department and for departmental managers, or the managing directors of subsidiary companies, to have full authority to authorize expenditure below these levels. The actual chosen limits depend on the size of the company and the general competence of line management, but care must be taken on three matters.

First, where say a factory manager has authority to authorize expenditures of £5,000 or less, it is not unknown, when a new installation costing £8,000 is wanted, to order it in two separate parts each costing less than £5,000, thus avoiding the central scrutiny altogether. This can partly be overcome by the common device of fixing an absolute sum which any executive can authorize personally in any one year. But it is as well to supplement this where necessary by sample checks, perhaps by an internal audit department where one exists.

A second and more important method of evading capital budgeting control, and a matter of serious importance in capital budgeting procedures, is the signing of long term contracts such as leases. An example might be a factory manager signing a ten year contract to purchase steam from an adjoining factory or a nearby power station at an annual cost below his personal authorization limit. Effective control can generally be achieved by requiring that all contractual payments beyond a given annual figure should receive prior investigation by the capital budgeting department and be subject (where appropriate) to a comparison with the purchasing alternatives.

The third matter to be considered is how to avoid recommending investments which are but the prelude to further investments each one of which appears to be attractive in its own right, but which taken together may be uneconomic. Where any given investment proposal is not complete in itself but merely part of an intended chain of further interdependent investments, then this fact must be clearly brought out so that the whole chain can properly be considered as one aggregate budget item. Thus any executive authorizing the start of a chain of interdependent investments should only do so if his expenditure limit suffices to cover the cost of the whole chain.

One general point on capital expenditure authorization limits should be made. Although a capital budgeting department will be directly concerned only with the projects costing more than the minimum authorized limits, its responsibility does not end there. It should be concerned to expound the general principles of vetting capital projects so that all minor capital expenditures are also adequately considered. This would be a suitable subject for internally run management training courses.

Consider now the recommended detailed capital proposal forms for the presentation of information.

Form A, set out below, contains a list of the basic information which may be required in the most complex of capital projects such as setting up a new subsidiary to handle a particular market or contract. Much of this information will be redundant or not apply to simpler capital projects - e.g. routine cost saving investments in an existing firm - but it will form a useful check-list for considering what will normally be required for the general run of projects undertaken by a firm.

FORM A

CAPITAL EXPENDITURE PROPOSAL
BASIC INFORMATION TO BE SUPPLIED

To apply to all capital expenditure proposals more than £x.
1. Reference No.
2. (a) Company and country of origin.
   (b) Location.
3. Brief description of the proposal, total *incremental* expenditures involved however financed, the estimated total or average *incremental* annual net cash flows (defined as profits before deducting interest payments, less tax when actually paid, plus depreciation less replacement capital expenditure, all on an *incremental* basis), and the estimated life of the project. Owners and acquisition terms where relevant.
4. Basic reasons for proposal including any intangible benefits or disadvantages likely to result.
5. Description of the process, plant, etc. including relevant details of patent position.

6. Availability of raw materials, plant, power, transport, housing, personnel, etc.
7. Market investigation into outlets for products, including likely range of output and selling prices and any effect on existing products of the Group.
8. Information and comments on inherent risks apart from those mentioned under 6 and 7 (see also 14 and 17b).
9. Legal and currency restrictions.
10. Statutory obligations.
11. Pollution, fire or other hazards.
12. Details of total capital expenditure to be incurred on fixed assets, broken down into main categories, and set out on a yearly or half-yearly basis – Form B(i). Details of the amount and timing of replacement capital expenditure.
13. Detailed breakdown of working capital estimate into stocks (inventories), debtors (accounts receivable), cash, and creditors (accounts payable), with a brief justification of the amounts involved, e.g. estimated stock turnover.
14. Details of estimated residual value of assets if project should be abandoned.
15. Detailed breakdown of proposed financing, including yearly or half-yearly breakdown of the investment of different funds into new equity funds, retained equity funds, proceeds from sale of surplus assets, and the various categories of loan finance. Details of loan interest and loan repayment terms. (Form B(ii)). Where it is proposed to purchase a new company partly or wholly with the shares of any Group company, a full justification of this and a rigorous comparison with the alternative of paying cash or raising loans. Similarly, where conversion options are proposed, full details and justification must be given.
16. Detailed operating cost estimates on an annual basis including start-up expenses. Costs, where possible, should be split down into fixed and variable categories. (Form C).
17. (a) Estimated Profit and Loss, and Source and Application of Funds statements, (Form D(i) and (ii) respectively, plus Balance Sheets where appropriate (e.g. when a new company is being formed to handle the project or when the effect of the project on the company's balance sheet will be significant) at useful intervals, e.g. at commencement of production and perhaps at five-yearly intervals thereafter.
    (b) Where any significant portion of the project's income is relatively free from risk details should be given.
18. Tax information should be included with full details of any unusual allowances being claimed, or wherever the annual tax liability shown in the Profit and Loss statement could not easily be reproduced in the central capital budgeting department.
19. Where there are viable alternative ways of undertaking a project the same details (3 – 18) should be given to permit an independent appraisal. This is particularly important when there is a choice of, say, type of plant, scale of output, etc., etc.
20. A brief explanation of why the project is being put forward at the present time, why it has not been put forward previously, and the likely consequences of postponement or rejection.
21. Where the project is such that acceptance may involve rejecting some other project or projects (i.e. mutually exclusive projects) details of the other project should be supplied in full to enable a comprehensive comparison to be made.
22. Where the project is part of an interdependent chain of projects full details of all the linked projects must be given.
23. Where it is proposed to enter into any medium or long term commitment, such as the charter of ships, hire of road vehicles, long term lease of buildings or facilities, or any form of long term contract for electricity, power, etc., full details must be given if the present value of such commitments, discounted at say, 6%, exceeds the limit of capital expenditure which can be sanctioned without central approval.

As we have stressed, this form comprises a basic guide to the relevant information for a major project and will require adaptation and supplementation to suit the needs of individual companies.

The remaining forms:

B. (i) Estimated Pre-Production Capital Expenditure
   (ii) Estimated Provision of Finance
C.   Estimated Annual Operating Costs.
D. (i) Forecast Profit and Loss Account.
   (ii) Forecast Source and Application of Funds.

are mostly based on standard accounting information, and are set out below. (No example of a balance sheet has been given as this would be no different to normal balance sheets.) They too are designed for a major project and would need scaling down for smaller projects. An example of these forms in use is given in Section 1 of Chapter 13.

FORM B
Project No. : ...

		Years		
	−4	−3	−2	−1

(i) *Estimated Pre-production Capital Expenditure*
  (a) Legal & Company Formation Expenses
  (b) Land & Property Acquisition
  (c) Fixed Asset Expenditures   (i)
     (broken down into significant (ii)
     categories)   (iii)
                     etc.
  (d) Planning & Administration Overheads
  (e) Loan Interest
  (f) Working Capital
  (g) Miscellaneous

Total Pre-Production Capital Expenditure

(ii) *Estimated Provision of Finance*
  (a) Equity Funds
  (b) Loans   (i)
     (including deferred interest where (ii)
     relevant)   (iii)
  (c) Bank Overdrafts
  (d) Other Short Term Loans, etc.
  (e) Miscellaneous

Total Finance Provided

FORM C
Project No.: ...
Estimated Annual Operating Costs

		Years			
	1	2	3	4	etc.

A. *Variable Cost of Production*
  Materials   (per unit)
  Direct Labour   (per unit)
  Power   (per unit)
  Packaging   (per unit)
  Other   (per unit)

B. *Variable Cost of Distribution*

Transport (per unit)

Export Duties (per unit)

Banking Charges, etc. (per unit)

Sales Commissions, etc. (per unit)

Other (per unit)

C. *Fixed Costs*

Production Overheads

Distribution Overheads

Administrative Overheads

Advertising, Sales Promotion, etc.

Start-Up Expenses

Total Costs of Output

Plus (Minus) Stockpile Requirements at cost

Total Cost of Sales

Volume of Sales

FORM D

Project No.: . . .

	Years				
	1	2	3	. . . n	Total

(i) *Forecast Profit and Loss Account*

   (a) Gross Sales Revenue

   (b) Less Cost of Sales (Form C)

   (c) Gross Operating Profit

Less:

   (d) Interest Payments

   (e) Depreciation

   (f) Taxation *Provided**

   (g) Net of Tax Profits

(ii) *Forecast Source and Application of Funds*

Sources

   (h) Net of Tax Profits – from (g)

   (i) Depreciation   – from (e)

   (j) Tax *Provided*   – from (f)

   (k) Decrease in Working Capital

   (l) Increase in Loans, Bank Overdrafts, etc.

   (m) Further Equity Funds (from elsewhere in the Company)

   (n) Sales of Surplus or Residual Assets

   (o) Total Sources of funds

Applications

   (p) Capital Replacement Expenditure

   (q) Tax *Payments*

   (r) Increase in Working Capital

   (s) Loans and Bank Overdraft Repayments, etc.

   (t) Surplus Available to Equity

   (u) Total Applications of Funds

* (Give full calculations separately.)

In compiling these forms several points must be borne in mind. All capital expenditures, costs, receipts, etc., should, of course, be compiled on an *incremental* basis (see Chapter 2, Section 2). Profits etc. are to be net of the effects caused in other parts of the business where sales etc. may be expected to change because of the project under consideration, etc.

The debt net of tax cash flow (where this is required) will be found by taking the loan interest payments, line (d), from the Profit and Loss Account less any tax due thereon, plus loan repayments, line (s), from the Application of Funds Statement. The equity net cash flow is line (t) from the latter statement. The combined net cash flow is found by adding together the debt and equity net cash flows.

Where a project is being screened initially, we recommend concentrating on the combined equity and debt net cash flow – that is, the *total* net cash flow, and comparing this with the firm's weighted average cost of capital where this is appropriate (i.e. where the debt and equity net cash flows form a fairly constant proportion of the total cash flow). Where the weighted average cost of capital is not appropriate, we recommend calculating the equity return separately (see Chapter 4, Section 4b).

For final – as opposed to initial – screening and presentation to top management, we would recommend using the return on total capital and (where it is significant) the return on the capital at risk as set out in Chapter 6, Section 4b. Also, where it is of material significance, to the acceptability of the project, the return on equity capital should be computed.

There is one final point which requires careful handling and that is how the project is financed. We have considered the case where a project requires some external financing for the sake of completeness. The capital budgeting department, in conjunction with the finance department, may well need to recommend some quite different form of financing from that proposed by a project's sponsors. Further, even if a project is to be mainly debt financed care must be exercised to determine how much is attributable to the project and how much to the debt raising capacity of other *existing* (see Chapter 4, Sections 6 and 8) assets. Similarly, even though a particular debt may not be repaid during a project's life, notional debt repayments may need to be calculated as set out in Section 8 of that chapter. This is a task for the department's financial specialist who will also be best suited to decide whether a detailed analysis of the equity cash flows is worth undertaking, given the future financing plans of the company.

6. POST MORTEMS

Post mortems (or post audit investigations) have in our view an essential function to play in capital budgeting decisions. It is generally the case, however, that post mortems are looked on with considerable disfavour in industry. They are sometimes held to discourage initiative and to produce a policy of overcaution (mistakes of omission rather than commision) and to give executives the sense of being 'hounded'. While there is a certain element of truth in this assessment of the situation, it is coloured by the strong emotional appeal it evokes of the image of untrammelled initiative and vigorous innovation contrasted with bureaucratic terrorism. A more realistic assessment of the situation would be to say that most investment proposals are of a kind that would safely pass even given the possibility of *post mortem* inquiries. Of the remaining projects that are likely to be put forward, a large proportion of them entirely deserve to be held in check and will be found to be basically unacceptable. Some of these proposals will be the result of unbalanced enthusiasms – which are an inevitable part of the generally desirable policy encouraging enthusiasm – and a proportion will often be the product of irresponsibility or internal power politics. Because these types of undesirable project are encouraged by the system itself, they will bulk too large in any capital budgeting system which has no effective post mortem procedure. Such a system will often *tend to discourage genuine worthwhile new initiatives*, for they will generally end by substituting for *post mortems* an inefficient general scepticism or an arbitrary cutting of investment budgets in order to exercise some control over the abuses to which such systems are inevitably prone. Alternatively, the sole check may be the consideration of the annual return on capital ratio for a whole factory or a subsidiary firm and this, as generally carried out (see Section 4 of Chapter 6), is unsatisfactory. Even when done properly (see Chapter 19, Section 1) it still has the disadvantage of lumping all projects together, thus losing the bad in the good.

On grounds of simple realism and efficiency therefore, we would recommend that a system of *post mortem* inquiries should be used. Apart from this control of abuses and inefficiency a significant advantage of this method is that it provides information on the errors of estimation involved in particular types of projects and on the judgment of individuals.

It would be wasteful and generally impractical for the system of *post mortem* inquiries to cover all capital projects and with little loss of control or information it can be based on samples of the investment projects accepted plus all major investments above a given level. At a relatively senior level, and independently of the department concerned with providing the basic data or analysis for a given project, a decision should be taken to have a *post mortem* enquiry on particular projects where there is any doubt concerning the efficiency with which the estimation and analysis have been performed, or where useful information and experience might result. Where administratively practical the *post mortem* should be performed by, or reviewed by, a team of experts independent of those from whom the project originated. This team should always contain one or two senior members of the capital budgeting department, but in the interests of the department's reputation for impartiality, it should never consist exclusively of such members.

The timing of a *post mortem* in relation to the commencement of the project being investigated will depend on the type of project. Some projects can be usefully investigated within 6–12 months of commencement, others not for several years. Essentially it is a matter of judgment by top management.

As regards projects involving relatively small amounts of capital, these too should be the subject of *post mortems* wherever the aggregate of such expenditure is significant. The sample of projects for the follow-up would of course be a much smaller proportion of the total of such projects than for projects involving relatively large amounts of expenditure.

As an additional method of controlling errors of omission we would suggest that in any firm there should be periodic presentations to senior management by interested departments of current investment opportunities, which although *prima facie* attractive, they are *not* recommending. Particular emphasis should be given here to new products or new developments generally. As a further check against errors of omission, questions should always be asked regarding projects currently recommended and which are now evidently very attractive, as to why they were not undertaken earlier.

7. GENERAL POINTS

If capital projects are to be efficiently analysed and financed, the departments concerned must be given sufficient time and resources. All too often these complex problems are subjected to lightning off the cuff decisions by senior management. Time is always held to be too precious for fuller consideration, yet the sums of money at stake can be enormous and are not seldom large. The scope for improved decisions foregone by insufficient consideration is such that few hurried top managers could justify taking the all too common short cuts. The provision of more time for fuller consideration is partly a matter for organization; partly for the intelligent anticipation of future information requirements (as in say a possible take-over). But still more is it a matter of the attitude of top managements who either do not know the scope for improvement (see reference 1), or who prefer to take major decisions in the exciting atmosphere of approaching deadlines, usually self imposed.

Even if there should be a dramatic improvement in this matter there will still be many occasions when time is unavoidably short and decisions must be quickly reached. It is in just these situations that a thorough knowledge of capital budgeting principles can be of most value in enabling an executive to concentrate on essentials, and to have short-cut methods at his fingertips. Of nowhere is this more true than at the negotiating table where concessions must be quickly sought and given. In view of this we would urge that at least one of the negotiating team should be a capital budgeting/financial specialist

REFERENCE

1. DONALD F. ISTVAN, *'Capital Expenditure Decisions – How They are made in Large Corporations'*. Indiana Business Reports, No. 33, Indiana University, 1961.

Part Two

Part Two

CHAPTER FIFTEEN
Optimal Financing

This chapter considers in some detail the problems of optimal financing. The first section deals with the optimal proportion of debt finance in the capital structure of the company. The second section deals with some problems of debt finance and in particular with conversion issues. The concluding section is an extended analysis of the effect of debt finance on the value of the firm's equity capital.

It will be convenient to consider first a simple but somewhat abstract financing situation in order to establish clearly certain basic points. Some of the very considerable complications met with in practice will then be introduced later. The first problem to be considered is the optimal proportion of debt and equity capital for a given firm.

1. THE OPTIMAL PROPORTIONS OF DEBT AND EQUITY

The object of raising debt capital is basically to provide finance on terms cheaper than those required by the equity shareholders. Essentially the firm is selling a certain proportion of its income as a prior charge to the debt holders in return for a capital sum. This sum is usually secured as a fixed or floating charge on the firm's assets. For this arrangement to be profitable to the equity shareholders the situation must evidently be that the debt holders are prepared to pay more for this amount and quality of income than it is worth to the equity shareholders.

Consider the case of a firm which currently is entirely equity financed. The management are considering methods of revising the financial structure of the company by raising debt capital. If the management want gearing, one method of obtaining this would be to make a debenture issue and then pay out the proceeds of the debenture issue to the equity shareholders in more dividends or even as a special reduction of the equity capital. A simpler method would be to issue free debenture stock (e.g. by capitalizing retained profits) to the existing shareholders who could then sell off the debentures for the same price as the firm would have obtained, thus avoiding the expense of raising the funds through the company and paying them out to the shareholders. In both cases the value of the equity of the company will fall because part of the equity income will have been ceded to the debenture holders. In both cases the shareholders will gain if debenture holders are willing to pay more for this (relatively risk free) income than it is worth to the equity shareholders. Thus, if the total value of the equity falls by £x, while the shareholders receive £y for their debentures, they will have gained £y − £x as a result of the additional gearing.

The grounds for assuming these markedly different demands for risk free income are as follows. Institutional factors cause the majority of lenders to place a high premium on relatively certain income, that is income from fixed interest securities. For example, insurance companies, pension funds, trustees, etc., have extensive contractual payments to meet in the future and, moreover, are engaged essentially in offering secure sources of income in the future. As a result they are willing to offer significantly more (i.e. offer more capital for a given amount of interest income) for relatively secure income than the majority of equity investors.

This situation is illustrated diagrammatically in Figure 15.1.

In Figure 15.1 the firm's total income is measured on the horizontal axis, and on the left vertical axis is measured the price per unit of income that equity shareholders are prepared to pay for different amounts of income, given that the balance of the income will be entirely absorbed by prior charge interest payments. The equity shareholders' demand curve with relation to these axes is the backward-sloping curve marked D_1. Thus for OL of equity income (with the balance LM being absorbed by interest charges) the equity shareholders are prepared to pay OP per unit of the equity income or a total of OP times OL.

This demand curve is drawn backward-sloping − i.e. with the equity shareholders prepared to pay more for each additional unit of income − on the assumption that, as the proportion of the total income sold as equity increases (and hence the proportion sold as interest charges decreases), the riskiness of the equity income decreases. In other words the *quality* of the equity income improves as its quantity increases. The curve implies that, if almost all the firm's income were absorbed in prior charges, the equity shareholders would consider the remaining income per unit virtually valueless because of the high degree of risk to which it was exposed. (The risks due to prior charges are discussed below.)

On the right hand vertical axis is given the price which the debenture holders are willing to pay per unit of prior charge income – that is, per £ of interest, given that the balance of the firm's income accrues to the equity shareholders. The demand curve of the debenture holders with relation to these axes is given by D_2. Thus if KM

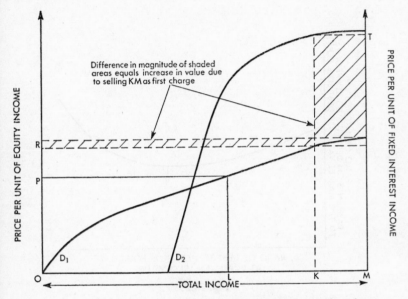

Fig. 15.1. D_1 is the demand curve of equity investors for a given income assuming that the balance KM is sold as a first charge
D_2 is the demand curve of debenture holders

is absorbed by interest charges the debenture holders would be prepared to pay MT per unit or a total of MT times KM. It should be noted that in the case of the debenture holders the demand curve slopes downward in the normal way as the quantity increases, for in their case the riskiness of their income *increases* with the proportion of the total sold as prior charges. This is simply because the firm could almost certainly meet a relatively small amount of prior charges in all circumstances, but might experience considerable difficulties in meeting a large proportion of prior charges in a period of poor profitability, thus threatening the security of the debenture holders.

The object of gearing must be to maximize the total capital value of the equity plus debt by choosing the best way of dividing the firm's total income between interest and equity income. In Figure 15.1 for example, selling the whole income as equity, would give a value to the equity of OR times OM. This could clearly be improved on if, as illustrated in the figure, KM were sold as a fixed charge to debenture holders.

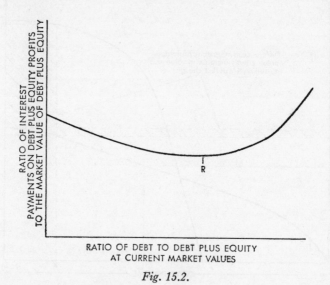

Fig. 15.2.

In terms of traditional theory, we can say that by increasing the proportion of debt capital the weighted average cost of capital can be reduced by introducing gearing. This situation is reflected in Figure 15.2. This is the counterpart of Figure 15.1 and shows on the vertical axis the weighted average cost of capital (defined as interest payments plus equity profits as a ratio or percentage of the total market value of the debt, including unquoted bank debt, etc., plus the equity). On the horizontal axis it shows the ratio of debt to debt plus equity capital measured at current market values. Conventionally this diagram is shown as U shaped, indicating that the weighted average cost of capital falls (hence the total value of the debt plus equity increases) with the ratio of debt to debt plus equity up to a certain point after which it decreases. On this basis the optimal point for the firm would be at the point R. At this point the weighted average cost would be at a minimum (the total value of debt plus equity would be maximized).

The reasons for average cost of capital falling to a minimum point have been discussed. Consider now the reasons why the cost of capital curve might curve upwards from this minimum point. Evidently for this to happen the total value of debt plus equity must fall as the amount of debt is increased. The total value of debt might fall because, by the firm increasing the proportion of debt from say 40% to 50%, the debenture holders would consider their interest income to be subject to a higher degree of risk. They may in extreme cases consider the existence of the firm to be threatened by the creation of additional prior charges, which, under adverse trading conditions, it might not be able to meet, even though such charges would be junior to their own. Similar considerations might influence the equity shareholders: they might feel that the firm could be forced into bankruptcy by failure to meet these heavy prior charges, or they might regard with disfavour the increased variability of their earnings relative to their average value.

As a practical matter it should be noted that a firm would have some difficulty in becoming overgeared. If a firm displayed signs of being overgeared, it is extremely likely that it would be required either to reduce its bank loans and other short term debt[1] or, for an expanding firm, that the rate of increase in debt would be slowed down. This would have the effect of causing the proportion of total debt to conform more closely to conventional standards. Similarly, as long term debt comes up for renewal, there will be pressure on a firm for a reduction in the total amount of its debt. This imposed reduction of debt results from the salient characteristic of the loan capital market, namely that if a firm's credit status is not good enough for it to qualify for interest rates within a limited conventional range, capital will not be advanced, or to put the point another way, the cost of loan capital becomes infinite and so the firm must reduce its indebtedness.

It should also be noted that, had a firm seriously reduced the total

---

[1] The importance of short term debt in gearing is frequently overlooked in this type of discussion. But it is often of significant proportions and certainly cannot be ignored in any discussion of risks to the equity from gearing. The relevance of lease commitments (see Chapter 8, Section 5) and the firm's cash position should also be considered.

value of its debt plus equity by overgearing, this would bring about its own remedy. For the firm would have created a situation in which the aggregates of its debt and equity were more valuable than the separate parts. It would then be profitable to another firm or institution to buy up all or most of the loan stock and equity of the company, for, given control of the loan stock, the purchaser is assured that the firm will not be pushed into liquidation by any third party owning loan stock and pressing its interest claims at a time when the company temporarily has inadequate profits or reserves to meet all its interest payments. A holding company, having acquired the loan stock and equity of the overgeared company, has effective ownership of its total income and can change the effective gearing as it chooses through its own (the purchasing company's) gearing.

Our own view on the shape of cost of capital curves is as follows. Conventional debt ratios in the majority of cases are extremely conservative. Relatively few firms ever reach the maximum debt permitted by these ratios. Considerably higher levels of indebtedness could be attained in the majority of cases without the equity shareholders feeling that the riskiness of their income had significantly increased. (Reasons for this contention are discussed in detail in Section 3 below.) Well before the equity shareholders considered that the riskiness of their income had increased significantly, the total value of the firm's debentures would begin to fall because of the extreme aversion to risk on the part of the debenture holders. This would precipitate a situation in which the firm would be called on to reduce its short term indebtedness and its longer term debt as it became due for renewal. Thus overgearing would tend to be automatically restricted. Where a firm actually becomes overgeared for a period this will generally be due to a fall in the value of its equity resulting from causes other than overgearing (e.g. a sharp decline in its profit prospects). The effect of this would probably be a period of imposed readjustment to 'normal' gearing and for the company to enjoy during this period a somewhat lower credit rating than in the past.

On these grounds we would suggest that the weighted average cost of capital curve is decreasing and is then flat over its relevant range, after which it rises – in short, the U shaped curve of conventional theory. It must be stressed, however, that we have no conclusive empirical evidence for this. Moreover, we consider that conclusive empirical evidence would be extremely difficult to obtain for reasons which are discussed in Section 3.

In Section 3 we shall also discuss in detail the contrary view to that put forward in the previous paragraphs, namely the view that the average cost of capital curve is flat throughout its length. The general subject is of somewhat specialist interest (and for this reason relegated to the latter part of this chapter) although less specialist readers may be interested in Section 3b dealing with the empirical data on which the contrary view is based, and in Section 3c discussing our reasons for supposing equity shareholders to be exposed to negligible risks from conventional levels of gearing.

2. SOME PROBLEMS OF DEBT FINANCE

Various types of debt have been discussed in the context of the general description given in Chapter 3 and in the context of specific capital budgeting problems in a number of chapters (notably 5, 8 and 13). In this section we shall briefly consider the place of different types of debt in the structure of a firm, and the conflict between gearing and self-financing, and finally consider in some detail the special problems of convertible debentures.

a. *The Choice between Long and Short Term Debt*

From the discussion of conventional financial ratios in Chapter 4, it was concluded that these implied that for a normal medium to large sized firm up to one-third of net assets could be financed by long term debt but that up to two-thirds of current assets could be financed by short term debt and a further one-twelfth by long term debt, making three-quarters in all. It is therefore possible to raise over twice the amount of debt on current assets by raising short term debt than by raising long term debt. In addition there is normally an interest differential in favour of short term debt. Efficient debt financing would therefore call for maximum short term debt consistent with an acceptable 'current' ratio, and then raising long term debt consistent with acceptable 'net worth' and 'times covered' ratios. A consideration to be borne in mind, however, is the riskiness – the impermanence – of short term debt capital in that it may be called in at a time when the firm is in financial difficulties and least able to repay. Given the limited amount of short term debt that can be raised while maintaining an acceptable current ratio, this additional risk of short term debt will not normally be a serious consideration.

b. *Specific versus General Debt Finance*

Specific debt finance (debt secured on specific assets) undoubtedly has many attractions to companies with marketable assets such as property, ships, etc., which are suitable for this type of capital raising. Interest rates are generally lower (especially where the debt consists of quoted mortgage debentures) and the amount of debt which may be raised may be appreciably higher than would be possible with a normal unsecured or floating charge debenture, since an opportunity for a more realistic valuation (sometimes asset by asset) presents itself. In addition, more security is offered than in the case of floating charge debentures which even on the same assets would represent a weaker legal form of security (see Chapter 8, Section 2). Specific debt in the form of mortgages on marketable assets, however, will normally be more expensive where the debt in question is unquoted, since the lenders will generally require some compensation for the absence of ready marketability. The advantage of such debt is that, as we have already noted, it may permit a higher level of gearing than less specific forms of debt. A slight additional advantage with debt of this kind is that it enables the firm to practise a degree of discrimination in the interest rates its pays, and to avoid the general uniform high rate it may be obliged to pay for a more general approach to the market, say, by a normal debenture issue. This will be particularly advantageous where the rate of interest required in the case of a general approach to the capital market significantly increases with the scale of the loan issue. The evident disadvantage of specific debt finance is that it may involve higher legal and administrative costs in the negotiation and documentation involved.

c. *Lease Finance*

This has already been considered at length in Chapter 8 in the discussion of 'Lease or Buy' and allied problems and will be only briefly considered here as a form of finance. It was suggested in Chapter 8 that lease projects (lease finance) should be analysed in terms of a normal cost saving investment, i.e. regarding the putting up of the capital to buy the asset as saving the lease commitments. Any adverse effect of the lease alternative on the normal borrowing of a firm could then be taken into account by including in the cost of the leasing alternative the gearing that would have to be forgone because of the presence of the lease commitment. General and therefore oversimplified comparisons between the cost of this type of finance and that of normal borrowing should be avoided as highly misleading.

d. *The Conflict between Gearing and High Retentions*

It is fairly common for firms which normally pursue a policy of markedly high retentions to find that this leads to conflict with a policy of high gearing. Thus, as the pace of capital investment slackens, a firm may amass considerable surplus cash from depreciation and other provisions and from retained profits. There are often thought to be substantial disadvantages in a policy of higher dividend distributions to alleviate the cash surplus. As a result there may be considerable pressure for the firm to back out of existing debt and certainly to avoid further borrowing. Thus high retentions and gearing appear to be in head on conflict. This complex problem is discussed in detail in Chapter 16.

e. *Convertible Loans* (*Convertibles*)

i. The simple case. Convertible loans are typically loans convertible on pre-determined terms on one or more specified future dates into the equity capital of the issuing company. It is preferable to consider first artificially simple cases in which uncertainty has been largely eliminated. Assume shares of the firm now stand at their nominal value of £1 each but that they are confidently expected by the market to rise to £1·25 at the end of four years. The dividend over the same period is expected to rise progressively by $\frac{1}{3}$% per year from 4% to about 5% (both after tax at the standard rate). Assume that a 20 year convertible loan is issued at par and bears 3% interest after tax at the standard rate, giving subscribers to the loan the right to convert into equities at the end of four years. What would the conversion terms have to be to make the conversion as attractive to an equity investor as immediate direct investment in the firm's equity? The relevant figures are set out in Table 15.1 for the investment of £100 now.

Table 15.1

£'s

Years	0 Capital Outlay	1	2	3	4	4 Capital Recovered
			Dividends/Interest			
Cash Flows						
Purchase of Shares now	−100	4·00	4·33	4·66	5·00	125
Purchase of Convertible Loan Stock	−100	3·00	3·00	3·00	3·00	X

2D

In order to establish the appropriate value of X, the value of £100 of the loan stock converted into equity at the end of the 4 years, it is necessary to make some assumptions concerning: (a) the rate of interest on comparable loans (i.e. loans with 16 years to redemption) which will prevail at the time of the conversion, and (b) the rate of discount which the equity shareholder applies to the future. The rate of interest at the time of the conversion is required in order to establish whether or not conversion will take place. If for example the yield to redemption on comparable 16 year loans had been reduced to 2% by the date of conversion, the loan stock would stand at £133 and evidently no one would convert unless the terms of the conversion were such as to make conversion from this figure the more attractive alternative. Normally conversion offers are pitched very near the going rate for normal loans of comparable security (the reasons for this are discussed below) and we shall assume that there is negligible change over the period in interest rates so that the loan stock at the time of conversion will be worth no more than its nominal value of £100.

If the equity investor discounts the future at 8% p.a., the problem is simply that of discovering that value of X which will bring the discounted series of cash flows A and B into equality. It is found in fact that $X = £129 \cdot 6$. In other words each £100 of loan stock when converted must be worth £129·6 of equity shares at the then current market valuation.

ii. Some general considerations affecting convertibles. We can use this simple example to throw some light on the factors affecting convertibles. As we have noted, these convertibles are usually pitched quite near the going rate of interest. It would be pointless to offer more than the going interest terms since for a reputable company this would lead to heavy over-subscription (besides setting an unwelcome precedent for the firm's other lenders) from the fixed interest market. Pitching the interest rate near the market level has the advantage that the firm will be able to draw capital for the issue from both the fixed interest capital market and the equity capital market. Any attempt to pitch the terms significantly below the going interest rate would mean that a firm would run the risk of losing substantially in support from the fixed interest capital market or being pushed into the alternative of trying to attract these investors by favourable conversion terms. There is reason to suppose that this would be very costly for the firm would be trying to compensate investors constitutionally averse to risk for the certain shortfall in interest obtained (compared with other debentures) by offering them a risky capital gain from their conversion rights. Conversely, equity investors are likely to attach relatively little importance to the security of income and capital but to be primarily interested in the conversion rights.

When the actual conversion date arises, then, in the circumstances of our example, the fixed interest investors will certainly convert, since they could then sell off their equity and purchase £129·6 of the loan stock of other firms (also offering 3%) with the proceeds. The situation is then that they will take advantage of the option when it materializes but will probably not value very highly the future risky prospect of receiving it. Hence, by this effectively joint approach to both the equity and fixed interest market, the firm is obliged to offer valuable conversion rights to tempt the equity investor but at the same time is obliged to give virtually the same rights to the fixed interest investor who values them considerably less. This is in conformity with the commonsense proposition that there are advantages in specialization, that is to tailoring particular capital raising operations to the interests of different investors: this after all is the reason why there are separate fixed interest and equity capital markets. If, of course, the firm were prepared to forgo support for the new issue from the primarily fixed interest investor it would be able to avoid the undue cost of offering terms to markedly disparate investors (the equity and fixed interest investors).

The possible advantages of convertibles are as follows. It is possible to argue that the market may contain a significant number of equity investors whose primary concern is to maintain the capital value of sums they now have available for investment. The potential new investor in the firm may expect that a firm's shares will oscillate in an uncertain way in the short run due to some highly unpredictable factors occurring in the immediate future; but once this period is over the investor may feel confident that it will then be clear that the firm's shares are or are not worth a given price. The conversion offer forms a bridge across this period of uncertainty and gives the investor an opportunity to 'maintain his capital intact' and then to convert the loan into ordinary shares if and when he is confident they will maintain their value. If the conversion offer is advantageous, then the loan stock will automatically rise to the level of its value when converted. Hence the investor has an assured minimum return plus the possibility of a capital gain. Under these circumstances the convertible might offer some positive advantage in enabling the firm to exercise a form of price discrimination in selling its future income. The extreme form of this price discrimination was illustrated in the case of normal gearing in Figure 15.1 of Section 1. In the present instance the firm might try to exploit differences in the equity market's assessment of the future prospects of the firm by selling the convertible to new shareholders for more than it is worth to the firm's old shareholders. This will increase the total value of the firm in much the same way as a normal debenture issue. The extent to which this type of discrimination would be profitable will obviously vary from case to case and no generalizations are possible.

There may also be a number of special circumstances which favour a convertible loan rather than separate issues of equity and loan capital. The first situation is one where long term interest rates are running at an exceptionally high level so that a firm would prefer to wait until a period of lower interest rates. If the firm has no other worthwhile sources of loan capital, and circumstances in the equity market are unpropitious for a new issue, it may be preferable to launch a convertible debenture conceding the high interest rate for a period but with the intention of enabling conversion at a fairly near date. It is questionable, however, in the absence of purely technical factors or market irrationality, whether the convertible loan, even under these conditions, offers any real advantages over a normal debenture plus equity issue. It would be equally open to most firms to offer a long term debenture with earlier redemption at a premium as an alternative to continuing the debenture with the high interest rates. If the convertible loan draws to any extent on money from the equity market it must be regarded as an equity investment by such investors. In the latter case it seems doubtful whether for a given amount of capital coming from the equity market this would not equally well be forthcoming on the basis of an equity issue offering comparable terms.

A purely institutional factor which may be of considerable importance in favouring convertibles is that they may enable institutions to circumvent restrictions on their investment policy. For example, where institutional restrictions result in what is thought by investment managers to be an unduly high proportion of fixed interest investment, the convertible may have the advantage of being a part equity investment which also meets institutional requirements as a fixed interest investment. On these grounds the convertible may attract

fixed interest money chafing at the constraint of institutional conservatism which is not shared by the investment managers directly
responsible for the investment funds.

While convertibles may afford advantages in certain circumstances,
there are reasons why investors should regard them with some
suspicion. It will not infrequently arise that whether or not the
share price rises to a level at which conversion is worthwhile will
be very much within the control of the firm itself. For example,
it would often be a relatively simple matter for a firm to increase
its share price appreciably by increasing the proportion of profits
distributed as dividends, issuing optimistic profit forecasts, resorting
to higher gearing, holding down salary increases or personnel
numbers, enforcing large cuts in stocks (inventories), etc. By reversal
of these same factors it would be possible for the firm to push its
share prices down. Any method of raising capital which creates
temptations for management deliberately to manipulate share prices
in a way that is not fully justified by the profitability of the firm
must be regarded with some misgivings – both by investors and
management.

iii. Analysing convertibles from the standpoint of a firm. Consider now
the method which the firm should use to set the terms of a convertible and the method of comparing this capital raising alternative
with other methods of capital raising.

Setting the terms of a convertible raises, as we have noted, certain
fundamental questions of commercial morality, given that the firm
may manipulate the share price to some degree and given also that
it could present an opportunity to exploit a market overvaluation
of the firm's share prospects. In this situation the firm could adopt
two basically different policies. The first would be to regard the
problem of setting the issue terms frankly as a battle of wits setting its own judgment as to the future share price against that of the
'new'[1] shareholders. (There would evidently be no point in trying to
exploit 'old' - that is, existing shareholders – who subscribe to the
new issue.) Following this policy the firm might reason that since the
market will gain if their expectations are correct it is entirely justified in trading on any errors in this estimate to enhance the position
of its present shareholders. For example, it might consider itself
justified in exploiting what it considers to be an overestimation of

[1] For suitable definitions of 'new' and 'old' shareholders see Section 1a
of Chapter 17.

its future share values in order to pitch the terms at a level which will ensure that no conversions in fact take place. Against a competent firm, however, the new shareholders would be engaged in an unequal struggle. Even supposing a firm does not succumb to the temptation to manipulate its share prices (by the methods touched on in the preceding sub-section) it might still have access to important information bearing on future profitability which it either cannot or will not disclose. Moreover, the firm could not successfully exploit the market in this way more than two or three times before the market (particularly the fixed interest market) was seriously discouraged from subscribing to further issues. For these reasons it would seem unlikely that firms would be prepared to adopt this policy for setting conversion terms.

The second policy would be for a firm to offer the market such terms that the yield to conversion at the conversion price offered (given the future share price as assessed by the firm) is a 'reasonable' return for the risks involved given the character of the main participants in the new issue. This is probably something like the policy that (implicitly) most firms pursue. As we have already noted, however, an issue which is intended to draw support from both the fixed interest and the equity capital market would usually necessitate offering terms that overcompensated both.

If the interest rate of the issue is very close to existing market rates of interest, a conversion at the price estimated by the firm would seem 'reasonable' terms to offer to those investors who are primarily interested in fixed interest investments. The holders of the convertible issue will have an opportunity to gain if the market price is higher at the date of conversion and no chance of loss – since they could always hold on to the loan stock if conversion was not attractive. For the equity type of investor, however, the situation is rather different. In order for him to find the offer attractive the terms would, as we have already noted, need to be considerably better, hence overcompensating the investor who is primarily interested in fixed interest investments. This, however, is inevitable with convertible issues aimed at drawing support from both fixed interest and equity markets.

When the conversion terms have been decided upon, there remains the problem of how these should be analysed in order to compare the convertible with any alternative. On a formal level the answer to this problem would appear to be as follows. A firm should set out the net of tax dividend cash flows (with of course the resultant dividends from reinvested profits) associated with the alternative policy – say a separate rights issue and straight debenture. From this it would need to calculate the net present value accruing to its *old* shareholders (that is their share of this stream of future dividends) less the additional capital which they will have subscribed to the new rights issue. The corresponding dividend stream should then be calculated for the convertible and the net present value accruing to the old shareholders calculated under this alternative. In this alternative a factor which would be taken into account would be the reduction of the dividend stream of the old shareholders resulting from the exercise of conversion rights at a later date. By comparing the two net present values the firm could formally ascertain which of the two courses of action would be most advantageous (i.e. maximize the net present value of its old shareholders). Needless to say the formal analysis poses a host of estimation problems particularly as to the amount which old shareholders might subscribe under the two alternatives. But broad assumptions might usefully limit the margin of error and clarify the important factors in the analysis.

3. THE EFFECT OF DEBT FINANCE ON THE COST OF EQUITY CAPITAL

a. *The Opposing Views*

In the opening section of this chapter we put forward the view that the riskiness of equity income (as subjectively assessed by equity shareholders) is not significantly affected by the amount of debt capital a firm raises, providing that such debt capital is not in excess of the amounts permitted by the conventional financial ratios appropriate to the industry concerned. This is largely the traditionalist view and also the view favoured by almost all of the authorities (see references [1] and [2]). We must now consider the opposing view which holds that the cost of capital to a firm (by cost is here meant the weighted average cost of debt and equity funds assuming appropriate conditions such that the concept is meaningful - see Chapter 4, Section 5) is independent of the amount of gearing or leverage involved. This view has been advanced by a number of writers over a considerable period, and has received support, albeit on very different grounds, in a brilliantly argued article by F. Modigliani and M. H. Miller, reference [3]. (Henceforth this latter view will be referred to as the MM view to distinguish it from the traditional view.)

For a firm which has more than the conventional acceptable proportion of debt capital, the traditional view would hold that if the proportion of debt capital was further increased the combined market value of that firm's debt and equity would tend to be constant or even fall. Put another way round, when debt becomes 'excessive' the income of the debenture holders and possibly the equity investor is held to be at such risk that the combined value of the debentures and the equity shares would tend either to remain constant or actually fall. In other words there is a point beyond which there is no advantage to be gained from the further issue of debt capital, and indeed there may be serious disadvantages involved such that the combined market value of a firm's debt and equity actually declines for the reasons briefly considered in Section 1. Thus past a certain proportion of debt, both schools would be in agreement as to the consequences. Disagreement centres around whether it is possible to borrow any debt at all without causing a corresponding decline in the value of the equity shares.

Before discussing the opposing views it must be pointed out that no conclusive statistical evidence is available to resolve the argument, nor is such evidence likely to become available. For any given set of firms in an industry so many factors bear concurrently on the market value of their debt and equity securities that it is not possible to speak with finality on the effect of gearing alone. Hence any realistic comparison is necessarily confined to a few firms of similar size and prospects in the same industry. As such samples are so small no conclusive valid generalizations are possible. Commentators are forced back on subjective views based on experience and on the interpretation of such evidence as is available. Thus, while we agree with the traditionalist view, we are conscious that this amounts to no more than a reasoned opinion.

One undisputed and definite advantage of debt capital so far as Britain and the United States are concerned is that there is a significant tax advantage to a firm in raising as large a proportion of debt capital as possible bearing in mind the other limiting factors such as conventional financial ratios. In the United States loan interest is a tax deductible expense from a firm's viewpoint, and with company tax currently exceeding 50% this is a significant advantage. In Britain loan interest is a tax deductible expense as far as profits tax is concerned. Profits tax is currently 15%, so the resultant saving, while significant, is not as important as in the United States. Where this tax advantage of debt capital exists, it pays a firm to raise as much debt capital as possible even if it raised it entirely from its own shareholders, as this maximizes the net of tax income a firm can pay out to the providers of its capital, that is, debt holders and shareholders combined. The tax advantage of gearing is fully conceded in the MM view in that to the extent that debt capital can be raised it lowers the net of tax weighted cost of capital. This advantage apart, however, gearing is held to be ineffective in lowering a firm's weighted average cost of capital.

A second definite advantage of raising debt capital arises from the existence of inflation. Providing a firm can maintain its gross income in real terms under inflationary conditions, the real income available to the equity shareholders is automatically increased as the burden of servicing debt capital necessarily falls. During prolonged inflation either the rate of interest on new debt issues rises to compensate for the expected rate of inflation, or the supply of debt capital contracts. Usually both these outcomes will occur simultaneously. But this does not prevent firms with debt capital benefiting substantially until these changes occur, which is typically a long time. A firm benefits from the lower cost of servicing debt until all its existing debt is repaid, a process which might take twenty years or more. Further, even when such changes in debt costs do occur they tend to be both too little and too late (see Chapter 6, Section 7).

These two advantages alone would be sufficient to justify any firm borrowing the maximum possible amounts of debt capital permitted by the conventional financial ratios, and in so doing it would lower its net of tax weighted average cost of capital, which is equivalent to securing a real benefit to the equity shareholders. But these two obvious advantages apart, how true is it that gearing offers no real advantages?

Before going on to this, however, we must first consider the empirical evidence offered by MM, since, if their empirical results cannot be successfully challenged, the validity of traditional theory must be seriously doubted, whatever non-quantitative arguments may be put forward in its support.

b. *The Empirical Evidence*

The empirical data used by MM consists of a sample of 43 public utilities and a sample of 42 oil companies, reproduced as Figures 15.3 and 15.4.

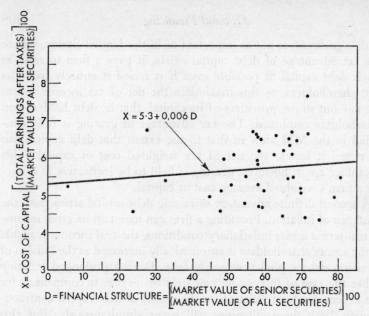

Fig. 15.3. *Cost of capital in relation to financial structure for 43 electric utilities, 1947–48*

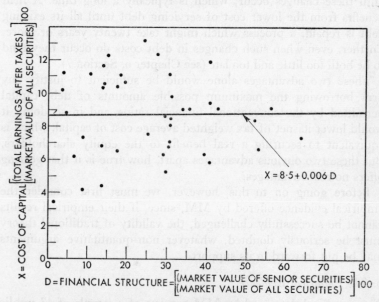

Fig. 15.4. *Cost of capital in relation to financial structure for 42 oil companies, 1953*

Figures 15.3, 15.4 are reproduced from Miller and Modigliani, *Amer. Econ. Rev.*, June 1958, by permission of the authors and the American Economic Association

The statistical analysis consists of an attempt to estimate our Figure 15.2, that is, the relationship between the weighted average cost of capital and the proportion of debt in the total capital structure. The second stage of the analysis is a regression between total shareholders' yield and the degree of gearing as measured by market value of debt to the market value of the equity shares. This is reproduced as Figures 15.5 and 15.6 below.

Our consideration of the data will be in terms of these last diagrams, since, if these diagrams had the shape indicated, this would imply an average cost of capital which was either horizontal or only slightly U shaped. We shall suggest that there are at least two other explanations for this apparent increase in the 'cost'[1] of equity, both of which are matters of common observation and are entirely consistent with traditional theory.

The first explanation is as follows. The reasons for firms showing relatively high current yields are usually that they have poor growth prospects, inefficient management, specific risks like known threats to their markets, etc. Given this high apparent cost of equity capital – which will usually be indicative of a very weak market in the equity shares of a firm – the firm should logically *prefer*, on grounds of traditional theory, to raise debt rather than equity capital. Adequate security for such debt raising will frequently exist despite relatively poor earnings for the equity. The effect of firms with a high equity cost of capital prefering to raise debt would evidently be an apparent correlation between these two characteristics as displayed in Figures 15.5 and 15.6. But the causality is entirely reversed from that required by the MM theory: here high gearing results *from* the high cost of equity capital, not vice versa.

The second explanation may be seen as follows. Suppose all firms were initially identical and started off with the same degree of gearing. Subsequently, however, some of the firms run into difficulties and make poorer profits and have poorer growth prospects than others. As a result, the value of the equity of these companies must fall to bring about a higher yield. This will make the companies highly geared by the criterion of market value of debt to market value of debt plus equity, hence producing an apparent correlation between high yield and high leverage – i.e. the firm would shift to the right

---

[1] Current yield is, of course, inadequate as a guide to the cost of equity capital for reasons which we have already considered in Section 4c, Chapter 1. For purposes of this discussion, however, we may take the current yield as an approximation.

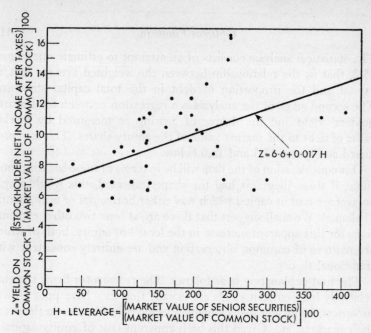

Fig. 15.5 Yield on common stock in relation to leverage for 43 electric utilities, 1947–48

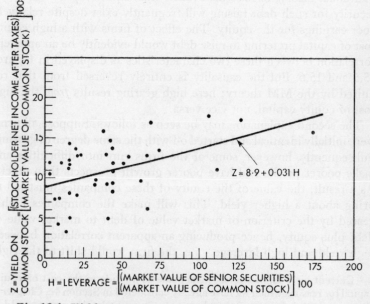

Fig. 15.6. Yield on common stock in relation to leverage for 42 oil companies, 1952–53

and higher up the diagram. The converse would apply to companies with exceptionally good profits, growth prospects, etc. This phenomenon certainly occurs and would tend to give rise to the data found in these empirical investigations. These two explanations are in our view more plausible interpretations of the data, thus the data neither confirm nor refute traditional theory.

Finally we should briefly mention some of the difficulties associated with this type of investigation, namely just what forms of gearing or more generally what fixed charges should be considered in this analysis. As we have already pointed out in our restatement of the traditional theory, if the risks attaching to the income stream are a primary consideration then some account must be taken of the short term debt of the company. Similarly – and this is of overwhelming importance in the case of the oil companies of Figure 15.6 – some account must be taken in the long term debt of the lease commitments of the firm, given their strong similarity to formal long term debt (see Chapter 8). Further, some account must be taken of the relative cash positions of the companies. This often varies appreciably from company to company, and where 'excessive', it is evidently a form of *negative* gearing.

c. *The MM Thesis Further Considered*

Let us consider the MM view more fully. Their basic position is summarized in the following three propositions:

Proposition I. The average cost of capital to any firm is completely independent of its capital structure and is equal to the capitalization rate of a pure equity stream of its risk class (defined below).

Proposition II. The expected yield r on the equity shares of a geared firm in a given risk class is equal to the appropriate rate of capitalization p on the equity shares of an ungeared firm in its risk class plus a premium which is a function of the financial risk of gearing. This premium is equal to the debt to equity ratio times the spread between p and the interest cost of debt money i. (The debt to equity ratio D/E is measured in terms of market value, thus $r = D/E(p-i)$.)

Proposition III. The cut-off point for investment in the firm will be p, the appropriate rate of capitalization in an ungeared firm in its risk class. It will be completely unaffected by the type of security used to finance the investment.

Thus the marginal cost of capital to a firm is equal to its average cost of capital which in turn is equal to the capitalization rate for an ungeared firm in the same risk class. By risk class is meant all the firms subject to the same risk, e.g. similar sized firms in the same industry.

In the MM analysis gearing is held to be ineffective in lowering the average cost of capital to a firm on the grounds that it is always possible for individual investors to borrow funds and substitute home-made gearing for gearing undertaken by firms. Thus any premium resulting from gearing by firms will be dissipated as a result of investors' activities in buying shares in ungeared firms partly financed by personal borrowings. Consider a simple example. Suppose there are two firms Geared Ltd. and Ungeared Ltd., identical in every respect save that the former is partly debt financed and the latter entirely equity financed. Their balance sheets are as follows:

Geared Ltd.

800,000 £1 Shares	800,000	Net Assets	1,000,000
200,000 6% Debentures	200,000		
	£1,000,000		£1,000,000

Ungeared Ltd.

1,000,000 £1 Shares	£1,000,000	Net Assets	£1,000,000

Ignoring tax, assume that both firms are estimated to have an annual income of £100,000 in perpetuity and that all income after paying out loan interest is paid out in dividends. Thus the dividend on Geared Ltd.'s shares

$$\frac{£100,000 - £12,000}{800,000} = £0{\cdot}11 \text{ per share}$$

and the dividend on Ungeared Ltd.'s shares is

$$\frac{£100,000}{1,000,000} = £0{\cdot}10 \text{ per share}$$

Suppose initially that both shares sell at a multiple of ten times earnings, thus a share in Geared Ltd. is worth £1·1 and a share in Ungeared Ltd. is worth only £1·0. The total market value of the two firms assuming the debentures to be standing at par would then be:

Geared Ltd.		Ungeared Ltd.	
800,000 Shares × £1·1	= 880,000	1,000,000 Shares × £1·0	= 1,000,000
200,000 Debentures at par	= 200,000		
	£1,080,000		

Suppose an investor holds 1,000 shares in Geared Ltd. on which he receives an annual income of £110. It would pay such an investor to sell the shares for £1,100, borrow £275 at 6% (MM assume investors to be able to borrow identical proportions to firms at identical interest rates), and purchase 1,375 shares in Ungeared Ltd. On these shares the investor would receive annually £137·5 gross, and after paying the loan interest of £16·5 (6% of £275) would receive an income of £121, an increase of £11 on the former investment. Faced with this opportunity investors would sell Geared Ltd.'s shares and buy Ungeared Ltd.'s shares until the premium on the former disappeared and the prices of both firm's shares were equal.

Given the MM assumptions, it would be profitable to buy up the shares in any ungeared (or *under*geared company) which stood at a discount compared with the shares in comparable fully geared firms. The effect of this would be to eliminate differences in share values resulting from differences in gearing. The point that should be noted is that MM do not *explicitly* dispute the effectiveness of gearing as such but *merely the value of a firm doing this itself, given that equity investors are assumed equally capable of doing it for themselves.* But it is essential to MM's argument that investors should prefer to exercise their gearing on the shares of Ungeared Ltd. rather than Geared Ltd. If they were indifferent which income stream – that of Geared Ltd. or that of Ungeared Ltd. – they geared up, there would evidently be no tendency for gearing to become equalized in the manner required for the validity of the theory.

The reason why investors should prefer to bring their 'home-made' gearing to bear on Ungeared rather than Geared Ltd. is that the income of the latter is assumed to be at *a significantly higher level of risk* than that of the former. Arguments of this type have been suggested by several writers, [4] and [5], and the main lines of reasoning would appear to be as follows. A firm raising debt capital creates interest charges which are a prior claim on its income. As a result the future income will be reduced by this constant amount of interest. Suppose we consider the riskiness of the shareholders' income (i.e. the income of the firm less interest) as measured by the ratio of the variability of the income relative to the mean value[1] of the income. We shall refer to this as the relative variability of the income. (As a statistical measure of the variability we might use the average of absolute deviation from the mean value.) Now it should be apparent that variability in this (or any other practical sense) will not be reduced by reducing future income in each year by a constant amount (the interest charge). The deviations would simply be around a different mean value. Since the mean value would be reduced, however, it follows that the relative variability – the riskiness of the shareholders' income – would be increased.

This line of reasoning has led to the proposition that the advantages of gearing in raising the return to equity (by the difference between earnings and interest on the debt capital) may be partially – if not completely – offset by the increased risk to which this return is exposed. The extreme form of the argument is illustrated by the data of Table 15.2 based on the previous example of Geared Ltd. and Ungeared Ltd. where both firm's income is now held to vary by $\pm £20,000$ around a mean value of £100,000 a year.

Table 15.2

	Ungeared Ltd.	Geared Ltd.
Debt	—	£200,000
Interest at 6%	—	£12,000
Earnings (Mean Value)	£100,000	£100,000
Net Earnings after deducting loan interest	£100,000	£88,000
Relative Variability of Net Earnings	±20%	±22·73%
Value of Shares	£1,000,000	£800,000
Mean Earnings as a percentage of Share value	10%	11%

In the extreme form of this argument it is alleged that because the totality of risk remains the same with or without gearing, the smaller equity investment in Geared Ltd., in return for higher net earnings, bears virtually all the risk associated with variation in earnings.

---

[1] MM specifically reject variability of earnings as a factor in uncertainty and consider uncertainty to be primarily a quality attaching to the subjective estimated mean value of earnings. As regards uncertainty due to gearing, it seems reasonable to suppose that this could be measured by our relative variability plus an additional risk factor for the eventuality that prior charges force the firm into liquidation.

Thus this greater risk exactly offsets the advantage of higher earnings in such a way that the market value of the equity plus debt in Geared Ltd. equals the market value of the equity of Ungeared Ltd.

It should be clear that if this extreme form of the argument were true all the MM propositions would automatically follow. There would be no real scope for 'home-made' gearing since all forms of gearing would be equally pointless. In our example of Geared and Ungeared Ltd., no advantage would follow from, say, institutions with access to debt capital (on the same terms as Geared Ltd.) buying up the shares of Ungeared Ltd. For, by hypothesis, the institutions would regard the income advantage arising from this gearing as being completely offset by the risk to which the institutions' income is subject because of the debt they have raised to acquire the shares.

As we have tried to show in the preceding analysis the MM propositions rest on two separate assumptions both of which must be true if their conclusions are to hold. These assumptions are:

(1) 'Home-made' gearing exists on the scale required;
(2) The risk differential between geared and ungeared firms is sufficient to cause investors with access to 'home-made' gearing to prefer the share of ungeared firms to such a degree as to cause an equalization of gearing for firms of the same risk class.

We suggest in what follows that assumption (2) is not true.

d. *Equalization of the Risks to the Equity from Gearing*

Consider now in more detail the two assumptions of 'home-made' gearing and the risk differential between geared and ungeared firms which, as we have shown above, underlie the MM analysis. The magnitude of the risk differential is, of course, of more general interest than for the part it plays in the MM analysis, since it bears on the *extent* to which gearing can reduce the cost of capital even if the traditional theory is broadly accepted. For this reason we shall consider the risk differential in some detail later.

That 'home-made' gearing exists in the United States on the scale required by the MM theory has been thoroughly questioned by Durand [6] and summarily denied by Weston [7]. It is certainly true that such conditions do not exist on any scale in Britain. A more plausible argument would be that some institutions provide supplementary gearing to the shares of undergeared companies. Investment trusts for example are normally free to raise substantial proportions of loan capital.[1]

Institutions such as pension funds, insurance companies, and unit trusts are normally ungeared for institutional reasons, but these could play their part in equalizing gearing in the ingenious way in which MM suggest private investors could do so without actually raising debt. Institutions or private investors holding a proportion of their portfolio in fixed interest securities are effectively gearing up other companies and are themselves *negatively* geared – i.e. are lenders, not borrowers, on fixed interest terms. Instead of borrowing themselves they can effectively gear up by reducing their own lending, that is, by reducing their holding of fixed interest securities and use the proceeds to buy equities. Thus these institutions could acquire shares of undergeared companies and gear up themselves in this indirect way.

If the MM theory were true, it is obvious that the institutions with their detailed knowledge and expert investment analysis would be prominent in consciously equalizing gearing in the way suggested by MM. In fact, if the MM theory were true, instead of being revolutionary it would be a commonplace of institutional investment policy. The incredulity with which experts close to the institutions have greeted the MM hypothesis thus constitutes in itself a fairly conclusive refutation of the theory – the institutions do *not* tend to equalize gearing. If the institutions do not play a prominent part in equalizing gearing it seems inconceiveable that private investors, ignoring the advice they would get from orthodox investment advisers, bring to bear the gearing required to equalize gearing throughout the whole economy.

We should note, however, that such indirect leverage is not a complete substitute from the viewpoint of the lender for actual debt instruments issued by a company. As regards the latter the lender would have the certainty that even in periods of poor profitability the company would do all in its power to meet its interest and debt repayment obligations, whereas an equity shareholder applying

---

[1] It should, however, be noted that a British investment trust, whose only income was from British companies on which profits tax had been paid, could not obtain profits tax relief (currently 15%) on its own debt capital. Thus such investment trusts could not fully reproduce the tax advantages to firms from gearing. A United States' regulated investment company could, however, fully reproduce the tax advantages of leverage by the individual firm.

'home-made leverage' would have the risk that in such periods the dividends on his shareholdings might be passed, leaving the shareholder to sell his shares on a weak market in order to meet his interest and debt repayment obligations.

In our view the assumption of 'home-made' gearing which has been strongly attacked can be defended as certainly being capable of existing on the scale required by the theory – if the stress is primarily on institutions providing the differential gearing. The theory fails, however, because its second main assumption – that the risk differential is sufficiently large to bring this differential gearing into play – is simply not true. The most obvious proof of this would be the fact that institutions who have the power to bring it into play and so equalize gearing do not in fact do so. It is impossible that while not doing this they should nevertheless seriously believe that geared firms were significantly more risky than ungeared. If they believe this, they would obviously tend to prefer the shares of ungeared firms, thus tending to bring about equalization of gearing. In our view the risk differential between firms with normal levels of gearing and entirely ungeared firms is too small to make the institutions exercise their gearing in favour of the ungeared firm and thus tend to equalize overall gearing. Our reasons for this view are as follows.[1]

First, the limitation of asset cover generally restricts total debt to 25%–35% of net assets for normal industrial concerns and this means that the times covered (ratio of profits to total interest payments) is 5 or more (see Chapter 4, Section 2). Hence only 20% or less of current earnings is typically being ceded to the debt holders in this way, and a proportion of this size is so small as to be unlikely to have any significant effect on the risk which the equity shareholders consider they are bearing on each unit of dividends they receive. A substantially larger burden of interest charges might perceptibly increase the risk of equity, but conventional ratios would appear in the majority of cases entirely to preclude borrowing of this magnitude.

Secondly, we should note that, although the relative variability of earnings may be increased by gearing, the effect on dividends will be very considerably attenuated by the normal endeavours of firms to maintain a stable dividend by varying their proportion of

---

[1] In what follows the argument is related to conditions in Britain although similar arguments could be made out for conditions in the United States.

retained profits. There is adequate scope for this in Britain,[1] since the market attaches considerably greater relative importance to dividends than earnings: this in itself would attenuate any adverse effect that gearing might have on the market price of the shares. (Also, since firms could draw on debt sources – if necessary becoming temporarily overgeared – to compensate for any shortfall in funds available for investment due to variations in retained earnings, this need be little handicap to the flow of investment.)

Thirdly, and perhaps most important of all, the main risk associated with a share under present-day conditions is that it will not achieve the growth prospects on which present share prices are based, and this risk is either independent of or more probably favourably affected by gearing.

We can look at the risk associated with a share as being due partly to the variability of net earnings around their present mean value and due partly to the risk associated with the relative variability of the trend in this mean value. This trend is normally expected to be upwards in an expanding economy. It is a well known fact that share prices at any given time are very much influenced by views about the future growth of dividends. Some growth of dividends is almost certain in an expanding economy where firms are – as is generally the case – retaining and reinvesting a large proportion of their earnings. We have already shown (see Section 4c of Chapter 1) that the yield on shares, (taking into account future capital appreciation) where dividends are expected to grow indefinitely at a constant compound rate, is the existing dividend yield plus the assumed compound rate of growth. In Britain at the end of 1962 share prices gave a gross of tax dividend yield of 4·7% while fixed interest securities gave a gross of tax yield of 5·4%. This disparity of the rates, taking into account the greater security afforded by fixed interest securities, implies that a compound growth of at least 3% was expected in dividends. The larger disparity in the United States (2.3%), suggests that appreciably greater growth of dividends is expected.

It would seem reasonable to assume that in the majority of cases the risks associated with the expected trend are considerably higher than risks associated with variability of present earnings around

[1] Over the period 1949–60, retained profits were consistently twice as large as net of tax dividends. (This is the correct comparison as no further income tax is payable on profits declared as dividends.) Source – Economic Trends No. 102 – April 1962 – Tables E and F.

their present mean level. But with a fixed proportion of debt financing it is difficult to see how debt financing could in any practical way *increase* the risks associated with the relative variability of the trend in dividends. This may be seen more clearly if we consider first the effect of an increase in the mean value of earnings of Ungeared Ltd., and Geared Ltd., if in neither case the increase in earnings is accompanied by an increase in direct capital raised, but rather is the result of retained earnings being reinvested profitably. In this case the shareholders of both firms will enjoy exactly the same increase in earnings (since no additional capital has been raised) subject to the same additional risk. Hence the *total* value of the shares of each firm should increase by the same amount. As there are fewer shares in the geared firm the value of each of its shares must, therefore, increase more than those of the ungeared firm. (Moreover, this gain would not be lost by any subsequent change in financial structure – e.g. issuing 'free' loan capital to existing equity shareholders in Geared Ltd.) The converse would, of course, occur if the firms suffered a fall in earnings, but the essential point is that there are fairly conclusive grounds for the assumption, in an economy which is expanding and in which firms are retaining and reinvesting a large proportion of their profits, that the risk of liquidation due to inability to meet prior charges is virtually eliminated and the major risk simply comprises errors in estimating the rate at which dividends will grow.

It is difficult to see in what practical circumstances this type of risk could be increased by the presence of debt capital in the firm's capital structure. Any purely temporary shortage of funds could be made up by raising funds from outside sources. Hence relative variability of profits around their existing mean value need not increase the risks associated with the growth of this mean value. A permanent fall in profitability which did not impair the firm's ability to meet interest charges would seem to affect geared and ungeared income streams alike as regards growth prospects.

In fact, if debt financing has any perceptible effect on the growth prospects of the firm there are grounds for supposing it to be favourable, for a firm prepared to make use of both the equity and debt capital market is in a far more flexible position for securing the funds required for expansion than a firm restricting itself to the equity market alone.

Finally, it must be borne in mind that shareholders are trying to assess the many different risks to which alternative shares are subject.

A large number of factors enters into any such comparison even within firms in the same industry – e.g. quality of management, cash reserves, profit history, size of firm, extent of diversification, etc. Moreover, a large amount of the relevant information simply is not available, e.g. turnover, margins on particular products, the hold of a firm on particular markets, development plans, etc. The introduction into this manifestly imperfect assessment of fine adjustments for the supposed risk associated with gearing would appear in the majority of cases somewhat absurd.

In summary, therefore, we would contend that for the majority of shares under present day conditions the main risk is the possible failure of shares to attain the trend in dividends on which the present share price is based. The implication of this and of our other arguments is that conventional levels of debt finance can at most have a marginal effect on a relatively small part of the risk borne by the equity shareholder, and that this effect itself may be offset by the advantages accruing from the greater flexibility afforded by utilization of the debt capital market.

REFERENCES

1. B. J. GRAHAM and D. L. DODD, in collaboration with C. TATHAM, *Security Analysis*, Third Edition, New York, 1951.
2. DAVID DURAND, 'Cost of Debt and Equity Funds for Business', *National Bureau of Economic Research*, 1952.
3. F. MODIGLIANI and M. H. MILLER, 'The Cost of Capital, Corporation Finance, and the Theory of Investment', *The American Economic Review*, June 1958.
4. F. B. ALLEN, 'Does Going into Debt Lower the Cost of Capital?', *Analysts' Journal*, August 1954.
5. R. SMITH, 'Cost of Capital in the Oil Industry', an unpublished study (1955), Carnegie Institute of Technology, Pittsburgh, 1955.
6. DAVID DURAND, 'The Cost of Capital in an Imperfect Market: a Reply to Modigliani and Miller', *The American Economic Review*, June 1959.
7. J. FRED WESTON, a review article in *Journal of Business*, April 1961, of 'The Management of Corporate Capital', edited by Ezra Solomons, a publication of the Graduate School of Business, University of Chicago, and published by the Free Press of Glencoe, Illinois, 1959. (References 2, 3 and 6 are published in this book.)

See also the rejoinder to Durand's second article (reference 6 above) by Messrs. Modigliani and Miller in *The American Economic Review*, September 1959.

CHAPTER SIXTEEN

Capital Budgeting under Cash Surplus Conditions

The purpose of this chapter is to consider the problems of optimal financing and the analysis of projects when a firm is in a temporary cash surplus position.

1. THE CASH SURPLUS PROBLEM AND POSSIBLE SOLUTIONS

It is fairly common for large firms to experience periods of temporary cash surplus when the total cash generated by retained profits and depreciation provisions is in excess of anticipated capital requirements. During periods of expansion a firm may pursue a sound investment policy which is entirely compatible with a large degree of self-financing so that the total of self-generated funds and the total of debt that can be raised by following a policy of high gearing, can all be invested at worthwhile rates of return. As the pace of expansion slackens, however, or as the firm passes through a phase of low replacement outlays, internally generated funds, given the existing policy on profit retentions, become excessive and the firm may move into a cash surplus position. The cash surplus makes it apparently pointless to raise further debt capital. Consequently the gearing of the company tends to run down, giving rise to the common phenomenon of profitable companies with large excess liquid assets and low gearing.

The 'obvious' solution to the problem would, of course, be that of paying out far more of the profits as dividends. Discriminating investors should obviously favour a firm which in periods of cash surplus paid out the surplus in special dividends. To some extent this policy of higher dividends is followed in periods of cash surplus but rarely on the scale required to avoid a continuing significant cash surplus over a number of years. But where the company is generating excess funds not out of profits but out of depreciation or other provisions, dividends would need to be in excess of current profits (i.e.

paid of out past retained profits), to alleviate the cash surplus; and few firms are prepared to consider such a policy.

There may well be special cases where a firm would be justified in withholding the surplus. This might arise where the cash surplus was of a very temporary nature so that paying it out now would involve making a new issue within two or three years to replace the cash so paid out – i.e. there would be an element of 'roundtripping' of the money. In normal circumstances new issue expenses, the necessity to reduce share prices to float the issue, and the possibly higher rates of taxation following on the distribution of dividends (this applies particularly where dividends are normally taxed again in the hands of shareholders as in the United States, see Chapter 3, Section 4), would be considerations justifying the retention of some or all of the cash surplus. More exactly, the financial justification for withholding the surplus cash must be that the difference between what the firm could obtain from its short run investment on the cash, plus the costs of 'roundtripping', and what the shareholders could obtain from short run investment of the cash, is positive.

Alternatively, the situation may be that over the period no worthwhile investments in other companies may be open to the equity shareholders. For example, it may be a reasonable view that equity prices are on a plateau at which they will remain for three years or so, or alternatively that the growth will be relatively small. On these grounds a firm may consider the opportunity cost of capital withheld from the shareholders in the short run to be significantly less than its long run average.

Finally, there may be special financial reasons justifying retention of the surplus cash. For example, the shares of the company may be thought to be seriously undervalued (see next chapter) or would become so in the event of a large new issue several years hence, so that the cost of capital provided by new issues at this later date would be exceptionally high compared with the cost of self finance even where the latter is held for a significant time in low yielding portfolio investments.

It should, however, be recognized that, even where the conditions we have stated for justifying the retention of surplus funds do not hold, many managements nevertheless retain surplus cash. There are numerous current examples of major firms with surplus cash being withheld from the shareholders.

The reasons for this are complicated and varied. To some degree almost certainly a management's sense of power and satisfaction in the obvious liquidity of its company plays a part, together with the saving thought that possibly some worthwhile investment opportunities may turn up. To some extent also the cash is regarded as a 'war chest' – a ready supply of cash in the eventuality that other companies with similar cash surpluses may use them to intensify competition. This increased competition may result in low profits and make it an inopportune time to try to raise further capital if this was required. Hence, a high level of liquidity is not without advantages.

But whatever the reasons for companies allowing cash surpluses to accumulate, only a minority ever seems to follow a policy of sufficiently high distributions required to reduce the cash surplus to zero. The majority persist in a cash surplus position unless an unduly low market value for their shares forces them to adopt a policy of higher distributions. If this is the case, the problem for optimal financing is to find some way of minimizing the costs to the shareholders of the firm being in a cash surplus.

We would suggest two policies which might be tried. The first concerns the gearing of undergeared firms in a cash surplus position. These firms could increase their gearing without difficulty by issuing free loan stock to their existing shareholders in the manner previously suggested in Chapter 4, Section 6. The firm would increase its gearing while the shareholders would receive the net proceeds of the sale of the loan which would be less than the fall in the value of their equity. If they did not wish to hold on to the loan stock they could sell it and invest the proceeds in other comparable equities.

The second policy concerns the use to which firms put their cash surplus. In the majority of cases the funds are kept in short dated securities. The reasons for this seem to be primarily organizational rather than financial. It results from a combination of conservative finance and the reluctance of top management to consider investing outside their own firm in the direct manner to which they have been accustomed. We would suggest that such a firm make a serious assessment of its financial needs and invest surplus cash according to the genuine requirements of its future needs. Where the cash is not required for three years or more, the firm should seriously consider investment in equities or any other form of finance which, over the period, offered a sufficient return commensurate with, or greater than, the risks involved. This policy admittedly involves taking risks, but equity shareholders may reasonably be presumed to prefer the normal risks and higher returns of equity investment to the security and low returns of fixed interest investments.

Moreover such a policy would be in keeping with the trend in recent years for firms to invest their liquidity reserves into longer dated fixed interest securities, and with the relative increase in the liquidity of equities due to the greater stability in national economies and the stock markets.

American firms have yet a third choice in that they are legally permitted to purchase their own shares. As long as a firm's shares are properly valued this is a desirable and efficient way of disposing of surplus cash, for by returning cash to shareholders, a firm is effectively re-investing funds at the shareholders' cost of capital.

2. ANALYSING CAPITAL PROJECTS UNDER CASH SURPLUS CONDITIONS

As we have noted, firms are generally unwilling to invest 'surplus' cash in securities other than treasury bills, short dated government securities or in other investments offering a high degree of security and liquidity even at the price of relatively low returns. Hence the *opportunity cost* of capital over this period, *given* that the decision has been taken not to distribute the surplus cash, may be relatively small. This has serious implications for the technique of analysing capital projects. The techniques to be described below follow logically from the decision to retain surplus cash in the business *whatever the reasons for so doing*. It is most important, given the decision to retain surplus cash, that the logic of the decision be followed through and appropriate modifications made to the method of analysing capital projects. Failure to do this may result in a serious degree of financial inefficiency.

a. *Analysis under Conditions of Equity Finance Only*

Gearing introduces some special complications into the analysis and for this reason we shall consider first the simple case of a firm entirely financed by equity capital and where all the surplus cash is invested in short dated fixed interest investments. The appropriate method of analysing projects under these conditions may be seen if we note that the situation is effectively identical with one in which the shareholders, for the period of the cash surplus, themselves had an opportunity cost of capital equal to that of the low yielding securities in which the firm will be investing its cash surplus. By its policy decision to retain the cash surplus the firm has effectively created a situation in which it offers the shareholders the choice between the money being invested on their behalf by the firm in low yielding short term investments or alternatively investing the money in the normal investments opportunities of the firm at whatever additional return can be obtained. Consider now the appropriate present value method for analysing projects under these conditions of the cost of capital. Let us assume that the period of cash surplus is expected to come to an end at the close of year k. By this time the firm may have to look to new equity issues for further sources of capital or retain more profits than would otherwise be the case. Alternatively, the firm may consider that, if at the end of year k it is still in a position of cash surplus, it will then substantially liberalize its dividend policy. This would effectively be the same as the firm finding investment opportunities offering the same rate of return as is open to its shareholders with the additional dividends.

Under these circumstances the appropriate discounting for the cash flows is that they should be discounted for k years at the rate which the firm could obtain on the alternative portfolio investment, and for the remaining period at the normal equity cost of capital rate. For example, suppose that the net of tax rate which the firm can earn on its portfolio investment is r_0, that its normal cost of capital is r_1, and that the period of cash surplus is expected to come to an end at the close of year 4 ($k = 4$). In this case a cash flow of say 100 at the end of year 7 would be discounted to have a present value of

$$\frac{100}{(1+r_0)^4(1+r_1)^3}.$$

The general present value formula under these circumstances is therefore:

$$R = \sum_{i=1}^{i=k} \frac{A_i}{(1+r_0)^i} + \sum_{i=k+1}^{i=n} \frac{A_i}{(1+r_0)^k(1+r_1)^{i-k}} - C \quad (16.1)$$

where the new symbols are as defined above.

b. *Analysis with Combined Debt and Equity Financing*

i. The short term debt case. Consider now the place of gearing in this analysis. Two main situations can be distinguished. The first is where a firm is using its cash surplus to reduce its short term borrowng – that is, the alternative investments open to the firm are such that it is more attractive to use the surplus cash, say, to reduce the bank overdraft in order to 'save' the interest charges. In this situation the marginal source of capital for new projects is ostensibly short term borrowing – that is, short term borrowing will be more than it otherwise would be if new investment projects are taken on.

This situation, however, is really one in which the firm is now undergeared as a result of using surplus equity capital to repay some borrowing. The additional short term borrowing could – and if the cash surplus position looks like continuing certainly should – be used to replace some of the equity in the capital structure of the company. The surplus equity which is replaced by the debt could be paid out in special additional dividends. On these grounds debt capital so raised must be considered as part of the funds available for distribution to the equity shareholders. As we have stressed before (Chapter 4, Section 8), it is not until debt raising is limited by the existing assets of the company that it can be considered in any way specifically attributable to the new proposed project.

As the firm emerges from the period of cash surplus and draws upon its borrowing powers it should again reach a position in which its borrowing is limited by its asset cover. At this time the written down assets of this particular project will genuinely enable some debt capital to be raised (or rather maintained) in the normal way. In this case we shall assume that the firm gets back into a position in which asset cover is the limiting factor by the end of year k. At this time there will be a genuinely higher level of debt than otherwise would be the case because of the extra assets available as debt cover from the project in question. For this reason we can take the debt inflow as being the normal proportion of debt to the written down value of assets of the project at the end of the year k and take this amount of debt in as an inflow at that time when evaluating the project. In the subsequent years there will be the normal debt and interest outflows to be deducted from the cash flows generated by the project. Consider an example.

Example 1. Consider a capital project involving an initial capital outlay of £1,000 and giving rise to annual end year cash flows of £142 for 10 years. The firm is at present in a cash surplus position but expects to be in a normal capital raising position by the end of year 4. Until this date the marginal sources of finance will be at an interest cost of 3% net of tax. The normal net of tax cost of equity capital is 9%, and under normal circumstances the firm raises 30% of its capital as debt. The *equity* cash flows are then as follows.

The cash flows for the first 3 years are simply the £142 since the assets of the project are not used to support debt capital. At the end of the 4th year the firm plans to raise debt and of this 30% will be attributable to the written-down book value of the project's assets at that time. We shall assume the assets to be depreciated linearly at £100 p.a. so that by the end of the 4th year the assets have a book value of £600 and hence can be used to support debt of £180. This makes the cash flow of the 4th year £142 + £180 = £322.

In the following year there are the normal debt outflows consequent on the asset being further depreciated. This debt outflow is 30% of £100 (the depreciation) and this outflow occurs in all years until the outflow of the 10th year reduces the debt to zero. The additional outflow of course includes interest payments at 3% on the outstanding balance of the debt. This is $0 \cdot 03 \times £180 = £5 \cdot 4$ at the end of year 5. At the end of year 6 it is $0 \cdot 03 \times £150 = £4 \cdot 5$, etc., etc. This procedure results in the net cash flows of Table 16.1 below.

Applying the present value formula above with $r_0 = 3\%$ and $r_1 = 9\%$, we find the net present value of the project to be:

$$£142 a_{3|3} + v_{4|3}(£322 + v_{1|9}£106 \cdot 6 \ldots + v_{6|9}£111 \cdot 1) - £1,000$$
$$= £121.$$

This net present value is to be interpreted in the normal way. In the absence of significant risks it indicates that the project is acceptable. If significant risks are involved in the project, this net present value must be measured against those risks to establish whether or not the project is acceptable.

ii. No short term debt: surplus cash held in portfolio investment. The situation in which a firm has no short term borrowing but holds a substantial portfolio of short term investments is the extreme case of that considered in the above discussion. It has 'surplus cash' to the extent both of this portfolio investment and of potential borrowing on the strength of its existing assets. If the marginal source of funds is from backing out of the low yielding portfolio investment, the rate of return on this low yielding investment is the appropriate value for r_0 in the preceding analysis which, with this numerical modification, holds in its entirety.

iii. Application of the yield method. The yield method can be generalized to cover the cost of capital conditions described above.

Table 16.1

£

Years	0	1	2	3	4	5	6	7	8	9	10
Initial cash outflow	−1,000										
Annual cash inflow	—	142	142	142	142	142	142	142	142	142	142
Debt inflow	—	—	—	—	180	—	—	—	—	—	—
Annual debt repayments	—	—	—	—	—	−30	−30	−30	−30	−30	−30
Interest at 3% on out-standing debt	—	—	—	—	—	−5.4	−4.5	−3.6	−2.7	−1.8	−0.9
Net cash flow	−1,000	142	142	142	322	106.6	107.5	108.4	109.3	110.2	111.1

The modified yield is the factor $(r_0 + d)$ in the following formula:

$$C = \sum_{i=1}^{i=k} \frac{A_i}{(1+r_0+d)^i} + \sum_{i=k+1}^{i=n} \frac{A_i}{(1+r_0+d)^k(1+r_1+d)^{i-k}}. \quad (16.2)$$

In this formula d is an unknown quantity determined by trial and error such that the future cash flows are discounted into equality with the initial capital outlay C. The yield return would then be described as $(r_0 + d)$ and be compared with r_0. (It could also be compared with r_1.) It is seen that from the nature of the calculation that d is the amount by which the return exceeds the cost of capital (r_0 for k years, and r_1 thereafter), and the modified yield, the return $(r_0 + d)$, is precisely analagous to the conventional yield return.

Example 2. Consider the data of the previous example. The modified yield in this case would be calculated as follows. It is seen from the present value of the previous calculation that, when d is 0, the net present value is £100·0. If the first trial value of d is 2%, the net present value applying (3% + 2%) becomes:

$$£142a_{3|5} + v_{4|5}(£322 + v_{1|11}£106\cdot6 \ldots + v_{6|11}£111\cdot1) - £1,000$$

$$= £30.$$

With $d = 4\%$, the net present value is $-£50$. Interpolating between these two values, d is found to be $2\frac{3}{4}\%$ and the modified yield is therefore $5\frac{3}{4}\%$. On this basis the project offers a return of $2\frac{3}{4}\%$ in excess of the cost of capital of 3% up to year 3 and thereafter 9%, which may well be sufficient compensation for the risks involved.

iv. Weighted average cost of capital approach. The above method has been applied to the equity cash flows, but it can be applied to the total cash flows using the weighted average cost of capital. In the preceding example the weighted average cost of capital would be taken as 3% for the first four years, since this is the cost of *all* the capital relating to this project over the first four years. Subsequent to this period, however, the firm reverts to its normal higher weighted average cost of capital which – recalling that 30% is debt capital – is given by $\cdot30 \times 3\% + \cdot70 \times 9\% = 7\cdot2\%$, or say 7%.

Formula (16.2) using $r_0 = 3$ and $r_1 = 7\%$ can now be applied to the total cash flows in the first and second lines of Table 6.1, namely $-£1,000$ followed by £142 for 10 years. The yield on these cash flows is found to be 5·4%, and d is therefore 2·4% above the cost of capital throughout the life of the project.

CONCLUSIONS

It is essential for a firm in a cash surplus position to follow through the logical consequences of its decision to withhold funds that could be distributed to shareholders, whether these funds are used in low yielding portfolio investments or used to back out of borrowing. The policy of cash surplus, however, frequently coexists with a refusal to countenance low yielding investments in the firm itself, or in any other low yielding commercial - as opposed to fixed interest portfolio – investment.

In some cases this inconsistency of policy is due simply to a failure to think through the logical consequences of a surplus cash position, combined with an absence of appropriate capital budgeting criteria to analyse projects under these conditions. It has been the object of the preceding sections to remedy this latter deficiency.

Frequently, however, this inconsistency of policy is due to a belief – sometimes not explicit – that it is a better policy to wait until more profitable investment opportunities materialize. But this reasoning is analogous to that of a shopkeeper, buying at one price and selling at another (higher) price, who holds on to stock bought cheaply in the past in the hope that the price at which he can sell will rise. If his selling price does rise by say £x he can make this additional profit of £x equally well by purchasing new stock and selling that. Compared with this policy, nothing extra is to be gained by holding on to the earlier, more cheaply purchased stock until the price rise materializes. The stock should be sold whenever it is possible to do so at more than its replacement price. The formulas given above in fact ensure that capital earns at least its 'replacement' cost.

CHAPTER SEVENTEEN

Cost of Capital and Analysis of Projects when Shares are Undervalued

The cost of capital to a firm and the appropriate method of discounting when the firm's shares are undervalued are two complex interrelated problems. Any direct method of solution involves considerable conceptual and mathematical difficulties. In the first section we shall outline the part of the solution to the problem which, on certain simplifying assumptions, is intuitively fairly obvious. In the next section we shall try to establish these results more formally, and finally develop them to establish the appropriate method of analysing capital projects under more general conditions.

The final section of the chapter is devoted to discussing a related problem, the relevance to project evaluation of the pattern of book profits (as opposed to discounted net cash flows) to which projects are estimated to give rise. It is sometimes held that for a firm to ignore the pattern of book profits may result - where book profits largely determine share prices - in inequitable treatment between short term and long term shareholders. It is appropriate to discuss this problem in this chapter since it can arise only when a firm's shares are incorrectly valued.

1. COST OF CAPITAL WHEN SHARES ARE UNDERVALUED

a. *Introduction*

The extensive discussion of the cost of capital in Part I was largely based on the assumption that the shares of a firm were correctly valued at the current market price. By correctly valued is meant that the yield (the discounted return of all future dividends) at the current market price is the same as shareholders could expect from comparable alternative investments. 'Correct' valuation implies perfect knowledge of the future for all investments which is of course unobtainable. In the absence of such knowledge the standard of 'correct' valuation for the shares of any given firm must generally be taken as the best estimate of the firm's management (see Chapter

3, Section 4d). As we have argued, since managements are more intimately concerned than the investing public with the opportunities open to their firms, and, perhaps more important, with their plans to exploit such opportunities, their estimates of future profits will generally be more accurate than the market's estimates.

While the assumption that the market value of a firm's shares is synonymous with the correct valuation is almost universal in the literature of finance and capital budgeting, it is common for shares to be incorrectly valued by a significant amount and not uncommon for them to be seriously undervalued. Serious overvaluation would seem to be more rare. The problem of shares being overvalued is not a difficult one for managements to deal with as an authoritative statement by them will usually suffice to force share prices down to a more realistic level. The following discussion is therefore entirely concerned with the more difficult problems raised by undervaluation. In this connection we would emphatically reiterate our view that when a management considers its firm's shares to be significantly undervalued they should, as a first priority, do everything in their power to raise the market value of their shares to the appropriate level. Their scope for so doing can be considerable. What follows is a discussion of how to measure a firm's cost of capital in the conditions where, temporarily at least, the management are unable to prevent the continuation of some significant degree of undervaluation.

It is in the nature of the undervaluation of a firm's shares that this can be only a temporary condition. If future earnings and dividends are going to be in excess of the market's current estimates, then when those earnings and dividends materialize the undervaluation will cease. In short, no share can be permanently undervalued. But where investment projects are a long time in coming to fruition the period of undervaluation can be correspondingly long.

A common situation giving rise to a temporarily high cost of capital is that of a temporary trade recession. These recessions are fairly common, indeed they are sometimes deliberately government induced, and are essentially temporary in duration. During the period of the recession, however, it is common for shares to be either undervalued or potentially so because of the withdrawal from the market of conservative investors especially the small private investors who may be unduly concerned with the short term outlook. Under these circumstances the market in a firm's shares is likely to be particularly weak so that if not already significantly undervalued it would rapidly become so if the firm attempted to make a new issue of equity capital. The cost of *new* equity capital (see below) during such periods is therefore temporarily at a high level. Within two or three years however the firm can normally expect to see its shares rise in value and the market 'harden' as the recessions come to an end.

Another fairly common undervaluation situation is where the market takes an exaggerated account of a firm's current low profits and inadequately assesses longer term profitability, or where the market fails to realize the full potential of new investment opportunities open to a firm, a common occurrence with progressive expanding companies. If a firm has sufficient grounds for preferring its own assessment of future profit prospects it will be led to expect a rise (or a recovery) in its share prices as the better profits materialize.

Essentially the same situation may exist even where, over the period, a firm sees no likelihood of a fall in the cost of externally raised equity capital but nevertheless expects that at a given future date internally generated or borrowed funds will be sufficient to meet all requirements. At this date, when the marginal finance comes from these sources, the cost of capital will fall to the level appropriate to these sources of finances.

In considering a firm's cost of capital during the period when its shares are undervalued it is also necessary to distinguish between existing funds and retained funds (the equity portion of the depreciation provision plus retained profits) on the one hand, and newly raised equity funds (rights issues and new issues) on the other. A firm is justified in regarding existing funds and retained funds as being available for reinvestment as long as they can earn a return equal to or in excess of that which the shareholders can obtain elsewhere, for this must always be to the benefit of the existing shareholders. In other words, the cost of capital to the firm for existing and retained funds is equal to the shareholders' cost of capital. As we have noted previously (Chapter 3, Section 4d), however, in the case of newly raised equity the cost of capital to the firm can exceed the shareholders' cost of capital. The reason for this is that to the extent that newly raised funds come from new shareholders such new shareholders are enabled to participate in the undervalued income prospects of the existing shareholders. If the existing shareholders are not to be worse off as a result, it is necessary that newly raised funds be invested to earn a return sufficiently above the existing shareholders' cost of capital to compensate them for the dilution of their existing undervalued income prospects. Thus, in these circumstances, the cost of capital to a firm exceeds the cost of capital to its shareholders.

There are two possible situations which need to be considered. In the first case the undervaluation may be fairly general, i.e. affecting most other shares as well to a similar degree. If this is the case then irrespective of the proportion of the new issue subscribed by new and old shareholders, it is the return on these foregone investments which set the cost of capital for the new issue. But in the second case, where the firm's shares are undervalued *relative* to other shares, the cost of capital to the firm – the rate of return it must earn on new projects – may be *higher* than the cost of capital to the individual shareholders, that is the rate of return which they could earn on alternative investments. For example, suppose that the normal market yield on shares (the normal cost of capital to the shareholders) is 10%, but that the firm's shares are relatively undervalued and a new issue could only be launched at a price which would give subscribers to the new issue a 15% yield. If all the new issue was subscribed by individuals who were not already shareholders the firm would clearly have to obtain at least 15% on the new capital raised if the new issue were not to be to the detriment of the old shareholders. In this case of *relative* undervaluation, therefore, the cost of capital to the firm is higher than the cost of capital to the shareholders.

It is of course true that any existing shareholder selling out during a period when the firm's shares are relatively undervalued, both loses by it and confers a corresponding windfall gain on the new shareholder, and this process goes on whether new capital is raised or not. But the actual raising of new capital aggravates this situation as it encourages many more new shareholders to participate cheaply in the undervalued income prospects of the existing shareholders than would otherwise do so.

Whether the undervaluation is general and applies to a wide range of shares or whether it applies only to the shares of the particular firm considering raising new capital only effects the cost of capital to the firm. But *given* the cost of capital in either case, the subsequent analysis of the effect of a changing cost of capital remains the same.

Finally, as undervaluation can be only a temporary condition, in determining the cost to a firm of raising new capital we are essentially determining at what rate of return the firm must be able to invest newly raised funds to justify raising such capital at a time of undervaluation as opposed to not raising any at all. Once this minimum rate of return is established it does *not* mean that it is necessarily in the interests of the shareholders to go ahead and raise the new capital providing it can be invested at this rate of return. It might be better still to wait until the undervaluation is reduced or eliminated.

In sum there are three problems: (1) what is the firm's cost of capital when its shares are undervalued relative to those of other firms'; (2) given the high cost of capital that may result from this or from general undervaluation of shares (e.g. during a recession), how is the generally temporary nature of this high cost of capital to be reflected in the analysis of capital projects financed with this capital; (3) by what criteria should the firm determine whether or not to postpone capital projects in order to avoid raising capital at the current high cost? These three problems will be analysed in this order and thus in the following sub-section we consider how the firm's cost of capital is determined by the proportions of the capital raised from outsiders and the proportion raised from existing shareholders. It will become apparent that in the relative undervaluation case the greater the proportion of capital raised from outsiders, the higher the rate of return it must earn if the interests of the existing shareholders are not to be impaired. Conversely, if all the new capital comes from the existing shareholders in strict proportion to their existing shareholdings, then it will be seen that it is sufficient to invest the new capital at the existing shareholders' cost of capital. In short, the cost of capital to a firm will vary according to the proportion of the new capital subscribed by existing shareholders and outsiders. In the case in which all other shares are undervalued to the same degree then, of course, the cost of capital will be the same whatever proportion of the capital is subscribed by new shareholders.

Before proceeding further, however, we need briefly to consider the definition of 'new' shareholders and 'old' shareholders. The need for such consideration will be apparent if the question is posed: is a shareholder, who at present owns only one share but who subscribes to almost all the shares of a proportionately large new issue, to be regarded as an 'old' or a 'new' shareholder? Where the shares of the company are significantly undervalued this single shareholder will make a handsome gain out of the new issue at the expense of all the other existing shareholders. It is unsatisfactory not to make any allowance for this one-sided gain merely because it accrues to an existing shareholder. The definition which we propose therefore, is as follows. Where a shareholder subscribes to a larger proportion of a new issue than he already owns of the existing shares of the company, this excess is to be regarded as capital subscribed by 'new' shareholders. Thus the extreme case of all the new shares being purchased by an individual at present owning no shares in the company should be considered as capital subscribed entirely by a 'new' shareholder; where a shareholder owns 10% of the existing shares and subscribes to 10% of the shares of the new issue all of this capital should be regarded as being subscribed by 'old' shareholders; where a shareholder subscribes to 10% of the new issue but at the moment owns only 3%, 7% of the capital subscribed by this shareholder should be regarded as coming from 'new' shareholders and 3% as coming from 'old' shareholders.

The proportionality criterion used in this definition would seem to be reasonable and fair, although in some circumstances other definitions might be more appropriate.[1] We would not, however, wish to minimize the obvious difficulties of estimating in advance what proportion of a new share issue would be subscribed by 'new' shareholders in the sense defined above. A great deal of research obviously needs to be done into the general question of subscriptions to new issues before any useful generalizations can be made. Forecasting the outcome, however, could be considerably assisted by careful discussion between representatives of a firm and its major shareholders, influential brokers, etc. This should enable a firm to judge with some degree of confidence the proportion of its shares it can expect to see taken up by the major institutions and larger private investors. As regards the smaller investors it would seem likely that their investment is primarily determined by availability of funds and general market sentiment at the time of the new issue and some estimate should be possible here.

b. *The Preliminary Analysis*

Where a firm is raising equity capital at a higher than normal cost (i.e. higher than the cost of capital to existing shareholders) in order to finance a project, the length of life of this project will be an

---

[1] A further refinement of the analysis would be to consider the *net* increase in 'new' shareholders induced by the new issue, insofar as some of these 'new' shareholders will become shareholders by subscribing to the new issue as an alternative to direct purchase of the existing shares of the firm. If the interest and publicity of a new issue is the main factor attracting new shareholders, however, the results of this approach should differ very little from that advocated in the text.

important consideration in analysing its attractiveness. For the firm is raising capital at a high cost which it effectively bears into perpetuity and it seems intuitively evident that a short term project must earn an exceptionally high return in its short life in order to offset this higher cost of capital which the firm will still be bearing long after this project has come to an end.

We shall denote this high cost of capital by r_1. In the remainder of Section 1 we shall assume that the firm's shares are only very temporarily undervalued and that the firm will soon be able to obtain equity funds at its normal cost of capital either externally by means of new issues or by internally generated funds. This normal cost of capital will be denoted by r_2. (r_2 is assumed to be the firm's *normal* cost of capital and hence also the shareholders' cost of capital.) Clearly firms would rarely raise new capital at the current onerous cost, say, r_1 (this is fully defined below) if this could be avoided by an insignificant delay in the raising of new funds. Our purpose in considering this unrealistic situation in which a firm is nevertheless contemplating raising capital on these onerous terms, is to establish the basis of analysis which can be extended to cover the case where the delay before the normal cost of capital r_2 becomes operative, is significant. This latter case is the subject of Section 2.

The assumption that in this simple case the normal cost of capital r_2 becomes operative almost immediately enables us to discount all *future* cash flows at this rate. Since the cost of raising capital now at r_1 is a perpetual burden (because a firm is assumed to go on indefinitely) it will be convenient to convert the future cash flows from all projects financed by this capital to an equivalent perpetuity. Thus, all the cash flows $A_1, A_2,..., A_n$ from a project financed in this way are discounted at r_2 to a present value P. The perpetuity having the same present value P is evidently r_2P. (It is appropriate to use r_2 as the rate of discount since we are here dealing with *future* cash flows arising over the period when r_2 is the operative cost of capital.) Since it is the equity capital which involves this high cost, it will be convenient to conduct the analysis in terms of the equity cash flows and it is these cash flows which are represented by the A_i's.

For a project to be acceptable it must give rise to a perpetuity equal to or more than the cost (borne in perpetuity) of the capital raised to finance it. Thus if a project has an initial capital cost C, and is financed at the high cost of capital r_1, then the perpetual annual cost of the financing is equivalent to r_1C. The present value now of the perpetuity r_2P is the amount of capital raised now which it would service, and as this capital costs r_1 per unit this is r_2P/r_1. Recalling now the definition of P, it follows that the present value now of any series of cash flows A_1, A_2 arising in the future is

$$C \leqslant \frac{r_2}{r_1} \sum_{i=1}^{i=n} \frac{A_i}{(1+r_2)^i}. \tag{17.1}$$

This is the basic formula on which all the succeeding analysis rests.

This convention of discussing the problem in terms of perpetuities in no way limits the generality of our conclusions, but it does provide a convenient and simplified basis for the analysis. This simple formula (17.1) makes clear the above divergence of the cost of capital to the firm and the cost of capital to the shareholders. The project would be acceptable to the shareholders themselves if it just showed a present value of C when discounted at the rate r_2. The firm, however, can raise capital to finance the project only at exceptionally onerous rate r_1 because of the undervaluation of its shares, and this is effectively being reflected in the fact that the normal present value of the project in (17.1) is being written down by r_2/r_1.

Consider now how r_1, the current high cost of long term capital, is determined.

i. The cost of equity capital (non-preferential rights issue).

Let us consider first the case in which old shareholders have no privileges compared with new shareholders in subscribing new capital – that is a new issue with no preferential rights. The cost of capital in this case, as in all cases, is the return which must be earned on the new capital to leave the total return to the old shareholders unimpaired. The solution to this problem will be apparent if we consider the share issue as constituted of two separate new issues, the first subscribed by old shareholders and the second subscribed by completely new shareholders, and consider the return which must be earned by each.

The capital issue subscribed by the old shareholders involves no future sharing with outsiders of the profits that would otherwise arise even without the new issue. It involves, as regards these profits, only a redivision between the existing shareholders. If we are concerned solely with maximizing the return to the aggregate required from the new capital subscribed by old shareholders, it is necessary merely to equal the return available to them from other investment opportunities which they have forgone to make this investment. The aggregate return to the old shareholders will be increased if the new capital subscribed by the old shareholders earns more than this return.

Because the firm's shares are undervalued, the return to be earned on the capital subscribed by the new shareholders must exceed the existing shareholders' cost of capital. As in the case when all the capital is subscribed by outsiders, this capital must be invested to yield a minimum return equal to the true (but, save by the firm's management, the unsuspected) yield on the firm's shares prior to the raising of further capital. Therefore in these circumstances the cost of capital r_1 is the two rates of return required by the two different types of capital weighted by their proportions in the total capital raised. The following example demonstrates the simple calculations involved.

Example 1. A firm contemplating a new issue estimates that at the *new* issue price its shares will have a true yield of 20 per cent on the existing share capital. The return which both new and existing shareholders can get elsewhere is assumed to be 10%. From past experience it is thought that about 50% of the new capital will be subscribed by the existing shareholders of the company. The cost of capital r_1 would therefore be estimated as follows:

$$r_1 = (0{\cdot}5 \times 10\%) + (0{\cdot}5 \times 20\%) = 15\%.$$

ii. Cost of capital under a rights issue. Rights issues were discussed in some detail in Chapter 3, Section 4e, and we shall only briefly recapitulate here. In a rights issue shares are normally sold at significantly less than the current market prices to the existing shareholders of the firm. The value of these preferential rights will depend on the market estimation of the future earnings (and dividend policy) on the enlarged share capital. Normally a firm will make some announcement of its expectations in this regard. Where the market estimates that the earnings and dividends on the new capital received by the firm will be the same as on the existing share capital (at the pre-issue price) the market price of the shares ex-rights (when the new issue has been taken up) will be given by the formula:

$$\text{Ex-rights price} = \text{pre-issue price} \times \frac{\text{no. old shares}}{\text{no. new} + \text{old shares}}$$

$$+ \text{issue price} \times \frac{\text{no. new shares}}{\text{no. new} + \text{old shares}}.$$

For example, in the case of a rights issue of 1 for 3 at 80s on shares that now stand at 100s the ex-rights price will be $(100s \times \frac{3}{4}) + (80s \times \frac{1}{4}) = 95s$. Shareholders who do not wish to subscribe could sell off their preferential rights at the difference between the issue price and the ex-rights price – in this example 5s per share. Rights from three shares would entitle the holder to subscribe or purchase the new shares at only 80s compared with the market price of 95s. At the price of 5s per share the rights on 3 shares are therefore worth exactly the saving they give rise to by enabling the holder of the rights to acquire one new share at the preferential price of 80s, and hence 5s per share will be the equilibrium price for the rights.

Where the shares are properly valued by the market both before and after the rights issue, the old shareholders neither gain nor lose by the new issue as long as they either subscribe for their rights or sell them off. They all receive 5s per share either in cash for their rights, or save this much by exercising their right, and this 5s per share exactly compensates them for the fall in the value of their existing shares – from 100s to the 95s at which they stand after the rights issue.

As we have argued, however, it frequently arises that a firm has good grounds for believing that the market has undervalued its shares, and in accepting the market valuation it runs the serious danger of not acting in the best interests of its shareholders in this critically important respect. The appropriate method of determining the cost of capital in this case is best seen from an example.

Example 2. Suppose, as above, that the firm makes a rights issue of 1 for 3 at 80s and that its present share price is 100s. The market imperfectly estimates the yield on the *pre-issue* prices to be the normal market yield of 8%, while the true yield at this price will be 16%. At the proposed issue price of 80s, therefore, the true yield will be 20 per cent.[1] The ex-rights price, as determined above, is 95s.

The costs of capital in this case is best ascertained by considering it as an extension of the case considered in the previous sub-section of a non-rights issue contributed partly by old and partly by new shareholders. If the cash received by the non-subscribing old

---

[1] In the remainder of this chapter we are assuming for simplicity that the true yield at the issue price compared to the true yield at the *pre-issue* price varies in the exact inverse proportion to the ratio of the issue price to the pre-issue price. In practice this would not always be so – see Section 4c of Chapter 1.

shareholders from the sale of their rights is ignored, it would appear that the issue can be regarded simply as a straight increase in the firm's share capital by $33\frac{1}{3}\%$ at the very low price of 80s. On this basis, if 60% of the new shares are subscribed by new shareholders, the cost of capital is the return which the firm expects to obtain on its existing share capital at the issue price (and without the proceeds of the new share issue) weighted by 0·6, and the rate of return which the old shareholders can obtain elsewhere weighted by 0·4. In this example the cost of capital r_1 would therefore be:

$$r_1 = (20\% \times 0·6) + (8\% \times 0·4) = 15·2\%.$$

In fact the firm could invest the proceeds of the share issue at a slightly lower return than this and still improve the position of the old shareholders since, in addition to the return being earned by the firm on the capital it receives, the old non-subscribing shareholders who have received a capital sum for their rights must also be earning a return from this element of capital, *and the return which the firm must earn on the marginal capital raised is reduced by this additional return.* Thus for each 80s received and invested by the firm, an additional return flowing to the shareholders is 8% on the 5s received per share by old shareholders in rights. The return required on the 80s actual capital received per new share issued by the firm is therefore:

$$\left(20\% \times \frac{48}{80}\right) + \left(8\% \times \frac{32}{80}\right) - \left(8\% \times \frac{5}{80}\right) = 14·7\%.$$

This can be formalized into the following *approximate* formula for the cost of capital r_1:

$$r_1 = \frac{mz}{w} + s\frac{(y-x)}{w} \qquad (17.2)$$

where m = the return to share capital at the *present contemplated issue price* but in the absence of the new share issue – i.e. the yield on the existing shares at the proposed issue price but prior to the new issue;

s = return which shareholders can obtain from alternative investments;

y = amount of new capital subscribed by old shareholders;

z = amount of new capital subscribed by new shareholders;

$w = y + z$ = total capital subscribed; and

x = amount of new capital paid to old shareholders for their rights.

As we have stressed, the analysis so far given applies strictly only to the case in which the cost of capital is expected to revert to normal at some time in the *immediate* future. That this is the case may be seen from considering the implications for the analysis of the firm's effective cost of capital remaining at its current high level for a number of years. For example, assume that projects started in any one of the years up to say year 6 must be financed by the raising of capital at the cost r_1 and must earn this high rate of return. Assume also that the firm's cost of capital reverts to its normal rate r_2 after year 6. If the firm is obliged to raise capital *now* at the current high cost to meet deficits in the capital budgets for each of these 6 years, then clearly, funds arising during this next 6 years are especially valuable (compared with funds arising *after* year 6) in that they could be used *to avoid raising permanent capital on these onerous terms* – that is, they would provide internally generated funds to reduce the amount of costly outside finance raised. But it is apparent that nothing of this is reflected in the above analysis. All the future funds are simply discounted at the firm's normal cost of capital (i.e. the shareholders' cost of capital), both before and after year 6, to arrive at the equivalent perpetuity which is then discounted at r_1. The error involved in using the method developed above would not be significant if the firm were only obliged to raise capital at these onerous terms to meet the capital requirements of, say, just one or two years ahead, but for longer periods the appropriate exact method is required.

The analysis is extended to cover this situation in Section 2 below. Before proceeding to this, however, we would stress that the basic formula derived above, namely (17.2), is only an approximation for determining a firm's cost of capital when new equity capital is being raised wholly or in part from new shareholders either by way of new (i.e. non-rights) issues or by rights issues. While it is a sufficiently accurate approximation for most practical purposes, especially when the proportion of new capital raised does not exceed 20% of the market value of the existing share capital, it is useful to have the correct and therefore the completely accurate formulae. The derivation of these rather more complex formulae is set out in Appendix A, which also contains two diagrams indicating the numerical effect of using formulae that take full account of the undervaluation of a firm's shares.

2. ANALYSIS OF PROJECTS WHEN A FIRM'S COST OF CAPITAL IS EXPECTED TO FALL AT A SIGNIFICANTLY DISTANT FUTURE DATE

a. *Introduction*

The results of the previous section strictly apply only when a firm's cost of capital is expected to revert to normal immediately, that is the firm's shares are assumed to be on the point of rising to the value which truly reflects future dividends. Evidently no firm in this position would consider raising new capital to finance projects on the onerous terms r_1 when after an insignificant delay new capital could be raised on normal terms at less cost to the old shareholders. Further no capital projects will have to be forgone for so short a postponement. In this section we are concerned to develop and generalize the results of the previous section to cover the more normal case in which the shares of a firm (which needs to raise new equity capital) are expected to be undervalued until some significantly delayed date in the future. Such a firm is faced with the choice of raising new equity capital now at a higher than normal cost, or postponing the commencement of certain projects until its shares rise to the value which truly reflects future prospects when the new equity capital can be raised at the normal cost.

The problem which a firm faces under these conditions are:

(i) establishing the profitability of projects if commenced *now* given the cost of equity capital at this time;

(ii) establishing the advantages of immediate commencement financed by raising equity capital now compared with raising equity capital and commencing the projects at a later date when the cost of the equity capital will have fallen.

Having established those projects which offer significant advantages if commenced immediately, a firm then needs to compare the aggregate amount of cash required for these projects with the aggregate of available funds (excluding the high cost equity which is to be provided by new issues). Debt capital can be deducted in the normal way from the cash flows of the projects which give rise to it. The resulting capital deficit is then the amount which the firm must consider raising by an equity issue.

In the following discussion, these problems – (i) and (ii) – are examined in the context of the cost of capital reverting to normal at some specific date in the future. It is of course unlikely that any very abrupt transition will occur, but it is merely necessary for the analysis for a firm to estimate the date by which the cost of capital will have reverted to a lower long term level, and where this is a date which the firm is prepared to consider as an acceptable alternative date for raising capital.

b. *Analysis*

Let us now consider how the analysis of the previous section can be modified to take this into account. Suppose we assume that a firm will be facing the need to raise fresh equity capital *now* to meet deficits in the capital budgets in *each* of the coming years 1, 2, and 3, but that after this last year it expects either that internally generated sources will be sufficient for all worthwhile investments, or that alternatively, its shares will have become properly valued and its cost of capital will fall to its normal long run level.

Before proceeding further with this analysis we must first expand our definition of r_1 to cover the present case. In Section 1, the cost of the capital subscribed by new shareholders was the discounted yield at the new issue price and assuming that the firm's cost of capital would revert to normal (i.e. r_2) in the immediate future. In the present case, where there is a delay of say k years before the firm's cost of capital reverts to normal, it will be convenient to consider the cost of capital provided by new shareholders in two parts. The first part is the cost of such capital over the years $0-k$ (defined below) and the second part is the cost of capital from end-year k onwards. This latter cost is defined as the discounted yield from end-year k onwards calculated on the *present* new issue price. Thus where $k = 3$ years, and assuming the present new issue price is £1·0, and the dividends for each of the first three years are £0·05, and from the fourth year $(k+1)$ onwards, £0·10, then the second part of the cost of capital is defined as the rate of discount which bring £0·10 (i.e. all future dividends) into equality with the new issue price of £1·0 *at end-year k*, and in this case is evidently 10%. It is this cost of capital which enters[1] into the formulae for r_1, and not the whole dividend yield from $t = 0$ onwards as in our previous case in which we were effectively taking k as being a time immediately after $t = 0$.

The analysis developed in the preceding sections clearly applies to

----

[1] It will be appreciated that, as before, r_1 is a weighted average cost of newly raised equity funds, weighted by the proportions of newly raised equity capital subscribed by new and old shareholders.

the situation which faces the firm at the end of year 3. In this year it is raising equity capital (or considering raising more in one of the earlier years) to provide for the requirements of year 3. Moreover, the cost of capital is expected to change to r_2 in the following year (year 4), hence it is appropriate to discount at the rate r_2, the normal long run cost of capital, in order to establish the high cost of capital r_1 for any project financed by the excessively costly funds of this current year. It follows that the results of formula (17.1) still hold in this case and, therefore, that the present value *at the end of year* 3 of any sum, say, A arising t years from year 3 is

$$\frac{r_2}{r_1} \frac{A}{(1 + r_2)^t}.$$

Another way of appreciating the logic of this is to reflect that any sum arising immediately before the end of year 3 can be used to avoid raising capital on the exceptionally onerous terms r_1 into perpetuity, while sums arising immediately after the end of year 3 come too late for this and can only be used to avoid raising capital at the normal rate r_2 (since the cost of capital has by then fallen to this level).

The analysis has so far established the means of reducing sums arising after the end of year $k = 3$ to their value immediately before the end of this year; we simply discount back to year 3 at the rate r_2, and then multiply by r_2/r_1. To complete the analysis we now need to establish the rate at which we should discount to reduce these sums at the end of year 3 back to their present value now at time $t = 0$. What this rate of discount should be will be apparent if we consider what rate of return would be required on a project with a life of k years or less; the life of such project terminates before the change in the cost of capital, hence all the complications ensuing from the changing cost of capital do not apply. The return required is clearly the weighted average as given by (17.2) except that m in that formula is now the dividend yield on the firm's shares at the new issue price and over the period 0 to k, while s is the yield that can be obtained in dividends and capital gains on alternative investments, over the period 0 to k. If this weighted average return is obtained then the investment will clearly provide sufficient profits to meet the claims of the new shareholders and an acceptable additional return to the old shareholders.

A qualification to this is that the weighted average return as given by (17.2) must be in excess of s, which implies that the firm's dividend yield m over the period 0 to k must be in excess of s; for if this condition is not met then it will evidently be impossible for the new investments which earn only a weighted average return less than s, to offer the return s on the capital subscribed by the old shareholders. In fact the return required and the rate of discount over the period 0 to k is either the rate given by (17.2) or s whichever is the higher. The following example illustrates the application of the formula (17.2) to the determination of the short term cost of capital.

Example 3. Suppose the case is as for Example 2 above, that is a 1 for 3 rights issue (60% subscribed by new shareholders and 40% by existing shareholders) at 80s on shares that at present stand at 100s. Suppose that the firm's cost of capital is likely to revert to normal by the beginning of year 4, and that the average dividend yield over this period is 5% after tax on the current share price of 100s. On the new issue price of 80s it is therefore $6\frac{1}{4}$%. Using this value for m in (17.2), and assuming that 5% is also the yield in dividends and capital gains obtainable on alternative investments over the period 0 to k, we find the short term cost of capital r_0 is:

$$r_0 = \left(6\tfrac{1}{4}\% \times \frac{48}{80}\right) + \left(5\% \times \frac{32-5}{80}\right)$$

$$= 3\cdot75\% + 1\cdot69\% = 5\cdot44\%.$$

These considerations establish the basis for the following formula for the present value R of a project financed under these conditions:

$$R = \sum_{i=1}^{i=k} \frac{A_i}{(1+r_0)^i} + \frac{r_2}{r_1(1+r_0)^k} \sum_{i=k+1}^{i=n} \frac{A_i}{(1+r_2)^{i-k}}. \qquad (17.3)$$

Where A_i is the cash flow of year i, k is the period at the end of which the cost of capital is expected to change from r_1 to r_2, r_0 is the short term cost of capital for the period 0–k, n is the life of the project, and C is the capital cost of the project. The formula involves no special computational problems and its application is illustrated in the following example.

Example 4. Consider the case of a project with an initial capital cost of £589,000, giving rise to an annual cash flow of £100,000 for ten years. At present the firm's shares are already somewhat under-valued and any new issue would need to be issued at the still lower price of £1·0 each, at which price they offer a true yield of $10\frac{3}{4}$%.

At this price the shares are subject to a significant degree of relative undervaluation as the shareholder's normal cost of capital is estimated at around 8%. The short term yield on alternative investments is estimated to be about 6%. The firm's current dividend is 7% of the proposed new issue price, i.e. £0·07, and is expected to remain at this level for 3 years, after which it will rise to £0·12 and stay at that level indefinitely. By then the firm's shares are expected to rise to reflect fully future dividends, thus the shares are expected to rise to £1·5 giving an 8% yield. In each of the next 3 years the firm expects to have substantial capital deficits which will justify raising further new equity capital despite the high cost of so doing. In these circumstances should the firm raise equity capital, by means of a new issue, to commence the project now? We shall examine two cases, (a) where all the new capital is to be raised from new shareholders, and (b) where 50% of the new capital is to be raised from new shareholders, the remainder coming from existing shareholders.

(a) The first step is to calculate the values of r_0 and r_1.

r_0 = the short term dividend yield on the firm's shares
  = 7%.

r_1 = the discounted dividend yield at the start of year 4 on the *present* share price = 12%.

r_2 is given as 8%.

Applying (17.3) to this data the present value R of the cash flows of the project is found to be as follows:

$$R = a_{3|7}£100,000 + \frac{0·08}{0·12}v_{3|7}(a_{7|8}£100,000)$$

$$= £546,000, \text{ to the nearest £000's.}$$

At this present value for the cash flows the project has a negative net present value of $-£43,000$ and should accordingly be rejected. The conventional yield on the project is 11%. If the cost of capital had been taken as the true discounted yield on the firm's shares ($10\frac{3}{4}$%), this would have falsely suggested that the project was acceptable.

(b) As above, the first step is to calculate the values of r_0 and r_1 when 50% of the new issue will be subscribed by the existing shareholders.

r_0 = the weighted average of the firm's short term dividend yield, and the short term yield available on alternative investments =

$$(50\% \times 7\%) + (50\% \times 6\%) = 6\tfrac{1}{2}\%.$$
Similarly, $r_1 = (50\% \times 12\%) + (50\% \times 8\%) = 10\%$.

Applying (17.3) to this data the present value R of the cash flows in these circumstances is found to be as follows:

$$R = a_{3|6\frac{1}{2}}£100,000 + \frac{0\cdot08}{0\cdot10}v_{3|6\frac{1}{2}}(a_{7|8}£100,000)$$

$$= £610,000 \text{ to the nearest } £000\text{'s}.$$

This gives a net present value of $+£21,000$ and the project should therefore be accepted. The higher present value results from the higher proportion of capital supplied by existing shareholders.

In this example it was assumed that the firm's shares were subject to *relative* undervaluation. While the cost of capital would be different, precisely the same numerical analysis would apply if shares were generally undervalued in the market.

So far we have made use of the method of present value in this analysis. Before proceeding further consider the application of the yield method.

c. *Modified Yield*

It is again possible to generalize the yield method to cover this situation. As we have argued before (Chapter 5, Section 1a) it is convenient to regard the excess of the discounted yield over the cost of capital as the premium paid for risk bearing. The relative value of the cash flows before and after the date at which the cost of capital changes is independent of this risk and the same relative valuation would apply to cash flows of any degree of risk. On these grounds it is possible to employ again the device used in Chapter 16, Section 2b (*iii*), increasing all the rates of discount shown in by a constant amount to obtain:

$$C = \sum_{i=1}^{i=k} \frac{A_i}{(1+r_0+d)^i} + \frac{r_2}{r_1(1+r_0+d)^k} \sum_{i=k+1}^{i=n} \frac{A_i}{(1+r_2+d)^{i-k}}. \quad (17.4)$$

Again the modified yield should be taken as $r_2 + d$ and compared with the normal cost of capital r_2. It should be appreciated, however, that d represents the excess of the modified yield over the cost of capital, both the short term cost of capital r_0, and the normal or long term cost of capital r_2.

The rate of return formulation provides a convenient basis for assessing the effect of a falling cost of capital. This is illustrated in Figures 17.1 and 17.2 where the cost of capital is expected to revert to normal at the end of year $k = 2$.

Both figures illustrate the effect of a falling cost of capital on projects each having constant annual net cash flows and a constant conventional discounted yield of 15%, but with lives varying from 5 to 25 years. In both figures $r_1 = 10\%$, but in Figure 17.1 $r_2 = 8\%$ and in Figure 17.2 $r_2 = 6\%$, thus Figure 17.2 assumes the greater degree of undervaluation. In both figures the value of $r_0 = r_2$.

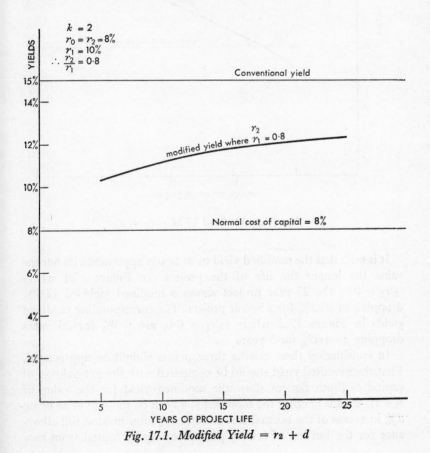

Fig. 17.1. *Modified Yield* $= r_2 + d$

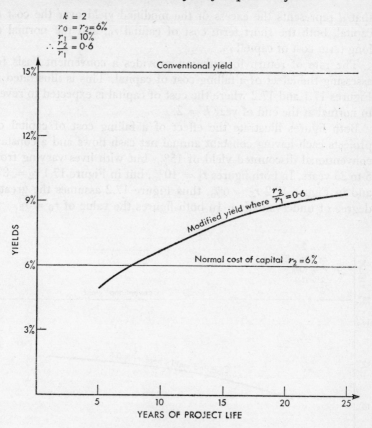

$$k = 2$$
$$r_0 = r_2 = 6\%$$
$$r_1 = 10\%$$
$$\therefore \frac{r_2}{r_1} = 0.6$$

Fig. 17.2. Modified Yield $= r_2 + d$

It is seen that the modified yield most nearly approaches its normal value the longer the life of the project. In Figure 17.1 where $r_2/r_1 = 0.8$, the 25-year project shows a modified yield of 12·4% dropping to 10·3% for a 5-year project. The corresponding modified yields in Figure 17.2 where $r_2/r_1 = 0.6$, are 9·3% for 25 years dropping to 4·9% for 5 years.

In considering these results three points should be appreciated. First the modified yield should be compared with the normal cost of capital r_2 (both figures show the modified yield for the value of $r_2 + d$). This is because the modified yield can be thought of as being $d\%$ in excess of the normal cost of capital r_2 after making full allowance for the burden of raising permanent equity capital from new shareholders on onerous terms. Second, the greater the degree of the undervaluation of shares the greater the difference between the modified yield and the conventional yield, thus the modified yields in Figure 17.2 are all less than the corresponding yields in Figure 17.1. Third, the shorter the life of the project for any given value of k, the greater the difference between the modified yield and the conventional yield. This is in accord with the commonsense belief that it can be very expensive to raise permanent capital on onerous terms to finance short term projects.

d. *Method of Analysis when* (17.3) *is Inapplicable*

Before examining the alternative policy of postponing commencement of the project to the beginning of year 4 $(k+1)$ when new equity capital can be raised on normal terms (8% in the example in (b) above), we must examine the consequences of the situation where the use of (17.3) results in few or no projects being acceptable, but where the number of projects which promise a conventional yield in excess of the shareholders' normal cost of capital exceeds the amount of internally generated funds. Consider how this comes about and the method of analysis required.

Initially a firm will consider projects on the basis of the cost of internally generated (plus borrowed) funds on the assumption that these sources will be sufficient. It may then find that the total capital requirements on this method of analysis in fact exceed the funds available and that it must consider raising fresh equity if it intends to undertake a capital programme of this size. The firm must then re-analyse its investment opportunities on the assumption that the high cost externally raised equity is the marginal source of funds and use the method of analysis developed above. If the acceptable projects on this method of analysis are sufficiently in excess of internally generated and borrowed funds to warrant a new equity issue then the method of analysis itself is validated: the marginal source of funds is clearly that assumed in the analysis.

It may be the case, however, that in applying this method of analysis the total budget requirements are so reduced by this more exacting criterion of acceptability that in fact no new issue of equity capital is justified. In this case the cost of capital to the firm lies somewhere in between the normal long run cost and the higher cost given by externally raised funds. The firm is essentially in a capital rationing situation since its marginal projects show returns in excess of the cost of internally generated plus loan funds, but are insufficiently attractive to meet the cost of the only other source of supply – externally raised equity.

Some of the problems of this type of capital rationing situation were discussed in Section 7 of Chapter 4. In the particular case now being considered we would suggest the following approach. Where the cost of capital is expected to revert to normal (to r_2) at the end of, say, k years (because of shares becoming correctly valued or internally generated funds being sufficient to meet requirements), different trial rates of discount r should be used over the period 0 to k (with r_2 used on all cash flows arising subsequent to this date) until a rate r is found which reduces the acceptable projects to a total which can be financed by the available funds generated internally or from loan sources. The value of r found by this process is the opportunity cost of capital over the period 0 to k.

e. *Immediate Commencement versus Postponement*

We have previously stressed the importance of timing in capital projects (see Section 1b (*ii*) of Chapter 5), that is choosing the best date of commencement. In situations such as that examined in sub-section (b) above, where the cost of capital is expected to change in the future, consideration of alternative dates of raising capital and commencing projects is of especial importance. This is illustrated by reconsidering Example 4.

Example 5. The firm is assumed to have a project costing £589,000 which gives rise to a constant annual cash flow of £100,000 for ten years. Taking the case – alternative (b) – where half the cost of new capital comes from new shareholders, and half from existing shareholders, the project was shown to have a net present value if commenced at once, of $+£21,000$. Consider the net present value if it is postponed 3 years to the start of year 4 by which time the firm's cost of capital reverts to normal.

We should apply (17.3) to this case, and take the same values as before, i.e. $r_0 = 6\frac{1}{2}\%$, $r_2 = 8\%$, and $r_1 = 10\%$.

Thus the present value from postponement becomes

$$R = v_{3|6\frac{1}{2}}\frac{0.08}{0.10}(a_{10|8}£100,000 - £589,000)$$

$$= £54,000 \text{ to the nearest } £000\text{'s.}$$

This substantially exceeds the net present value which would arise with immediate commencement, hence the project should be postponed.

We have here taken the capital cost and net cash flows of the project as unchanged by postponement although clearly in practice both values could change. Where this is likely the method should still be applied but to the changed figures appropriate to the later commencement date.

If the method of analysis applied to ascertain which projects are acceptable for immediate commencement results in a reduction of the present capital requirements to an amount covered by internally generated sources, then again we have the situation where the method of analysis when shares are temporarily undervalued has been shown to be inapplicable to the situation being considered. The appropriate method of analysis is then that given at the end of sub-section (d). Where the situation is one of short run capital rationing of the type described there it will still be found useful to consider the possibility of postponing projects. This would be achieved using the method of present value and the short run opportunity cost of capital for discounting cash flows over the period 0 to k.

In all the preceding examples it was assumed that each project could be considered separately and independently of all its possible replacements. In the case of a project which has a number of foreseeable replacements these should be considered as one project for the purposes of the above analysis. A further discussion and a numerical example of this case will be found in reference [1].

3. THE RELEVANCE OF BOOK PROFITS
TO THE SELECTION OF CAPITAL PROJECTS

Throughout the preceding chapters the stress has been on analysing capital projects on the basis of the net cash flows to which projects give rise. Thus we have ignored the element of reported or book profits (i.e. the increased profits which will be recorded in the *published* accounts of a firm as a result of accepting projects) as such. We must now consider whether or not this ignoring of book profits is of any consequence to shareholders.

Continuing the assumption of Chapter 3, let us assume that a given firm's shareholders are fairly homogeneous and that a return of 10% represents their net of tax investment opportunities elsewhere, i.e. 10% is the shareholders' cost of capital. Consider now how the interests of a shareholder would be affected if the firm decides to retain certain profits which could be distributed as dividends to invest in a profitable project promising a 15% net of tax yield with say a three-year gestation period. During the three years the project has no earnings but thereafter it is highly profitable. Is it necessarily in the interest of all shareholders that the firm should accept this project to be financed from retained earnings?

If we assume that prior to the contemplation of this new project the shares of the company are correctly valued at the current market price then accepting the new project will be in the interests of all shareholders providing that, once accepted, the shares rise sufficiently in price to reflect the prospective earnings of the new project. But if the share price fails to rise sufficiently such that the shares are undervalued, say perhaps for the whole of the gestation period, then accepting the new project will not necessarily be in the interests of all the shareholders. Those shareholders selling out prior to the share price reflecting its true value could lose thereby. In short, because book profits during the gestation period do not reflect future profit prospects, the firm's shares could be temporarily undervalued and acceptance of the project in such circumstances could result in a conflict of interest between the short term and the long term shareholder.

It is important to be clear about the exact conditions which would cause a short term shareholder to lose by the firm accepting the new project rather than increasing dividends. If the value of the shares, after the new project is accepted, equals or exceeds the value the shares would otherwise have had *plus* the increased dividend that non-acceptance would have permitted (the new project is assumed to be financed from retained profits), then the short term shareholder will not lose by the firm accepting the new project. It is thus not a necessary condition that the firm's shares *fully* reflect future prospects, merely that their value is such that a short term shareholder disposing of his shares prior to the time the shares are again fully valued does not lose thereby. It can be shown that this condition is met so long as the market judges that the profits retained can be invested to earn at least 10%, i.e. the yield on the firm's existing business at the current market price. To the extent that the market judges the yield on the extra retained profits to exceed 10%, a short term shareholder will be better off as a result of the new project being accepted. By selling out in such circumstances prior to the time the shares are again properly valued a short term shareholder will not get the price he should on his shares, but he will nevertheless get a better price than if the new project had not been accepted. In short, the market must judge the extra retained profits to be invested at less than the current prospective discounted yield (here assumed to be 10%) before a conflict of interest arises between the short term and the long term shareholders. To the extent that market prices are overinfluenced by current earnings and dividends then investment in projects with a significant gestation period is likely to have this result. We have so far considered the problem from the viewpoint of the short term shareholder not *losing* by a firm's acceptance of a long term project. But equally, there is the problem of deciding whether a firm should accept a short term project which would boost the short term share value but which might be to the detriment of the long term shareholders.

How best to balance the conflict of interest which can arise between short term and long term shareholders (or indeed between any groups of shareholders, e.g. those in a high tax bracket and those who pay little or no tax) is essentially a matter of opinion. It is possible to argue that decisions should be taken simply on the basis of what a firm's management deems to be the majority interest, or that some mixed policy should be followed whereby some attention is given to the claims and interests of any substantial minority or minorities.[1]

The former policy, of considering only the majority interest, is straightforward enough, but the latter policy involves many practical difficulties some of which will be briefly considered.

Application of a policy of paying some attention to the needs of short term shareholders (presuming them to be in a minority) suggests that the following additional restraints should be imposed on the investment programme of the firm. Suppose a proportion of the shareholders (henceforward referred to as short term shareholders) will sell their shares in year k. Each year (in the absence of further shareholders' capital being raised directly) we should regard this proportion of capital invested as being provided by the short term shareholders. This proportion of the capital investment each year will give rise to a series of cash flows and these will normally increase as each year more capital attributable to the short-term shareholders is retained from profits and invested up to year k. In this year the short term shareholder will sell out. The cash flows up

---

[1] All these arguments presuppose that a firm's management knows the interests of different groups of shareholders, e.g. the tax bracket of shareholders, the proportion who hold shares for different periods, etc., etc.

to year k will of course arise jointly from the short term and long term shareholders retained earnings. But the short term shareholders get only their proportion of those profits plus a terminal incremental capital gain which is the result of market forces acting on the *changed* series of cash flows (or rather reported profits in this case) resulting from the investment on behalf of the short term investors.

In order for the retention of the short term shareholders profits to be 'justified', the share of the series of capital outlays, and the resulting cash flows plus the capital gain, must be such that when discounted at the rate equal to that of other opportunities open to the shareholder they show a positive net present value. This overall policy would, of course, be applied to the aggregate net cash flows in each year and the changes in share prices resulting from these cash flows.

The immediate difficulty arises that the imposition of this restraint on behalf of the short term shareholders may operate to the detriment of the long term shareholders. For example, it could be that if very few worthwhile short term investments are available, and in order to satisfy the basic constraint, the firm would be required to accept projects which, while showing worth-while return in the short run, displayed an inadequate return in the longer term. In effect, the firm would be using these projects to transfer some of the profits that would otherwise accrue to the long term shareholders to the short term shareholders.

The same problem in a more severe form would arise if a firm tried to pursue the policy of giving both the long term and short term shareholders an equal return. This policy would require that the investments attributable to, and the cash flows and capital gains accruing to the short term shareholders, should offer the same discounted return as the same inflows and outflows relating to the long term shareholders. Again, if relatively few worth-while projects were available so that, say, the short term shareholders with the existing investment programme stood to receive a lower discounted return, the firm would be impelled to rectify this by taking on short term projects which would increase short term profitability at the expense of long term profits.

It is probable that, in principle, a firm would never accept projects showing what would otherwise be an inadequate return, simply because it would tend to make the return between short and long term shareholders more equitable. What a firm could do would be to exert pressure on those responsible for capital expenditure and other programmes affecting profitability, to look more carefully for the type of projects required to result in a more equitable distribution of gain between the different types of shareholder. In addition, a firm could distribute a greater proportion of its profits during the gestation period as an indication of its confidence in the profitability of these investments, where, as is normally the case, this greater payout would increase share prices.

It is possible that despite both these measures there may be substantial inequality of return between short term and long term shareholders or even a situation in which one of the two groups of shareholders suffers a definite loss through the retention of profits attributable to it being invested in projects which are primarily in the interests of the other group of shareholders. It seems highly probable in such a case that a firm would accept this position rather than pursue the only alternative, which would be that of taking fundamentally unacceptable projects simply in the interests of equity between the different types of shareholders. If a firm did in fact follow this policy it could well impair the soundness of the company and might well be acting against the interests of the community in general by a misallocation of resources.

The conclusion would therefore seem to be the following. First that the discounted yield return should be used to decide whether or not projects are 'acceptable' at all. (By 'acceptable' is meant acceptable to long term shareholders who are likely to be, and are here assumed to be, in a majority. Automatically any projects which were profitable in the short term without poor offsetting profits in the long term, and which would thus lead to an improvement in the position of the short term shareholders, would be accepted by this criterion.) At the later stage of looking at the aggregate cash flows and estimates of the proportion of shareholders likely to sell out in different years and estimating the share prices in those years, the returns accruing to the different categories of shareholders should be scrutinized. In the event that what is considered to be a serious inequality between the returns accruing to the different categories of shareholders emerges, then a firm should search more intensively for the types of project which would reduce the disparity in return between the different categories of shareholders, subject to the general restraint that the projects in question meet the basic criterion of being acceptable to the long term shareholders.

REFERENCE

1. A. J. MERRETT and ALLEN SYKES, 'The Rate of Interest and the Timing of Capital Projects', *The Manchester School*, September 1961.

APPENDIX A

THE DERIVATION OF COST OF CAPITAL UNDER CONDITIONS OF VERY SHORT TERM UNDERVALUATION

In Section 1 the approximate general formulae (17.2), was developed to determine the cost of capital to a firm when its shares were very temporarily undervalued, but when it was nevertheless raising equity capital wholly or partly from new shareholders. This appendix continues the analysis where Section 1 left off, and consists of the mathematical derivation of the correct formulae to which (17.2) approximates.

To proceed further we now need to consider the problem mathematically. Consider the following expression for the *change* in the old shareholders net present value brought about by raising new capital of w:

$$\frac{(s+y)}{r_2(s+w)}[A+f(w)] - \frac{A}{r_2} - (y-x) \qquad (17.5)$$

where A = net profit *on a perpetuity basis* without the new issue, i.e. the net profit of the firm's *existing* business,

    s = value of existing shares (at the new issue price),

    z = amount of the new issue subscribed by new shareholders,

    y = amount of the new issue subscribed by old shareholders,

    $w = y+z$ = total new capital subscribed,

    x = amount received in rights by old shareholders,

  $f(w)$ = net profit *on a perpetuity basis* on the new capital w, and

    r_2 = normal cost of capital to the firm and thus the cost of capital to the old shareholders.

The term in square brackets and its multiplier represent the net present value in perpetuity of the income received by the old shareholders. The A/r_2 is the present value which would accrue to the old shareholders without the new issue, and $y-x$ is the net capital (net of the amount received in rights) put up by the old shareholders as a result of the new issue.

Consider now the conditions which must obtain as regards the amount of capital raised and the return on marginal projects if the net present value of the old shareholders is to be maximized. To establish this we maximize with respect to w, the amount of new capital raised. It is then found that for the shareholders' net present value to be at a maximum the following conditions[1] must hold:

$$f'(w) = [A+f(w)]\left[\frac{1}{k} - \frac{p}{s+y}\right] + \frac{r_2k}{s+y}\left\{1 - \frac{1}{k}\left[d+z\left(1 - \frac{d}{k}\right) - pd\right]\right\} \quad (17.6)$$

where all the symbols are as defined for (17.5) save for $f'(w)$ = rate of return on the marginal project considered for inclusion in the investment programme,

$k = s+w$,
c = value of existing shares before the new issue,
$d = c+w$, and
$p = y/w$, the proportion of capital subscribed by old shareholders.

The equation assumes that the value of the rights – x in (17.5) – is determined by the formula given in Section 1(b) (*ii*) above. In the non-rights case the condition for a maximum net present value is that

$$f'(w) = [A+f(w)]\left[\frac{1}{k} - \frac{p}{s+y}\right] + \frac{pkr_2}{s+y}. \quad (17.7)$$

The equation for both cases states that, for the old shareholders' net present value to be maximized, the rate of return on the marginal project must equal the right-hand side of the respective equations. Before considering the equations further an example may help to make their numerical significance more clear.

Example 6. The basic data of the example is set out in Table 17.2 below.

Table 17.2

(in £000's)

Project	a Capital Cost	b Cumulative Capital Cost = w	c Annual Equivalent Net Profit on a Perpetuity Basis	d Total Cumulative Profit = $f(w)$ on new investment	e Marginal Return $f'(w) = c/a$
1	100	100	30·0	30·0	·30
2	40	140	10·8	40·8	·27
3	60	200	15·0	55·8	·25
4	80	280	16·0	71·8	·20
5	50	330	7·5	79·3	·15

[1] These are obtained by assuming that the conditions described in Section 1(b) (*ii*) hold as regards the market valuation of rights and maximising (17.5) with respect to w.

The market, which normally values the firm's shares on a 10% yield basis, expects that without the new issue the firm's future earnings will be £100,000 p.a. in perpetuity whereas the firm estimates them to be £200,000 p.a. The new issue gives no preferential rights to existing shareholders, and at the proposed new issue price values the existing shares at £1m (the market's capitalized value of estimated future earnings) at which price the firm estimate the true yield is 20%. The proportion of capital subscribed by the old shareholders is assumed to be constant at 25%. The market presumes the new capital will be invested to earn the same return as it estimates the existing capital is earning, i.e. 10%. The projects which the firm is considering for inclusion in its capital programme are set out in the last column of the table in descending order of their rate of return.

Figure 17.3 shows the solution to equation (17.7) for this particular case. On the horizontal axis is shown w the total amount of capital raised,

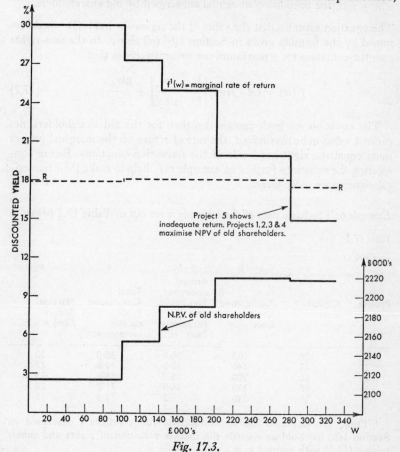

Fig. 17.3.

while the vertical axis shows the discounted yield. The line RR shows the right-hand side of equation (17.7) for successive values of w. The line marked $f'(w)$ is simply the marginal rate of return for the successive projects 1, 2, 3, 4, etc., as given in column (d) of Table 17.2. The two lines are seen to intersect at the point where $w = £280,000$. This shows that this value of w satisfies equation (17.7) and therefore that this value of w (and the series of capital products financed with this new capital) is the new capital issue which will maximize the net present value to the old shareholders. This fact is confirmed by the values of the old shareholders' net present value given as line NPV on the same figure.

We must now consider equation (17.6) in more detail. The first point to note is that for relatively small new issues, i.e. as w tends to zero the equation (17.6) is identical to (17.2). The second point to observe is that equations (17.6) and (17.7) both assume that the proportion p of the new capital coming from the old shareholders remains constant. It is quite possible in certain cases that this assumption will not hold. In such cases the factor p in these equations should be replaced by the proportion of the *marginal* amount of new capital subscribed by old shareholders. Thus in our preceding example in moving from $w = $ say $£140,000$ to $w = £200,000$ in order to obtain the $£60,000$ required finance for project 3, the value of p used in equation (17.7) to obtain the line RR in Figure 17.3 should be the proportion of this $£60,000$ contributed by old shareholders.

From an examination of the formulae and a consideration of particular cases, it is found that some useful generalizations can be made. As we have seen, where the new issue is relatively small the equations reduce to the simple general approximation (17.2). Where the issue is relatively large this will also generally suffice as good approximation as a result of off-setting factors. If all the new projects earned the same or lower rate of return as that on the existing shares (at the new issue price) then the right-hand sides of both (17.6) and (17.7) would tend to decline with w. This is illustrated for (17.6) Figure 17.4.

This depicts the right-hand side of equation (17.6) for two different rights issues, the first for a rights issue at a price equal to 50%, and the second equal to 80% of the existing share price. In both cases the existing number of shares is assumed to be 1 million and to stand at a market price of £1 each. At this price the true yield on the shares is 20% although that estimated by the market is only 10% – the normal market yield for the shares – hence the shares stand at only half their correct valuation. All the new capital is assumed to be invested at 20% into perpetuity, that is $f(w) = 0 \cdot 2w$, and 40% is assumed to be subscribed by old shareholders.

Both curves are seen to fall with increasing values of w although the fall is much less marked in the case where the new issue is at the more likely price of 80% of the existing share price. The lines more closely approximate to a horizontal straight line the nearer the new issue price is to the existing share price and the nearer the latter is to the true valuation

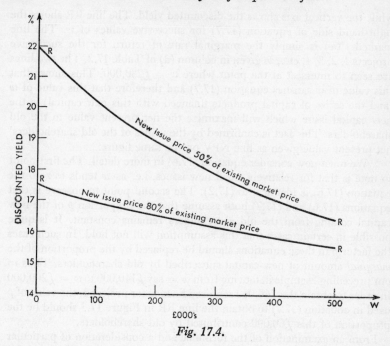

Fig. 17.4.

of the shares. In the extreme case of a rights issue where the shares are correctly valued, the line is of course an exactly horizontal straight line whatever the new issue price. Higher rates of return on the new projects – and at least some of the new projects will show such returns – will tend to arrest this decline. This is to be expected. If the new projects are very profitable and are accepted, then to the extent this is unrecognized by the market, they increase the extent to which the firm's shares are under-valued, hence increasing the rate of return which any further new project must earn to improve the new present value of the old shareholders. It is reasonable also to suppose that the proportion of new capital coming from the old shareholders will fall as the size of the new issue increases – it is certainly not likely to increase. The effect of this falling value of p is to increase the rate of return which a project must exceed before it will increase the net present value of the old shareholders. Given these off-setting tendencies formula (17.2) will generally be a quite adequate work-ing approximation providing the new issue is relatively small only or medium sized, or the degree of undervaluation is not too great.

A difficulty to which we must briefly refer is that of discontinuity. It may sometimes be the case that the firm has only a series of relatively large projects and in this case, if the curve RR of Figure 17.3 is falling relatively steeply, it may indicate as a maximum point a value of w that is impractical given that the particular project which this rate of return requires capital considerably in excess of *w*. In these cases the simplest procedure would be to make a straightforward computation of the present value of the old shareholders, from (17.5), and then determine directly from this the series of projects which gives the maximum. It may be helpful in any case *in the final stages* of any analysis to compute the net present value accruing to the old shareholders in order to ascertain the actual magnitude of gain where this needs to be weighed against imponderable factors such as the uncertainty of the estimates of the new issue price, etc.

CHAPTER EIGHTEEN

The General Principles of Valuation

Many capital budgeting problems necessitate an economically viable method of valuing assets. When a firm transfers an asset from an existing use to a new project, or when an asset is likely to outlast the project on which it will be employed, it is important as such times to be able to value the assets concerned. The same basic asset valuations are required for many other purposes such as determining insurance values and as a basis for depreciation policy. In addition, the problem of asset valuation logically interlocks with the common capital budgeting problem of determining the optimal life for assets. This chapter is concerned with developing a method of asset valuation and its applications to the problems mentioned is the subject of the next chapter. In particular the following chapter will illustrate the connections between valuation, depreciation policy in a firm's accounts and replacement of assets and concludes the analysis by setting forth an integrated depreciation valuation and replacement policy (the I.D.V.R.).

1. DEFINITION OF VALUE CONCEPTS

Throughout this chapter we shall use the following general definition of value: *The value of an asset to a firm is the sum of money which would just compensate the firm for its loss in stated conditions, given the action that will be taken by the firm to minimize this loss*. This definition is inevitably very general and much of this and the next chapter will be taken up with drawing out its implications and extending it to cover special valuation problems. Consider first the valuations (or limits to value) which under different conditions are commonly placed on assets. These values are replacement cost, resale value, and the discounted value of the future net cash flows attributable to ownership of an asset.

In the case of an asset which a firm would want to replace the upper limit to its value is set by replacement cost – providing instantaneous replacement is possible. Where, for whatever reason, an asset cannot be immediately replaced by an identical asset (or at least cannot be replaced prior to the next occasion on which it is required), its value is not adequately measured solely by reference to the installed price of a replacement. To this price must be added an allowance for the inconvenience and loss of revenue caused by being temporarily without the use of the asset. Thus if a new taxi cab is destroyed and a replacement cannot be delivered for a month, then the destroyed taxi should be valued at replacement cost plus one month's loss of net of tax earnings. This difference between value and replacement cost in such conditions will be referred to as the revenue factor. We can now rephrase our statement concerning the upper limit to asset value. Whenever a firm would replace an asset, the upper limit to its value is set by the replacement cost of a similar asset plus the revenue factor, the value of which will depend on the losses and inconvenience arising during the period between the loss of the asset and the installation of its replacement.

If replacement cost plus the revenue factor set the normal upper limit to the value of an asset, the lower limit is set by its resale value. Resale value is defined as being net of all scrapping or selling costs, and also net of any tax allowances or charges consequent upon resale. No asset can be worth less than its net disposable value, as an asset owner can always realize such a value by selling the asset. If a firm is about to sell an asset then clearly its value is its resale value.

The third assessment of value, the discounted value of the future net cash flows attributable to ownership of an asset, needs no introduction in this book. Its measurement in practice is often difficult because the net cash flows attributable to the asset are the joint product of one or more other assets. The concept however is clear enough. It should also be noted that when an asset cannot be, or will not be replaced, it is usually the sole measure of value, at least when this value exceeds resale value.

In practice it is usually the case that this discounted value significantly exceeds replacement cost. For example, whenever an asset is purchased its discounted value should be in excess of its replacement cost (i.e. the purchase price) otherwise the purchase would not be economic. For the greater part of any asset's life the discounted value of its future services will exceed the replacement cost of a similar second-hand asset. But as the asset approaches the end of its life the discounted value will fall below the replacement cost, and eventually it will also fall below resale value. When this happens it signals the end of the asset's life, and it should be disposed of. In measuring the discounted value of the services to be attributed to an asset account must be taken of the effect on its value of a newer more efficient asset. Whenever such an asset makes its appearance it reduces the value of all existing assets designed to provide the same services, and can thus shorten their economic lives. A sufficiently large increase in the relative efficiency of new assets would cause all existing assets to be scrapped at once, that is it would cause the discounted value of the services of all the existing assets to fall below their residual values now that the new asset is available. This problem of obsolescence is a complex one, and is considered more fully at the end of the next chapter.

This illustrates the significance of discounted value, because it is a comparison of this value with cost which determines whether any asset is bought, and a comparison with resale value which determines when any asset is sold. It is thus a concept which enters implicitly into every rational purchase and sale decision. While to measure it exactly is often difficult, in practice it usually suffices to know whether it significantly exceeds either replacement cost or resale value.

In the light of the definition of value previously given, let us consider the validity and usefulness of these three concepts. Which concept is applicable depends on (a) the use to which a firm intends to put the asset and (b) the policy which a firm would follow if it did not possess the asset in question. Consider each of the three values in turn.

Suppose a firm is just on the point of disposing of an asset and the asset is destroyed. In these circumstances the value lost is the resale value and no more as no earnings have been sacrificed nor any inconvenience caused. In the case where an asset has been bought new, and it is destroyed, then assuming the firm would replace it, the value lost is the replacement cost of a new asset plus the appropriate inconvenience factor. Similarly, where an asset is destroyed which the firm does not intend to replace, but which it would have continued to operate for a few more years, the value lost is the discounted net cash flow which could have been attributed to the asset including its eventual residual value when scrapped.

We have so far shown that the three common values, resale, replacement and the present value of future services from special cases of the general definition of value, given that the policy of a firm is respectively to sell, replace (with an identical asset) or forgo ownership entirely in the event of the asset being destroyed. Suppose, however, a firm's policy would be to replace an existing old asset with a possibly quite different new asset should the old asset be destroyed. Clearly the destroyed asset is hardly likely to be worth as much as the replacement cost of a new asset, especially if the new asset incorporates any improved features, but it is obviously worth more than its resale value or the firm would have sold it. Nor, assuming the asset could be replaced by a similar second-hand asset (and this alternative seldom exists in practice save for a limited range of assets such as ships, buildings, and vehicles) would this second-hand replacement cost be relevant (save as an upper limit) to determining the value lost if the most favourable action taken to redeem that loss would be to replace with a new asset. Thus, the relevant criteria for valuing the asset must be to establish exactly what net cash flows the firm would be involved in from losing the asset and replacing it with a new one.

Possession of an asset gives rise to a certain net cash flow in the future, while *not* possessing it and taking some course of action (such as buying a new asset) to minimize the effect of non-possession, gives rise to a different future net cash flow. From this it is clear that the value of the asset is the present value of the difference between the two net cash flows. As the asset under discussion will be replaced if destroyed, and as the firm's gross income will be unaffected, the difference in the net cash flows results entirely from the difference in the two streams of costs (both capital outlays and all relevant running or operating costs). Consider now the method for establishing these cost differences.[1]

To simplify the initial analysis of the two cost streams let us assume (a) that there will be a perpetual succession of replacements for the present asset, and (b) that all these replacements will have operating and capital costs etc., which are identical with one another – although they may differ from those of the existing asset. It will be shown later that these assumptions can all be relaxed to allow for greater realism without substantially impairing the conclusions.

Suppose a firm to have an existing asset whose total economic life from the time it was bought new to the time it will be replaced is z years, of which k years remain. The cost of operating this asset for k more years, then replacing it with new assets at intervals of n years thereafter, and operating those successors is given in Table 18.1 below. In this example k is taken as 3 years and n as 10 years.

[1] Another approach to this problem is given in Section 2. By making use of a simple example as well as algebraic formulae it should be more comprehensible to non-mathematical readers.

470   *The Finance and Analysis of Capital Projects*

(For convenience all cost outlays and running costs are assumed to occur end year in *all* the examples in this chapter.)[1]

A sufficient practical approximation for most purposes is to multiply the operating costs by $(1 + r/2)$, where r is the firm's cost of capital, on the assumption that operating costs arise mid-year on average and must be grossed up by half a year's 'interest'.

Table 18.1

0	1	2	3	4	13	14	23	24...etc.
Years			k	$k+1$	$k+n$	$k+n+1$	$k+2n$	$k+2n+1...$
Net Costs $-D_1$	D_2	(D_k+C-S_k)	R_1	(R_n+C-S_n)	R_1	(R_n+C-S_n)	R_1	

(C = the capital cost of a new asset replacement; S_i = the residual value of an asset when scrapped in year i of its life or in the case of the existing asset in year i of its *remaining* life; R_i = the annual cost of operating a new asset in year i of its life; and D_i = the annual cost of operating the existing asset in year i of its *remaining* life.)

Thus, up to year k the firm is involved only in the annual operating costs (including all repairs etc.) of its existing asset in producing its required output. These are denoted by D_1 to D_k. At the end of year k the old asset is sold for S_k, and a replacement costing C is bought. This new asset (and all its assumed identical successors) may show considerable operating economies compared to the existing asset being replaced, or it may give rise to a more valuable output (less rejects etc.) which can be considered as the exact equivalent of a lower operating cost. These net operating costs are denoted as R_1 for the first year of operating the replacement, R_2 for the second etc. At the end of n years the first replacement is scrapped for S_n and an identical replacement costing C is bought and this pattern is repeated every n years for ever.

A similar table can be drawn up setting out the costs the firm would be involved in if it did not possess the existing asset. This is set out in Table 18.2 below.

Table 18.2

0	1	2	...10	11	12	...20	21...etc.
Year			n	$n+1$	$n+2$	$2n$	$2n+1...$etc.
Net Costs C	R_1	R_2	(R_n+C-S_n)	R_1	R_2	(R_n+C-S_n)	R_1

[1] Where in fact operating costs are spread fairly evenly over the year – as is typically the case – then they should be converted to a year end equivalent by the methods set out in Chapter 1, Section 7.

As the firm needs the services provided by the existing asset, if it were deprived of the asset it would immediately buy another new asset. This table assumes that the asset being bought at the present time is identical to that being bought at the end of year k in Table 18.1. Similarly, all the replacements are assumed to be identical. In consequence, the cash flows of Table 18.2 are identical to those of Table 18.1 from year $k+1$ onwards. Year k is different in Table 18.1 from year 0 in Table 18.2 as the latter contains only the cash outflow C.

We have defined the present value of the asset as being the present value of the difference between the cash flows of Table 18.2 and the cash flows of Table 18.1 since this is essentially the loss in which the firm would be involved if there were an entirely uncompensated for expropriation of the old asset. To arrive at the formula for the value of the asset it will be convenient to calculate separately the present value of the cash flows of the two tables and then to subtract that of Table 18.1 from Table 18.2.

Reducing this series of net costs to a present value will be simplified if we first reduce all the operating costs R_1, R_2, etc., to their present value at the beginning of the life of the asset to which they refer and let

$$R(n) = \sum_{i=1}^{i=n} \frac{R_i}{(1+r)^i} .$$

Similarly, by reducing the residual value S_n to its present value equivalent $S_n(1+r)^{-n}$, and denoting this as $S(n)$ we can simplify the series of cost outlays. Then, as a result of these simplifications the Table 18.2 series of cash flows can be rewritten as

Table 18.3

	0	1	2	... 10	11	12	... 20	21 etc.
Years				n	$n+1$	$n+2$	$2n$	$2n+1$
Net Costs	$C+R(n)-S(n)$	0	0	$C+R(n)-S(n)$	0	0	$C+R(n)-S(n)$	0

This series is seen to be a periodic payment of $[C+R(n)-S(n)]$ every n years in perpetuity. Now the present value of any sum, say A, into perpetuity at intervals of k years beginning k years from now is given by equation (1.6) as $A/[(1+r)^k-1]$. Hence the periodic payment of $[C+R(n)-S(n)]$ beginning *one period* (i.e. n years) from now has a present value of

$$\frac{C+R(n)-S(n)}{(1+r)^n-1}.$$

As the series commences immediately with an initial payment of $[C+R(n)-S(n)]$ the total present value is

$$V(n) = [C+R(n)-S(n)] + \frac{[C+R(n)-S(n)]}{(1+r)^n-1}$$

therefore

$$V(n) = \frac{[C+R(n)-S(n)](1+r)^n}{(1+r)^n-1}.$$

hence

$$V(n) = \frac{[C+R(n)-S(n)]}{1-(1+r)^{-n}}. \tag{18.1}$$

This result can now be applied to work out the present value of the series of Table 18.1. This series consists of two parts. The first part is the series of Table 18.3 delayed k years. Hence multiplying the present value of the series of Table 18.3 by $(1+r)^{-k}$ we obtain the present value of this part of the series of Table 18.1 as:

$$\frac{[C+R(n)-S(n)](1+r)^{-k}}{1-(1+r)^{-n}}.$$

The remaining part of the series of Table 18.1 consists of the operating costs of the existing assets, D_1 to D_k, and the residual value S_k recovered at the end of year k. As before, if we take the present value of this series as

$$D(k) = \sum_{i=1}^{i=k} \frac{D_i}{(1+r)^i}, \quad \text{and} \quad \frac{S_k}{(1+r)^k}$$

as $S(k)$, the present value of the whole series of Table 18.1 can be written as:

$$V(k) = \frac{[C+R(n)-S(n)](1+r)^{-k}}{1-(1+r)^{-n}} + D(k) - S(k). \tag{18.2}$$

From the basic definition of value, the value of the existing asset is the difference between the two series, that is (18.1)–(18.2). Subtracting one from the other we obtain the value of an asset in year j of its life ($j = z-k$) as $V(j) = V(n)-V(k)$ therefore

$$V(j) = \frac{[C+R(n)-S(n)]}{1-(1+r)^{-n}} - \frac{[C+R(n)-S(n)](1+r)^{-k}}{1-(1+r)^{-n}} - D(k)+S(k)$$

therefore

$$V(j)=[C+ R(n)- S(n)]\frac{[1-(1+r)^{-k}]}{1-(1+r)^{-n}} - D(k)+ S(k) \ . \tag{18.3}$$

It can be seen that in cases where the value of the asset is fairly obvious the formula (18.3) gives the expected result. For example, if the asset has just been acquired and is brand new, the value given by the formula is exactly its replacement cost new, C, since in this case the remaining life, k, of the 'old' asset equals, n, the life of a new asset and all the remaining terms cancel out as by definition $D(k) = R(n)$, and $S(k) = S(n)$. At the end of the asset's life $k = 0$ and (18.3) results in a valuation equal to the resale value $S(k)$, since again all the terms apart from $S(k)$ cancel out.

Although we have derived (18.3) on fairly restrictive assumptions, in particular the assumption of a perpetual succession of replacements with an identical life, it will be found to hold as an accurate approximation in a wide variety of cases. For instance, the only difficulty in determining a general expression for the value of an asset where it is required for only a limited period is in determining the policy of a firm in the event of losing possession of the asset. Suppose, for example, that an asset has a normal working life of 10 years, is now 4 years old and the firm owning it expects to need this sort of asset for only a further 16 years. If the existing asset were suddenly destroyed, what would be the policy of the firm as regards replacement? One new replacement would last only 10 years – too short a period. One replacement now followed by a further replacement 10 years hence would last 20 years – too long a period. Given any specific policy, however, it is a simple matter to arrive at a valuation formula on precisely the same basis as (18.3).

It is a relatively simple matter to prove that if, where the firm requires the asset for a very limited number of years, it can acquire the asset (or its services by, say, 'leasing') for the odd number of years at a cost equal to the value of an asset with this number of years of remaining life, then the general valuation formula holds for the existing asset.[1] In the example of the firm requiring an asset for 16 years only, the formula (18.3) would hold exactly (as regards the existing asset) if 10 years hence the firm could acquire the services of a similar asset for the remaining six years costing the value of an asset with six years of life remaining as given by the valuation formula (see the next section where the relation of the formula to second-hand market values is developed). This statement can be extended further to show that the valuation formula will hold if the net present value of the services provided by the asset are equal to the value of the asset for the odd number of years. For if this were the case the firm would be no worse off if it simply declined to replace or purchase a similar second-hand asset for the odd number of years at the end of its period of use for an asset of this type (the 6 years from the 10th year onwards in the preceding example). The alternative (18.3) would also hold exactly if the firm could sell the second replacement bought new at the valuation given by (18.3) at the end of the sixth year of its life when the firm no longer has a use for it (see next section).

Recalling that we are considering costs and values several years hence, it would appear probable that one of these conditions would hold on many occasions, at least to the degree of accuracy required to make the valuation formula (18.3) a sufficiently accurate approximation to the particular special valuation formula appropriate to the special cases being considered. For these reasons we shall refer to (18.3) as the *general valuation formula*. By applying the formula a method of valuation is provided for an asset at each stage of its life under a wide range of conditions which arise in practice. Moreover, as will be shown later, this is the definition of value which (with some minor adjustments) is required for a wide range of practical purposes, including the price at which the firm should be prepared to sell and also to insure the assets (see Section 1 of next Chapter).

Having derived the general valuation formula by the cost minimization approach, we turn now to another method of derivation

---

[1] This can be proved by taking the cost arising from immediate loss of the asset as the cost of a series of new replacements plus the cost of a second-hand asset (or its services) for the remaining odd period of years. The series of costs arising from continued possession of the old asset is similarly defined where the number of years for which the asset is required is not exactly divisible by n. Taking the difference in these present costs, formula (18.3) is obtained.

based on valuing an asset to its owner for any year of its economic life. This approach, which is illustrated by a simple 2 year arithmetic example, is based on the second-hand value of an asset assuming a *perfect* second-hand market existed. It should be a more readily comprehensible approach for non-mathematicians than that developed in this section. In addition, it throws useful light on the theory of second-hand values and the connection between the general valuation formula (18.3), and sinking fund depreciation.

2. ASSESSING THE CHANGES IN AN ASSET'S VALUE OVER ITS LIFE

Most assets decline in value over time. In many cases this is largely attributable to wear and tear, and maintenance and repair costs tending to increase, while the quality of its services tend to fall. Finally, an asset may decline in value because of obsolescence, either through an improved method of making the same end product (*production* obsolescence) or because an improved substitute tends to replace the end product itself (*product* obsolescence). This section considers these effects with the exception of obsolescence which is considered in the next chapter.

a. *Valuing an Asset with Constant Operating Costs and giving a Constant Quality of Service*

i. *No residual value.* First consider the decline in value of an asset unaffected by obsolescence, rising repair costs, or a fall in the quality of services. How will such an asset fall in value over its economic life? Suppose the asset costs £210, has an economic life of 2 years and a scrap value of zero. Suppose further that there is a perfect second-hand market for the asset (which assumes perfect knowledge and no buying or selling costs) and that all buyers and sellers have an equal and constant capital cost of 10%. (It is necessary to know this cost because buying assets with different lives will lock up different amounts of capital, a factor which must be taken into account.) We can determine the value of the asset after a year by finding the equilibrium price for second-hand assets. At this price, those wishing to have the use of an asset of this type will be indifferent between buying a new asset and buying a second-hand asset. Let C_0 be the cost of the asset new, C_1 its second-hand value after 1 year and C_2 its second-hand value after 2 years (zero in this case). Then if a buyer purchases a second-hand asset the cost of a year's services from it will be simply $(C_1 - C_2)$. If a new asset is bought, however, the cost will be the initial purchase price less the second-hand value after 1 year $= (C_0 - C_1)$. But by purchasing a new asset the buyer will have locked up extra capital over the year and in so doing will have forfeited a year's income at his cost of capital. Thus the total cost of buying a new asset for a year is

$$C_0 - C_1 + rC_0$$
$$= (1+r)C_0 - C_1.$$

Similarly the total cost of owning a second-hand asset in the second year

$$= C_1 - C_2 + rC_1 = (1+r)C_1 - C_2.$$

As assets are assumed to give identical services over all their working lives the equilibrium prices must be such that the cost of owning the asset for a year is the same regardless of whether a new or second-hand asset is purchased, hence

$$(1+r)C_0 - C_1 = (1+r)C_1 - C_2$$

or

$$C_1 - C_2 = (1+r)(C_0 - C_1).$$

As $C_0 = £210$, $C_2 = 0$, and $r = 10\%$, this reduces to

$$C_1 = 1 \cdot 1(£210 - C_1)$$

therefore

$$C_1 = £110.$$

This can be seen to be the correct answer. If the asset is bought second-hand for £110, then, as it has no scrap value at the end of the year, £110 represents the cost of having the use of its services for a year. To this must be added the end year interest cost of £11 (10% of £110) representing the interest on the capital tied up in the asset – making the total cost £121. If the asset is bought new, however, it costs £100 in depreciation (the initial cost – £210 – less the value that would be recovered at the end of the year through resale – £110). But as using a new asset locks up £210 of capital for a year then to the depreciation cost must be added the 'interest' forgone at 10% = £21. Thus the total cost involved in using the new asset can be seen to be £121 also. (This can also be demonstrated by considering the present value of the cash flows involved. Purchasing a second-hand asset costs £110 now. Purchasing a new asset cost £210 but £110 could be recovered a year hence. The present value at 10% of £110 a year hence is £100. Thus the .present value cost of buying a new asset is £210 − £100 = £110, the same as for a second-hand asset.)

It can also be seen that the value of the asset is declining by the amount of a cumulative sinking fund calculated at a 10% rate. (A full discussion of sinking funds is given in Section 3a of Chapter 1.) Thus the annual sinking fund instalment necessary to recover the initial capital C_0 is simply $C_0/s_{n|r}$, see formula (1.11)

$$= \frac{£210}{s_{2|10}} = £100.$$

Subtracting this sinking fund depreciation charge from the initial capital cost £210, we get the value of the asset after 1 year, namely £110. Subtracting £100 *plus* the 'interest' of £10 accumulating in the sinking fund during the second year from this £110 value at the end of the first year, we get the value of the asset at the end of the second year, namely zero.

From the simple two year example it is clear that the decline in value each year is $(1+r)$ times the decline in value of the previous year. Hence if D_i is the decline in value of the i'th year, then $D_i = (1+r)^i D_1$. Since the asset falls in value to zero by the end of its life, the sum of D_i's must equal the full cost of the asset, that is $\Sigma(1+r)^i D_1 = C$. This can be written as $s_{n|r} D_1 = C$. From this last expression it is seen that $D_1 = C/s_{n|r}$ – the expression for the annual sinking fund payment required to amortize C over n years at the interest rate r. From this and the preceding results it is seen that the cumulative fall in value of the asset over say j years is the sum of the D_i's to date, that is

$$\sum_{i=1}^{i=j} (1+r)^i D_1 = s_{n|j} D_1.$$

The last expression is seen to be the value of the sinking fund at the end of year j thus proving the general proposition that the value of the asset at any time is its initial capital cost less the accumulated sinking fund depreciation.

As a formula for valuing the asset the result is that

$$V(j) = C - \frac{C}{s_{n|r}} s_{j|r}$$

$$= C\left[1 - \frac{(1+r)^j - 1}{(1+r)^n - 1}\right]$$

$$= C\left[\frac{1 - (1+r)^{-(n-j)}}{1 - (1+r)^{-n}}\right].$$

To avoid using the clumsy term $(n-j)$, let this term be denoted by k, that is the number of remaining years of life the asset has before it will be scrapped (see Section 1). Therefore,

$$V(j) = C\left[\frac{1 - (1+r)^{-k}}{1 - (1+r)^n}\right]. \tag{18.4}$$

Thus, when an asset gives equal services for every year of its life at no increase in cost, it is seen that the asset falls more in value each year of its life due to the effect of the 'interest' factor. In short it will give rise to a *convex* depreciation curve.

Consider now the allowance to be made in the above formula if the asset has a residual value at the end of its useful life.

ii. Allowing for residual value. Whenever the asset has a residual value S at the end of its life then it is evident that the effective capital cost in purchasing a new asset is not C, but C less the present value of the eventual residual value, that is $C - S(1+r)^{-n}$. At the end of any year j this residual value will be worth $S(1+r)^{-k}$. If we define $S(1+r)^{-n}$ as (Sn), and $S(1+r)^{-k}$ as $S(k)$ then the above formula can be rewritten as

$$V(j) = [C - S(n)]\left[\frac{1 - (1+r)^{-k}}{1 - (1+r)^{-n}}\right] + S(k). \tag{18.5}$$

Applying this to a 2 year example where $C = £331$ and $S = £121$ (making the depreciable capital £210 as before), $j = 1$, $r = 10\%$, then $V(j) = £231$ (to the nearest £). The present value of buying a new asset for a year's use is therefore $£331 - (£231/1 \cdot 1) = £221$. Similarly, the present value of buying a one year old asset for a year's use is $£231 - (£121/1 \cdot 1) = £221$ also. Hence £231 is seen to be equilibrium price of a one year old asset.

b. *Valuing an Asset with Rising Operating Costs*

The older most assets become the more costly they are to run as more maintenance is required to prevent breakdowns and repairs are needed more frequently. The quality of the service rendered may also begin to fall. It is convenient to consider all these factors as increases in operating costs per period. In the case of repairs and maintenance this is straightforward enough. In the case of a declining quality of service it is necessary to estimate the losses in which this may involve the firm. There may be increased wastage of materials, a fall in the rate of production, and possibly some direct loss of revenue or customer goodwill due to relatively inferior products. All of these should be estimated for each year the asset is kept in production.

Assuming such a schedule of operating costs by periods has been drawn up for an asset, how does this affect its value? This value can be determined as before by assuming there is a perfect second-hand market for the asset in question and determining what the second-hand values must be under equilibrium conditions. Making use of the previous example, suppose an asset costs £210 new, that it has a life of 2 years and a residual value of zero, and that its operating costs are £30 in the first year and £70 in the second year. Ignoring for the moment the effect of the cost of capital, what will be the equilibrium price of the asset after 1 year so that buyers are indifferent whether they buy new or second-hand assets?

For buyers to be indifferent between the two, the cost of owning and operating new and second-hand assets must be constant. Ignoring for the moment interest tied up in capital and any final residual value, these costs must just be depreciation and operating costs. Let C_0 = initial cost, and C_1 the unknown capital cost of a second-hand asset after 1 year, etc. and R_1 = the operating costs in year 1, and R_2 the operating costs in year 2, etc. Then

$$C_0 - C_1 + R_1 = C_1 - C_2 + R_2$$

therefore

$$£210 - C_1 + £30 = C_1 - 0 + £70$$

therefore

$$C_1 = £85.$$

This can be seen to be correct. At this value after 1 year the cost of a new asset for 1 year is £125 depreciation plus £30 operating costs $= £155$: for a second hand asset it is $£85$ depreciation plus $£70$ operating costs $= £155$ also. Thus the effect of rising operating costs is to increase the fall in the asset's value (depreciation) in the early years at the expense of the later years. It results in a *concave* depreciation curve.

It is now useful to modify this approach and to incorporate the effect of interest on the capital tied up in the two assets. Combining the equations developed in (a) above with those just developed, and assuming all costs to arise end year,[1] it is seen that

$$(1+r)C_0 - C_1 + R_1 = (1+r)C_1 - C_2 + R_2.$$

Substituting for all the known values with $r = 10\%$ therefore

$$1 \cdot 1(£210) - C_1 + £30 = 1 \cdot 1 C_1 - 0 + £70.$$

therefore

$$C_1 = £91 \text{ (to the nearest } £).$$

At this value of the asset after a year it can be seen that a buyer would be indifferent between buying a new and a second-hand asset.

A second-hand asset would cost $£91$ in depreciation plus $£70$ in operating costs, plus $£9$ in interest $= £170$ (to the nearest $£$). A new asset would cost $£119$ in depreciation, $£30$ in operating costs and $£21$ in interest, $= £170$ also.

The effect of including the allowance for the cost of capital is thus to reduce the concavity of the depreciation curve affected by using operating costs alone, although in this example the reduction is small.

The three different depreciation curves may be compared diagrammatically as follows.

In practice, for many assets, the effect of rising operating costs will more than outweigh the effect of allowing for interest on the extra capital tied up in the earlier years, and the depreciation curve will be concave, indicating that the asset gives more valuable services in the earlier years of its life than the later years.

Having considered the effect of both rising operating costs and interest on capital combined the next step is to incorporate this into the general formula being developed. When an asset is purchased new to be operated for its full life then the buyer is effectively undertaking a capital outlay plus a series of annual operating costs. Thus

[1] See the second footnote in Sub-section 1(a).

the effective capital cost is $C + R(n)$, where $R(n)$ is defined as the present value of all future operating costs (on a year end equivalent basis) over the life of the asset, that is as

$$\sum_{i=1}^{i=n} \frac{R_i}{(1+r)^i}$$

where R_i = operating costs in year i. (Where the operating costs are rising either at a linear or a compound rate, resort should be made to the short-cut formulas of Chapter 1, Section 2c.)

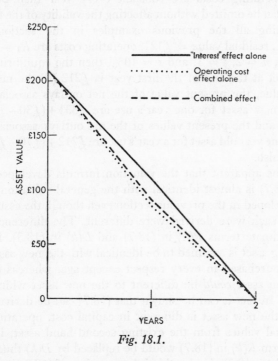

Fig. 18.1.

At the end of any year j, the firm has yet to bear the operating costs over k years, the remainder of the asset's life. These operating costs have a present value *at the end of year j* of

$$R(k) = \sum_{i=j+1}^{i=n} \frac{R_i}{(1+r)^{i-j}}.$$

Thus the valuation formula (18.4) can be modified to give the value of an asset with rising operating costs at end year j as

$$V(j) = [C+R(n)]\left[\frac{1-(1+r)^{-k}}{1-(1+r)^{-n}}\right] - R(k). \qquad (18.6)$$

And incorporating the allowance for residual value (18.5) we obtain the comprehensive valuation formula

$$V(j) = [C+R(n)-S(n)]\left[\frac{1-(1+r)^{-k}}{1-(1+r)^{-n}}\right] - R(k) + S(k). \qquad (18.7)$$

(Where operating costs are constant every year then both $R(n)$ and $R(k)$ can be omitted without affecting the validity of the formula.)

Combining all the previous examples in the section, where $C = £331$, residual value $= £121$, operating costs are $R_1 = £30$ and $R_2 = £70$, $n = 2$, $j = 1$, and $r = 10\%$, then the equilibrium value of the asset at the end of the first year is £212 (to the nearest £). At this value, the present value of the net outlays associated with buying a new asset for one year's use are $£331+(£30-£212)/1\cdot1$ $= £165\frac{1}{2}$, and the present values of the net outlays associated with buying a one year old asset for a year's use are $£212+(£70-£121)/1\cdot1$ $= £165\frac{1}{2}$ also.

It will be apparent that the valuation formula developed in this section (18.7) is almost identical with the general valuation formula (18.3) developed in the previous section even though the assumptions on which each were derived were different. The difference lies in the penultimate terms $R(k)$ in (18.7) and $D(k)$ in (18.3). In (18.7) the existing asset is assumed to be identical with the new asset which could be purchased in every respect except age, whereas in (18.3) the existing asset *could* be different to the new asset which would replace it. In fact it can be shown that (18.7) can be derived afresh assuming the new asset is different in capital cost, operating costs, and residual values from the existing second-hand asset, in which case the term $R(k)$ in (18.7) would be replaced by $D(k)$ thus making it identical to (18.3). Under this interpretation of (18.3) it gives the second-hand value of any asset in year j of its life assuming a perfect second-hand market and assuming the availability of a new asset costing C, with different operating costs and residual values. Hence we have yet another useful interpretation of the general valuation formula (18.3).

Given these two derivations of (18.3) what is their interrelationship? In Section 1 we considered how to value an existing asset which would be replaced at the end of its life by an infinite chain of replacements identical with one another. This result holds whatever prices the second-hand market gives rise to. In this section we have considered what the equilibrium second-hand price of an asset would have to be in a market with no buying or selling costs (i.e. the buying price being exactly equal to the selling price) such that any buyer who wished to have the services of such an asset for a limited period would be indifferent between the latest model new asset and any second-hand asset which was not obsolete. That two seemingly different approaches give rise to identical valuation formulae suggest there must be a link between them, and indeed there is. By assuming a perfect second-hand market for a given asset we are assuming that there is a continuing demand for assets performing the type of service of which the given asset is capable, and that as all buyers and sellers are assumed to have the same cost of capital, the value of an asset of any given age will be the same for all buyers and all sellers. For this reason, the value of an asset of any given age to any owner who requires the use of its services for only a limited period becomes identical with that of an owner who will go on replacing the asset indefinitely. But it is not a necessary condition for this result that some participants have a permanent need for the present model of the asset being valued, or indeed for the latest model available new. All the conclusions so far reached would follow if instead of a perpetual succession of identical assets it was merely the case that new assets identical to those now being used were still being purchased at the end of the life of the longest lived of the present assets.

One point needs emphasizing here. It may be objected that both valuation approaches seem to depend on there being no further obsolescence in the assets being considered. Both formulae take full account of the decline in value of existing assets brought about by the improved efficiency characteristics of the latest available new model, but make no provision for the possibility of future models (as yet unavailable) being better still and so likely to affect the value of at least some of the existing assets (the younger assets with the longer expectations of economic life) before they reach the end of their currently forecast lives. This difficulty is fully considered in the next chapter where the formulae are modified to allow for the effect of likely *future* obsolescence. But two points can be made at this stage. First, where improvements in the efficiency of future models is relatively slow (the common situation) the effect on the present value of existing assets is not usually significant bearing in mind the effect of discounting. Second, when no improved model will appear during the lifetime of the latest available model if bought new, then future obsolescence has no effect on the value of any existing assets.

One other link between the two approaches to the general valuation formula deserves brief consideration. Assuming no second-hand market exists at all, so that if an asset is destroyed prior to the end of its life the owner must replace it with a new one, we have shown in Section 1 what value the owner should place on the asset at the time it is destroyed (18.3). This value can be calculated for every year of an asset's economic life hence it gives the economically meaningful valuation or depreciation curve for any asset over its life and this indeed is one of the important uses to which the general valuation formula can be put (see Section 1 of the next chapter). In short, it represents the value at which the asset should notionally change hands at the year end. In drawing up the relevant costs of a particular year an asset owner is concerned to value depreciable assets both at the start and the end, and both prices must be economically meaningful if costs are to be measured fairly between one year and another. Thus the correct value represents the 'price' at which any asset should notionally be sold by its owner in one year, to its owner in the next year. As the owner is typically the same each year there is both complete knowledge and no buying or selling costs – the two conditions necessary for a perfect second-hand market. Hence the notional annual transfer price can be likened to the price which would prevail in a perfect second-hand market.

c. *Conclusion*

One important conclusion follows from the argument developed in this section. Where there exists a good second-hand market for any asset, second-hand prices should tend to the values where the total costs involved in owning any asset (running costs, repairs, declining efficiency, and interest on capital employed) will be constant, despite the age or model of the asset.

REFERENCES

J. C. BONBRIGHT, *Valuation of Property*, McGraw-Hill, 1937.
A. J. MERRETT and G. BANNOCK, *Business Economics and Statistics*, Hutchinson, 1962, Chapter 2.

CHAPTER NINETEEN

Valuation, Depreciation and Replacement

1. APPLICATIONS OF THE GENERAL VALUATION FORMULA

The general valuation formula developed in the previous chapter has many useful applications to business problems and it is to these we now turn, ignoring for the moment the possibility of *future* obsolescence, which is discussed in the second section of this chapter. The first three uses to be considered are calculating an asset's depreciation charges, choosing the optimal life for any asset in given conditions, and making the optimal choice of asset when alternatives exist. These three topics are considered ignoring any complications that may be introduced by tax allowances, etc. Then the effect of taxation on asset values is examined and the general valuation formula is modified to accord with the conclusions reached. In the light of this, the problems of estimating depreciation, optimal life and optimal asset choice are briefly reconsidered.

The remaining topics considered include valuations for insurance purposes, the validity of the ratio of annual profits to capital for control purposes, the effect of inflation on asset values and depreciation, and the valuation of residual assets.

a. *Calculating Annual Depreciation Charges Ignoring Tax Complications*)

One obvious use of the general valuation formula (18.3) is to draw up the likely decline in asset value over time, that is, to determine the annual depreciation charge in a meaningful way, always assuming the asset will in fact be replaced.[1]

Example 1. Consider a very simple example of an asset with an economic life of 6 years costing £1,000 and having a zero residual

---

[1] Where an asset will not be replaced, it falls in value by the decline in the present value of the future net cash flows attributable to it. Even in this case the general valuation formula will give a sufficiently accurate approximation of an asset's value under a wide variety of conditions – see Section 1 of the previous chapter.

value. The firm has a cost of capital of 8%. Tax complications will be ignored. Three variations of this example will be considered:

  (i) Constant operating costs of £100 a year;
 (ii) Constant operating costs of £100 a year plus a major repair (or replacement) of £400 at the end of year 3; and
(iii) Rising annual operating costs of £100 in year 1 rising by £25 increments to £225 in year 6.

As before, all costs are taken as being year end equivalents. Given this information, the end year values of the asset under these different conditions can be calculated and this in done in Table 19.1 below.

Table 19.1

End Year Asset Values

End Year	(i) Constant Operating Costs	(ii) Constant Operating Costs Plus £400 Repair End Year 3	(iii) Rising Operating Costs
	£	£	£
0	1,000	1,000	1,000
1	864	795	807
2	717	574	623
3	558	335	450
3*	n.a.	735	n.a.
4	386	508	288
5	200	264	138
6	0	0	0

*(Asset value after £400 repairs expenditure).

The same information is perhaps better displayed in graphical form and this is done in Figure 19.1 below. In addition, the depreciation curve resulting from the use of the straight line depreciation method is shown for comparison.

Where operating costs (including increasing inefficiency) are constant (V_1), the asset declines more steeply with every passing year by the amount of a cumulative sinking fund, giving rise to a convex curve. The higher a firm's cost of capital the more convex the curve. Where operating costs rise sufficiently steeply over the asset's life to overcome the effect of 'interest' on capital invested (V_4), the asset declines more steeply in its early years and less steeply later on (as in the case of vehicles), resulting in a concave curve. The more operating costs increase with age, the more concave the curve. These two curves appear on either side of the straight line depreciation curve V_2), probably the most common method of depreciation. It is interesting to note that for the straight line depreciation 'curve' to accord with the economically meaningful curve, operating costs would have to be increasing by exactly the same amount as interest accumulating in a notional sinking fund.

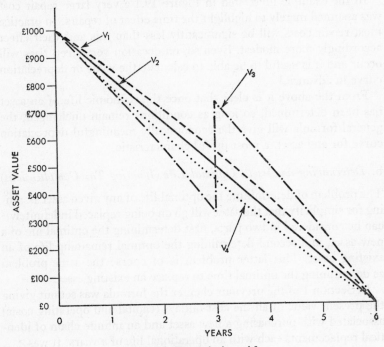

Fig. 19.1. Depreciation with

$V_1 = $ *No repair cost constant operating costs* - - - - - - - - -

$V_2 = $ *Straight line depreciation* ——————

$V_3 = $ *Depreciation allowing for £400 repair cost end year 3* · — · — · — · —

$V_4 = $ *Depreciation with no repair cost but rising operating cost* ......

The curve V_3 shows a steeper decline than the others prior to the heavy repair cost outlay, and at the time of the repair cost it rises vertically by £400 to reflect the enhanced value of the repairs. Thereafter it falls more steeply again. This conforms with common sense as any asset is more valuable after a major overhaul or replacement. Also this steep rise accords with the conduct of accountants who make provisions for major repairs in advance, capitalize the repairs when they occur, and then write them off over the remainder of the asset's lives.

In the example illustrated in Figure 19.1 a very large repair cost was assumed merely to highlight the time effect of repairs. In practice most repair costs will be significantly less than this and their effect accordingly more modest. Even so, on occasion very steep rises will occur and it is useful to be able to calculate the value or depreciation curve in advance.[1]

From the above it is clear that once the economic life of an asset has been determined, so long as conditions remain unchanged, the general formula will give the economically meaningful depreciation curve for any asset, a most useful characteristic.

b. *Determining an Asset's Optimal Life (Ignoring Tax Complications)*

The problem of determining the optimal life of any given asset assuming for simplicity that the asset will go on being replaced indefinitely,[2] can be considered in two parts, first determining the optimal life of a new asset, and second determining the optimal remaining life of an existing asset. This latter problem is of course the same problem as determining the optimal time to replace an existing asset.

In Section 1 of the previous chapter the formula was set out giving the present value of all the cost outlays (capital and operating costs) associated with purchasing a new asset and an infinite chain of identical replacements each with an operational life of n years. It was

$$V(n) = \frac{[C + R(n) - S(n)]}{1 - (1+r)^{-n}} . \tag{18.1}$$

---

[1] The curve V_1 represents the decline in value of an asset when no repair costs arise. If such an asset did have an *unforeseen* breakdown at the end of the third year (i.e. a breakdown which did not normally occur in assets of this type) that cost £400, then this would not cause the depreciation curve of the asset to conform to V_3. An asset cannot increase in value by the amount of the repair cost above the value of a similar asset. The value of such an asset prior to the repair is £400 less than the V_1 curve – i.e. £158. The repair expenditure merely restores the damaged asset to the same value as similar assets which have not broken down, – i.e. to £558.

[2] Where an asset will not be replaced at all, its optimal life is that which maximizes the present value of its future net cash flow. Where the asset will be followed by a limited number of replacements the method here developed will apply providing that the conditions described at the end of Section 1 of the previous chapter obtain.

The optimal life of such a new asset is the value of *n* which reduces this formula to a minimum. As operating costs (which have been defined in the previous chapter to include any decline in operating efficiency, decline in quality of output etc.) typically rise with age, it seldom pays to run an asset for its maximum *physical* or *technical* life. (The terms 'physical' and 'technical' life, which are here taken as synonymous, are defined below.) Given a schedule of annual repair and operating costs and annual residual values, it is possible to determine when it pays to scrap an asset and replace it with a new one.

If repair and operating costs are constant, then however small the initial cost of an asset, there would be no point in ever replacing it unless it became obsolescent (this term is defined in Section 2b below). But in the absence of obsolescence, the important factor determining the optimal life of most assets is the eventual rise in repair and operating costs. 'Physical' life or 'technical' life are terms to which it is difficult to attach a precise meaning. If cost is no object, most assets could be continuously repaired and have a virtually infinite life, although it might result in every single part of the asset being physically replaced at regular intervals. But for most assets this continuous replacement and indefinite life are quite impractical. There comes a time when the repairs are so large and complicated to carry out that, without doing any cost estimates, it is clear that the repairs are not justified and may even prove impossible to carry out. When an asset reaches this condition, which is easier to recognize in practice than to describe in the abstract, we shall refer to it as having reached the end of its physical or technical life. In short, we are really stating that almost without exception most industrial assets do not have continuously constant repair and operating costs. The time comes when an asset will fail to function without a major repair, and it is this factor, an eventually rising repair cost, which determines the maximum useful life, that is, the maximum physical or technical life, of almost any asset.

Given the necessary information on repair and operating costs the computational task of determining optimal life is relatively simple. It is merely necessary to sketch out the value of (18.1) at, say, three year intervals beginning with the year in which repair and operating costs begin to rise significantly, to narrow down the period in which the minimum occurs, and then make year by year calculations in this area. Where an asset will require a major repair or replacement outlay in a given year, it is worth comparing the life of the asset for the period ending just *prior* to this expenditure, with the full physical life of the asset to determine whether such expenditure would be justified. In some cases it is possible to foresee the pattern of repair cost fairly definitely in advance, for example in the case of trucks, ships, aircraft, etc., or where a policy of scheduled preventive maintenance is followed. In other cases only the general outline of repair costs can be foreseen before an asset is purchased or in the early years of its life.

The two main purposes for which the optimal life will be needed are first in determining the time span of, and hence partly the desirability of, new investment involving the new assets. Secondly it may be required in determining the value of an existing asset (the method of doing this is described below).

It will be found that in both these uses of the optimal life, the results are relatively insensitive to errors in the data required for estimating optimal life, hence no great refinement of forecasting will normally be required.

To calculate the optimal remaining life for an existing asset is just a bit more difficult. It involves finding how many more years it pays to go on operating an existing asset before replacing it with a new asset or a *newer* second-hand asset. We will here consider only the problem of replacing with a new asset as this is the most common situation.[1] Before the optimal life of an existing asset can be determined, the optimal life of its new replacement must first be determined as this effects the time when it pays to scrap the existing asset. Thus the same steps just outlined for calculating the optimal life of a new asset must be gone through for the replacement. This done, the optimal life for an existing asset is the value of k which minimizes the formula (18.2) developed in Section 1 of the previous chapter, that is which minimizes the value of

$$V(k) = \frac{[C + R(n) - S(n)](1+r)^{-k}}{1 - (1+r)^{-n}} + D(k) - S(k) \qquad (18.2)$$

[1] Where an active second-hand market exists and a firm is prepared to consider purchasing second-hand, the optimal life of the optimal replacement must first be determined – i.e. to determine if a second-hand asset of any given age, run for a given period, is a better purchase than a new asset run for its optimal period. This is found in the same manner just described for new assets – i.e. using (18.1) but where C is taken as the price of a second-hand asset. Should it prove to be the case that second-hand replacement is the optimal policy, the problem of valuing the existing asset is identical to that involved in replacing it with a new asset. Only the value of $[C + R(n) - Sn]$ will be different.

As before, the curve of (18.3) for an asset's full remaining physical life should be plotted where the resale value of the asset in any year of its remaining physical life is likely to be greater than the value calculated from the general valuation formula. This can only arise if the resale value of the asset prior to the end of its physical life is likely to exceed the final residual value significantly. Where this is not the case, the next step is to consider repair and operating costs. Where these are fairly constant the optimal life, as in the case of a new asset, will equal physical life. If operating costs rise steeply, then values of k should be calculated from this time to the end of the asset's physical life.

All the above presupposes that, in choosing an asset's optimal life, full consideration is given to the intensity with which the asset is utilized where the possibility of different rates of utilization exist. For most assets maximum utilization will be the optimal choice, providing the repair and maintenance costs involved are not prohibitive – see reference [1].

c. *Determining the Optimal Choice of Asset* (*Ignoring Tax Complications*)

A common capital budgeting problem is that of choosing between plants with different capital and operating costs, capacity, and durability. The procedure is quite straightforward where the asset is required to produce a fairly *constant* output. Suppose a firm is choosing between putting up a large single plant of type A, or two smaller plants of type B with different cost characteristics. To choose between them the firm must first apply the formula (18.1) to each alternative separately to determine their optimal lives. It will be apparent that the optimal choice of asset cannot be determined without first determining the optimal life of the alternative assets or combinations of assets. This done, it should choose whichever alternative results in the lower value of $V(n)$. If there are more than two choices the formula should be applied to each separate alternative, and the one giving the lowest value of $V(n)$ should be chosen.

Where output is likely to increase the problem becomes one of choosing the best initial plant (which can be considered to have a constant output and can therefore be chosen by the method just indicated) coupled with choosing the optimal time and the optimal plant for expansion, a subject already dealt with in Chapter 9.

d. *The Effect of Taxation on Asset Values*

i. Effect on the general valuation formula. So far in the development of the formulae we have ignored the effect of taxes. But the purchase of assets usually gives rise to capital allowances, operating costs can usually be set off against taxable income, and the disposal of an asset usually has tax consequences also. These complications are all fairly straightforward to handle. All the factors in the general valuation formula (18.3) developed in the previous chapter should be considered on a net of tax basis. (In this, and what follows, we are, of course, assuming that there will always be sufficient taxable income to enable all tax allowances to be fully offset.)

The initial capital outlay C is usually unaffected because any capital allowances to which it gives rise usually occur with a time lag. These capital allowances should be considered annually when they arise and be netted off against annual operating costs. Thus if an asset costs £1,000 and gives rise to a capital allowance of £100 a year for 10 years, and a tax rate of 40% is in force collected one year in arrears, these annual operating costs should be reduced by £40 for 10 years, starting with the annual equivalent operating costs, at the end of the first year. The annual operating costs, which will usually be allowable expenses for tax purposes, should also be taken on a net of tax basis, allowing for any delay in tax payments.[1] Finally, the residual value of the asset should be taken net of any balancing charges or allowances, again corrected for any delay in tax payments or refunds.[1]

From this it will be apparent that tax allowances may have a significant bearing on asset valuation. That this is so is in conformity with common sense. Assets with identical capital and operating costs, lives and residual values but which attract different tax allowances will not be of identical cost to a firm. Thus henceforth all the terms in the general valuation formula will be deemed to be on a full net of tax basis, including, of course, the cost of capital.

Consider now the effect of taxation upon asset values. Ignoring

---

[1] Full accuracy requires that the delay in tax payments be allowed for. Thus if operating costs are £80, and tax 40% collected a year later, then the first operating cost should be considered as £80, and all subsequent ones as £80 − £32 = £48, with a refund of £32 the year after the asset is disposed of. In practice such pedantic accuracy will seldom be justified and all costs can be taken net of tax as though taxes were collected without any delay. Thus operating costs could be considered as £48 net throughout.

for the moment any capital or residual balancing allowances (or charges), the effect on operating costs alone is to reduce their net burden. Where operating costs are constant this will have no effect on the valuation curve over an asset's life: where operating costs are rising with time, however, being able to offset them against tax will attenuate their effect, that is, it will raise the valuation curve throughout its length and reduce it concavity.

As regards residual values, where the residual value equals the written down value for tax purposes there will be no effect. Where the residual value exceeds the tax value a balancing charge will be levied which will, therefore, reduce the net realized residual value and so lower the valuation curve throughout its length. Conversely, where the tax value exceeds the residual value the firm can claim a balancing allowance which increases the net realized residual value and so raises the valuation curve throughout its length.

Capital allowances vary in their effect. Where the capital allowance is constant for every year, it is akin to the tax allowance on constant operating costs, that is, it has no effect on the valuation curve. Where the capital allowances are heavier in the early years (as is typically the case with investment and initial allowances and use of the reducing balance method) then if this exactly offsets rising net of tax operating costs, the effect is to raise the valuation curve to the shape resulting from the interest effect alone, that is to raise the curve to a convex shape. Where capital allowances are heavily concentrated in the early years of an asset's life in such a way that combining such allowances with net of tax operating costs results in the annual burden of running the asset *increasing* over the asset's life, the valuation curve is depressed into a more concave shape. To be more exact, the valuation curve drawn on the basis of annual asset values *after* claiming the capital allowance becomes more concave. The actual valuation curve falls vertically by the amount of tax saved just after the receipt of the tax saving allowance. The effect is exactly opposite to that given by a repair outlay – see curve V_3 of Figure 19.1. To illustrate this effect let us reconsider Example 1 given in a. above. Suppose we consider case *iii*, which assumed rising operating costs but no major repair outlays. Assume this case (curve V_4 of Figure 19.1) represented the depreciation curve calculated on the basis of net of tax operating costs but with no capital allowances. Let us now consider the effect of capital allowances concentrated in the early years of the asset's life. Suppose the firm owning the asset is subject to a 50% tax rate and could write off 60% of the capital cost at the end of the first year, and the remaining 40% at the end of the second. (This is an extreme example but it highlights the effect of the capital allowances.) This is equivalent to reducing operating costs by two lump sum payments of £300 at the end of the first year and £200 at the end of the second. The effect is illustrated below by curve V_5 in Figure 19.2 - curve V_4 is reproduced for comparison.

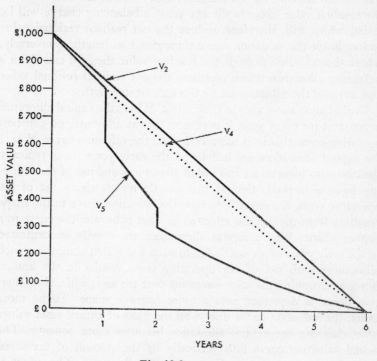

Fig. 19.2.

V_2 = *Straight line depreciation* ————

V_4 = *Depreciation with rising*
net of tax operating costs
but no capital allowances ......

V_5 = *Depreciation curve*
V_4 *with capital allowances* ————

The effect of the capital allowances is clearly seen from the comparison of the curve V_5 with V_4. When the capital allowances are received (end years 1 and 2) the curve falls vertically, and its overall concavity is increased.[1]

From the above analysis it is apparent that taxes can have a very significant bearing on asset valuation and one that should be specifically taken into account, especially the effect of capital allowances when these are concentrated in the early years of an asset's life.

ii. Resale values and insurance values. Two further points need to be noticed as regards the effect of taxation on asset values. The first point is that balancing allowances may make the actual price at which a firm would be indifferent to selling an asset differ from the value given by the general valuation formula (18.3). For this latter value is the sum which a firm would require to compensate it for complete and *uncompensated* loss of an asset. But some compensation for total loss of an asset will often follow in the shape of balancing allowances – the right to set off against tax the written down tax value of the asset. Thus, if a firm sold an asset for the value given by (18.3), this would exactly compensate it for loss of the asset if there were no further tax consequences whatever – i.e. if the sum received was not taxed and all capital allowances on the old asset ceased forthwith. This in fact would only occur if the asset were sold for exactly its written down tax value. If it were sold for more than this then the Revenue would tax this difference. Hence if the valuation given by (18.3) is £X in excess of its written down tax value, the asset would need to be sold for its written down tax value plus £X grossed up to offset the taxation which would be levied on this sum. This total sum is the true resale value of the asset to the firm. Thus if (18.3) gave a value less than the written down tax value of the asset then the resale value say P of the asset to the firm in any year j would be

$$P = \frac{V(j) - tW}{1 - t}. \tag{19.1}$$

[1] It should be noticed that the curve V_5 does not fall by the full value of the tax refunds – £300 at the end of year 1 and £200 at the end of year 2 – but by these amounts less the operating costs – £100 for year 1 and £125 for year 2. This arises because the operating costs are the year-end equivalents of the continuous weekly or monthly operating costs and are thus deemed to occur end year when they have the same effect as a repair cost at that time. Had the curve been drawn to show continuous values as opposed to year end values, at the end of years 1 and 2 the curve would have fallen by the full amount of the tax refund.

where t is the tax rate and W the written down tax value of the asset. This resale value of the asset follows immediately from the proposition that the resale price plus the balancing allowance must equal the value of the asset $V(j)$, that is $V(j) = P + t(W - P)$. (It is assumed that the resale price would not exceed the initial capital cost since any *excess* of the former over latter would not normally be subject to a balancing allowance. The adjustment required to allow for the few cases when this assumption is not true should be fairly obvious.)

This analysis now enables the insurance values of assets to be determined, that is, the sums at which to insure assets where a firm's policy is to insure them for the sums which (net of all tax effects) would just compensate the firm for the loss of the assets. The tax authorities normally treat insurance compensation for destruction of assets as if the assets had been sold for the sum in question and the normal tax balancing charges or allowances follow. From this it will be clear that the correct insurance values for the assets are precisely the same values as determined in (19.1) above for resale values.

We turn now to reconsidering depreciation policy, the choice of optimal asset life, and the optimal choice of assets in the light of the effects of taxation.

e. *The Consequences of Allowing for the Taxation Effect on Asset Values*

i. Depreciation policy. As tax allowances affect the economic value of an asset to the firm it is necessary to calculate the valuation curve or depreciation curve using the general valuation formula (18.3) on a net of tax basis. This, as will be shown later (Sub-section f), is the correct asset value for use in control purposes when comparing annual *net of tax* profits to capital employed.

It may be objected that allowing for tax effects, particularly capital allowances, results in distortion of an asset's 'real' value. Thus the asset, represented by curve V_5 in Figure 19.2 above, is just as efficient at the beginning of year 2 as at the end of year 1 despite the steep fall in 'value' which it is suggested occurs between the two times separated by a single day. The answer is that while the asset is *technically* as efficient as before its *economic* value to the firm is less because by the beginning of the second year the first year's capital allowance has been claimed (i.e. the tax authority has effectively made a payment to the firm) and once claimed cannot be claimed again. The firm is exactly as well off on both dates. At the end of year 1 it has an asset worth £X: at the beginning of year 2 it has the same asset now worth £Y plus a sum of money just claimed from the tax authority of £$(X - Y)$. In short, assets should be depreciated to reflect the effect of claimed capital allowances.

An important advantage of using this depreciation procedure is that it would automatically fulfil – and to a considerably more effective degree – the intended function of tax equalization accounts, namely that of removing from the profit and loss account the 'distorting' effect due to tax depreciation differing from accounting depreciation. The proposed depreciation procedure will automatically 'smooth out' of income the distorting effects of irregular tax depreciation (as well as both the British type investment allowances and American tax credit) by varying the depreciation charged thus maintaining the return on capital constant (see Example 3 below).

ii. The choice of optimal life. It will be found that on a significant number of occasions that the use of the optimizing formulas (18.1) and (18.2) on a net of tax basis will affect the optimal life of both new and existing assets. In most cases where this happens the effect will be to reduce optimal asset life, particularly in the case where large capital allowances are concentrated in the early years of an asset's life. This can be seen by comparing curves V_4 and V_5 in Figure 19.2. Curve V_5, which reflects the effect of large capital allowances in the first two years of an asset's life, is significantly lower than curve V_4. This suggests that if the firm were to be deprived of the asset any time after the second capital allowance had been claimed (i.e. from the beginning of year 3 onwards) its loss would be much less than if there were no capital allowances. This arises because the net cost of buying a capital asset is significantly reduced (by the present value of the capital allowances) and where the operating costs of such an asset rise steeply with age it can pay to scrap the asset earlier to avoid the last years of high operating costs. That this is so can be demonstrated by taking an extreme case. If an asset attracted an immediate 100% capital allowance and the effective tax rate was 99%, the net cost to the owner would be 1% of the asset's price. If operating costs rose every year an asset was used, then as soon as the operating costs of a year exceeded those of the previous year by more than 1% of the asset's price, it would pay to scrap that asset and replace it with a new one.

That this effect is not confined to extreme cases can be illustrated from the following three year example.

Example 2. A new asset costs £1,000, has a physical life of 3 years, and a zero scrap value. Its *net of tax* annual operating costs (year end equivalents) are £100 for years 1 and 2 and £500 for the third and final year. The firm's net of tax cost of capital is 8%. When there are no tax allowances it can be shown that the optimal life of the asset is the full 3 years.

Substituting in

$$V(n) = \frac{[C+R(n)-S(n)]}{1-(1+r)^{-n}} \tag{18.1}$$

for values of n of 2 and 3 (there is no need to consider 1 year as the operating costs do not rise in year 2, thus indicating the optimal life cannot be less than 2 years — see b above), it is seen that $V(3) = £7,640$ compared to $V(2) = £8,250$, thus proving 3 years is the optimal life. But if the firm has an effective tax rate of 50% and is allowed to write off 50% of capital cost at the end of year 1, $33\frac{1}{3}\%$ at the end of year 2, and the balance $16\frac{2}{3}\%$ at the end of year 3 the optimal life becomes 2 years instead of 3, thus proving that capital allowances can affect optimal life. The arithmetic of the example is as follows.

Using formula (18.1) and combining the annual net of tax allowances with the annual operating costs it transpires that $V(2) = £5,170$ while $V(3) = £5,500$. (This presumes that for a 2 year life the firm could claim by the end of year 3 a balancing allowance for the $16\frac{2}{3}\%$ written down value of the asset at the end of year 2.)

iii. The optimal choice of asset. In the same way as the valuation formulae affect the optimal life of assets, so too can they affect the optimal choice of assets, and all such calculations need to be done on the full net of tax bases.

f. *The Annual Return on Capital Ratio*

One of the most common profitability tests applied both to firms in general and to parts of firms to indicate general efficiency is the annual return on capital employed ratio. We have already had occasion (Chapter 7, Section 4) to point out the weakness of this test based as it is on the results of a single year and often arbitrary asset valuations. It is, however, an interesting property of the general valuation formula (18.3) that it results in the meaningful valuation of assets for use in computing this ratio. Thus, if an asset gives rise to a *constant* gross cash flow (i.e. constant revenue or gross earnings) in every year of its life then it can be shown that the return on capital ratio will also be constant indicating that profitability is constant from year to year.

Example 3. Consider a simple two year example (used in Section 2 of the previous chapter), where an asset costs £331, has a two year life, a residual value of £121, operating costs equivalent to £30 at the end of the first year and £70 at the end of the second and where the relevant cost of capital is 10%. This resulted in the asset being valued by (18.3) at £212 at the end of the first year, thus giving rise to depreciation of £331 − £212 = £119 in the first year, and of £212 − £121 = £91 in the second year. Suppose this asset gave rise to a gross cash flow equivalent to £215 at the end of each of the two years. It emerges that the ratio of net profit to capital employed is 20% for both years as long as the cumulative sinking fund is included in the capital employed and the annual sinking fund interest is added to the net cash flow.

Years		1		2
Gross Cash Flow		£215		£215
Less (i) Depreciation	−£119		−£91	
(ii) Operating Costs	− 30		− 70	
		−149		−161
		£66		£ 54
Plus Sinking Fund Interest		—		12*
Annual Profit		£66		£ 66
Capital Employed −				
Year end Asset Value		£212		£121
Plus Sinking Fund		119		210
Total		£331		£331
Annual Return on Capital		£66/£331 = 20%		£66/£331 = 20%

* (10% on first year's depreciation of £119 = £12 to nearest £. This could of course be subtracted from the second year's depreciation charge of £91 to give the *net* sinking fund instalment of £79 that would then have to be set aside to recover the *depreciable* portion of the original investment, i.e. the initial cost less residual value = £331 − £121 = £210.)

The reason for this is apparent. Using the general valuation formula (18.3) has resulted in total annual costs being constant (see previous chapter, Section 2). As total capital employed consists of the written down value of the asset plus the accumulated sinking fund, it too must be a constant equal to the initial capital investment.

Hence, where the gross cash flow is also constant, profit must also be constant, and with it the ratio of net profit to capital.

It may be objected that, in practice, sinking funds are not set up and so to include a cumulative sinking fund in with capital employed, and its 'interest' in with profits is not possible. This ignores, however, that depreciation funds generated by a project are typically re-invested in the business. As long as these funds are invested to yield an average return equal to the cost of capital, the result is equivalent to setting up a sinking fund, and so the interpretation given above still holds.

All this can be shown to apply when the further complications such as taxes on profits and capital allowances (which affect asset valuation – see e. above) are taken into account. Thus, if annual *net of tax* profits are compared with capital employed with all assets valued according to the general valuation formula, it will indicate a constant profitability where the firm's gross of tax earnings are also constant. If it is desired to use the annual return on capital ratio this is the way it should be calculated to avoid distortions due merely to the method of calculation used. To use gross of tax profits and assets valued on a depreciation basis which ignores the effect of using operating costs, 'interest' charges on capital employed, capital allowances, and residual values, etc., is to risk fluctuations in the control data on profitability due more to arithmetic than economics.

g. *Allowing for Residual Asset Values*

Included in the net cash flows attributable to any project should be the residual value of any assets outlasting the project (Chapter 2, Section 2a, *ii*). There will be occasions when these residual values are quite significant as will often be the case when land and property are involved. Further, the importance of residual values in the risk assessment of potentially short lived projects has also been stressed (Chapter 6, Section 4b, *ii*).

The estimation of a residual asset value depends on the use to which a firm will put the asset when freed from the existing project. Where it has no further use for it, the asset is worth its net resale value only. But where the firm can make use of the asset, its value should be calculated from the general valuation formula (18.3). This will, of course, involve estimating the optimal life of the asset as set out in b. and e, *ii* above. This 'value in use' should then be compared to the net resale value, and whichever is higher will represent the residual value of the asset to the firm.

2. EXTENSIONS OF THE ANALYSIS

In this concluding section we shall consider some extensions of the analysis developed in this and the preceding chapter, and in particular the problems of allowing for changing capital and operating costs on successive asset replacements and for the impact of *future* obsolescence.

a. *Changing Costs*

Changes in the capital or operating costs of an asset are evidently identical in their economic impact on the life and value of an asset whether the changing costs are due to simple price changes on an otherwise unchanged asset, or due to changes in the technical character of the asset. For this reason the analysis developed in this sub-section overlaps with that of obsolescence which is considered subsequently.

Consider first the case of inflation in the capital and operating cost of an asset. In the absence of technical obsolescence the most common situation will probably be where the capital cost of an asset increases at approximately the same rate as the general price level— i.e. continues at about the same price in *real* terms. Capital allowances, however, are fixed in the money terms of the date on which the asset was acquired. In strict accuracy, therefore, to make optimal life calculations, etc. in real terms, it is necessary (see Chapter 6, Section 7) to increase the rate of discount applied to the capital allowances by the rate of inflation. This, however, will rarely be of any numerical importance, and so this refinement can usually be ignored. As regards operating costs it is quite possible where they include a large proportion of labour costs that they will increase at a faster rate than the general price level. This will make each new replacement begin life with a higher level of operating cost in real terms than its predecessor. If over the life of an asset operating and repair costs remained constant but the life of the asset was simply terminated by the need for a major repair, this inflation in operating and repair costs will not affect the asset's optimal life since these increased costs cannot be reduced by switching to a new asset. Where an asset has *progressively* increasing repair and operating costs over its life and this gradual rise brings about the end of the asset's economic life, inflation in these costs will tend to shorten its economic life. For in this case the difference in repair costs (recalling that it is these differences which determine the economic life) will be progressively increasing each year in real terms because they are growing at a faster rate than the general price level.

It is, of course, possible that the cost of an asset will rise relative to the general price level while the annual operating and repair costs merely remain constant in real terms. In so far as this occurred it would evidently tend to make replacements less and less frequent because of their increasing capital cost. Similarly, if the real cost of an asset fell consistently this would evidently tend to make replacements occur more often, as is demonstrated by the motor car over the last half century. (Other factors were important here too, but evidently the increasing cheapness of cars had a major influence.)

Where it is possible to estimate these changes in costs to a useful degree of accuracy (or where it simply desired to ascertain the sensitiveness of the result to specific assumptions) the following approximation can be used. It can be shown that the effect of assuming a succession of identical replacements *after* the first replacement (that is, the asset currently being purchased new) will generally involve negligible error where an asset has a life of, say, 10 years or more. Given this basis, *the optimal life* of the *second* replacement asset can be estimated on the assumption that it will be followed by a succession of identical replacements with all the particular characteristics that it is estimated will obtain with this second replacement. Having determined this optimal life by the methods already developed above, it is a simple matter to add to the present value of this series the present value arising from the first replacement, and determine by trial the life of the first replacement which minimizes this *combined* present value. Formally the optimal life m of the first asset, that is, the asset being bought now is, the value of m which minimizes

$$V(m, n) = C_1 + D(m) - S(m) + \frac{V(n)}{(1+r)^m} \qquad (19.2)$$

where $V(m, n)$ is the present cost of the whole series of replacements;

C_1 is the capital cost of the first replacement asset to be purchased;

m is the optimal life of this first asset;

$D(m)$ is the present value of operating and repair costs of this first asset;

$S(m)$ is the present cost of the resale value of this first asset at the end of m years; and

$V(n)$ is as defined in (18.3) above, namely the present cost of the second and succeeding generations of assets operated for their *optimal* life at the start of the series.

A useful point to note about (19.2) is that the optimal life of all the assets is *independent* of the price paid for the first of the series (as this is constant for all values of m and n), and depends merely on the future residual values and the *future* costs that will be incurred after the first asset has been acquired. The reason for this is not hard to see. Assuming residual values to be constant, the only costs which can be minimized are the future costs; these can be minimized by taking the optimal time to replace the eventually cheaper assets as yet not acquired. The first asset's capital cost (C_1) in (19.2), is not a *future* cost but an *immediate* inescapable cost that cannot in any way be minimized by varying the optimal life of future assets. Another way of appreciating the same point is to reflect that immediately after purchasing the asset the price paid for it would be of historical interest only and irrelevant to determining its optimal life. But its optimal life must remain the same as previously calculated, hence the cost of the first asset must have been irrelevant to determining its optimal life in the first place. It is the capital cost of the subsequent replacements that are relevant.

The following example illustrates some of these points and the application of (19.2).

Example 4. Suppose a firm is considering acquiring an asset (which will continue to be replaced indefinitely) which has an initial capital cost (C_1) of £10,000, and annual net of tax operating costs (end year equivalents) estimated at £1,000 for the first four years of its life, rising by £250 a year for every year thereafter due to increasing repairs and inefficiencies. It is estimated that the manufacturer will be able to bring the price of this model down to £7,000 some five years hence. The residual values of all the models are assumed to be zero. Given these facts, and assuming the firm's cost of capital is 8% net of tax, what is the optimal life of the first asset?

To answer this question we must first apply (18.1) in the normal way to the data given on the second asset costing £7,000 to determine its optimal life. This is found to be 9 years, and $V(n) = V(9) = £30,682$. Putting this result and the data on the first asset into (19.2) we must determine the value of m which minimizes the following expression:

$$V(m, n) = \pounds 10,000 + R(m) + \frac{\pounds 30,682}{1 \cdot 08^m}$$

with the minimum value of m being fixed, of course, at 5 years, the time at which the cheaper model will be available. The value of m minimizing the above is found to be 9 years also. This confirms the proposition previously noted that where residual values are constant in future (as they are in this example where the residual values of all of the assets are assumed to be zero), and the operating costs on all future assets are identical to one another and to those of the asset currently being purchased, the optimal life of the first or current asset is equal to the optimal life of all the future identical replacements. The capital cost of the first asset is quite irrelevant because, given that the firm wishes to purchase currently an asset of this type to be replaced indefinitely, it is inescapable.

It should be noted that, if the capital cost of all future replacements is expected to remain constant at the price of the current asset ($\pounds 10,000$), the optimal life of the current and all subsequent assets would be 11 years. Thus the 30% fall in capital costs makes it worth replacing the asset, and all its successors, two years earlier.

The results of the above calculations are only an approximation which depends on the validity of using the formula (18.1) to assess the cost of all subsequent replacements, that is, depending on the validity of the assumption that all the assets purchased after the current asset will have identical costs, etc., to one another. A check on the importance of this assumption is to calculate the percentage of the present value of future costs arising from the current asset together with its first replacement as a proportion of total future costs including all the subsequent replacements. It is found in this case to be 75%, thus clearly indicating the relative unimportance of the subsequent replacements to the accuracy of the result found.

The data provided from this approximation readily extends to provide valuations of the new asset throughout its life. In the same way that the general valuation formula (18.3) was found by taking $V(n) - V(k) = V(j)$, in the present case $V(j)$ represents the value of the first of the series of assets in the j'th year.

Once the optimal life of the first asset has been determined, it is then possible to determine its value to the firm throughout its economic life assuming the data remain constant. This is done by determining what action the firm would take if deprived of the first asset. Until the cheaper new asset (i.e. cheaper in capital cost and/or operating costs) becomes available the firm would have to replace with a new asset with costs identical to the existing asset. In these circumstances the value of the first asset in any year j of its life in this period would be

$$V(j) = V(m, n) - D(k) + S(k) - \frac{V(n)}{(1+r)^k} \qquad (19.3)$$

where $V(m, n)$ is as defined by (19.2),[1] $V(n)$ is the present value of the new series of replacements by the cheaper new asset as used in (19.2) and defined by (18.1), and k is defined as $(m-j)$ on the assumption that at the end of k years the firm would be able to replace with the cheaper new asset. Once the cheaper new asset is available (assuming it pays to continue to operate the existing asset rather than scrap it at once) then the value of the existing asset becomes

$$V(j) = V(n) - D(k) + S(k) - \frac{V(n)}{(1+r)^k}$$

which is the same as (18.3).

(The extensions to cover other choices, e.g. replacing with a second-hand asset to bridge the gap before the cheaper new asset is available, should be apparent.)

b. *Obsolescence*

For our purposes we may broadly define obsolescence as any change in the technical characteristics of new assets which enhances their value relative to old assets. We are primarily concerned here with *production* or technical obsolescence as opposed to *product* obsolescence although the latter type of obsolescence differs only in its complexity from production obsolescence. For example, the value to a firm of body dies designed to produce a particular model of car, when this model has been partly superseded by a rival's new model, can still be computed by the methods developed above. Essentially the poor selling qualities of the old assets result in a loss of profits which can be regarded as an increased cost of the 'old' assets compared with new assets (new body dies to produce a new model).

---

[1] It should be noted that where it would pay to scrap the existing asset sooner if the cheaper new asset could be made available sooner, and then the value of $V(m, n)$ would need recalculating.

To deal with this subject exhaustively would be outside the compass of this book and we shall only attempt a few generalizations which may aid order of magnitude thinking about this complex subject. From the general definition of value (and all too familiar experience) the effect of improved operating or selling characteristics (where these are not offset by increased costs) is to cause a fall in the value of an existing asset since the gains from immediate purchase of a new asset are increased by its improved characteristics. For this reason, of course, the economic life of existing assets will be reduced. Similarly, the economic life of the new asset will be reduced in turn if further improvements are made. Where obsolescence takes the form of a new capital process of lower initial capital cost, its effect is of course, identical to that of a simple reduction in the price of the old assets which were formerly being produced, and this situation has already been discussed in a. above. Another aspect of obsolescence is the reductions in operating and repair costs of successive generations of assets. Given estimates of the likely cost characteristics of the second generation of assets it is quite simple to cope with the problem of valuation and determining optimal life by the approximative method of the previous section. The following example illustrates the approach.

Example 5. Suppose a firm is considering purchasing an asset, which it will continue to replace indefinitely, which has an initial capital cost, C_1, of £7,000. Annual (year end equivalent) net of tax operating costs are as for the previous example *4* in a. above, namely £1,000 for the first four years rising by £250 a year for every subsequent year due to increasing repairs and inefficiencies. It is forecast that an improved model of this asset will be available in five years time with the same capital cost of £7,000, but with improved operating characteristics such that annual operating costs will be £500 less in *every* year of the asset's life compared to the current model. The residual values of all the models are assumed to be zero. Given these facts, and assuming the firm's cost of capital is 8% net of tax, what is the economic life of the first asset?

In the absence of an improved model the economic life of the first asset would be 9 years, as worked out previously using (18.1). But the existence of an improved model may well effect this. To find out if this is so the first step is to determine the optimal life of the forecast improved model available five years hence assuming, as before, that it will be replaced by models identical to it in all respects (i.e. costs, etc.). Using (18.1), this optimal life is found to be 9 years also, and the value of $V(n) = V(9) = £24,430$.

(It is interesting to note that the optimal life of the improved model, assuming no further improvements, is identical to what the optimal life of the existing model would be assuming no further improvements in its successors. This results from the fact that *relative* increase in operating costs with time is the same in both cases.)

Having determined the optimal life of the new model, the optimal life for the existing model is found from inserting the relevant data in (19.2) and determining the value of m which minimizes the expression, with the minimum value of m being, of course, 5 years, the time from which the new model will be available. Thus, substituting into (19.2) we obtain:

$$V(m, n) = £7,000 + R(m) + \frac{£24,430}{1 \cdot 08^m}.$$

The value of m which minimizes the above is 7 years. It is also found that the capital and operating costs of the first asset plus the first replacement by an asset of the new type account for 73% of the total present value of the total costs of the whole series of perpetual replacements. From this it is clear that the optimal life for the first asset will be very insensitive to changes in the cost characteristics of the replacements subsequent to the first asset of the new type. Where the rate of technical improvement (measured by its economic importance) follows certain regular patterns, it is possible to develop a general formula for the cost of the series of replacement assets and for the value of existing assets. The simplest case is that of what we shall call linear obsolescence. This is where assets show a continuing and constant reduction in operating costs with each successive generation of assets. In this situation if each year assets have operating costs £a less than those of the preceding year the operating costs of an asset 10 years old would be $10a$ less than assets currently available.[1]

Generally it is, of course, impossible to predict the pattern of cost obsolescence further than the next generation of assets – beyond saying that whatever the pattern of obsolescence it must ultimately slow down or stop or the cost of owning and operating the asset will become negative! Given this, and the overwhelming importance of the first and second generation of assets in determining optimal

---

[1] A formula for this case is given in reference (2).

life and valuation, it is preferable to concentrate attention on the first generation replacement, using the approximation (19.2), rather than rely on unfounded perpetual extrapolation of past trends.

It is also important to be careful not to overestimate the importance of obsolescence as a factor affecting asset valuation and optimal life. The effect of obsolescence on optimal life depends to a large degree on the pattern of repair and operating costs, including any fall in the quality of output. It may be that such costs are so decisively the effective limiting factor on an asset's life that obsolescence has no effect whatever. This will be seen fairly obviously if we take the case of an asset with no *rising* repair or operating costs but whose otherwise perpetual life was reduced to, say, 20 years by obsolesence. If, however, it is assumed that a major repair is required, say, in the 10th year such that even without the technical improvements in new assets it is cheaper (in terms of immediate capital outlay) to buy a new asset than repair the old a firm will obviously scrap the existing asset in its 10th year. Thus obsolescence, which, in the absence of *rising* repair and operating costs, would be a potent factor determining the economic life of the asset, may effectively be forestalled by the decisive importance of major repairs.

Again it is important in assessing obsolescence not to be misled by the extreme cases of major obsolescence: the exceptional events in this case can seem very normal from the mere fact that the exceptional events are remembered when the more commonplace are forgotten.

3. AN INTEGRATED DEPRECIATION, VALUATION AND REPLACEMENT POLICY – (IDVR)

The past two chapters have been concerned with establishing and demonstrating the detailed economic logic of asset valuation, depreciation and replacement, given the requisite cost information estimates. This has enabled us to see the logical structure of the problem more clearly and to assess the likely importance of errors in the relevant data. At this stage we can draw together the threads of discussion and consider an administrative procedure for an integrated depreciation, valuation and replacement policy (henceforth referred to as IDVR) with the limited information normally available.

The reliability of the cost data estimates will of course vary appreciably from asset to asset. For many assets (particularly those with fairly active second hand markets), such as most types of commercial vehicles, ships and aircraft, fairly complete and reliable estimates can be made. For other assets it may not be possible to do more than guess at some increasing pattern of costs with the assets' lives being terminated at some estimated future date by 'unforeseen' factors (e.g. major repairs or obsolescence). For an asset of the first type we recommend using the appropriate formula to establish its estimated optimal remaining life together with the present valuation and the appropriate related annual depreciation charges associated with this life. For an asset of the second type we would recommend initially using the best available intuitively estimated maximum life, and employing this in the appropriate formulae to calculate the present valuation and the appropriate related annual depreciation charges.

The computations involved can be performed cheaply and conveniently on a computor using a simple standard programme. This enables the IDVR procedure to be used for the routine purpose of producing depreciation charges for the annual accounts. The data on the individual assets should be revised at, say, 5–7 year intervals (a shorter period might be appropriate for some types of assets) in the light of the lastest cost estimates, and *ad hoc* whenever a major new development indicates an asset might profitably be replaced earlier than previously foreseen. This procedure, which is equivalent to ranging shots at a constantly moving target, enables a firm systematically to 'home in' on the optimal date for replacing its assets thus maintaining its assets at peak economic efficiency. Further it results in realistic asset valuations and depreciation policies, abolishing the need for time consuming tax equalization accounts and making for more meaningful statements of reported income.

REFERENCES

1. DAVID SOLOMONS, 'The Determination of Asset Values', *Journal of Business*, Volume XXXV, January 1962.
2. A. J. MERRETT and G. BANNOCK, *Business Economics and Statistics*, Chapter 2, Hutchinson, 1962.

Appendix Table A

Appendix Table A   The Present Value of 1

$$v_{n|r} = (1+r)^{-n}$$

Year	1	2	3	4	5	Percentage 6	7	8	9	10
1	0.990099	0.980392	0.970874	0.961538	0.952381	0.943396	0.934579	0.925926	0.917431	0.909091
2	0.980296	0.961169	0.942596	0.924556	0.907029	0.889996	0.873439	0.857339	0.841680	0.826446
3	0.970590	0.942322	0.915142	0.888996	0.863838	0.839619	0.816298	0.793832	0.772183	0.751315
4	0.960980	0.923845	0.888487	0.854804	0.822702	0.792094	0.762895	0.735030	0.708425	0.683013
5	0.951466	0.905731	0.862609	0.821927	0.783526	0.747258	0.712986	0.680583	0.649931	0.620921
6	0.942045	0.887971	0.837484	0.790315	0.746215	0.704961	0.666342	0.630170	0.596267	0.564474
7	0.932718	0.870560	0.813092	0.759918	0.710681	0.665057	0.622750	0.583490	0.547034	0.513158
8	0.923483	0.853490	0.789409	0.730690	0.676839	0.627412	0.582009	0.540269	0.501866	0.466507
9	0.914340	0.836755	0.766417	0.702587	0.644609	0.591898	0.543934	0.500249	0.460428	0.424098
10	0.905287	0.820348	0.744094	0.675564	0.613913	0.558395	0.508349	0.463193	0.422411	0.385543
11	0.896324	0.804263	0.722421	0.649581	0.584679	0.526788	0.475093	0.428883	0.387533	0.350494
12	0.887449	0.788493	0.701380	0.624597	0.556837	0.496969	0.444012	0.397114	0.355535	0.318631
13	0.878663	0.773033	0.680951	0.600574	0.530321	0.468839	0.414964	0.367698	0.326179	0.289664
14	0.869963	0.757875	0.661118	0.577475	0.505068	0.442301	0.387817	0.340461	0.299246	0.263331
15	0.861349	0.743015	0.641862	0.555265	0.481017	0.417265	0.362446	0.315242	0.274538	0.239392
16	0.852821	0.728446	0.623167	0.533908	0.458112	0.393646	0.338735	0.291890	0.251870	0.217629
17	0.844377	0.714163	0.605016	0.513373	0.436297	0.371364	0.316574	0.270269	0.231073	0.197845
18	0.836017	0.700159	0.587395	0.493628	0.415521	0.350344	0.295864	0.250249	0.211994	0.179859
19	0.827740	0.686431	0.570286	0.474642	0.395734	0.330513	0.276508	0.231712	0.194490	0.163508
20	0.819544	0.672971	0.553676	0.456387	0.376889	0.311805	0.258419	0.214548	0.178431	0.148644
21	0.811430	0.659776	0.537549	0.438834	0.358942	0.294155	0.241513	0.198656	0.163698	0.135131
22	0.803396	0.646839	0.521893	0.421955	0.341850	0.277505	0.225713	0.183941	0.150182	0.122846

23	0·795442	0·634156	0·506692	0·405726	0·325571	0·261797	0·210947	0·170315	0·137781	0·111678
24	0·787566	0·621721	0·491934	0·390121	0·310068	0·246979	0·197147	0·157699	0·126405	0·101526
25	0·779768	0·609531	0·477606	0·375117	0·295303	0·232999	0·184249	0·146018	0·115968	0·092296
26	0·772048	0·597579	0·463695	0·360689	0·281241	0·219810	0·172195	0·135202	0·106393	0·083905
27	0·764404	0·585862	0·450189	0·346817	0·267848	0·207368	0·160930	0·125187	0·097608	0·076278
28	0·756836	0·574375	0·437077	0·333477	0·255094	0·195630	0·150402	0·115914	0·089548	0·069343
29	0·749342	0·563112	0·424346	0·320651	0·242946	0·184557	0·140563	0·107328	0·082155	0·063039
30	0·741923	0·552071	0·411987	0·308319	0·231377	0·174110	0·131367	0·099377	0·075371	0·057309
31	0·734577	0·541246	0·399987	0·296460	0·220359	0·164255	0·122773	0·092016	0·069148	0·052099
32	0·727304	0·530633	0·388337	0·285058	0·209866	0·154957	0·114741	0·085200	0·063438	0·047362
33	0·720103	0·520229	0·377026	0·274094	0·199873	0·146186	0·107235	0·078889	0·058200	0·043057
34	0·712973	0·510028	0·366045	0·263552	0·190355	0·137912	0·100219	0·073045	0·053395	0·039143
35	0·705914	0·500028	0·355383	0·253415	0·181290	0·130105	0·093663	0·067635	0·048986	0·035584
36	0·698925	0·490223	0·345032	0·243669	0·172657	0·122741	0·087535	0·062625	0·044941	0·032349
37	0·692005	0·480611	0·334983	0·234297	0·164436	0·115793	0·081809	0·057986	0·041231	0·029408
38	0·685153	0·471187	0·325226	0·225285	0·156605	0·109239	0·076457	0·053690	0·037826	0·026735
39	0·678370	0·461948	0·315754	0·216621	0·149148	0·103056	0·071455	0·049713	0·034703	0·024304
40	0·671653	0·452890	0·306557	0·208289	0·142046	0·097222	0·066780	0·046031	0·031838	0·022095
41	0·665003	0·444010	0·297628	0·200278	0·135282	0·091719	0·062412	0·042621	0·029209	0·020086
42	0·658419	0·435304	0·288959	0·192575	0·128840	0·086527	0·058329	0·039464	0·026797	0·018260
43	0·651900	0·426769	0·280543	0·185168	0·122704	0·081630	0·054513	0·036541	0·024584	0·016600
44	0·645445	0·418401	0·272372	0·178046	0·116861	0·077009	0·050946	0·033834	0·022555	0·015091
45	0·639055	0·410197	0·264439	0·171198	0·111297	0·072650	0·047613	0·031328	0·020692	0·013719
46	0·632728	0·402154	0·256737	0·164614	0·105997	0·068538	0·044499	0·029007	0·018984	0·012472
47	0·626463	0·394268	0·249259	0·158283	0·100949	0·064658	0·041587	0·026859	0·017416	0·011338
48	0·620260	0·386538	0·241999	0·152195	0·096142	0·060998	0·038867	0·024869	0·015978	0·010307
49	0·614119	0·378958	0·234950	0·146341	0·091564	0·057546	0·036324	0·023027	0·014659	0·009370
50	0·608039	0·371528	0·228107	0·140713	0·087204	0·054288	0·033948	0·021321	0·013449	0·008519

Appendix Table A

Appendix Table A The present value of 1

$$v_{n|r} = (1+r)^{-n}$$

Percentage

Year	11	12	13	14	15	16	17	18	19	20
1	0·900901	0·892857	0·884956	0·877193	0·869565	0·862069	0·854701	0·847458	0·840336	0·833333
2	0·811622	0·797194	0·783147	0·769468	0·756144	0·743163	0·730514	0·718184	0·706165	0·694444
3	0·731191	0·711780	0·693050	0·674972	0·657516	0·640658	0·624371	0·608631	0·593416	0·578704
4	0·658731	0·635518	0·613319	0·592080	0·571753	0·552291	0·533650	0·515789	0·498669	0·482253
5	0·593451	0·567427	0·542760	0·519369	0·497177	0·476113	0·456111	0·437109	0·419049	0·401878
6	0·534641	0·506631	0·480319	0·455587	0·432328	0·410442	0·389839	0·370432	0·352142	0·334898
7	0·481658	0·452349	0·425061	0·399637	0·375937	0·353830	0·333195	0·313925	0·295918	0·279082
8	0·433926	0·403883	0·376160	0·350559	0·326902	0·305025	0·284782	0·266038	0·248671	0·232568
9	0·390925	0·360610	0·332885	0·307508	0·284262	0·262953	0·243404	0·225456	0·208967	0·193807
10	0·352184	0·321973	0·294588	0·269744	0·247185	0·226684	0·208037	0·191064	0·175602	0·161506
11	0·317283	0·287476	0·260698	0·236617	0·214943	0·195417	0·177810	0·161919	0·147565	0·134588
12	0·285841	0·256675	0·230706	0·207559	0·186907	0·168463	0·151974	0·137220	0·124004	0·112157
13	0·257514	0·229174	0·204165	0·182069	0·162528	0·145227	0·129892	0·116288	0·104205	0·093464
14	0·231995	0·204620	0·180677	0·159710	0·141329	0·125195	0·111019	0·098549	0·087567	0·077887
15	0·209004	0·182696	0·159891	0·140096	0·122894	0·107927	0·094888	0·083516	0·073586	0·064905
16	0·188292	0·163122	0·141496	0·122892	0·106865	0·093041	0·081101	0·070776	0·061837	0·054088
17	0·169633	0·145644	0·125218	0·107800	0·092926	0·080207	0·069317	0·059980	0·051964	0·045073
18	0·152822	0·130040	0·110812	0·094561	0·080805	0·069144	0·059245	0·050830	0·043667	0·037561
19	0·137678	0·116107	0·098064	0·082948	0·070265	0·059607	0·050637	0·043077	0·036695	0·031301
20	0·124034	0·103667	0·086782	0·072762	0·061100	0·051385	0·043280	0·036506	0·030836	0·026084
21	0·111742	0·092560	0·076798	0·063826	0·053131	0·044298	0·036991	0·030937	0·025913	0·021737
22	0·100669	0·082643	0·067963	0·055988	0·046201	0·038188	0·031616	0·026218	0·021775	0·018114

23	0.090693	0.073788	0.060144	0.049112	0.040174	0.032920	0.027022	0.022218	0.018299	0.015095
24	0.081705	0.065882	0.053225	0.043081	0.034934	0.028380	0.023096	0.018829	0.015377	0.012579
25	0.073608	0.058823	0.047102	0.037790	0.030378	0.024465	0.019740	0.015957	0.012922	0.010483
26	0.066314	0.052521	0.041683	0.033149	0.026415	0.021091	0.016872	0.013523	0.010859	0.008735
27	0.059742	0.046894	0.036888	0.029078	0.022970	0.018182	0.014421	0.011460	0.009125	0.007280
28	0.053822	0.041869	0.032644	0.025507	0.019974	0.015674	0.012325	0.009712	0.007668	0.006066
29	0.048488	0.037383	0.028889	0.022375	0.017369	0.013512	0.010534	0.008230	0.006444	0.005055
30	0.043683	0.033378	0.025565	0.019627	0.015103	0.011648	0.009004	0.006975	0.005415	0.004213
31	0.039354	0.029802	0.022624	0.017217	0.013133	0.010042	0.007696	0.005911	0.004550	0.003511
32	0.035454	0.026609	0.020021	0.015102	0.011420	0.008657	0.006577	0.005009	0.003824	0.002926
33	0.031940	0.023758	0.017718	0.013248	0.009931	0.007463	0.005622	0.004245	0.003213	0.002438
34	0.028775	0.021212	0.015680	0.011621	0.008635	0.006433	0.004805	0.003598	0.002700	0.002032
35	0.025924	0.018940	0.013876	0.010194	0.007509	0.005546	0.004107	0.003049	0.002269	0.001693
36	0.023355	0.016910	0.012279	0.008942	0.006529	0.004781	0.003510	0.002584	0.001907	0.001411
37	0.021040	0.015098	0.010867	0.007844	0.005678	0.004121	0.003000	0.002190	0.001602	0.001176
38	0.018955	0.013481	0.009617	0.006880	0.004937	0.003553	0.002564	0.001856	0.001347	0.000980
39	0.017077	0.012036	0.008510	0.006035	0.004293	0.003063	0.002192	0.001573	0.001132	0.000816
40	0.015384	0.010747	0.007531	0.005294	0.003733	0.002640	0.001873	0.001333	0.000951	0.000680
41	0.013860	0.009595	0.006665	0.004644	0.003246	0.002276	0.001601	0.001129	0.000799	0.000576
42	0.012486	0.008567	0.005898	0.004074	0.002823	0.001962	0.001368	0.000957	0.000671	0.000472
43	0.011249	0.007649	0.005219	0.003573	0.002455	0.001692	0.001170	0.000811	0.000564	0.000394
44	0.010134	0.006830	0.004619	0.003135	0.002134	0.001458	0.001000	0.000687	0.000474	0.000328
45	0.009130	0.006098	0.004088	0.002750	0.001856	0.001257	0.000854	0.000583	0.000398	0.000273
46	0.008225	0.005445	0.003617	0.002412	0.001614	0.001084	0.000730	0.000494	0.000335	0.000228
47	0.007410	0.004861	0.003201	0.002116	0.001403	0.000934	0.000624	0.000418	0.000281	0.000190
48	0.006676	0.004340	0.002833	0.001856	0.001220	0.000805	0.000533	0.000355	0.000236	0.000158
49	0.006014	0.003875	0.002507	0.001628	0.001061	0.000694	0.000456	0.000300	0.000199	0.000132
50	0.005418	0.003460	0.002219	0.001428	0.000923	0.000599	0.000390	0.000255	0.000167	0.000110

Appendix Table A   The present value of 1

$$v_{n|r} = (1+r)^{-n}$$

Year	Percentage									
	21	22	23	24	25	26	27	28	29	30
1	0·826446	0·819672	0·813008	0·806452	0·800000	0·793651	0·787402	0·781250	0·775194	0·769231
2	0·683013	0·671862	0·660982	0·650364	0·640000	0·629882	0·620001	0·610352	0·600925	0·591716
3	0·564474	0·550707	0·537384	0·524487	0·512000	0·499906	0·488190	0·476837	0·465834	0·455166
4	0·466507	0·451399	0·436897	0·422974	0·409600	0·396751	0·384402	0·372529	0·361111	0·350128
5	0·385543	0·369999	0·355201	0·341108	0·327680	0·314882	0·302678	0·291038	0·279931	0·269329
6	0·318631	0·303278	0·288781	0·275087	0·262144	0·249906	0·238329	0·227374	0·217001	0·207176
7	0·263331	0·248589	0·234782	0·221844	0·209715	0·198338	0·187661	0·177636	0·168218	0·159366
8	0·217629	0·203761	0·190879	0·178907	0·167772	0·157411	0·147765	0·138778	0·130401	0·122589
9	0·179859	0·167017	0·155187	0·144280	0·134218	0·124930	0·116350	0·108420	0·101086	0·094300
10	0·148644	0·136899	0·126168	0·116354	0·107374	0·099150	0·091614	0·084703	0·078362	0·072538
11	0·122846	0·112213	0·102576	0·093834	0·085899	0·078691	0·072137	0·066174	0·060745	0·055799
12	0·101526	0·091978	0·083395	0·075673	0·068719	0·062453	0·056801	0·051699	0·047089	0·042922
13	0·083905	0·075391	0·067801	0·061026	0·054976	0·049566	0·044725	0·040390	0·036503	0·033017
14	0·069343	0·061796	0·055122	0·049215	0·043980	0·039338	0·035217	0·031554	0·028297	0·025398
15	0·057309	0·050653	0·044815	0·039689	0·035184	0·031221	0·027730	0·024652	0·021936	0·019537
16	0·047362	0·041519	0·036435	0·032008	0·028147	0·024778	0·021834	0·019259	0·017005	0·015028
17	0·039143	0·034032	0·029622	0·025813	0·022518	0·019665	0·017192	0·015046	0·013182	0·011560
18	0·032349	0·027895	0·024083	0·020817	0·018014	0·015607	0·013537	0·011755	0·010218	0·008892
19	0·026735	0·022865	0·019580	0·016788	0·014412	0·012387	0·010659	0·009184	0·007921	0·006840
20	0·022095	0·018741	0·015918	0·013538	0·011529	0·009831	0·008393	0·007175	0·006141	0·005262
21	0·018260	0·015362	0·012942	0·010918	0·009223	0·007802	0·006609	0·005605	0·004760	0·004048
22	0·015091	0·012592	0·010522	0·008805	0·007379	0·006192	0·005204	0·004379	0·003690	0·003113
23	0·012472	0·010321	0·008554	0·007101	0·005903	0·004914	0·004097	0·003421	0·002860	0·002395

24	0·010307	0·008460	0·006955	0·005726	0·004722	0·003900	0·003226	0·002673	0·002217	0·001842
25	0·008519	0·006934	0·005654	0·004618	0·003778	0·003096	0·002540	0·002088	0·001719	0·001417
26	0·007040	0·005684	0·004597	0·003724	0·003022	0·002457	0·002000	0·001631	0·001333	0·001090
27	0·005818	0·004659	0·003737	0·003003	0·002418	0·001950	0·001575	0·001274	0·001033	0·000839
28	0·004809	0·003819	0·003038	0·002422	0·001934	0·001547	0·001240	0·000996	0·000801	0·000645
29	0·003974	0·003130	0·002470	0·001953	0·001547	0·001228	0·000977	0·000778	0·000621	0·000496
30	0·003284	0·002566	0·002008	0·001575	0·001238	0·000975	0·000769	0·000608	0·000481	0·000382
31	0·002714	0·002103	0·001633	0·001270	0·000990	0·000774	0·000605	0·000475	0·000373	0·000294
32	0·002243	0·001724	0·001328	0·001024	0·000792	0·000614	0·000477	0·000371	0·000289	0·000226
33	0·001854	0·001413	0·001079	0·000826	0·000634	0·000487	0·000375	0·000290	0·000224	0·000174
34	0·001532	0·001158	0·000877	0·000666	0·000507	0·000387	0·000296	0·000226	0·000174	0·000134
35	0·001266	0·000949	0·000713	0·000537	0·000406	0·000307	0·000233	0·000177	0·000135	0·000103
36	0·001046	0·000778	0·000580	0·000433	0·000325	0·000244	0·000183	0·000138	0·000104	0·791 4*
37	0·000865	0·000638	0·000472	0·000349	0·000260	0·000193	0·000144	0·000108	0·809 4*	0·608 4
38	0·000715	0·000523	0·000383	0·000282	0·000208	0·000153	0·000114	0·843 4*	0·627 4	0·468 4
39	0·000591	0·000429	0·000312	0·000227	0·000166	0·000122	0·895 4*	0·659 4	0·486 4	0·360 4
40	0·000488	0·000351	0·000253	0·000183	0·000133	0·966 4*	0·704 4	0·515 4	0·377 4	0·277 4
41	0·000403	0·000288	0·000206	0·000148	0·000106	0·767 4	0·555 4	0·402 4	0·292 4	0·213 4
42	0·000333	0·000236	0·000167	0·000119	0·851 4*	0·609 4	0·437 4	0·314 4	0·227 4	0·164 4
43	0·000276	0·000193	0·000136	0·961 4*	0·681 4	0·483 4	0·344 4	0·245 4	0·176 4	0·126 4
44	0·000228	0·000159	0·000111	0·775 4	0·544 4	0·383 4	0·271 4	0·192 4	0·136 4	0·969 5
45	0·000188	0·000130	0·900 4*	0·625 4	0·436 4	0·304 4	0·213 4	0·150 4	0·106 4	0·746 5
46	0·000156	0·000107	0·732 4	0·504 4	0·348 4	0·242 4	0·168 4	0·117 4	0·818 5	0·574 5
47	0·000129	0·873 4*	0·595 4	0·407 4	0·279 4	0·192 4	0·132 4	0·914 5	0·634 5	0·441 5
48	0·000106	0·716 4	0·484 4	0·328 4	0·223 4	0·152 4	0·104 4	0·714 5	0·492 5	0·339 5
49	0·878 4*	0·587 4	0·393 4	0·264 4	0·178 4	0·121 4	0·820 5	0·558 5	0·381 5	0·261 5
50	0·726 4	0·481 4	0·320 4	0·213 4	0·143 4	0·958 5	0·645 5	0·436 5	0·295 5	0·201 5

* The final digit is the power of 10 by which the given tabular value has to be divided.

Appendix Table A   The present value of 1

$$v_{n|r} = (1+r)^{-n}$$

Year	Percentage									
	31	32	33	34	35	36	37	38	39	40
1	0·763359	0·757576	0·751880	0·744269	0·740741	0·735294	0·729927	0·724638	0·719424	0·714286
2	0·582717	0·573921	0·565323	0·556917	0·548697	0·540657	0·532793	0·525100	0·517572	0·510204
3	0·444822	0·434789	0·425055	0·415610	0·406442	0·397542	0·388900	0·380507	0·372354	0·364431
4	0·339559	0·329385	0·319590	0·310156	0·301068	0·292310	0·283869	0·275730	0·267880	0·260308
5	0·259205	0·249534	0·240293	0·231460	0·223014	0·214934	0·207204	0·199804	0·192720	0·185934
6	0·197866	0·189041	0·180672	0·172731	0·165195	0·158040	0·151243	0·144786	0·138647	0·132810
7	0·151043	0·143213	0·135843	0·128904	0·122367	0·116206	0·110397	0·104917	0·099746	0·094865
8	0·115300	0·108495	0·102138	0·096197	0·090642	0·085445	0·080582	0·076027	0·071760	0·067760
9	0·088015	0·082193	0·076795	0·071789	0·067142	0·062828	0·058819	0·055092	0·051626	0·048400
10	0·067187	0·062267	0·057741	0·053574	0·049735	0·046197	0·042933	0·039922	0·037141	0·034572
11	0·051288	0·047172	0·043414	0·039980	0·036841	0·033968	0·031338	0·028929	0·026720	0·024694
12	0·039151	0·035737	0·032642	0·029836	0·027289	0·024977	0·022875	0·020963	0·019223	0·017639
13	0·029886	0·027073	0·024543	0·022266	0·020214	0·018365	0·016697	0·015190	0·013830	0·012599
14	0·022814	0·020510	0·018453	0·016616	0·014974	0·013504	0·012187	0·011008	0·009949	0·008999
15	0·017415	0·015538	0·013875	0·012400	0·011092	0·009929	0·008896	0·007977	0·007158	0·006428
16	0·013294	0·011771	0·010432	0·009254	0·008216	0·007301	0·006493	0·005780	0·005149	0·004591
17	0·010148	0·008918	0·007844	0·006906	0·006086	0·005368	0·004740	0·004188	0·003705	0·003280
18	0·007747	0·006756	0·005898	0·005154	0·004508	0·003947	0·003460	0·003035	0·002665	0·002343
19	0·005914	0·005118	0·004434	0·003846	0·003339	0·002902	0·002525	0·002199	0·001917	0·001673
20	0·004514	0·003877	0·003334	0·002870	0·002474	0·002134	0·001843	0·001594	0·001379	0·001195
21	0·003446	0·002937	0·002507	0·002142	0·001832	0·001569	0·001345	0·001155	0·000992	0·000854
22	0·002630	0·002225	0·001885	0·001598	0·001357	0·001154	0·000982	0·000837	0·000714	0·000610
23	0·002008	0·001686	0·001417	0·001193	0·001005	0·000848	0·000717	0·000606	0·000514	0·000436

24	0.001533	0.001277	0.001066	0.000890	0.000745	0.000624	0.000523	0.000439	0.000370	0.000311
25	0.001170	0.000968	0.000801	0.000664	0.000552	0.000459	0.000382	0.000318	0.000266	0.000222
26	0.000893	0.000733	0.000602	0.000496	0.000409	0.000337	0.000279	0.000231	0.000191	0.000159
27	0.000682	0.000555	0.000453	0.000370	0.000303	0.000248	0.000203	0.000167	0.000138	0.000113
28	0.000520	0.000421	0.000341	0.000276	0.000224	0.000182	0.000149	0.000121	0.990 4*	0.810 4*
29	0.000397	0.000319	0.000256	0.000206	0.000166	0.000134	0.000108	0.878 4*	0.712 4	0.578 4
30	0.000303	0.000241	0.000193	0.000154	0.000123	0.986 4*	0.791 4*	0.636 4	0.512 4	0.413 4
31	0.000232	0.000183	0.000145	0.000115	0.911 4*	0.725 4	0.578 4	0.461 4	0.369 4	0.295 4
32	0.000177	0.000139	0.000109	0.856 4*	0.675 4	0.533 4	0.422 4	0.334 4	0.265 4	0.211 4
33	0.000135	0.000105	0.818 4*	0.639 4*	0.500 4	0.392 4	0.308 4	0.242 4	0.191 4	0.151 4
34	0.000103	0.795 4*	0.615 4	0.477 4	0.370 4	0.288 4	0.225 4	0.175 4	0.137 4	0.108 4
35	0.786 4*	0.602 4	0.463 4	0.356 4	0.274 4	0.212 4	0.164 4	0.127 4	0.987 5	0.768 5
36	0.600 4	0.456 4	0.348 4	0.266 4	0.203 4	0.156 4	0.120 4	0.921 5	0.710 5	0.549 5
37	0.458 4	0.346 4	0.262 4	0.198 4	0.151 4	0.115 4	0.874 5	0.668 5	0.511 5	0.392 5
38	0.350 4	0.262 4	0.197 4	0.148 4	0.112 4	0.842 5	0.638 5	0.484 5	0.368 5	0.280 5
39	0.267 4	0.198 4	0.148 4	0.110 4	0.826 5	0.619 5	0.465 5	0.351 5	0.264 5	0.200 5
40	0.204 4	0.150 4	0.111 4	0.824 5	0.612 5	0.455 5	0.340 5	0.254 5	0.190 5	0.143 5
41	0.156 4	0.114 4	0.836 5	0.615 5	0.453 5	0.335 5	0.248 5	0.184 5	0.137 5	0.102 5
42	0.119 4	0.863 5	0.628 5	0.459 5	0.336 5	0.246 5	0.181 5	0.133 5	0.985 6	0.729 6
43	0.906 5	0.654 5	0.472 5	0.342 5	0.249 5	0.181 5	0.132 5	0.966 6	0.709 6	0.521 6
44	0.692 5	0.495 5	0.355 5	0.255 5	0.184 5	0.133 5	0.964 6	0.700 6	0.510 6	0.372 6
45	0.528 5	0.375 5	0.267 5	0.191 5	0.136 5	0.979 6	0.704 6	0.508 6	0.367 6	0.266 6
46	0.403 5	0.284 5	0.201 5	0.142 5	0.101 5	0.720 6	0.514 6	0.368 6	0.264 6	0.190 6
47	0.308 5	0.215 5	0.151 5	0.106 5	0.749 6	0.529 6	0.375 6	0.266 6	0.190 6	0.136 6
48	0.235 5	0.163 5	0.114 5	0.792 6	0.555 6	0.389 6	0.274 6	0.193 6	0.137 6	0.968 7
49	0.179 5	0.124 5	0.854 6	0.591 6	0.411 6	0.286 6	0.200 6	0.140 6	0.982 7	0.691 7
50	0.137 5	0.936 6	0.642 6	0.441 6	0.304 6	0.210 6	0.146 6	0.101 6	0.707 7	0.494 7

* The final digit is the power of 10 by which the given tabular value has to be divided.

Appendix Table A

$$v_{n|r} = (1+r)^{-n}$$

Appendix Table A   The present value of 1

Year	41	42	43	44	Percentage 45	46	47	48	49	50
1	0·709220	0·704225	0·699301	0·694444	0·689655	0·684932	0·680272	0·675676	0·671141	0·666667
2	0·502993	0·495933	0·489021	0·482253	0·475624	0·469131	0·462770	0·456538	0·450430	0·444444
3	0·356732	0·349249	0·341973	0·334898	0·328017	0·321323	0·314810	0·308471	0·302302	0·296296
4	0·253002	0·245950	0·239142	0·232568	0·226218	0·220084	0·214156	0·208427	0·202887	0·197531
5	0·179434	0·173204	0·167232	0·161506	0·156013	0·150743	0·145684	0·140829	0·136166	0·131687
6	0·127258	0·121975	0·116946	0·112157	0·107595	0·103248	0·099105	0·095155	0·091387	0·087791
7	0·090254	0·085898	0·081780	0·077887	0·074203	0·070718	0·067418	0·064294	0·061333	0·058528
8	0·064010	0·060491	0·057189	0·054088	0·051175	0·048437	0·045863	0·043442	0·041163	0·039018
9	0·045397	0·042600	0·039992	0·037561	0·035293	0·033176	0·031199	0·029352	0·027626	0·026012
10	0·032197	0·030000	0·027967	0·026084	0·024340	0·022723	0·021224	0·019833	0·018541	0·017342
11	0·022834	0·021127	0·019557	0·018114	0·016786	0·015564	0·014438	0·013401	0·012444	0·011561
12	0·016195	0·014878	0·013676	0·012579	0·011577	0·010660	0·009822	0·009054	0·008352	0·007707
13	0·011486	0·010477	0·009564	0·008735	0·007984	0·007302	0·006682	0·006118	0·005605	0·005138
14	0·008146	0·007378	0·006688	0·006066	0·005506	0·005001	0·004545	0·004134	0·003762	0·003425
15	0·005777	0·005196	0·004677	0·004213	0·003797	0·003425	0·003092	0·002793	0·002525	0·002284
16	0·004097	0·003659	0·003271	0·002926	0·002619	0·002346	0·002103	0·001887	0·001694	0·001522
17	0·002906	0·002577	0·002287	0·002032	0·001806	0·001607	0·001431	0·001275	0·001137	0·001015
18	0·002061	0·001815	0·001599	0·001411	0·001246	0·001101	0·000973	0·000862	0·000763	0·000677
19	0·001462	0·001278	0·001118	0·000980	0·000859	0·000754	0·000662	0·000582	0·000512	0·000451
20	0·001037	0·000900	0·000782	0·000680	0·000592	0·000516	0·000450	0·000393	0·000344	0·000301
21	0·000735	0·000634	0·000547	0·000472	0·000409	0·000354	0·000306	0·000266	0·000231	0·000200
22	0·000521	0·000446	0·000382	0·000328	0·000282	0·000242	0·000208	0·000180	0·000155	0·000134
23	0·000370	0·000314	0·000267	0·000228	0·000194	0·000166	0·000142	0·000121	0·000104	0·891 4*

24	0.000262	0.000221	0.000187	0.000158	0.000134	0.000114	0.965 4*	0.820 4*	0.697 4*	0.594 4
25	0.000186	0.000156	0.000131	0.000110	0.924 4*	0.778 4*	0.656 4	0.554 4	0.468 4	0.396 4
26	0.000132	0.000110	0.915 4*	0.763 4*	0.637 4	0.533 4	0.446 4	0.374 4	0.314 4	0.264 4
27	0.936 4*	0.773 4*	0.640 4	0.530 4	0.440 4	0.365 4	0.304 4	0.253 4	0.211 4	0.176 4
28	0.664 4	0.544 4	0.447 4	0.368 4	0.303 4	0.250 4	0.207 4	0.171 4	0.142 4	0.117 5
29	0.471 4	0.383 4	0.313 4	0.256 4	0.209 4	0.171 4	0.141 4	0.115 4	0.950 5	0.782 5
30	0.334 4	0.270 4	0.219 4	0.177 4	0.144 4	0.117 4	0.956 5	0.780 5	0.637 5	0.522 5
31	0.237 4	0.190 4	0.153 4	0.123 4	0.994 5	0.804 5	0.650 5	0.527 5	0.428 5	0.348 5
32	0.168 4	0.134 4	0.107 4	0.856 5	0.686 5	0.550 5	0.442 5	0.356 5	0.287 5	0.232 5
33	0.119 4	0.943 5	0.748 5	0.594 5	0.473 5	0.377 5	0.301 5	0.241 5	0.193 5	0.155 5
34	0.844 5	0.664 5	0.523 5	0.413 5	0.326 5	0.258 5	0.205 5	0.163 5	0.129 5	0.103 5
35	0.599 5	0.468 5	0.366 5	0.287 5	0.225 5	0.177 5	0.139 5	0.110 5	0.868 6	0.687 6
36	0.425 5	0.329 5	0.256 5	0.199 5	0.155 5	0.121 5	0.947 6	0.742 6	0.582 6	0.458 6
37	0.301 5	0.232 5	0.179 5	0.138 5	0.107 5	0.830 6	0.645 6	0.502 6	0.391 6	0.305 6
38	0.214 5	0.163 5	0.125 5	0.960 6	0.738 6	0.568 6	0.438 6	0.339 6	0.262 6	0.203 6
39	0.152 5	0.115 5	0.875 6	0.667 6	0.509 6	0.389 6	0.298 6	0.229 6	0.176 6	0.136 6
40	0.107 5	0.810 6	0.612 6	0.463 6	0.351 6	0.267 6	0.203 6	0.155 6	0.118 6	0.904 7
41	0.762 6	0.570 6	0.428 6	0.321 6	0.242 6	0.183 6	0.138 6	0.105 6	0.793 7	0.603 7
42	0.541 6	0.402 6	0.299 6	0.223 6	0.167 6	0.125 6	0.939 7	0.706 7	0.532 7	0.402 7
43	0.383 6	0.283 6	0.209 6	0.155 6	0.115 6	0.857 7	0.639 7	0.477 7	0.357 7	0.268 7
44	0.272 6	0.199 6	0.146 6	0.108 6	0.794 7	0.587 7	0.435 7	0.322 7	0.240 7	0.179 7
45	0.193 6	0.140 6	0.102 6	0.748 7	0.548 7	0.402 7	0.296 7	0.218 7	0.161 7	0.119 7
46	0.137 6	0.988 7	0.715 7	0.519 7	0.378 7	0.275 7	0.201 7	0.147 7	0.108 7	0.794 8
47	0.970 7	0.696 7	0.500 7	0.361 7	0.260 7	0.189 7	0.137 7	0.995 8	0.725 8	0.529 8
48	0.688 7	0.490 7	0.350 7	0.250 7	0.180 7	0.129 7	0.931 8	0.672 8	0.486 8	0.353 8
49	0.488 7	0.345 7	0.245 7	0.174 7	0.124 7	0.885 8	0.633 8	0.454 8	0.326 8	0.235 8
50	0.346 7	0.243 7	0.171 7	0.121 7	0.854 8	0.606 8	0.431 8	0.307 8	0.219 8	0.157 8

* The final digit is the power of 10 by which the given tabular value has to be divided.

Appendix Table B

Appendix Table B   The present value of 1 per annum

$$a_{\overline{n}|r} = \frac{1-(1+r)^{-n}}{r}$$

Year	Percentage									
	1	2	3	4	5	6	7	8	9	10
1	0·990099	0·980392	0·970874	0·961538	0·952381	0·943396	0·934579	0·925926	0·917431	0·909091
2	1·97040	1·94156	1·91347	1·88609	1·85941	1·83339	1·80802	1·78326	1·75911	1·73554
3	2·94099	2·88388	2·82861	2·77509	2·72325	2·67301	2·62432	2·57710	2·53129	2·48685
4	3·90197	3·80773	3·71710	3·62990	3·54595	3·46511	3·38721	3·31213	3·23972	3·16987
5	4·85343	4·71346	4·57971	4·45182	4·32948	4·21236	4·10020	3·99271	3·88965	3·79079
6	5·79548	5·60143	5·41719	5·24214	5·07569	4·91732	4·76654	4·62288	4·48592	4·35526
7	6·72819	6·47199	6·23028	6·00205	5·78637	5·58238	5·38929	5·20637	5·03295	4·86842
8	7·65168	7·32548	7·01969	6·73274	6·46321	6·20979	5·97130	5·74664	5·53482	5·33493
9	8·56602	8·16224	7·78611	7·43533	7·10782	6·80169	6·51523	6·24689	5·99525	5·75902
10	9·47130	8·98259	8·53020	8·11090	7·72173	7·36009	7·02358	6·71008	6·41766	6·14457
11	10·3676	9·78685	9·25262	8·76048	8·30641	7·88687	7·49867	7·13896	6·80519	6·49506
12	11·2551	10·5753	9·95400	9·38507	8·86325	8·38384	7·94269	7·53608	7·16073	6·81369
13	12·1337	11·3484	10·6350	9·98565	9·39357	8·85268	8·35765	7·90378	7·48690	7·10336
14	13·0037	12·1062	11·2961	10·5631	9·89864	9·29498	8·74547	8·24424	7·78615	7·36669
15	13·8651	12·8493	11·9379	11·1184	10·3797	9·71225	9·10791	8·55948	8·06069	7·60608
16	14·7179	13·5777	12·5611	11·6523	10·8378	10·1059	9·44665	8·85137	8·31256	7·82371
17	15·5623	14·2919	13·1661	12·1657	11·2741	10·4773	9·76322	9·12164	8·54363	8·02155
18	16·3983	14·9920	13·7535	12·6593	11·6896	10·8276	10·0591	9·37189	8·75563	8·20141
19	17·2260	15·6785	14·3238	13·1339	12·0853	11·1581	10·3356	9·60360	8·95011	8·36492
20	18·0456	16·3514	14·8775	13·5903	12·4622	11·4699	10·5940	9·81815	9·12855	8·51356
21	18·8570	17·0112	15·4150	14·0292	12·8212	11·7641	10·8355	10·0168	9·29224	8·64869
22	19·6604	17·6580	15·9369	14·4511	13·1630	12·0416	11·0612	10·2007	9·44243	8·77154

23	8·88322	9·58021	10·3711	11·2722	12·3034	13·4886	14·8568	16·4436	18·2922	20·4558
24	8·98474	9·70661	10·5288	11·4693	12·5504	13·7986	15·2470	16·9355	18·9139	21·2434
25	9·07704	9·82258	10·6748	11·6536	12·7834	14·0939	15·6221	17·4131	19·5235	22·0232
26	9·16095	9·92897	10·8100	11·8258	13·0032	14·3752	15·9828	17·8768	20·1210	22·7952
27	9·23722	10·0266	10·9352	11·9867	13·2105	14·6430	16·3296	18·3270	20·7069	23·5596
28	9·30657	10·1161	11·0511	12·1371	13·4062	14·8981	16·6631	18·7641	21·2813	24·3164
29	9·36961	10·1983	11·1584	12·2777	13·5907	15·1411	16·9837	19·1885	21·8444	25·0658
30	9·42691	10·2737	11·2578	12·4090	13·7648	15·3725	17·2920	19·6004	22·3965	25·8077
31	9·47901	10·3428	11·3498	12·5318	13·9291	15·5928	17·5885	20·0004	22·9377	26·5423
32	9·52638	10·4062	11·4350	12·6466	14·0840	15·8027	17·8736	20·3888	23·4683	27·2696
33	9·56943	10·4644	11·5139	12·7538	14·2302	16·0025	18·1476	20·7658	23·9886	27·9897
34	9·60857	10·5178	11·5869	12·8540	14·3681	16·1929	18·4112	21·1318	24·4986	28·7027
35	9·64416	10·5668	11·6546	12·9477	14·4982	16·3742	18·6646	21·4872	24·9986	29·4086
36	9·67651	10·6118	11·7172	13·0352	14·6210	16·5469	18·9083	21·8323	25·4888	30·1075
37	9·70592	10·6530	11·7752	13·1170	14·7368	16·7113	19·1426	22·1672	25·9695	30·7995
38	9·73265	10·6908	11·8289	13·1935	14·8460	16·8679	19·3679	22·4925	26·4406	31·4847
39	9·75696	10·7255	11·8786	13·2649	14·9491	17·0170	19·5845	22·8082	26·9026	32·1630
40	9·77905	10·7574	11·9246	13·3317	15·0463	17·1591	19·7928	23·1148	27·3555	32·8347
41	9·79914	10·7866	11·9672	13·3941	15·1380	17·2944	19·9931	23·4124	27·7995	33·4997
42	9·81740	10·8134	12·0067	13·4524	15·2245	17·4232	20·1856	23·7014	28·2348	34·1581
43	9·83400	10·8380	12·0432	13·5070	15·3062	17·5459	20·3708	23·9819	28·6616	34·8100
44	9·84909	10·8605	12·0771	13·5579	15·3832	17·6628	20·5488	24·2543	29·0800	35·4555
45	9·86281	10·8812	12·1084	13·6055	15·4558	17·7741	20·7200	24·5187	29·4902	36·0945
46	9·87528	10·9002	12·1374	13·6500	15·5244	17·8801	20·8847	24·7754	29·8923	36·7272
47	9·88662	10·9176	12·1643	13·6916	15·5890	17·9810	21·0429	25·0247	30·2866	37·3537
48	9·89693	10·9336	12·1891	13·7305	15·6500	18·0772	21·1951	25·2667	30·6731	37·9740
49	9·90630	10·9482	12·2122	13·7668	15·7076	18·1687	21·3415	25·5017	31·0521	38·5881
50	9·91481	10·9617	12·2335	13·8007	15·7619	18·2559	21·4822	25·7298	31·4236	39·1961

Appendix Table B   *The present value of 1 per annum*

$$a_{n|r} = \frac{1-(1+r)^{-n}}{r}$$

Year	Percentage									
	11	12	13	14	15	16	17	18	19	20
1	0·900901	0·892857	0·884956	0·877193	0·869565	0·862069	0·854701	0·847458	0·840336	0·833333
2	1·71252	1·69005	1·66810	1·64666	1·62571	1·60523	1·58521	1·56564	1·54650	1·52778
3	2·44371	2·40183	2·36115	2·32163	2·28323	2·24589	2·20958	2·17427	2·13992	2·10648
4	3·10245	3·03735	2·97447	2·91371	2·85498	2·79818	2·74324	2·69006	2·63859	2·58873
5	3·69590	3·60478	3·51723	3·43308	3·35216	3·27429	3·19935	3·12717	3·05763	2·99061
6	4·23054	4·11141	3·99755	3·88867	3·78448	3·68474	3·58918	3·49760	3·40978	3·32551
7	4·71220	4·56376	4·42261	4·28830	4·16042	4·03857	3·92238	3·81153	3·70570	3·60459
8	5·14612	4·96764	4·79877	4·63886	4·48732	4·34359	4·20716	4·07757	3·95437	3·83716
9	5·53705	5·32825	5·13166	4·94637	4·77158	4·60654	4·45057	4·30302	4·16333	4·03097
10	5·88923	5·65022	5·42624	5·21612	5·01877	4·83323	4·65860	4·49409	4·33893	4·19247
11	6·20652	5·93770	5·68694	5·45273	5·23371	5·02864	4·83641	4·65601	4·48650	4·32706
12	6·49236	6·19437	5·91765	5·66029	5·42062	5·19711	4·98839	4·79322	4·61050	4·43922
13	6·74987	6·42355	6·12181	5·84236	5·58315	5·34233	5·11828	4·90951	4·71471	4·53268
14	6·98187	6·62817	6·30249	6·00207	5·72448	5·46753	5·22930	5·00806	4·80228	4·61057
15	7·19087	6·81086	6·46238	6·14217	5·84737	5·57546	5·32419	5·09158	4·87586	4·67547
16	7·37916	6·97399	6·60388	6·26506	5·95423	5·66850	5·40529	5·16235	4·93770	4·72956
17	7·54879	7·11963	6·72909	6·37286	6·04716	5·74870	5·47461	5·22233	4·98966	4·77463
18	7·70162	7·24967	6·83991	6·46742	6·12797	5·81785	5·53385	5·27316	5·03333	4·81219
19	7·83929	7·36578	6·93797	6·55037	6·19823	5·87746	5·58449	5·31624	5·07003	4·84350
20	7·96333	7·46944	7·02475	6·62313	6·25933	5·92884	5·62777	5·35275	5·10086	4·86958
21	8·07507	7·56200	7·10155	6·68696	6·31246	5·97314	5·66476	5·38368	5·12677	4·89132
22	8·17574	7·64465	7·16951	6·74294	6·35866	6·01133	5·69637	5·40990	5·14855	4·90943

23	4·92453	5·16685	5·43212	5·72340	6·04425	6·39884	6·79206	7·22966	7·71843	8·26643
24	4·93710	5·18223	5·45095	5·74649	6·07263	6·43377	6·83514	7·28288	7·78432	8·34814
25	4·94759	5·19515	5·46691	5·76623	6·09709	6·46415	6·87293	7·32998	7·84314	8·42174
26	4·95632	5·20601	5·48043	5·78311	6·11818	6·49056	6·90608	7·37167	7·89566	8·48806
27	4·96360	5·21513	5·49189	5·79753	6·13636	6·51353	6·93515	7·40856	7·94255	8·54780
28	4·96967	5·22280	5·50160	5·80985	6·15204	6·53351	6·96066	7·44120	7·98442	8·60162
29	4·97472	5·22924	5·50983	5·82039	6·16555	6·55088	6·98304	7·47009	8·02181	8·65011
30	4·97894	5·23466	5·51681	5·82939	6·17720	6·56598	7·00266	7·49565	8·05518	8·69379
31	4·98245	5·23921	5·52272	5·83709	6·18724	6·57911	7·01988	7·51828	8·08499	8·73315
32	4·98537	5·24303	5·52773	5·84366	6·19590	6·59053	7·03498	7·53830	8·11159	8·76860
33	4·98781	5·24625	5·53197	5·84928	6·20336	6·60046	7·04823	7·55602	8·13535	8·80054
34	4·98984	5·24895	5·53557	5·85409	6·20979	6·60910	7·05985	7·57170	8·15656	8·82932
35	4·99154	5·25122	5·53862	5·85820	6·21534	6·61661	7·07005	7·58557	8·17550	8·85524
36	4·99295	5·25312	5·54120	5·86171	6·22012	6·62314	7·07899	7·59785	8·19241	8·87859
37	4·99412	5·25472	5·54339	5·86471	6·22424	6·62881	7·08683	7·60872	8·20751	8·89963
38	4·99510	5·25607	5·54525	5·86727	6·22779	6·63375	7·09371	7·61833	8·22099	8·91859
39	4·99592	5·25720	5·54682	5·86946	6·23086	6·63805	7·09975	7·62684	8·23303	8·93567
40	4·99660	5·25815	5·54815	5·87133	6·23350	6·64178	7·10504	7·63438	8·24378	8·95105
41	4·99717	5·25895	5·54928	5·87294	6·23577	6·64502	7·10969	7·64104	8·25337	8·96491
42	4·99764	5·25962	5·55024	5·87430	6·23774	6·64785	7·11376	7·64694	8·26194	8·97740
43	4·99803	5·26019	5·55105	5·87547	6·23943	6·65030	7·11733	7·65216	8·26959	8·98865
44	4·99836	5·26066	5·55174	5·87647	6·24089	6·65244	7·12047	7·65678	8·27642	8·99878
45	4·99863	5·26106	5·55232	5·87733	6·24214	6·65429	7·12322	7·66086	8·28252	9·00791
46	4·99886	5·26140	5·55281	5·87806	6·24323	6·65591	7·12563	7·66448	8·28796	9·01614
47	4·99905	5·26168	5·55323	5·87868	6·24416	6·65731	7·12774	7·66768	8·29282	9·02355
48	4·99921	5·26191	5·55359	5·87922	6·24497	6·65853	7·12960	7·67052	8·29716	9·03022
49	4·99934	5·26211	5·55389	5·87967	6·24566	6·65959	7·13123	7·67302	8·30104	9·03624
50	4·99945	5·26228	5·55414	5·88006	6·24626	6·66051	7·13266	7·67524	8·30450	9·04165

Appendix Table B

Appendix Table B   The present value of 1 per annum

$$a_{n|r} = \frac{1-(1+r)^{-n}}{r}$$

Year	Percentage									
	21	22	23	24	25	26	27	28	29	30
1	0.826446	0.819672	0.813008	0.806452	0.800000	0.793651	0.787402	0.781250	0.775194	0.769231
2	1.50946	1.49153	1.47399	1.45682	1.44000	1.42353	1.40740	1.39160	1.37612	1.36095
3	2.07393	2.04224	2.01137	1.98130	1.95200	1.92344	1.89559	1.86844	1.84195	1.81611
4	2.54044	2.49364	2.44827	2.40428	2.36160	2.32019	2.27999	2.24097	2.20306	2.16624
5	2.92598	2.86364	2.80347	2.74538	2.68928	2.63507	2.58267	2.53201	2.48300	2.43557
6	3.24462	3.16692	3.09225	3.02047	2.95142	2.88498	2.82100	2.75938	2.70000	2.64275
7	3.50795	3.41551	3.32704	3.24232	3.16114	3.08331	3.00866	2.93702	2.86821	2.80211
8	3.72558	3.61927	3.51792	3.42122	3.32891	3.24073	3.15643	3.07579	2.99862	2.92470
9	3.90543	3.78628	3.67310	3.56550	3.46313	3.36566	3.27278	3.18421	3.09970	3.01900
10	4.05408	3.92318	3.79927	3.68186	3.57050	3.46481	3.36439	3.26892	3.17806	3.09154
11	4.17692	4.03540	3.90185	3.77569	3.65640	3.54350	3.43653	3.33509	3.23381	3.14734
12	4.27845	4.12737	3.98524	3.85136	3.72512	3.60595	3.49333	3.38679	3.28590	3.19026
13	4.36235	4.20277	4.05304	3.91239	3.78010	3.65552	3.53806	3.42718	3.32240	3.22328
14	4.43170	4.26456	4.10816	3.96160	3.82408	3.69485	3.57327	3.45873	3.35070	3.24867
15	4.48901	4.31522	4.15298	4.00129	3.85926	3.72607	3.60100	3.48339	3.37264	3.26821
16	4.53637	4.35673	4.18941	4.03330	3.88741	3.75085	3.62284	3.50265	3.38964	3.28324
17	4.57551	4.39077	4.21904	4.05911	3.90993	3.77052	3.64003	3.51769	3.40282	3.29480
18	4.60786	4.41866	4.24312	4.07993	3.92794	3.78613	3.65357	3.52945	3.41304	3.30369
19	4.63460	4.44152	4.26270	4.09672	3.94235	3.79851	3.66422	3.53863	3.42096	3.31053
20	4.65669	4.46027	4.27862	4.11026	3.95388	3.80834	3.67262	3.54580	3.42710	3.31579
21	4.67495	4.47563	4.29156	4.12117	3.96311	3.81615	3.67923	3.55141	3.43186	3.31984
22	4.69004	4.48822	4.30208	4.12998	3.97049	3.82234	3.68443	3.55579	3.43555	3.32296

23	3.32535	3.43841	3.55921	3.68853	3.82725	3.97639	4.13708	4.31063	4.49854	4.70251
24	3.32719	3.44063	3.56188	3.69175	3.83115	3.98111	4.14281	4.31759	4.50700	4.71282
25	3.32861	3.44235	3.56397	3.69429	3.83425	3.98489	4.14742	4.32324	4.51393	4.72134
26	3.32970	3.44368	3.56560	3.69630	3.83670	3.98791	4.15115	4.32784	4.51962	4.72838
27	3.33054	3.44471	3.56688	3.69787	3.83865	3.99033	4.15415	4.33158	4.52428	4.73420
28	3.33118	3.44551	3.56787	3.69911	3.84020	3.99226	4.15657	4.33462	4.52810	4.73901
29	3.33168	3.44614	3.56865	3.70009	3.84143	3.99381	4.15853	4.33709	4.53123	4.74298
30	3.33206	3.44662	3.56926	3.70086	3.84240	3.99505	4.16010	4.33909	4.53379	4.74627
31	3.33235	3.44699	3.56973	3.70146	3.84318	3.99604	4.16137	4.34073	4.53590	4.74898
32	3.33258	3.44728	3.57010	3.70194	3.84379	3.99683	4.16240	4.34205	4.53762	4.75122
33	3.33275	3.44750	3.57039	3.70231	3.84428	3.99746	4.16322	4.34313	4.53903	4.75308
34	3.33289	3.44768	3.57062	3.70261	3.84467	3.99797	4.16389	4.34401	4.54019	4.75461
35	3.33299	3.44781	3.57080	3.70284	3.84497	3.99838	4.16443	4.34472	4.54114	4.75588
36	3.33307	3.44792	3.57094	3.70302	3.84522	3.99870	4.16486	4.34530	4.54192	4.75692
37	3.33313	3.44800	3.57104	3.70317	3.84541	3.99896	4.16521	4.34578	4.54256	4.75779
38	3.33318	3.44806	3.57113	3.70328	3.84556	3.99917	4.16549	4.34616	5.54308	4.75850
39	3.33321	3.44811	3.57119	3.70337	3.84569	3.99934	4.16572	4.34647	4.54351	4.75909
40	3.33324	3.44815	3.57124	3.70344	3.84578	3.99947	4.16590	4.34672	4.54386	4.75958
41	3.33326	3.44818	3.57128	3.70350	3.84586	3.99957	4.16605	4.34693	4.54415	4.75998
42	3.33328	3.44820	3.57132	3.70354	3.84592	3.99966	4.16617	4.34710	4.54438	4.76032
43	3.33329	3.44822	3.57134	3.70358	3.84597	3.99973	4.16627	4.34723	4.54458	4.76059
44	3.33330	3.44823	3.57136	3.70360	3.84601	3.99978	4.16634	4.34734	4.54473	4.76082
45	3.33331	3.44824	3.57138	3.70362	3.84604	3.99983	4.16641	4.34743	4.54486	4.76101
46	3.33331	3.44825	3.57139	3.70364	3.84606	3.99986	4.16646	4.34751	4.54497	4.76116
47	3.33332	3.44825	3.57140	3.70365	3.84608	3.99989	4.16650	4.34757	5.54506	4.76129
48	3.33332	3.44826	3.57140	3.70367	3.84610	3.99991	4.16653	4.34762	4.54513	4.76140
49	3.33332	3.44826	3.57141	3.70367	3.84611	3.99993	4.16656	4.34766	4.54519	4.76149
50	3.33333	3.44827	3.57141	3.70368	3.84612	3.99994	4.16658	4.34769	4.54524	4.76156

Appendix Table B

Appendix Table B The present value of 1 per annum

$$a_{\overline{n}|r} = \frac{1-(1+r)^{-n}}{r}$$

Year	Percentage									
	31	32	33	34	35	36	37	38	39	40
1	0.763359	0.757576	0.751880	0.746269	0.740741	0.735294	0.729927	0.724638	0.719424	0.714286
2	1.34608	1.33150	1.31720	1.30319	1.28944	1.27595	1.26272	1.24974	1.23700	1.22449
3	1.79090	1.76629	1.74226	1.71880	1.69588	1.67349	1.65162	1.63024	1.60935	1.58892
4	2.13046	2.09567	2.06185	2.02895	1.99695	1.96580	1.93549	1.90597	1.87723	1.84923
5	2.38966	2.34521	2.30214	2.26041	2.21996	2.18074	2.14269	2.10578	2.06995	2.03516
6	2.58753	2.53425	2.48281	2.43314	2.38516	2.33878	2.29394	2.25056	2.20860	2.16797
7	2.73857	2.67746	2.61866	2.56205	2.50752	2.45498	2.40433	2.35548	2.30834	2.26284
8	2.85387	2.78595	2.72079	2.65824	2.59817	2.54043	2.48491	2.43151	2.38010	2.33060
9	2.94189	2.86815	2.79759	2.73003	2.66531	2.60326	2.54373	2.48660	2.43173	2.37900
10	3.00907	2.93041	2.85533	2.78361	2.71504	2.64945	2.58667	2.52652	2.46887	2.41357
11	3.06036	2.97759	2.89874	2.82359	2.75188	2.68342	2.61800	2.55545	2.49559	2.43826
12	3.09951	3.01332	2.93139	2.85342	2.77917	2.70840	2.64088	2.57641	2.51481	2.45590
13	3.12940	3.04040	2.95593	2.87569	2.79939	2.72676	2.65758	2.59160	2.52864	2.46850
14	3.15221	3.06091	2.97438	2.89231	2.81436	2.74027	2.66976	2.60261	2.53859	2.47750
15	3.16963	3.07644	2.98826	2.90471	2.82545	2.75020	2.67866	2.61059	2.54575	2.48393
16	3.18292	3.08822	2.99869	2.91396	2.83367	2.75750	2.68515	2.61637	2.55090	2.48852
17	3.19307	3.09713	3.00653	2.92087	2.83975	2.76287	2.68989	2.62056	2.55460	2.49180
18	3.20082	3.10389	3.01243	2.92602	2.84426	2.76681	2.69335	2.62359	2.55727	2.49414
19	3.20673	3.10901	3.01687	2.92986	2.84760	2.76972	2.69588	2.62579	2.55919	2.49582
20	3.21124	3.11288	3.02020	2.93273	2.85008	2.77185	2.69772	2.62738	2.56057	2.49701
21	3.21469	3.11582	3.02271	2.93488	2.85191	2.77342	2.69907	2.62854	2.56156	2.49787
22	3.21732	3.11805	3.02459	2.93648	2.85327	2.77457	2.70005	2.62938	2.56227	2.49848

23	2·49891	2·56279	2·62998	2·70077	2·77542	2·85427	2·93767	3·02601	3·11973	3·21933
24	2·49922	2·56316	2·63042	2·70129	2·77604	2·85502	2·93856	3·02707	3·12101	3·22086
25	2·49944	2·56342	2·63074	2·70167	2·77650	2·85557	2·93922	3·02788	3·12198	3·22203
26	2·49960	2·56361	2·63097	2·70195	2·77684	2·85598	2·93972	3·02848	3·12271	3·22293
27	2·49972	2·56375	2·63114	2·70215	2·77709	2·85628	2·94009	3·02893	3·12326	3·22361
28	2·49980	2·56385	2·63126	2·70230	2·77727	2·85650	2·94036	3·02927	3·12369	3·22413
29	2·49986	2·56392	2·63135	2·70241	2·77741	2·85667	2·94057	3·02953	3·12400	3·22452
30	2·49990	2·56397	2·63141	2·70249	2·77750	2·85679	2·94072	3·02972	3·12425	3·22483
31	2·49993	2·56401	2·63146	2·70255	2·77758	2·85688	2·94084	3·02986	3·12443	3·22506
32	2·49995	2·56403	2·63149	2·70259	2·77763	2·85695	2·94092	3·02997	3·12457	3·22524
33	2·49996	2·56405	2·63152	2·70262	2·77767	2·85700	2·94099	3·03006	3·12467	3·22537
34	2·49997	2·56407	2·63153	2·70264	2·77770	2·85704	2·94104	3·03012	3·12475	3·22547
35	2·49998	2·56408	2·63155	2·70266	2·77772	2·85706	2·94107	3·03016	3·12481	3·22555
36	2·49999	2·56408	2·63156	2·70267	2·77773	2·85708	2·94110	3·03020	3·12486	3·22561
37	2·49999	2·56409	2·63157	2·70268	2·77775	2·85710	2·94112	3·03022	3·12489	3·22566
38	2·49999	2·56409	2·63157	2·70269	2·77775	2·85711	2·94113	3·03024	3·12492	3·22569
39	2·50000	2·56410	2·63157	2·70269	2·77776	2·85712	2·94114	3·03026	3·12494	3·22572
40	2·50000	2·56410	2·63157	2·70269	2·77777	2·85713	2·94115	3·03027	3·12495	3·22574
41	2·50000	2·56410	2·63157	2·70270	2·77777	2·85713	2·94116	3·03028	3·12496	3·22576
42	2·50000	2·56410	2·63158	2·70270	2·77777	2·85713	2·94116	3·03028	3·12497	3·22577
43	2·50000	2·56410	2·63158	2·70270	2·77777	2·85714	2·94117	3·03029	3·12498	3·22578
44	2·50000	2·56410	2·63158	2·70270	2·77777	2·85714	2·94117	3·03029	3·12498	3·22578
45	2·50000	2·56410	2·63158	2·70270	2·77778	2·85714	2·94117	3·03030	3·12499	3·22579
46	2·50000	2·56410	2·63158	2·70270	2·77778	2·85714	2·94117	3·03030	3·12499	3·22580
47	2·50000	2·56410	2·63158	2·70270	2·77778	2·85714	2·94117	3·03030	3·12499	3·22580
48	2·50000	2·56410	2·63158	2·70270	2·77778	2·85714	2·94117	3·03030	3·12500	3·22580
49	2·50000	2·56410	2·63158	2·70270	2·77778	2·85714	2·94117	3·03030	3·12500	3·22580
50	2·50000	2·56410	2·63158	2·70270	2·77778	2·85714	2·94118	3·03030	3·12500	3·22580

Appendix Table B

Appendix Table B The present value of 1 per annum

$$a_{\overline{n}|r} = \frac{1-(1+r)^{-n}}{r}$$

Year	Percentage									
	41	42	43	44	45	46	47	48	49	50
1	0·709220	0·704225	0·699301	0·694444	0·689655	0·684932	0·680272	0·675676	0·671141	0·666667
2	1·21221	1·20016	1·18832	1·17670	1·16528	1·15406	1·14304	1·13221	1·12157	1·11111
3	1·56895	1·54941	1·53030	1·51160	1·49330	1·47539	1·45785	1·44068	1·42387	1·40741
4	1·82195	1·79536	1·76944	1·74416	1·71951	1·69547	1·67201	1·64911	1·62676	1·60494
5	2·00138	1·96856	1·93667	1·90567	1·87553	1·84621	1·81769	1·78994	1·76293	1·73663
6	2·12864	2·09054	2·05361	2·01783	1·98312	1·94946	1·91680	1·88509	1·85431	1·82442
7	2·21889	2·17643	2·13540	2·09571	2·05733	2·02018	1·98422	1·94939	1·91565	1·88294
8	2·28290	2·23693	2·19258	2·14980	2·10850	2·06862	2·03008	1·99283	1·95681	1·92196
9	2·32830	2·27952	2·23258	2·18736	2·14379	2·10179	2·06128	2·02218	1·98444	1·94798
10	2·36050	2·30952	2·26054	2·21345	2·16813	2·12451	2·08250	2·04202	2·00298	1·96532
11	2·38333	2·33065	2·28010	2·23156	2·18492	2·14008	2·09694	2·05542	2·01542	1·97688
12	2·39953	2·34553	2·29378	2·24414	2·19650	2·15074	2·10676	2·06447	2·02377	1·98459
13	2·41101	2·35601	2·30334	2·25287	2·20448	2·15804	2·11344	2·07059	2·02938	1·98972
14	2·41916	2·36338	2·31003	2·25894	2·20999	2·16304	2·11799	2·07472	2·03314	1·99315
15	2·42493	2·36858	2·31470	2·26315	2·21378	2·16647	2·12108	2·07751	2·03566	1·99543
16	2·42903	2·37224	2·31798	2·26608	2·21640	2·16881	2·12318	2·07940	2·03736	1·99696
17	2·43194	2·37482	2·32026	2·26811	2·21821	2·17042	2·12462	2·08068	2·03850	1·99797
18	2·43400	2·37663	2·32186	2·26952	2·21945	2·17152	2·12559	2·08154	2·03926	1·99865
19	2·43546	2·37791	2·32298	2·27050	2·22031	2·17227	2·12625	2·08212	2·03977	1·99910
20	2·43650	2·37881	2·32376	2·27118	2·22091	2·17279	2·12670	2·08251	2·04011	1·99940
21	2·43723	2·37944	2·32431	2·27165	2·22131	2·17314	2·12701	2·08278	2·04035	1·99960
22	2·43775	2·37989	2·32469	2·27198	2·22160	2·17339	2·12722	2·08296	2·04050	1·99973

23	2·43812	2·38020	2·32496	2·27221	2·22179	2·17355	2·12736	2·08308	2·04060	1·99982
24	2·43838	2·38043	2·32515	2·27237	2·22192	2·17367	2·12745	2·08316	2·04067	1·99988
25	2·43857	2·38058	2·32528	2·27248	2·22202	2·17374	2·12752	2·08322	2·04072	1·99992
26	2·43870	2·38069	2·32537	2·27255	2·22208	2·17380	2·12756	2·08326	2·04075	1·99995
27	2·43880	2·38077	2·32543	2·27261	2·22212	2·17383	2·12759	2·08328	2·04077	1·99996
28	2·43886	2·38082	2·32548	2·27264	2·22215	2·17386	2·12762	2·08330	2·04079	1·99998
29	2·43891	2·38086	2·32551	2·27267	2·22218	2·17388	2·12763	2·08331	2·04080	1·99998
30	2·43894	2·38089	2·32553	2·27269	2·22219	2·17389	2·12764	2·08332	2·04080	1·99999
31	2·43897	2·38091	2·32555	2·27270	2·22220	2·17390	2·12765	2·08332	2·04081	1·99999
32	2·43898	2·38092	2·32556	2·27271	2·22221	2·17390	2·12765	2·08333	2·04081	2·00000
33	2·43900	2·38093	2·32556	2·27271	2·22221	2·17390	2·12765	2·08333	2·04081	2·00000
34	2·43900	2·38094	2·32557	2·27272	2·22221	2·17391	2·12766	2·08333	2·04081	2·00000
35	2·43901	2·38094	2·32557	2·27272	2·22222	2·17391	2·12766	2·08333	2·04081	2·00000
36	2·43901	2·38094	2·32558	2·27272	2·22222	2·17391	2·12766	2·08333	2·04082	2·00000
37	2·43902	2·38095	2·32558	2·27272	2·22222	2·17391	2·12766	2·08333	2·04082	2·00000
38	2·43902	2·38095	2·32558	2·27273	2·22222	2·17391	2·12766	2·08333	2·04082	2·00000
39	2·43902	2·38095	2·32558	2·27273	2·22222	2·17391	2·12766	2·08333	2·04082	2·00000
40	2·43902	2·38095	2·32558	2·27273	2·22222	2·17391	2·12766	2·08333	2·04082	2·00000
41	2·43902	2·38095	2·32558	2·27273	2·22222	2·17391	2·12766	2·08333	2·04082	2·00000
42	2·43902	2·38095	2·32558	2·27273	2·22222	2·17391	2·12766	2·08333	2·04082	2·00000
43	2·43902	2·38095	2·32558	2·27273	2·22222	2·17391	2·12766	2·08333	2·04082	2·00000
44	2·43902	2·38095	2·32558	2·27273	2·22222	2·17391	2·12766	2·08333	2·04082	2·00000
45	2·43902	2·38095	2·32558	2·27273	2·22222	2·17391	2·12766	2·08333	2·04082	2·00000
46	2·43902	2·38095	2·32558	2·27273	2·22222	2·17391	2·12766	2·08333	2·04082	2·00000
47	2·43902	2·38095	2·32558	2·27273	2·22222	2·17391	2·12766	2·08333	2·04082	2·00000
48	2·43902	2·38095	2·32558	2·27273	2·22222	2·17391	2·12766	2·08333	2·04082	2·00000
49	2·43902	2·38095	2·32558	2·27273	2·22222	2·17391	2·12766	2·08333	2·04082	2·00000
50	2·43902	2·38095	2·32558	2·27273	2·22222	2·17391	2·12766	2·08333	2·04082	2·00000

Appendix Table C

Appendix Table C *The amount of 1 per annum*

$$s_{n|r} = \frac{(1+r)^n - 1}{r}$$

Year	Percentage									
	1	2	3	4	5	6	7	8	9	10
1	1·00000	1·00000	1·00000	1·00000	1·00000	1·00000	1·00000	1·00000	1·00000	1·00000
2	2·01000	2·02000	2·03000	2·04000	2·05000	2·06000	2·07000	2·08000	2·09000	2·10000
3	3·03010	3·06040	3·09090	3·12160	3·15250	3·18360	3·21490	3·24640	3·27810	3·31000
4	4·06040	4·12161	4·18363	4·24646	4·31012	4·37462	4·43994	4·50611	4·57313	4·64100
5	5·10101	5·20404	5·30914	5·41632	5·52563	5·63709	5·75074	5·86660	5·98471	6·10510
6	6·15202	6·30812	6·46841	6·63298	6·80191	6·97532	7·15329	7·33593	7·52333	7·71561
7	7·21354	7·43428	7·66246	7·89829	8·14201	8·39384	8·65402	8·92280	9·20043	9·48717
8	8·28567	8·58297	8·89234	9·21423	9·54911	9·89747	10·2598	10·6366	11·0285	11·4359
9	9·36853	9·75463	10·1591	10·5828	11·0266	11·4913	11·9780	12·4876	13·0210	13·5795
10	10·4622	10·9497	11·4639	12·0061	12·5779	13·1808	13·8164	14·4866	15·1929	15·9374
11	11·5668	12·1687	12·8078	13·4864	14·2068	14·9716	15·7836	16·6455	17·5603	18·5312
12	12·6825	13·4121	14·1920	15·0258	15·9171	16·8699	17·8885	18·9771	20·1407	21·3843
13	13·8093	14·6803	15·6178	16·6268	17·7130	18·8821	20·1406	21·4953	22·9534	24·5227
14	14·9474	15·9739	17·0863	18·2919	19·5986	21·0151	22·5505	24·2149	26·0192	27·9750
15	16·0969	17·2934	18·5989	20·0236	21·5786	23·2760	25·1290	27·1521	29·3609	31·7725
16	17·2579	18·6393	20·1569	21·8245	23·6575	25·6725	27·8881	30·3243	33·0034	35·9497
17	18·4304	20·0121	21·7616	23·6975	25·8404	28·2129	30·8402	33·7502	36·9737	40·5447
18	19·6147	21·4123	23·4144	25·6454	28·1324	30·9057	33·9990	37·4502	41·3013	45·5992
19	20·8109	22·8406	25·1169	27·6712	30·5390	33·7600	37·3790	41·4463	46·0185	51·1591
20	22·0190	24·2974	26·8704	29·7781	33·0660	36·7856	40·9955	45·7620	51·1601	57·2750
21	23·2392	25·7833	28·6765	31·9692	35·7193	39·9927	44·8652	50·4229	56·7645	64·0025
22	24·4716	27·2990	30·5368	34·2480	38·5052	43·3923	49·0057	55·4568	62·8733	71·4027

23	25·7163	28·8450	32·4529	36·6179	41·4305	46·9958	53·4361	60·8933	69·5319	79·5430
24	26·9735	30·4219	34·4265	39·0826	44·5020	50·8156	58·1767	66·7648	76·7898	88·4973
25	28·2432	32·0303	36·4593	41·6459	47·7271	54·8645	63·2490	73·1059	84·7009	98·3471
26	29·5256	33·6709	38·5530	44·3117	51·1135	59·1564	68·6765	79·9544	93·3240	109·182
27	30·8209	35·3443	40·7096	47·0842	54·6691	63·7058	74·4838	87·3508	102·723	121·100
28	32·1291	37·0512	42·9309	49·9676	58·4026	68·5281	80·6977	95·3388	112·968	134·210
29	33·4504	38·7922	45·2189	52·9663	62·3227	73·6398	87·3465	103·966	124·135	148·631
30	34·7849	40·5681	47·5754	56·0849	66·4388	79·0582	94·4608	113·283	136·308	164·494
31	36·1327	42·3794	50·0027	59·3283	70·7608	84·8017	102·073	123·346	149·575	181·943
32	37·4941	44·2270	52·5028	62·7015	75·2988	90·8898	110·218	134·214	164·037	201·138
33	38·8690	46·1116	55·0778	66·2095	80·0638	97·3432	118·933	145·951	179·800	222·252
34	40·2577	48·0338	57·7302	69·8579	85·0670	104·184	128·259	158·627	196·982	245·477
35	41·6603	49·9945	60·4621	73·6522	90·3203	111·435	138·237	172·317	215·711	271·024
36	43·0769	51·9944	63·2759	77·5983	95·8363	119·121	148·913	187·102	236·125	299·127
37	44·5076	54·0343	66·1742	81·7022	101·628	127·268	160·337	203·070	258·376	330·039
38	45·9527	56·1149	69·1594	85·9703	107·710	135·904	172·561	220·316	282·630	364·043
39	47·4123	58·2372	72·2342	90·4091	114·095	145·058	185·640	238·941	309·066	401·448
40	48·8864	60·4020	75·4013	95·0255	120·800	154·762	199·635	259·057	337·882	442·593
41	50·3752	62·6100	78·6633	99·8265	127·840	165·048	214·610	280·781	369·292	487·852
42	51·8790	64·8622	82·0232	104·820	135·232	175·951	230·632	304·244	403·528	537·637
43	53·3978	67·1595	85·4839	110·012	142·993	187·508	247·776	329·583	440·846	592·401
44	54·9318	69·5027	89·0484	115·413	151·143	199·758	266·121	356·950	481·522	652·641
45	56·4811	71·8927	92·7199	121·029	159·700	212·744	285·749	386·506	525·859	718·905
46	58·0459	74·3306	96·5015	126·871	168·685	226·508	306·752	418·426	574·186	791·795
47	59·6263	76·8172	100·397	132·945	178·119	241·099	329·224	452·900	626·863	871·975
48	61·2226	79·3535	104·408	139·263	188·025	256·565	353·270	490·132	684·280	960·172
49	62·8348	81·9406	108·541	145·834	198·427	272·958	378·999	530·343	746·866	1057·19
50	64·4632	84·5794	112·797	152·667	209·348	290·336	406·529	573·770	815·084	1163·91

Appendix Table C

Appendix Table C   The amount of 1 per annum

$$s_{\overline{n}|r} = \frac{(1+r)^n - 1}{r}$$

Year	Percentage									
	11	12	13	14	15	16	17	18	19	20
1	1·00000	1·00000	1·00000	1·00000	1·00000	1·00000	1·00000	1·00000	1·00000	1·00000
2	2·11000	2·12000	2·13000	2·14000	2·15000	2·16000	2·17000	2·18000	2·19000	2·20000
3	3·34210	3·37440	3·40690	3·43960	3·47250	3·50560	3·53890	3·57240	3·60610	3·64000
4	4·70973	4·77933	4·84980	4·92114	4·99337	5·06650	5·14051	5·21543	5·29126	5·36800
5	6·22780	6·35285	6·48027	6·61010	6·74238	6·87714	7·01440	7·15421	7·29660	7·44160
6	7·91286	8·11519	8·32271	8·53552	8·75374	8·97748	9·20685	9·44197	9·68295	9·92992
7	9·78327	10·0890	10·4047	10·7305	11·0668	11·4139	11·7720	12·1415	12·5227	12·9159
8	11·8594	12·2997	12·7573	13·2328	13·7268	14·2401	14·7733	15·3270	15·9020	16·4991
9	14·1640	14·7757	15·4157	16·0853	16·7858	17·5185	18·2847	19·0859	19·9234	20·7989
10	16·7220	17·5487	18·4197	19·3373	20·3037	21·3215	22·3931	23·5213	24·7089	25·9587
11	19·5614	20·6546	21·8143	23·0445	24·3493	25·7329	27·1999	28·7551	30·4035	32·1504
12	22·7132	24·1331	25·6502	27·2707	29·0017	30·8502	32·8239	34·9311	37·1802	39·5805
13	26·2116	28·0291	29·9847	32·0887	34·3519	36·7862	39·4040	42·2187	45·2445	48·4966
14	30·0949	32·3926	34·8827	37·5811	40·5047	43·6720	47·1027	50·8180	54·8409	59·1959
15	34·4054	37·2797	40·4175	43·8424	47·5804	51·6595	56·1101	60·9653	66·2607	72·0351
16	39·1899	42·7533	46·6717	50·9804	55·7175	60·9250	66·6488	72·9390	79·8502	87·4421
17	44·5008	48·8837	53·7391	59·1176	65·0751	71·6730	78·9792	87·0680	96·0218	105·931
18	50·3959	55·7497	61·7251	68·3941	75·8364	84·1407	93·4056	103·740	115·266	128·117
19	56·9395	63·4397	70·7494	78·9692	88·2118	98·6032	110·285	123·414	138·166	154·740
20	64·2028	72·0524	80·9468	91·0249	102·444	115·380	130·033	146·628	165·418	186·688
21	72·2651	81·6987	92·4699	104·768	118·810	134·841	153·139	174·021	197·847	225·026
22	81·2143	92·5026	105·491	120·436	137·632	157·415	180·172	206·345	236·438	271·031

23	91·1479	104·603	120·205	138·297	159·276	183·601	211·801	244·487	282·362	326·237
24	102·174	118·155	136·831	158·659	184·168	213·978	248·808	289·494	337·010	392·484
25	114·413	133·334	155·620	181·871	212·793	249·214	292·105	342·603	402·042	471·981
26	127·999	150·334	176·850	208·333	245·712	290·088	342·763	405·272	479·431	567·377
27	143·079	169·374	200·841	238·499	283·569	337·502	402·032	479·221	571·522	681·853
28	159·817	190·699	227·950	272·889	327·104	392·503	471·378	566·481	681·112	819·223
29	178·397	214·583	258·583	312·094	377·170	456·303	552·512	669·447	811·523	984·068
30	199·021	241·333	293·199	356·787	434·745	530·312	647·439	790·948	966·712	1181·88
31	221·913	271·293	332·315	407·737	500·957	616·162	758·504	934·319	1151·39	1419·26
32	247·324	304·848	376·516	465·820	577·100	715·747	888·449	1103·50	1371·15	1704·11
33	275·529	342·429	426·463	532·035	664·666	831·267	1040·49	1303·13	1632·67	2045·93
34	306·837	384·521	482·903	607·520	765·365	965·270	1218·37	1538·69	1943·88	2456·12
35	341·590	431·663	546·681	693·573	881·170	1120·71	1426·49	1816·65	2314·21	2948·34
36	380·164	484·463	618·749	791·673	1014·35	1301·03	1669·99	2144·65	2754·91	3539·01
37	422·982	543·599	700·187	903·507	1167·50	1510·19	1954·89	2531·69	3279·35	4247·81
38	470·511	609·831	792·211	1031·00	1343·62	1752·82	2288·23	2988·39	3903·42	5098·37
39	523·267	684·010	896·198	1176·34	1546·17	2034·27	2678·22	3527·30	4646·07	6119·05
40	581·826	767·091	1013·70	1342·03	1779·09	2360·76	3134·52	4163·21	5529·83	7343·86
41	646·827	860·142	1146·49	1530·91	2046·95	2739·48	3668·39	4913·59	6581·50	8813·63
42	718·978	964·359	1296·53	1746·24	2355·00	3178·79	4293·02	5799·04	7832·98	10577·4
43	799·065	1081·08	1466·08	1991·71	2709·25	3688·40	5023·83	6843·86	9322·25	12693·8
44	887·963	1211·81	1657·67	2271·55	3116·63	4279·55	5878·88	8076·76	11094·5	15233·6
45	986·639	1358·23	1874·16	2590·56	3585·13	4965·27	6879·29	9531·58	13203·4	18281·3
46	1096·17	1522·22	2118·81	2954·24	4123·90	5760·72	8049·77	11248·3	15713·1	21938·6
47	1217·75	1705·88	2395·25	3368·84	4743·48	6683·43	9419·23	13273·9	18699·6	26327·3
48	1352·70	1911·59	2707·63	3841·48	5456·00	7753·78	11021·5	15664·3	22253·5	31593·7
49	1502·50	2141·98	3060·63	4380·28	6275·41	8995·39	12896·2	18484·8	26482·6	37913·5
50	1668·77	2400·02	3459·51	4994·52	7217·12	10435·6	15089·5	21813·1	31515·3	45497·2

Appendix Table C

Appendix Table C   The amount of 1 per annum

$$s_{n|r} = \frac{(1+r)^n - 1}{r}$$

Year	21	22	23	24	25	26	27	28	29	30
1	1·00000	1·00000	1·00000	1·00000	1·00000	1·00000	1·00000	1·00000	1·00000	1·00000
2	2·21000	2·22000	2·23000	2·24000	2·25000	2·26000	2·27000	2·28000	2·29000	2·30000
3	3·67410	3·70840	3·74290	3·77760	3·81250	3·84760	3·88290	3·91840	3·95410	3·99000
4	5·44566	5·52425	5·60377	5·68422	5·76562	5·84798	5·93128	6·01555	6·10079	6·18700
5	7·58925	7·73958	7·89263	8·04844	8·20703	8·36845	8·53273	8·69991	8·87002	9·04310
6	10·1830	10·4423	10·7079	10·9801	11·2588	11·5442	11·8366	12·1359	12·4423	12·7560
7	13·3214	13·7396	14·1708	14·6153	15·0735	15·5458	16·0324	16·5339	17·0506	17·5828
8	17·1189	17·7623	18·4300	19·1229	19·8419	20·5876	21·3612	22·1634	22·9953	23·8577
9	21·7139	22·6700	23·6690	24·7125	25·8023	26·9404	28·1287	29·3692	30·6639	32·0150
10	27·2738	28·6574	30·1128	31·6434	33·2529	34·9449	36·7235	38·5926	40·5564	42·6195
11	34·0013	35·9620	38·0388	40·2379	42·5661	45·0306	47·6388	50·3985	53·3178	56·4053
12	42·1416	44·8737	47·7877	50·8950	54·2077	57·7386	61·5013	65·5100	69·7800	74·3270
13	51·9913	55·7459	59·7788	64·1097	68·7596	73·7506	79·1066	84·8529	91·0161	97·6250
14	63·9095	69·0100	74·5280	80·4961	86·9495	93·9258	101·465	109·612	118·411	127·913
15	78·3305	85·1922	92·6694	100·815	109·687	119·347	129·861	141·303	153·750	167·286
16	95·7799	104·935	114·983	126·011	138·109	151·377	165·924	181·868	199·337	218·472
17	116·894	129·020	142·430	157·253	173·636	191·735	211·723	233·791	258·145	285·014
18	142·441	158·405	176·188	195·994	218·045	242·585	269·888	300·252	334·007	371·518
19	173·354	194·254	217·712	244·033	273·556	306·658	343·758	385·323	431·870	483·973
20	210·758	237·989	268·785	303·601	342·945	387·389	437·573	494·213	558·112	630·165
21	256·018	291·347	331·606	377·465	429·681	489·110	556·717	633·593	720·964	820·215
22	310·781	356·443	408·875	469·056	538·101	617·278	708·031	811·999	931·044	1067·28

Percentage

23	377·045	435·861	503·917	582·630	673·626	778·771	900·199	1040·36	1202·05	1388·46
24	457·225	532·750	620·817	723·461	843·033	982·251	1144·25	1332·66	1551·64	1806·00
25	554·242	650·955	764·605	898·092	1054·79	1238·64	1454·20	1706·80	2002·62	2348·80
26	671·633	795·165	941·465	1114·63	1319·49	1561·68	1847·84	2185·71	2584·37	3054·44
27	813·676	971·102	1159·00	1383·15	1650·36	1968·72	2347·75	2798·71	3334·84	3971·78
28	985·548	1185·74	1426·57	1716·10	2063·95	2481·59	2982·64	3583·34	4302·95	5164·31
29	1193·51	1447·61	1755·68	2128·96	2580·94	3127·80	3788·96	4587·68	5551·80	6714·60
30	1445·15	1767·08	2160·49	2640·92	3227·17	3942·03	4812·98	5873·23	7162·82	8729·99
31	1749·63	2156·84	2658·40	3275·74	4034·97	4967·95	6113·48	7518·74	9241·04	11350·0
32	2118·06	2632·34	3270·84	4062·91	5044·71	6260·62	7765·12	9624·98	11921·9	14756·0
33	2563·85	3212·46	4024·13	5039·01	6306·89	7889·38	9862·70	12321·0	15380·3	19183·8
34	3103·25	3920·20	4950·68	6249·38	7884·61	9941·62	12526·6	15771·8	19841·6	24939·9
35	3755·94	4783·64	6090·33	7750·23	9856·76	12527·4	15909·8	20189·0	25596·7	32422·9
36	4545·68	5837·05	7492·11	9611·28	12322·0	15785·6	20206·5	25842·9	33020·7	42150·7
37	5501·28	7122·20	9216·30	11919·0	15403·4	19890·8	25663·2	33079·9	42597·7	54796·9
38	6657·55	8690·08	11337·0	14780·5	19255·3	25063·4	32593·3	42343·2	54952·0	71237·0
39	8056·63	10602·9	13945·6	18328·9	24070·1	31580·9	41394·5	54200·4	70889·1	92609·1
40	9749·52	12936·5	17154·0	22728·8	30088·7	39793·0	52572·0	69377·5	91448·0	120393·0
41	11797·9	15783·6	21100·5	28184·7	37611·8	50140·2	66767·4	88804·1	117969·0	156512·0
42	14276·5	19257·0	25954·6	34950·0	47015·8	63177·6	84795·6	113670·0	152181·0	203466·0
43	17275·6	23494·5	31925·1	43339·1	58770·7	79604·8	107691·0	145499·0	196314·0	264507·0
44	20904·4	28664·3	39268·9	53741·4	73464·4	100303·0	136769·0	186240·0	253246·0	343860·0
45	25295·3	34971·4	48301·8	66640·4	91831·5	126383·0	173698·0	238388·0	326689·0	447019·0
46	30608·4	42666·1	59412·2	82635·1	114790·0	159243·0	220597·0	305137·0	421430·0	581126·0
47	37037·1	52053·7	73078·0	102468·0	143489·0	200648·0	280160·0	390577·0	543645·0	755465·0
48	44815·9	63506·5	89886·9	127062·0	179362·0	252817·0	355804·0	499939·0	701303·0	982106·0
49	54228·3	77478·9	110562·0	157558·0	224204·0	318550·0	451872·0	639923·0	904682·0	1276740·0
50	65617·2	94525·3	135992·0	195373·0	280256·0	401374·0	573878·0	819103·0	1167040·0	1659760·0

Appendix Table C   The amount of 1 per annum

$$s_{n|r} = \frac{(1+r)^n - 1}{r}$$

Percentage

Year	31	32	33	34	35	36	37	38	39	40
1	1·00000	1·00000	1·00000	1·00000	1·00000	1·00000	1·00000	1·00000	1·00000	1·00000
2	2·31000	2·32000	2·33000	2·34000	2·35000	2·36000	2·37000	2·38000	2·39000	2·40000
3	4·02610	4·06240	4·09890	4·13560	4·17250	4·20960	4·24690	4·28440	4·32210	4·36000
4	6·27419	6·36237	6·45154	6·54170	6·63288	6·72506	6·81825	6·91247	7·00772	7·10400
5	9·21919	9·39833	9·58054	9·76588	9·95438	10·1461	10·3410	10·5392	10·7407	10·9456
6	13·0771	13·4058	13·7421	14·0863	14·4384	14·7987	15·1672	15·5441	15·9296	16·3238
7	18·1311	18·6956	19·2770	19·8756	20·4919	21·1262	21·7790	22·4509	23·1422	23·8534
8	24·7517	25·6782	26·6384	27·6333	28·6640	29·7316	30·8373	31·9822	33·1676	34·3947
9	33·4247	34·8953	36·4291	38·0287	39·6964	41·4350	43·2471	45·1354	47·1030	49·1526
10	44·7864	47·0618	49·4507	51·9584	54·5902	57·3516	60·2485	63·2869	66·4731	69·8137
11	59·6701	63·1215	66·7695	70·6243	74·6967	78·9982	83·5404	88·3359	93·3977	98·7391
12	79·1679	84·3204	89·8034	95·6365	101·841	108·437	115·450	122·904	130·823	139·235
13	104·710	112·303	120·439	129·153	138·485	148·475	159·167	170·607	182·844	195·929
14	138·170	149·240	161·183	174·065	187·954	202·926	219·059	236·438	255·153	275·300
15	182·003	197·997	215·374	234·247	254·738	276·979	301·111	327·284	355·662	386·420
16	239·423	262·356	287·447	314·891	344·897	377·692	413·522	452·652	495·370	541·988
17	314·645	347·309	383·305	422·954	466·611	514·661	567·524	625·659	689·565	759·784
18	413·185	459·449	510·795	567·758	630·925	700·939	778·509	864·410	959·495	1064·70
19	542·272	607·472	680·358	761·796	852·748	954·277	1067·56	1193·89	1334·70	1491·58
20	711·376	802·863	905·876	1021·81	1152·21	1298·82	1463·55	1648·56	1856·23	2089·21
21	932·903	1060·78	1205·81	1370·22	1556·48	1767·39	2006·07	2276·02	2581·16	2925·89
22	1223·10	1401·23	1604·73	1837·10	2102·25	2404·65	2749·31	3141·90	3588·81	4097·24

23	1603·26	1850·62	2135·30	2462·71	2839·04	3271·33	3767·56	4336·83	4989·45	5737·14
24	2101·28	2443·82	2840·94	3301·03	3833·71	4450·00	5162·55	5985·82	6936·34	8033·00
25	2753·67	3226·84	3779·45	4424·38	5176·50	6053·00	7073·70	8261·43	9642·51	11247·2
26	3608·31	4260·43	5027·67	5929·67	6989·28	8233·09	9691·97	11401·8	13404·1	15747·1
27	4727·89	5624·77	6687·81	7946·76	9436·53	11198·0	13279·0	15735·4	18632·7	22046·9
28	6194·53	7425·70	8895·78	10649·7	12740·3	15230·3	18193·2	21715·9	25900·4	30866·7
29	8115·84	9802·92	11832·4	14271·5	17200·4	20714·2	24925·7	29969·0	36002·6	43214·3
30	10632·7	12940·9	15738·1	19124·9	23221·6	28172·3	34149·2	41358·2	50044·6	60501·1
31	13929·9	17082·9	20932·6	25628·3	31350·1	38315·3	46785·4	57075·3	69563·0	84702·5
32	18249·2	22550·5	27841·4	34342·9	42323·7	52109·8	64097·1	78764·9	96693·5	118585·0
33	23907·4	29767·6	37030·1	46020·5	57137·9	70870·3	87814·0	108697·0	134405·0	166019·0
34	31319·7	39294·3	49251·0	61668·5	77137·2	96384·6	120306·0	150002·0	186824·0	232428·0
35	41029·8	51869·4	65504·8	82636·8	104136·0	131084·0	164820·0	207004·0	259686·0	325400·0
36	53750·1	68468·6	87122·4	110734·0	140585·0	178275·0	225805·0	285667·0	360965·0	455561·0
37	70413·6	90379·6	115874·0	148385·0	189791·0	242456·0	309354·0	394221·0	501742·0	637787·0
38	92242·8	119302·0	154113·0	198837·0	256218·0	329741·0	423816·0	544026·0	697423·0	892903·0
39	120839·0	157480·0	204972·0	266442·0	345896·0	448448·0	580629·0	750757·0	969419·0	1250060·0
40	158300·0	207874·0	272613·0	357034·0	466960·0	609890·0	795462·0	1036050·0	1347490·0	1750090·0
41	207374·0	274395·0	362577·0	478426·0	630398·0	829452·0	1089780·0	1429740·0	1873020·0	2450130·0
42	271661·0	362202·0	482228·0	641092·0	851038·0	1128060·0	1493010·0	1973050·0	2603490·0	3430180·0
43	355877·0	478108·0	641364·0	859065·0	1148900·0	1534160·0	2045420·0	2722810·0	3618860·0	4802260·0
44	466200·0	631104·0	853015·0	1151150·0	1551020·0	2086450·0	2802220·0	3757470·0	5030210·0	6723160·0
45	610723·0	833058·0	1134510·0	1542540·0	2093880·0	2837580·0	3839050·0	5185310·0	6992000·0	9412420·0
46	800048·0	1099640·0	1508900·0	2067000·0	2826730·0	3859110·0	5259500·0	7155730·0	9718880·0	13177400·0
47	1048060·0	1451520·0	2006840·0	2769790·0	3816090·0	5248390·0	7205510·0	9874910·0	13509200·0	18448400·0
48	1372590·0	1916010·0	2669100·0	3711510·0	5151720·0	7137810·0	9871550·0	13627400·0	18777800·0	25827700·0
49	1798590·0	2529140·0	3549900·0	4973430·0	6954830·0	9707420·0	13524000·0	18805800·0	26101200·0	36158800·0
50	2356150·0	3338460·0	4721370·0	6664400·0	9389020·0	13202100·0	18527900·0	25952000·0	36280700·0	50622300·0

Appendix Table C

Appendix Table C The amount of 1 per annum

$$s_{\overline{n}|r} = \frac{(1+r)^n - 1}{r}$$

Year	Percentage									
	41	42	43	44	45	46	47	48	49	50
1	1·00000	1·00000	1·00000	1·00000	1·00000	1·00000	1·00000	1·00000	1·00000	1·00000
2	2·41000	2·42000	2·43000	2·44000	2·45000	2·46000	2·47000	2·48000	2·49000	2·50000
3	4·39810	4·43640	4·47490	4·51360	4·55250	4·59160	4·63090	4·67040	4·71010	4·75000
4	7·20132	7·29969	7·39911	7·49958	7·60113	7·70374	7·80742	7·91219	8·01805	8·12500
5	11·1539	11·3656	11·5807	11·7994	12·0216	12·2475	12·4769	12·7100	12·9469	13·1875
6	16·7269	17·1391	17·5604	17·9911	18·4314	18·8813	19·3411	19·8109	20·2909	20·7812
7	24·5850	25·3375	26·1114	26·9072	27·7255	28·5667	29·4314	30·3201	31·2334	32·1719
8	35·6648	36·9793	38·3393	39·7464	41·2019	42·7073	44·2641	45·8737	47·5378	49·2578
9	51·2874	53·5106	55·8252	58·2248	60·7428	63·3527	66·0682	68·8931	71·8313	74·8867
10	73·3153	76·9850	80·8301	84·8582	89·0771	93·4950	98·1203	102·962	108·029	113·330
11	104·375	110·319	116·587	123·196	130·162	137·503	145·237	153·383	161·963	170·995
12	148·168	157·653	167·719	178·402	189·735	201·754	214·498	228·008	242·324	257·493
13	209·917	224·867	240·839	257·899	276·115	295·561	316·312	338·451	362·063	387·239
14	296·983	320·311	345·400	372·374	401·367	432·519	465·979	501·908	540·474	581·859
15	419·746	455·841	494·921	537·219	582·982	632·477	685·989	743·823	806·306	873·788
16	592·842	648·294	708·738	774·595	846·324	924·417	1009·40	1101·86	1202·40	1311·68
17	836·907	921·578	1014·49	1116·42	1228·17	1350·65	1484·82	1631·75	1792·57	1968·52
18	1181·04	1309·64	1451·73	1608·64	1781·85	1972·95	2183·69	2415·99	2671·93	2953·78
19	1666·26	1860·69	2076·97	2317·44	2584·68	2881·50	3211·03	3576·67	3982·18	4431·68
20	2350·43	2643·18	2971·07	3338·12	3748·78	4207·99	4721·21	5294·47	5934·44	6648·51
21	3315·11	3754·31	4249·63	4807·89	5436·73	6144·67	6941·18	7836·81	8843·32	9973·77
22	4675·31	5332·13	6077·97	6924·36	7884·26	8972·22	10204·5	11599·5	13177·5	14961·7

23	6593·18	7572·62	8692·49	9972·08	11433·2	13100·4	15001·7	17168·2	19635·5	22443·5
24	9297·39	10754·1	12431·3	14360·8	16579·1	19127·6	22053·4	25410·0	29258·0	33666·2
25	13110·3	15271·8	17777·7	20680·5	24040·7	27927·4	32419·6	37607·8	43595·4	50500·3
26	18486·5	21687·0	25423·1	29781·0	34860·0	40774·9	47657·7	55660·5	64958·1	75751·5
27	26067·0	30796·6	36356·1	42885·6	50548·1	59532·4	70057·9	82378·5	96788·6	113628·0
28	36755·5	43732·1	51990·2	61756·3	73295·7	86918·3	102986·0	121921·0	144216·0	170443·0
29	51826·3	62100·6	74346·9	88930·0	106280·0	126902·0	151391·0	180444·0	214883·0	255666·0
30	73076·0	88183·9	106317·0	128060·0	154107·0	185278·0	222545·0	267059·0	320176·0	383500·0
31	103038·0	125222·0	152034·0	184408·0	223456·0	270506·0	327142·0	395248·0	477064·0	575251·0
32	145285·0	177816·0	217410·0	265548·0	324012·0	394940·0	480900·0	584968·0	710826·0	862878·0
33	204853·0	252500·0	310898·0	382390·0	469818·0	576613·0	706924·0	865754·0	1059130·0	1294320·0
34	288843·0	358551·0	444585·0	550643·0	681237·0	841857·0	1039180·0	1281320·0	1578110·0	1941480·0
35	407270·0	509144·0	635757·0	792927·0	987794·0	1229110·0	1527600·0	1896350·0	2351380·0	2912220·0
36	574252·0	722986·0	909134·0	1141820·0	1432300·0	1794500·0	2245570·0	2806600·0	3503560·0	4368330·0
37	809696·0	1026640·0	1300060·0	1644220·0	2076840·0	2619980·0	3300980·0	4153770·0	5220300·0	6552490·0
38	1141670·0	1457830·0	1859090·0	2367670·0	3011420·0	3825170·0	4852450·0	6147570·0	7778250·0	9828740·0
39	1609760·0	2070120·0	2658500·0	3409450·0	4366560·0	5584750·0	7133100·0	9098410·0	11589600·0	14743100·0
40	2269760·0	2939570·0	3801660·0	4906100·0	6331510·0	8153730·0	10485700·0	13465700·0	17268500·0	22114700·0
41	3200360·0	4174190·0	5436370·0	7069840·0	9180690·0	11904400·0	15413900·0	19929200·0	25730100·0	33172000·0
42	4512510·0	5927360·0	7774010·0	10180600·0	13312000·0	17380500·0	22658400·0	29495200·0	38337800·0	49758000·0
43	6362650·0	8416850·0	11116800·0	14660000·0	19302400·0	25375500·0	33307900·0	43652800·0	57123300·0	74637000·0
44	8971330·0	11951900·0	15897100·0	21110400·0	27988500·0	37048300·0	48962600·0	64606200·0	85113700·0	111955000·0
45	12649600·0	16971700·0	22732800·0	30399000·0	40583300·0	54090500·0	71975100·0	95617200·0	126819000·0	167933000·0
46	17835900·0	24099900·0	32507900·0	43774600·0	58845800·0	78972100·0	105803000·0	141513000·0	188961000·0	251900000·0
47	25148600·0	34221800·0	46486300·0	63035400·0	85326400·0	115299000·0	155531000·0	209440000·0	281552000·0	377850000·0
48	35459600·0	48595000·0	66475500·0	90771000·0	123723000·0	168337000·0	228631000·0	309971000·0	419512000·0	566775000·0
49	49998000·0	69004800·0	95059900·0	130710000·0	179399000·0	245772000·0	336087000·0	458757000·0	625073000·0	850162000·0
50	70497200·0	97986900·0	135936000·0	188223000·0	260128000·0	358827000·0	494048000·0	678961000·0	931359000·0	1275240000·0

Index

accounting principles, 102 *et seq.*
Allen, F. B., 415, 422
annual allowance, 52
annual capital charge, *see* discounting methods
annual depreciation charge, *see* depreciation
annual return on capital, 237
annuities, *see* present value
Anthony, R. N., 268
Armstrong, F. E., 102
asset cover, 115
assets, 104
  optimal life, 488
  optimal choice, 491
  residual value, 50, 478–9
  value, 44, 302–3, 466
  value formulae, 473 *et seq.*
AVCO (Average Cost), *see* stock valuation

Bailey, M. J., 160, 171
balance sheet, 104–7
balancing allowance, 52
bank borrowing, 61–3
Bank of England, 295
Bannock, G., 302, 309, 484, 507, 509
Bates, G. E., 27, 32
Berliner Method, 345
Bellmore, D. H., 70, 102
Bierman, H., 57, 120, 147
bills of exchange, 63
Bonbright, J. C., 484
bond rate, 18
bonds, 65
bonus issues, 95
book profits, 455–9
Boulding, K., 36
break-up value, 303
British Petroleum, 67
Bryce, M. D., 364, 371
budget categories, 378–80
Bull, G., 297, 309
Burns, D., xii

capital:
  allowances, 52
  budgeting dept., 373
  gains, 72
  rationing, 139–42
  recovery period, *see* payback
  outlays, 43
Carter, C. F., 185, 218
cash flows, *see* net cash flows
Childs, J. F., 114
Common Market, 294
compensating balances, 61

computers, applications of, 375, 509
confidence level, 185
continuous compounding, 26
convertible loans, 66, 401 *et seq.*
cost minimization, 292–3
cost of capital:
  bank borrowing, 61–3
  bills of exchange, 63–4
  bonus issues, 95–7
  curves, 398
  debentures, 65–7
  deferred tax, 64
  depreciation provision, 81
  determination of, 73 *et seq.*
  equity, 69 *et seq.*
  inflation effects on, 213–4
  interest, 40–1
  long term loans, 65–7
  medium term loans, 65–7
  new issues, 82–6, 440
  preference shares, 67–8
  retained profits, 79
  rights issues, 87 *et seq.*, 441
  shareholders, 75–7
  short term funds, 60–4
  trade credit, 60–1
  undervalued shares, 433 *et seq.*
  weighted average, 118 *et seq.*, 363, 396 *et seq.*, 431
cost saving investments, 209–10, 243–4
Courtaulds, 77, 136
current assets, 104
current ratio, 62, 109. *See also* financial ratios
cut-off rate, 227

Daily Herald, 296
Daily Mirror, 296
Dean, J., xv, 36, 221, 234–5, 240
debenture:
  bonds, 65
  fixed charge, 248
  floating charge, 65, 248
  holders, 393–4
  mortgage, 65
  trust deed, 65
debt:
  capital, 393–4
  finance, 135–8, 407 *et seq.*
  raising potential, 115–8
Decision Theory, 185
deferred tax, *see* taxation
demand curves for different shares of a firm's income, 394–5
depreciation:
  annual charge, 485
  provision, 47, 142–7

depreciation, *cont.*
  sinking fund method, 40
devaluation, 368
differential yield, *see* yield
discount market, 295
discount periods, 27–8
discounted yield, *see* yield
discounting methods, 33 *et seq.*
  comparison of, 149
dividend policy, 336
dividend yield, *see* yield
Dodd, D. L., 70, 101, 407, 422
Donaldson, G., 117, 147
Dougall, H. E., 232, 234, 240
Durand, D., 407, 417, 422

earnings yield, *see* yield
Edey, H. C., 107, 346, 347
effective annual equivalent rate of
  interest, 60
  on bank overdraft
effective net of tax factor, 244
effective rate, 25
English Channel, 234
equity:
  capital, 69
  net cash flows, 122–4
  supply curves, 98–101
  yields, 199
Eximbank, 364
ex-rights share price, 87
extended yield, *see* yield

Finance Act 1961, 364
finance of overseas subsidiaries, 364–6
financial policy, 377
financial ratios, 109 *et seq.*, 261, 399
  of American companies, 112–4
  of British companies, 114
FIFO (First In First Out), *see* stock
  valuation
Fisher, I., 36
fixed charged debentures, *see* debentures
floating charge debentures, *see* debentures

Gant, D. R., 268
gearing, 396
General Motors, 113
G.P.O. (General Post Office), 294
goodwill, 333
Gordon, M. J., 22, 32, 233, 240
Graham, B. J., 70, 101, 407, 422
Griesinger, F. K., 268

Harold, G., 70, 102
Hayes, D. A., 70, 102
head office problem, 276 *et seq.*
Henderson, R. F., 86, 102
Hummel, P. M., 32

I.C.I. (Imperial Chemical Industries),
  67, 77, 136
incremental yield, *see* yield
inflation, 213 *et seq.*
  effects on: debt finance, 409
  leasing, 254–8
  take-overs, 340
initial allowance, 52
institutional lenders, 58, 108–9, 404,
  418
intangible assets, 104
IDVR (Integrated depreciation, valuation and replacement), 508–9
International Finance Corporation, 364
interpolation, 17, 31
intersection of opportunities, 289
investment, 212
  allowance, 52
  rate, *see* yield rate
Istvan, D. F., 390

Jenkins Committee Report, 261

Keynes, 36

Laski, D. J., 163
LIFO (Last In First Out), *see* stock
  valuation
Leach, W. A., 170, 171, 268
lease:
  financial implications, 260 *et seq.*
  general points, 258–9
  finance, 400
  inflation, 254–8
  return on project, 265
  specific debt finance, 248 *et seq.*
leaseback
  comparison with debt, 252
  cost of capital, 244–6
  cost saving investment, 247
liabilities, 104–5

marginal projects, 125
marginal source of finance, 121
market research, 302
McDowell, I., 289, 293
Meredith, G. P., 185, 218
mergers, 294 *et seq.*
Merrett, A. J., 170, 171, 221, 240, 302,
  309, 484, 507, 509
method of averages, 19
Miller, M. H. & Modigliani, F.,   407
  422
  thesis, 413–7
mining companies, 81, 348–9
MM, *see* Miller
modified yield, *see* yield
Moody's 125 Industrials, 114
mortgage bonds, 65
mortgage debentures, 65
multiple yields, 62

nationalized industries, 69, 240, 372
necessity-postponability, 235
net cash flows, 43, 45
net of tax returns, 70
net present value, 131, *See also* discounting methods
new issues, 82–6
NP, *see* necessity postponability
NPV, *see* net present value

obsolescence, 505–6
Odhams Press, 296
operations research, 375
opportunity value, 46, 278
optimal timing, 278 *et seq.*
optimal size, 288
overseas earnings, 367

Paish, F. W., 64, 101
Parkinson, H., 70, 102
payback, 200, 228 *et seq.*
  applications, 233–4
  assessing risk and liquidity, 230–1
  calculation, 205–6
  diagrammatic presentation, 207
  drawbacks, 201, 232–3
PEP, xii, xx
perpetuities, *see* present value
personnel problems, 297, 306–7
post audit, 388–9
post mortem, *see* post audit
preference shares, 67, 305–6
present value of:
  annuities, 7
  perpetuities, 8
  regular cash flows, 3–11
  tax allowances on capital expenditure, 51–4
presentation of information, 380 *et seq.*
privileged subscriptions, *see* rights issues
profit and loss account, 103
property analysis, 170
PV, *see* present value

Rate of Return, 219 *et seq.*, 345
ratios, *see* financial ratios
residual debt financing, 137
return on capital, 387
  risk, 190
  total, 187, 194
revaluation, 368
rights issues, 87
risk, 149, 416
  effect on lease or buy decisions, 243
  policy, 377
  probability analysis, 182
  sources of, 180
RR, *see* Rate of Return

scrip issues, *see* bonus issues
SEC (Securities Exchange Commissions), 77, 86, 92, 260

Seebeck, C. L., 32
SFR, *see* sinking fund return
Shackle, G. L. S., 185, 218
Shapiro, E., 22, 32
share capital, 104
Shell Petroleum Ltd., 69
short term funds, 60–4
sinking fund return, 165 *et seq.*
Smidt, S., 57, 120, 147
Smith, R., 415, 422
Solomon, Ezra, 98, 171, 422
Solomons, D., 491, 509
Soper, C. S., 162, 171
specific debt finance, 247, 400
state industries, 69. *See also* nationalized industries
stock appreciation, 310
stock dividends, 95
stock splits, *see* bonus issues
stock valuation, 104
stockpile, calculation of, 356
'Super' Profits Method, 345
Sykes, Allen, 170, 171, 221, 240

take-overs:
  additional debt finance, 330
  asset evaluation, 302–3
  effect of inflation, 340
  example, 311 *et seq.*
  financial considerations, 304–6
  future income, 299–302
  gearing, 304
  legal considerations, 307
  personnel problems, 306–7
  price of similar firms, 344
  tax aspects, 304
  terms, 331 *et seq.*
Tanker Finance Ltd., 69
taxation, 42, 46, 79
  allowances, formulae for, 52–7
  asset valuation, 492 *et seq.*
  bonus share issues, 96
  debt finance, 408
  deferred payments, 64
  depreciation policy, 496
  dividends, 70, 74
  finance of overseas subsidiaries, 364
  leases, 243–4
  preference dividends, 67
  take-overs and mergers, 297
Terborgh, G., xv, 227, 230, 240
terminal values, 12 *et seq.*
times covers, *see* financial ratios
trade credits, 60
trade investments, 104

undervalued shares, 75, 434
Unit Trusts, British, 73

Vancil, R. F., 268
Vauxhall Motors, 113
Vice, A., 297, 309

Watson, J. F., 297, 309
weighted average cost of capital, *see*
    cost of capital
Wenham, E. G., 170, 171, 268
Weston, J. F., 417, 422
Which?, 73
withholding tax, 366
working capital, 49
World Bank, 364

yearly discounting, accuracy of, 29

yield:
    differential, 37
    discounted, 21
    dividend, 19 *et seq.*, 70
    earnings, 19 *et seq.*, 70
    incremental, 154
    modified, 450
    rate, 15
    to redemption on a bond, 18, 36
yield method, 429–31. *See also* dis-
    counting methods
    disadvantages, 150–7
    extended, 159, 163, 171